50 YEARS

lonely planet

OF TRAVEL



# ENGLAND

The Lake District, Cumbria & Northeast England p517

Yorkshire p433

Manchester, Liverpool & Northwest England p482

Birmingham & the Midlands p362

Cambridge & East Anglia p329

Oxford, The Cotswolds & The Thames Valley p178

LONDON P50

Bristol, Bath & Southwest England p221

Canterbury & the Southeast p139

Devon & Cornwall p276

Joe Bindloss, Isabel Albiston, Olly Berry, Keith Drew, Sarah Irving, Lauren Keith, James March, Hugh McNaughtan, Lorna Parkes, Tasmin Waby

# CONTENTS

## Plan Your Trip



## The Guide

Canterbury (p144)

Bath (p233)

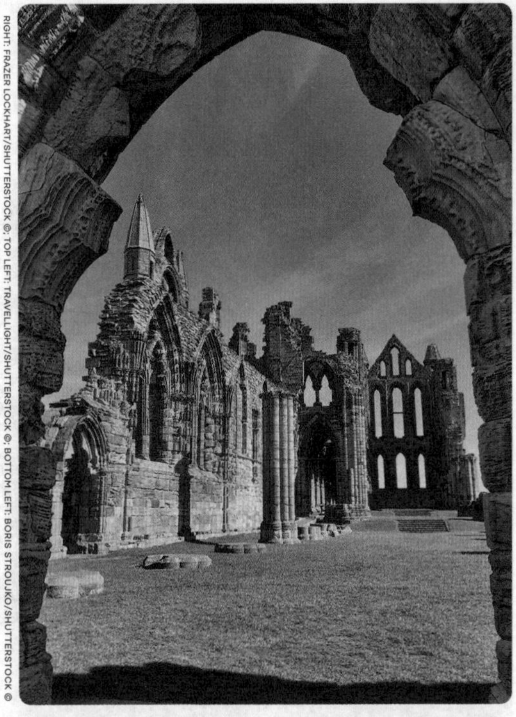

Whitby Abbey (p461)

## Toolkit



## Storybook

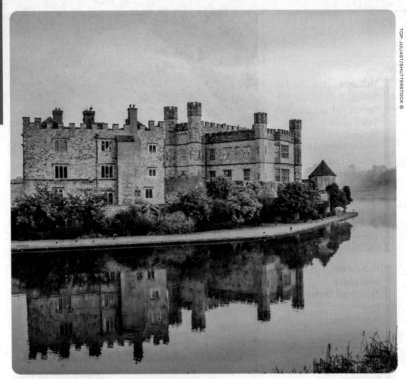

Leeds Castle (p151)

# ENGLAND

## THE JOURNEY BEGINS HERE

I've been lucky enough to work all over the world, from Australia to the Himalayas, but I always feel drawn back to England. I spent years of my childhood in Suffolk, searching for fossils and stone tools on empty beaches, and upped sticks to London as a graduate, where something just clicked.

What is the appeal of this idiosyncratic island? The history, as much as anything else. The house where I spent my school years had medieval charms against witches in the chimney, and corn dollies popped up all over the village in summer – a tradition dating back to pagan times.

Whether you're exploring a castle or sinking a pint in a pub that hosted union meetings during the Industrial Revolution, England's history seeps out of the stonework. Best of all, it's a history that's constantly in flux, as new locals arrive from across the world, adding new chapters to the national story.

**My favourite experience** is paddleboarding from Dedham to Flatford – this stretch of the River Stour has hardly changed since I used to kayak here aged seven.

**Joe Bindloss**

*@joe_on_travel*

## WHO GOES WHERE

### Our writers and experts choose the places which, for them, define England

KELLYGARCIAPHOTO.COM/GETTY IMAGES ©

Brighton is a city where people are not afraid to be themselves, and this freedom of expression allows creativity to thrive. The hopeful optimism underlying the city's positive actions towards embracing diversity and combating climate change represents the best of England to me. Perhaps it's all the fresh sea air and wholesome vegetarian food, but this is a place that feels alive. When there's a gale blowing, grab your kit and go kitesurfing.

**Isabel Albiston**

@isabel_albiston

*Isabel is a writer who spends as much time as she can in St Leonards on the East Sussex coast.*

HUYSMAN GEERT/SHUTTERSTOCK ©

For me, nowhere sums up the wildness – and the weirdness – of Cornwall quite like the far west, specifically the Penwith peninsula. It's stark, strange, windswept and littered with mysterious ancient monuments, and it has some of the most jaw-dropping stretches of coastline anywhere in Britain. I've lost count of how many times I've travelled the coast around Zennor, Pendeen and Botallack, but I never get tired of it. It's magic.

**Oliver Berry**

@olivertomberry

*Oliver Berry is a travel and nature writer based in Cornwall, and the co-author of all our previous Devon and Cornwall guides.*

GORDON BELL/SHUTTERSTOCK ©

There is no mistaking that water plays a significant role in the makeup of the northwest of England. From the Irish Sea hugging the Isle of Man, the Mersey kissing the Wirral and the canal 36 miles to the inland port at Manchester, our waterways tell the story of the region's wealth, development, dark past and decline. Walk along the promenade in New Brighton (p551) to see Liverpool's changing skyline, from the dockland cranes to the Three Graces.

**Sarah Irving**

*Sarah is a writer about travel, culture and the outdoors who is especially interested in a destination's overlooked and unusual features.*

Exmoor is one of my favourite places to walk in England. There's so much natural diversity in a relatively small area. There are some lovely trails across the moors, but nothing beats a salt-stung hike along England's highest cliffs. Every rise reveals a view more frammable than the last. I've walked Exmoor's entire coastline, but the memory that always jumps out is swooping down Countisbury Hill to Lynmouth, the harbour twinkling far below in the afternoon sun.

MILAN RADEMAKERS/SHUTTERSTOCK ©

**Keith Drew**

*@keithdrewtravel*

*Keith is a travel writer who grew up in Somerset and is currently walking the South West Coast Path. For more on Exmoor, go to page 248.*

Those big moments of a trip to London – the itinerary highlights like Big Ben and St Paul's Cathedral – leave an impression. After a decade here, I still pinch myself every time I walk across Waterloo Bridge. But the stories you take home come from the quiet places, unexpected connections and Londoners' up-for-it-all attitude. Perhaps it's cliché, but Samuel Johnson was right: 'When a man is tired of London, he is tired of life; for there is in London all that life can afford'.

FIIPHOTO/SHUTTERSTOCK ©

**Lauren Keith**

*@noplacelike_it*

*Lauren is a travel writer and adopted Londoner who loves shining the spotlight on obscure and off-beat places.*

The 'city of 1000 trades' was Birmingham's evocative nickname during the Industrial Revolution, though most of its howling foundries have long since disappeared. However, the city's handsome Jewellery Quarter neighbourhood – my own neighbourhood – still retains many of its old Georgian houses and Victorian factories, but now dotted with low-lit bars and friendly cafes. I love walking from languid St Paul's Square up past the cast-iron Chamberlain Clock, where the ghosts of Birmingham's mighty past mingle with a dynamic, youthful city.

KIEV.VICTOR/SHUTTERSTOCK ©

**James March**

*@jmarchtravel*

*James is a travel writer based in Birmingham.*

ASHLEY COOPER/GETTY IMAGES ©

Bamburgh Castle is an icon of the northeast. Sitting atop Great Whin Sill, a shelf of volcanic dolerite running through Northumbria, Cumbria and Durham, it's been central to thousands of years of its history. Overlooking a dramatic coast and the Farne Islands, this hill has been occupied by the Normans, Anglo-Saxons, Britons and prehistoric 'Northumbrians'. It's usually been crowned with an emphatic fortress like the Norman one that stands there to this day.

**Hugh McNaughton**

***Hugh is a former English lecturer who managed to massage his love of writing, travel and history into his day job.***

JOE DANIEL PRICE/GETTY IMAGES ©

There is something magical about the descent into the village Robin Hood's Bay – a stroll so steep that it requires serious concentration. Spindly cobbled lanes lead to cosy pubs and hidden fisher cottages that once stashed smugglers' contraband along the wild, contrary Yorkshire Coast. As the North Sea rears into view at the very bottom of the village, it's hard to avoid the temptation of a pint in The Bay Hotel before clambering over the beach, poking in the rockpools to find salt-encrusted crabs.

**Lorna Parkes**

*@Lorna_Explorer*

*Lorna is a travel journalist, food lover and adopted Yorkshire lass.*

DAVID HUGHES/SHUTTERSTOCK ©

In the Thames Valley, at the base of the Chiltern Hills, the awe-inspiring Windsor Castle overlooks a passing parade of river boats. Historic villages brim with world-class dining and friendly pubs. You can kayak, stand up paddleborad, or swim in the river near Hurley Lock, and walk its meandering riverside path. But best of all, the Thames Valley is so accessible, with trains zipping into London, and Heathrow 45 miles down the road.

**Tasmin Waby**

*Tasmin is a writer and editor who pens articles and guidebooks for Lonely Planet, while bringing up two future explorers of the world, in her chosen home city: London.*

Perth
Dundee
Stirling
Isle of Jura
Loch Lomond
Glasgow
Edinburgh
Berwick-upon-Tweed
Isle of Arran
SCOTLAND
Mull of Kintyre
North Sea
Tan Hill Inn
Sip a pint in England's highest pub (p452)
Scafell Pike
Conquer England's highest mountain (p542)
Hadrian's Wall
Carlisle
Newcastle-upon-Tyne
Durham
Whitby Abbey
Walk in the footsteps of Dracula (p461
Keswick
The Pennines
Darlington
Middlesbrough
Belfast
Whitehaven
Ambleside
IRELAND
Isle of Man
Ramsey
Douglas
Scarborough
Castle Howard
Get the Bridgerton vibe amid lavish gardens (p446)
Harrogate
York
Manchester's Museums
Industrial history and more (p490)
Blackpool
Leeds
Hull
Huddersfield
Liverpool
Manchester
ENGLAND
Stockport
Warrington
Dublin
Irish Sea
Bangor
Llandudno
Buxton
Sheffield
Lincoln
Skegness
North Norfolk Seafood
Sample all the ocean's bounty (p354)
Stoke-on-Trent
Nottingham

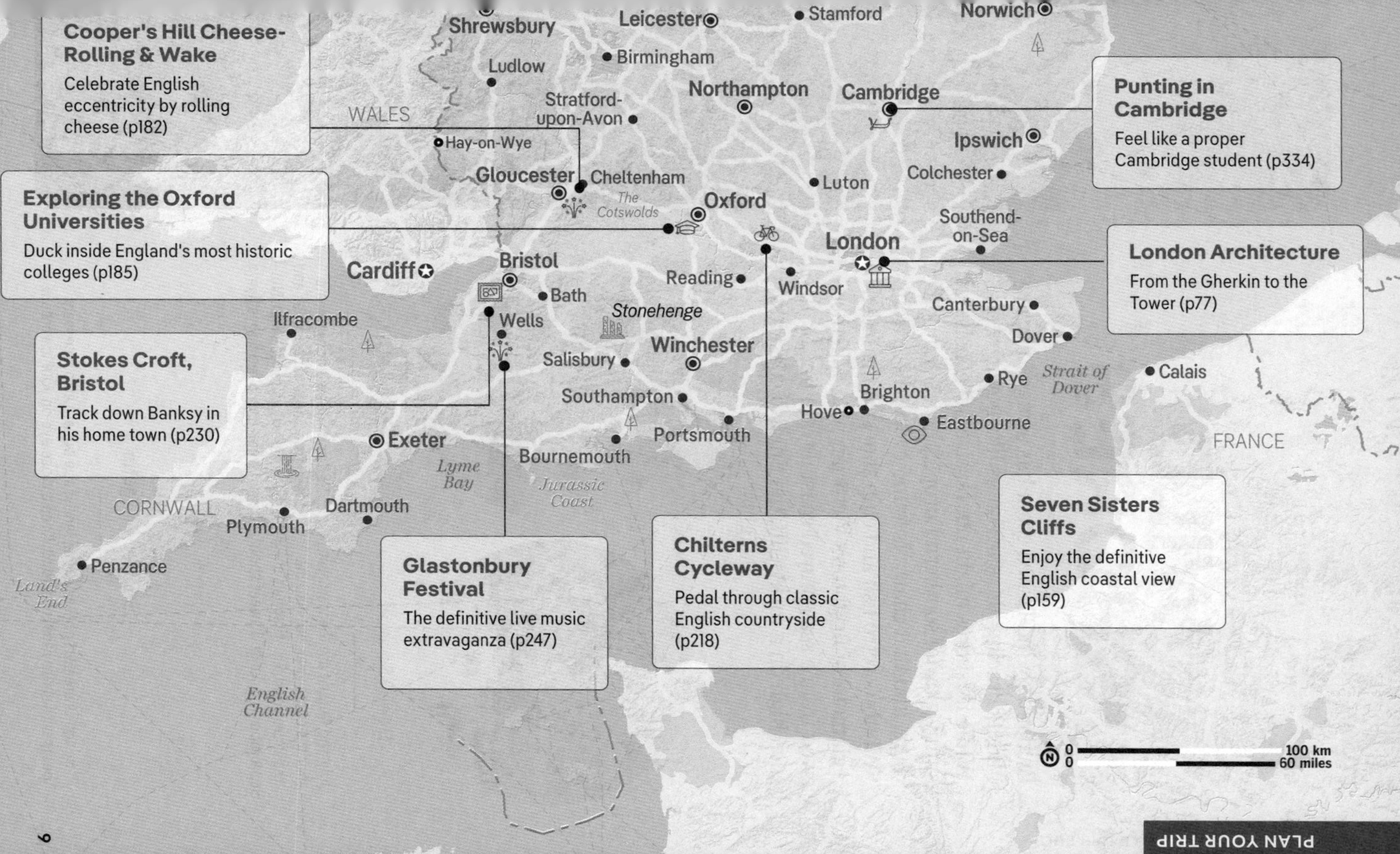
Cooper's Hill Cheese-Rolling & Wake
Celebrate English eccentricity by rolling cheese (p182)
Exploring the Oxford Universities
Duck inside England's most historic colleges (p185)
Stokes Croft, Bristol
Track down Banksy in his home town (p230)
Glastonbury Festival
The definitive live music extravaganza (p247)
Chilterns Cycleway
Pedal through classic English countryside (p218)
Seven Sisters Cliffs
Enjoy the definitive English coastal view (p159)
London Architecture
From the Gherkin to the Tower (p77)
Punting in Cambridge
Feel like a proper Cambridge student (p334)
Shrewsbury
Leicester
Stamford
Norwich
Ludlow
Birmingham
Northampton
Cambridge
WALES
Stratford-upon-Avon
Hay-on-Wye
Ipswich
Gloucester
Cheltenham
Luton
Colchester
The Cotswolds
Oxford
Southend-on-Sea
London
Cardiff
Bristol
Reading
Windsor
Bath
Canterbury
Stonehenge
Ilfracombe
Wells
Winchester
Dover
Salisbury
Calais
Rye
Strait of Dover
Brighton
Southampton
Hove
Eastbourne
Portsmouth
Exeter
FRANCE
Lyme Bay
Bournemouth
Jurassic Coast
CORNWALL
Dartmouth
Plymouth
Penzance
Land's End
English Channel
0 100 km
0 60 miles

# WILD SHORES

England's wind-lashed coast has a rugged beauty and its bracing air rejuvenates like nowhere else. While its shores might not receive the consistent sunny glow of southern Europe, there's character here, and that charm is found everywhere from Whitby's retro fish and chip shops to the faded glamour of Brighton's Victorian pier. Whether viewed from a sea-sprayed coastal train line or an old bench high on a rocky cliff, the English coast always delights.

## Beach Season

July and August are the warmest months of the year, but also the most crowded. The first half of September is a coastal sweet spot.

## Staying Safe

Red and yellow flags indicate lifeguarded areas of beaches and are the safest places to swim. Never swim when only a red flag is flying.

## Sneaky Seagulls

Seagulls are part of the coastal landscape but are also incessant pests with sharp radars for food. Keep a close eye on your ice cream.

TERRY YARROW/SHUTTERSTOCK © LEFT: LUCYON/SHUTTERSTOCK ©, MARK BENNETTS/SHUTTERSTOCK ©

Durdle Door, Jurassic Coast

## BEST COASTAL EXPERIENCES

Hunt for fossilised ammonites among the scattered rocks of Dorset's 185-million-year-old **Jurassic Coast** ❶ (p270)

Spot puffins and many other birds at the beautiful windswept **RSPB Bempton Cliffs reserve** ❷ (p476)

Catch a wild wave when surfing at Newquay's famous **Fistral Beach** ❸ (p306)

See Anthony Gormley's ethereal **Another Place sculptures** ❹ emerge from beneath the shores of Crosby Beach on Merseyside (p509)

Hike the epic clifftops of the **Seven Sisters** ❺ from Beachy Head to Eastbourne (p159)

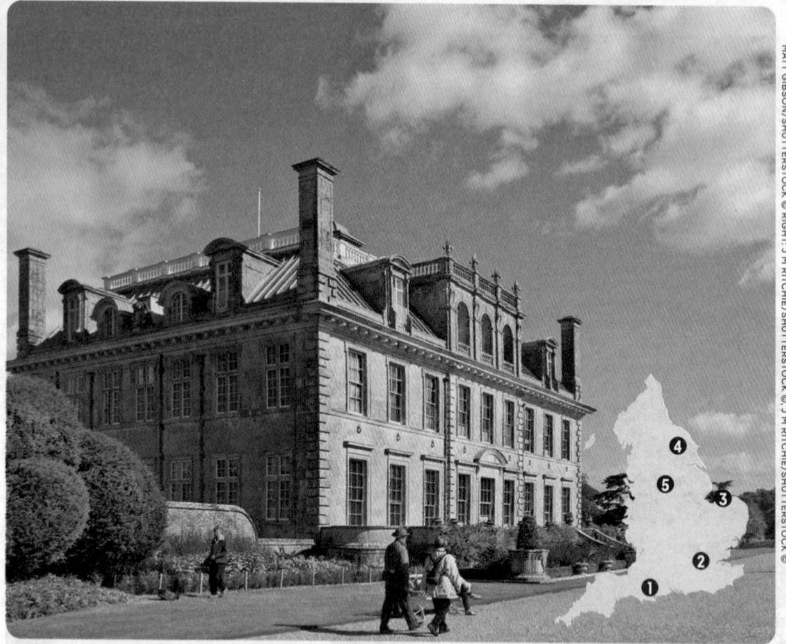



Kingston Lacy

# OPULENT ABODES

With fairytale architecture and rich histories, stately homes are a never-ending source of fascination and around 3000 remain in the UK, many of which you'll find in England's pastoral countryside. Most are open for anyone wanting to know what it's like to own lavish furniture, glamorous ballrooms and maybe have a maze in the back garden.

## Take a Tour

Guided tours are a good way to put these luxurious surroundings into some context and to learn a few quirky stories and tales.

## Slavery Links

While these homes were status symbols for some of England's wealthiest families, that wealth can often, unfortunately, be linked back to the slave trade.

## BEST STATELY HOME EXPERIENCES

Take in superb paintings and the greatest private collection of Egyptian artefacts in the UK at **Kingston Lacy** ❶ (p265)

Rub shoulders with royalty and admire paintings by Rubens, Van Dyck and Canaletto amid the grandiose corridors of **Buckingham Palace** ❷ (p61)

Wander the elegant gardens and stunning rooms of the 18th-century Neo-Palladian **Holkham Hall** ❸ (p353)

Visit **Castle Howard** ❹ and its vast landscaped gardens to see where Brideshead Revisited and Bridgerton were filmed (p446)

Explore the 16th-century Long Gallery and medieval chapel at Derbyshire's **Haddon Hall** ❺, the oldest parts of which date back to the 11th century (p410)

# THE PERFECT POUR

The pub was – and still is – the anchor for many English communities and a crisp pint of beer or cider their salvation. But beer has evolved, and the country's favourite drink now comes in a riot of different styles and flavours. So sample stouts, sours and IPAs in modern taphouses, rural country pubs and everything in-between.

### Multiple Choice

The city in England with the most pubs per sq mile is Portsmouth with 12 – almost double the number in London.

### A Tight Squeeze

Confirmed by the Guinness Book of Records, the smallest pub in England is The Nutshell in Suffolk. The bar measures a cosy 15ft by 7ft.

### Ale Accompaniments

Bar snacks are a nice addition to a good pub session. A bag of crisps or the odd-sounding but tasty pork scratchings go well.

### BEST DRINKING EXPERIENCES

Enjoy a tipple or two of **scrumpy cider ❶**, freshly pressed from the bountiful apple orchards of central and south Somerset (p244)

Take a tour of the many real ale pubs of **Derby ❷**, a city sometimes referred to as the 'Real Ale Capital of England' (p423)

Roll through the brewery bars and bottle shops lining the stretch of historic railway arches making up London's **Bermondsey Beer Mile ❸** (p120)

Spend the night at England's highest pub, the remote **Tan Hill Inn ❹** high up in the Yorkshire Dales (p452)

Sample a few beers in the Cornish sun at the 13th-century **Pandora Inn ❺** with its striking thatched roof (p321)

# FANTASTIC FESTIVITIES

England's long winter means festival season is being salivated over as soon as the days begin to brighten. So between May and September, England's streets, parks and virtually anywhere with enough room for a tent and a stage morph into a mass of sizzling food, lively music and good vibes. From bumping urban hip-hop revelry to rural pork pie festivals, no aspect of English life is beyond a summer celebration, so dive in.

### At Glasto

Glastonbury is England's most famous music festival, though you'll need to plan months in advance (and have a bit of luck) to snag a ticket.

### Drink Water

Festivals can be long and boozy affairs so drink water and stay hydrated throughout the day, especially in hot weather.

### Celebrate Literature

Though held in Wales, the Hay Literature festival is one of the UK's greatest festivals and is a stone's throw over the border from Herefordshire.

JACEK WOJNAROWSKI/SHUTTERSTOCK © LEFT: RAGGEDSTONE/SHUTTERSTOCK ©, DAVE SMITH 1965/SHUTTERSTOCK ©

## BEST FESTIVAL EXPERIENCES

Marvel at the sight of 100-plus hot-air balloons floating above the city at the **Bristol International Balloon Fiesta** ❶ (p231)

Watch the manic racing and collisions at **The Bumps** ❷, Cambridge's busy rowing races on the River Cam each May (p340)

Spend the Spring Bank Holiday watching the downhill cheese chase at the bizarre **Cooper's Hill Cheese Rolling & Wake** ❸ (p182)

Sing along to maritime music at the **Falmouth International Sea Shanty Festival** ❹, Europe's largest free nautical song festival (p281)

Head to the majestic North York Moors and taste the fine culinary offerings at the **Malton Food Lovers Festival** ❺ (p447)

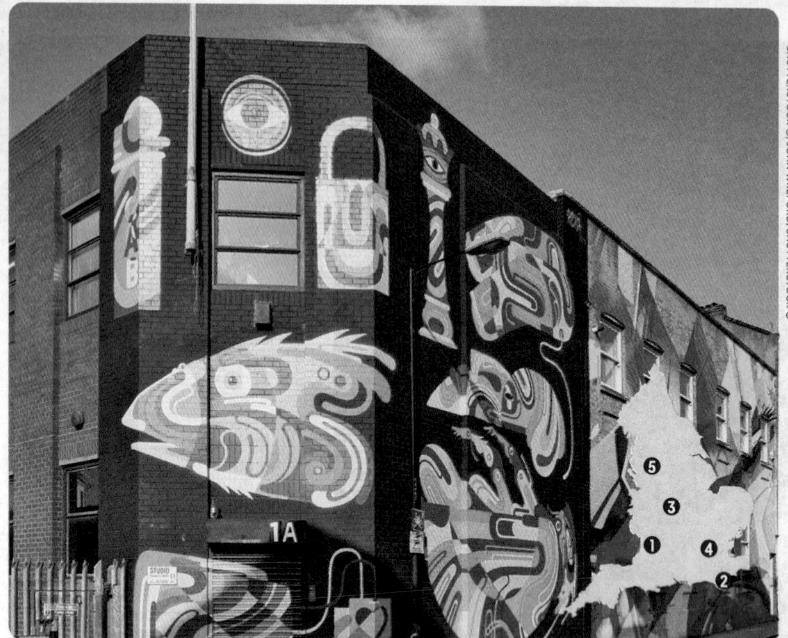




Shoreditch street art

# A SPLASH OF COLOUR

From Banksy to Burne-Jones, the canon of English art is wide and it's not always simply the domain of hushed galleries either. Art in England is found everywhere, from graffiti in disused railway arches to bold murals on the sides of houses. Sometimes you just need to know where to look.

## Royal Replications

The most painted monarch in English history is Charles I, with over 200 examples (most famously on horseback).

## Take Advantage

Enjoy street art when you can – it may not always be there if you return to the same location at a later date.

## BEST ART EXPERIENCES

Track down a Banksy mural in the backstreets of **Stokes Croft** ❶ on a street-art walking tour of Bristol (p230)

Visit three award-winning galleries across 18 miles of cinematic coastline on the Hastings to **Eastbourne Art Trail** ❷ (p160)

Stroll a languid canal towpath all the way to Birmingham's underrated art deco **Barber Institute of Fine Arts** ❸ (p372)

Explore the gaudy graffiti and political street-art murals of **Brick Lane and Shoreditch** ❹ in London (p94)

View the extensive and eclectic wallpaper collection of Manchester's **Whitworth Art Gallery** ❺ (p492)

# TWO-WHEEL TRAILS

From repurposed railway lines to gentle country lanes, England is a perfect place to get outdoors and roll through some delightful landscapes. The summer months are especially good for cycling and, thanks to the country's high density, many of the best trails are located near towns so planning for bike hire and accommodation is simple.

## Safety First

It goes without saying, but always wear a helmet and be aware of cars, especially on narrow winding country lanes.

## Help on Hills

E-bikes are more popular than ever and are useful on hills and gradients, especially for less experienced cyclists or when covering great distances.

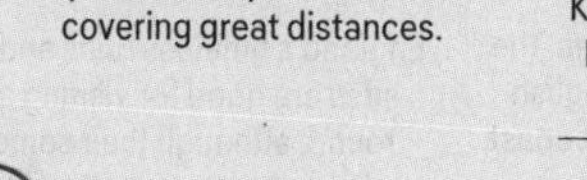

## Cycle Paths

The UK's National Cycle Network has 5220 miles (8400km) of traffic-free paths, alongside 7519 miles (12,101km) on-road.

## BEST CYCLING EXPERIENCES

See the sights of **Bristol** ❶ from its excellent network of cycle lanes, exactly what you'd expect from the UK's first Cycling City (p226)

Cycle through the rolling hills of Derbyshire and see **Derwent Reservoir** ❷, the famous practice site of the legendary Dambusters (p409)

Feel the sea breeze on a Kent coast cycling tour from **Ramsgate to Whitstable** ❸ (p148)

Take the family mountain biking on the 12-mile **Swale Trail** ❹ through some of the prettiest parts of the Yorkshire Dales (p452)

Pass by ancient beech forests along winding country lanes on the **Chilterns Cycleway** ❺ (p219)

# GHOSTS OF THE PAST

From marauding Roman armies to the spectre of Luftwaffe bombers in the night sky, England has seen conflict spanning centuries but what remains are some unique and often spectacular ruins. Many are now open to the public up and down the country and are well worth a visit for a macabre window into some brutal periods throughout English history. From crumbling castles to bomb-flattened cathedrals, these sights are both bizarre and beautiful.

### Roman Landfall

A strange land across the sea, the Romans first arrived on English shores in 55 BCE on the Kent coast.

### Wrap Up

England's timeless ruins and historic sites are good for visiting all year round, although their sometimes skeletal appearances will mean wrapping up warm in winter.

### Fine Fettle

There are over 100 castle ruins in England still remaining. Yet the oldest and largest castle – Windsor Castle – is still in fine condition.

FULCANELLI/SHUTTERSTOCK © LEFT: FOTOGENIX/SHUTTERSTOCK ©, VALERIIAARNAUD/SHUTTERSTOCK ©

## BEST RUINED HISTORY EXPERIENCES

Explore the mythical ruins of **Glastonbury Abbey** ❶, believed to be the final resting place of King Arthur and Queen Guinevere (p246)

Wander the strange green overgrown ruins of London's 900-year-old **St Dunstan in the East** church ❷ (p78)

Delve into the Isle of Wight's unheralded Roman history by seeing the ornate mosaic floors at **Brading Roman Villa** ❸ (p177)

Stand amid the macabre fragmented remains of **Coventry Cathedral** ❹, the victim of German bombing during the WWII (p385)

Admire the gaunt headland ruins of **Whitby Abbey** ❺ – which was the inspiration behind *Dracula*; it's a crucial destination after Stoker stayed here (p461)

**Oyster**

# A TASTE OF THE DEEP

While fish and chips might be ubiquitous across England, there's just something magical about enjoying the quintessential English dish while the sea breeze blows. This is a maritime country, so head to the coast and enjoy as much great seafood as possible, from syrupy oysters in Whitstable to succulent lobsters in Northumberland.

## Seafood shacks

Lead by Riley's Fish Shack in Tynemouth, beachfront seafood shacks are becoming popular and offer quality coastal dining without having to book a table.

## Sample Cornwall

With its deep fishing heritage and tradition, the southwestern region of Cornwall has some of the finest seafood in England.

## BEST SEAFOOD EXPERIENCES

Tuck into flavoursome fish, home-grown oysters and spicy crab (of course) at the chilled-out **Crab House Café** ❶ on the Isle of Portland (p272)

Enjoy famous **Whitby fish and chips** ❷ but also don't miss Whitby crab, mackerel fishing trips and North Sea lobsters (p462)

Sample everything from crab to shrimp at the many delightful stops on the **North Norfolk Coast** ❸ (p354)

Experience sublime Michelin-star seafood at Nathan Outlaw's magnificent restaurant in the picturesque Cornish village of **Port Isaac** ❹ (p305)

Pick up some smoked kippers at **L Robson & Sons** ❺, the famous smokehouse in the northern fishing village of Craster (p575)

# ABOVE THE CLOUDS

When thinking about hiking in England, the yawning valleys, hazy hills and craggy summits of the Lake District typically spring to mind, yet the country is blessed with wild landscapes and cinematic vistas up and down the country. So consider lesser-known spots too, such as the Shropshire Hills or the South Downs.

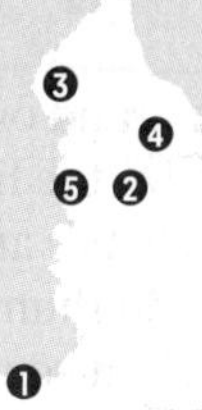

### High Point

Located in the Lake District, Scafell Pike is England's tallest mountain, at an elevation of 978m (3209ft) above sea level.

### Pack Well

For longer hikes, make sure to pack waterproof clothes, a water bottle, snacks, a portable phone charger and sunscreen if the weather is hot.

### Bridleways

Public Bridleways are marked with a blue arrow and are open to walkers, cyclists and horse riders.

### BEST HIKING EXPERIENCES

Hike up through the heather to the trig point atop **Dunkery Beacon** ❶, the highest part of Exmoor, for views across the Bristol Channel to South Wales (p251)

Take in panoramic views and air crash remains from the 510m-high summit of **Mam Tor** ❷ in the Peak District (p409)

Attempt to climb the mighty **Scafell Pike** ❸ in the Lake District, England's highest mountain (p542)

Try your luck at the **Yorkshire Three Peaks Challenge** ❹ by climbing the rugged mountains of Whernside, Ingleborough and Pen-y-ghent (p453)

Follow the grand ridge of sandstone along the **Cheshire Sandstone Trail** ❺, rising dramatically from Frodsham to Whitchurch (p502)

# TURN UP THE VOLUME

From grand ornate concert halls to small sweaty rock clubs, the live music scene in England comes in many shapes and sizes. And it was amid the sticky floors and thumping speakers of those ecstatic club nights that some of the greatest English bands cut their teeth, from The Beatles at Liverpool's Cavern Club to The Who and the Sex Pistols at London's 100 Club. Book tickets and feel the thrill of live music.

### Seasonal Shows

Use summer to enjoy live music outdoors at England's many festivals, and winter's cold nights as a chance to explore the club scene.

### Performing History

Dating back to 1859, Wilton's Music Hall in Shadwell, London, is England's oldest surviving music hall and still hosts performances today.

### Backroom Gigs

Many pubs in England host gigs either in backrooms or upstairs, so keep an eye out for them wherever you're travelling.

The Cavern Club

## BEST MUSICAL EXPERIENCES

Buckle up for the rollercoaster ride of legendary music sets and carnival sideshows that make up the world-famous **Glastonbury Festival of Contemporary Performing Arts** ❶ (p247)

Look out for the neon lights of **Ronnie Scott's Jazz Club** ❷ in London, then step downstairs for the world's finest jazz sounds (p69)

Head to the **Glyndebourne Festival** ❸ near Lewes for classical music, sparkling wine, country picnics and general English eccentricity (p159)

Soak up the frenetic atmosphere at Nottingham's **Rock City** ❹, the famous venue that's hosted everyone from U2 to David Bowie (p419)

See where it all began for the Fab Four at Liverpool's **Cavern Club** ❺, an intimate venue packed with Beatles memorabilia (p508)

VALERIE2000/SHUTTERSTOCK © RIGHT: IAN LUCK/SHUTTERSTOCK ©, CARON BADKIN/SHUTTERSTOCK ©

Salisbury Cathedral

# GRAND DESIGNS

Now dominated by angular skyscraper The Shard, a cursory glance at London's gleaming skyline shows how much English architecture has changed in recent years. But this is a country that's been producing architectural wonders for centuries, so explore soaring Gothic cathedrals, epic viaducts and opulent palaces alongside more modern curiosities. Just remember to look up.

### Sky-High Shard

At 309m (1016ft) high, The Shard is the UK's tallest building. The viewing gallery on Level 72 is The Shard's highest public level.

### Brutalism

Following post-war austerity, the brutalist architecture style became popular and these polarising concrete edifices are still visible within England's large urban centres today.

### BEST ARCHITECTURE EXPERIENCES

Gaze up at the dizzying spire of **Salisbury Cathedral** ❶, the tallest in the UK – and still supported within by ancient wooden scaffolding (p254)

See the modern face of the City of London and skyscrapers like the **Cheesegrater**, the **Gherkin** and the **Walkie Talkie** ❷ (p77)

Take in the cavernous size and reverberating acoustics at Buxton's historic **Devonshire Dome** ❸ (p410)

Stroll through romantic England at **Lavenham Village** ❹ and its charming half-timbered medieval cottages (p360)

Relax in stunning spas amid Italian mosaic floors and curving Islamic arches at **Harrogate Turkish Baths** ❺ (p455)

# INTO THE BLUE

While an island nation, England's landscape is pierced by miles of rivers, canals and streams. For many, they're an escape into a world of tranquility, especially when gliding on a narrowboat. For others, they're a thrilling opportunity to hit the water in a canoe or kayak. Pick your poison and explore England's many waterways.

### Snaking Severn

At 220 miles (354km) long, the River Severn is the UK's longest river, starting in Wales' Cambrian Mountains and finishing in the Bristol Channel.

### Numerous Names

Confusingly, there are multiple rivers with the same name. England has four River Avons, four River Derwents and two River Ouses.

### Canal Preparation

If you're planning to hire a canal boat, do some research on how to operate locks if it's your first time.

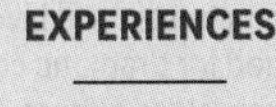

### BEST BOATING EXPERIENCES

Experience the Venetian-esque tradition of **punting in Cambridge** ❶, as you drift by manicured lawns and exquisite architecture (p334)

Tour **Canterbury's old waterways** ❷ and pass medieval bridges, ancient walls and half-timbered houses (p341)

Hire a rowing or motor boat and meander up and down the **Thames** at Oxford, Marlow or Henley ❸ (p215)

Glide by forested hillsides, waterside villages and pioneering 18th-century mills at **Derbyshire's Derwent Valley Mills** ❹ (p415)

Learn about can life at the **National Waterways Museum** ❺, where the Manchester Ship Canal meets the River Mersey (p510)

# REGIONS & CITIES

Find the places that tick all your boxes.

## The Lakes, Cumbria & Northumberland

**THE BLEAK AND THE BEAUTIFUL**

The Lake District is England's most famous outdoor hub, but be ready to share the trails with a crowd in summer. Bring extra camera cards for the historic sights and epic mountaintop views. Over on the east coast, Newcastle is the stepping-off point for Hadrian's Wall and the dramatic Northumberland coast.

p517

## Manchester, Liverpool & Northwest England

**REVOLUTION, SCIENCE AND MUSI**

Football and music fans go weak at the knees at the mention of Manchester and Liverpool, gateway cities for a region famed for dramatic coastal scenery, Tudor history and working-class culture. Don't limit your explorations to the mainland – the Isle of Man offers Unesco-listed landscapes, quirky museums and wildlife encounters.

p482

## Birmingham & the Midlands

**HEARTLANDS, HILLS AND HISTORY**

England's second biggest city, Birmingham is a lively base for exploring the industrious Midlands, the crucible of the Industrial Revolution. There's history here by the shed-load, from Shakespeare's Stratford to soaring cathedrals, castles and stately homes, plus uplifting green spaces in the Peak District and the Shropshire and Malvern hills.

p362

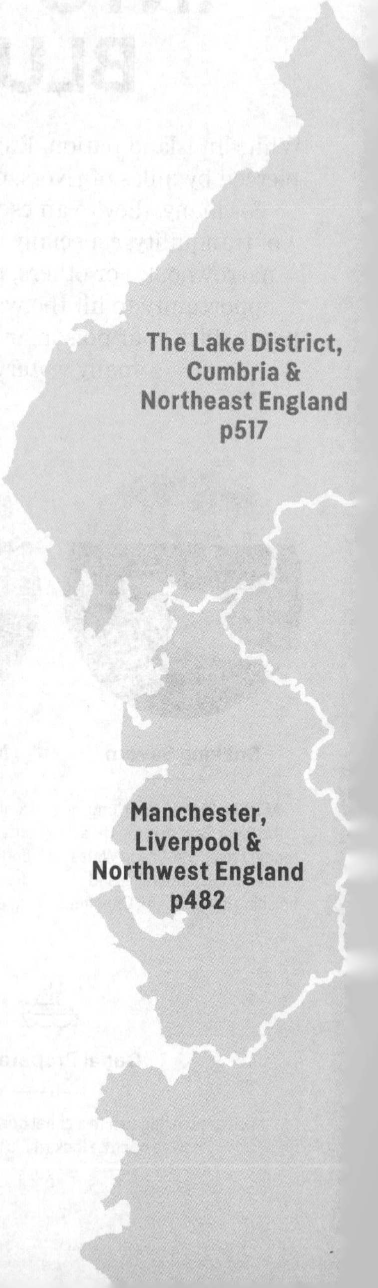

The Lake District, Cumbria & Northeast England
p517

Manchester, Liverpool & Northwest England
p482

## Yorkshire

**GRIT, GLAMOUR AND WILD PLACES**

For many locals, Yorkshire is England. The sprawling industrial cities of Leeds, Bradford, Sheffield and York are dwarfed by the green expanses of the North York Moors and Yorkshire Dales, and history spills out of the landscape at every turn. Mix up Pennine hikes with trips to castles, stately homes and beaches.

**p433**

## Cambridge & East Anglia

**QUINTESSENTIALLY ENGLISH SCENES**

England's 'wild east' is a beguiling mix of medieval towns and peaceful backwaters, where you can jump from top-end gastronomy in Cambridge and Norwich to fish and chip suppers on the Suffolk and Norfolk coast in a single afternoon. Bring an appetite for the region's famous seafood.

p329

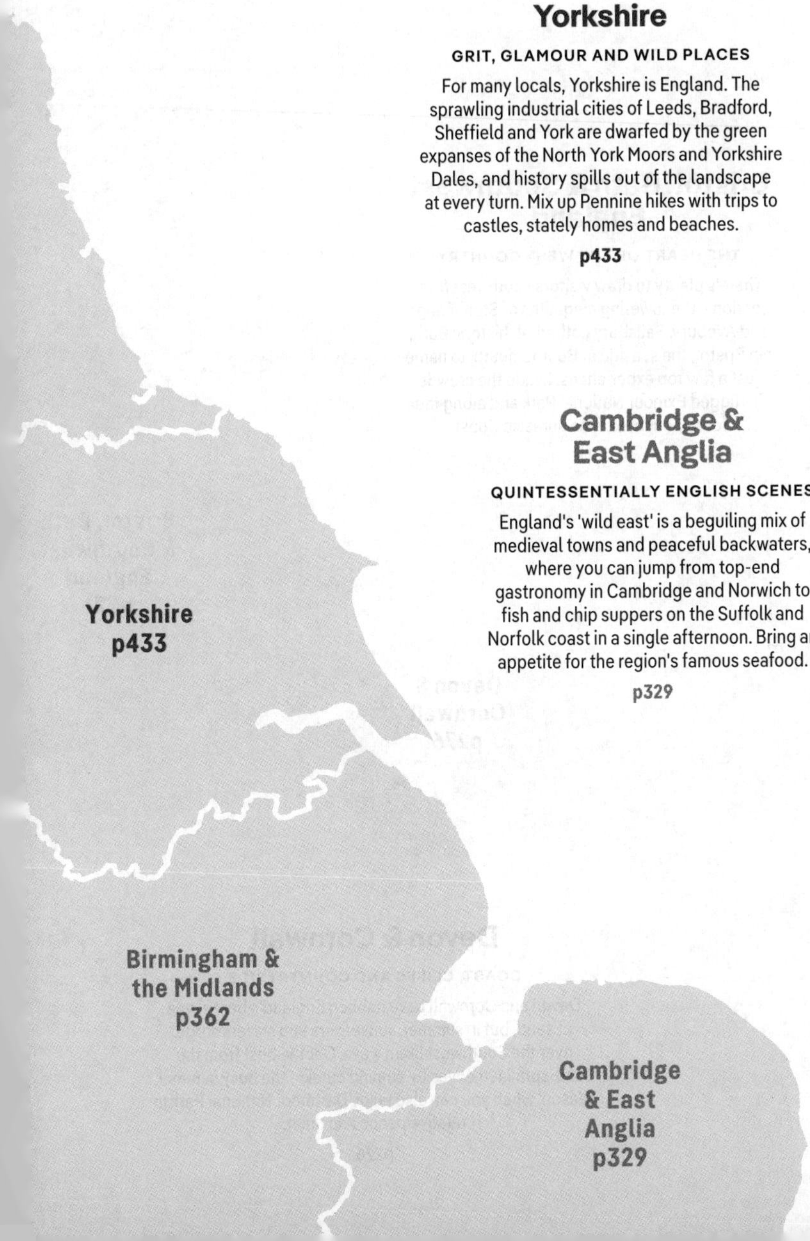

## Bristol, Bath & Southwest England

**THE HEART OF THE WEST COUNTRY**

There's plenty to draw visitors southwest from London – the towering megaliths of Stonehenge and Avebury, Salisbury cathedral, historic Bath, hip Bristol, the seaside at Bournemouth, to name just a few top experiences. Evade the crowds in rugged Exmoor National Park and along the fossil beaches of the Jurassic Coast.

p221

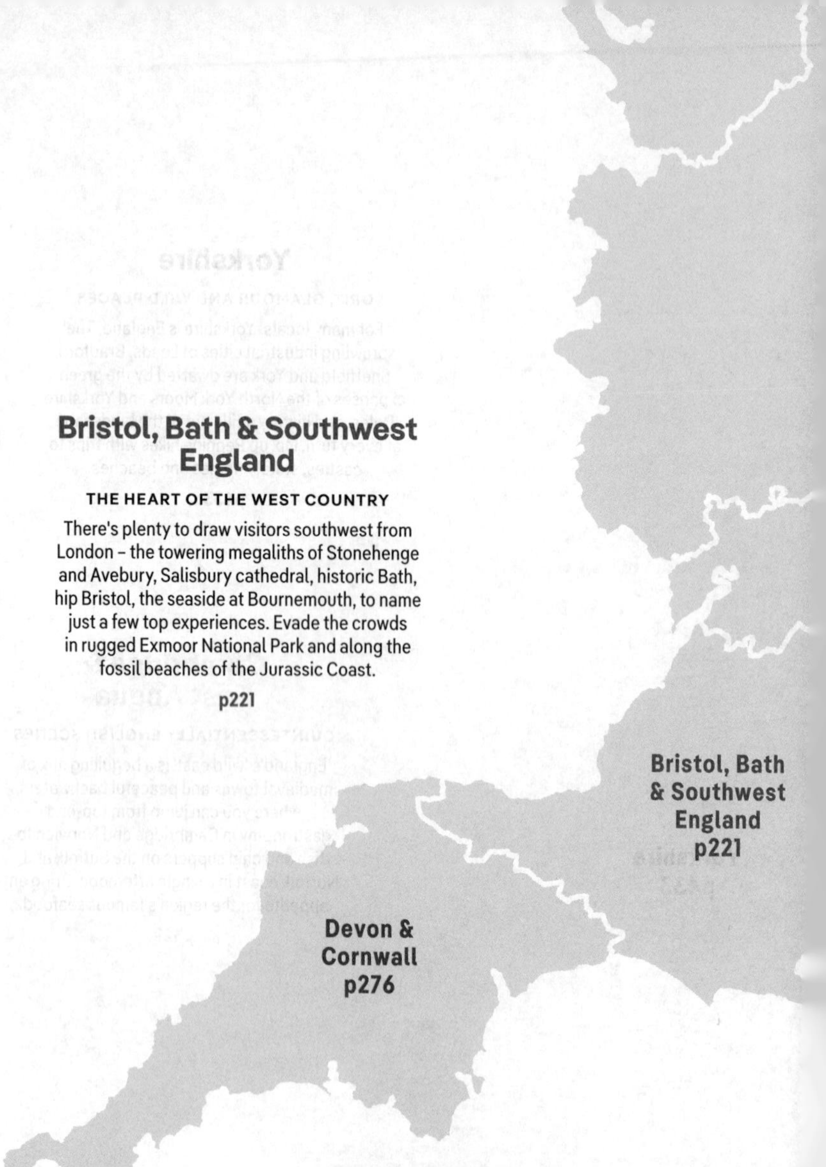

Bristol, Bath & Southwest England p221

Devon & Cornwall p276

## Devon & Cornwall

**COAST, CLIFFS AND COUNTRYSIDE**

Devon and Cornwall have nabbed England's best strips of sand, but in summer, sunseekers and surfers surge over the Southwest like a wave. Get the best from the sand-sprinkled coves by coming outside the busy summer season, when you can also enjoy Dartmoor National Park in relative peace and quiet.

p276

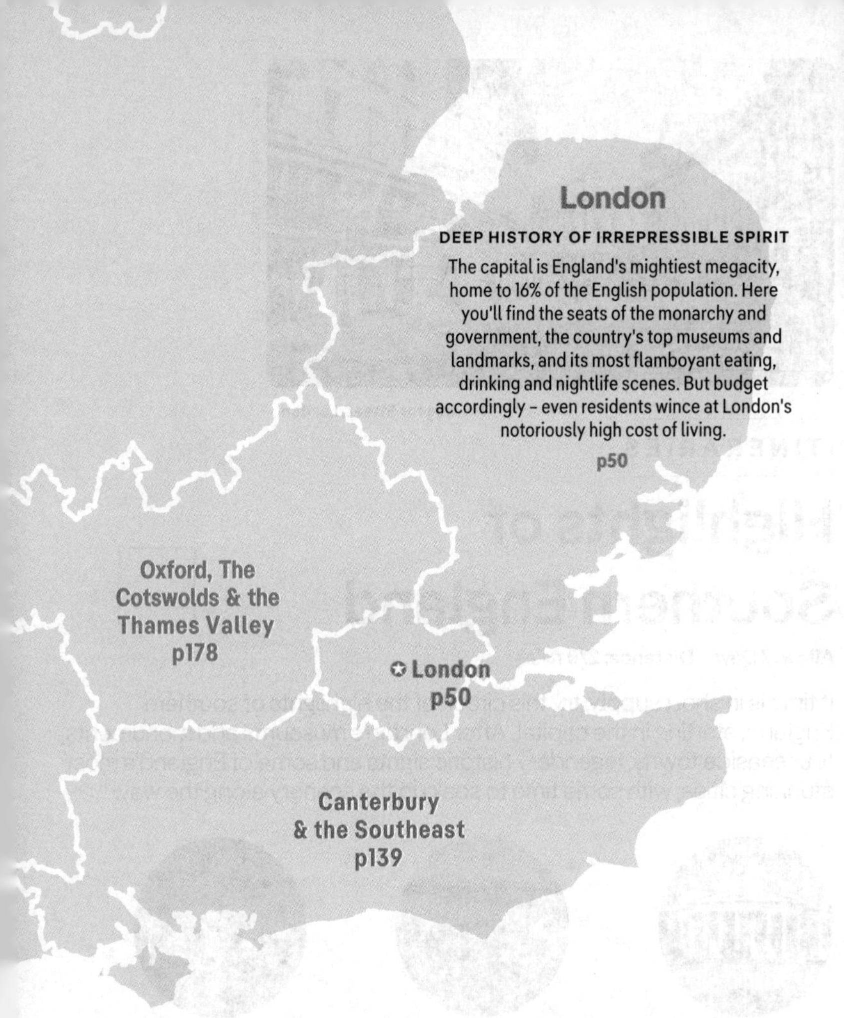

## London

**DEEP HISTORY OF IRREPRESSIBLE SPIRIT**

The capital is England's mightiest megacity, home to 16% of the English population. Here you'll find the seats of the monarchy and government, the country's top museums and landmarks, and its most flamboyant eating, drinking and nightlife scenes. But budget accordingly – even residents wince at London's notoriously high cost of living.

p50

Oxford, The Cotswolds & the Thames Valley
p178

London
p50

Canterbury & the Southeast
p139

## Oxford, The Cotswolds & the Thames Valley

**HISTORY AND HONEY-HUED VILLAGES**

Arguably England's most elegant city, Oxford is the ideal hub for a deep dive into the England you've seen showcased in a hundred period dramas. This is an area of historic country houses, picturesque Cotswolds villages, rolling countryside and yet more classically English experiences in Cheltenham and Windsor.

p178

## Canterbury & the Southeast

**CLIFFS, CASTLES AND COASTAL TOWNS**

Canterbury is the most famous of the historic cities dotted around southeast England. Chalk grasslands roll out towards the south coast, ending abruptly at the white cliffs. Here you'll find Brighton, the walking trails of the North and South Downs, the Isle of Wight, seafaring Portsmouth and abundant historic sights.

p139

CEDRIC WEBER/SHUTTERSTOCK ©

Regent Street, London

ITINERARIES

# Highlights of Southern England

**Allow:** 7 Days **Distance:** 270 miles

If time is in short supply, try this circuit of the highlights of southern England, starting in the capital. After London's museums and monuments, tour seaside towns, legendary historic sights and some of England's most stunning cities, with some time to soak up the scenery along the way.

1

### LONDON 2 DAYS

The capital (p50) has it all – amazing free museums, magnificent monuments, royal memorabilia, stellar nightlife, spectacular shopping and to-die-for dining at every price point. There are lush green spaces where you can escape the London crowds. Whatever else you do, devote a day to the British Museum and the Kensington Museums and you'll leave full of knowledge about this history-steeped island.

*1½ hours*

2

### BRIGHTON 1 DAY

The English seaside is something else – a burst of colour and noise that is as much about what goes on behind the beach as what happens on the shore. An easy train ride from London will plonk you amid the seagulls and slot machines of Brighton (p153), the setting for some of England's most boisterous and inclusive nightlife. You might even find time to look at the sea!

*2 hours*

3

### STONEHENGE 1 DAY

Stonehenge (p257) isn't quite the same spiritual encounter with the ages that it once was, but this looming circle of standing stones is still a remarkable place to consider how England's history has been shaped over the centuries. Come for the summer solstice to see Stonehenge at its most uninhibited.

*1 hour*

***Detour:** Tack on a visit to nearby Avebury for more neolithic history without the hordes. 3 hours. 1 hour*



DAN BRECKWOLDT/SHUTTERSTOCK ©, MICHAELASBEST/SHUTTERSTOCK ©, WILLIAM TOTI/500PX ©

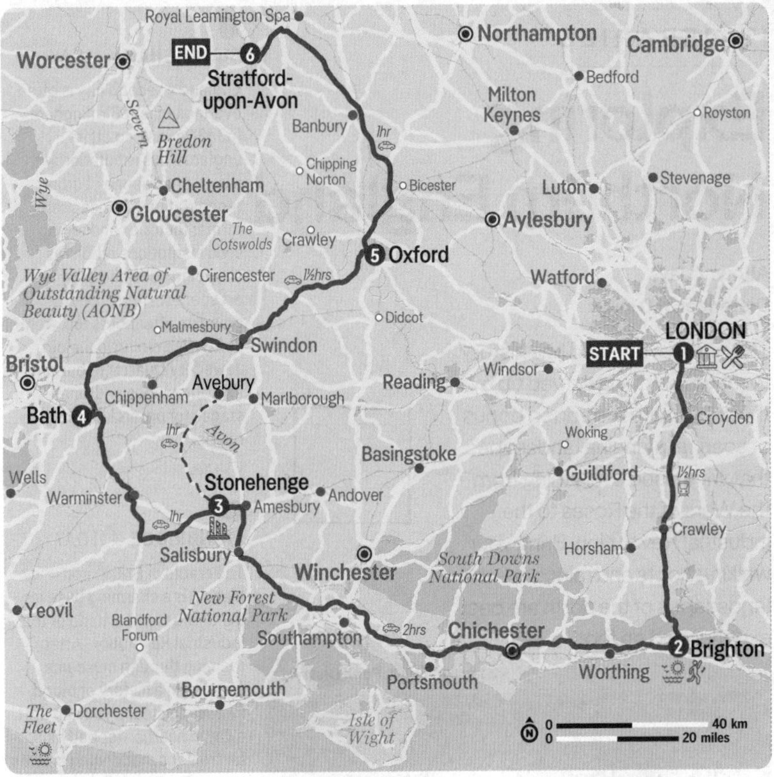

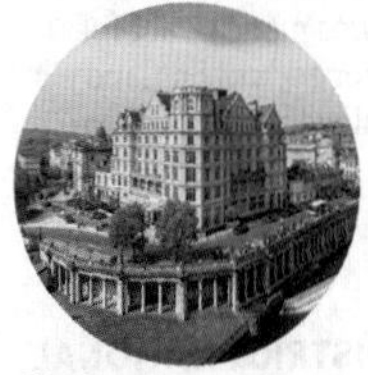

4

### BATH 1 DAY

Hewn from soft, golden limestone, the World Heritage-listed city of Bath (p233) is a true beauty. The Romans were the first to develop the hot springs bubbling under the Somerset hills, but it was the Georgians who transformed the streets of Bath into the height of period glamour. Despite the swirling crowds, visiting still feels a bit like being whisked away into an English historical drama.

*1½ hours*

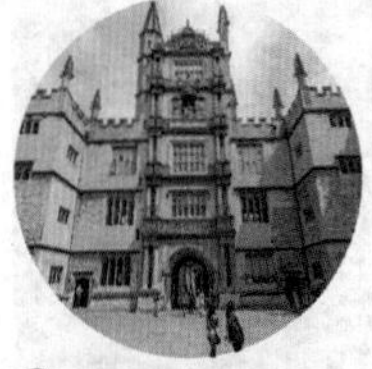

5

### OXFORD 1 DAY

For an experience as English as high tea, it's a close call between Oxford and Cambridge. But we nominate Oxford (p184) for its proximity to the picturesque villages of the Cotswolds. In the city, though, all eyes are on the historic colleges, with their ancient chapels, heirloom libraries and arcane traditions. Rent a bicycle to explore and feel like an Oxford don for the day.

*1 hour*

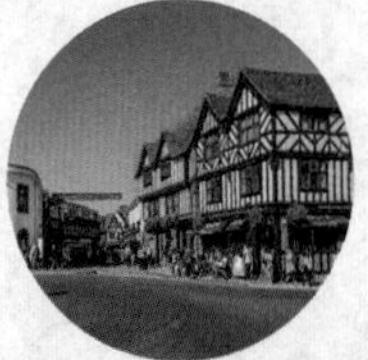

6

### STRATFORD-UPON-AVON 1 DAY

If you can leave Stratford-upon-Avon (p383) without buying at least a Shakespeare pencil, you've done well. The hometown of England's most celebrated playwright isn't shy about exploiting its literary heritage, but after touring the half-timbered homes where the Bard lived and wrote, and seeing a show by the Royal Shakespeare Company on its home stage, we suspect you won't mind.

ALEXEY FEDORENKO/SHUTTERSTOCK ©, CHRISTIAN MUELLER/SHUTTERSTOCK ©, CLAUDIO DIVIZIA/SHUTTERSTOCK ©

ITINERARIES

# Exploring Northern England

**Allow:** 7 days

**Distance:** 350 miles

The north of England has history to match anything served up by the south, with the added bonus of soaring, plunging landscapes that witnessed everything from the Wars of the Roses to the Industrial Revolution. Bring your walking boots and raincoat – the landscapes of the north are best experienced on foot.

Stanage Edge, Peak District

VALDIS SKUDRE/SHUTTERSTOCK ©

1

## BIRMINGHAM 1 DAY

England's second city is often overlooked, but Birmingham (p368) is shaking off its unglamorous reputation with a bold programme of urban regeneration that has seen former factories and fading civic institutions reborn as shopping hubs and edgy art spaces. There's plenty going on after hours too, from Indian fine dining in the old Jewellery Quarter to buzzing microbreweries and small stages for up-and-coming bands.

*1 hour*

2

## IRONBRIDGE 1 DAY

The cradle of British iron-making is a charming base for exploring the heartland of the Industrial Revolution. After roaming through museums steeped in a history of blood, sweat and steam, you can drift away in heather-topped hills, far from the maddening crowds. In between are delightful small towns made beautiful by the proceeds of England's industrial great leap forward. (p396)

*2 hours*

3

## PEAK DISTRICT NATIONAL PARK 1 DAY

Walkers and climbers gather like moths around a flame in the purple moorlands of the Peak District (p407), where stone-walled towns and disused railways lines reinvented as cycle paths provide easy access to inimitable English views from the higher ground. Scattered around the hills are lavish stately homes whose grandeur stands in marked contrast with the austere cathedrals to industry all around.

*1½ hour*

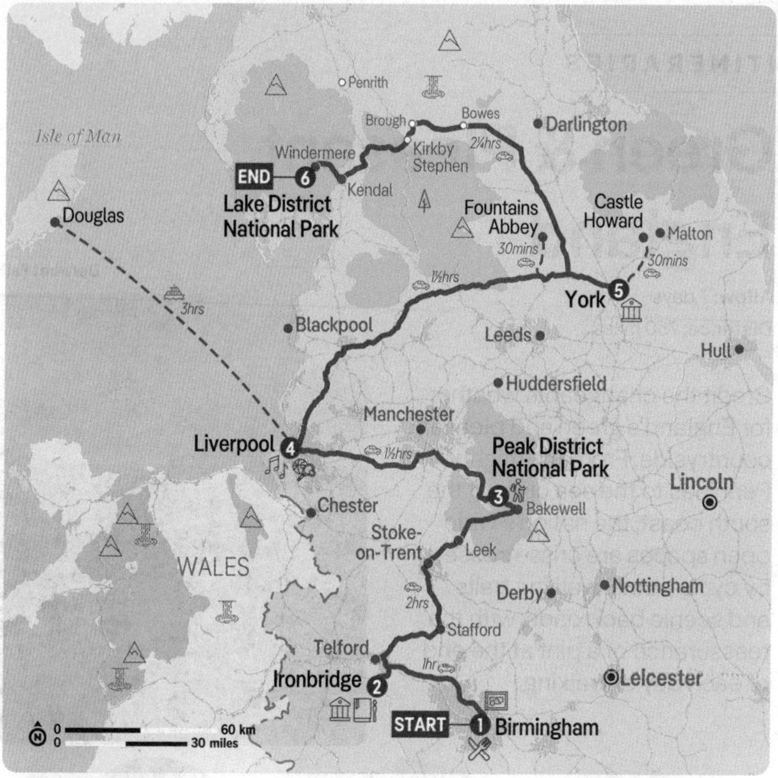

❹
### LIVERPOOL ⏱1 DAY

Come to Liverpool (p504) for the Beatles but stay for the grand architecture, the dockland history and the genre-busting museums. Football fans go football crazy at Anfield, while gourmets eat their fill in a city that is boldly throwing off the stereotypes.

*1½ hour*

***Detour:** A 55-mile ferry ride from Liverpool, the Isle of Man is Unesco-listed for its rugged, wave-carved coastline. 5 hours 3 hours*

❺
### YORK ⏱1 DAY

Timeless York (p438) serves up the best of Yorkshire on a platter – rich history, cosy pubs, a grand cathedral, Tudor and Viking treasures, the country's best railway museum and the green spaces of the Yorkshire Dales and North York Moors within easy striking distance of the city centre.

*2¼ hour*

***Detour:** Use York as an atmospheric base for a day trip to Castle Howard or Fountains Abbey. 4 hours 30 minutes*

❻
### LAKE DISTRICT NATIONAL PARK ⏱2 DAYS

The fame of England's best-loved national park (p550) precedes it, but the crowds do little to mar the grandeur of the mountains, lakes and valleys on all sides. This is the country's favourite place to take a walk, so expect some company on the treks up Helvellyn, Scafell Pike and the Old Man of Coniston. Come in spring or autumn to enjoy the scenery with smaller crowds.

ITINERARIES

# Green & Pleasant England

**Allow:** 7 days

**Distance:** 750 miles

Credit the changeable weather for England's green and pleasant countryside. From the mighty Pennines to the sea cliffs of the south coast, the nation's wide open spaces are criss-crossed by cycle paths, walking trails and scenic backroads, with the reassurance of a pint at the end of each day of walking.

Derwent Fells

## 1 DARTMOOR NATIONAL PARK 1 DAY

Start the journey into England's wild side in one of the country's most dramatic national parks (p295)– an elemental landscape of stunted forests, exposed hillsides and tortured granite tors. Within day-tripping distance of Devon's beaches and Cornwall's surf breaks, Dartmoor is a place for wild walks followed by a restorative beverage in a trinket-filled country pub on the park fringes.

*3 hours*

## 2 SOUTH DOWNS WAY 1 DAY

Linking Eastbourne and Winchester, the South Downs Way (p159) winds across a petrified wave of chalk hills, with birds of prey hovering overhead and epic coastal views from atop the white cliffs. For maximum drama, concentrate on the section between Eastbourne and Alfriston, where lighthouses dot the trail and the landscape plummets dizzyingly down to a sparkling sea at Beachy Head.

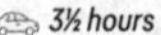

## 3 RSPB MINSMERE 1 DAY

For birders, there's nowhere better than Minsmere, a serene sweep of marshes and reed beds tucked between the charming seaside towns of Aldeburgh and Southwold (p356). In this waterlogged wonderland, bordered by silent beaches, bitterns boom, marsh harriers swoop and curlews call. Bird numbers peak in the spring and summer so bring your binoculars and tick off some serious British birdlife.

*5 hours.*

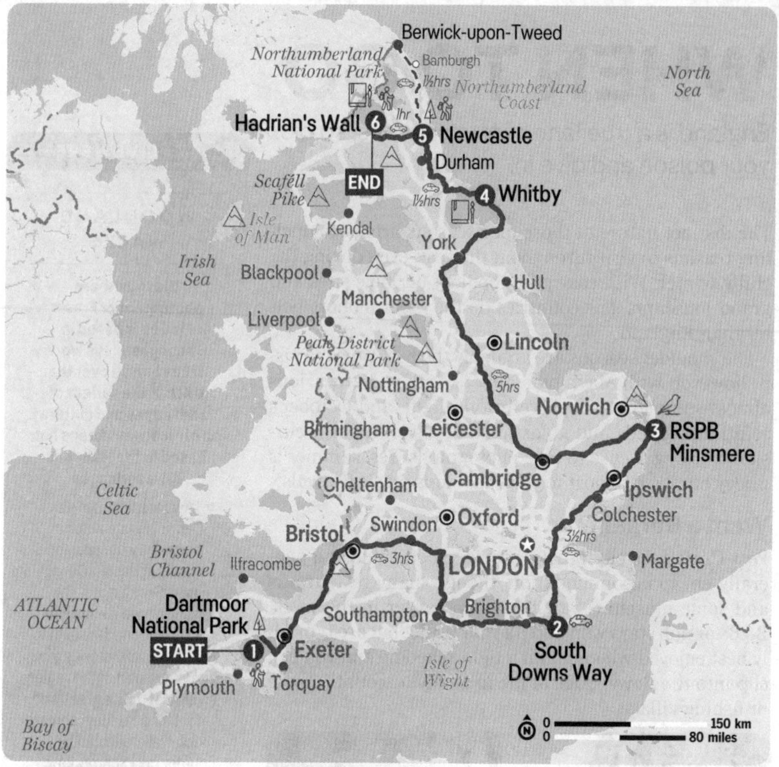

Berwick-upon-Tweed
Northumberland National Park
Bamburgh
1½hrs
Northumberland Coast
North Sea
1hr
Hadrian's Wall 6
5 Newcastle
END
Durham
Scafell Pike
½hrs
4 Whitby
Isle of Man
Kendal
York
Irish Sea
Blackpool
Hull
Manchester
Liverpool
Peak District National Park
Lincoln
Nottingham
5hrs
Norwich
Birmingham
Leicester
3 RSPB Minsmere
Cambridge
Celtic Sea
Cheltenham
Ipswich
Colchester
Oxford
Swindon
Bristol
3½hrs
Bristol Channel
3hrs
Ilfracombe
LONDON
Margate
ATLANTIC OCEAN
Dartmoor National Park
Southampton
Brighton
2 South Downs Way
START 1
Exeter
Isle of Wight
Plymouth
Torquay
Bay of Biscay
0 150 km
0 80 miles

4

**WHITBY** 1 DAY

Whitby (p460) serves up a sampling platter of scenery, history and literary connections. Above the stone-built harbour and the town's long, sandy beach, the spectral remains of Whitby Abbey are a pilgrimage destination for *Dracula* fans, while inland, North York Moors National Park beckons to walkers and mountain bikers. Add in the country's best fish and chips and you've got one epic day at the seaside.

*1½ hours.*

5

**NEWCASTLE** 2 DAYS

Compared to the Lake District, Northumberland National Park is blissfully uncrowded, and fun-filled Newcastle (p555) is the ideal base. Devote one day to the 'toon', with its proud northern heritage, and another to day trips into the greenery.

*1 hour*

***Detour:*** *As well as Northumberland National Park, consider a day trip to Durham or the scenic coastline between Bamburgh and Berwick-upon-Tweed. 3 hours 30 minutes-1½ hours*

6

**HADRIAN'S WALL** 1 DAY

It takes a week to walk the full length of Hadrian's Wall (p567), but you can get a taste of the drama of this famous fortification by sticking to the central section, where the wall strains over a chain of rolling hills. Focus on the trail between the Housesteads and Chesters forts, where timeworn ruins reveal the scale of this epic Roman endeavour.

# WHEN TO GO

England is a true land of four seasons, so pick your poison and dive in.

The distinct nature of those four seasons brings compelling reasons to visit throughout the year, even during the chilly winter. With cosy pubs, opulent heritage sites and grand museums, few countries do the great indoors better than England.

The shoulder seasons are arguably the best times to visit, however, with May's blooming flowers and gregarious almost-summer atmosphere in full flight, and October's scintillating reds and golds making any outdoor excursion one long excuse to take photographs. Yes, summer is pricey but it's also host to some fabulous music festivals.

## Want a Bargain?

Post-Christmas city breaks provide good value and generally cheap accommodation, though many restaurants and some museums won't be open earlier in the week. B&Bs or pub stays won't break your wallet but are typically best enjoyed when not on a tight schedule and you can slip into the slower pace of life in an idyllic country town or fishing village.

WILLIAM BARTON/SHUTTERSTOCK ©

Regent St (p68)

I LIVE HERE

### WOODLAND WALKS

**Glasgow-born photographer Fraser McGee is based in Birmingham. His work takes him all over the UK, but the variety of landscapes and culture on offer always keeps him based in the Midlands @frasermcgee**

'I love visiting the Peak District in late autumn, especially the ancient woods of Padley Gorge near Grindleford. The moss-covered twisted trees and abandoned Industrial Revolution mill stones give this unique part of the region an almost-Tolkien feel, and is ideal for a Sunday morning dog walk followed by a country pub Sunday lunch. November is the ideal month to see those autumnal colours at their best, and the 18th-century Chequers Inn at nearby Froggatt Edge does a great roast with fine local ales too.'

### RAINY DAYS

The Lake District is England's wettest region, receiving an average of 130in (330cm) of rain each year. Seathwaite – a village in the Lake District – is the wettest inhabited place in the UK.

## Weather Through the Year

| JANUARY | FEBRUARY | MARCH | APRIL | MAY | JUNE |
|---|---|---|---|---|---|
| Ave. daytime max: **8°C** | Ave. daytime max: **9°C** | Ave. daytime max: **12°C** | Ave. daytime max: **16°C** | Ave. daytime max: **18°C** | Ave. daytime max: **21°C** |
| Days of rainfall: **12** | Days of rainfall: **10** | Days of rainfall: **9** | Days of rainfall: **9** | Days of rainfall: **8** | Days of rainfall: **8** |

### LONDON'S URBAN HEAT ISLAND

London is subject to a phenomenon known as the 'urban heat island' – where high concentrations of heat-absorbing materials such as roads, pavements and buildings lead to significantly warmer temperatures than in surrounding areas.

## Big Bash Festivals

**Glastonbury** Nearly a quarter of a million people descend on Worthy Farm to catch the big-name acts performing at this monster music festival (p247). **June**

Running since 1769, the **London Summer Exhibition** in Mayfair showcases a smorgasbord of art, including prints, painting, film and photography, architecture and sculpture. **June & July**

**Brighton Pride** is one of the year's biggest LGBTIQ+ events and this colourful three-day celebration features live performances, a parade through the city centre, an Arts & Film Festival and a Pride Dog Show. **August**

Brilliantly bookish conversations abound for 10 days at the **Cheltenham Literature Festival**, which attracts some of the world's biggest names speaking at over 500 events. **October**

### I LIVE HERE

### SUMMER WAVES

**Nick Hounsfield is a Bristol-based surfer, social entrepreneur and founder of *The Wave*, the first inland surfing destination of its kind @wavemakernick**

'The South West coastline, and especially North Devon and Cornwall, holds a special place in my heart and is somewhere I've escaped to every summer since childhood. I love spending time in and around the water, whether that's surfing at some of the secret spots around St Ives, fishing off the rocks at Trevone or watching the sun slip down on the vast horizon at the end of the day – it's my medicine and always resets me, putting a massive smile on my face.'

## Local & Quirkier Festivals

Wrap up and head to the **North York Moors & Yorkshire Dales Dark Skies Festival** (p467) for some of England's clearest and most entrancing evenings. Activities include astrophotography workshops, stargazing safaris, children's trails and mindful experiences. **February**

Thought to have Pagan origins, the **Padstow 'Obby 'Oss** celebration is a bizarre street procession with two people dressed as horses (osses) accompanied by traditional music provided by drums and accordion, as well as costumed dancers. **May**

The **Robin Hood Festival** (p424) takes place (unsurprisingly) in Sherwood Forest and features Medieval re-enactments, jousting, swordplay lessons, open-air theatre performances and archery at Major Oak. **July**

England's biggest bonfire night celebration of its kind, **Bonfire Night** in Lewes (p159) sees a series of torchlit processions through the town's narrow streets alongside spectacular firework displays. **November**

### THE WARMING GULF STREAM EFFECT

Western Cornwall and the Isles of Scilly sit on the eastern edge of the Gulf Stream and thus enjoy a mild maritime climate, warmer winters and more hours of sunshine than the rest of England.

| JULY | AUGUST | SEPTEMBER | OCTOBER | NOVEMBER | DECEMBER |
|---|---|---|---|---|---|
| Ave. daytime max: **24°C** | Ave. daytime max: **22°C** | Ave. daytime max: **20°C** | Ave. daytime max: **16°C** | Ave. daytime max: **12°C** | Ave. daytime max: **9°C** |
| Days of rainfall: **7** | Days of rainfall: **8** | Days of rainfall: **8** | Days of rainfall: **11** | Days of rainfall: **11** | Days of rainfall: **11** |

LEFT: DANIEL LIMPI/EYEEM/GETTY IMAGES © RIGHT: SEE-SAW FILMS/ALBUM/ALAMY STOCK PHOTO ©

# GET PREPARED FOR ENGLAND

Useful things to load in your bag, your ears and your brain.

## Clothes

**Layers** Preparing for all types of weather is an essential part of the English experience. England's maritime location in the North Atlantic means that even in summer biting winds and untimely rain showers can unexpectedly scupper a balmy afternoon. So if you're carrying a backpack, make the most of its space and pack a jumper or hoodie and a waterproof jacket.

**Walking boots** For a small densely populated country, England has a lot of wild coast and rural countryside where waterproof walking boots will be essential for a comfortable experience.

**Hats** A thick-knitted hat will be your best friend if you're visiting between November and March.

### Manners

Sometimes polite to a fault, the English are orderly queuers. **If you jump a line, expect stern looks** and grumbling at the very least.

Like their Canadian cousins, the English have a **confusing habit of apologising** with a quick 'sorry' even if they're not in the wrong.

The English **don't usually tip bar staff**, but not leaving something after a meal may be considered rude.

**Umbrella** Outside the summer months, a small umbrella may be worth bringing. Most city centre hotels should provide complimentary umbrellas, however, if the heavens do open.

## READ

**Girl, Woman, Other** (Bernardine Evaristo; 2019) Booker Prize-winning novel following the lives and struggles of 12 people – most of whom are black women – in modern Britain.

**Empireland** (Sathnam Sanghera; 2021) An impassioned and deeply personal journey through Britain's imperial past and present that, Sanghera argues, still shapes English society today.

**Middle England** (Jonathan Coe; 2018) A funny and compelling state-of-the-nation novel offering a multilayered portrait of pre- and post-Brexit Britain at its most confused.

**Watching the English** (Kate Fox; 2014) A revealing and fascinating anthropological look at the quirks, habits and behaviour of English people.

### Words

**Alright** is a quick way of asking, 'How are you?'. Often just the single word is used as a question, with an inflection at the end. Can also be used to say 'hello'.

**Sorry** is a formal apology used in many situations. For example, if you bump into somebody (a frequent occurrence in London). You might also hear 'pardon' used in the same manner.

**Mate** is a common form of address and term of endearment with friends. Generally used in informal situations, and can sometimes be interchanged with more region-specific words like 'pal' in the north or 'geezer' in the south.

**Cheers** is used as a toast or to raise a glass (as the rest of the English-speaking world does), but it is also frequently used to say 'thanks'.

**Excuse me** is a formal way of getting somebody's attention. Always useful, whether you're trying to signal a waiter at a restaurant or an attendant at a ticket office.

**Quid** is common informal slang for the currency, the British Pound.

**Take-out coffee** is often heard at cafes, and is the equivalent of the American English of coffee 'to-go'.

**Tube** is the alternate (and quicker) way of saying Underground, when discussing London's famous underground metro system.

**Footie** is a shorter way of referring to football, England's national sporting obsession and is often used in regards to the Premier League. As in, 'You watching the footie tonight?'.

## WATCH

**This Is England** (2006) Drama about Northern England's working-class youth and its various subcultures in the turbulent 1980s.

**The Office** (2001–2003) Iconic mockumentary comedy about the minutiae and frivolity of life in a tepid English office environment.

**The Crown** (2016–present) Historic drama about England's most famous family, during the reign and life of Queen Elizabeth II.

**Peaky Blinders** (2013–2022) Crime series set in 1920s Birmingham following a gang loosely based on a real-life gang.

**Heartstopper** (2022–present) Uplifting coming-of-age drama (pictured) that positively represents a full spectrum of LGBTIQ+ identities.

## LISTEN

**Sgt Pepper's Lonely Hearts Club Band** (The Beatles; 1967) Groundbreaking combination of rock, pop, music hall, vaudeville, jazz, blues and Indian styles from England's greatest musical export.

**Kiwanuka** (Michael Kiwanuka; 2019) Winner of the 2020 Mercury Prize, Kiwanuka's third album is an expansive career-defining, genre-straddling masterpiece.

**Whatever People Say I Am, That's What I'm Not** (Arctic Monkeys; 2006) Killer indie tunes paired with witty observations of English youth culture that still sounds fresh today.

**Prioritise Pleasure** (Self Esteem; 2021) Rebecca Taylor brings big pop anthems with dark witty lyrics addressing institutional sexism, street harassment, insecurity and much more.

CIVIL/SHUTTERSTOCK ©

Scotch eggs

# THE FOOD SCENE

## Making the most of its abundant produce and vast coastline, English restaurants now offer some of Europe's finest eating experiences.

Stereotypes about the English are sometimes painfully true, though the one about the poor quality of English food can be consigned to history. Where once complex gastronomy was an afterthought, the country is now awash with sublime restaurants offering a strong emphasis on fresh locally grown ingredients, amid an ever-expanding array of Michelin stars.

As a windswept northern European nation, a hearty base of meat and potatoes has been the standard starting point for English cuisine and this is still the case for quintessential favourites like Sunday roasts and fish and chips. However, with the global influx of England's migrant population, this has now evolved into a much broader palette.

And in recent years, young chefs have been showcasing their creativity at street food festivals and open-air markets, bringing unique flavours and interpretations to wider audiences. There's now an expectation of quality, from the freshest produce to well-crafted textures and colours to add balance. England is serious about food and can't wait to show you why.

### Evolution at Home

English homecooking is all about warmth and comfort, and historically that has meant a reliance on meat, pastry and root vegetables. Hearty classics include sausage and mash, steak and kidney pie and shepherd's pie.

MARCIN JUCHA/SHUTTERSTOCK ©

Battenberg cake

However, England's increasingly multicultural population means a world of techniques, ingredients and flavours have been brought into its homes, adding a whole new dimension to English cooking. Turmeric and cumin from India, honey beans and yarri from west Africa, pimentón from Spain, ackee from Jamaica, soy sauce from China and the aromas of much more now pour out of kitchens up and down the country.

**CURRIES & AFTERNOON TEA**

For more information on food, see p586

## Vegetarians & Vegans

England isn't as wedded to meat as some of its European neighbours, but this is still a pastoral farming nation with meat and dairy products at its core. That said, vegetarian and vegan options have never been better and England's meat-free landscape now includes vegan cafes, vegetarian-only pizza joints and far more accommodating menus at pubs and restaurants.

Indian, Thai, Bangladeshi and Chinese restaurants are plentiful and sometimes will have over half their menus crammed with delicious veggie dishes. Even classic full English breakfasts and Sunday roasts will easily be converted to meat-free, either on the menu or simply just by asking.

## At the Coast

With almost 3000 miles of coastline, seafood has formed a huge part of English cuisine that goes far beyond the traditional staple of fish and chips. From Whitstable oysters to freshly caught Northumberland lobster, the English coast is a diverse gastronomic canvas rich for exploring throughout the year.

Cornwall is particularly well-known for its seafood and the far-flung county in the southwest is well worth the journey. Make sure to sample shellfish platters, john dory, Porthilly rock oysters, Cornish crab and the bizarrely titled Stargazy Pie.

DRONG/SHUTTERSTOCK ©

Cornish pasty

PADMAYOGINI/SHUTTERSTOCK ©

### FOOD & DRINK FESTIVALS

**Big Apple** Visit busy cideries and take in rolling orchard views while sampling local cider and perry at this harvest-time Herefordshire festival in October.

**Isle of Man Food & Drink Festival** Explore the finest Manx cooking and produce every September on the island in the Irish Sea.

**Yorkshire Dales Cheese Festival** A celebration of Yorkshire's cheese in the home of Wensleydale with artisan cheesemakers every October.

**Porthleven Food Festival** Three-day April feast showcasing the best in Cornish produce and flavours.

**Whitstable Oyster Festival** (pictured) Celebrate summer on the north Kent coast in oyster-obsessed Whitstable.

**Beer on the Wye** Riverside beer festival in Hereford every July serving up ales of myriad styles and strengths.

## Specialities

### Sweet Treats

**Battenburg cake** Check-pattern sponge cake wrapped in marzipan.
**Arctic roll** Vanilla ice-cream cake in a thin layer of sponge.
**Sticky toffee pudding** Sponge cake drowned in toffee sauce.
**Mince pie** Sweet fruit pie often served at Christmas.
**Flapjack** Sweet chewy oat bar.

### Local Favourites

**Cornish pasty** Shortcrust pastry filled with beef and vegetables.
**Balti** Fiery one-pot curry found across Birmingham.
**Scouse** Hearty Liverpudlian stew.
**Pie and mash** Traditional working-class London meal.

### Cheap Treats

**Sausage roll** Sausage meat enclosed in puffed pastry.
**Scotch egg** Boiled egg cloaked in sausage meat and breadcrumbs.
**Chip butty** A sandwich filled with chips.
**Pork pie** Cold pork wrapped in crimped pastry.

Marmite

### Dare to Try

**Black pudding** A type of sausage made from pig's blood. The latter – unsurprisingly – can be off-putting to many, until they try it.
**Jellied eels** Traditional dish born in London's East End. Its appearance is arguably even more off-putting than its name.
**Mushy peas** Marrowfat peas soaked in water, creating a thick, green paste. Classic accompaniment to fish and chips in northern England.
**Marmite** Salty spread made from yeast extract. As the slogan goes, you either love it or hate it.
**Stargazy pie** Fish pie from Cornwall with sardine heads poking out through the pastry. Pure nightmare fuel.

### MEALS OF A LIFETIME

**Opheem** (p372) Chef Aktar Islam's progressive Indian cuisine is a window into Birmingham's gastronomic evolution and the city's newest Michelin-star restaurant.

**Emily Scott** (p305)Surfing scenes and coastal views pair up nicely with chef Emily Scott's sublime local seafood menu plucked straight from the waters off Newquay in Cornwall.

**Menu Gordon Jones** (p237) The eponymous chef at this Bath restaurant chooses what you'll be eating (and drinking). It's off-beat, experimental cooking at its best.

**Black Swan at Oldstead** (p446) An old country pub nestled on the edge of the North York Moors driven by produce from their farm to craft stunning modern British cuisine.

### THE YEAR IN FOOD

**SPRING**

Spring's shoots bring a plethora of green vegetables like cabbage, kale and asparagus. It's a good time to hit the coast too and enjoy seafood like Cornish crab before the crowds of summer appear.

**SUMMER**

While lighter foods like green beans, courgettes and fresh peas seem perfect for summer, salad season is balanced out by the English thirst for a sizzling BBQ loaded with beef steaks, sausages and lamb chops.

**AUTUMN**

Harvest season is a great time to explore the colourful countryside, especially towards the apple orchards of the southwest where the cider is flowing. Look out for root vegetables and, of course, pumpkins.

**WINTER**

The dark winter months are when the hearty English classics thrive. Warming dishes stuffed with meat, vegetables and pastry like shepherd's pie, sausage and mash and Lancashire hotpot are perfect for toasty nights in.



I WEI HUANG/SHUTTERSTOCK ©, SMPOLY/SHUTTERSTOCK ©, PETER TURNER PHOTOGRAPHY/SHUTTERSTOCK ©, ISTETIANA/SHUTTERSTOCK ©

Lancashire hotpot

LEFT: SHINAI79/SHUTTERSTOCK © RIGHT: OLGABOMBOLOGNA/SHUTTERSTOCK ©

JAZZLOVE/SHUTTERSTOCK ©

Stanage Edge (p410)

# THE OUTDOORS

From wild coasts to blustery green summits, England's pastoral landscape changes with the seasons and brings an ever-evolving challenge to intrepid adventurers.

An island nation, England's temperate maritime climate means that outdoor activities are available all year round, usually without worry of extreme weather. With 2,748 miles (4422km) of coastline, walks along England's wind-whipped shores, particularly around the Jurassic Coast, are seductive, while the cinematic hills and valleys of the Peak District and Lake District offer widescreen hikes with magnificent views. Cycling in these climes is exceptional too, though a roll through England's chocolate box villages and hamlets can be just as rewarding.

## Walking & Hiking

Even if it doesn't possess the soaring peaks of its Alpine European neighbours, England's rolling landscape brings some spectacular walks, and its trails are ideal – for the most part – to walkers of all ages and abilities throughout the year. England's density also means many are within easy reach of large urban centres. And while grandiose hikes are always a satisfying challenge, don't forget to mix these up with lush forest trails including stops for beers in quaint countryside villages to truly make the most of your time crossing this ancient land. Just remember to stick to official tracks, as 92% of the English countryside is private and off-limits for walkers.

Autumn and its brilliant red and gold canvas is perhaps the prettiest time of year for walking, though May's returning warmth, bright foliage and jovial beer gardens makes

**Wild Outdoor Options**

**ROCK CLIMBING**
Scale the long-famous gritstone outcrop of **Stanage Edge** in the Peak District (p410).

**MOUNTAIN BIKING**
Hit the dirt on the many spectacular trails cutting through **Yorkshire's dales and moors** (p457).

**WINDSURFING**
Set up sail and scoot across the water at blustery **Portland Harbour** (p273).

### FAMILY ADVENTURES

**Glide through Birmingham's historic canals** on an eco-friendly electric boat from **GoBoat (p371)** in Brindley Place.

**Dare to explore the Forbidden Corner** (p456), a large folly garden of spine-chilling installations above and below ground on the edge of the Yorkshire Dales.

**Take the kids out on a day boat** (or kayak, for the more adventurous) through the charming rivers of the **Norfolk Broads (p251)**.

Go off-road in search of magnificent red-deer stags on a **wildlife safari across the heathlands of Exmoor** (p249).

**Search for fairies** amid the green foliage and woodland beauty of **Summerhill Glen** (p514) on the Isle of Man.

for an alluring combination and might be ideal to avoid the summer crowds. Put on your boots, pack for all weather possibilities (this is Britain, after all) and explore this green and pleasant land.

## Cycling

The English countryside's languid lanes and gentle hills are a perfect match for the casual cyclist, though it's certainly a good idea to wait for the clearer and warmer skies of summer before putting foot to pedal. While popular places like the Cotswolds are the romantic embodiment of this, look out for the generally flat disused former railway lines that often weave through some stunning and easily reachable landscapes. From crossing Victorian viaducts on Derbyshire's Monsal Trail to leafy coastal routes like Cornwall's Camel Trail, they make cycling adventures possible for everyone.

For those who need a bigger challenge, there are plentiful grand circuits like the Lake District's 65km Lakeland Loop. Yorkshire's swooping Settle Circular is of a similar leg-aching length, and is wisely attacked across a couple of days to make the most of the county's picturesque village pitstops. England's car-centric culture makes city cycling more trouble than it's worth, though the likes of bike-friendly Bristol and Cambridge are trying to change that image.

**Surfing, Fistral Beach (p306)**

## Surfing

You don't need the balmy heat of California or Hawaii to have a good time surfing, and England's eclectic coastline offers challenges in waves (pun intended). The wild windswept beaches of the southwest, and Cornwall in particular, are the English surfing epicentre and the North Atlantic pummels the coast with unrelenting breaks. Head to Newquay for the fullest experience.

Wetsuits are a must for those brave enough to hit the waves during winter, while the most pleasant (and crowded) conditions will be between June and August. Hit the untamed and feral shores of Northumberland for a more offbeat blast.

**CAVING**
Pack a torch to explore the evocatively named **Thor's Cave** in Staffordshire (p422).

**WILD SWIMMING**
Brave the cold and get away from London's hum by going wild swimming in **Hampstead Heath** (p457).

**LONG-DISTANCE HIKING**
Cross the 34-mile Cheshire Sandstone Trail for some fabulous views over the **Cheshire Plains** (p502).

**FISHING**
Slow down in the **Lake District** and set up a quiet spot to fish for pike, roach, eels and salmon (p524).

# ACTION AREAS

Where to find England's best outdoor activities.

### Surfing

1. Newquay (p306)
2. Croyde (p298)
3. Severn Bore (p209)
4. Cromer (p352)
5. Whitby (p462)
6. Long Sands Beach (p560)

### Cycling

1. Brighton Pier to Saltdean Pool (p156)
2. Camel Trail (p302)
3. Strawberry Line Path (p241)
4. Chilterns Cycleway (p218)
5. Buttertubs Pass (p452)
6. Curlew Cycle Route (p565)

### Walking/Hiking

1. Seven Sisters Cliff Walk (p159)
2. Dartmoor Tors (p295)
3. Mam Tor (p409)
4. Malham Cove (p450)
5. Ribble Valley (p498)
6. Great Langdale (p540)

## Swimming

1. Hampstead Heath (p106)
2. Jubilee Pool Penzance (p315)
3. Porthcurno (p314)
4. Durdle Door (p272)
5. Cirenchester Open Air Swimming Pool (p203)
6. Janet's Foss Waterfall (p451)
7. Port St Mary (p515)

## National Parks

1. South Downs National Park (p159)
2. Peak District National Park (p407)
3. Exmoor National Park (p252)
4. Yorkshire Dales Nationl Park (p449)
5. Lake District National Park (p552)
6. Northumberland National Park (p564)

ENGLAND

# THE GUIDE



Lake District National Park (p550)

# LONDON

## DEEP HISTORY OF IRREPRESSIBLE SPIRIT

London's story started nearly 2000 years ago, and the city's history is displayed through instantly recognisable landmarks, such as St Paul's Cathedral and Big Ben.

London's architecture tells a unique and beguiling biography; tireless innovation is built into the city's fabric. The capital's deep-rooted past is accented by modern structures – the Shard, the Gherkin and Tate Modern – but it never drowns out London's centuries-old narrative. Major projects continue to move London forward, such as the 2022 opening of the Elizabeth line, the 73-mile east–west railway that extends across the capital and into neighbouring counties. The regenerated Battersea Power Station, a 1940s power plant turned shopping centre, became accessible to the public for the first time in 2022 and still has many of its industrial features preserved.

London is a city of concrete plans but also of ideas and the imagination – whether it's theatrical innovation, contemporary art, pioneering music, cutting-edge design or global cuisine. It's a place where wide-open vistas and sight-packed, high-density streets exist in unison. Add in charming parks, historic neighbourhoods, leafy suburbs and tranquil riverbanks and you have, quite simply, one of the world's great metropolises.

A cosmopolitan dynamism makes London one of the planet's most international cities, yet one that remains intrinsically British. This diverse city is deeply multicultural, with two of five Londoners foreign-born, representing 270 nationalities and speaking 300 languages. The UK may have voted for Brexit, but the majority of Londoners didn't.

With a population nearing 10 million, London feels huge, and that can be hard to wrap your head around at first, but it becomes manageable if you treat it as the locals do: as a series of villages. This is indeed how London grew up – and grew out – as smaller communities became absorbed into the land-hungry city, and it's still noticeable along the mini high streets, with their clusters of restaurants, shops and bars. But even in central areas deemed 'touristy', Londoners can be found. You might be eavesdropping on gossiping politicos in a Westminster pub or queuing behind them at a pocket-sized restaurant in Soho.

Never settling or sitting still, London has it all: major museums, endless art galleries, renowned attractions, sweeping parks and riverside panoramas. How can you help but fall in love?

LAZYLLAMA/SHUTTERSTOCK ©

### THE MAIN AREAS

**THE WEST END**
Famous London sights and cultural experiences. p56

**THE CITY**
The capital's historic heart. p71

**THE SOUTH BANK**
River-hugging hub of theatre and art. p81

**SHOREDITCH & EAST LONDON**
Late nights at hip hangouts. p91

**CAMDEN & NORTH LONDON**
Urban village energy. p100

ALEXANDER SPATARI/GETTY IMAGES ©

Above: Regent Street (p68); left: King's Royal Guard

# Find Your Way

London is a huge and sprawling city, but the public transport network is generally a well-oiled machine that runs reliably. London's main sights are clustered around the West End, the South Bank and the City of London, and if you plan well, you'll mostly be relying on your own two feet.

Camden & North London
p100

**FROM THE AIRPORT**

London has six airports in all corners of the capital, though some use the 'London' label cheekily (London Southend is 40 miles away). London City and Heathrow are on the London Underground network. Trains and (slower but cheaper) bus services head to central London from all airports.

Notting Hill & West London
p121

The West End
p56

Science Museum

Natural History Museum

**LONDON UNDERGROUND**

The London Underground, which includes the London Overground, Docklands Light Railway (DLR) and the Elizabeth line, is the fastest and most efficient way of getting around town. Some stations are much closer together in reality than they are on the map.

**BUS**

London's red double-decker buses afford great views of the city, but the going can be slow because of traffic jams and people getting off and on at every stop. The bus network is extensive, but it's sometimes quicker to walk.

Richmond & Southwest London
p128

**Shoreditch & East London**

p91

London City (3mi)

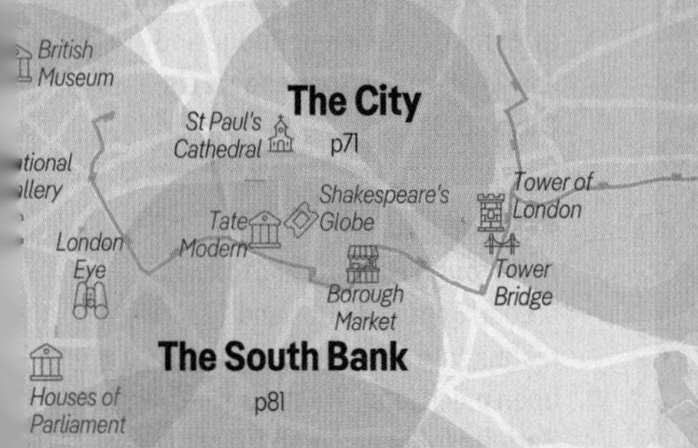


**Greenwich**

p109

Painted Hall

National Maritime Museum

Royal Observatory

**Peckham & South London**

p113

**WALK**

To explore London's neighbourhoods, you can't beat walking, though the winding streets require a good map or GPS. In central London, bridges cross the Thames at regular intervals. It can be quicker to walk than catch the Tube or bus for short distances.

Gatwick (23mi)

# Plan Your Days

Put on your comfy (but still slightly stylish) shoes and grab everything you need for a full day out in London. Your capital itinerary packs in plenty.

PPTARA/SHUTTERSTOCK ©
View from London Eye (p84)

## Day 1

### Morning

- Get your bearings at **Trafalgar Sq** (p60). See superb art in the **National Gallery** (p66) then walk down Whitehall past **No 10 Downing St** (p69) to the **Houses of Parliament** and **Big Ben** (p61). **Westminster Abbey** (p57) is nearby.

### Afternoon

- Cross Westminster Bridge to the **London Eye** (p84) then stroll the South Bank to **Tate Modern** (p83). Admire **St Paul's Cathedral** (p76) from Millennium Bridge and see what's on at **Shakespeare's Globe** (p84).

### Evening

- **Borough Market** (p86) closes around 5pm, but pubs and restaurants around its edges are open much later. Try the queue at **Padella** (p85) and grab a pint at historic **George Inn** (p87).

### YOU'LL ALSO WANT TO

Dig deeper into London's neighbourhoods, save brain power for museums big and small, and kick back with a beer after a sightseeing-packed day out.

### EXPLORE SOUTH KENSINGTON'S MUSEUMS

Visit the big three: the **Natural History Museum**, the **Science Museum** and the **Victoria & Albert Museum**.

### SHOP AT THE MARKETS

Explore London's famous markets: West London's **Portobello Road Market**, North London's **Camden Market**, and East London's **Upmarket**.

### RELAX IN A PARK

**Hyde Park** is the largest in central London, but it's got nothing on 1000-hectare **Richmond Park**, dotted with deer herds.


ILEANA_BT/SHUTTERSTOCK ©, WILLIAM PERUGINI/SHUTTERSTOCK/SHUTTERSTOCK ©,ALEXANDRE ROTENBERG/SHUTTERSTOCK ©

## Day 2

### Morning

● Lay siege to the **Tower of London** (p73) early. Take a tour with a Beefeater and marvel at the Crown Jewels. Admire Tower Bridge from the ramparts.

### Afternoon

● Source lunch from **Leadenhall Market** (p80) or the **Bloomberg Arcade** (p80) before walking to **St Paul's Cathedral** (p76). Soak up the interior splendour and climb up to see the city outside the dome.

### Evening

● Enjoy dinner in **Chinatown** (p70); from here, the West End is your oyster: grab a cocktail at **Swift** (p67) in Soho, head to the **theatre** (p85) or watch a street performance in **Covent Garden** (p61).

## Day 3

### Morning

● Spend the morning perusing the vast collection at the **British Museum** (p60).

### Afternoon

● Make your way to the river and hop on a boat from any central London pier towards Greenwich. Grab lunch at **Greenwich Market** (p112) while deciding what to tackle: the **Painted Hall** (p111), **Royal Observatory** (p110) and **National Maritime Museum** (p112) are all strong contenders.

### Evening

● Take a sunset boat ride on the river to Tower Pier and head towards Spitalfields for dinner at **Som Saa** (p97). Recount your day over top-notch cocktails at **Discount Suit Company** (p98) before setting off on a Shoreditch bar crawl.

### DRINK AT A LONDON BREWERY

Crawl the **Bermondsey Beer Mile**, sip a canalside pint at **Crate**, see what's brewing in Deptford's **Villages** and **Little Faith**.

### FIND AN HISTORIC PUB

Soak up the atmosphere and the suds in the City of London's beautiful banks-turned-bars, including **Counting House** and **Trading House**.

### DINE & DRINK IN SOUTH LONDON

When standard market sellers have closed, tiny bars and restaurants are still doing a roaring trade in **Brixton** and **Tooting**.

### SEE STATELY HOMES

Step into the past in southwest London's exquisite country estates, such as **Strawberry Hill House** and **Syon House**.

# THE WEST END

## FAMOUS LONDON SIGHTS AND CULTURAL EXPERIENCES

Home to many of London's famous museums, attractions and important royal locations, the West End packs in the lion's share of the capital's big-name sights. Throw in an excellent food scene, a thriving theatre district and top shopping streets, and it's no surprise that the West End throngs with big-city energy day and night. But that's not to say you won't also find quiet corners and delightful parks. At the heart of the city in terms of both sightseeing and geography, it's a neighbourhood that demands – and deserves – all the time you can give it.

The West End is a vague term – any Londoner will give you their own take on which neighbourhoods it does and doesn't include – but what is striking is its variety: from reverential quiet in literary Bloomsbury and legal-hub Holborn to late-night revelry in Soho and the vibrant shopping streets around Oxford Circus and Piccadilly Circus.

### TOP TIP

While the West End is well served by the London Underground, the Tube isn't always the best way to get around. Most sights are within walking distance of one another, and you'll get a much better sense of the area's atmosphere on foot.

**Buckingham Palace (p61)**

## Westminster Abbey

CHURCH OF CORONATIONS AND COMMEMORATIONS

Westminster Abbey is of such royal and national importance that it's hard to overstress its symbolic value or imagine its equivalent anywhere else in the world. Except for Edward V (murdered) and Edward VIII (abdicated), every English sovereign has been crowned here since William the Conqueror in 1066. Sixteen royals have been married here, and many have been buried here – Queen Elizabeth II's funeral took place in the Abbey in 2022 (she's buried at Windsor Castle).

A splendid mixture of architectural styles, Westminster Abbey is considered the finest example of early English Gothic. Much of the Abbey's architecture is from the 13th century, but it was founded much earlier, in 960 CE. Never a cathedral (the seat of a bishop), Westminster Abbey is a 'royal peculiar' administered by the Crown. At the heart of the Abbey is the beautifully tiled sanctuary, the stage for coronations, royal weddings and funerals.

Apart from the royal graves, keep an eye out for the many famous commoners interred here, especially in **Poets' Corner**, where you'll find the gravestones of Geoffrey Chaucer, Charles Dickens and Alfred Tennyson, as well as memorials to the other greats, such as William Shakespeare and Jane Austen. Sir Isaac Newton, Charles Darwin and the ashes of Stephen Hawking are interred in **Scientists' Corner** near the north aisle of the nave.

### ABBEY EXTRAS

Audio guides are included in the ticket price, but to get more out of your visit, book in advance to join a **verger-led tour**, which includes access to usually off-limits spaces, such as the shrine of Edward the Confessor and the Quire stalls.

Opened in 2018, the **Queen's Diamond Jubilee Galleries** are a museum space located in the medieval triforium, the arched gallery above the nave. Highlights are the graffiti-inscribed chair used for the coronation of Mary II and the 13th-century Westminster Retable, England's oldest surviving altarpiece.

**Isaac Newton monument and grave**

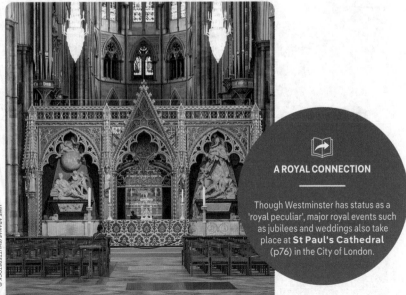

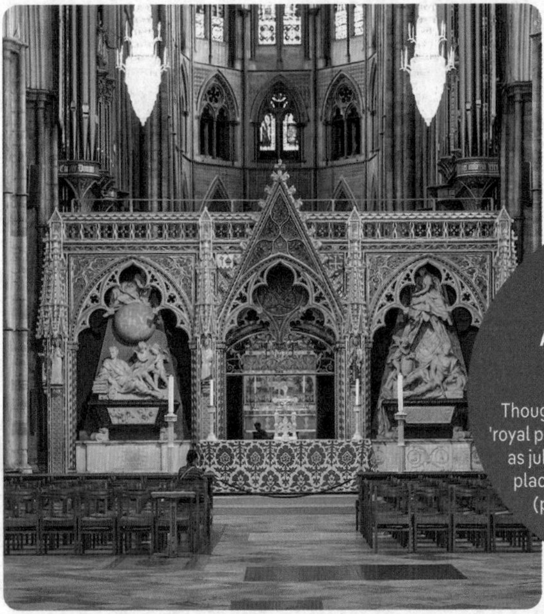

### A ROYAL CONNECTION

Though Westminster has status as a 'royal peculiar', major royal events such as jubilees and weddings also take place at **St Paul's Cathedral** (p76) in the City of London.

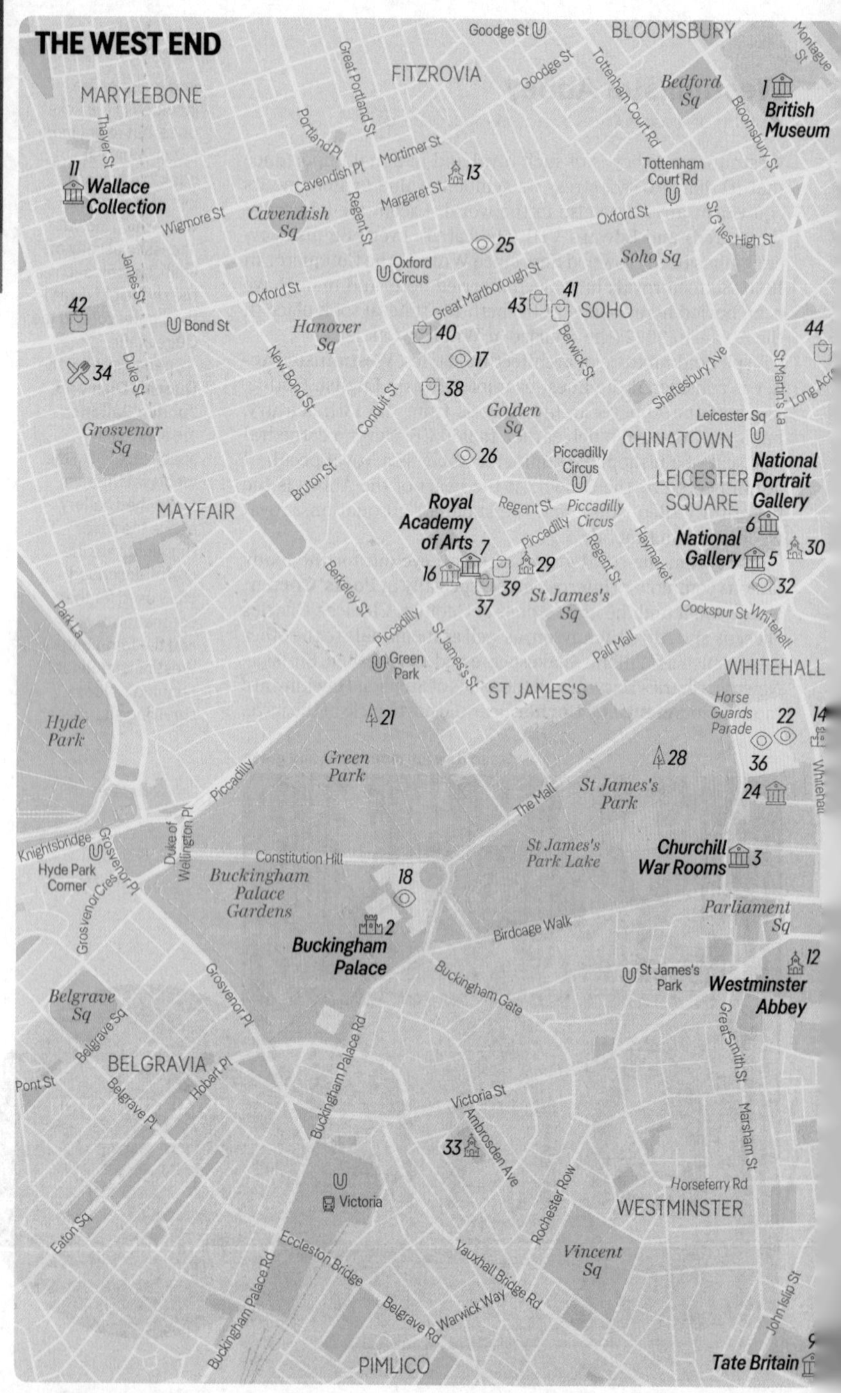
THE WEST END
MARYLEBONE
FITZROVIA
BLOOMSBURY
SOHO
CHINATOWN
LEICESTER SQUARE
MAYFAIR
ST JAMES'S
WHITEHALL
BELGRAVIA
WESTMINSTER
PIMLICO
1 British Museum
2 Buckingham Palace
3 Churchill War Rooms
5 National Gallery
6 National Portrait Gallery
7 Royal Academy of Arts
11 Wallace Collection
12 Westminster Abbey
Tate Britain
Hyde Park
Green Park
St James's Park
St James's Park Lake
Buckingham Palace Gardens
Grosvenor Sq
Cavendish Sq
Hanover Sq
Golden Sq
Soho Sq
Bedford Sq
St James's Sq
Parliament Sq
Belgrave Sq
Vincent Sq
Horse Guards Parade
Goodge St
Tottenham Court Rd
Oxford Circus
Bond St
Leicester Sq
Piccadilly Circus
Green Park
Hyde Park Corner
St James's Park
Victoria
Oxford St
Regent St
Piccadilly
The Mall
Pall Mall
Constitution Hill
Birdcage Walk
Whitehall
Victoria St
Horseferry Rd
Vauxhall Bridge Rd
Buckingham Palace Rd
Grosvenor Pl
Park La
Shaftesbury Ave
Charing Cross Rd
Haymarket
Cockspur St
New Bond St
Conduit St
Bruton St
Berkeley St
St James's St
Great Portland St
Portland Pl
Cavendish Pl
Mortimer St
Margaret St
Great Marlborough St
Berwick St
Wigmore St
James St
Duke St
Thayer St
Goodge St
Tottenham Court Rd
Bloomsbury St
St Giles High St
Montague St
St Martin's La
Long Acre
Knightsbridge
Grosvenor Cres
Duke of Wellington Pl
Buckingham Gate
Great Smith St
Marsham St
Ambrosden Ave
Rochester Row
Eccleston Bridge
Belgrave Rd
Warwick Way
John Islip St
Pont St
Belgrave Pl
Hobart Pl
Eaton Sq

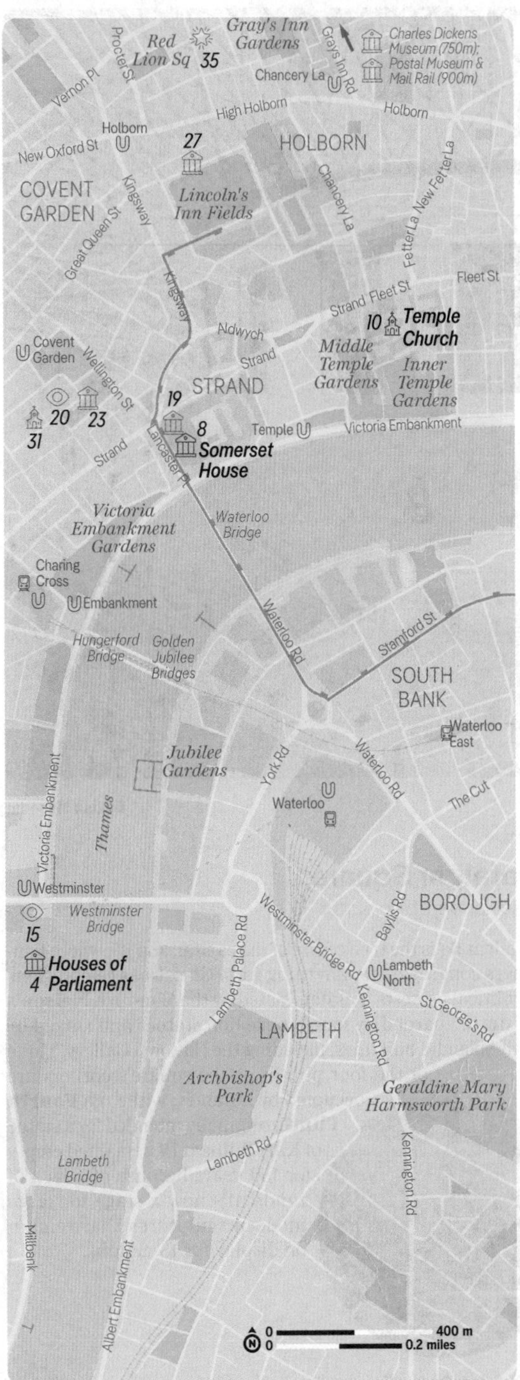


**HIGHLIGHTS**

**1** British Museum
**2** Buckingham Palace
**3** Churchill War Rooms
**4** Houses of Parliament
**5** National Gallery
**6** National Portrait Gallery
**7** Royal Academy of Arts
**8** Somerset House
**9** Tate Britain
**10** Temple Church
**11** Wallace Collection
**12** Westminster Abbey

**SIGHTS**

**13** All Saints Margaret Street
**14** Banqueting House
**15** Big Ben
**16** Burlington Arcade
**17** Carnaby St
**18** Changing the Guard
**19** Courtauld Gallery
**20** Covent Garden Piazza
**21** Green Park
**22** Horse Guards Parade
**23** London Transport Museum
**24** No 10 Downing Street
**25** Oxford St
**26** Regent Street
**27** Sir John Soane's Museum
**28** St James's Park
**29** St James's Piccadilly
**30** St Martin-in-the-Fields
**31** St Paul's Church
**32** Trafalgar Square
**33** Westminster Cathedral

**EATING**

**34** Mercato Mayfair

**ENTERTAINMENT**

**35** Novelty Automation
**36** Trooping the Colour

**SHOPPING**

**37** Fortnum & Mason
**38** Hamleys
**39** Hatchards
**40** Liberty
**41** Reckless Records
**42** Selfridges
**43** Sister Ray
**44** Stanfords

## British Museum

ARTEFACTS OF THE WORLD

The **British Museum** is the country's most popular museum (around 5.8 million visitors annually) and one of the world's oldest (opened in 1759). It houses – sometimes controversially – some of the most important pieces of human history, such as the **Rosetta Stone**, the key to deciphering Egyptian hieroglyphs; and the Parthenon sculptures, taken from Athens' Acropolis by Lord Elgin (British ambassador to the Ottoman Empire). The vast Etruscan, Greek, Roman, European, Asian and Islamic galleries carry on humanity's story.

Starting in 1753 with a 'cabinet of curiosities' sold to the nation by physician and collector Sir Hans Sloane, the collection mushroomed over the ensuing years through acquisitions, bequests and the indiscriminate plundering of the empire. The grand Enlightenment Gallery was the first section of the redesigned museum to be built in 1823.

About 80,000 objects are on display at a time (from the collection of eight million). The museum is huge, so avoid overwhelm by picking a gallery or theme for your visit or taking a tour.

British Museum

TOP: CHRISDORNEY/SHUTTERSTOCK ©, ARCHITECTS: FOSTER + PARTNERS; BOTTOM: LUNAMARINA/SHUTTERSTOCK ©

## Trafalgar Square

AT THE CENTRE OF LONDON

Trafalgar Sq is the true centre of the capital, and it's where Londoners congregate for anything from Christmas celebrations to political protests. It is dominated by the 52m-high **Nelson's Column**, guarded by four bronze lion statues and ringed by many splendid buildings, including the National Gallery. Three of the four plinths at the square's corners are occupied by notables, while the **Fourth Plinth**, originally intended for a statue of King William IV, remained empty for 150 years because of a lack of funds. It's now a stage for large modern sculptures that remain on display for 18 months.

Trafalgar Square lion

## Covent Garden

HISTORIC MARKET GOES MODERN

London's wholesale fruit-and-vegetable market until 1974 is now mostly the preserve of visitors, who flock to Covent Garden to shop among the quaint Italian-style arcades, eat and drink in the myriad cafes and restaurants, and browse through eclectic stalls in the Apple Market. The West Piazza, the open square in front of St Paul's Church, sees street performers encircled by enthralled crowds. It's a long-standing tradition: even Samuel Pepys' diary from 1662 mentions an Italian puppet play he watched here with a character named Punch.

Covent Garden

## Houses of Parliament & Big Ben

THE HEART OF UK DEMOCRACY

Both the elected House of Commons and the House of Lords, who are appointed or hereditary, sit in the sumptuous Houses of Parliament, a mostly mid-19th century neogothic confection with a few sections that survived a 1834 fire. The building's most famous feature is its clock tower, Elizabeth Tower – it's often called Big Ben, but that's actually the 13.7-tonne bell inside the tower.

Get tickets for a guided or self-paced tour, ideally in advance because they often happen only once a week (on Saturdays). UK residents can request a free guided tour through their MP or a member of the House of Lords.

Elizabeth Tower (Big Ben)

## Buckingham Palace

THE PREMIER ROYAL RESIDENCE

Built in 1703 for the Duke of Buckingham and then purchased by King George III, Buckingham Palace has been the Royal Family's London lodgings since 1837 when Queen Victoria moved in. Commoners can get a peek at the State Rooms – a mere 19 of the palace's 775 rooms – from mid-July to September when the monarch is on summer holiday. They are just as sumptuous as you'd imagine, dripping with over-the-top decor and hung with priceless art.

Even if you're visiting outside of summer, it's worth stopping by, especially on Sundays when the Mall is closed to vehicle traffic. **Changing the Guard**, when soldiers in bright-red uniforms and bearskin hats parade down the Mall and into Buckingham Palace, is madly popular with tourists.

# The British Museum

## A HALF-DAY TOUR

With about 80,000 artefacts on display, the British Museum is so vast and comprehensive that it can be daunting to visit. To avoid a frustrating trip – and getting lost on the way to the Egyptian mummies – set out on this half-day exploration, which takes in some of the museum's most important objects. If you want to see and learn more, download the British Museum app to your phone before you arrive.

A good starting point is the ❶ **Rosetta Stone**, the key that cracked the code to ancient Egypt's hieroglyphs. Nearby treasures from Assyria – an ancient civilisation centred in Mesopotamia between the Tigris and Euphrates rivers – including the colossal ❷ **Winged Bulls from Khorsabad**, give way to the ❸ **Parthenon Sculptures**, high points of classical Greek art. Be sure to see the monumental frieze celebrating the birth of Athena. En route

**Winged Bulls of Khorsabad**
This awesome pair of gypsum winged bulls with human heads once guarded the entrance to the palace of Assyrian King Sargon II at Khorsabad in Mesopotamia, a cradle of civilisation in present-day Iraq.

**Parthenon Sculptures**
The Parthenon, a white marble temple dedicated to the goddess Athena, was part of a fortified citadel on the Acropolis in Athens. Interactive displays explain how dozens of 5th-century sculptures once fitted together.

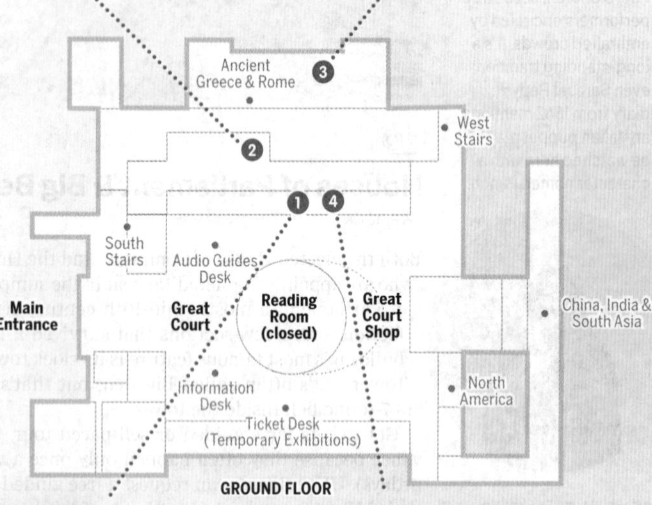


**Bust of Ramses II**
The most impressive sculpture in the Egyptian galleries, this 7250kg bust of Ramses the Great, scourge of the Israelites in the Book of Exodus, inspired Percy Bysshe Shelley's poem 'Ozymandius'.

**Rosetta Stone**
Written in hieroglyphic, demotic (cursive ancient Egyptian script used for everyday needs) and ancient Greek, the 762kg stone contains a decree celebrating the one-year anniversary of Ptolemy V's coronation.

to the West Stairs is a huge ❹ **Bust of Ramses II**, just a hint of the large collection of ❺ **Egyptian mummies** upstairs. The Romans introduce visitors to the early Britain galleries via the rich ❻ **Mildenhall Treasure**. The Anglo-Saxon ❼ **Sutton Hoo Ship Burial** and the medieval ❽ **Lewis Chessmen** follow.

## EATING OPTIONS

**Court Cafe** At the northern end of the Great Court; takeaway counters with salads and sandwiches; communal tables.

**Pizzeria** Out of the way off Room 12; quieter; children's menu available.

**Great Court Restaurant** Upstairs overlooking the former Reading Room; sit-down meals.



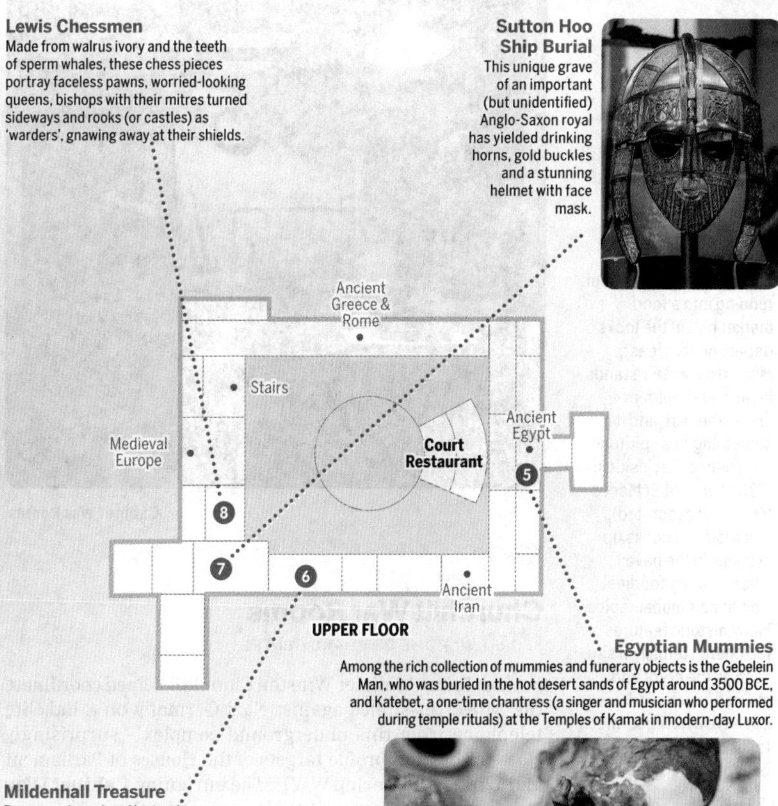


**Lewis Chessmen**
Made from walrus ivory and the teeth of sperm whales, these chess pieces portray faceless pawns, worried-looking queens, bishops with their mitres turned sideways and rooks (or castles) as 'warders', gnawing away at their shields.

**Sutton Hoo Ship Burial**
This unique grave of an important (but unidentified) Anglo-Saxon royal has yielded drinking horns, gold buckles and a stunning helmet with face mask.

MAVRITSINA IRINA/SHUTTERSTOCK ©

**Egyptian Mummies**
Among the rich collection of mummies and funerary objects is the Gebelein Man, who was buried in the hot desert sands of Egypt around 3500 BCE, and Katebet, a one-time chantress (a singer and musician who performed during temple rituals) at the Temples of Kamak in modern-day Luxor.

**Mildenhall Treasure**
Roman gods such as Neptune and Bacchus share space with early Christian symbols like the *chi-rho* (short for 'Christ') on almost three dozen silver bowls, plates and spoons used during the last days of the Roman Empire in Britain.

ILEANA_BT / SHUTTERSTOCK ©

London Transport Museum

## London Transport Museum

LONDON ON THE MOVE

Housed in Covent Garden's former flower-market building, the captivating London Transport Museum looks at how the capital developed as a result of better transport. It's stuffed full of horse-drawn omnibuses, vintage London Underground carriages with heritage maps, and old double-decker buses (some of which you can clamber through, making this something of a kids' playground). The gift shop sells great London souvenirs, such as retro Tube posters and pillows made from the same fabric as the train seats.

## Mercato Mayfair

TEMPLE OF TASTE

You can hardly turn a corner in London without running into a food market but, in the looks department at least, **Mercato Mayfair** stands head and shoulders above the rest, and it's something of a spiritual experience. Set inside the 1828 church of St Mark's (now deconsecrated), this food hall cooks up cuisines in the nave, where hungry foodies wait at communal tables. Many historic features of the church remain in situ, such as the crypt and stained-glass windows, but have a new gourmet focus, such as the craft beer bar that pours pints brewed in the church's basement.

Cabinet War Rooms

## Churchill War Rooms

SECRET WARTIME COMMAND CENTRE

Former Prime Minister Winston Churchill helped coordinate the Allied resistance against Nazi Germany on a Bakelite telephone from this underground complex – surprisingly close to the high-profile targets of the Houses of Parliament and Whitehall – during WWII. The intriguing **Cabinet War Rooms** remain much as they were when the lights were switched off in 1945, capturing the drama and dogged spirit of the time. Sleeping quarters butt up against meeting rooms and the mess hall, and the small space surely magnified the personality of the stubborn wartime leader. The modern multimedia **Churchill Museum** affords insights into his life and includes some arresting artefacts, such as his velvet one-piece boiler suit and some half-smoked cigars.

Fortnum & Mason

### BEST PLACES FOR AFTERNOON TEA

**Foyer & Reading Room at Claridge's**
Nibble traditional sandwiches and warm scones in Art-Deco surrounds below a Dale Chihuly glass sculpture. £££

**Oscar Wilde Lounge at Hotel Café Royal**
Pick from more than 25 teas at this gilt-and-parquet venue once patronised by its namesake writer. £££

**Fortnum & Mason**
Take afternoon tea where Queen Elizabeth II did in 2012: the Diamond Jubilee Tea Salon. £££

**Dean Street Townhouse**
Relax on velvet-upholstered furniture near a roaring fireplace and enjoy cakes and gin-and-tonic cucumber sandwiches. £££

**Wolseley**
Erstwhile car showroom transformed into opulent Viennese-style brasserie; golden chandeliers and stunning black-and-white tiled floors. £££

## MORE IN THE WEST END

# A Night Out at the Theatre

SETTING THE STAGE

The West End is London's main theatre district, with more than 40 stages showing everything from old-school classics (often starring well-known actors) to raise-the-roof musicals and new dramas. Going to the theatre is very much a must-do London experience, but as with many of the best things in the capital, life belongs to the organised. To see what's on during your visit check websites such as **London Theatre** (londontheatre.co.uk). For famous productions, subscribe to its newsletter for alerts on the next ticket release to get good seats at the best price. Book well ahead for popular shows and buy directly from the venue. For last-minute (including day-of) tickets and lottery giveaways for sold-out shows, try **TodayTix** (todaytix.com) or visit the **TKTS** booth in person in Leicester Sq. Don't buy tickets from random strangers online; it's almost always a scam.

### WHERE TO EAT IN THE WEST END

**Kanada-Ya**
In the debate over London's best ramen, we're still voting for this one. £

**Pollen Street Social**
Chef Jason Atherton's haute cuisine (Michelin-starred within six months of opening) is a worthy splurge. £££

**Rules**
Posh, very British establishment that lays claim to being London's oldest restaurant (1798). £££

**BEST INTERNATIONAL CUISINE IN THE WEST END**

**Palomar**
Levantine restaurant resembling a 1930s diner, with expert chefs behind the central zinc bar. ££

**Lina Stores**
Longtime Soho deli that also dishes up perfect handmade pasta to drooling diners. £

**Dishoom**
Successful mini-chain that gives new life to the disappearing Iranian cafes of Bombay. £

**Hoppers**
Sri Lankan bowl-shaped hoppers (fermented-rice pancakes) served with curries and chutneys. £

**Kiln**
Tiny Thai grill producing innovative small plates from wood-burning kilns in its long, narrow kitchen. ££

DANIEL LANGE/SHUTTERSTOCK ©

**St John Soane's Museum**

## The Novelty of Automation

PLAYING GAMES

A short walk from Holborn station, **Novelty Automation** is an eccentric home-made arcade of coin-operated satirical machines, combining vintage seaside charm with the trials and tribulations of modern times. Games include building your own reactor ('Free edible nuclear waste every time!') and using a crane to sneak coins into the City of London without being spotted by regulators.

## Art in the West End

THE COUNTRY'S BEST COLLECTION

The West End has some of London's – and the UK's – most impressive and important art institutions. With more than 2300 European masterpieces in its collection, the **National Gallery** is one of the world's great galleries, with masterpieces by Leonardo da Vinci, Michelangelo, Titian and Vincent van Gogh. Next door is the National Portrait Gallery (reopening in 2023 after a three-year renovation and expansion), full of paintings of familiar faces, such as royals, scientists, politicians and celebrities.

**WHERE TO EAT IN THE WEST END**

**Mortimer House Kitchen**
The Med meets the Middle East in this Art-Deco dining room. ££

**Berenjak**
Soho's interpretation of Tehran's hole-in-the-wall kebab houses is a triumph. ££

**Spring**
Sustainable restaurant in a restored Victorian drawing room at Somerset House. £££

**Somerset House** was designed in 1775 for government departments and royal societies and now contains galleries that encircle a lovely open courtyard; the **Courtauld Gallery** hosts a small but exceptional Impressionist collection, while the **Embankment Galleries** feature temporary exhibitions. **Royal Academy of Arts** is Britain's oldest society devoted to fine arts, founded in 1768. Its collection of drawings, paintings, architectural designs, photographs and sculptures comes from past and present Royal Academicians, but its famous **Summer Exhibition** showcases contemporary art for sale by both unknown and established artists.

**Tate Britain** celebrates British art from 1500 to the present, including pieces from William Hogarth, Thomas Gainsborough and John Constable, as well as modern and contemporary pieces from Lucian Freud, Barbara Hepworth and Gillian Ayres. Arguably London's finest smaller gallery, the **Wallace Collection** is an enthralling glimpse into 18th-century aristocratic life. The sumptuously restored Italianate mansion houses incredible 17th- and 18th-century paintings, porcelain, artefacts and furniture.

### BEST SPOTS FOR A CLASSY COCKTAIL

**Connaught Bar**
Lavish Art-Deco design, faultless service and even a travelling martini trolley.

**American Bar**
London's oldest cocktail bar, serves a £5000 sazerac with cognac from 1858.

**Artesian**
Multi-award-winning cocktails at a sumptuous bar at The Langham hotel.

**DUKES Bar**
Gentlemen's-club-like ambience, where white-jacketed masters mix up martinis and more.

**Rivoli Bar**
Art-deco marvel at The Ritz: all camphor wood, illuminated Lalique glass and golden ceiling domes.

**sketch**
The three-Michelin-starred restaurant, bar with self-playing piano, and toilets inside egg-shaped pods defy definition.

## Beyond the British Museum

MUST-VISIT BUT LESS OBVIOUS MUSEUMS

The West End has a clutch of smaller, more niche museums that are happy to show off their quirky side.

Built in 1927 to beat traffic congestion, the Post Office Railway was a subterranean train line that moved four million pieces of mail beneath the streets every day until it was shuttered in 2003. Revamped and opened to the public, **Mail Rail** now delivers visitors around the tracks below the largest sorting office, in trains based on the original designs. Tickets include access to the **Postal Museum** across the street.

**Sir John Soane's Museum** is one of the most atmospheric in London. Set inside the architect's Georgian home, which he bequeathed to the nation on the condition that it remain untouched after his death, the museum brims with Soane's collection of art and archaeological purchases.

Writer Charles Dickens lived in a Georgian terraced house east of Bloomsbury for just 2½ years (1837–39), now the **Charles Dickens Museum**. Each of the dozen rooms are evocative of life in Victorian times. Though many places in London claim to have a Dickens connection, this address is his sole surviving residence in town.

### WHERE TO DRINK IN THE WEST END

**Purl**
Foams, aromas, unlikely garnishes and bespoke glassware give cocktails an air of discovery.

**Cahoots**
Looking like a disused Underground station, this bar channels the WWII spirit of London.

**Swift**
Superior cocktail bar with over 250 whiskies; often on lists of the world's best bars.

### THE WEST END'S LGBTIQ+ SCENE

LGBTIQ+ bars are dotted around London, but Soho's gay village, centred on Old Compton St, still has the best concentration of spots. **Duke of Wellington** brings in a bearded, fun-loving gay crowd. **Village** is up for a party any night of the week, with a schedule of karaoke nights and go-go-dancers.

The lesbian scene has few venues of its own, but **She Soho** is a notable exception and hosts events and party nights in a friendly and unpretentious atmosphere.

London's massive **Pride** parade paints the town pink in late June/early July and takes over major streets in the West End. North of Russell Sq, **Gay's the Word** is the UK's first specifically gay and lesbian bookstore.

LAUREN KEITH/LONELY PLANET ©

Carnaby St

## London Shopping Streets & Department Stores

READY, SET, SPEND

The West End's shopping scene, London's retail nexus, hardly needs a formal introduction. Pedestrianised **Carnaby St** has a mix of chain and indie shops, while **Oxford St** and **Regent St** are busy with flagship shops and luxe department stores, such as Selfridges – opened in 1909 and set in a grand columned building – and Liberty, which lures in shoppers with its Tudor Revival facade. Hamleys, the biggest and oldest toy emporium in the world, houses six floors of fun.

**Covent Garden** is also beset with well-known labels, but the shops are smaller and counterbalanced by indie boutiques and vintage stores. Trading since 1853, Stanfords is the ultimate travel bookshop and a destination in its own right.

Luxury gets turned up a notch on **Piccadilly**, home to Fortnum & Mason, the 'royals' grocery store,' where staff still wear old-fashioned tailcoats. Hatchards, the UK's oldest bookshop, dates to 1797 and has been crammed into a five-storey Georgian building for more than 200 years. The 1819 Burlington Arcade is an old-school covered shopping alley for the wealthy. It's most famous for the Burlington Beadles, uniformed guards

### WHERE TO DRINK IN THE WEST END

**Attendant**
Abandoned Victorian public toilet turned coffee shop. Grab a stool at the urinal.

**Princess Louise**
Pressed-tin ceilings, handsome tiling, mirrors and a central horseshoe bar in a 1872 pub.

**Lamb**
Frosted-glass 'snob screens' concealed genteel Victorian drinkers from staff at this pub on Lamb's Conduit St.

who keep an eye out for such offences as chewing gum, opening umbrellas or anything that could lower the tone.

**Soho** is the spot for vinyl shops (Sister Ray and Reckless Records), bookstores and some arty independents.

## Power & Politics

IN THE FOOTSTEPS OF AUTHORITY

Westminster is deeply connected to both the government and the monarchy, with a number of important spots along **Whitehall**, which runs between Downing St and Trafalgar Sq. No 10 Downing St has been the prime minister's London residence since the late-19th century. Just a minute's walk up the street, Banqueting House is the sole surviving section of the Tudor Whitehall Palace (1532). Its ceilings have huge oil paintings by Peter Paul Rubens.

Across Whitehall, **Horse Guards Parade** is a large open area for royal ceremonies. Catch a less-crowded version of Buckingham Palace's Changing the Guard as the Household Cavalry swaps soldiers at 11am from Monday to Saturday and at 10am on Sunday. Trooping the Colour, the ceremonial celebration of the monarch's birthday takes place here in June, regardless of the actual date of the monarch's birthday.

Walk through Horse Guards Parade to reach **St James's Park**, a small but well-manicured spot. The lake brims with waterfowl, including the famous pelicans, introduced to the park in 1664 as a gift from the Russian ambassador to King Charles II. The picture-perfect sight of Buckingham Palace from the Blue Bridge spanning the central lake is the best you'll find. Head towards Buckingham Palace and across the Mall to find **Green Par**k, the smallest of the eight Royal Parks but somehow never as crowded as St James's.

## West End Churches

CITY SANCTUARIES

While Westminster Abbey understandably steals the show, the West End has many more beautiful churches worth a visit (and most are much cheaper!). Some also have live music and candlelit events.

Not to be confused with the Abbey, **Westminster Cathedral** has a distinctive candy-striped red-brick and white-stone exterior, plus a 83m-tall bell tower with a viewing platform. The sparse interior remains largely unfinished, after funds ran out in the early 20th century, but mosaics dazzle from the altar and side chapels.

### BEST LIVE MUSIC IN THE WEST END

**Ronnie Scott's**
Legendary lounge that's hosted such luminaries as Miles Davis, Charlie Parker, Ella Fitzgerald and Count Basie.

**Royal Opera House**
Classic productions with a modern touch put on by world-class performers.

**Wigmore Hall**
Classical music venue, with more than 460 concerts a year in a 1901 piano showroom.

**100 Club**
Rock-leaning heritage London venue at the same address since 1942.

**PizzaExpress Jazz Club**
Mediocre chain pizza place meets smooth sax with incredible results; there's live music every night.

### CAPITAL OF CREATIVITY

Art is everywhere in London; don't miss major galleries like the **Victoria & Albert** (p124), which houses the largest collection of decorative arts, or **Tate Modern** (p83)on South Bank .

### WHERE TO SHOP IN THE WEST END

**Daunt Books**
The Marylebone location is the Edwardian original, with oak panels, galleries and gorgeous skylights.

**Twinings**
Oldest company in London still trading on the same site; a staggering selection of teas.

**James Smith & Sons Umbrellas**
Fighting the British weather since 1857 with elegant umbrellas, plus walking sticks and canes.

WILLIAM BARTON/SHUTTERSTOCK ©

Chinatown

### CHINATOWN

Although not as big as Chinatowns in some other world-class cities, London's version is a lively quarter with red lanterns strung up across the streets, and restaurants, noodle shops and Asian supermarkets aplenty. Entrances on Girard St, Macclesfield St and Wardour St are marked with red-pillared gates.

At **Beijing Dumpling**, the stars of the show are kneaded behind the steamy front window: tiny dough pockets ready to be made into xiaolongbao (soup dumplings). Decorated in vintage communist kitsch, **Baozi Inn** serves Beijing- and Chengdu-style street food. **Four Seasons** is famous for its roast duck, and **Opium** dishes out dim sum alongside knockout cocktails. Across Shaftesbury Ave, **Bar Shu** has possibly the best Sichuan food in London.

Off Trafalgar Sq, **St Martin-in-the-Fields** is the parish church to the royal family, and a delightful fusion of neoclassical and baroque. It's well known for its classical music concerts, many by candlelight. **St James's Piccadilly**, the only church Christopher Wren built from scratch, stages lunchtime and evening pay-what-you-can performances.

Just a few streets back from busy Oxford and Regent Sts, **All Saints Margaret Street** is one of the country's best examples of High Victorian Gothic architecture, with extraordinary tiling and exquisite stained glass.

The magnificent **Temple Church** was built by the secretive Knights Templar, an order of crusading monks founded in the 12th century to protect pilgrims travelling to and from the holy lands. Thought to be modelled after the Church of the Holy Sepulchre in Jerusalem, it was heavily damaged by WWII bombings. Today the sprawling oasis of fine buildings offers a rare traffic-free green space.

### TO MARKET

Oxford St is Europe's busiest shopping street. If you've got more to spend, check out what's for sale at London's famous **Portobello Road Market** p125) and **Camden Market** (p101).

### WHERE TO SHOP IN THE WEST END

**Benjamin Pollock's Toyshop**
Victorian paper theatres, wooden marionettes, finger puppets and antique teddy bears.

**Algerian Coffee Stores**
Caffeinating Soho since 1887; huge selection of coffee beans and tea in an old-school storefront.

**Milroy's of Soho**
Every bottle at this whisky shop is handpicked; sample some in the secret behind-the-bookcase bar.

# THE CITY

## THE CAPITAL'S HISTORIC HEART

The Romans founded the town of Londinium in 47 CE, and this area has been inhabited continuously ever since. The settlement changed hands several times as empires got invaded and faded, and the deep layers of this 2000-year history are revealed in the neighbourhood's architecture, street names, tourist attractions and quiet corners. The current millennium has seen a profusion of skyscrapers sprout, a visual contrast to famous historic sites such as the Tower of London and St Paul's Cathedral. Today, more than half a million people work in the City of London, but only about 7400 live here.

For its small size, the City of London – also known as the Square Mile – punches well above its weight for must-see sights. Combine the classics with lesser-known churches and alleyways to get the full experience. The delightful Museum of London is slated to open at its new home in Smithfield in 2026.

### TOP TIP

To appreciate this area's industrious buzz, visit on a weekday when everything is open. The neighbourhood largely empties in the evening as workers retreat to the suburbs. Weekends have traditionally been quiet – a brilliant time for nearly people-free explorations, but that's slowly changing as bars and restaurants adjust their hours beyond the 9 to 5.

**The City skyscrapers**

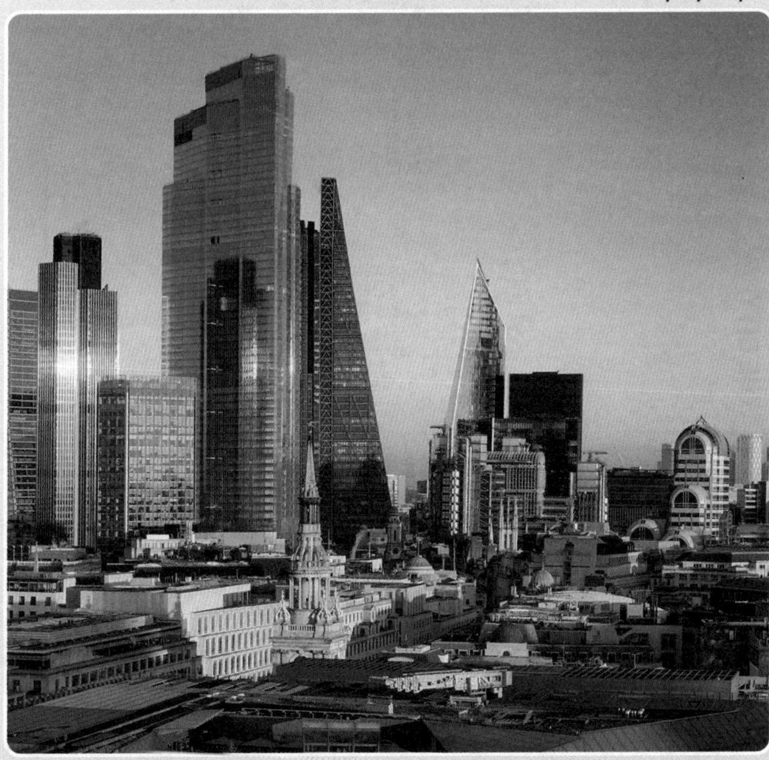

# THE CITY

**HIGHLIGHTS**
**1** Sky Garden
**2** St Paul's Cathedral
**3** Tower of London

**SIGHTS**
**4** Barbican
**5** Barbican Art Gallery
**6** Barbican Conservatory
**7** Curve
**8** Garden at 120
**9** St Bride's
**10** St Dunstan in the East
**11** St Mary Aldermary
**12** St Vedast -alias-Foster

**ACTIVITIES, COURSES & TOURS**
**13** Shoreditch Street Art Tours

**EATING**
**14** Bob Bob Cité
**15** City Social
**16** Duck & Waffle
**17** Sushisamba

**DRINKING & NIGHTLIFE**
**18** Black Parrot
**19** City of London Distillery
**20** Gobpsy
**21** Jamaica Wine House
**22** Merchant House
**23** Sabine Rooftop Bar
**24** Searcys at the Gherkin

**ENTERTAINMENT**
**25** Barbican Centre

**SHOPPING**
**26** One New Change

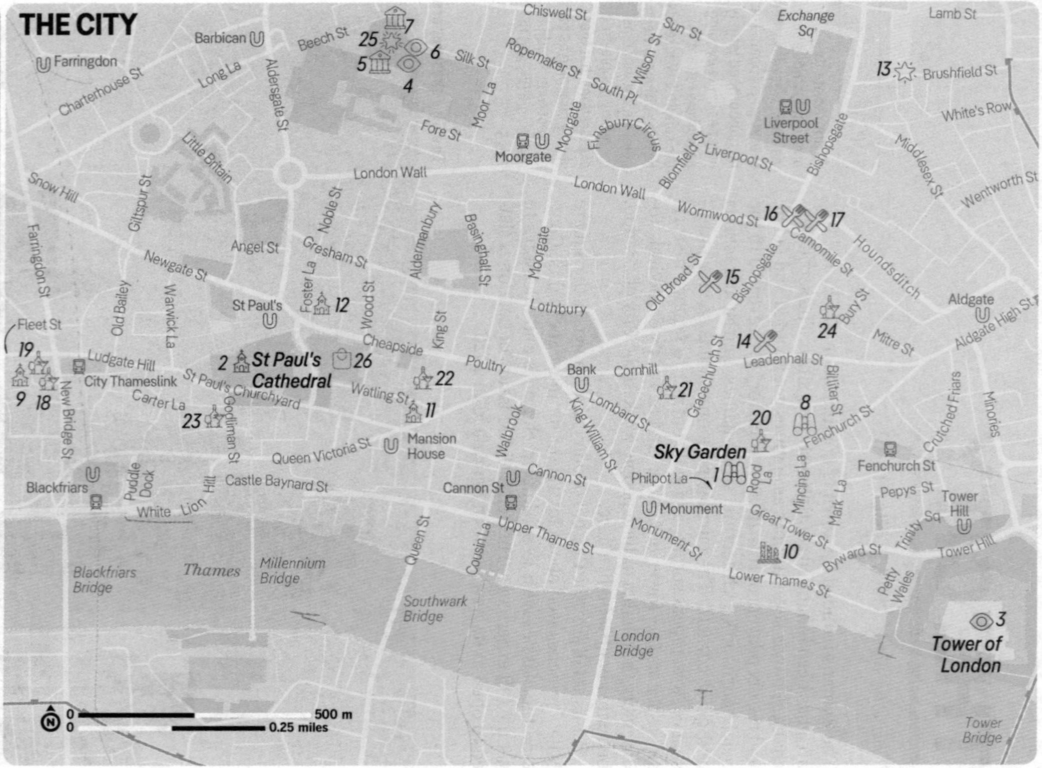

## Sky Garden

GREENERY UP IN THE GODS

The ferns, fig trees and purple African lilies that clamber up the final three skyscraping storeys of 20 Fenchurch St (the building better known as the 'Walkie Talkie') are mere wallflowers at this 155m-high rooftop garden – it's the extraordinary 360-degree views of London that make this spot so popular. The Sky Garden has front-row seats overlooking the Shard and vistas that gallop for miles east and west. The space includes a restaurant, a brasserie and two bars. It's free to visit, but you must book online in advance.

Sky Garden

ARCHITECT: RAFAEL VIÑOLY PAJOR PAWEL/SHUTTERSTOCK ©

## Tower of London

BLOODY INTRIGUING

The unmissable Tower of London offers a window into 1000 years of gruesome and compelling history. A former royal residence, treasury, mint, armoury and zoo, it's perhaps most remembered as the prison where a king, three queens and many nobles – including Anne Boleyn and Catherine Howard, Henry VIII's second and fifth wives – met their deaths. The immaculately dressed Yeomen Warders (better known as the Beefeaters) live on site, protecting the spectacular Crown Jewels – which contain the biggest diamonds in the world – and leading tours of the Tower.

Look out for the Tower's famous ravens. Legend says should they leave, the kingdom will fall. Spare birds are kept in the aviary, and their wing feathers are clipped in case they get any ideas.

## Barbican

CULTURE IN THE CITY

The architectural value of this huge pitted concrete brutalist housing estate divides Londoners, but the Barbican remains a sought-after place to live as well as the City's preeminent cultural centre. Public spaces include a quirky conservatory and the Barbican Centre theatres, cinema and two art galleries: Barbican Art Gallery and the Curve. Navigating the Barbican, designed to be a car-free urban neighbourhood, requires reliance on a network of elevated paths that didn't fully come to fruition. Find your bearings by signing up for an architecture tour.

The whole site makes for a fascinating stroll, especially around the fountain-studded central lake.

# Tower of London

## TACKLING THE TOWER

Although it's usually less busy in the late afternoon, don't leave your assault on the Tower until too late in the day. You could easily spend hours here and not see it all. Start by getting your bearings on a tour with a Yeoman Warder (Beefeater); they are included in the cost of admission, entertaining and the easiest way to access the ❶ **Chapel Royal of St Peter ad Vincula**, which is where they finish.

When you leave the chapel, the ❷ **Scaffold Site** is directly in front. The building immediately to your left is Waterloo Barracks, where the ❸ **Crown Jewels** are housed. These are a highlight of a Tower visit, so keep an eye on the entrance and pick a time to visit when it looks relatively quiet. Once inside, take things at your own pace. Slow-moving travelators shunt you past the dozen or so crowns that are the treasury's centrepieces, but feel free to double-back for a second or even third pass.

Allow plenty of time for the ❹ **White Tower**, the core of the whole complex, starting with the exhibition of royal armour. As you continue on to the 1st floor, keep an eye out for ❺ **St John's Chapel**.

The famous ❻ **ravens** can be seen in the courtyard south of the White Tower. Next, visit the ❼ **Bloody Tower** and the torture displays in the dungeon of the Wakefield Tower. Head next through the towers that formed the ❽ **Medieval Palace**, then take the ❾ **East Wall Walk** to get a feel for the castle's mighty battlements. Spend the rest of your time poking around the many other fascinating nooks and crannies of the Tower complex.

### BEAT THE QUEUES

➡ Buy tickets online, avoid weekends and aim to be at the Tower first thing in the morning, when queues are shortest.

➡ The London Pass (www.londonpass.com) allows you to jump the queues and visit the Tower (plus some other 80 attractions) as often as you like.

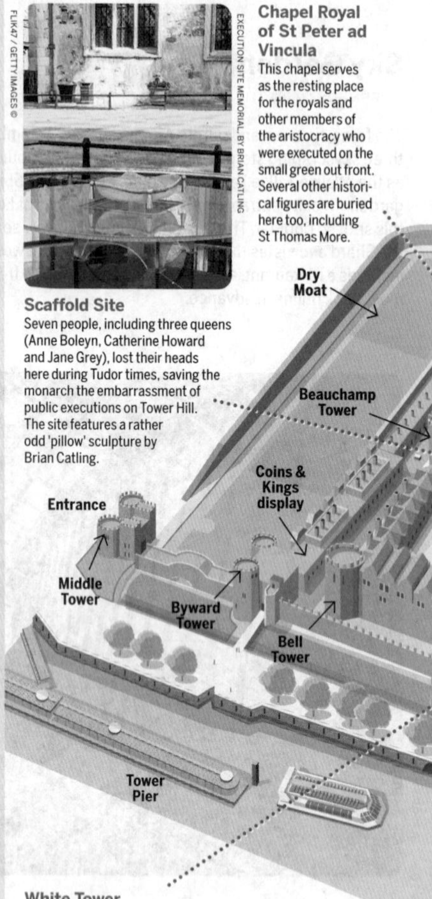


FLIK47 / GETTY IMAGES ©

EXECUTION SITE MEMORIAL BY BRIAN CATLING

**Chapel Royal of St Peter ad Vincula**
This chapel serves as the resting place for the royals and other members of the aristocracy who were executed on the small green out front. Several other historical figures are buried here too, including St Thomas More.

**Scaffold Site**
Seven people, including three queens (Anne Boleyn, Catherine Howard and Jane Grey), lost their heads here during Tudor times, saving the monarch the embarrassment of public executions on Tower Hill. The site features a rather odd 'pillow' sculpture by Brian Catling.

**White Tower**
Much of the White Tower is taken up with an exhibition on 500 years of royal armour. Look for the virtually cuboid suit made to match Henry VIII's large body, complete with an oversized armoured codpiece to protect, ahem, the crown jewels.

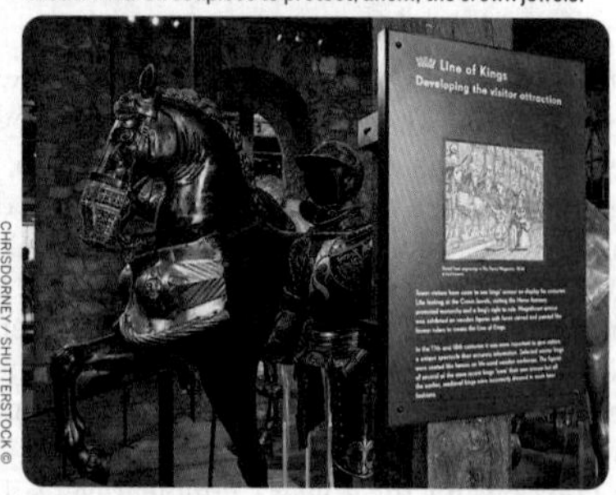


CHRISDORNEY / SHUTTERSTOCK ©

### St John's Chapel
The White Tower's unadorned chapel dates from 1080, making it the oldest surviving Christian place of worship in London.

JOSEPH M. ARSENEAU / SHUTTERSTOCK ©

### Crown Jewels
When it's not being worn for ceremonies of state, the sovereign's bling is kept here. Among the 23,578 gems, look out for the 530-carat Great Star of Africa diamond at the top of the Sovereign's Sceptre with Cross, the largest part of what was then the largest diamond ever found.

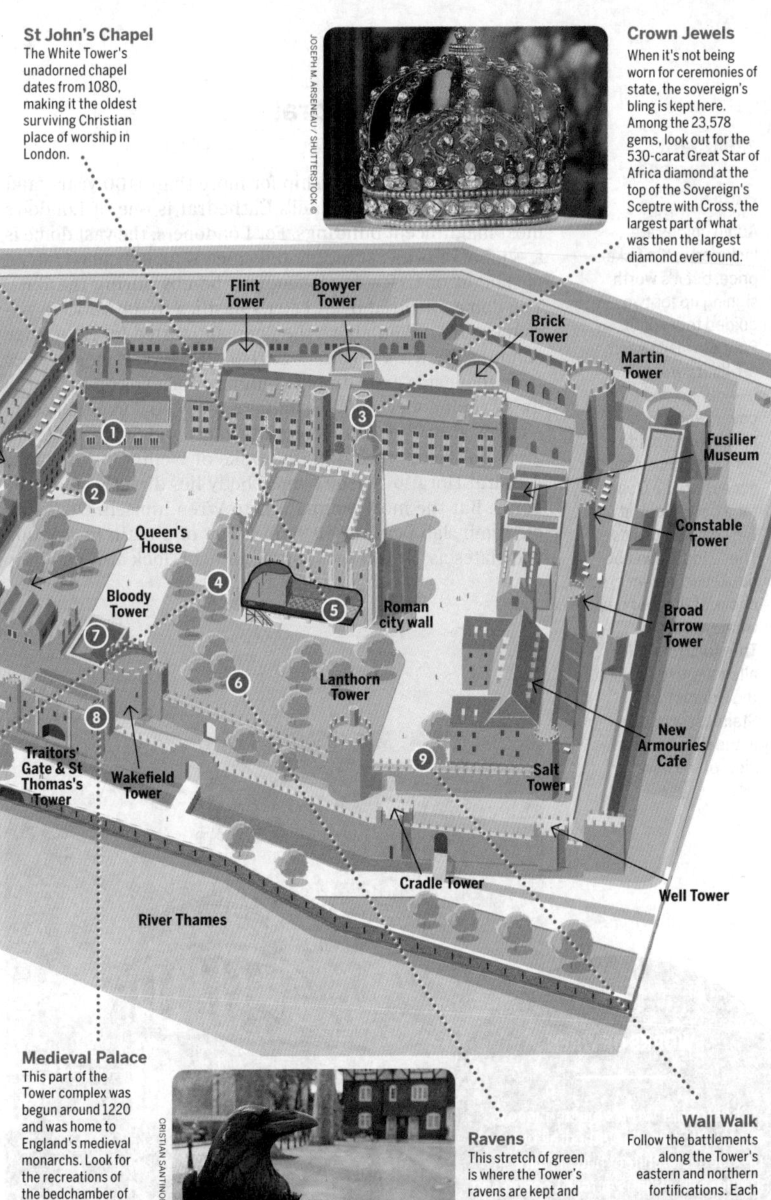


### Medieval Palace
This part of the Tower complex was begun around 1220 and was home to England's medieval monarchs. Look for the recreations of the bedchamber of Edward I (1272–1307) in St Thomas's Tower and the throne room of his father, Henry III (1216–72) in the Wakefield Tower.

CRISTIAN SANTINON / SHUTTERSTOCK ©

### Ravens
This stretch of green is where the Tower's ravens are kept and fed on raw meat and blood-soaked biscuits. According to legend, if the ravens depart the fortress, the Tower and the kingdom will fall.

### Wall Walk
Follow the battlements along the Tower's eastern and northern fortifications. Each of the towers along the way has themed displays, covering everything from the royal menagerie to the Tower during WWI.

## St Paul's Cathedral

SAINTLY SYMBOL OF LONDON'S RESILIENCE

A place of Christian worship for more than 1400 years (and pagan before that), St Paul's Cathedral is one of London's most magnificent buildings. For Londoners, the vast dome is a symbol of pride, standing tall since 1710 and surviving an onslaught of Luftwaffe incendiary bombs during the Blitz. The dome, inspired by St Peter's Basilica in the Vatican, rises more than 85m above the floor, supported by eight huge columns. Viewing architect Christopher Wren's masterpiece from the inside and climbing hundreds of steps up to the top for sweeping views of the capital is a celestial experience.

Below, the crypt has memorials to around 300 of Britain's great and good, including the Duke of Wellington and Vice Admiral Horatio Nelson, whose body lies directly below the dome. But the most poignant is to Wren himself. On a simple tomb slab bearing his name, part of a Latin inscription translates as: 'If you seek his monument, look around you'.

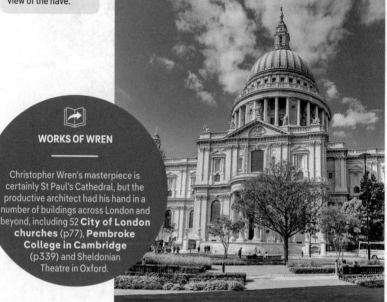

### BEHIND THE SCENES OF ST PAUL'S

Audio guides are included in the ticket price, but it's worth signing up for two guided tours of St Paul's to visit usually off-limits areas. Free 1½-hour guided tours cover similar ground as the audio guide, with the bonus of accessing the Quire for a better look at the ceiling mosaics. These tours can't be booked in advance, so check at the tour desk when you arrive. The Triforium Tour (£10) allows you to descend the Geometric Staircase and take in the BBC-exclusive view of the nave.

**St Paul's Cathedral**

JANIS LACIS/SHUTTERSTOCK ©

### WORKS OF WREN

Christopher Wren's masterpiece is certainly St Paul's Cathedral, but the productive architect had his hand in a number of buildings across London and beyond, including 52 **City of London churches** (p77), **Pembroke College in Cambridge** (p339) and Sheldonian Theatre in Oxford.

LOIS GOBE/SHUTTERSTOCK ©

Vaulted ceiling, St Mary Aldermary

## KNOW YOUR NICKNAMES: CITY OF LONDON'S NOTABLE BUILDINGS

The Walkie Talkie isn't the only City skyscraper with a silly name. Developers generally decide to name these towers after their addresses, but Londoners ensure that something much more memorable sticks.

The 180m-tall **Gherkin** (30 St Mary Axe) gets its nickname from its distinctive pickle-shaped design. The **Cheesegrater** (officially the Leadenhall Building) has a slanted profile to preserve the sightline to St Paul's Cathedral, a legally protected view. The Lloyd's Building is sometimes known as the **Inside Out Building** because its ducts, vents and lifts are on the exterior (an architectural style called Bowellism). The **Scalpel**, the nickname given to a 38-storey skyscraper, proved so fitting that developers ditched its official name of 52 Lime St.

MORE IN THE CITY OF LONDON

# City of London churches

IN THE SPIRIT OF THE CITY

Before the Great Fire in 1666, the Square Mile had 111 churches wedged into its narrow streets, but 86 of them, including old St Paul's, were lost in the inferno, and more were later shattered in the Blitz. Today, in the shadow of rebuilt St Paul's Cathedral, 47 of these centuries-old stone churches, many also designed by St Paul's architect Christopher Wren, have survived the odds and remain integral pieces of the financial district's fabric. Sandwiched between modern high-rises, these churches remain peaceful oases.

Built in 1682, **St Mary Aldermary** is not only one of the most architecturally impressive, with its immaculate fan vaulted ceiling, but also one you'll want to linger in longer: a coffee shop serves good brews in the apse. **St Vedast-alias-Foster** is easy to hurry past at ground level, but there's a hidden alleyway garden and 17th-century-style plaster ceiling detailed with gold and varnished aluminium leaf. Printing presses on Fleet St stopped in the 1980s, but **St Bride's** is still called the 'journalists' church'. Its distinctive steeple is said to have

**CITY ACCOMMODATION WITH A STORY**

**Ned**
Former Midland Bank with *Great Gatsby* lobby vibe and a bar in the old safe. **£££**

**Andaz Liverpool Street**
The modern rooms belie that they sit above a secret Masonic temple in the basement. **£££**

**London St Paul's YHA**
Hostel housed in the former boarding school for St Paul's Cathedral choirboys. **£**

## HIDDEN SPOTS IN THE CITY

**Moira Cameron** is the first female Yeoman Warder and lived inside the Tower of London for 15 years. She shares her favourite hidden places in the Square Mile.

**London Mithraeum**
If ancient Roman history is your thing, then the London Mithraeum should be on your list. It's free to visit and houses the fabulously displayed Temple of Mithras. Give yourself some time to check out the incredible wall of artefacts, too.

**St Dunstan in the East**
For a little peace and quiet in the busy City of London, make your way to the church garden at St Dunstan in the East. Grab a cuppa and spend some time in this haven just off Idol Ln.

LAUREN KEITH/LONELY PLANET ©

**Sushisamba terrace**

inspired tiered wedding cakes. Bombed in the Blitz, the ruins of 12th-century **St Dunstan in the East** have been left to the elements, resulting in a beautifully sombre public garden sprouting below the miraculously intact steeple and amid the blackened walls, with ivy crawling through the skeletal windows.

## Getting High in the City

HEAD IN THE CLOUDS

Construction in the ancient City of London continues apace, and a bumper crop of modern skyscrapers show off London's architecture through floor-to-ceiling windows and perfectly perched outdoor terraces.

Survey the kingdom from **Duck & Waffle**, the highest 24-hour restaurant in town (on the 40th floor). Just below, **Sushisamba**'s 38th-floor terrace is the loftiest outdoor dining space in Europe. **City Social** pairs sublime skyscraper views from its 24th-floor digs with Michelin-starred cuisine served in an Art-Deco interior. The top floors of the **Gherkin** building were once reserved as a private members' club, but now anyone dressed to impress is invited into Searcys at the Gherkin. It might not be at the top elevation-wise, but three floors up the **Cheesegrat-**

### CITY ACCOMMODATION WITH A STORY

**Four Seasons Hotel at Ten Trinity Square**
Once Port of London Authority HQ, with a columned facade and statue of Fr Thames. £££

**Threadneedles**
Victorian-era bank-turned-hotel with grand domed lobby that uses the old banking counter as the bar. £££

**Counting House**
Rooms above a convivial pub in what used to be an 1895 gentlemen's club. £££

**er** building is Bob Bob Ricard City, an outpost of the restaurant that made the 'Press for Champagne' button a quintessential over-the-top London experience.

If your credit limit is in danger, **Garden at 120**, London's largest roof garden, is a 15th-floor pocket park paradise. Its mid-rise vantage point gives a unique perspective on nearby skyscrapers. Booking isn't required, making this a good alternative if you can't get into the **Sky Garden**. A free viewing platform at **One New Change** rewards with up-close views of St Paul's Cathedral; take the lift to the 6th floor. To see it from a slightly different angle over a drink, head to **Sabine Rooftop Bar**.

## Lost in the City Lanes

SEE WHERE A STROLL TAKES YOU

The City of London is the oldest part of the capital, and its labyrinthine street layout hides secretive passageways that are a delight to explore.

Down a quiet alleyway parallel to Fleet St, **Black Parrot** is a rum-obsessed bar that puts a London twist on the vivacious Caribbean spirit. Around the corner on Bride Ln, **City of London Distillery** was the first gin distillery opened in this district for nearly 200 years. North of Mansion House Tube station, seek out **Merchant House,** a well-hidden and well-stocked bar with some 600 whiskies, 400 rums and 400 gins on a seemingly forgotten alleyway. It even has a speakeasy within the speakeasy: the **Brig**, London's smallest bar. For £65 per person per hour, couples or small groups get their own private bartender and all drinks included.

East of Bank Tube station, **Jamaica Wine House** stands on the site of London's first coffee house (1652), frequented by diarist Samuel Pepys. To get under the skin of this section of City alleys, sign up for the **Coffeehouse Tour** with Unreal City Audio to learn how the drink fuelled the British empire, and even sample some 17th-century-style 'bitter Mohammedan gruel' yourself.

Even the busy streets of the City hide prizes. In the shadow of the Walkie Talkie building, the **Gobpsy** speakeasy has no signage at street level, so be ready to duck into a barbershop and descend the stairs.

**ROMAN RUINS**

Londinium was the second capital of Roman Britain, and the Romans laid their foundations across the country. The best places to witness Roman history are the gorgeous Roman baths in **Bath** (p233) and along the country-belting **Hadrian's Wall** (p567).

### BEST HISTORIC PUBS IN THE CITY OF LONDON

**Blackfriar**
Friar-themed Art-Nouveau signage, decor and mosaics at this pub built atop a medieval Dominican monastery.

**Counting House**
Bank-turned-beer-stop with a grand wooden staircase and painted ceilings edged with gold-coloured crown moulding.

**Viaduct Tavern**
Etched-glass panes and blood-red embossed vines adorn one of the City's only remaining Victorian gin palaces.

**Trading House**
Formerly the Bank of New Zealand, with tiered chandeliers, dark wood and high barrel-vaulted ceiling.

**Jamaica Wine House**
On the site of London's first coffee house site (1652); look for the huge streetlamp down an alley.

### WHERE TO EAT IN THE CITY OF LONDON

**Sweetings**
London's oldest seafood restaurant, dating to 1889, with service from white-aproned staff at narrow counters. **££**

**Duck & Waffle**
Dine on the namesake dish with an unbeatable view from the highest restaurant in town. **££**

**Hawksmoor Guildhall**
Sunday roasts and perfectly prepared steak; subterranean spot with parquet floors and maroon leather seating. **££**

## FROM THE ROMANS TO THE RECENT WALKING TOUR

Today's City of London is about the same size as Roman Londinium, and this walk saunters through many of the key stages of the area's history.

From St Paul's Tube station, exit onto Cheapside. These roads were once London's markets, indicated by street names such as Milk St and Honey Ln. Still a hub of commerce, the modern **1 One New Change** shopping centre has arguably the City's richest view of St Paul's Cathedral; take the lift up to the public roof terrace for a free peek.

Leave the shopping centre on Bread St, turn left on Watling St and then cross Queen Victoria St into **2 Bloomberg Arcade**, lined with restaurants. Left on Walbrook is **3 London Mithraeum**, a Roman cult temple dedicated to the bull-slaying god Mithras. Make your way to the Bank junction, pausing to admire the imposing Bank of England – and visiting the **4 Bank of England Museum** – before ducking into the **5 Royal Exchange** for a Fortnum & Mason cup of tea. East on Cornhill is the splendid 19th-century **6 Leadenhall Market**, roughly where the Roman forum once stood. Meander past shops that inspired Diagon Alley in *Harry Potter*.

Head south on Gracechurch St to the **7 Monument to the Great Fire of London**, climbing 311 stairs to the top before the views snatch your breath away again. Leave via Monument St and turn left at St Dunstan's Hill, where the bombed-out **8 St Dunstan in the East** church stands as a stark reminder of the Blitz.

Head down the hill and then turn left on Lower Thames St, and in a few minutes you'll bump into the moat guarding the **9 Tower of London**. Walk towards the river to spot **10 Tower Bridge** and its sky-blue suspension struts.

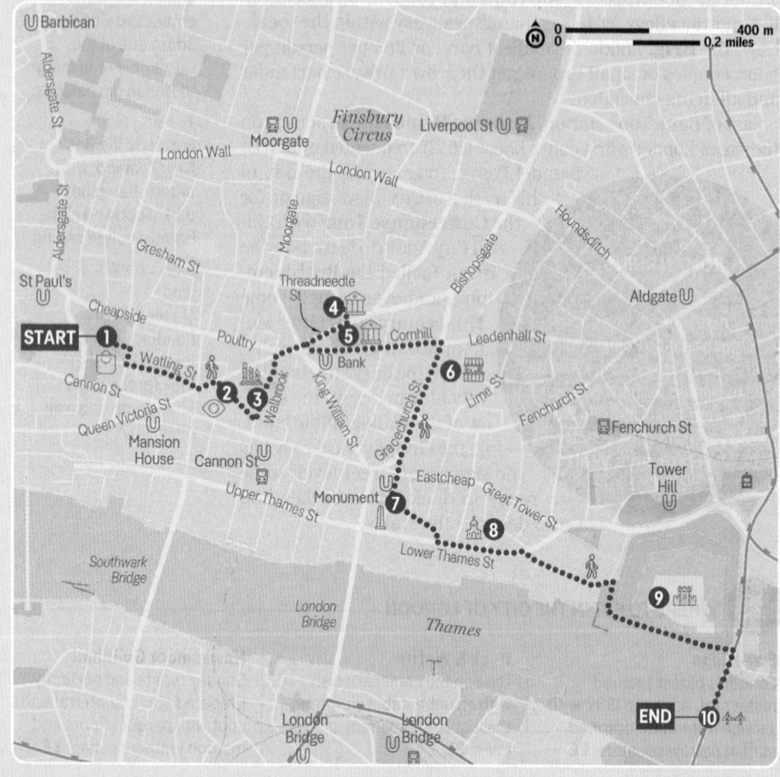

# THE SOUTH BANK

## RIVER-HUGGING HUB OF THEATRE AND ART

Across the river and away from the naysayers in the buttoned-down City of London, playful South Bank has been a destination for entertainment since the Middle Ages. It's still a must-visit area for lovers of art, culture and architecture. This district has a dense concentration of theatres, including the reconstructed Shakespeare's Globe, the UK's largest cinema screen at the BFI and the huge Southbank Centre complex that's Europe's largest arts venue. Thanks to the huge drawcard sights that stretch out along the riverside between Westminster Bridge and Tower Bridge, South Bank is a tourist-friendly and heavily visited neighbourhood. Christmas Day might be the only quiet time in its calendar.

The presence of Borough Market established South Bank's foodie credentials centuries ago, and now even more street-food markets and restaurants are setting up shop on the market fringes and side streets.

### TOP TIP

Exploring South Bank on foot is best. Simply walking along the River Thames between Westminster Bridge and London Bridge takes you past the London Eye, Southbank Centre, Tate Modern, Shakespeare's Globe and Borough Market. You also get views of the City of London, Tower Bridge and the Tower of London across the water.

**Tower Bridge**

## THE SOUTH BANK

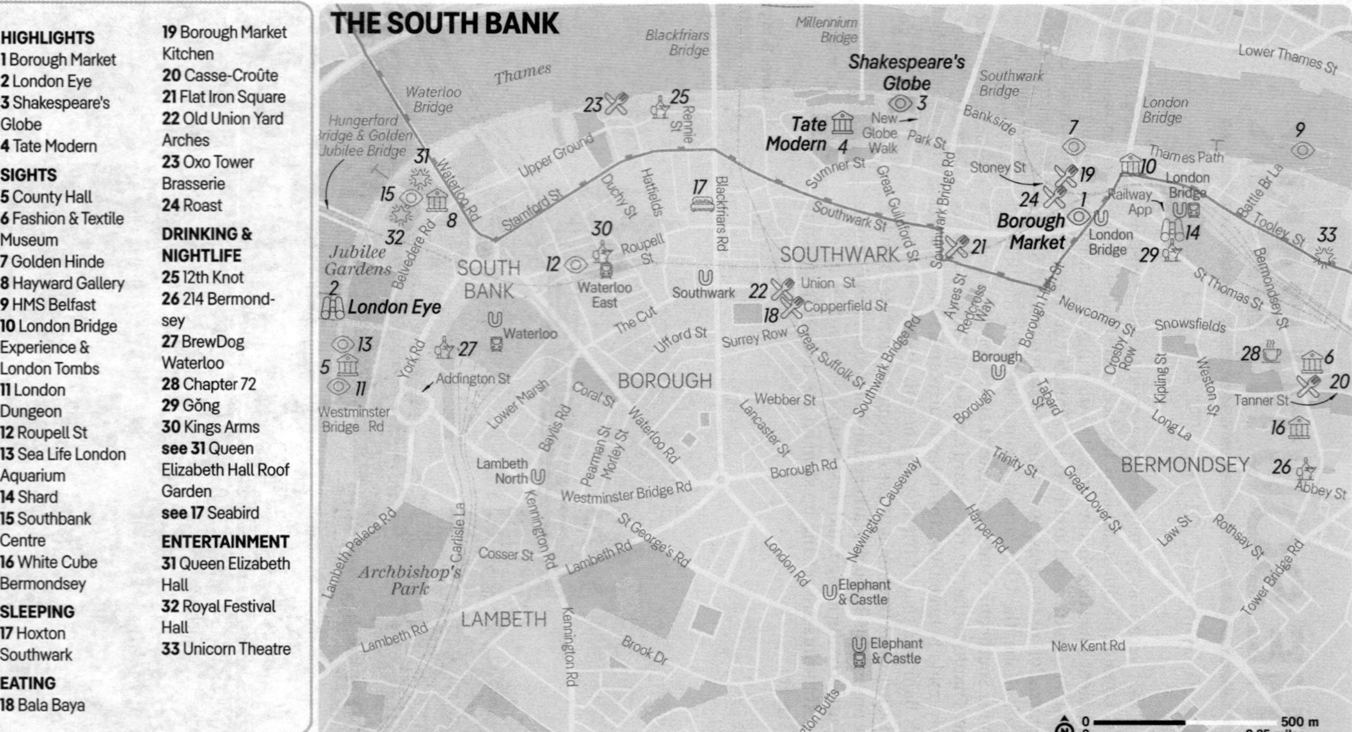


**HIGHLIGHTS**
**1** Borough Market
**2** London Eye
**3** Shakespeare's Globe
**4** Tate Modern

**SIGHTS**
**5** County Hall
**6** Fashion & Textile Museum
**7** Golden Hinde
**8** Hayward Gallery
**9** HMS Belfast
**10** London Bridge Experience & London Tombs
**11** London Dungeon
**12** Roupell St
**13** Sea Life London Aquarium
**14** Shard
**15** Southbank Centre
**16** White Cube Bermondsey

**SLEEPING**
**17** Hoxton Southwark

**EATING**
**18** Bala Baya
**19** Borough Market Kitchen
**20** Casse-Croûte
**21** Flat Iron Square
**22** Old Union Yard Arches
**23** Oxo Tower Brasserie
**24** Roast

**DRINKING & NIGHTLIFE**
**25** 12th Knot
**26** 214 Bermondsey
**27** BrewDog Waterloo
**28** Chapter 72
**29** Gŏng
**30** Kings Arms
**see 31** Queen Elizabeth Hall Roof Garden
**see 17** Seabird

**ENTERTAINMENT**
**31** Queen Elizabeth Hall
**32** Royal Festival Hall
**33** Unicorn Theatre

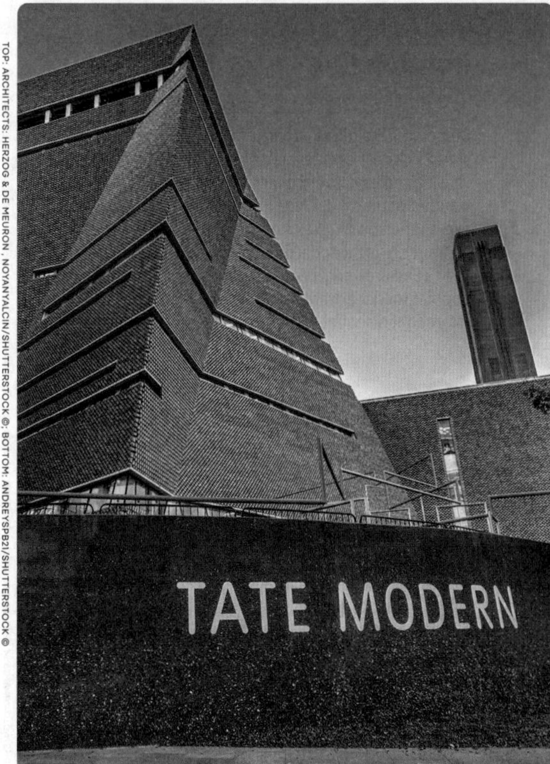


## Tate Modern

ART IN A FORMER POWER STATION

One of London's most impressive attractions, this outstanding modern- and contemporary-art gallery is housed in the creatively revamped Bankside Power Station. A spellbinding synthesis of modern art and industrial brick design, Tate Modern has been extraordinarily successful in bringing challenging work to the masses, through both its free permanent collection and its fee-charged temporary exhibitions. The curators have at their disposal more than 60,000 works by Henri Matisse, Andy Warhol, Mark Rothko, Jackson Pollock, Barbara Hepworth, Damien Hirst, Rebecca Horn and many more big names. The 10-storey Blavatnik Building extension, opened in 2016, increased exhibition space by 60%.

Borough Market

## Borough Market

A FOODIE FEAST

For a thousand years, a market has existed at the southern end of London Bridge, making this still-busy ancient gathering point a superb spectacle. Overflowing with small shops, food stalls cooking in close quarters and wholesale greengrocers catering to London's top-end restaurants, Borough Market makes a delicious lunch stop, afternoon grazing session or pure dinner-party inspiration.

The market specialises in high-end fresh (and often local) products. Wander through the maze of assorted fruit and vegetable stalls, cheesemongers, butchers, fishmongers and bakeries, as well as delis and gourmet stalls that sell spices, nuts, preserves and condiments.

When you're ready to dig in and dine, take your pick from the many food stalls clustered in the tucked-away **Borough Market Kitchen** area off Winchester Walk, an expansion opened in 2019 in a former car park. If you prefer to take a seat, plenty of brick-and-mortar restaurants line the market's edges on side streets, under railway arches or – in the case of **Roast** – even have a perch in the rafters.

London Eye

## London Eye

PANORAMIC VIEWS FROM A LONDON LANDMARK

Standing 135m high in a fairly flat city, the London Eye is the world's largest cantilevered observation wheel and affords views 25 miles in every direction (as far as Windsor Castle), weather permitting. A ride in one of the 32 glass-enclosed eye-shaped pods takes a gracefully slow 30 minutes. The London Eye is the focal point of the capital's midnight New Year's Eve fireworks display, and it's one of the UK's most popular tourist attractions. Book tickets online in advance for a slight discount or fast-track entry.

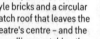

## Shakespeare's Globe

ALL THE WORLD'S A STAGE

Designed to resemble the 16th-century original as closely as possible, the reconstructed Shakespeare's Globe was built with 600 oak pegs (there's not a nail or screw in the house), specially fired Tudor-style bricks and a circular thatch roof that leaves the theatre's centre – and the groundlings watching the performance – vulnerable to the elements. Despite Shakespeare's popularity, the original Globe Theatre was demolished by the Puritans in 1644. If you're not able to get tickets for a show, guided tours take in the architecture and give access to the exhibition space, with displays on Shakespeare, life in Bankside and theatre in the 17th century.

Shakespeare's Globe

## Southbank Centre

EUROPE'S BIGGEST ART SPACE

It's easy to get wrapped up – and lost – in Southbank Centre, made up of three brutalist buildings that stretch across 7 riverside hectares. With cafes, restaurants, shops and bars, this complex is always a hive of activity, from the singing lift up to the 6th floor to teenage skateboarders doing tricks in the Undercroft.

Royal Festival Hall, home to four resident orchestras, is one of the best places in London to hear modern and classical music, poetry and spoken-word performances. Queen Elizabeth Hall has a smaller-scale but still full programme of gigs, talks, dance performances and music. In summer, don't miss the plant-strewn cafe-bar on the roof. The Hayward Gallery hosts a handful of contemporary art exhibitions every year.

WILLIAM BARTON/SHUTTERSTOCK ©

The Old Vic

MORE IN SOUTH BANK

## Seeing South Bank from Above

SUCH GREAT HEIGHTS

South Bank has a growing bouquet of lofty restaurants, bars and attractions to showcase the impressive views of the river and the city beyond.

The dramatic splinter-like form of the **Shard** has become an icon of the city and is one of the tallest buildings in Europe. The scene from the 244m-high viewing platforms on floors 69 and 72 is unique, but it comes at an equally lofty price. To take in the view over a memorable meal or drink, visit one of the building's restaurants or bars. **GŎNG** is the highest, on the 52nd floor.

On the 12th floor of luxe Sea Containers hotel, **12th Knot is** a showstopper, with knockout views of the city and a table-width outdoor roof terrace to boot.

Atop the Hoxton Southwark hotel, sleek **Seabird** has palm-filled indoor and outdoor spaces with vantage points of St Paul's from wicker-seat comfort.

The prominent **Oxo Tower** has an 8th-floor brasserie – run by posh department store Harvey Nichols – and the stunning

### BEST THEATRES BEYOND THE GLOBE

**Old Vic**
Thousand-seater nonprofit theatre going strong for more than 200 years.

**Young Vic**
Groundbreaking stage that's as much about showcasing and discovering new talent as people discovering theatre.

**Bridge Theatre**
Opened in 2017; London's first new major theatre in 80 years.

**National Theatre**
The country's flagship theatre, which delivers up to 25 shows a year.

**Vaults**
Supper clubs, live performances and alt art in converted railway arches under Waterloo station.

### WHERE TO EAT INTERNATIONALLY ON THE SOUTH BANK

**Padella**
The best pasta this side of Italy; the *pici cacio e pepe* is a must-try. £

**Bala Baya**
A love letter to Tel Aviv; Israeli chef at the helm and many veggie choices. £££

**Arabica Bar & Kitchen**
Classic Middle Eastern favourites served mezze-style; round up a group to sample and share. £

**BEST FOOD MARKETS BEYOND BOROUGH**

**Flat Iron Square**
Industrial-chic food court in railway arches and surrounding outside space; pizza, game burgers, Lebanese, Venezuelan.

**Vinegar Yard**
Equal parts street food market, bar, vintage shopping and art installation. Huge outdoor space.

**Lower Marsh Market**
Food and bric-a-brac market selling dishes ranging from curry to falafel. Saturdays feature clothing and craft.

glassed-in terrace provides a front-row seat to stellar city views. But you don't have to handsomely pay for it: the lift also grants access to a free viewing gallery.

If you want to savour the city scene without the distraction of dinner and drinks, book a 'flight' on the **London Eye**.

## Backstreets of South Bank

A PEEK INTO LONDON'S PAST

The River Thames and its conga line of absorbing attractions along the South Bank hog the attention of most visitors to this neighbourhood, but a short stroll inland reveals a quieter but just as fascinating side of the capital.

Since the Victorian era, South Bank and wider South London have been crisscrossed by elevated railways, but over time many of the viaducts were rendered inaccessible by new construction and forgotten. Now local community organisations have developed the **Low Line**, a network of shops, restaurants, bars and cultural spaces in the once abandoned arches. There's some on-the-ground signage and an online map (lowline.london), but the Low Line is still a work in progress. Without a map, the route isn't always obvious, but you can see plenty is happening in Flat Iron Square, **Borough Market** and the **Old Union Yard Arches**, where restaurant Bala Baya is located.

Near Waterloo East station, **Roupell St** is an astonishingly pretty row of low-rise workers' cottages, all sooty bricks and brightly painted doors, dating back to the 1820s. The street is so uniform it looks like a film set – and is often used as one. The same architecture extends to Theed and Whittlesey Sts, which run parallel to Roupell St to the north. Admire the architecture from the **Kings Arms**, a neighbourhood boozer that's retained original features, such as the working fireplace in winter.

**ON THE UP**

Get another perspective on the capital's skyline across the river in the City of London. See the city from 40th-floor **Duck & Waffle** (p79) or an up-close view of St Paul's Cathedral from the free public viewing terrace at **One New Change** (p79).

## Strolling Bermondsey St

ARTS, EATS AND DRINKS

Despite being only about 500m long, Bermondsey St, south of the London Bridge railway tracks, has an impressive density of things to do.

Once an area made wealthy from wool trading, tanneries and leatherworking, it still retains a flavour of creativity. The **Fashion & Textile Museum** showcases quarterly temporary exhibitions that have included retrospectives on Swedish fashion, the evolution of underwear and 20th-century

**WHERE TO EAT INTERNATIONALLY ON THE SOUTH BANK**

**Texas Joe's**
Authentic Lone Star barbecue from a Dallas expat on a Bermondsey backstreet. ££

**Juma Kitchen**
Iraqi kebabs and meaty dumplings from a stall behind the main area of Borough Market. £

**Casa do Frango**
This is the spot for *peri-peri frango* (charcoal-grilled chicken brushed in the peppery sauce). ££

Lower Marsh Market

art in textiles. **White Cube Bermondsey** impresses with its large exhibition spaces, which lend themselves to monumental pieces or expansive installations using several mediums.

Bermondsey St also has plenty of places to pause for a drink or linger over a meal. So typical is the French interior of **Casse-Croûte** that you'll have to keep reminding yourself that you are in London and not in Paris. The daily changing menu, written on a chalkboard only in French, is quintessential hearty countryside fare. **Chapter 72**, a cafe-cocktail bar, can do anything with espresso, and it's so dedicated to coffee that it even runs an espresso-martini masterclass. Something of a speakeasy but with none of the pretentiousness, **214 Bermondsey** is hidden below the Flour & Grape restaurant and lists more than 100 gins, served splashed with its own house-made craft tonic or expertly fashioned into a cocktail of your choosing. It also offers three-glass gin flights with the labels removed so you have to guess what's what.

## BEST PLACES FOR A DRINK IN THE SOUTH BANK

**Lyaness**
Cocktails of oddball ingredients (oyster honey and blood curaçao) from famous mixologist Mr Lyan.

**Rake**
London's original craft beer bar, with an astonishing selection that includes rare brews.

**George Inn**
Magnificent 1677 galleried coaching inn that's the last of its kind in London.

**Understudy**
This National Theatre bar spills out on the huge waterfront terrace, perfect for people-watching.

**Kings Arms**
Charming neighbourhood boozer serving traditional ales and bottled beers on old-school Roupell St.

## WHERE TO FIND BRITISH DISHES ON THE SOUTH BANK

**Anchor & Hope**
Excellent gastro-pub started by former chefs from nose-to-tail pioneer St JOHN. ££

**Skylon**
Retro-futuristic decor and a season-driven menu of contemporary British cuisine. £££

**Swan at the Globe**
Perfect pre-theatre dinner of British dishes in refined surrounds with river views. ££

# The River Thames

## CENTRAL LONDON ALONG THE WATER

London's history has always been determined by the Thames. The city was founded as a Roman port nearly 2000 years ago, and over the centuries since then, many of the capital's landmarks have lined the river's banks. Going for a walk or on a boat trip is a great way to see the attractions.

If you don't want to walk, the best place to board is Westminster Pier, from where boats head downstream to the original City of London, now the skyscraper-dominated financial district and beyond. Across the river, the South Bank boasts as many top attractions as its northern counterpart, including the slender Shard, one of the tallest buildings in Europe.

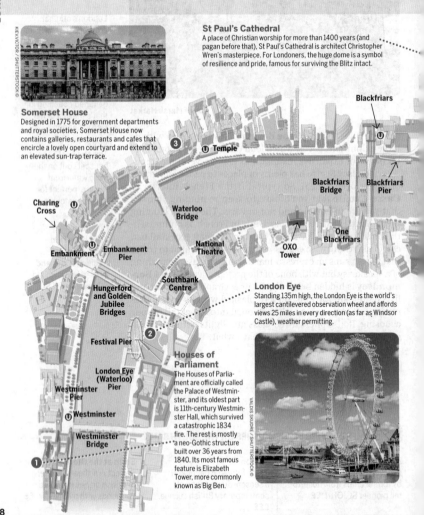

KIEVVICTOR / SHUTTERSTOCK ©

**Somerset House**
Designed in 1775 for government departments and royal societies, Somerset House now contains galleries, restaurants and cafes that encircle a lovely open courtyard and extend to an elevated sun-trap terrace.

**St Paul's Cathedral**
A place of Christian worship for more than 1400 years (and pagan before that), St Paul's Cathedral is architect Christopher Wren's masterpiece. For Londoners, the huge dome is a symbol of resilience and pride, famous for surviving the Blitz intact.

**London Eye**
Standing 135m high, the London Eye is the world's largest cantilevered observation wheel and affords views 25 miles in every direction (as far as Windsor Castle), weather permitting.

**Houses of Parliament**
The Houses of Parliament are officially called the Palace of Westminster, and its oldest part is 11th-century Westminster Hall, which survived a catastrophic 1834 fire. The rest is mostly a neo-Gothic structure built over 36 years from 1840. Its most famous feature is Elizabeth Tower, more commonly known as Big Ben.

VALDIS SKUDRE / SHUTTERSTOCK ©

From west to east, the highlights to look out for on both sides are the ❶ **Houses of Parliament**, the ❷ **London Eye**, ❸ **Somerset House**, ❹ **St Paul's Cathedral**, the ❺ **Tate Modern**, ❻ **Shakespeare's Globe**, the ❼ **Tower of London** and ❽ **Tower Bridge**.

In addition to covering this central section of the Thames, boats can also be taken upstream as far as Kew and

## RIDING THE RIVERBOAT

Thames Clippers operates riverboats approximately every 20 minutes between Westminster and Greenwich, with less frequent services to piers further east and west. You can buy tickets at the piers, but for a discount on the boat ticket price, buy online or use an Oyster or contactless payment card.

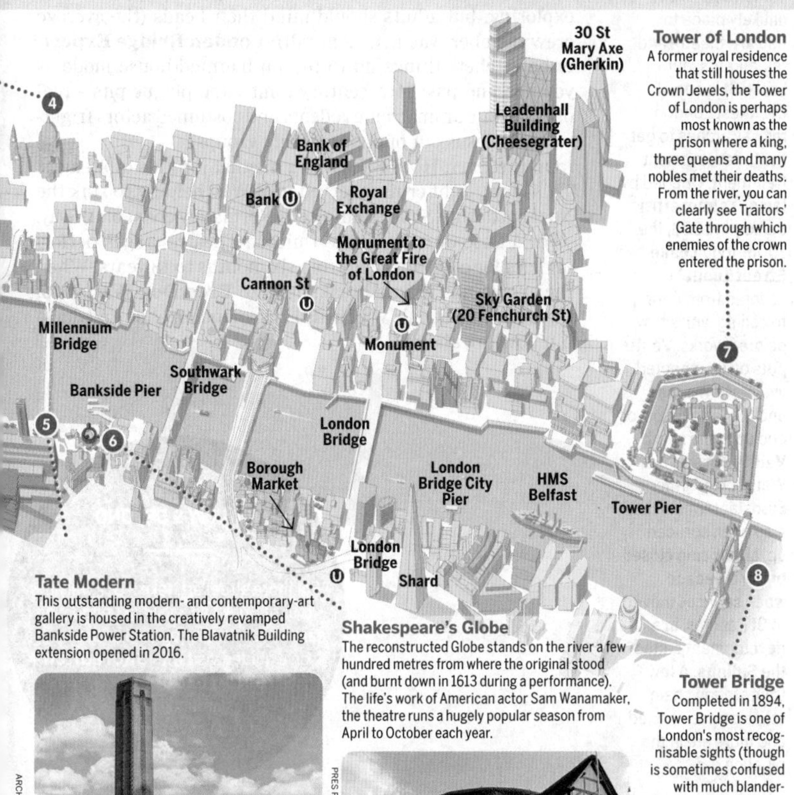


**Tower of London**
A former royal residence that still houses the Crown Jewels, the Tower of London is perhaps most known as the prison where a king, three queens and many nobles met their deaths. From the river, you can clearly see Traitors' Gate through which enemies of the crown entered the prison.

**Tate Modern**
This outstanding modern- and contemporary-art gallery is housed in the creatively revamped Bankside Power Station. The Blavatnik Building extension opened in 2016.



**Shakespeare's Globe**
The reconstructed Globe stands on the river a few hundred metres from where the original stood (and burnt down in 1613 during a performance). The life's work of American actor Sam Wanamaker, the theatre runs a hugely popular season from April to October each year.



**Tower Bridge**
Completed in 1894, Tower Bridge is one of London's most recognisable sights (though is sometimes confused with much blander-looking London Bridge to the west). The roadway across the bridge is still raised around 1000 times a year for boats coming into the capital.

## The South Bank for Families

FUN FOR ALL AGES

South Bank is a particularly fun-filled neighbourhood if you're visiting London with kids, with plenty to entertain the whole family.

County Hall has a number of kid-focused attractions. At **London Dungeon**, shuffle through themed rooms where actors, often covered in fake blood, tell creepy stories and goad visitors. It's spooky, interactive and fun if you like jumping out of your skin. **Sea Life London Aquarium** is mostly geared towards children and has a shark tunnel, a ray lagoon and gentoo penguin enclosures.

Head towards London Bridge to board a replica of Francis Drake's **Golden Hinde**, a 16th-century warship. Kids love exploring, but adults should mind their heads (the average crew member was just 1.6m tall). **London Bridge Experience** ratchets things up to full-on haunted-house mode as you descend past 14th-century tombs and plague pits – real ones – while animatronic rodents and costumed actors frighten the bejesus out of unsuspecting groups.

On the river, HMS Belfast is a magnet for kids of all ages. This large, light cruiser served in WWII, helping to sink the Nazi battleship *Sand* shelling the Normandy coast on D-Day.

For a dose of culture, the Unicorn Theatre stages performances for children aged from six months to 18 years. When the grown-ups need a break, head to **BrewDog Waterloo**, the UK's largest pub, which also has an indoor slide and duckpin bowling alley.

### LEAKE STREET ARCHES & WATERLOO SIDINGS

A grungy road under Waterloo station seems an unlikely place to find art, theatre and restaurants, but Leake St is one of the latest London railway arches to get the redevelopment treatment. Opened by famous street artist Banksy in 2008, the 200m-long **Leake Street Tunnel** is covered from floor to ceiling with spray-painted works. **Vaults** puts on unexpected live performances, and the leftover props end up in the nearby **Vaulty Towers** bar. Waterloo's former Eurostar terminal has also been spruced up, after being closed off for a decade when services moved to St Pancras, in a development called the **Sidings**. A few train station chain staples have opened and more are in the pipeline.

### BANKSY & BEYOND

For more street art, take a DIY walking tour of Brick Lane, in East London, or learn about the stories behind the pieces on a guided visit with **Shoreditch Street Art Tours** (p94). The buildings around Hackney Wick station have also been used as canvases.

### WHERE TO FIND BRITISH DISHES ON THE SOUTH BANK

**Market Porter**
Pie/fish and chips in the upstairs dining room – or 6am pints with market workers. **££**

**Fountain & Ink**
Convivial spot serving pub food and craft beer to a jolly after-work crowd. **££**

**Founder's Arms**
Standard pub offerings elevated by prime riverside seating that's a welcome summer sun trap. **££**

# SHOREDITCH & EAST LONDON

## LATE NIGHTS AT HIP HANGOUTS

Once a poorer working-class neighbourhood on the fringes of the well-to-do city, East London has transformed yet again, repurposing its abandoned factories, crumbling historic buildings and disused docklands into late-night clubs, fascinating museums and swish cocktail bars. This area has a long history of migration, and a diverse patchwork of people still call this neighbourhood home. Far from simply being a historical repository, this district is the heart of London's creative industry that's actively shaping the next chapter in the capital's history. If it's happening in London, it's happening here.

Shoreditch knows how to throw a party, and this neighbourhood's dancing shoes are always on. Before your night out, scour the many markets and indie shops around Spitalfields and Brick Lane for unique and vintage finds. While East London doesn't have any big-name sights, its smaller museums focus on the ordinary instead of the aristocratic, providing a counterbalance of narratives in the capital's story.

### TOP TIP

The East End's bounty of markets around Spitalfields, Brick Lane and Columbia Rd is in full swing on Sundays, the best day to join the crowds shrugging off their hangovers on a consumerist crawl. Saturdays bring out the stalls of Broadway Market in Hackney.

Spitalfields Market

# SHOREDITCH & EAST LONDON

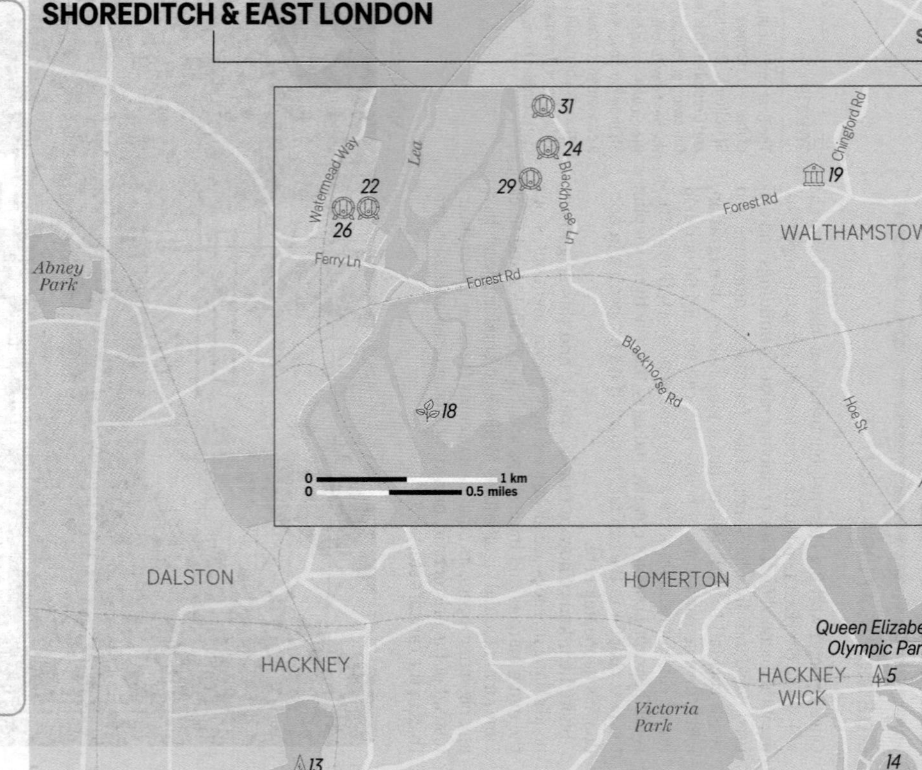


**HIGHLIGHTS**
**1** Broadway Market
**2** Columbia Road Flower Market
**3** Museum of London Docklands
**4** Old Spitalfields Market
**5** Queen Elizabeth Olympic Park
**6** Whitechapel Gallery

**SIGHTS**
**7** ArcelorMittal Orbit
**8** Christ Church Spitalfields
**9** Crossrail Place Roof Garden
**10** Dennis Severs' House
**11** God's Own Junkyard
**12** London Aquatics Centre
**13** London Fields
**14** London Stadium
**15** Museum of the Home
**16** Old Truman Brewery
**17** Victoria Park
**18** Walthamstow Wetlands
**19** William Morris Gallery

**EATING**
**20** Market Halls Cargo
**21** MMy Wood Wharf

**DRINKING & NIGHTLIFE**
**22** Beavertown
**23** Captain Kidd
**24** Exale
**see 11** Mother's Ruin
**25** Pillars
**26** Pressure Drop
**27** Prospect of Whitby
**28** Shoreditch Street Art Tours
**29** Signature
**30** Town of Ramsgate
**see 25** Trap Taproom
**31** Wild Card

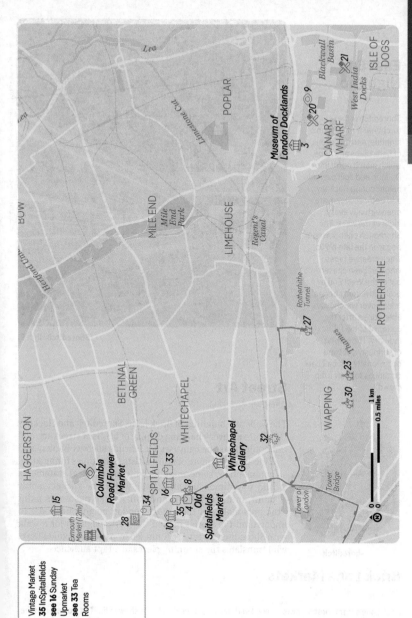

Brewery
**ENTERTAIN-MENT**
**32** Wilton's
**SHOPPING**
**33** Backyard Market
**34** Boxpark
**see 16** Brick Lane
Vintage Market
**35** InSpitalfields
**see 16** Sunday Upmarket
**see 33** Tea Rooms

HAGGERSTON
BOW
Hertford Union
Lea
15
Exmouth Market (1.2mi)
2
**Columbia Road Flower Market**
BETHNAL GREEN
28
34
SPITALFIELDS
10
16
33
35
4
8
**Old Spitalfields Market**
WHITECHAPEL
6
**Whitechapel Gallery**
MILE END
Mile End Park
Limestone Cut
LIMEHOUSE
POPLAR
Regent's Canal
32
**Museum of London Docklands**
3
20
9
Tower of London
27
Rotherhithe Tunnel
Tower Bridge
WAPPING
30
23
Thames
CANARY WHARF
Blackwall Basin
21
West India Docks
ISLE OF DOGS
ROTHERHITHE
0 1 km
0 0.5 miles

## East End Nightlife

GOING OUT OUT

Shoreditch is the torchbearer of London's nightlife, and its dozens of bars, clubs and pubs, which march north into Dalston and spill over into neighbouring Hackney and Bethnal Green, are open virtually every night of the week. The Shoreditch phenomenon began in the late 1990s, when creative types who had been chased out of the West End by prohibitive rents began taking over warehouses abandoned after the collapse of the fabrics industry. The surplus of seriously cool and occasionally oddball bars continues to draw a hip crowd.

**Shoreditch High St**

## Street Art

OPEN-AIR ART GALLERY

The walls and buildings of Brick Lane, Shoreditch and Hackney Wick are an ever-changing display of brilliant street art, and moonlight as the canvases for legends such as Banksy and Eine as well as more obscure artists. Sometimes funny social commentary, sometimes hard-hitting political statements and sometimes just an artistic whim, the stickers, spray paint, mini sculptures and collage-like paste-ups paint the personality of these East London neighbourhoods. To understand the stories behind the works, sign up for a walk with Shoreditch Street Art Tours, led by passionate guide Dave, who translates the stunning pieces to a rapt audience.

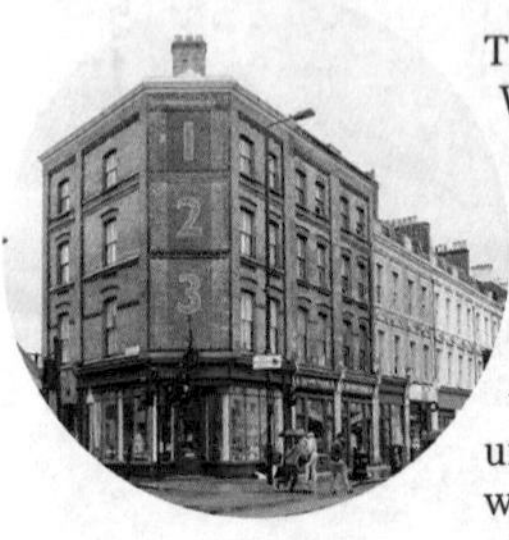

**Shoreditch**

## Brick Lane Markets

ON A SHOPPING SPREE

Brick Lane's **Upmarket** sprawls among the beautiful brick buildings of the Old Truman Brewery on both sides of Brick Lane between Hanbury and Buxton Sts. Vintage fiends, fashionistas and foodies will be occupied for hours – it's a buzzing place to while away a weekend. Traders serve drool-inducing fare in the glass-sided building on the corner of Brick Lane and Hanbury St, while shoppers rummage through the racks at **Brick Lane Vintage Market** (open daily) in the basement. Bric-a-brac and fashion accessories are on show in the **Tea Rooms** and the **Backyard Market**. The world's first pop-up mall, **Boxpark**, just outside Shoreditch High Street station, is a shopping and street-food enclave made from upcycled shipping containers.

## Wilton's Music Hall

WORLD'S LAST SURVIVING GRAND MUSIC HALL

Built in 1859 as a place for working-class East Enders to experience West End entertainment, the glorious Wilton's Music Hall once again puts on hundreds of performances a year, from comedy and classical music to theatre and opera. After a stint as a Methodist Mission and decades of dereliction and decay, it was saved and done up just enough to preserve its shabby-chic beauty. Even if you're not attending a performance, it's worth grabbing a drink in the bar to get a taste of the atmosphere.

Saturday Market, Victoria Park

Vintage Fair, Wilton's Music Hall

## Victoria Park

THE PEOPLE'S PARK

Victoria Park's 86-hectare leafy expanse of ornamental lakes, monuments, tennis courts, flowerbeds and lawns opened in 1845. It was the first public park in the East End, given the go-ahead after a local MP presented Queen Victoria with a petition of 30,000 signatures. A weekly farmers' market with hot food stalls takes place on Sundays, and warm weather brings out ice-cream vans and music festivals. It's lined on two sides with canals – Regent's Canal to the west and Hertford Union Canal to the south – which are lovely to walk along.

## Queen Elizabeth Olympic Park

AFTER THE 2012 GAMES

The centrepiece of London's 2012 Olympic Games, the 227-hectare Queen Elizabeth Olympic Park includes the main Olympic venues as well as playgrounds, walking and cycling trails, gardens and a diverse mix of wetland, woodland, meadow and other wildlife habitats. The main focal point is **London Stadium**, now the home ground for West Ham United FC. Other signature buildings include the Zaha Hadid–designed **London Aquatics Centre** and the twisted-steel **ArcelorMittal Orbit**. This 115m-high sculpture is in essence an artwork, but at the 80m mark it also offers an impressive panorama from a mirrored viewing platform. A dramatic tunnel slide running down the tower is the world's highest and longest, coiling 178m down to ground level.

## BEST PLACES TO STAY OUT LATE IN SHOREDITCH & EAST LONDON

**Beigel Bake**
Relic of the Jewish East End that's still serving dirt-cheap bagels around the clock.

**XOYO**
No-frills basement venue with resident DJs and late-night gigs.

**Bethnal Green Working Men's Club**
Off-the-wall club nights, from cabaret and drag shows to burlesque and bake-offs, in an LGBTIQ+-friendly venue.

**◆■● (A Bar with Shapes for a Name)**
Signposted with shapes instead of words, this Bauhaus minimalist bar is open until 3am daily.

ARCHITECTS: FOSTER + PARTNERS, 4KCLIPS/SHUTTERSTOCK ©

Crossrail Place Roof Garden

### TASTE OF LOCAL LONDON

If you're not in London over a weekend, you can still sample the local market atmosphere in South London. Go shopping or visit one of the many bars and restaurants in **Brixton Village** (p117), **Pop Brixton** (p119) or **Tooting Market** (p119).

## MORE IN SHOREDITCH & EAST LONDON

# Exploring Georgian Spitalfields

MULTICULTURALISM THROUGH THE CENTURIES

Crowded around its famous market and grand parish church, Spitalfields has long been one of the capital's most diverse areas. Waves of Huguenot (French Protestant), Jewish, Irish and, more recently, Indian and Bangladeshi immigrants have made Spitalfields their home. A walk along **Brick Lane** is the best way to experience the sights, sounds and smells of Bangladeshi London, but to get a sense of what Georgian Spitalfields was like, branch off to Princelet, Fournier, Elder and Wilkes Sts. Having fled persecution in France, the Huguenots set up shop here from the late 17th century, practising their trade of silk weaving. Step into this world at **Dennis Severs' House**, set up as if a Huguenot family has just walked out the door. Each of the 10 rooms is stuffed with the minutiae of everyday life from centuries past: half-drunk cups of tea, emptied but gleaming wet oyster shells and, in perhaps unnecessary attention to detail, a used chamber pot by the bed.

## WHERE TO EAT IN SHOREDITCH & EAST LONDON

**Breddos Tacos**
From car-park origins to serving some of London's best Mexican food in a permanent Clerkenwell outlet. **£**

**Clove Club**
Started life as a supper club in a London flat; now a Michelin-starred restaurant. **£££**

**St JOHN**
Pioneers of the nose-to-tail food movement in the UK, with a daily changing menu. **££**

## A Window into Ordinary Life

THERE'S NO PLACE LIKE HOME

Beautiful ivy-clad brick almshouses built in 1714 as a home for poor pensioners now house the delightful free-to-visit **Museum of the Home** (formerly the Geffrye Museum). A series of rooms show how Londoners have furnished and decorated their homes over the last 400 years, from a 1630s dining room to a 1998 loft apartment. The attention to detail is impressive, down to the crumbs on the floor of the 1930s bachelor pad.

## London's Trading Powerhouse

DERELICT DOCKS DONE UP

From the 1500s to the mid-20th century, **Canary Wharf** and London's **Docklands** were the hub of the British Empire and its enormous global trade. Cargo landed at these docks from around the world, but after WWII bombings and technological and political changes, the docks began to close in the 1960s. Today's financial district skyscrapers in Canary Wharf emerged from a 1980s government-sponsored overhaul. **Museum of London Docklands**, housed in an 1802 warehouse, charts the fascinating history of the docks' decline and resurrection.

Despite the soullessness that can come with an office-heavy district, the radical redevelopment of Canary Wharf is impressive. Public art decorates elevated walkways and pedestrianised streets, and the free **Crossrail Place Roof Garden** injects a dose of much-needed plant life into the place. Two market-style food courts have moved in to feed the masses: **Market Halls Cargo** near the Canary Wharf Elizabeth line station and **MMy Wood Wharf**.

For a more atmospheric picture of the past, head just around the river bend to **Wapping** (pronounced 'whopping'). This neighbourhood still has plenty of early-19th-century warehouses and old-school riverside pubs, such as the **Prospect of Whitby** (opened in 1520), **Captain Kidd** (named after a pirate hanged here in 1701) and **Town of Ramsgate** (built in 1545 on the foundations of an even older pub).

## Off the Beaten Track in Walthamstow & Tottenham

WORTH A TRIP

At the northeastern end of the Victoria line, unassuming Walthamstow has plenty to shout about. Fans of the Arts and Crafts movement should visit the **William Morris Gallery**,

### JACK THE RIPPER

Perhaps the best-known serial killer in the world, the never-identified Jack the Ripper brutally murdered numerous women who lived and worked in the impoverished East End in the 1880s.

Though Whitechapel's slums and working-class history have been almost entirely cleared away, Jack the Ripper walking tours remain a shockingly popular way to 'see' East London. These walks, sometimes led by costumed and 'bloodied' guides, tend to focus on the gruesome details of the savage murders, but **Look Up London** (https://lookup.london) turns these tours on their head with a 'Feminist Jack the Ripper Tour', which centres the stories of the victims whose lives were cut short as well as the achievements of East End women today.

**Som Saa**
Crowdfunded to open in an old Spitalfields fabric warehouse. Authentic Thai curries and grilled meats. ££

**Barge East**
Hundred-tonne barge sailed from the Netherlands to offer seasonal fare and drinks with waterside views. ££

**Mangal II**
Top-notch Turkish in simple surrounds on Stoke Newington Rd. ££

## RYAN CHETIYA-WARDANA'S FAVOURITE HAUNTS

**Ryan Chetiyawardana** (aka Mr Lyan), the world's most awarded bartender and owner of Seed Library and Lyaness, has lived and worked in East London for more than 15 years. *@mrlyan*

**Lyle's**
Shows off modern British food at its best. James Lowe ran St JOHN, a temple to British cooking, just down the road, but with Lyle's, he's brought his own distinct style.

**Happiness Forgets**
An intimate basement bar on Hoxton Sq, this neighbourhood spot has a global outlook and brings amazing creativity to a wider audience.

**Jolene**
Serves great tea and coffee to take away, but the sandwiches, cakes and baked goods are the real stars of the show. Pray there's Guinness cake when you go.

Whitechapel Gallery

TOP: TUPUNGATO/SHUTTERSTOCK ©; BOTTOM: JOE DUNCKLEY/SHUTTERSTOCK ©

home of the designer who founded renowned interior design company Morris & Co which created famous patterned wallpapers. To the west, the pleasantly incongruous Walthamstow Wetlands claim 211 hectares of natural tranquillity across 10 reservoirs surrounded by walking paths.

Walthamstow and nearby Tottenham, across the River Lea, have exciting drinking destinations set on otherwise dull industrial estates. Between Walthamstow Central and Wood Street stations, two breweries (**Wild Card** and **Pillars**), a cider taproom (**Trap Taproom**), a gin distillery (**Mother's Ruin**) and the neon nirvana of **God's Own Junkyard**, where you can grab a drink and wander among the art, bring life to Ravenswood Industrial Estate. These neighbourhoods even have the beginnings of their own 'beer mile' to rival Bermondsey (p120). As yet, it's still informal enough that the name hasn't even been decided (Blackhorse Beer Mile? Tottenham Beer Mile?), but its breweries are worth tracking down. **Beavertown** is the one most familiar to hopheads, but make time for **Pressure Drop**, **Exale** and **Signature** as well.

### WHERE TO DRINK IN SHOREDITCH & EAST LONDON

**Nightjar**
Bona fide speakeasy pouring award-winning libations behind a gold-knobbed door.

**Crate Brewery**
Craft beer brewed in a canalside Victorian warehouse in Hackney Wick.

**Discount Suit Company**
Speakeasy (originally a suit company storeroom) tucked away like a hidden-seam on old Petticoat Ln.

## Cutting-Edge Exhibitions

ART WITH AN EDGE

A firm favourite of art students, the groundbreaking **Whitechapel Gallery** doesn't have a permanent collection but hosts edgy exhibitions of contemporary art. It made its name by staging exhibitions of both established and emerging artists, including the first UK shows by Pablo Picasso, Jackson Pollock, Mark Rothko and Frida Kahlo.

## Markets Beyond Brick Lane

EAST LONDON ORIGINALS

East London is a top neighbourhood for discovering cool boutiques and market stalls that showcase up-and-coming designers, not to mention endless vintage shops.

Traders have been hawking their wares at **Old Spitalfields Market** since 1638. Sundays are the biggest days, but Thursdays are good for antiques and vintage, and crates of vinyl take over on the first and second Fridays of the month. The market upped its foodie credentials with the **Kitchens**, a collection of food counters serving street food at the heart of the market. **InSpitalfields** has a good selection of non-tacky London-themed souvenirs.

A wonderful explosion of colour and life, the Sunday-only **Columbia Road Flower Market** sells a beautiful array of flowers, pot plants and everything you need for the garden. It's a lot of fun and the best place to hear proper Cockney barrow-boy banter ('We got flowers cheap enough for ya muvver-in-law's grave!'). About a 15-minute walk to the northeast, **Broadway Market** has been around since the late 19th century, and the focus these days is artisan food, handmade gifts and unique clothing. Stock up on edible treats then head to **London Fields** for a picnic. In Clerkenwell, **Exmouth Market** is lined with restaurants, pubs, boutique shops and weekday lunchtime food stalls.

Exmouth Market

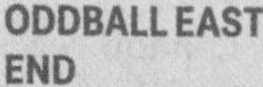

**ODDBALL EAST END**

**Dans Le Noir**
The experience of dining in the pitch black is exhilarating and, dare we say, eye-opening.

**MEATliquor**
Temple to the burger gods, somewhat sacrilegiously set in the former Hoxton Market Christian Mission.

**Viktor Wynd Museum of Curiosities, Fine Art & Natural History**
Cabinet of curiosities: pickled genitals, dodo bones, celebrity excrement and Pablo Escobar's gilded hippo skull.

**Satan's Whiskers**
Small neon red lettering is the only sign you're entering a world-class cocktail bar.

**Cocktail Trading Co**
Unrivalled cocktail concoctions, such as bottles presented in envelopes and ice as big as Rubik's Cubes.

**Netil360**
Rooftop cafe-bar with incredible views. Telescopes get you better acquainted with workers in 'the Gherkin'.

# CAMDEN & NORTH LONDON

## URBAN VILLAGE ENERGY

North London reveals competing personalities depending on where exactly you land. Urban renewal has spruced up King's Cross, once an industrial wasteland that's now a great place to hang out for an alfresco lunch, an ice cream or a drink in renovated historic buildings. Intoxicating Camden heaves with shoppers at its uber-popular markets, and lovers of live music rock out at its glut of gig venues. But other areas, such as Hampstead and Alexandra Palace, retain a quieter village vibe, even though these once small settlements on London's periphery were long ago sucked into the capital's ever-expanding orbit.

While King's Cross and Camden have a more restless urban energy, North London neighbourhoods just beyond the centre are laid-back, leafy and green, home to wonderfully wild parks and overgrown historic cemeteries. Stunning architecture from across the centuries underscores North London's well-heeled past and its forward-looking attitude.

### TOP TIP

To see just how well North London infuses its neighbourhoods with urban nature, take a walk. Hampstead Heath perfectly pairs wild woodlands with scenes of distant skyscrapers. Regent's Canal, once a lifeline for industry, is now a favourite close-to-home getaway for Londoners, providing a quiet walk away from car traffic.

**Camden**

VALDIS SKUDRE/SHUTTERSTOCK ©

King's Cross station

## Warner Bros Studio Tour: The Making of Harry Potter & Platform 9¾

DON'T LET THE MUGGLES GET YOU DOWN

Whether you're a fair-weather fan or a full-on Potterhead, North London has two major points of pilgrimage for Harry Potter addicts.

The *Harry Potter* films were shot on set about 20 miles northwest of London, and you can see the custom-made costumes, sets and props on the **Warner Bros Studio Tour: The Making of Harry Potter.** Large hangars contain interior sets – Dumbledore's office, the Gryffindor common room – and an outdoor section features even more.

You must book tickets online in advance, and allow at least three hours to do it justice. Golden Tours offer a tickets-and-transfer bus package, or catch a train from London Euston to Watford Junction and then take a 15-minute shuttle bus or taxi.

Euston is half a mile west of the real King's Cross station, which features in the books. You'll find platform 9¾ at King's Cross; look for the queue in the departures terminal forming around a luggage trolley half disappearing into the wall.

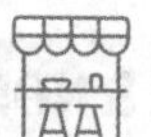

## Camden Market

SHOPPERS' PARADISE

Although – or perhaps because – it stopped being cutting-edge several thousand cheap leather jackets ago, Camden Market attracts millions of visitors and is one of London's most popular attractions. What started out as a collection of craft stalls beside Camden Lock now extends most of the way from Camden Town tube station to Chalk Farm tube station. You'll find a bit of everything: clothes (of variable quality), bags, jewellery, arts and crafts, candles, incense and myriad decorative titbits. Some side streets, such as Inverness St south of the canal, are lined with stalls selling cheap T-shirts, hats and plastic bangles.

Warner Bros Studio

# CAMDEN & NORTH LONDON

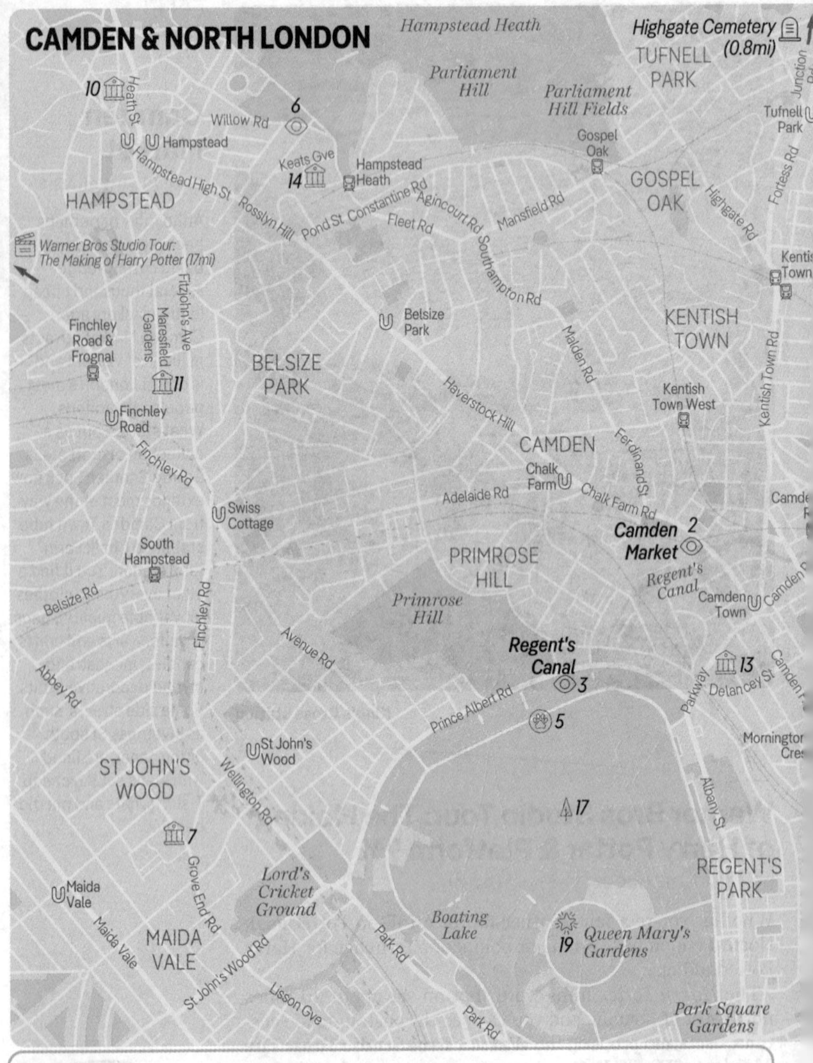


**HIGHLIGHTS**
**1** British Library
**2** Camden Market
**3** Regent's Canal
**4** Wellcome Collection
**5** ZSL London Zoo

**SIGHTS**
**6** 2 Willow Road
**7** Abbey Road Studios
**8** Coal Drops Yard
**9** Estorick Collection of Modern Italian Art
**10** Fenton House
**11** Freud Museum
**12** Granary Square
**13** Jewish Museum London
**14** Keats House
**15** King's Cross Station
**16** London Canal Museum
**17** Regent's Park
**18** St Pancras Station & Hotel

**ENTERTAINMENT**
**19** Regent's Park Open Air Theatre

**SHOPPING**
**20** Harry Potter Shop at Platform 9¾

Alexandra Palace (3mi)
Clissold Park
Arsenal
Abney Park Cemetery (1mi)
Tollington Rd
Hornsey Rd
Highbury Gve
Green Lanes
Parkhurst Rd
Camden Rd
Holloway Rd
HIGHBURY
TUFNELL PARK
Brecknock Rd
Caledonian Rd
Holloway Rd
Leighton Rd
Camden Rd
LOWER HOLLOWAY
Liverpool Rd
Holloway Rd
Highbury Fields
Torriano Ave
Camden Park Rd
York Way
Caledonian Rd
Canonbury
St Paul's Rd
BARNSBURY
Highbury & Islington
St Paul's Rd
New River
Caledonian Park
9
Caledonian Rd & Barnsbury
Liverpool Rd
Upper St
Canonbury Rd
Essex Rd
ISLINGTON
Essex Rd
New North Rd
York Way
St Pancras Way
Barnard Park
Essex Rd
CAMDEN TOWN
8
Copenhagen St
KING'S CROSS
12
Eagle Wharf Rd
16
Pancras Rd
Caledonian Rd
Upper St
Wenlock Basin
City Road Basin
Shepherdess Walk
Oakley Sq
20
York Way
Pancras Rd
PENTONVILLE
Angel
St Pancras International (Eurostar)
Pentonville Rd
Goswell Rd
Eversholt St
15
King's Cross
18
SOMERS TOWN
King's Cross St Pancras
City Rd
1
British Library
Euston
Swinton St
King's Cross Rd
Rosebery Ave
St John St
FINSBURY
Lever St
Bath St
Euston Rd
Grays Inn Rd
Judd St
4
Euston Sq
Wellcome Collection
Calthorpe St
Woburn Pl
Hunter St
Guildford St
CLERKENWELL
0 500 m
0 0.25 miles

Keats House (p108)

ALEX_MASTRO/SHUTTERSTOCK ©

Coal Drops Yard

## Coal Drops Yard & Granary Square

THE NEW FACE OF KING'S CROSS

Post-industrial King's Cross used to be somewhere you went *through* rather than *to*, but its regeneration has breathed new life into its once forgotten corners. North of King's Cross station, Coal Drops Yard is a double-level shopping and eating arcade made up of beautifully restored 1850s buildings. Next door, positioned on a sharp bend in the Regent's Canal, Granary Sq has a fountain made of 1080 individually lit water jets, which pulse and dance in sequence. On warm days, it becomes a busy urban beach.

## British Library

WRITTEN REPOSITORY OF THE WORLD

Completed in 1998, the British Library is home to some of the greatest treasures of the written word, including the *Codex Sinaiticus* (the first complete text of the New Testament), Leonardo da Vinci's notebooks and two copies of the Magna Carta (1215). The most precious manuscripts are held in the Sir John Ritblat Treasures Gallery, including stunningly illustrated religious texts, Shakespeare's First Folio (1623), a Gutenberg Bible from 1455, a copy of *The Diamond Sutra* in Chinese dating to 868 – the world's oldest block-printed book – as well as handwritten lyrics by the Beatles and the score to Handel's *Messiah*.

British Library

## Highgate Cemetery

GOTHIC VICTORIAN VALHALLA

A wonderland of shrouded urns, broken columns, sleeping angels and Egyptian-style tombs, Highgate Cemetery spreads over 20 wild and atmospheric hectares. On the eastern side, pay your respects to the graves of Karl Marx and Mary Ann Evans (better known as novelist George Eliot). The real highlight is the West Cemetery, where a maze of winding paths leads to rings of tombs that flank a circular path, called the Circle of Lebanon. Highgate remains a working cemetery. More recent high-profile interments include singer George Michael and Russian dissident Alexander Litvinenko, who died under sinister circumstances after drinking polonium-laced tea. His body was still so radioactive that he had to be buried in a special lead-lined coffin.

MAGDANATKA/SHUTTERSTOCK ©

Holly Bush

**BEST PUBS IN NORTH LONDON**

**Holly Bush**
Grade II-listed Georgian pub with an antique interior in a secluded hilltop location.

**Edinboro Castle**
Camden staple with a fun atmosphere, full menu and a huge beer garden.

**Flask**
Perfect place for a pint while walking between Hampstead Heath and Highgate Cemetery.

**Spaniards Inn**
Dating from 1585, this historic tavern has more character than a West End musical.

**Lock Tavern**
A Camden institution, with a beer garden and roof terrace to watch the market throngs.

MORE IN CAMDEN & NORTH LONDON

## Quirky Museums in North London

CULTURAL CACHE OF CAMDEN AND BEYOND

North London's smaller museums offer intriguing perspectives for those curious to dig into the capital's culture beyond the big institutions.

South of Euston station, the **Wellcome Collection** focuses on the intersection of art, science and medicine. At its heart is Sir Henry Wellcome's collection of (at times controversial) medical curiosities. The **London Canal Museum**, in the backstreets of King's Cross, traces the history of London's canal network in a former ice storage warehouse from 1857.

Sigmund Freud lived the last year of his life in a house off Finchley Rd that's now the **Freud Museum**. The psychiatrist's study still has his famous couch. In the heart of Camden Town, the **Jewish Museum** has displays about beliefs and rituals, the history of Jewish people in Britain and the Holocaust. The **Estorick Collection of Modern Italian Art**, in a Georgian townhouse near Highbury & Islington station, is the only gallery in Britain devoted to Italian art.

**WHERE TO GET A DRINK IN NORTH LONDON**

**Booking Office 1869**
Show-stopping red-brick bar in the former St Pancras railway station booking office.

**69 Colebrooke Row**
The 'bar with no name' mixes up delightful cocktails with ambitious flavours.

**Rooftop at The Standard**
Dreamy views of St Pancras station and the city from on high.

## HAMPSTEAD HEATH WALKING TOUR

Hampstead Heath covers 320 hectares in rolling woodlands and wild meadows. It feels a million miles away from central London, but you can catch sight of the city from its hilltops.

Take the London Overground to Hampstead Heath station. Follow the street called Parliament Hill into the park to start your climb up to the 1 **Parliament Hill Viewpoint** for a panoramic scene of the city.

A spider web of trails to the north leads to three bathing ponds (a 2 **mixed pond** to the west and 3 **men's** and 4 **women's** to the east). The men's and women's ponds are open year-round for cold-water swimming enthusiasts and are supervised by lifeguards. If you want to take a dip, BYO swimsuit and towel.

Traverse the heath to its northern edge and find the 18th-century 5 **Kenwood House**. The free-to-visit gallery contains a magnificent collection of art, including paintings by Rembrandt, Constable, Turner, Gainsborough and Vermeer.

Once you've had your fill of fresh air and culture, head to one of the wonderful pubs around Hampstead Heath for a restorative pint. Exit the heath via the Kenwood House car park and walk southwest along Hampstead Ln. At the heath's edge is the 1585 6 **Spaniards Inn**, where Romantic poets Keats and Byron and artist Sir Joshua Reynolds all paused for a drink.

Walk or take bus 210 to the Jack Straw's Castle stop and walk through the historic neighbourhood of Hampstead. Loved by artists in the interwar years, it has retained a bohemian feel, with sumptuous houses, leafy streets, cafes and lovely boutiques. Finish with a gastro-pub dinner at the secluded 7 **Holly Bush**, a Grade II–listed pub with a splendid antique interior.

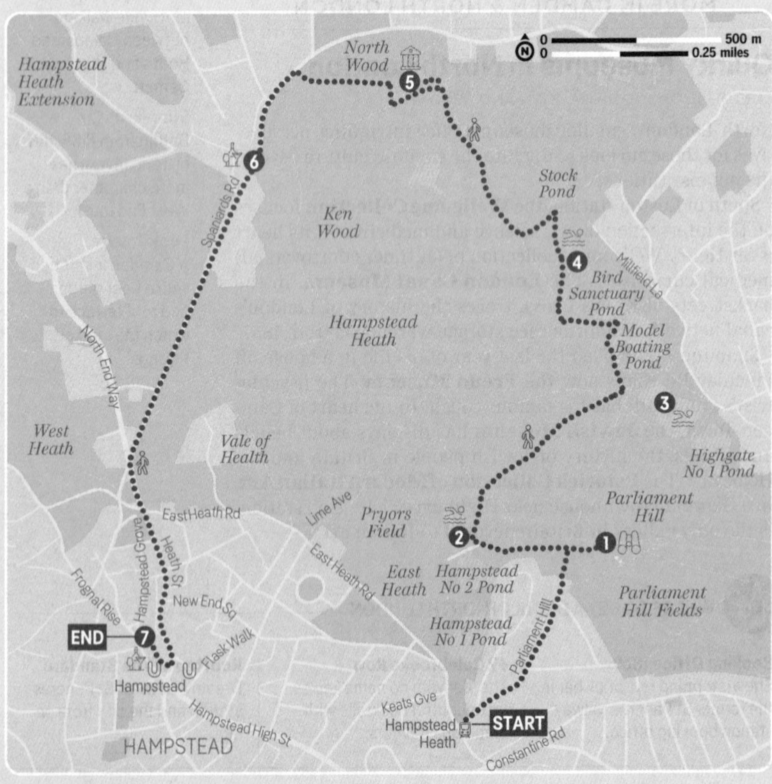

Abbey Road Studios

## Abbey Road Studios

MAGICAL MYSTERY TOUR

Beatles aficionados can't visit London without making a pilgrimage to the famous **Abbey Road** recording studios in St John's Wood. The studios themselves are off-limits, so you'll have to content yourself with examining the decades of fan graffiti on the fence outside and strolling across the zebra crossing to re-enact the cover of the fab four's 1969 masterpiece *Abbey Road*.

## Parks & Open Spaces

GET INTO THE GREEN

North London is blessed with a bounty of parks besides Hampstead Heath, and if the sun's shining, you should drop any plans you've made and make a beeline for one.

**Regent's Park** is one of central London's loveliest. Queen Mary's Gardens, towards the south of the park, are particularly pretty, especially in June when the roses are in bloom. Performances take place here in an open-air theatre during summer. The park's northwestern side is edged by Regent's Canal, and you can walk its towpath west to Little Venice or

### BEST PLACES FOR LIVE MUSIC

**Scala**
Intimate gigs and dance-happy club nights in a 1920s cinema.

**Green Note**
One of the best places to see live folk and world music. Performances every night.

**Jazz Cafe**
Jazz is only a small slice of the offering; there's also funk, hip-hop, R&B and soul.

**Dublin Castle**
Live punk and alternative bands play most nights in this comfortingly grungy pub's back room.

**Union Chapel**
Atmospheric music venue in a still-used chapel from 1877.

### WHERE TO GET A DRINK IN NORTH LONDON

**Ladies & Gentlemen**
Public toilets turned into a top-notch cocktail bar.

**Euston Tap**
Pub with craft beer and cask ales inside a monumental stone gatehouse.

**Little Creatures**
Australia-born brewery now making beer near Regent's Canal.

east to Camden Town, King's Cross, Victoria Park and even all the way to the Thames. **ZSL London Zoo** takes over Regent Park's northeastern corner. Opened in 1828, it's the oldest in the world. The emphasis nowadays is firmly on conservation, breeding and education, with fewer animals and bigger enclosures.

**Abney Park Cemetery** has become a delightfully overgrown ruin that's now a managed wilderness, providing an important urban habitat for birds, butterflies and bugs. The derelict chapel at its centre could be straight out of a horror film, and the atmosphere of the whole place is rather spooky. The 79-hectare park spilling down the hillside from Alexandra Palace has sweeping views of the city unfurling at its feet.

**BEST PLACES TO EAT IN NORTH LONDON**

**Ottolenghi**
Fresh ingredients whipped into eastern Mediterranean dishes and salads from the famous Jerusalem-born chef. ££

**Roti King**
Flaky Malaysian flatbread served with curry or stuffed with tasty fillings. £

**Camden Lock Market & West Yard**
Dozens of food stalls offering international cuisines, from French and Argentinian to Japanese and Caribbean. £

**Trullo**
Homemade pasta, charcoal grilled meat and fish, and all-Italian wine list. ££

**Duke of Cambridge**
The UK's first certified organic pub tucked down a side street in Islington. ££

## Notable North London Architecture

BEAUTIFUL BUILDINGS AND HISTORIC HOMES

Affluent Hampstead has long been associated with artists and intellectuals, and some of their homes are now open as museums.

One of the oldest houses in Hampstead, evocative **Fenton House**, a 1686 merchant's residence, has fine collections of porcelain, keyboard instruments, Georgian furniture and period art. Regency-style **Keats House** was the home of the golden boy of the Romantic poets, John Keats, from 1818 to 1820, and he wrote many celebrated poems here.

For fans of modernist architecture, a look inside **2 Willow Road**, designed by Ernő Goldfinger in 1939, is a treat, with its lived-in feel and clever spiral staircase. For more on modernism, stop by **Isokon Gallery**, a museum in the former garage of the first modernist block of flats in Britain. Residents included author Agatha Christie and Walter Gropius, founder of the Bauhaus movement.

Even the area's twinned transport hubs are beauty spots. Tour Gothic **St Pancras** (1868) and see the hotel's grand staircase that featured in a Spice Girls video. A major 2012 refurbishment of **King's Cross station** opened a new departures terminal under a roof of a curving web of steel.

A few miles northeast of Hampstead is **Alexandra Palace** (1873). In 1936, Ally Pally was the scene of the world's first TV transmission.

**WHERE TO SHOP BEYOND CAMDEN MARKET**

**Camden Passage Market**
A cobbled lane in Islington lined with antique stores, vintage-clothing boutiques and cafes.

**Word on the Water**
Secondhand bookshop on a restored 1920s Dutch barge on Regent's Canal.

**Harry Potter Shop at Platform 9¾**
Wood-panelled store stocking wands, Hogwarts house jumpers and books.

# GREENWICH

## SEAFARING HISTORY WHERE TIME BEGINS

If Greenwich's grand sights belonged to a British town beyond the capital, they would elevate it to one of the top destinations in the UK. That they belong to a district of London naturally makes this quaint Unesco-listed area a must-see neighbourhood.

Regal historic Greenwich (pronounced '*gren*-itch') complements its riverside village feel with grand architecture, vibrant markets, grassy parkland and cosy pubs. Most visitors dedicate only a day to Greenwich, but it's a lot of culture and history to pack into a single session, with the Royal Observatory, Queen's House, National Maritime Museum and Old Royal Naval College demanding several hours each. The Painted Hall, covered in huge murals, is unmissable. Fortunately, all of Greenwich's big-hitting sights are within an easily walkable area.

For a more local look at this part of London, venture to edgy Deptford or high-rise-ridden North Greenwich, both rapidly developing in very different ways.

### TOP TIP

While it's possible to get here by train or Docklands Light Railway (DLR), why not arrive on, under or over the water? Thames Clippers services dock at Greenwich Pier, while the London Cable Car soars 90m high before landing in North Greenwich. The Greenwich Foot Tunnel (1902) dives below the surface.



**Queen's House, Greenwich**

## GREENWICH

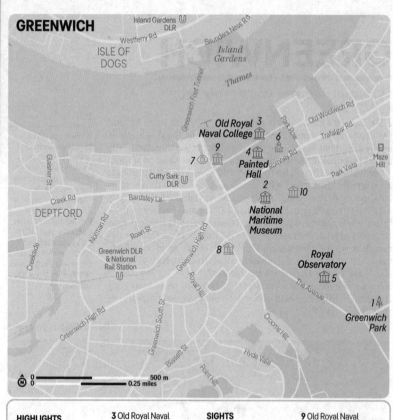

Island Gardens DLR
Westferry Rd
Saunders Ness Rd
ISLE OF DOGS
Island Gardens
Thames
Greenwich Foot Tunnel
Old Royal Naval College 3
Park Row
Old Woolwich Rd
Trafalgar Rd
6
9
4 Painted Hall
Romney Rd
7
Maze Hill
Park Vista
Glaisher St
Cutty Sark DLR
2 National Maritime Museum
10
Creek Rd
Bardsley La
DEPTFORD
Norman Rd
Roan St
Greenwich High Rd
8
Creekside
Greenwich DLR & National Rail Station
Royal Observatory 5
Royal Hill
The Avenue
1 Greenwich Park
Greenwich High Rd
Greenwich South St
Crooms Hill
Blissett St
Hyde Vale
Point Hill
0 500 m
0 0.25 miles

**HIGHLIGHTS**
**1** Greenwich Park
**2** National Maritime Museum
**3** Old Royal Naval College
**4** Painted Hall
**5** Royal Observatory

**SIGHTS**
**6** Chapel of St Peter & St Paul
**7** Cutty Sark
**8** Fan Museum
**9** Old Royal Naval College Visitor Centre
**10** Queen's House

## Royal Observatory & Greenwich Park

HOME OF GREENWICH MEAN TIME

Rising like a beacon of time atop Greenwich Park, the Royal Observatory is home to the prime meridian (longitude 0° 0' 0"). Tickets include access to the Christopher Wren–designed Flamsteed House and the Meridian Courtyard, where you can stand with your feet straddling the eastern and western hemispheres. You can also see the Great Equatorial Telescope (1893) inside the onion-domed observatory and explore space and time in the museum galleries.

Pause in Greenwich Park (covering 74 hectares, the oldest enclosed Royal Park) for views of Canary Wharf (p97) – the financial district across the Thames – from the crown of the hill.

**Royal Observatory**

Painted Hall

## Painted Hall & Old Royal Naval College

GREENWICH'S GRANDEST ARCHITECTURAL ICON

King William III and Queen Mary II commissioned Christopher Wren to construct a naval hospital here in 1692, and the resulting structure is a masterpiece of baroque architecture. It's now home to the University of Greenwich and Trinity Laban Conservatoire of Music and Dance, but the grounds and some buildings are open to the public.

Designed as a dining room for retired and disabled sailors, the Painted Hall is an over-the-top banqueting space that's covered floor to ceiling with the largest painting in Europe. It took artist Sir James Thornhill 19 years and three monarch changes to complete.

Included in the Painted Hall admission ticket is a worthwhile 45-minute tour of the grounds, taking visitors to hard-to-find areas, such as the Victorian skittle alley. Tours start inside the Old Royal Naval College Visitor Centre, which contains artefacts from King Henry VIII's old palace.

Don't miss the beautiful 1742 Chapel of St Peter & St Paul which is decorated in an elaborate rococo style and has an astonishing ceiling painted in cream and light blue.

## DISCOVERING DEPTFORD

Once an important and wealthy dockyard and shipbuilding centre, Deptford is now a district in transition.

From Greenwich, walk along the river and cross Deptford Creek on the swing bridge. A **statue of Peter the Great** near the Thames recalls the Russian tsar's 1698 visit to Deptford to learn about developments in shipbuilding. To the southwest, **Albury St** is lined with early Georgian buildings that once housed Deptford's naval officers, allegedly including Lord Nelson and his lover Lady Hamilton.

On the southern side of the train line is **Deptford Market Yard**, which has resurrected the once abandoned railway arches. Get a taste of what's brewing at **Villages** before venturing south to sample more at **Little Faith**.

NUI7711/SHUTTERSTOCK ©

Cutty Sark

MORE IN GREENWICH

# Museums of Maritime Greenwich

INTO CHARTED WATERS

Greenwich's clutch of museums naturally steers toward ships and seafaring, but artsy types will find plenty to fawn over, too.

Narrating the long, briny and eventful history of nautical Britain, the excellent **National Maritime Museum** has three floors of engrossing exhibits. Highlights include JMW Turner's huge oil painting *Battle of Trafalgar* (1824), the 19m-long gilded state barge built in 1732 for the Prince of Wales, and the colourful figureheads installed on the ground floor.

Next door, **Queen's House** was the UK's first classical building, and it's as enticing for its form as for its art collection. Many pieces on display are portraits and have an unsurprising maritime bent. The helix-shaped Tulip Stairs are a favourite photo op.

The **Cutty Sark**, the last of the great clipper ships to sail between China and England in the 19th century, longingly faces the Thames from its dry dock. It was launched in 1869 and carried almost 4.5 million kg of tea in just seven years of service.

Fans of fans should seek out the small **Fan Museum**, up a quiet neighbourhood side street near Greenwich Park. It has thousands of historic and modern fans from around the world, including ivory, tortoiseshell, peacock-feather and folded-fabric examples.

## SAIL AWAY

Dive deeper into naval history at **HMS Belfast** (p90), aboard **HMS Victory** (p170) – Lord Nelson's flagship at the Battle of Trafalgar – or see the **Mary Rose** (p170), the favourite ship of Henry VIII.

## WHERE TO EAT IN GREENWICH

**Greenwich Market**
Browse handmade jewellery and prints; feast on homemade cakes, locally sourced oysters and filled churros. £

**Goddards at Greenwich**
A Greenwich institution since 1890 that serves classic dishes of pie, mash and jellied eels. £

**Trafalgar Tavern**
An elegant tavern with crystal chandeliers, nautical decor and big windows overlooking the Thames. ££

# PECKHAM & SOUTH LONDON

## LAID-BACK LOCAL LIFE

Beyond a few worthwhile museums and galleries, sightseeing is not why you've come to South London. These neighbourhoods, born from leafy Victorian suburbs, retain their distinct village-like feel, with fantastic central markets – now becoming increasingly gentrified – and a more relaxed Londoners-at-leisure charm.

Come nightfall, Brixton, Peckham and Clapham in particular are ready to stay up late, happily stealing some jewels from Shoreditch's nightlife crown. There's a fierce pride that comes with living 'saff' (south) of the river and an authentic sense of community that can be tapped into even on a short visit.

Things in South London can be quiet during the week. Some must-visit markets, like the one on Maltby St, only come to life at weekends (Saturdays especially). Railways have made tracks through this part of the capital, and breweries, bars and restaurants have turned once dingy brick arches into their hip new homes.

### TOP TIP

Plan your time in South London in advance. There's a lot of ground to cover, and occasionally poor public transport links can suck up a lot of time. Monday is the quietest day of the week – good for peaceful exploration but a challenge to find an open restaurant.

**Clapham Common**

DALIU/SHUTTERSTOCK ©

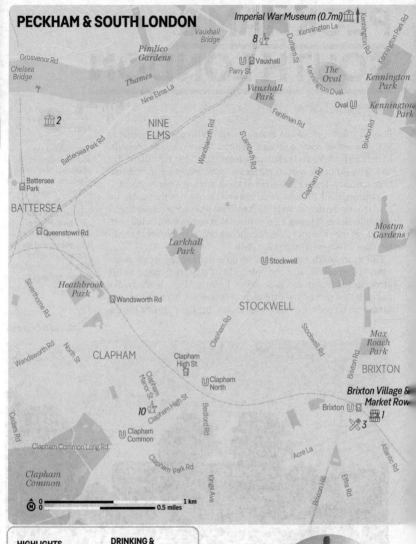

# PECKHAM & SOUTH LONDON

Imperial War Museum (0.7mi)
Vauxhall Bridge
Pimlico Gardens
Grosvenor Rd
Chelsea Bridge
Thames
Nine Elms La
8
Vauxhall
Parry St
Kennington La
Durham St
Kennington Rd
Kennington Park Rd
The Oval
Kennington Oval
Vauxhall Park
Kennington Park
Oval
Fentiman Rd
2
NINE ELMS
Battersea Park Rd
Wandsworth Rd
S Lambeth Rd
Brixton Rd
Clapham Rd
Battersea Park
BATTERSEA
Queenstown Rd
Larkhall Park
Mostyn Gardens
Stockwell
Silverthorne Rd
Heathbrook Park
Wandsworth Rd
STOCKWELL
Clapham Rd
Stockwell Rd
Max Roach Park
Wandsworth Rd
North St
CLAPHAM
Clapham High St
Clapham North
Clapham Manor St
Brixton Rd
BRIXTON
Brixton Village & Market Row
Brixton
1
3
10
Clapham High St
Bedford Rd
Cedars Rd
Clapham Common
Clapham Common Long Rd
Clapham Park Rd
Acre La
Atlantic Rd
Clapham Common
Kings Ave
Brixton Hill
Effra Rd
0 1 km
0 0.5 miles

**HIGHLIGHTS**
**1** Brixton Village & Market Row

**SIGHTS**
**2** Battersea Power Station

**EATING**
**3** Franco Manca
**see 1** Honest Burgers

**DRINKING & NIGHTLIFE**
**4** Bussey Rooftop Bar
**5** Forza Wine
**6** Four Quarters
**7** Frank's
**8** Royal Vauxhall Tavern
**9** Skylight Peckham
**10** Two Brewers

**Battersea Power Station (p116)**

**ARCHITECTURE EYE CANDY**

Some of London's most beautiful buildings aren't necessarily the obvious ones in the skyline. Elsewhere, dozens of **City of London churches** (p77) get lost among the skyscrapers, and Southwest London hides lovely stately homes, such as **Syon House** (p135).

TOP: CKTRAVELS.COM/SHUTTERSTOCK ©, BOTTOM: ANNAJ77/SHUTTERSTOCK ©

Horniman Museum

## Horniman Museum

ECLECTIC HISTORIC COLLECTION

This 1901 Art-Nouveau building, with its clock tower and mosaics, was specially designed to house the collection of wealthy Victorian tea merchant Frederick John Horniman. The core of the museum is the Natural History Gallery, which contains taxidermied animals displayed in old-school glass cases, including the famous overstuffed walrus that doesn't have any wrinkles. The museum is set on 6.5 hectares of gardens with views of central London. Paths circle around the gardens, including the Horniman Nature Trail, along an abandoned railway line turned into wild woodlands and the Animal Walk, which goes past enclosures of alpacas, guinea pigs and rabbits.

## Imperial War Museum

RIVETING INSIGHTS INTO CONFLICT

Fronted by an intimidating pair of 15in naval guns and a piece of the Berlin Wall, the state-of-the-art Imperial War Museum is housed in what was the Bethlem Royal Hospital, a psychiatric facility also known as Bedlam. The museum's focus is on WWI and WWII, which each have a dedicated gallery. It's an insightful experience as there's great emphasis on storytelling through individual testimonies, which are often as enlightening as they are poignant. One of the most challenging sections is the extensive and harrowing Holocaust Galleries.

Imperial War Museum

## Battersea Power Station

A LONDON LANDMARK RESURRECTED

Battersea Power Station is one of South London's best-known buildings, and in 2022 it opened to the public for the first time as what's perhaps the capital's most gorgeous shopping centre. It also includes luxury flats and the London HQ of Apple. Built in 1933 by Giles Gilbert Scott, who also designed the iconic red telephone box and the sibling power station converted into the Tate Modern, Battersea Power Station was snuffed out in 1983 only to enter a decades-long existential limbo. Admire its revitalised industrial interior over a cocktail at **Control Room B** or survey London from above aboard **Lift 109**, a glass-sided elevator that climbs to the top of the northwest chimney for a 360-degree view of the capital.

## Dulwich Picture Gallery

OLD MASTERS IN AN INTIMATE SETTING

The world's first purpose-built public art gallery, the Dulwich Picture Gallery was designed by architect Sir John Soane (architect of the Bank of England) and opened in 1817 to house nearby Dulwich College's collection of paintings. This gallery has a remarkable set of works by the old masters, including works by Rembrandt, Rubens, Gainsborough, Poussin and Canaletto. Unusually, the gallery also includes a mausoleum for its founders, lit by a moody *lumière mystérieuse* (mysterious light) created with tinted glass placed among the pictures.

**Dulwich Picture Gallery**

**Eltham Palace**

TOP RIGHT: JONO PHOTOGRAPHY/SHUTTERSTOCK ©, RIGHT: WIRESTOCK CREATORS/SHUTTERSTOCK ©

## Eltham Palace

ART DECO MOD MEETS MEDIEVAL MANOR

About 30 minutes southeast from London Bridge station by train, this gorgeous 1930s art-deco mansion was built by Stephen Courtauld, whose family made a fortune in the rayon (artificial silk) industry, and his wife Virginia (Ginie) as a country estate for entertaining guests. Its sleek interior design features high-tech amenities of the time, such as telephones, electrically synchronised clocks, a built-in vacuum system and a boiler with enough hot water for 12 baths at the same time. The 'modern' mansion is attached to the remnants of a medieval royal estate, the boyhood home of Henry VIII before the Tudors decamped to Greenwich.

Don't miss the Map Room where the couple plotted their extensive travels, unveiled after 70 years of being covered by wallpaper.

## Brixton Village & Market Row

GO FULL GLUTTON

Pack a second stomach because South London will satiate your appetite. This revitalised covered market, once the dilapidated 1930s Granville Arcade, has enjoyed an eye-catching renaissance. More than 130 traders have set up shop, including Brixton originals **Franco Manca** and **Honest Burgers**, which have since successfully spiralled into mini London chains. Coffee shops, West African fabric stores and numerous restaurants cohabit with halal butchers, greengrocers and bazaars, and happily some retain the neighbourhood's Afro-Caribbean flavour. Just outside on Electric Ave, Brixton Market showcases the neighbourhood's richness. Jamaican fish and fruits are stacked high, and shoppers leaf through racks of vintage and knock-off fashion.

## WE LIVE HERE: BEST PUBS IN SOUTH LONDON

**Andrew Grumbridge** and **Vincent Raison**, co-founders of pub-loving South London slacker community Deserter, pick their favourite watering holes. *@deserterblog*

**Blythe Hill Tavern**
At this wood-panelled cracker, staff wear a collar and tie, but don't let that put you off. The vibe is relaxed and the beer impeccably kept.

**Mayflower**
This cosy, barely lit pub is named after the ship that carried the Pilgrims to America. Though if this pub was as good then as it is now, it's a wonder they left at all.

**Shirker's Rest**
Hands up, we have an interest in this one. We transformed an old solicitor's office into a friendly micropub to give something back to society.

Mayflower

MORE IN PECKHAM & SOUTH LONDON

## Going out in South London

NIGHTLIFE ACROSS THE NEIGHBOURHOODS

South London's nightlife options are as diverse as its neighbourhoods. With a plethora of pop-ups and rooftops, Peckham guarantees a great night out. **Frank's** is a summer alfresco favourite: drink in the views (and something stronger) from its perch on the top floor of a multistorey car park. Across the railway, the **Bussey Rooftop Bar**, atop a former cricket-bat factory, is the highest in the 'hood. **Forza Wine**, the next roof over, has a mix of indoor and outdoor space on top of a refurbished Edwardian building. Back on ground level, **Four Quarters** tempts nerds to lose an entire evening in its arcade bar. North of busy Peckham High St, **Skylight Peckham** is a high-up delight at all hours, from bottomless brunch to lazy afternoons of skyline gazing to late-night dance parties to DJs and live music.

**Elephant and Castle** keeps the music going with two mega clubs. **Ministry of Sound** put four bars, three dance floors and more than 60 speakers in an abandoned bus garage.

### WHERE TO EAT IN PECKHAM & SOUTH LONDON

**Brunswick House**
Part restaurant, part architectural salvage in a lone Georgian house lying between Vauxhall high-rises. ££

**Smoke & Salt**
Understated dishes prepared using back-to-basics techniques on Tooting High St. ££

**Bar Tozino**
Superb tapas and wine bar in a converted railway arch along Maltby Street Market. ££

**Corsica Studios** is where the weekend never dies: its licence extends to 6am on Fridays and Saturdays.

Vauxhall and Clapham have an established LGBTIQ+ nightlife scene. **Royal Vauxhall Tavern** is a gay landmark with cabaret and performances every night of the week. **Two Brewers** is a dancing madhouse on weekends.

## Finding 'Old London' in Shad Thames & Rotherhithe

STEP BACK IN TIME

For one of London's most perfect examples of time travel, step into **Shad Thames**, a small neighbourhood east of Tower Bridge. Once the largest warehouse complex in the city, the beige-brick converted factories, which once stored coffee, tea and spices, still line the narrow cobbled lanes, as industrial cranes and iron footbridges loom overhead. Secretive staircases, such as **Horsleydown Steps**, provide prized views of Tower Bridge and the river. Take the pedestrian-only bridge over **St Saviour's Dock** for a picturesque view of the seemingly unchanged waterside wharves.

Follow Bermondsey Wall and Chambers St east to find the neighbourhood of **Rotherhithe**, tucked in a bend of the River Thames. Once an important port, Rotherhithe had working docks until the 1970s, and similar to Shad Thames, its architectural heritage is well preserved in its cobblestone streets and mighty warehouses with in-situ industrial features. A stop at the 16th-century **Mayflower** is a must; it's one of London's most atmospheric pubs. It's named after the vessel which set sail from Rotherhithe in 1620, taking the Pilgrims to North America.

Pop Brixton

### MUST-EAT MARKETS & FOOD HALLS

**Pop Brixton**
Semi-permanent shipping container pop-up of 100% independently owned restaurants, bars and shops. £

**Peckham Levels**
Street-food stalls on 6th floor of a former car park with views of London's skyscrapers. £

**Mercato Metropolitano**
Food hall inside a disused paper factory with skylight windows and loads of outdoor space. £

**Maltby Street Market**
Restaurants and food stalls set up alongside and under railway arches leading from London Bridge. £

**Tooting Market & Broadway Market Tooting**
Top-notch tiny restaurants and bars next to nail salons and Caribbean and African grocers. £

**Kudu**
Menu of South African flavours made with inventive ingredients at this family-run Peckham spot. ££

**Paladar**
Fantastic Elephant & Castle restaurant serving Latin American cuisine stretching from Cuba to Colombia. ££

**Chez Bruce**
Opposite leafy Wandsworth Common; a sophisticated Michelin-starred restaurant far off the tourist track. £££

## BERMONDSEY BEER MILE WALKING TOUR

London's craft-beer revival is in full swing, with Bermondsey at its epicentre. Some two dozen breweries and taprooms have sprung up along a disjointed stretch of railway arches. Most are working breweries and limit hours to the weekends.

Start your session with a legendary doughnut from 1 **St JOHN Bakery** and take a seat among the stacks of wooden barrels at 2 **London Beer Factory**. For a more substantial brunch, pass under the tracks at Tanner St to find 3 **Maltby Street Market**. At the end of the market is 4 **Hiver**, which infuses IPAs, ales and blondes with local honey. Head under the railway to 5 **Anspach & Hobday** and sample its flagship beer, a dark coffee-chocolate porter, a style that originated in this neighbourhood in the 18th century. Wind back through the arches to 6 **Cloudwater**, the London taproom of a Manchester-based brewery. Next door is the ever-experimental 7 **Brew By Numbers**, with its 'scientific' branding. Continue southeast on Enid St to 8 **Kernel Arch 7 Taproom**, the first brewery to set up under the railway line. Grab Kernel's beloved Table Beer, a surprisingly hoppy sessionable American pale ale.

Food trucks often set up shop outside the breweries on Enid St, so grab a bite and prepare for the sobering half-mile trek along the arches and through industrial estates for a heavy dose of American hops at 9 **Partizan**. After one last jaunt through the arches, turn left into the security-gated Bermondsey Trading Estate. The prize is at the end of the long, winding road: the done-up taproom of 10 **Fourpure**, with suspended egg chairs, trailing vines and much to choose from on its 43 craft-beer taps. South Bermondsey and Surrey Quays stations are within stumbling distance.

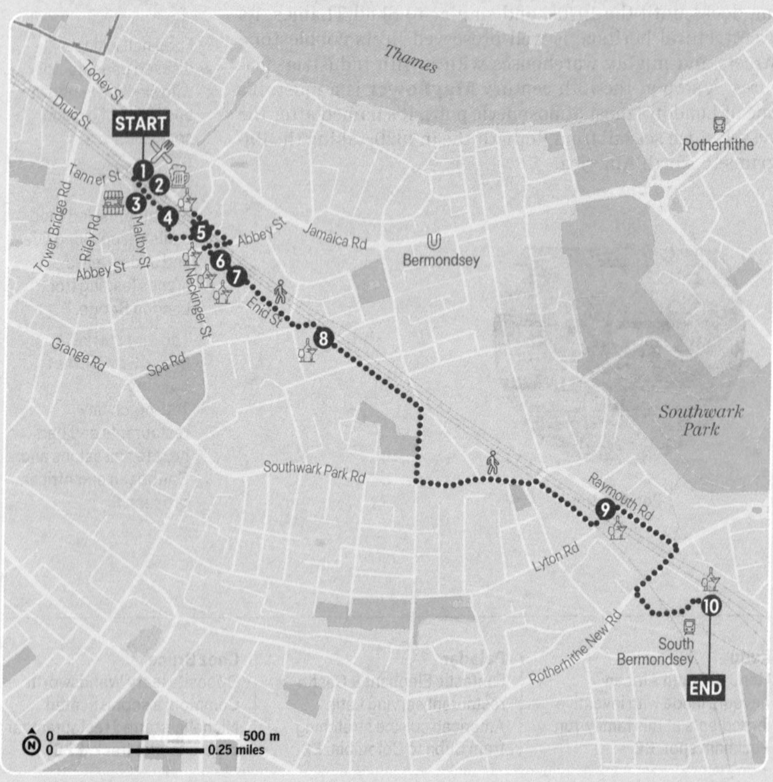

# NOTTING HILL & WEST LONDON

## FAMOUSLY FASHIONABLE MARKETS, MUSEUMS AND PARKS

Well-groomed West London is among the capital's handsomest districts. Its polished architecture and elegant ambience attract shoppers to its high-end department stores in Knightsbridge, vintage hunters to its street markets in Notting Hill, families and culture vultures to its galleries and historic house museums in South Kensington, and night owls to its see-and-be-seen bars in Chelsea. Brightly painted houses on Lancaster Rd and Colville Tce line up like crayons in a box, and the wisteria-clad houses down cobbled mews are some of the capital's most coveted real estate.

The huge acreage of Hyde Park, big enough to contain an entire royal residence as well as plenty of hidden corners and historic oddities, provides some breathing room, as do the relaxed canals in Little Venice. Still a bastion of Black culture, Notting Hill Carnival is Europe's biggest street festival over the August bank holiday weekend.

### TOP TIP

To witness royal pageantry with a smaller crowd than at Buckingham Palace, catch the King's Life Guard departing Hyde Park Barracks for Horse Guards Parade at 10.28am on weekdays, a ritual that dates to 1660. They troop via Hyde Park Corner and under Wellington Arch, Constitution Hill and the Mall.

**Harrods (p126)**

# NOTTING HILL & WEST LONDON

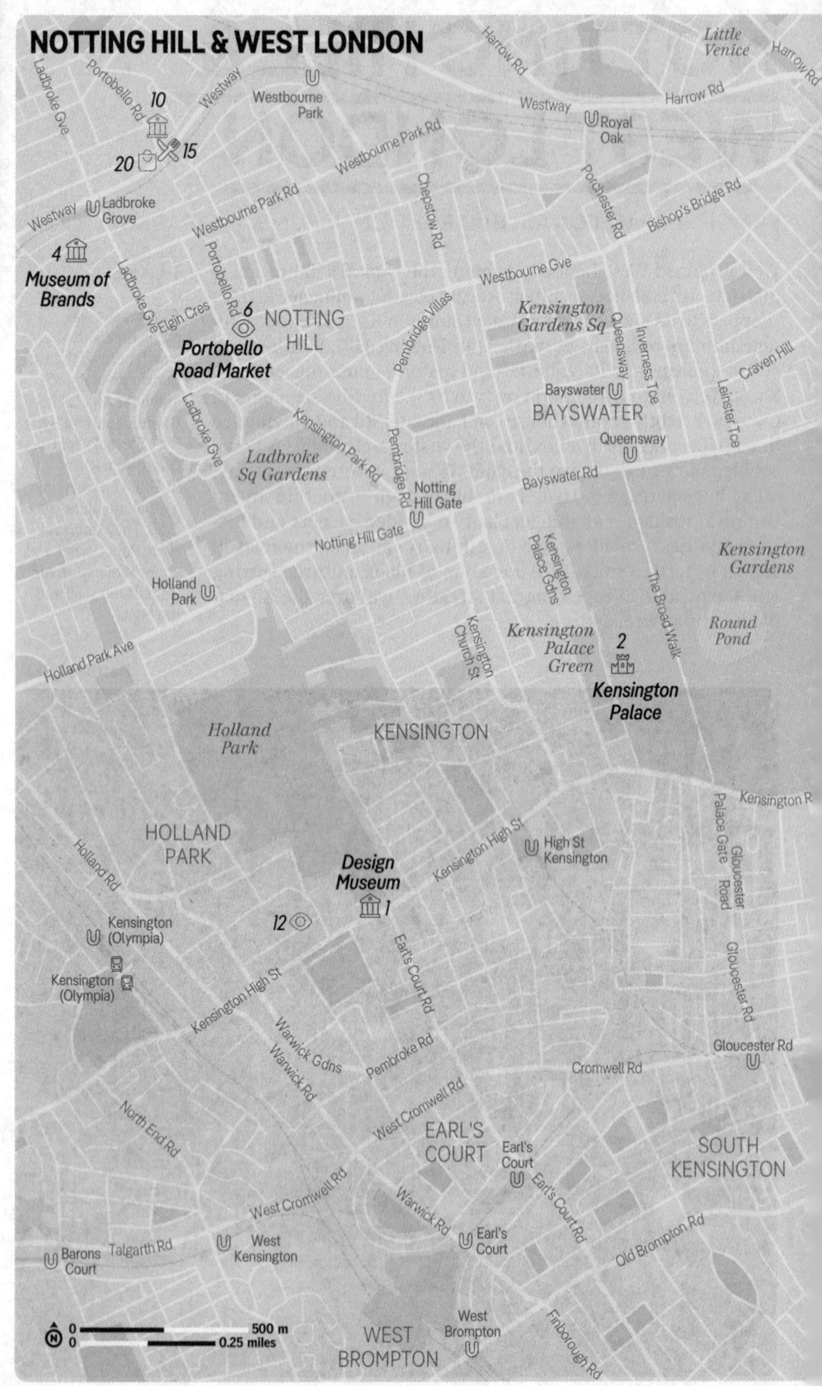
Museum of Brands
Portobello Road Market
NOTTING HILL
Kensington Gardens Sq
BAYSWATER
Ladbroke Sq Gardens
Kensington Gardens
Round Pond
Kensington Palace Green
Kensington Palace
Holland Park
KENSINGTON
HOLLAND PARK
Design Museum
EARL'S COURT
SOUTH KENSINGTON
WEST BROMPTON
Little Venice
Westbourne Park
Royal Oak
Ladbroke Grove
Bayswater
Queensway
Notting Hill Gate
Holland Park
High St Kensington
Kensington (Olympia)
Gloucester Rd
Earl's Court
West Kensington
Barons Court
West Brompton
Harrow Rd
Westway
Westbourne Park Rd
Chepstow Rd
Porchester Rd
Bishop's Bridge Rd
Westbourne Gve
Ladbroke Gve
Portobello Rd
Elgin Cres
Pembridge Villas
Queensway
Inverness Tce
Leinster Tce
Craven Hill
Kensington Park Rd
Pembridge Rd
Bayswater Rd
Notting Hill Gate
Kensington Palace Gdns
The Broad Walk
Kensington Church St
Holland Park Ave
Kensington Rd
Palace Gate
Gloucester Road
Kensington High St
Holland Rd
Earl's Court Rd
Gloucester Rd
Warwick Gdns
Warwick Rd
Pembroke Rd
Cromwell Rd
West Cromwell Rd
North End Rd
Talgarth Rd
Old Brompton Rd
Finborough Rd
0 500 m
0 0.25 miles

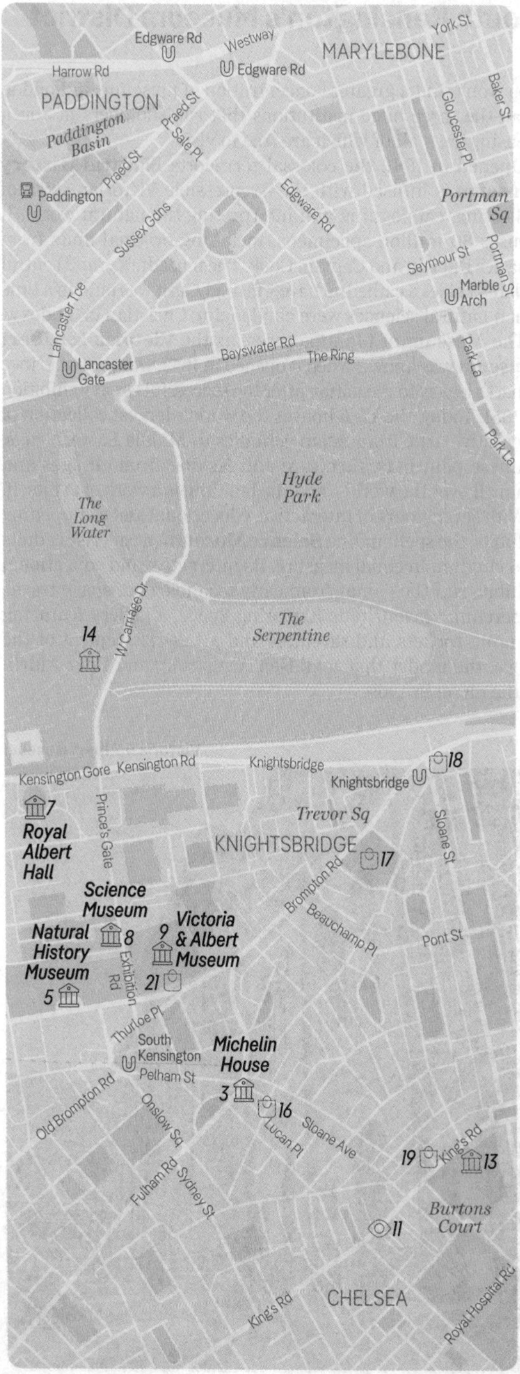

Edgware Rd
Westway
York St
MARYLEBONE
Harrow Rd
Edgware Rd
PADDINGTON
Paddington Basin
Praed St
Sale Pl
Baker St
Gloucester Pl
Praed St
Paddington
Edgware Rd
Portman Sq
Sussex Gdns
Seymour St
Portman St
Marble Arch
Lancaster Tce
Bayswater Rd
The Ring
Park La
Lancaster Gate
Park La
Hyde Park
The Long Water
The Serpentine
W Carriage Dr
14
Kensington Gore
Kensington Rd
Knightsbridge
Knightsbridge
18
7
Royal Albert Hall
Prince's Gate
Trevor Sq
Sloane St
KNIGHTSBRIDGE
17
Brompton Rd
Science Museum
Beauchamp Pl
Natural History Museum
8
9
Victoria & Albert Museum
Pont St
Exhibition Rd
21
5
Thurloe Pl
South Kensington
Michelin House
Pelham St
3
16
Old Brompton Rd
Onslow Sq
Sloane Ave
Lucan Pl
19
King's Rd
13
Fulham Rd
Sydney St
Burtons Court
11
CHELSEA
King's Rd
Royal Hospital Rd

**HIGHLIGHTS**
**1** Design Museum
**2** Kensington Palace
**3** Michelin House
**4** Museum of Brands
**5** Natural History Museum
**6** Portobello Road Market
**7** Royal Albert Hall
**8** Science Museum
**9** Victoria & Albert Museum

**SIGHTS**
**10** Graffik Gallery
**11** King's Road
**12** Leighton House
**13** Saatchi Gallery
**14** Serpentine Gallery

**EATING**
**15** Acklam Village Market

**SHOPPING**
**16** Conran Shop
**17** Harrods
**18** Harvey Nichols
**19** John Sandoe Books
**20** Portobello Green Arcade
**21** V&A Shop

**Michelin House building (p126)**

# South Kensington's Museum District

A CLUSTER OF CULTURE

You won't find a greater concentration of museums in London than the three huge institutions that rub shoulders in South Kensington – all of which are free to visit.

Opened in 1881, the colossal terracotta **Natural History Museum** is infused with the irrepressible Victorian spirit of collecting, cataloguing and interpreting the natural world. It houses 80 million specimens, including original finds from Charles Darwin and Captain Cook. The museum's grand central hall resembles a cathedral nave – fittingly, as it was built in a time when natural sciences were challenging Christian orthodoxy.

The Museum of Manufactures, as the **Victoria & Albert Museum** was known when it opened in 1852, was part of Prince Albert's legacy to the nation after the successful Great Exhibition of 1851. Today, the V&A houses the world's largest collection of decorative arts, from Asian ceramics to Middle Eastern rugs, Chinese paintings, furniture and fashion from all ages and from all over the world – and the building is a work of art itself.

With seven floors of interactive, educational and eye-opening exhibits, the spellbinding **Science Museum** mesmerises adults and children in equal measure. Its interactive and educational exhibits run the gamut from early technology to space travel. A perennial favourite is Exploring Space, a gallery featuring genuine rockets and satellites and a full-size replica of the *Eagle*, the lander that took Neil Armstrong and Buzz Aldrin to the moon in 1969.

**HYDE PARK**

Hyde Park is central London's largest green space, seized by Henry VIII from Westminster Abbey in 1536 and turned into an aristocratic hunting ground. These days, it's a place to stroll and picnic, boat on the Serpentine lake, or catch a concert, outdoor film or winter funfair.

The park's vast scale hides quiet corners and surprises, such as the Holocaust Memorial Garden, a Victorian-era pet cemetery and Speakers' Corner, where those ranting on their soapboxes once included Karl Marx, Vladimir Lenin and George Orwell.

**Victoria & Albert Museum**

LAUREN KEITH/LONELY PLANET ©

## Royal Albert Hall

BRITAIN'S MOST FAMOUS CONCERT VENUE

This red-brick elliptical amphitheatre, built in 1871 and encircled with a 244m-long mosaic frieze depicting the 'Triumph of Arts and Letters', hosts nearly 400 live performances every year, including ballet, concerts of all musical genres, and film screenings with live orchestral accompaniment, but it's best known as the venue for the BBC's Promenade Concerts (the Proms) in summer. If you're not here for a show, you can get the story of the building and its acoustic 'mushrooms' on a guided tour.

Royal Albert Hall

## Kensington Palace

PEEK INSIDE A ROYAL RESIDENCE

Constructed in 1605, Kensington Palace became the favourite royal abode under William and Mary of Orange in 1689 and remained so until George III became king and relocated to Buckingham Palace. Today, it remains a residence for high-ranking royals, including the Duke and Duchess of Cambridge (Prince William and Princess Kate), but a large part of the palace is open to the public. Don't miss the lavishly decorated Cupola Room in the King's State Apartments, ornate historic furniture in the slightly more restrained Queen's State Apartments and the rooms where Victoria was born and lived until she became queen.

Kensington Palace

## Portobello Road Market

NOTTING HILL'S LEGENDARY SHOPPING STREET

Buzzing Portobello Road Market is one of London's most-loved places to browse an eclectic mix of antiques, curios, and vintage and 'firsthand' fashion. Market stalls stretch for more than a mile along Portobello Road and spill into nearby streets. The market is at its busiest best on Saturdays, when some 1500 vendors compete for shoppers' attention, but come early or be prepared to use your elbows. Fridays are a close second. The stalls disappear on Sundays, but some of the brick-and-mortar shops are open.

Underneath the Westway, **Portobello Green Arcade** is home to clothing and jewellery designers, vinyl merchants and indie shops. Fuel up at the street food stalls of nearby **Acklam Village Market**, with treats from across the globe.

## BEST PLACES TO EAT IN WEST LONDON

**Rabbit**
Flavours of the English countryside at this farm-to-fork restaurant from three brothers on King's Rd. ££

**V&A Cafe**
Tea and cake in extraordinarily decorated Morris, Gamble and Poynter Rooms, often to piano accompaniment. £

**Dinner by Heston Blumenthal**
Two-Michelin-starred gastronomic tour de force through British culinary history. Dishes carry dates to explain context. £££

**Market Halls Victoria**
Buzzing food stalls transforming a transport hub: eight kitchens, communal tables and a roof terrace. £

TOM EVERSLEY/SHUTTERSTOCK ©

Design Museum

MORE IN NOTTING HILL & WEST LONDON

# Destination Shopping in West London

LUXE FASHION FINDS TO OFFBEAT BUYS

Portobello Road Market isn't the only place that will give your wallet a workout in West London. Head to Knightsbridge to shop at its famous luxury department stores. **Harrods** has eight floors of fashion, food and homewares reached by the kitschy 'Egyptian escalator'. **Harvey Nichols** is London's temple of high fashion, with an excellent range of denim and a massive makeup hall that includes exclusive lines.

For more astonishing architecture and cool finds, head to **Conran Shop** for kitchenware, children's toys, coffee-table books and greeting cards. It's housed in the magnificent Art-Nouveau Michelin House, built as the tyre company's UK headquarters in 1911. The famed roly-poly Michelin Man (Bibendum) appears in the stained-glass windows, and the lobby is decorated with tiles illustrating early-20th-century cars.

A short walk to the south is the chic King's Rd in Chelsea, lined with designer stores, specialist sellers and charity shops that resemble fashion boutiques. Detour down Blacklands Tce

## WHERE TO GET A DRINK IN NOTTING HILL & WEST LONDON

**Paradise by Way of Kensal Green**
Bar-gastropub done up with eclectic religious paintings, taxidermy and dense drapes.

**Troubadour**
Convivial boho bar-cafe that's seen performances by Adele, Joni Mitchell, Jimi Hendrix and Bob Dylan.

**Churchill Arms**
Pub covered in colourful flowers on the outside and filled with Winston Churchill memorabilia inside.

to find charming **John Sandoe Books** in an 18th-century building, the perfect antidote to impersonal book superstores.

Don't overlook West London's **museum gift shops** for unique souvenirs. Given their focus on art and creativity, the shops at the V&A and the Design Museum have particularly wonderful selections.

## Creative Culture of West London

ART OUTSIDE THE BIG INSTITUTIONS

Beyond the V&A, West London has a creative cache of house museums and galleries that promise to surprise and inspire.

The slick, free-to-visit **Design Museum** is dedicated to the role of design in everyday life, displayed through 1000 objects, from historic London Underground maps to 1980s Apple computers. Its small permanent collection is complemented by a revolving programme of special exhibitions. A five-minute walk west leads to Leighton House, home of artist Frederic, Lord Leighton (1830–96), president of the Royal Academy for 18 years and the only British artist ever raised to the peerage. The highlight is the domed, mosque-like Arab Hall, with walls covered in colourful tilework.

The quirky **Museum of Brands** is a nostalgic shrine to consumer culture. Walk through the time tunnel from the Victorian era to the modern day and giggle over adverts, postcards and toys that you'll soon start recognising from your childhood.

In Hyde Park, the free **Serpentine Gallery** is one of London's most important contemporary-art galleries. Damien Hirst, Louise Bourgeois, Tomoko Takahashi and Jeff Koons have all exhibited here.

The **Saatchi Gallery** hosts temporary exhibitions of experimental work. It's just off the shop-happy King's Rd, so if you're still looking to spend, check out the gift shop's arty souvenirs. At some exhibitions, you buy straight from the gallery walls. **Graffik Gallery** is one of the first galleries in London to take street art seriously. You can purchase pieces by such legends as Banksy, Dotmaster and Stik or join a hands-on spray-paint workshop.

### LONDON BREWS

Even for craft beer lovers, it's a stretch to complete the entire Bermondsey Beer Mile in one go. But when you're ready for more local brews, head to the industrial estates of **Walthamstow** (p97) or **Crate** (p98) in Hackney Wick.

### BEST OFF-THE-BEATEN-TRACK SIGHTS

**Chelsea Physic Garden**
Established in 1673, London's oldest botanic garden contains 5000 different edible, poisonous and pharmaceutical plants.

**Kensal Green Cemetery**
Once England's most fashionable necropolis, Gothic Kensal Green was first of London's 'Magnificent Seven' cemeteries.

**Little Venice**
Junction of Regent's Canal and Grand Union Canal; overseen by beautiful mansions, navigated by narrowboats.

**Apsley House**
Home of the 1st Duke of Wellington, with china, silver, paintings and the Duke's death mask.

**Trailer Happiness**
Retro tiki bar in a Portobello Road basement; rum cocktails mixed by London's best bartenders.

**Aerial Rooftop**
Outdoor bar with a retractable roof that overlooks the BBC's redeveloped Television Centre.

**Little Yellow Door**
Enter the brightly painted unmarked door to find a homely cocktail lounge/well-designed living room.

# RICHMOND & SOUTHWEST LONDON

## A LEAFIER SIDE OF THE CITY

Home to the capital's largest Royal Park and a botanical garden with the most extensive collection of plants on the planet, Richmond and Southwest London feel a world away from the urban jungle. This district was once the reserve of royal residences and stately country homes. Some survive in splendid grandeur, and the place retains a refined air – even now, Richmond ranks as one of the least impoverished of London's 32 boroughs.

Life here revolves around laid-back outdoor activities, from deer-spotting strolls in Richmond Park and getting a tree's-eye view from the canopy at Kew Gardens to walking the Thames Path and pausing for a pint at a pub. Some of the capital's most charming riverside pubs can be found on both banks of the Thames.

### TOP TIP

Southwest London is one of the top neighbourhoods to explore the capital's greener side, and late spring and summer are the times to see it at its blooming best. The colder, darker months come with colour-changing autumn foliage, an ice rink at Hampton Court Palace, winter illumination trails and Christmas markets.

**Treetop walkway, Kew Gardens**

ALEX SEGRE/SHUTTERSTOCK ©

## Richmond Park

BIGGEST URBAN PARK IN EUROPE

Encompassing almost 1000 hectares, Richmond Park has formal gardens and ancient oaks but is perhaps best known for its 600-strong herd of red and fallow deer, which have roamed freely since 1637. The park's rambling wilderness is perfect for a quiet walk or picnic. The vista from Richmond Hill has inspired painters and poets for centuries, and it's the only view in England protected by an act of Parliament. Flower fans should visit Isabella Plantation, a stunning garden blooming with rhododendrons, azaleas and camellias in April and May.

**Richmond Park**

## Kew Gardens

PRESERVING THE PLANET'S PLANTS

In 1759, botanists began collecting specimens from around the world to plant in the 3-hectare Royal Botanic Gardens at Kew. They never stopped collecting, and the gardens, which have blossomed to 130 hectares, provide the largest living plant collection on Earth, certified by Guinness World Records in 2022. Highlights include the steamy Victorian-era Palm House, a hothouse of iron and curved sheets of glass; the biome-spanning Princess of Wales Conservatory; the bright red-brick 1631 Kew Palace, formerly King George III's country retreat; the Temperate House, the world's largest surviving Victorian glasshouse; and the 18m-high Treetop Walkway.

**Lily House, Kew Gardens**

## Hampton Court Palace

GRAND ROYAL RESIDENCE OF HENRY VIII

The largest Tudor structure in England, Hampton Court Palace was given to the famously egotistical Henry VIII in 1529 by his chancellor. Hampton Court was already one of Europe's most sophisticated palaces when Christopher Wren designed an extension in the 17th century. The result is a beautiful blend of Gothic, Tudor and baroque architecture, shown off in spectacular fashion in the Great Hall, with its hammer-beam roof that appears to drip, stalactite-like, with crown-shaped ornaments, and the tapestry- and mural-covered state apartments.

You could easily spend a day exploring the palace and its extensive gardens that contain a 320-year old hedge maze, the world's largest grapevine, and fruit and vegetable beds that once fed the royal family.

# Hampton Court Palace

## A DAY AT THE TUDOR PALACE

Hampton Court Palace and its huge gardens can feel like a maze – even outside of the actual labyrinth. It helps to understand how the palace has grown over the centuries and how successive royal occupants embellished Hampton Court to suit their purposes and to reflect the style of the time.

As soon as he had his royal hands upon the palace from Cardinal Thomas Wolsey, Henry VIII began expanding the 1 **Tudor architecture**, adding the 2 **Great Hall**, the exquisite 3 **Chapel Royal**, the opulent Great Watching Chamber and the gigantic 4 **Henry VIII's Kitchens**. By 1540 it had become one of the grandest and most sophisticated palaces in Europe. James I kept things ticking over, while Charles I added a new tennis court and did some serious art-collecting, including pieces that can be seen in the 5 **Cumberland Art Gallery**.

PETER FIELDS / ALAMY STOCK PHOTO ©

**7 The Maze**

*Around 150m north of the main building*

Created from hornbeam and yew and planted around 1700, the maze covers a third of an acre within the famous palace gardens. A must-see conclusion to Hampton Court, it takes the average visitor about 20 minutes to reach the centre.

### OPEN FOR INSPECTION

The palace was opened to the public by Queen Victoria in 1838.

**Henry VIII's Kitchens**

These vast kitchens were the engine room of the palace and had a staff of 200 people. Six spit-rack-equipped fireplaces ensured roast meat was always on the menu (to the tune of 8200 sheep and 1240 oxen per year).

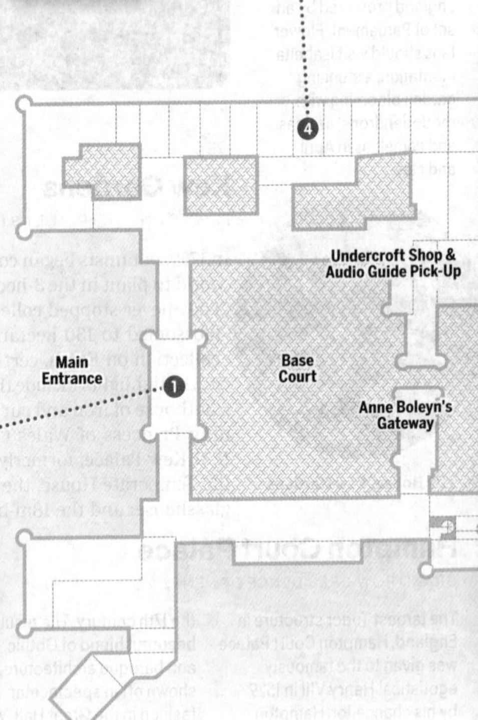


**Tudor Architecture**

Dating to 1515, the palace serves as one of the finest examples of Tudor architecture in the nation. Cardinal Thomas Wolsey was responsible for transforming what was originally a grand medieval manor house into a stunning Tudor palace.

KIEVVICTOR / SHUTTERSTOCK ©

After the Civil War, puritanical Oliver Cromwell warmed to his own regal proclivities, spending weekends in the comfort of the former queen's bedroom. In the late 17th century William and Mary employed Christopher Wren to expand the palace in a baroque style, chiefly William III's Apartments, reached by the **6 King's Staircase**. William III also commissioned the world-famous **7 maze**.

## TOP TIPS

➡ Book online for cheaper prices and guaranteed entry. Annual membership allows unlimited admission to five royal palaces in London.

➡ Give yourself plenty of time. You can easily spend a day enjoying the full range of sights and the extensive gardens.

➡ Audio guides are included in the ticket price. Pick one up from the Undercroft shop.

PLUSONE / SHUTTERSTOCK ©

### Great Hall

This grand dining hall is the defining room of the palace, displaying what is considered England's finest hammer-beam roof. The walls are covered in 16th-century Flemish tapestries that depict the story of Abraham, and the space is lit by exquisite stained-glass windows.

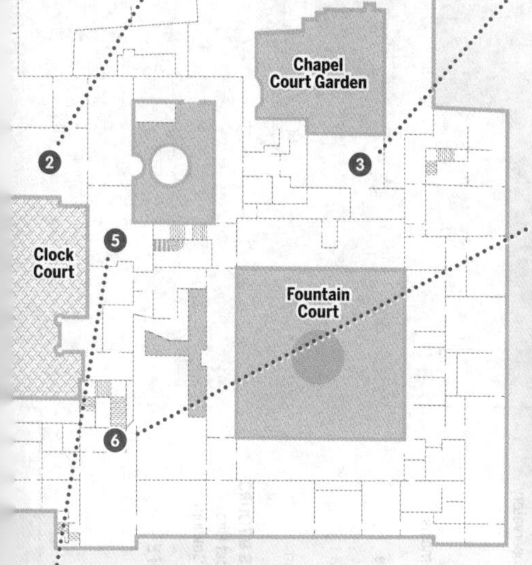


### Chapel Royal

The blue and gold vaulted ceiling is one of the palace's most beautiful features, and you can get an up-high view of it from the Royal Pew, accessed via Henry VII's Apartments. It's still a working chapel, so it's closed on Sundays and other holy days.

### King's Staircase

Painted by Italian artist Antonio Verrio, the King's Staircase is a suitably bombastic prelude to William III's Apartments. The artwork adulates William III by elevating him above a cohort of Roman emporors.

GORDON BELL / SHUTTERSTOCK ©

### Cumberland Art Gallery

This gallery shows a rotating election of artworks, mostly from the Royal Collection. William Kent designed the rooms in the 1730s for the Duke of Cumberland.

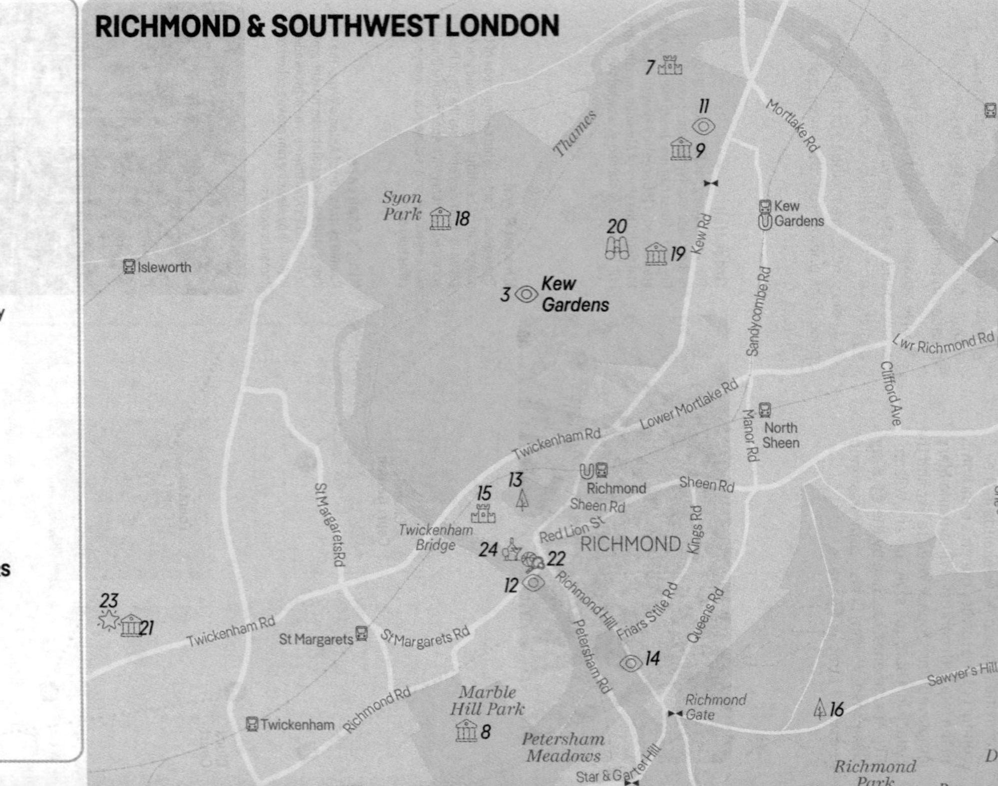


**HIGHLIGHTS**
**1** Hampton Court Palace
**2** Hampton Court Palace Maze
**3** Kew Gardens

**SIGHTS**
**4** Chiswick House
**5** Ham House
**6** Isabella Plantation
**7** Kew Palace
**8** Marble Hill House
**9** Palm House
**10** Pembroke Lodge
**11** Princess of Wales Conservatory
**12** Richmond Bridge
**13** Richmond Green
**14** Richmond Hill
**15** Richmond Palace Remains
**16** Richmond Park
**17** Strawberry Hill House
**18** Syon House
**19** Temperate House
**20** Treetop Walkway
**21** World Rugby Museum

**ACTIVITIES, COURSES & TOURS**
**22** Richmond Bridge Boat Hire
**23** Twickenham Rugby Stadium

**DRINKING & NIGHTLIFE**
**24** White Cross

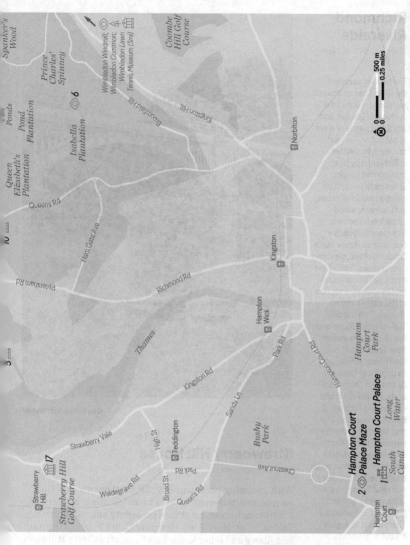

Strawberry Hill
17
Strawberry Hill Golf Course
Strawberry Vale
Waldegrave Rd
High St
Broad St
Teddington
Park Rd
Queen's Rd
Petersham Rd
Queens Rd
Queen Elizabeth's Plantation
Ponds
Pond Plantation
Prince Charles' Spinney
Spanker's Wood
Isabella Plantation
6
Ham Gate Ave
Wimbledon Windmill; Wimbledon Common; Wimbledon Lawn Tennis Museum (3mi)
Thames
Richmond Rd
Kingston Rd
Broomfield Hill
Kingston Hill
Coombe Hill Golf Course
Sandy Ln
Bushy Park
Chestnut Ave
Hampton Wick
Park Rd
Kingston
Norbiton
Hampton Court Rd
2 Hampton Court Palace Maze
1 Hampton Court Palace
Hampton Court
Hampton Court Park
South Canal
Long Water
0 500 m
0 0.25 miles

Chiswick House (p136)

ANTHONY SHAW PHOTOGRAPHY/SHUTTERSTOCK ©

## Richmond Riverside

ADVENTURES ALONG THE WATER

The bucolic stretch of the River Thames around Richmond is one of the prettiest in London, and you'll find plenty of ways to get out on – or next to – the water. Arrive in Richmond by boat from central London or navigate yourself by hiring a traditional rowing skiff, kayak or stand-up paddleboard near Richmond Bridge, the five-span structure that's London's oldest surviving river crossing. Follow the river's gentle curves on foot by walking a section of the water-hugging Thames Path National Trail, of which Richmond has 21 miles. Downriver from Teddington Lock, the Thames is tidal, and its depth can fluctuate by up to 7m twice a day as the water rolls in and out. Around Richmond Bridge, shops, bars and restaurants line the river's eastern edge, perfect for catching the sun or watching the action on the water. The White Cross pub even has separate entrances for low and high tides, but when the Thames is at its highest, it's out of bounds to those not willing to wade. Wellies are provided.

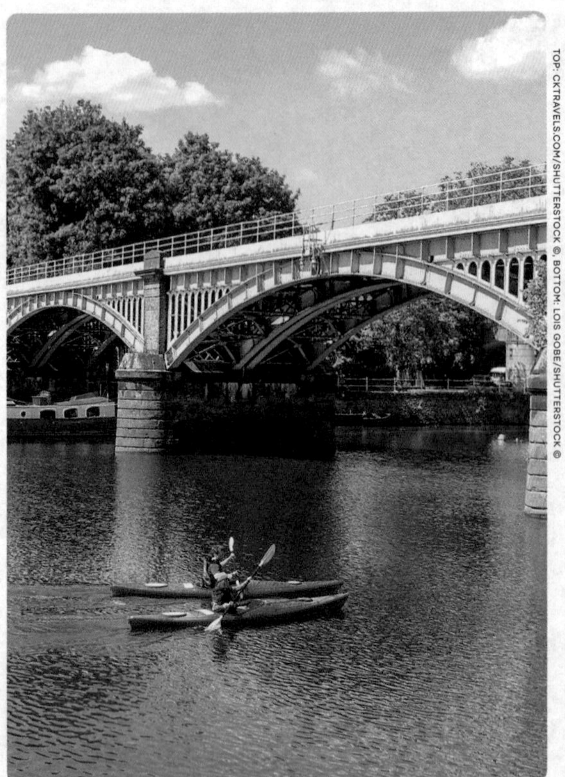

Canoeing, Richmond

## Strawberry Hill House

A GOTHIC ARCHITECTURAL FANTASY

With gleaming snow-white walls, battlements and Gothic turrets, this 18th-century villa in Twickenham appears like a hallucination in an otherwise sedate suburban setting. Taking inspiration from Hampton Court Palace, Westminster Abbey and other iconic buildings, Strawberry Hill is an architectural hotchpotch dreamt up by art historian, writer and politician Horace Walpole, son of the first British prime minister and author of the world's first Gothic novel. The building is a marvel, decked out in stained-glass windows, pointed-arch bookcases and elaborate fireplaces, and reaches its pinnacle in the gallery, with its magnificent fan-vaulted ceiling made of gilded papier-mâché.

Strawberry Hill House

Ham House

## MORE IN RICHMOND & SOUTHWEST LONDON

# Stately Homes of the Southwest

MAGNIFICENT HISTORIC MANORS

Before suburban London gobbled up this stretch of countryside, wealthy families – some of whom made their fortunes from the transatlantic trade of enslaved Africans – constructed stately homes along the bucolic banks of the Thames.

Once a medieval abbey, **Syon House** was dissolved on the orders of Henry VIII and rebuilt into a residence, today owned by the Duke of Northumberland. Extensively remodelled by Robert Adam in 1762, the elegant rooms took inspiration from classical Rome, revealed in the basilica-domed entry hall and the State Dining Room lined with Corinthian columns and marble statues of ancient Roman deities.

Red-brick **Ham House** was built in 1610 by an Elizabethan courtier and later sold to the first Earl of Dysart. The carved Great Staircase leads to decadent drawing rooms, state apartments and galleries with paintings by Constable, Reynolds and Van Dyck.

## UNFORGETTABLE DINING IN RICHMOND

**Erik Rivas**, a local food blogger, has lived with his wife and daughter in Richmond for five years. Combining his passion for food and southwest London, he shares his top tips for the best local food. *@richmonderfoodie*

**Al Boccon Di' Vino**
This cosy Italian restaurant feels like you're eating at your grandparents' house. The dishes are endless, and the atmosphere is convivial. Everyone eats the same menu together, and staff ring a bell before serving the main course.

**Chatora**
Every dish is presented beautifully by expert chefs, from the food down to carefully chosen tableware. Try their slow-cooked lamb shank rogan josh. It's my favourite dish, and (I hear) the owner's, too.

## WHERE TO EAT IN RICHMOND & SOUTHWEST LONDON

**Petersham Nurseries Cafe**
Michelin-listed upscale restaurant in a greenhouse that takes sustainability seriously. **£££**

**Chez Lindsay**
An appetising slice of France serving wholesome cuisine from Brittany in a down-to-earth atmosphere. **£££**

**Gelateria Danieli**
Handmade ice cream in delicious flavours, including Bakewell tart, Kinder Bueno, biscotti and honeycomb. **£**

**SPORTING SOUTHWEST LONDON**

For two weeks each June and July, sports fans turn their attention to **Wimbledon** for the world's oldest tennis tournament, hosted here since 1877. Most tickets are allocated through a famously oversubscribed public ballot, or you can queue for a chance to watch same-day matches. For an up-close experience outside of tournament time, visit the Wimbledon Lawn Tennis Museum to see Centre Court from the 360-degree viewing box.

Twickenham Rugby Stadium is the home of English rugby union. Tickets for international matches are hard to obtain, but **guided tours** grant access to usually off-limits areas, such as the England Changing Room and Players Tunnel. Tour tickets include entry to the World Rugby Museum, which features 41,000 items of rugby memorabilia.

Cross the Thames for just £1 by private ferry to reach **Marble Hill House**, the comparatively more modest 18th-century home of Henrietta Howard, Countess of Suffolk. She sought a space away from her abusive husband and quietly built this rural retreat, a highly unusual move at the time. Its restrained interiors show off paintings, porcelain and the trimmings of a well-to-do life.

In 1729, the third Earl of Burlington constructed **Chiswick House**, a grand neo-Palladian pile. The eye-catching interior includes the richly decorated Blue Velvet Room with a stunningly painted ceiling and the Gallery designed to evoke a Roman bathhouse.

## Wide Open Spaces

LONDON GONE WILD

London became the world's first National Park City in 2019. For an urban introduction, head to **Richmond Green**, ringed with mansions and delightful pubs. In the Middle Ages, jousting tournaments were held here, and today it's an absolute picture on a sunny day. The nearby remains of Richmond Palace – the main entrance and red-brick gatehouse – date to 1501. Henry VII's arms are visible above the main gate, and Elizabeth I died here in 1603.

When you're ready to go wild, lace up your boots and hike section 6 of the **Capital Ring**, a 15-part, 78-mile London-encircling walking route. This part starts in Wimbledon Park and threads its way to Richmond Park, past the 1817 octagonal **Wimbledon Windmill Museum** in Wimbledon Common; **Pembroke Lodge**, originally a one-room cottage that housed the park's mole-catcher but expanded into a grand home for the Countess of Pembroke in 1796; and **King Henry's Mound**, which has a legally protected view of St Paul's Cathedral, 12 miles away (you'll need to look through the on-site telescope to see it).

At 7.3 miles, this is one of the longest segments of the Capital Ring, and despite the number of opportunities to stop for cream tea, it's one of the most delightfully wild stretches.

**COUNTRY PILES**

Plenty more stately homes lie just outside of London, including **Highclere Castle** (p193), where *Downton Abbey* was filmed; Hever Castle in Kent; and the art-deco-meets-medieval **Eltham Palace** (p117), just 30 minutes from London Bridge station.

**WHERE TO DRINK IN RICHMOND & SOUTHWEST LONDON**

**White Swan**
Traditional pub overlooking a quiet section of the Thames, which laps at the tables at high tide.

**Tap on the Line**
At Kew Gardens station – the only pub right next to a London Tube platform.

**Prince's Head**
Cosy 300-year-old pub overlooking Richmond Green, with lively outdoor tables perfect for people watching.

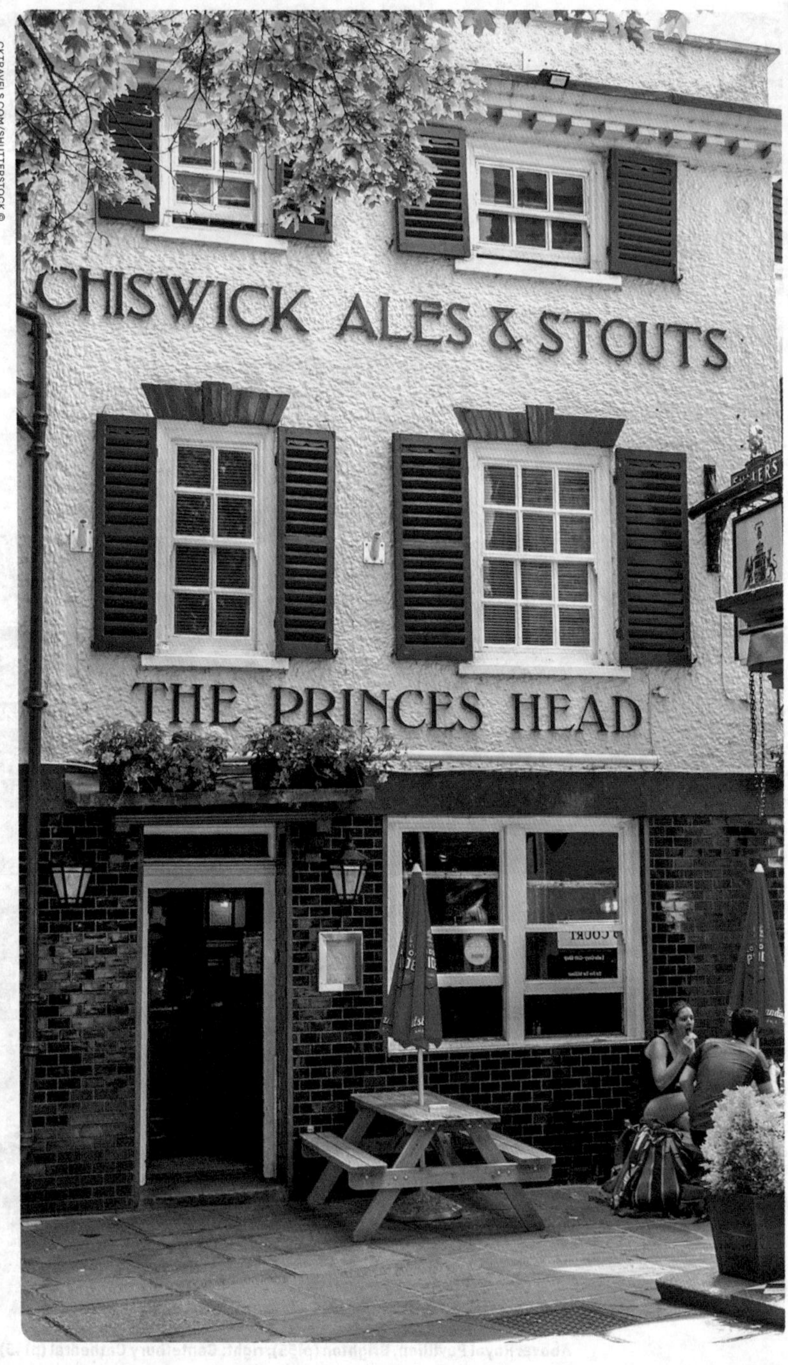




Prince's Head

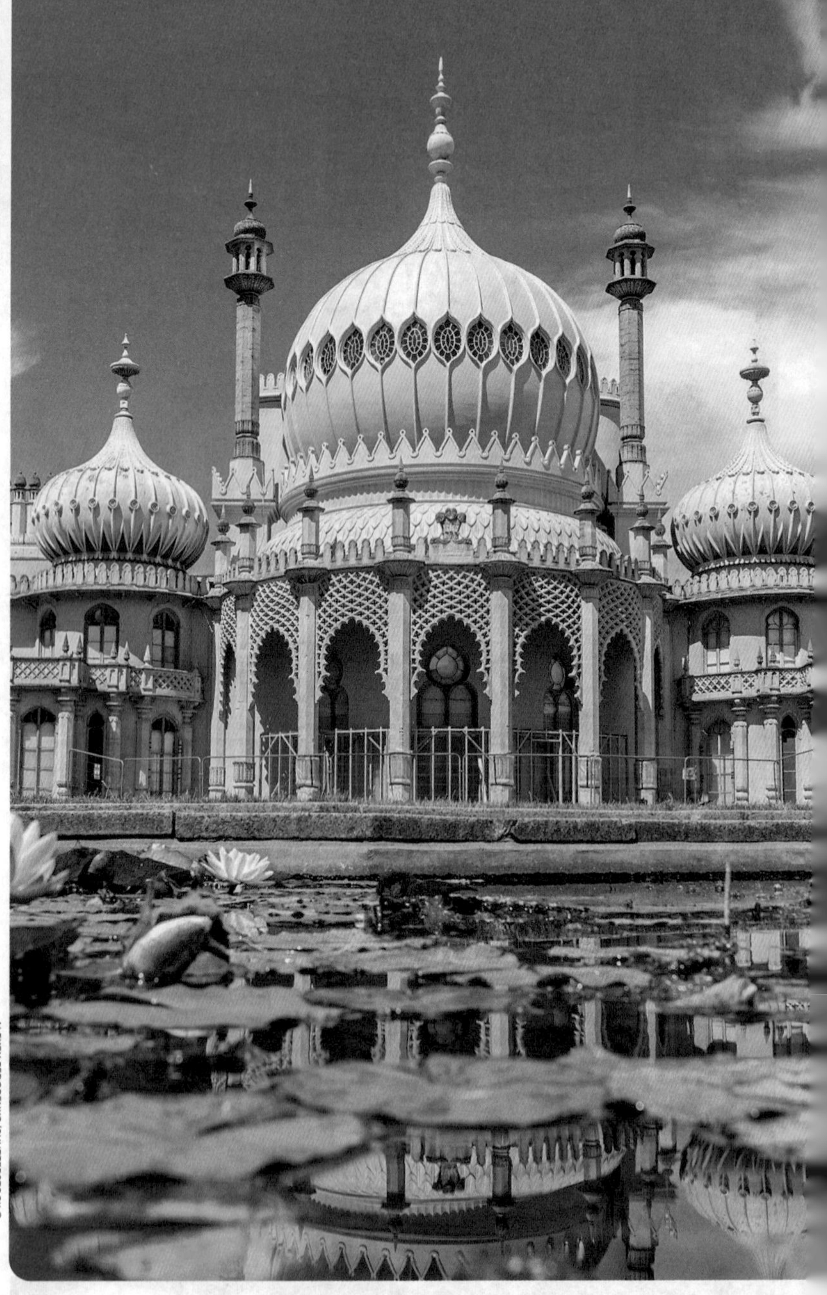

ALEXEY FEDORENKO/SHUTTERSTOCK ©

Above: Royal Pavillion, Brighton (p155); right: Canterbury Cathedral (p145)

# CANTERBURY & THE SOUTHEAST

## CLIFFS, CASTLES AND COASTAL TOWNS

With miles of coastline to explore, the southeast is a region of cathedral cities, countryside walks and vibrant seaside towns.

England's sunny southeast is the corner of the country where the coastline comes closest to the Continent. Historically, the area has been the frontline of defence against invasion, a past which has left reminders in the form of Norman castles and naval shipyards. The region's strategic position is brought into full focus at Dover Castle, where, from Roman times to the Cold War, the occupiers have prepared for the event of an attack.

Millions of people a year make the journey to visit the venerable cathedral in Canterbury, the spiritual heart of England and an ancient pilgrimage site. Elsewhere in the region, Winchester and Chichester – also cities dominated by their historic cathedrals – have personalities of their own. Several of the southeast's coastal towns reflect a journey from thriving Victorian resorts through harder times in the late 20th century to recent regeneration. Brighton, Margate, Folkestone and Hastings are home to burgeoning creative communities, art galleries, independent shops and excellent restaurants. However social issues associated with unemployment, poverty, and homelessness persist in these towns.

Beyond the urban centres are the rolling chalk downs and ancient woodlands of the countryside, interspersed with grand country houses and medieval villages with historic pubs. From the South Downs to the New Forest, there are more walking and cycling trails here than most people could manage in a lifetime.



### THE MAIN AREAS

# Find Your Way

The southeast covers the area between London and the south coast, encompassing the counties of Kent, East and West Sussex, Surrey and Hampshire. We've picked the places that best capture the region's history, culture and natural beauty.

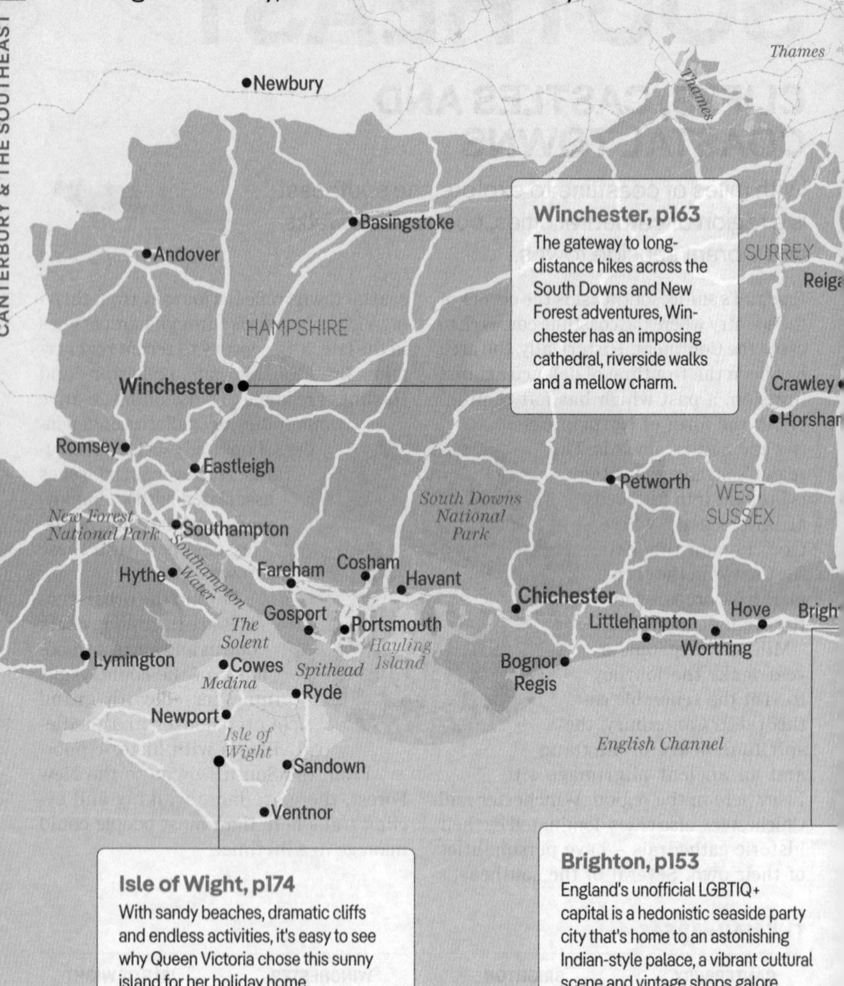


**Winchester, p163**
The gateway to long-distance hikes across the South Downs and New Forest adventures, Winchester has an imposing cathedral, riverside walks and a mellow charm.

**Isle of Wight, p174**
With sandy beaches, dramatic cliffs and endless activities, it's easy to see why Queen Victoria chose this sunny island for her holiday home.

**Brighton, p153**
England's unofficial LGBTIQ+ capital is a hedonistic seaside party city that's home to an astonishing Indian-style palace, a vibrant cultural scene and vintage shops galore.

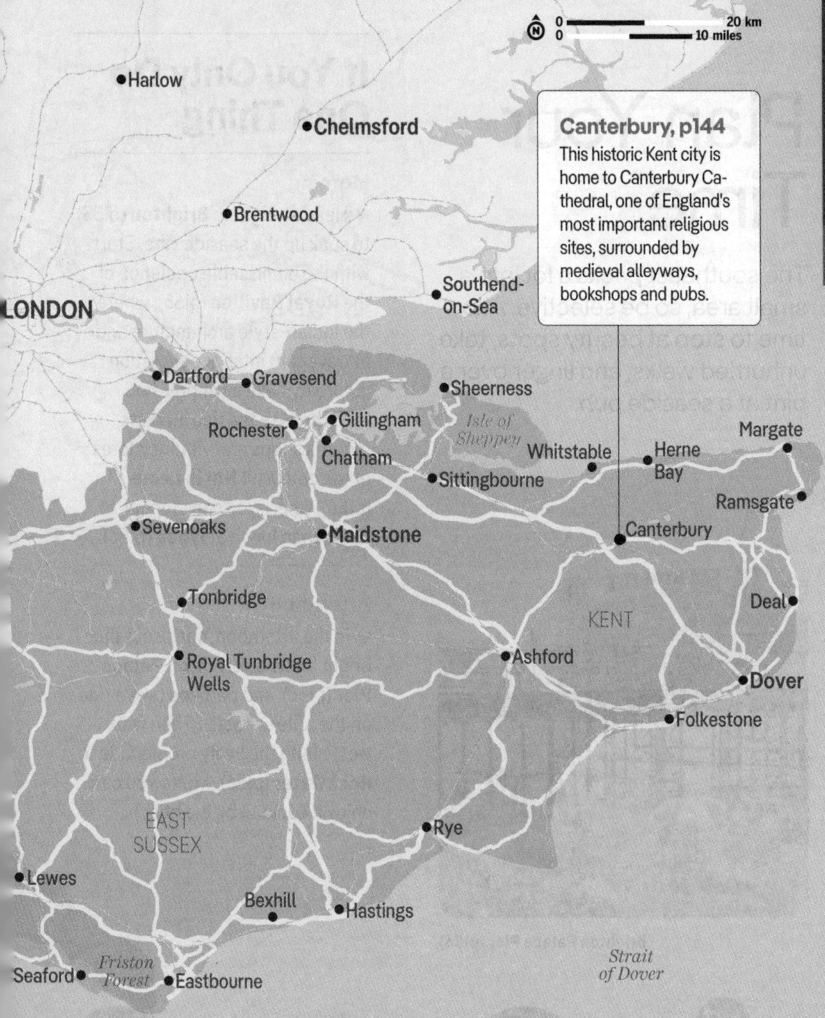

0 20 km
0 10 miles

Harlow
Chelmsford
Brentwood
Southend-on-Sea
LONDON
Dartford
Gravesend
Sheerness
Rochester
Gillingham
Chatham
Isle of Sheppey
Whitstable
Herne Bay
Margate
Sittingbourne
Ramsgate
Sevenoaks
Maidstone
Canterbury
Tonbridge
Deal
KENT
Ashford
Royal Tunbridge Wells
Dover
Folkestone
EAST SUSSEX
Rye
Lewes
Bexhill
Hastings
Friston Forest
Seaford
Eastbourne
Strait of Dover

**Canterbury, p144**
This historic Kent city is home to Canterbury Cathedral, one of England's most important religious sites, surrounded by medieval alleyways, bookshops and pubs.

**CAR**

Car is a generally the easiest way to get around the southeast, particularly in rural areas, and driving affords more freedom to make unscheduled stops. However, parking can be expensive in urban centres and traffic can be heavy on the coast.

**BUS**

For short journeys and for trips outside the region's main towns, buses are usually the best option if you don't have a car. Buses are often cheaper than trains. Most bus companies accept contactless payments by card.

**TRAIN**

It's easy to reach the area's main hubs by train from London. The ease of travelling between regional towns depends on the train line; if the journey involves several changes there may be a more direct route by bus.

# Plan Your Time

The southeast packs a lot into a small area, so be selective. Allow time to stop at beauty spots, take unhurried walks, and linger over a pint at a seaside pub.

SAKARES JERDNAPAPAN/SHUTTERSTOCK ©

Brighton Palace Pier (p156)

## If You Only Do One Thing

### Morning

- Head straight to **Brighton** (p153) to soak up the seaside vibe. Start with the unmissable opulence of the **Royal Pavilion** (p155), where the Indian-style architecture and extravagant interior decoration is sure to make an impression. Next, browse the flea markets, records shops and vintage stores of the colourful **North Laine** (p155), where you can stop for a vegetarian lunch at **Iydea** (p156).

### Afternoon

- In the afternoon, check out the bright lights of **Brighton Palace Pier** (p156), and perhaps take a ride on the roller-coaster. Then walk west along the lively promenade to **Rockwater** (p156), where you can enjoy a cocktail by the beach.

### Seasonal Highlights

The southeast is England's sunniest corner. From crisp winter mornings to long summer nights, each season has its highlights. Autumn transforms the countryside into a palette of russets and gold.

**MAY**

Performers from around the globe arrive in Brighton for the annual three-week long **arts festival**.

**JUNE**

Wildflowers are in bloom but the summer crowds have not yet descended; the perfect time to **hike** the South Downs.

**AUGUST**

Beaches fill up with day-trippers from London. Brighton celebrates **Pride** with a rainbow-hued parade, concerts and parties.

PHILIP REEVE/SHUTTERSTOCK ©, DMITRY NAUMOV/SHUTTERSTOCK ©, EYEMATTER/SHUTTERSTOCK ©

## 4 Days to Travel Around

After a day in Brighton, head east along the coast to the **Seven Sisters Country Park** (p159), where you can hike over the dramatic chalk cliffs to Eastbourne, home to **Towner Art Gallery** (p160). From here, make a stop to explore **Rye's** (p1620) cobbled streets and medieval buildings, before continuing on to **Canterbury** (p144).

Spend some time absorbing the history of **Canterbury Cathedral** (p145), and feast on local produce at the **Goods Shed** (p145). Next up, take the train to Ramsgate and explore the Kent coast on a **cycling tour** (p148) to Whitstable, stopping at Broadstairs and Margate along the way.

## A Week-Long Stay

Start in **Canterbury** (p144) and take a day trip to discover more of **Kent** (p149). Next head to **Brighton** (p153) for some seaside fun. Travel west along the coast to **Chichester** (p166) – explore the city centre on a **walking tour** (p169) – and on to **Portsmouth Historic Harbour** (p168), where the Tudor ship the *Mary Rose* is a must-see.

From Portsmouth, take the ferry to the **Isle of Wight** (p174), and marvel at the isle's **coastline** (p177), before catching the boat from Yarmouth to Lymington in the **New Forest** (p171). Enjoy a Forest walk or cycle, before finishing your trip in the cathedral city of **Winchester** (p163).

**SEPTEMBER**

The weather is still warm but the beaches are quieter, making this an excellent time to visit the **coast**.

**OCTOBER**

A good time to see **starling murmurations**. The re-enactment of the **Battle of Hastings** commemorates the events of 1066.

**NOVEMBER**

The skies turn red as the country's biggest **bonfire** celebrations are held in Lewes in East Sussex.

**DECEMBER**

Winchester gets into the festive spirit with a **Christmas market** and ice rink at the cathedral.

London
Canterbury

# CANTERBURY

Canterbury is a city built around its cathedral. The World Heritage–listed site that dominates the city centre is both one of England's top tourist attractions and a holy place of worship. It is a vast edifice crammed with enthralling stories, arresting architecture and an enduring sense of spirituality. But some visitors also pick up on ominous undertones of violence: the cathedral is the site of one of the most notorious murders in English history, the assassination of Archbishop Thomas Becket in 1170. Surrounding the cathedral complex are alleyways lined with medieval timber-framed buildings that further evoke tales of pilgrims.

But Canterbury is not a city stuck in the past. These days, it's a busy place with an energetic student population, good restaurants and an outstanding arts venue, the Marlowe Theatre. Canterbury's pubs are the perfect place to sample local beers and soak up the city vibe.

**TOP TIP**

Pilgrims may no longer flock here in their thousands, but tourists certainly do. Be sure to book ahead for the best hotels and restaurants. It is also best to book tours in advance, especially in summer. The tourist office, located in Beaney House, can help with bookings.

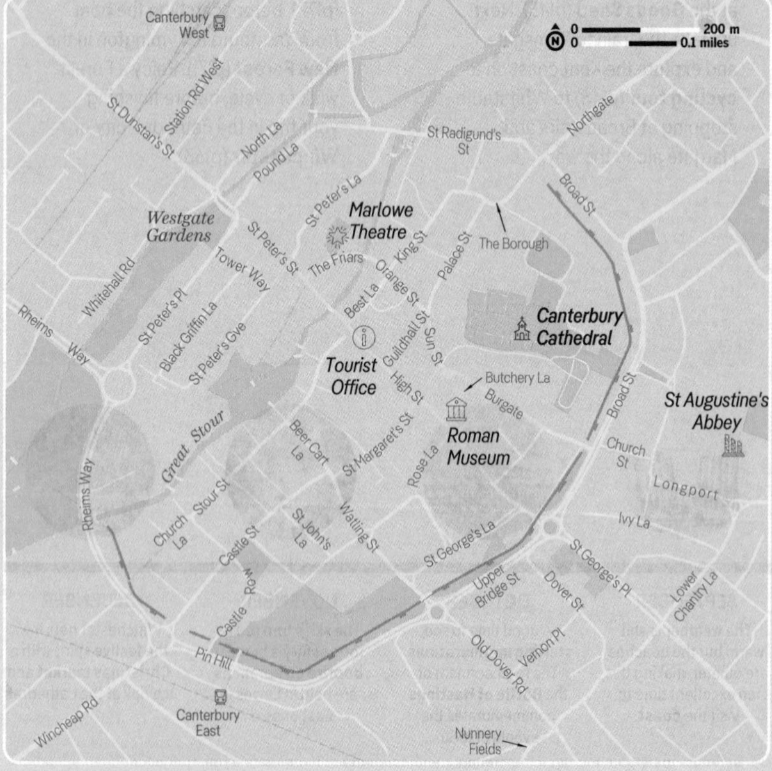

PHILIP BIRD LRPS CPAGB/SHUTTERSTOCK ©

Canterbury Cathedral

## Uncovering the Past at Canterbury Cathedral

EXPLORING ENGLAND'S SPIRITUAL HEART

**Canterbury Cathedral** is considered by many to be one of Europe's finest, but the Church of England mother church (the spiritual head of the Anglican church) is so rich in historical significance that taking it all in may feel overwhelming. For those keen to learn all they can, guided tours offer a comprehensive explanation of the many treasures and architectural details that tell the story of the cathedral's 1400-year history. However, exploring the cathedral and precincts alone offers the chance to experience moments of peace away from the crowds, and to connect with the spirituality of the site.

The **Cathedral ticket office** is next to the early Tudor-era Christ Church Gate. Pop upstairs in the ticket office building for a view of the cathedral exterior, which is mostly Gothic in style. Before entering the cathedral at the southwest porch, walk further around to the left (the cathedral's westernmost side) to view statues of historical figures in the exterior niches, which include Queen Elizabeth II and Prince Philip, added in 2015.

Once inside, the signposted visitor route offers information about the cathedral's most important details. Don't miss the Martyrdom, the spot where Becket was murdered by two of Henry II's knights; today it is marked by a flickering candle and a strikingly modern altar.

The atmosphere changes in the cavernous crypt, in which silence is requested. This was the only space to survive the

### BEST FOOD & DRINK IN CANTERBURY

**Refectory Kitchen**
Friendly cafe serving healthy meals and all-day breakfasts. £

**Goods Shed**
An atmospheric indoor farmers market, food hall and restaurant rolled into one. ££

**Foundry**
A microbrewery and distillery offering excellent craft beers and pub food in an industrial setting. ££

**Parrot**
Dating back to 1370, this snug pub serves local ales; has upstairs dining room. ££

**Bridge Arms**
This outstanding gastropub is located just south of Canterbury in the village of Bridge. £££

### WHERE TO STAY IN CANTERBURY

**ABode Canterbury**
A centrally located boutique hotel with nicely decorated rooms, a Champagne bar and good restaurant. ££

**House of Agnes**
B&B with mixture of old rooms in original inn and modern rooms in newer annex. ££

**Pig at Bridge Place**
A characterful hotel in a renovated period house located on the outskirts of Canterbury. £££

devastating fire of 1174, which destroyed the rest of the building. The original site of Becket's tomb is marked by *Transport*, a striking sculpture by Antony Gormley, completed in 2010, of a floating figure composed of 19th-century handmade nails that were previously in the cathedral's roof. Elsewhere in the crypt look for carvings of mythical figures among the forest of pillars, and stop to take in the beautiful 12th-century wall murals in St Gabriel's Chapel.

Religious services at the cathedral are open to anybody wishing to attend, without charge. Many people find Evensong, during which hymns are sung by the cathedral choir, to be a particularly moving service.

### THE CANTERBURY TALES

After the gruesome murder of Archbishop Thomas Becket in Canterbury Cathedral, Becket's tomb became the most popular pilgrimage site in medieval England. These days the well-trodden route from London is best remembered as the subject of Geoffrey Chaucer's *The Canterbury Tales*.

Written between 1387 and his death in 1400, in Middle English, *The Canterbury Tales* is an unfinished series of 24 vivid stories told by a party of pilgrims. Chaucer created the illusion that the pilgrims, not Chaucer (though he appears in the tales as himself), are narrating the stories, which are entertaining yarns of adultery, debauchery, crime, and romance, stuffed with Chaucer's witty observations about human nature.

## Medieval Alleys, Ancient Walls & Waterways

TRACKING CANTERBURY'S PAST & PRESENT

From Canterbury West station, enter the city centre through the archway of the medieval **Westgate Tower** and head to the bridge to book a spot on a **river tour** along the River Stour, ducking under bridges along the way.

Once back on dry land, look for the life-size bronze **statue of Chaucer** on Best Lane, then get lost in the warren of alleyways. Many of the crooked medieval buildings would once have hosted visiting pilgrims. To delve deeper still into Canterbury's past, stop at the **Roman Museum** on Butchery Lane for a subterranean stroll around a reconstructed Roman marketplace. The museum highlight is an almost intact Roman soldier's helmet dating from Caesar's invasion.

Nearby are the ruins of St Augustine's Abbey, which were destroyed during Henry VIII's Dissolution of the Monasteries in the 16th century. At Burgate, follow the city walls south through **Dane John Gardens** and climb the **mound** for views back across the city to the cathedral.

### CATHEDRAL CITIES

Like Canterbury, **Winchester** (p163) and **Chichester** (p166) are cities centred around significant cathedrals. Though they receive fewer visitors than Canterbury Cathedral, they each have a distinct history and atmosphere.

### GETTING AROUND

Canterbury has two railway stations, Canterbury East and Canterbury West. Trains from London Victoria arrive at Canterbury East, while trains from London's Charing Cross and St Pancras stations arrive at Canterbury West; the stations are about 1 mile apart and both within walking distance of the city centre. The fastest connection to London is the high-speed service to London St Pancras (one hour).

If arriving by car, Castle St car park is well located on the edge of the historic city centre. Many of the roads near the cathedral are pedestrianised. The city centre is compact and walkable.

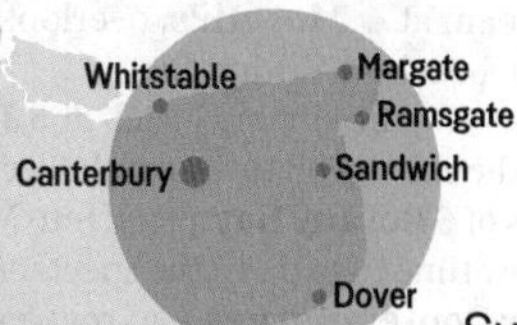

Whitstable
Margate
Ramsgate
Canterbury
Sandwich
Dover

# Beyond Canterbury

## Surrounding Canterbury, the Kent countryside is a wonder of castles and country houses, vineyards, and sunny seaside towns.

Within easy reach of Canterbury, the Kent coastline is lined with sandy bucket-and-spade beaches, chalk cliffs and a series of coastal towns each with distinct personalities, from old-school Broadstairs to hip Margate to lively Ramsgate. Creativity thrives in these coastal communities in the form of burgeoning visual arts scenes, experimental music festivals and innovative restaurants.

Away from the vibrant urban centres, rural Kent evokes the England of romcoms, with sun-dappled tree-lined lanes, crooked country pubs and charming villages. This rural idyll is home to fruit-laden orchards, vineyards, grand country houses and historic castles. Churchill was so fond of his Kentish home that he remarked, 'A day away from Chartwell is a day wasted'.

### TOP TIP

On summer weekends traffic to the Kent coast can reach a standstill. To avoid the queues, take the train or cycle.

Broadstairs

CHRISTINE BIRD/SHUTTERSTOCK ©

## THE KENT COAST: RAMSGATE TO WHITSTABLE CYCLING TOUR

This jaunt along the Kent coast follows the signposted and mostly off-road National Cycle Network route 15 (25 miles). Ramsgate and Whitstable have train connections to Canterbury and London.

The lively town of Ramsgate, with its sandy beaches and cosmopolitan cafes, makes a great starting point. Pick up the Viking Coastal Trail section of route 15 and set off along the coast towards 1 **Ramsgate Harbour**. Rounding the corner towards Broadstairs, the trail passes through 2 **King George VI Memorial Park**. Look out for the 19th-century, curved Italianate Greenhouse. Here the garden tearoom (open in summer only) serves thick slices of homemade cake.

Continue pedalling over the cliffs to Broadstairs, a quaint resort that plays the Victorian nostalgia card at every opportunity. Charles Dickens spent most summers here between 1837 and 1859; find out more at the 3 **Dickens House Museum**. Stop for ice cream at 4 **Morelli's**, overlooking the sandy beach at Viking Bay.

After passing the surfing beach at 5 **Joss Bay** and the equally picturesque chalk cliffs and sands of 6 **Botany Bay**, pedal into Margate. Allow time to explore the spectacular 7 **Turner Contemporary** and rejuvenated Dreamland amusement park.

Continue west past 8 **St Mildred's Bay**, taking in the views from the clifftops, and continue along the seawall to the peaceful ruins of a medieval church, 9 **Reculver Towers**. Follow the coastline past 10 **Herne Bay Pier** and admire its helter-skelter before continuing on to Whitstable, a favoured spot for day-trippers. Rest your legs and feast on fresh local seafood in the lively 11 **Whitstable Harbour**, where oysters have been harvested since Roman times, before passing weatherboard houses, narrow alleyways and galleries on your way uptown to the station.

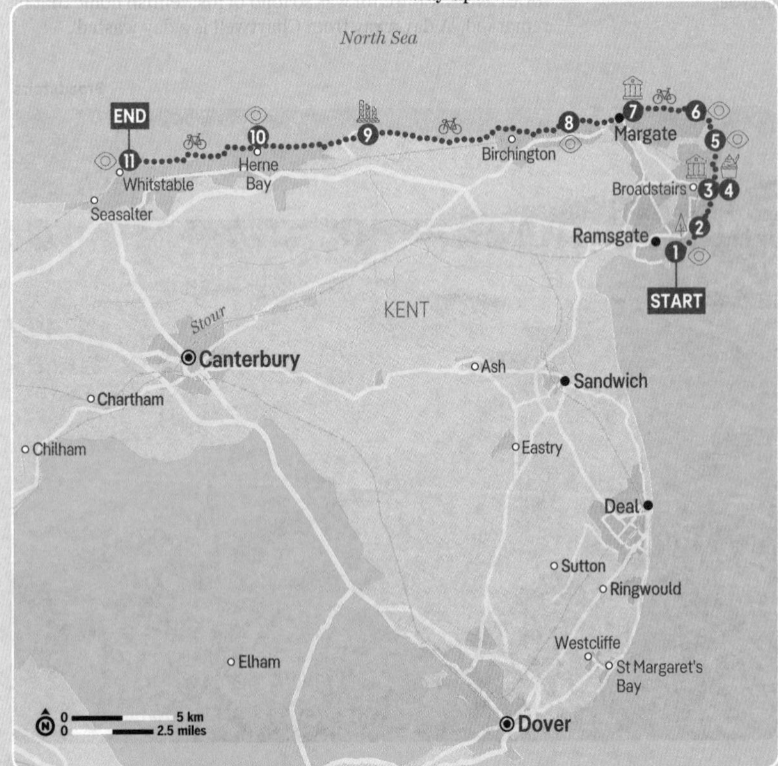

ALANMORRIS/SHUTTERSTOCK ©

Reculver Towers

## Medieval Sandwich

KENT'S LIVING MUSEUM

During its heyday, Sandwich was an important port (the harbour silted up in the 16th century) and England's fourth city, but these days the place feels more like a living museum. Only 35 minutes from Canterbury by bus, the best way to experience Sandwich is to wander its maze of medieval streets, camera in hand, and take in the charm.

At the waterfront, where the **old toll bridge** over the River Stour marks the entrance into town, several pubs here make a pleasant spot for a drink. From the bridge, a walking trail follows the river east to **Sandwich Marina**.

Head up St Peter's St to **St Peter's Church**, where you can climb the tower for rooftop views. The Dutch gable on the church and the ornate brickwork of many other buildings in town reflects the influence of Flemish refugees who settled in the town in the 16th century. Make your way past half-timbered houses to the **Guildhall Museum**, where the highlight is a copy of the Magna Carta, discovered in Sandwich's archives in 2015.

### THE TURNER CONTEMPORARY'S EFFECT ON MARGATE

Since the blockbuster Turner Contemporary art gallery was opened in 2011 by Tracey Emin, who grew up in Margate, more than 3.5 million visitors have come to see exhibitions featuring the work of artists such as Grayson Perry, Ai Weiwei and JMW Turner himself (the gallery is located on the site of the seafront guesthouse where Turner used to stay).

Intended as a catalyst for regeneration, the gallery has undoubtedly had an effect on the town's creative sector, with visual artists and musicians taking advantage of low-priced local studio space and the sense of community. However, despite the growth of Margate's arts scene, the town continues to experience high levels of youth unemployment and child poverty.

### WHERE TO EAT IN KENT

**Peter's Fish Factory**
Popular Margate fish and chips shop. Grab an outside table or eat on the beach. £

**Wyatt & Jones**
Family-run restaurant in Broadstairs serving small plates made with carefully sourced ingredients. ££

**Angela's**
Sustainable seafood restaurant in Margate with daily menu based on the catch of the day. ££

**BEST PUBS ON THE KENT COAST**

**Old Neptune** White-boarded pub located right on the Whitstable beach, with live music at weekends.

**Belle Vue Tavern** This pub near Ramsgate has a terrace with spectacular views of the coast.

**Lifeboat** Cosy Margate pub with a wide range of local ales and craft beers.

**Zetland Arms** A beachside pub in Deal serving Shepherd Neame beers and local seafood.

**Chapel Bar & Bookshop** This place in Broadstairs is a chapel, bar and bookshop in one.

LUKE VILE/SHUTTERSTOCK ©

Chartwell House

## Winetasting in Kent

SIPPING ENGLISH WINE

English wine was once widely derided, but due to warmer temperatures and the efforts of determined winemakers, Kentish wine is gaining in reputation. An hour's drive from Canterbury, several of Kent's vineyards are located close to each other in charmingly bucolic settings, and visiting the vineyards takes you into beautiful countryside you might not otherwise have reason to explore. Book ahead for guided tours of any of the vineyards.

Start at **Balfour** winery, a high-tech, modern operation on the Hush Heath Estate. Here you can sample Balfour's Brut Rosé, which is served to first-class passengers on British Airways flights. A full estate tour includes a guided walk and a tasting of six wines, or pick up a map for a self-guided walk around the vines and through ancient oak woodland. A restaurant overlooks the vines and serves sharing platters of Kentish charcuterie and cheeses.

At **Biddenden,** the signature grape is ortega. As well as wine, the shop also sells Biddenden ciders, local honey and other Kentish produce. Finally, **Chapel Down** winery is a

**WHERE TO EAT IN KENT**

**Stark** This Michelin-starred restaurant in Broadstairs serves a seasonal six-course tasting menu. **£££**

**Fordwich Arms** Expect peaceful riverside dining and dishes that are works of art at this Michelin-starred restaurant. **£££**

**Sportsman** This gastropub serves good-value Michelin-starred food in a stripped-back setting. **£££**

lovely spot for a guided tour and tasting (Tenterden Estate Bacchus is a good one to try), but it's not necessary to book a tour to walk through the vineyard; maps are available.

## Chartwell, Churchill's Beloved Country Home

ENTERING CHURCHILL'S PRIVATE HOME

An hour's drive from Canterbury by car, and now under the care of the National Trust, Sir Winston Churchill's home from 1924 until his death in 1965 offers a breathtakingly intimate insight into the life of England's cigar-chomping former prime minister. Churchill's deep connection to his family home can be felt in every corner of the estate, from the wall he built in the garden, to the studio where he painted (where many of his paintings are displayed and his cigar still sits in an ashtray), to the replicas of the treehouses he built for his children. The house itself is full of mementos, and guides do a great job explaining the significance of personal items. Upstairs beneath Tudor rafters is Churchill's desk and the ship-deck wooden floor he paced while thinking.

For a chance to view Churchill's bedroom, book a place on an after-hours highlights tour. You might even catch a glimpse of Jock VII, a cat who lives at the house to fulfill the Churchill family request that there always be a marmalade cat called Jock in residence.

**NORTH DOWNS WAY**

The 153-mile North Downs walking trail begins near Farnham in Surrey, but one of its most beautiful sections runs from near Ashford to the trail endpoint in Dover. Near here the route passes through **Samphire Hoe** country park, a ledge of parkland created between the cliffs and the sea using chalk excavated during the construction of the Channel Tunnel. The **East Kent Loop** extends the trail as far as Canterbury.

## A Moated Marvel

EMBRACING HISTORY AT LEEDS CASTLE

Forty minutes' drive from Canterbury, romantic **Leeds Castle** and its extensive grounds make for a great family day out. Built on Norman foundations and home to several medieval queens, including Henry VIII's first wife Catherine of Aragon, Leeds Castle is not stuck in the past. The focus here is on fun, from the cinematic talking heads of queens relating their stories, to falconry displays, to a hedge maze, overseen by a grassy bank from which fellow travellers can shout directions.

The castle interior reflects the renovations undertaken by its last owner, the high-society hostess Ladie Baillie, when the castle was infamous for its raucous parties attended by the likes of Errol Flynn and John F Kennedy. Up the beautiful carved-wood spiral staircase, Lady Baillie's private rooms are a castle highlight.

**WHERE TO STAY IN KENT**

**Dover Adventure Backpackers**
This friendly hostel has a terrace with views of the White Cliffs. £

**Royal Harbour Hotel**
Occupying two Regency townhouses on a seafront crescent, this Ramsgate hotel has glorious harbour views. ££

**Reading Rooms**
Luxury two-room B&B in an 18th-century townhouse located in a tranquil Margate square. £££

## BEST SEASIDE PUBLIC ART IN KENT

**Folkestone**
Download the Creative Folkestone map of the Folkestone Artworks exhibition, which includes more than 70 outdoor contemporary pieces by artists including Tracey Emin and Antony Gormley. Don't miss Cornelia Parker's *Folkestone Mermaid* (2011) at Sunny Sands beach, Lubaina Himid's *Jelly Mould Pavilion* (2017) on the seafront boardwalk, and Richard Woods' playful *Holiday Home* (2017) at the harbour, a comment on housing inequalities.

**Ramsgate**
Look out for a bronze bust of Vincent van Gogh by Anthony Padgett, a brick three-piece suite by Rodney Harris, and the installation *Beacons*, created by Conrad Shawcross in collaboration with local schoolchildren.

**Margate**
Keep your eyes peeled for numerous pieces commissioned by Turner Contemporary and a wealth of street art.

# Unravelling Layers of History in Dover

CASTLE, SECRET TUNNELS & CLIFFS

Spending a day in Dover, 30 minutes from Canterbury by train, offers an introduction to 2000 years of English history and a chance to connect to the emblematic significance and natural beauty of Dover's white cliffs.

**Dover Castle** sits on the clifftop overlooking the channel and ferry port at the point of the shortest sea crossing to mainland Europe. The site is vast, so allow several hours to explore. Begin your visit at the castle highlight, the **secret wartime tunnels** that were excavated to house troops during the Napoleonic Wars and later used as a command post and a hospital during WWII. A guided tour makes use of creative audiovisuals to tell the story of Operation Dynamo, code name for the evacuation of thousands of soldiers from Dunkirk that was directed from the tunnels. A second tour takes in the sights, sounds and smells of the wartime hospital housed.

From here, pass the complex's earliest building – the remains of a **Roman lighthouse** – and peek inside the **Saxon church**, before exploring the 12th-century **Great Tower**, where interactive exhibits take visitors back to the time of Henry II.

The experience of visiting the castle gives a sense of Dover's historical significance at the front line of England's defence. From here, head 1 mile east to the National Trust–managed **White Cliffs**. Follow the path along the clifftops for a bracing 2-mile walk to the **South Foreland Lighthouse,** where you can eat at the cafe's picnic tables looking out towards France.

Dover Castle

### GETTING AROUND

Kent's coastal towns are well connected by train and bus with London and Canterbury. Taking public transport also saves on car-park costs. However, public transport to rural areas is less frequent, and the villages in and around the Kent Downs are best reached by car or by bike.

London
Brighton

# BRIGHTON

Ever since the 19th century, when Prince George hosted all-night parties at his opulent Royal Pavilion pleasure palace, Brighton has embraced hedonism. Brighton has a history of providing space for alternative forms of self-expression, and the punk scene that thrived in the 1970s and 1980s has had a lasting effect on the city's culture. Home to England's biggest gay scene, Brighton is a place that invites people to be themselves.

A colourful city with a vibe that veers towards the outrageous, this is where burlesque meets contemporary design. It's also a city that is big on all things eco-conscious; Brighton has been represented by the Green Party MP Caroline Lucas since 2010. Here living ethically is approached in a characteristically fun way, with vegan restaurants, vintage clothes shops and cyclepaths galore.

Brighton's pebble beach is one of its biggest draws, and when the sun comes out the crowds descend.

### TOP TIP

For the inside track on Brighton's best food and drink, join a culinary walk around town with **Brighton Food Tours**. The VIB (Very Independent Brighton) tour runs year-round on Friday and Saturday and is a great way to discover the town's street-food vendors and local producers.

**Brighton Pier**

**HIGHLIGHTS**
1 Brighton Dome
2 Royal Pavilion

**SIGHTS**
3 Brighton Marina
4 Brighton Museum & Art Gallery
5 Pavilion Gardens

**ACTIVITIES & TOURS**
6 Saltdean Lido
7 Undercliff Walk

**SHOPPING**
8 Black Mocha
9 Blackout Shop
10 DOWSE
11 Lanes
12 North Laine Bazaar
13 Resident Music
14 Snoopers Paradise

# BRIGHTON

See Enlargement
Brighton
English Channel
0 1 km
0 0.5 miles

Enlargement
Gloucester Rd
Over St
Kemp St
Kensington Gdns
York Pl
Frederick St
Foundry St
Cheltenham Pl
Gloucester Pl
Grand Pde
Morley St
Queens Rd
Upper Gardner St
North Rd
Victoria Gardens
Church St
Regent St
Marlborough Pl
Kingswood St
Windsor Rd
Portland St
Brighton Dome
North St
Bond St
New Rd
Royal Pavilion
William St
Duke St
THE LANES
Edward St
Princes St
Old Steine
George St
Market St
Castle Sq
Ship St
Bartholomews
0 200 m
0 0.1 miles

Royal Pavilion

GOGAI8128/SHUTTERSTOCK ©

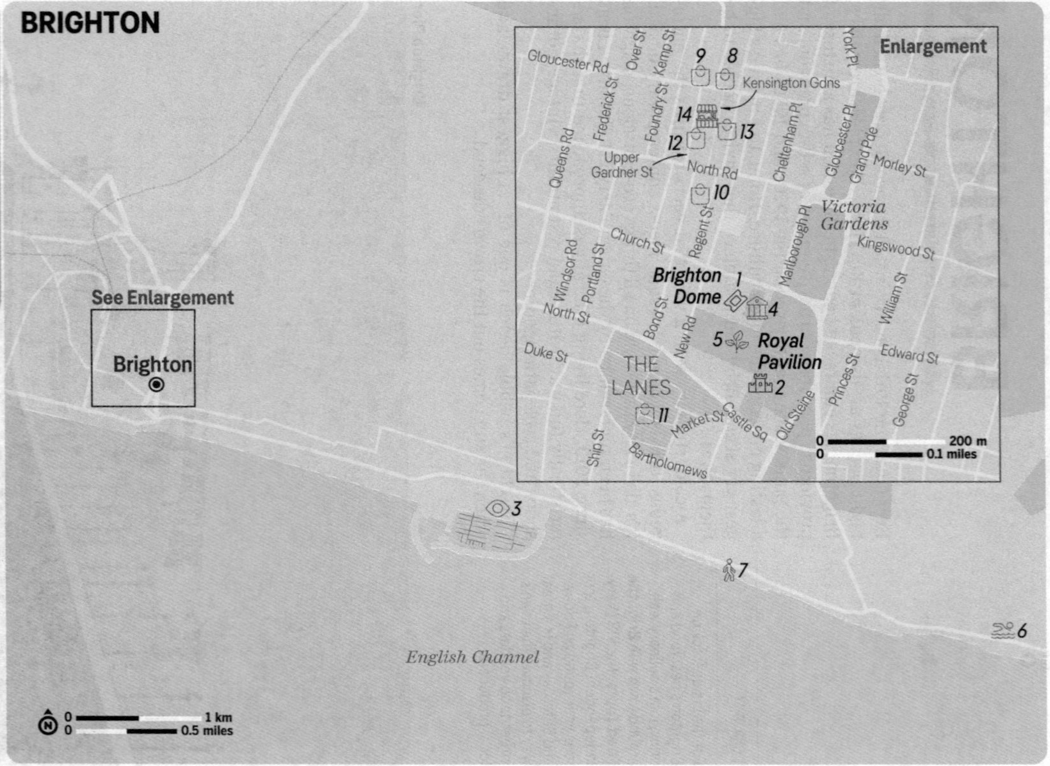

## A Life of Hedonistic Excess

BRIGHTON'S MUST-SEE PARTY PALACE

Walking down from the train station, the first glimpse of the astonishing 19th-century Indian-inspired architecture to come is the magnificent **Brighton Dome**, now a concert hall and theatre. Beyond the dome lies the ostentatious former party palace of King George IV, the **Royal Pavilion** itself. Meticulously planned to wow visitors at every turn, the pavilion interior is an outlandish fantasy decorated with hand-painted Chinese wallpaper and mirrors to trick the eye. The banqueting room is something to behold, with its centrepiece dragon chandelier and table set for a feast: French chef Antonin Carême's menu card speaks of hedonistic excess. Audio guides tell evocative tales of the palace's heyday. Don't miss the fascinating exhibition of photographs depicting the Royal Pavilion during its time as a hospital for Indian soldiers during WWII.

The Royal Pavilion's former stable blocks, constructed in the same opulent Regency style, now house **Brighton Museum** and **Art Gallery**. Highlights include the collection of Egyptian artefacts and the architectural details of the interior domes and glazed wall tiles of the building itself. Look out for Grayson Perry's *Difficult Background* (2001), a ceramic depicting the effect of war on children.

Allow time to wander the serpentine paths of the **gardens**, which are free to enter and offer wonderful views of the Royal Pavilion buildings.

## Retail Therapy in the Lanes

HUNTING FOR VINTAGE FINDS

The tightly packed **Lanes** form Brighton's popular shopping district. Every twist and turn is packed with jewellers, gift shops, cafes and boutiques, selling everything from upcycled furniture to vegan shoes. Just south of the Brighton train station, the **North Laine** area has a number of partially pedestrianised streets with colourful murals and a more bohemian vibe.

The flea market **Snoopers Paradise** and nearby **North Laine Bazaar** are fun places to search for retro collectibles and vintage clothes, records and books. Music lovers could spend hours browsing the vinyl at **Resident Music**, where you might even catch a band playing in-store. For beautiful

### LGBTIQ+ BRIGHTON

**Ophelia Payne**, a drag performer and singer, shares her tips. *@thisisopheliapayne*

The LGBTIQ+ community is almost spoilt for choice with community friendly bars. The hub of gay Brighton is **St James's St**, where you can walk from one gay bar to the next. Don't miss **Bar Broadway** on Steine St. Nearby is the gay nightclub **Club Revenge**.

In Kemptown, the wonderful **Arcobaleno** is a family-run bar, restaurant and LGBTIQ+ community space, with great food and cocktails and themed live entertainment most weekends.

For shows, check what's on at **Ironworks Studios**. **Proud Cabaret** and **The Walrus** both host drag brunches.

Along the seafront on Marine Pde you'll find **R-Bar**, **Charles Street Tap**, **Centre Stage** and **Legends**.

### WHERE TO STAY IN BRIGHTON

**YHA Brighton**
In an excellent location near the pier, this hostel has good-value dorm beds and private rooms. **£**

**27 Brighton**
Superbly decorated B&B with a George IV theme; some rooms have sea views. **££**

**Hotel Una**
Individually decorated rooms in a Regency townhouse full of period features. **£££**

**BEST RESTAURANTS IN BRIGHTON & HOVE**

**Iydea**
Generous vegetarian curries, enchiladas, quiches and salads. £

**Terre à Terre**
Beautiful and inventive vegetarian tapas served in a laid-back setting. ££

**Wild Flor**
Relaxed restaurant serving creative plates made with Sussex ingredients. ££

**Rockwater**
Restaurant and bar; wonderful for a rooftop cocktail or cosy indoor meal. ££

**Little Fish Market**
Chef Duncan Ray's Hove restaurant offers a set taster menu of exquisite seafood dishes. £££

TOMS AUZINS/SHUTTERSTOCK ©

**Undercliff walk**

handmade ceramics and textiles, head to **Dowse**. Nearby is the kitsch emporium **Blackout Shop.** For the best hot chocolate in town, stop at **Black Mocha**.

## Join the Party at Brighton's Seafront

CYCLING FROM PIER TO POOL

The seafront at Brighton and Hove is an active place, with joggers and dog-walkers zipping along the promenade, past buzzing bars, beachside volleyball games and tarot-card readers. At **Brighton Palace Pier**, the screams of thrill-seekers compete with the crashing of waves; take a stroll past doughnut stands and arcade games to the pier-end **viewing platform**.

A 5-mile traffic-free bike ride to Saltdean is a great way to take it all in. Follow the cyclepath east to Brighton Marina and continue along the **Undercliff Walk** (cycling permitted), a 3-mile path between the cliffs and the sea. At Saltdean beach, look for **Saltdean Lido**, an appealingly retro 1930s outdoor pool complex that's open in the summer (book ahead).

**GETTING AROUND**

Trains connect Brighton with London, stopping at Gatwick Airport. Parking is expensive in the city centre; consider using the free Park & Ride at Withdean. Brighton has a bike share programme as well as several bike rental shops.

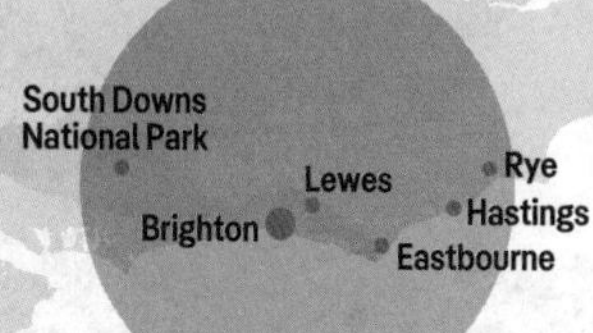

# Beyond Brighton

**Explore the stunning stretch of coast where the rolling hills of the South Downs National Park meet the sea.**

The area surrounding Brighton offers many varied options for exploration. There is the chance to get active and traverse the area's walking and cycling trails, stopping at beaches that beckon you to take a dip in the sea. History enthusiasts can visit sites at the centre of the 1066 Norman invasion; art lovers can discover the work of artists inspired by the East Sussex light; and fans of opera won't want to miss Glyndebourne. But getting to know the area really requires nothing more than joining in with the activities that make daily life here seem enviable: strolling the seafront at sunset and striking up conversations in cafes and pubs.

**TOP TIP**

Secure 33% discounts on most rail fares in the southeast by purchasing a Network Railcard (valid for one year).

**South Devon poppyfield**

### WHY I LOVE THE SOUTH DOWNS NATIONAL PARK

**Isabel Albiston,**
Lonely Planet writer

When I'm staying in St Leonard's I love to go for walks along the coast. The big skies, ever-changing light and the sound of waves lapping over shingle beaches make striding along the seafront a meditative experience. The exhilarating hike over the Seven Sisters and Beachy Head is my favourite local hike. The clifftops are carpeted in spongy, vibrant green grass that reaches right up to the sheer drop of the cliff edge. The nearest road is a mile back from the path, so the only sounds are of the wind, sea, birds, and other walkers.

DAVID C TOMLINSON/GETTY IMAGES ©

**Seven Sisters**

## A Look Around Lewes

HISTORIC COUNTRY TOWN

An affluent town with a turbulent past, Lewes makes an easy day trip (15 minutes by train) from Brighton. At the top of Lewes' Georgian-building-lined high street sits **Lewes Castle**, where two towers offer views over the town to the South Downs. Off the main drag, there's a more intimate atmosphere as you descend into twisting narrow streets called 'twittens'. For an inside glimpse into Lewes' medieval past, visit the early 16th-century **Anne of Cleves timber-framed house** (Henry VIII's fourth wife owned but never lived in the house). Stroll through **Southover Grange Gardens** and past the ruins of the **Priory of St Pancras**, then cool off with a dip in **Pells Pool**, a historic lido (book ahead). Stop by the shop at **Harvey's Brewery** to pick up traditionally brewed ales and local Sussex wines.

### WHERE TO STAY IN EAST SUSSEX

**YHA South Downs**
Farmhouse in the South Downs National Park, with dorm beds, private rooms and a campsite. £

**Old Rectory**
This B&B in a Hastings period home has an honesty bar and a walled garden. ££

**Dubois Bed & Breakfast**
Good value, cosy rooms in a peaceful Victorian house in Lewes. ££

## Catch an Opera at Glyndebourne

ARIAS, PICNICS & SPARKLING WINE

Thirty minutes by train and bus from Brighton, and surrounded by the rolling hills of the South Downs, **Glyndebourne opera house** hosts an annual festival that has an atmosphere of old-fashioned English eccentricity. When, in 1934, science teacher John Christie and his opera-singer wife Audrey Mildmay decided to build a 1200-seat opera house in the middle of the Sussex countryside, it seemed a magnificent folly. But now Glyndebourne is one of England's best venues for the lyric arts during the festival season, from May to August. Tickets usually sell out within days of going on sale in March. Dress up, and bring a picnic to eat in the grounds during the 1½-hour interval.

## Hike the Seven Sisters Cliffs

SPECTACULAR COASTAL WALK

Encompassing rolling chalk downs, ancient woodland and stunning views, the **South Downs National Park** is traversed by a 100-mile off-road walking and cycling trail from Winchester to Eastbourne.

Many sections of the trail make excellent day hikes. Five miles north of Brighton is the popular beauty spot the **Devil's Dyke**, a deep, wide dry valley full of wildflowers. From here you can hike 7 miles east to **Ditchling Beacon**, one of the highest points on South Downs Way, with far-reaching views.

But perhaps the most beautiful walk on the South Downs Way is the trail's final 10-mile section over the Seven Sisters chalk cliffs to Eastbourne. This route is only accessible to walkers; cyclists follow an alternative trail from Alfriston to Eastbourne. Check the maps and pick up snacks at the **Seven Sisters Country Park** visitor centre (55 minutes by bus from Brighton). For the best views (and knockout photos) of the cliffs, take a detour along the west bank of Cuckmere River and climb up **Seafood Head**. At low tide you can walk east along the beach at the mouth of the river, without having to retrace your steps.

From here the trail is an exhilarating roller-coaster of steep inclines and declines over the undulating cliffs. To your right, the sheer chalk cliff face plunges into the churning sea below. Stop at the cafe at **Birling Gap**, before tackling the final climb up to **Beachy Head**, the highest point of the cliffs. Then it's all downhill into Eastbourne.

### LEWES BONFIRES

On 5 November, thousands of people descend on Lewes to watch the street carnival, fireworks displays, processions of torchbearers, and effigies going up in flames in bonfires around town. Six separate bonfire societies hold celebrations, each with its own traditions, costumes and marching bands.

Though the night officially commemorates the uncovering of the Gunpowder Plot in 1605, it has come to represent a form of dissent and protest, with effigies based on the most villainous politicians and public figures of the moment. The processions and bonfires are ticketed events.

### ARTY COASTAL TOWNS

For more contemporary art by the sea, don't miss Margate's **Turner Contemporary** (p149) and Chichester's **Pallant House Gallery** (p169).

**Gallivant**
Camber Sands hotel with high-end design, a destination restaurant, and a host of activities. **£££**

**Jeake's House**
Known for its excellent breakfasts, this splendid Rye hotel occupies a characterful 17th-century townhouse. **£££**

**Belle Tout Lighthouse**
A decommissioned lighthouse on the clifftop at Beachy Head, with six creatively decorated B&B rooms. **£££**

### STARLING MURMURATIONS ON THE SUSSEX COAST

The sight of thousands of starlings swooping and rising as one is truly mesmerising and one of nature's most breathtaking spectacles. Starling murmurations are believed to be a tactic to deter predators and protect the birds within one confusing, swirling mass.

The best time to see murmurations is at dusk during the autumn and winter months. Particularly dramatic displays are often seen near the piers in Eastbourne, Hastings and Brighton, where some 40,000 starlings gather at the skeletal remains of the derelict West Pier.

PHILIP REEVE/SHUTTERSTOCK ©

**Starling murmurations, Brighton**

## Hastings to Eastbourne Art Trail

EXPLORING COASTAL GALLERIES

Hastings is home to a community of artists whose work can be viewed in small independent galleries such as **Rebel Gallery** and the **Dirty Old Gallery**. **Hastings Contemporary** houses temporary exhibitions in a black-tiled building that was designed to blend in with the adjacent black clapboard Net Huts of the Stade. The 6-mile stretch of coast between Hastings Stade and Bexhill-on-Sea makes a great walk, passing the renovated **Hastings Pier** on the way.

In St Leonards-on-Sea, there is a cluster of galleries worth exploring near the seafront, including **Kino** and **Project 78**. At Marina car park, look for the **mural by Bansky** on the concrete steps down to the beach.

In Bexhill, the **De La Warr Pavilion** is a restored Grade I-listed modernist marvel on the seafront and a must-see for fans of art deco architecture. The building, designed in 1935, today serves as a contemporary arts centre and concert venue.

Twelve miles west of Bexhill (20 minutes by train), Eastbourne's **Towner Art Gallery** is one of the southeast's most exciting exhibition spaces. The gallery's colourful exterior is by German artist Lothar Götz.

### WHERE TO DRINK IN EAST SUSSEX

**Crown**
Friendly pub in Hastings with a good drinks selection and local art on the walls.

**Cactus Hound Bar**
Choose from over 40 tequilas or order a cocktail at this relaxed St Leonards bar.

**Mermaid Inn**
Few inns can claim to be as atmospheric as this Rye establishment, dating from 1420.

Pevensey Castle

## On the Trail of William the Conqueror

TRACKING THE EVENTS OF 1066

In 1066, Duke William of Normandy's landing at Pevensey and the defeat of King Harold in the Battle of Hastings forever changed the course of English history. You can discover more about the Norman conquest at the sites where the momentous events took place.

The dramatic ruins of **Pevensey Castle** (one hour by train from Brighton) mark the spot where William and his army landed in 1066, two weeks before the battle. He wasted no time in setting up a base, establishing a castle within the sturdy Roman walls that still stand today. Ten miles northeast is the site where William and King Harold met on 14 October 1066, in an exceptionally bloody day-long battle in which Harold was killed, opening the way for William to be crowned king. In penance for the battle's bloodshed, King William built an abbey on the same sight. Today, the battlefield and monastery ruins can be visited at **Battle Abbey**. Watch the evocative video recounting the events of the day before walking around the battlefield itself; an audio guide makes it possible to imagine the events unfolding before you.

### EAST SUSSEX RAMBLES

**Eileen Swift** is a retired teacher and a member of a local walking club, who lives in Hastings.

My absolute favourite place to walk is **Hastings Country Park Nature Reserve**. It has stunning coastal views as well as beautiful ancient gill woodland. There are many different tracks you can take depending on how fit you are – some paths are quite challenging (the Bale House Visitor Centre at Fairlight can provide information).

If you are lucky enough to be there when there is a spring tide, you may be able to view the dramatic sandstone cliffs from the shoreline or even head out to **Pett Level** where you can walk along the beach to see the sunken forest. You might even find the dinosaur footprints there (the footprints of at least seven dinosaur species were first seen in the eroding the cliffs in 2018).

**Cock Inn**
Pub near Lewes with cask-conditioned real ales and a range of guest beers on tap.

**Hanushka Coffee House**
Cosy book-lined Hastings coffee shop with two branches, each full of browsable titles.

**Lamb Inn**
This ancient Eastbourne institution has been plonking Sussex ales on the bar for eight centuries.

**BEST RESTAURANTS IN EAST SUSSEX**

**Goat Ledge**
This beachside shack in St Leonards, near Hastings, sells popular fresh fish sandwiches. £

**Rock a Nore Kitchen**
Tiny restaurant in Hastings Stade with daily catch from Hastings' fishing fleet on the menu. ££

**Fig**
Rye cafe with excellent vegan and vegetarian options on its menu of creative, healthy dishes. ££

**Skylark**
Relaxed Eastbourne cafe and restaurant serving brunches, lunches and candlelit evening meals. ££

**Farmyard**
This St Leonards restaurant and wine shop serves local produce in atmospheric surroundings. £££

Every October, Battle Abbey hosts a two-day re-enactment of the battle in its original location, complete with horses and live commentary that tracks the battle's progress. History enthusiasts stay in period-style tents in Norman and Saxon camps, cooking food on open fires and practising traditional crafts; visitors are free to walk through the camps and ask questions.

The **1066 Country Walk** is a 31-mile trail from Pevensey via Battle to Rye. Along the way are 10 sculptures inspired by the Bayeux Tapestry.

## Cobbled Streets, Crooked Houses & Salt Marshes

IN THE FOOTSTEPS OF SMUGGLERS

Two hours by train from Brighton, **Rye**'s cobbled lanes, mysterious passageways and crooked half-timbered buildings seem to whisper tales of smugglers and intrigue; some are even said to be haunted. A good place to start exploring is **Mermaid St**, where the timber-framed houses have names such as 'The House with Two Front Doors'. At the top of the hill, take a look around **Lamb House**, a Georgian townhouse that was once the home of writer Henry James. **Rye Castle** houses a ramshackle but charming museum that includes a recreation of the cell of the women's prison and a medieval medicinal herb garden.

From Rye, it's a pleasant 3-mile walk along the River Rother to **Camber Sands**, a gorgeous expanse of dunes and beach that's ideal for picnicking. At nearby Northpoint Water lake, **Rye Watersports** offers lessons and equipment rental.

On the other side of the river is **Rye Harbour Nature Reserve**, a unique mosaic of habitats, including shingle ridges, salt marsh and reedbeds. The reserve is home to more than 4500 recorded species of plants and animals, including important colonies of little, common and Sandwich terns. The cafe at the **Discovery Centre** looks out over the reserve, which is traversed by boardwalk paths. You can extend your walk as far as the tiny medieval town of **Winchelsea**, which is connected by bus to Hastings and Rye.

**GETTING AROUND**

Trains connect Brighton with Eastbourne and Hastings, which has onwards connections to Battle and Rye. The 12X bus between Brighton and Eastbourne stops at Seven Sisters Country Park.

# WINCHESTER

Now a relatively small, prosperous, and mellow city, Winchester was once the capital of England. The Romans built a settlement here that was then the country's fifth largest town, but the city really took off when powerful bishops moved their seat to Winchester in the 7th century. Later, King Alfred the Great made it his capital.

Though Winchester is no longer a centre of political power, there is an enduring sense of pride in the city's historical importance. Here the old England of public schools, military regiments and Anglican bishops meets bohemian Winchester's music scene and creative arts venues.

Winchester also has strong literary links. John Keats wrote poetry inspired by walks through the city's tranquil water meadows, while Jane Austen is buried in the awesome Winchester Cathedral. Near the cathedral, the house where Austen died in 1817 is marked with a plaque.

**TOP TIP**

Winchester city centre can be tackled on foot. The trailhead for the South Downs Way walking and cycling route is in the east of town. If you are planning to explore Winchester's surrounds on two wheels, it's best to contact rental companies in advance to reserve a bike.

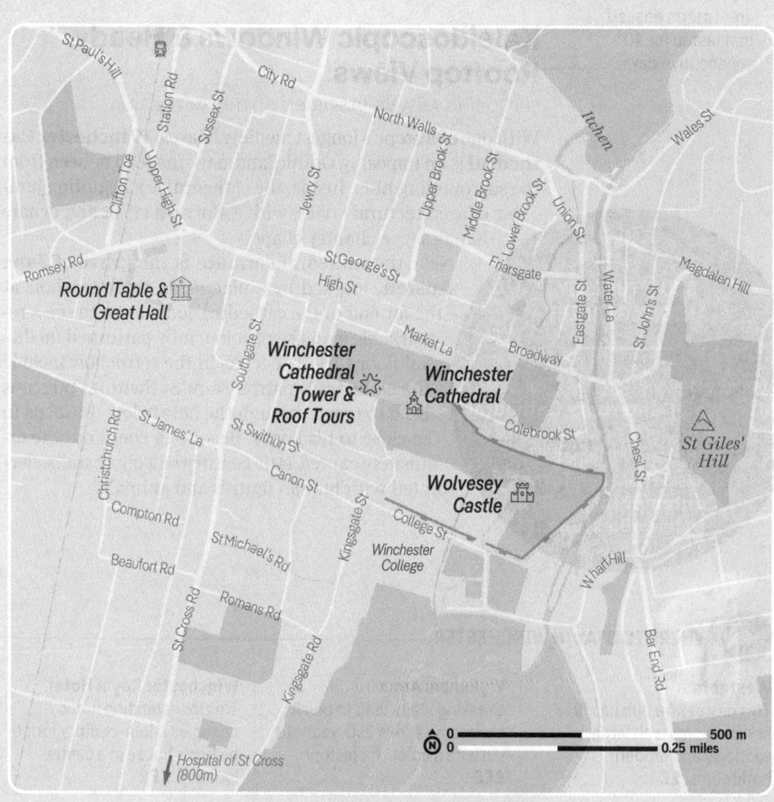

**RAIN ON ST SWITHIN'S DAY**

According to folklore, if it rains on St Swithin's Day (15 July), it will rain for the next 40 days and nights. The story behind the myth is that St Swithin, a 9th-century bishop of Winchester, requested to be buried outside where the rain and steps of passersby would fall on his grave. After his body was moved inside one 15 July, legend has it that a great storm ensued that lasted for 40 consecutive days.

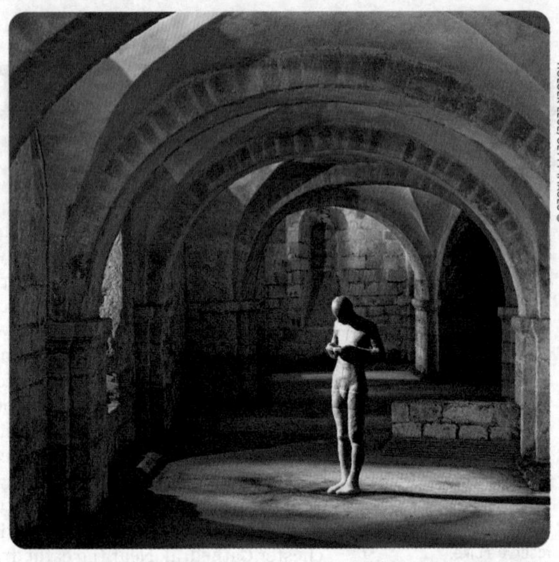

HOLGER LEUE/GETTY IMAGES ©

Crypt, Winchester Cathedral

## Kaleidoscopic Windows & Heady Rooftop Views

EXPLORING AN AWE-INSPIRING GOTHIC CATHEDRAL

With one of Europe's longest medieval naves, **Winchester Cathedral** is an imposing Gothic landmark that can be seen from the surrounding hills. Inside, the cathedral is a beguiling jumble of architectural styles, with a Norman crypt and ornate Renaissance chantry chapels.

Near the cathedral entrance is the **grave of Jane Austen,** marked by a plaque. In the retrochoir at the far end of the cathedral, look down to see a remarkable expanse of colourfully patterned medieval floor tiles. The icons in the retrochoir include the cathedral's patron saint St Swithin; pilgrims used to crawl through the hole below the icons to be close to his bones. Be sure to check out the exquisitely carved 14th-century oak choir stalls, decorated with human figures and animals.

**SCULPTURES BY ANTONY GORMLEY**

Another of Antony Gormley's sculptures can be seen in **Canterbury Cathedral** (p145). Look for his iconic *Another Time* figures submerged in the sea outside Margate's **Turner Contemporary** (p149) and in **Folkestone** (p152).

### WHERE TO STAY IN WINCHESTER

**Westgate**
This city centre pub has 10 stylish rooms with large windows and modern bathrooms. **££**

**Wykeham Arms**
Creaking stairs lead to plush bedrooms at this 250-year-old inn with a colourful history. **£££**

**Winchester Royal Hotel**
This longstanding hotel occupies a 16th-century former bishop's house in a central location. **£££**

One of the cathedral's most striking features is the abstract patchwork of the West Window: after the original stained glass window was destroyed by Parliamentary troops during the English Civil War, the current window was created in 1660 using fragments of shattered glass.

In the cathedral crypt is *Sound II,* an enigmatic life-size lead statue of a contemplative man by Antony Gormley, who used his own body to cast the piece. The crypt is vulnerable to flooding, during which times the figure stands in water. Tower and roof tours take you along the full length of the nave and past the bell chamber.

The cathedral's tree-fringed lawns are tranquil spots to take time out, especially on the quieter south side beyond the cloisters.

## Knights of the Round Table

TAKING INSPIRATION FROM KING ARTHUR

Hanging on the wall of the **Great Hall** – the only part of the 11th-century Winchester Castle to have survived destruction at the hands of Oliver Cromwell – is a large wooden replica of King Arthur's round table, with mysterious origins. It's now thought to have been constructed in the late 13th century, possibly as part of an 'Arthurian' tournament to celebrate the wedding engagement of one of Edward I's children. But Thomas Malory, a 15th-century chronicler of the Arthurian legend, believed the table to be a 6th-century original, dating from the time when legends say Arthur was king (historians can't confirm whether Arthur really existed). Henry VIII later had the table painted, adding a Tudor rose and an image of himself.

## A Stroll around Town

WINCHESTER'S RIVERSIDE WALKS

Winchester's walks include the mile-long **Keats Walk** through the water meadows to the Hospital of St Cross. Its beauty is said to have prompted the poet to pen the ode *To Autumn;* pick up the trail near Wolvesey Castle, the crumbling remains of the 12th-century home of the Bishop of Winchester. From St Cross, you can continue along the trail for another mile to reach **St Catherine's Hill**; climb to the tops for views of the Itchen Valley.

### BEST BARS & RESTAURANTS IN WINCHESTER

**Josie's**
Arrive early at weekends to bag a table at this cafe serving Winchester's best brunches. £

**Overdraft**
With DJ decks, craft beer on tap and tacos, Overdraft offers a fun dining experience. ££

**Chesil Rectory**
In a 15th-century timber-framed building, this restaurant serves modern British dishes. £££

**Black Boy**
Open fires, random antiques and a magical beer garden make this a legendary local.

**Hyde Tavern**
This surprising local hangout hosts beer competitions, folk jam sessions and performances by renowned musicians.

### GETTING AROUND

Trains to Winchester leave from London Waterloo. There are Park & Ride car parks to the south and east of the city centre.

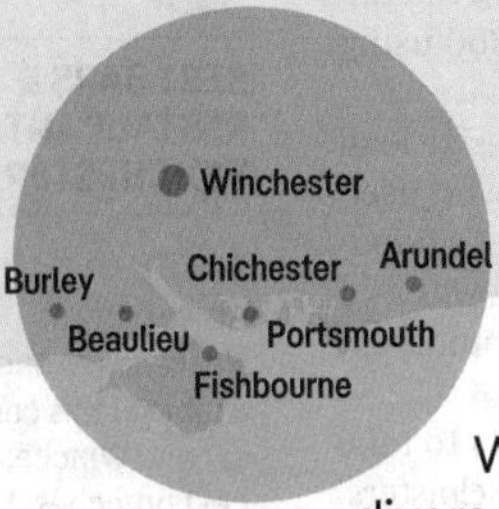

Winchester
Burley
Chichester
Arundel
Beaulieu
Portsmouth
Fishbourne

# Beyond Winchester

## Winchester's surrounds offer trails through diverse countryside, with a dash of naval history, a castle and an artsy Cathedral city.

Winchester is surrounded by opportunities to embrace nature, with walking and cycling trails through diverse habitats that promise close encounters with wildlife at every turn. The city is the gateway to the rolling chalk hills of the South Downs National Park to the east and to the woodlands and heathlands of the Surrey Hills in the North Downs. To the southwest of the city is the New Forest National Park, where ponies wander the scrubland and deer hide among the trees.

But the area has no shortage of culture. An important city since Roman times, Chichester has a vibrant arts scene centred around its Festival Theatre and galleries. Nearby, Arundel's castle and antiques shops seems stuck in another time.

**TOP TIP**

One of the best ways to explore is by train and bike. Bring your bike onboard or hire from a rental shop.

Chichester (p169)

LANAG/SHUTTERSTOCK ©

Box Hill

## Surrey Hills & Gardens

HIKES, VIEWS & MAGNIFICENT GARDENS

The Surrey Hills Area of Outstanding Natural Beauty, one to 1½ hours by car from Winchester, encompasses a variety of woodlands, lowland heathlands, and wildflower-rich grasslands, traversed by walking and cycling trails. Much of the area is managed by the National Trust.

You don't need to walk far to see the famous views from **Box Hill**, the setting of the picnic in Jane Austen's *Emma*. Waymarked trails here range from the gentle to the challenging. At Easter you can roll decorated eggs down Box Hill.

In Hindhead, the **Devil's Punch Bowl** is a scenic valley scooped out of the verdant Surrey Hills, with trails through heather and dense woodland, and across fields and crystal-clear streams. The area is particularly beautiful in autumn.

Nearby is the fabulous **RHS Wisley**, a wonderland of flowers, bushes, borders and trees planted in a themed garden. Keep an eye out for riveting pieces of sculpture along the way, including an astonishing metal horse's head near Battleston Hill.

### SURREY HILLS WILDLIFE

The Surrey Hills provide an important habitat for a number of butterflies, including the elusive purple emperor, Adonis blue, holly blue, and bright yellow brimstone. Some years, hundreds of painted lady butterflies arrive from North Africa; other years there are none at all.

The lowland heaths of the western Surrey Hills, characterised by heathers, gorses and grasses, are home to species of birds including the Dartford warbler. Listen out for the call of the nightingale in areas of thick, dense scrub.

### WHERE TO EAT & DRINK IN SURREY

**Swan Inn**
Ideal for walks in the hills, Swan Inn in Chiddingfold has a bar, restaurant and rooms.

**Anchor**
This pub and restaurant in the village of Ripley is full of beams and fireplaces.

**Fox Revived**
This Norwood Hill pub has a range of ales, bistro-style food and views of the hills.

### BEST PLACES TO EAT & DRINK IN PORTSMOUTH

**Feed**
Breakfasts and burgers are the order of the day at this popular Portsmouth cafe. £

**Abarbistro**
This bistro and bar is a laid-back spot to soak up local life. ££

**Still & West**
A waterside pub serving a menu of gastropub fare, Sunday roasts and sandwiches. ££

**Old Customs House**
On Gunwharf Quay, this nautical establishment serves refined pub classics and speciality beers and ales. ££

ARCHITECTS: WILKINSON EYRE, RON ELLIS/SHUTTERSTOCK ©

Mary Rose Museum

## Boarding Battleships of the Past

DISCOVERING ENGLAND'S NAVAL HISTORY

**Portsmouth Historic Dockyard**, one hour by train from Winchester, is both an active naval base and the site of a number of historic warships and maritime museums. The complex has more attractions than it's possible to visit in a single day, so be strategic.

The best place to start is at the harbour's star attraction: the **Mary Rose Museum**. It houses the wreck of Henry VIII's flagship, which sank off the coast of Portsmouth while fighting the French in 1545. The vessel's starboard side was submerged in mud and silt, keeping out oxygen and wood-attacking sea creatures. When the *Mary Rose* was raised from the seabed in 1982, the starboard side and its contents had remained remarkably intact.

The Mary Rose Museum begins with an audiovisual experience that puts the ship in its Tudor context. The ship itself, in its dramatically lit, humidity-controlled chamber, is an awesome sight. The museum route takes you on a tour through the decks, passing the surgeon's and carpenter's cabins and the huge brass cauldrons of the cook's galley. On each level, galleries display clothes, shoes, coins, musical instruments and other personal

**NELSON'S FLEET**

You can learn more about Admiral Nelson onboard his flagship HMS *Victory* (which was built in Chatham, not Buckler's Hard) at **Portsmouth Historic Dockyard** (p168).

### WHERE TO STAY IN WEST SUSSEX

**Arden Guest House**
This friendly B&B is located just over the river from Arundel historical centre. ££

**Chichester Harbour Hotel**
A Georgian hotel in Chichester city centre, with a good restaurant and bar. £££

**East Walls Hotel**
Family run hotel in Chichester with antique furniture and four-poster beds. £££

## ART & HISTORY IN CHICHESTER WALKING TOUR

Chichester, one hour by train from Winchester, is a lively town still almost encircled by its ancient city walls. Explore Chichester's history and arts scene on this city-centre walk.

Begin at **1 Chichester Cathedral**, unusual for its detached medieval **2 bell tower**. Next to the tower is a statue of St Richard, a 13th-century bishop and patron saint of Sussex. Inside the cathedral, three storeys of beautiful arches sweep upwards. Take a look at the 12th-century Romanesque reliefs, a glassed-over section of Roman mosaic flooring, and a stained glass window by artist Marc Chagall, which was installed in 1978. At the Arundel tomb, take a moment to read the poem by Philip Larkin, inspired by the figures' clasped hands.

Continue walking around the south side of the cathedral down Richard's Walk and turn right to reach **3 Bishop's Palace Gardens**. Follow the path west through the gardens to reach the Roman **4 city walls**. Crossing West St, follow the walls walk through **5 Priory Park** and past the independent **6 New Park Cinema**. Turn right at East St and walk to the **7 Market Cross**, built in 1501 to provide shelter to market traders. From here take a detour up North St to the corner of Crane St to see the ceramic tile relief of the Roman goddess **8 Minerva** surrounded by local birds.

Return to the Market Cross and walk back along East St. Turn right onto North Pallant and look for murals of a **9 watchdog** by Belgian artist Joachim, and distinctive **10 stick figures** by Stik. Soon you'll reach the Queen Anne mansion and 21st-century wing of **11 Pallant House Gallery**, which houses a superb collection of modern and contemporary work. Allow plenty of time to look around.

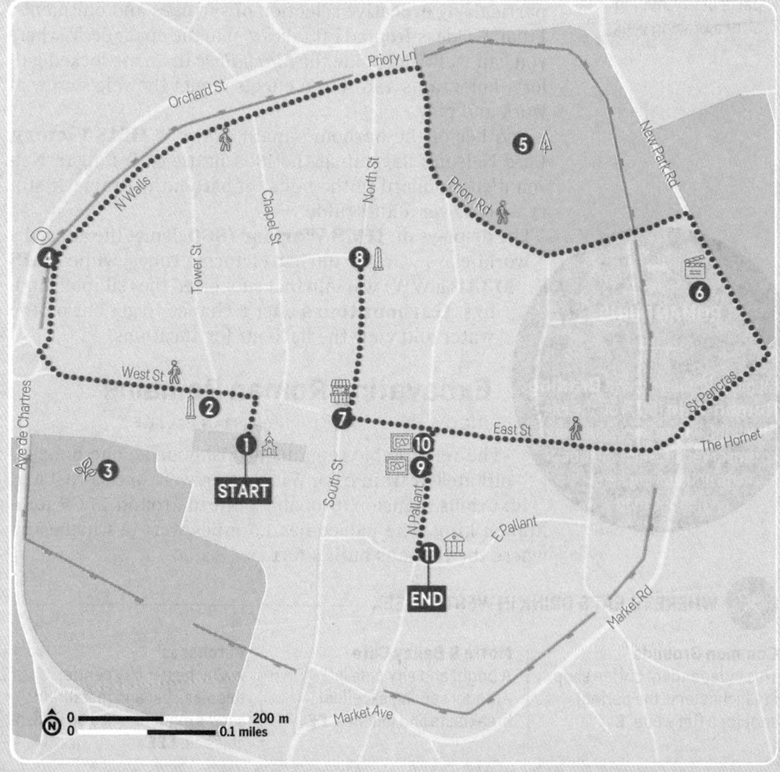

**WINTER WONDERLANDS**

In late November and December, the grounds of Winchester Cathedral host a magical German-style Christmas market. Wooden chalet stalls, fairy lights, mulled wine and carol singers create a festive atmosphere. Best of all is the ice rink, where you can skate in the shadow of the cathedral.

Winter can also be a beautiful time to visit the New Forest. The area's cosy pubs with roaring log fires look particularly inviting after a bracing walk.

ARCHITECT: KEITH WILLIAMS , VIEW PICTURES/GETTY IMAGES ©

Novium Museum

objects found in the wreck; the surgeon's chest contains a particularly evocative selection of syringes and ointments. Finally, a glass-fronted lift takes you to the upper deck, where you can walk alongside the *Mary Rose* in an air-locked gallery; holograms and sound effects depict the ship's crew at work and play.

Another of the harbour's main draws is **HMS Victory**, Lord Nelson's flagship at the 1805 Battle of Trafalgar. Nelson died on board in the midst of battle; the dramatic story is told over audio guide.

The displays on **HMS Warrior 1860** depict life aboard a world-class warship during Victorian times, while **HMS M33** is a WWI warship that supported the Gallipoli landings. **Harbour tours** offer a chance to get out on the water and view the harbour fortifications.

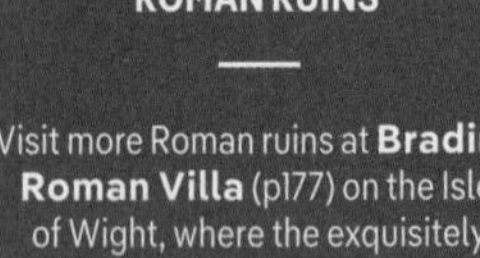

**ROMAN RUINS**

Visit more Roman ruins at **Brading Roman Villa** (p177) on the Isle of Wight, where the exquisitely preserved mosaics include an unusual cockerel-headed man.

## Excavating Roman Remains

UNCOVERING FISHBOURNE ROMAN PALACE

The remarkable remains at Fishbourne, one hour 20 minutes by train from Winchester, were once a vast and luxurious mansion, probably built in around 75 CE for a Roman king. The palace lies 1.5 miles west of Chichester, where the Romans built a fort.

### WHERE TO EAT & DRINK IN WEST SUSSEX

**Common Grounds**
This independent coffee shop in Chichester is the perfect spot for a flat white. **£**

**Motte & Bailey Cafe**
A bright and airy cafe in Arundel serving excellent breakfasts and lunches. **££**

**Purchases**
In Chichester city centre, this sleek bar and restaurant serves modern takes on British classics. **£££**

The site's museum tells the story of the villa's unlikely discovery in the 1960s: it was chanced upon during the laying of a new water main. The subsequent excavation was a community effort, which is documented with evocative photographs of volunteers at the dig.

The centrepiece is a spectacular mosaic floor depicting Cupid riding a dolphin, flanked by seahorses and panthers. Take time to stroll through the replanted Roman gardens and imagine life at the palace during Roman times.

In Chichester city centre, **Novium Museum** was built to preserve and display the remains of Roman baths, discovered in the 1970s.

**BEST GALLERIES & SHOPS IN ARUNDEL**

**Arundel Contemporary**
Carefully selected and curated pieces displayed over two floors of an elegant Victorian townhouse.

**Kim's Bookshop**
Hard-to-find vintage and collectible titles alongside newly released books. There is a second branch in Chichester.

**Pallant of Arundel**
Specialist food shop and deli selling Sussex wines, beers and cheeses; also sandwiches and pastries.

## Life in an English Castle

EXPLORING TIME-WARPED ARUNDEL CASTLE

**Arundel Castle**, 1½ hours by train from Winchester, rises above the River Arun and the surrounding plains like an illustration from a book of fairy tales. A castle was first built here in the 11th century, but the current building was mostly constructed between 1718 and 1900. It is still the home of the current Duke of Norfolk, who lives in a private section of the castle; the halls and bedrooms that visitors can see are also used by the family on occasion.

There are panoramic views over the West Sussex countryside from the restored **castle keep**. In the main part of the castle are Victorian-style bedrooms with extravagantly sized bathrooms, and the colossal **Baron's Hall**. Perhaps the most impressive room is the Gothic library, fitted out in carved Honduras mahogany. The room dates from 1800 and houses around 10,000 books. The castle halls are filled with elaborate taxidermy.

In the castle grounds, take time to look at the carved stone tombs in the **Fitzalan Chapel**. The **formal gardens** are spectacular and not to be missed; there is a cafe there if you want to linger.

If you can't get enough of the castle's whimsical beauty, go for a swim at **Arundel Lido**, which has fabulous castle views.

## New Forest Nature Trails

VIEWING FOREST WILDLIFE

Encompassing a mix of ancient woodlands, open heathlands and wetlands, the **New Forest National Park**, 30 minutes by train from Winchester, is an important conservation area that's home to many rare species of plants. A number of endangered ground-nesting birds, including curlews, come to

**WERE TO STAY IN THE NEW FOREST**

**Teddy's Farm**
Bring your own or stay in a pre-pitched bell tent at this peaceful, gorgeous campsite. £

**Master Builder's House Hotel**
A beautifully restored 18th-century hotel on the banks of the River Beaulieu in Buckler's Hard. ££

**Pig**
One of the New Forest's classiest hotels has the air of an elegant country-house retreat. £££

## NEW FOREST ADVENTURES

**Jenny Clark**, founder of The Wild Times Yoga & Adventure Retreats, shares her tips. Instagram: *@thewildtimesco*

Pick up a picnic from **Noohn** cafe in Burley before heading out on a forest walk. Some of my favourites are around **Rhinefield Arboretum**, **Hawkhill**, **Longslade Bottom** and along the river from **OberCorner** to the **Oak Inn** at Bank for a great Sunday lunch. Stroll along the seawall at **Keyhaven** for some bird-watching and views of the Isle of Wight, or jump on the little ferry to historic **Hurst Castle** before visiting the **Gun Inn's** sunny garden for a drink or a meal. I often take my retreat guests to Keyhaven to go paddleboarding or swimming.

Rockford Common, New Forest National Park

the Forest to breed, and a population of goshawks (birds of prey) nest in the area's trees. The Forest is also home to free-roaming animals, including ponies, cattle, pigs and donkeys, who belong to local families. The animals often wander onto the roads, so drive carefully.

Cycling is a wonderful way to experience the Forest. A good place to pick up the trails is the village of **Burley**, known for its witchy associations and home to the shop **Coven of Witches**, purveyors of crystals and spell kits. The bike rental shop there offers route cards with details of a range of trails; several include optional detours via local pubs. One of the best sections goes into the heart of the forest in the **South Oakley Inclosure**, through a deer sanctuary (the Forest is home to five species of wild deer) and along Bolderwood Ornamental Dr.

### WHERE TO DRINK IN THE NEW FOREST

**Wash House**
Micro ale pub in Milford-on-Sea serving local craft ales, ciders, spirits and wine.

**White Buck**
Pub near Burley with beer garden for the summer and cosy fireplaces for the winter.

**King's Head**
Traditional pub in Lymington; ceiling beams made from Napoleonic ships, real ales on tap.

You can also cycle from one Forest village to the next: scenic loops connect Brockenhurst with Lymington, Burley, Lyndhurst and Beaulieu.

## Historic Riverside Shipyard

THE RIVER BEAULIEU'S SECRETS

In the east of the New Forest, the pretty villages of **Beaulieu** and Buckler's Hard, 50 minutes' drive from Winchester, are linked by a 2-mile riverside walk. Beaulieu's star attraction is the theme-park-esque **National Motor Museum** complex, featuring a vintage car museum, stately home and a 13th-century abbey, traversed by a monorail.

The riverside walk is part of a nature reserve that protects the area's shingle banks and salt marshes, which are a habitat for breeding birds and wild fowl. The wetland habitats at **Keeping Marsh** support diverse wildlife. Birds to look out for include kestrels, skylarks, reed warblers, redshanks and lapwings. The path also passes through an area of ancient, semi-natural woodland (not quite primary forest, but still a rare habitat).

**Buckler's Hard** is a picturesque hamlet of 18th-century cottages. It was once the location of a secret boatyard, where several warships that fought under Nelson's command in the Battle of Trafalgar were built. The **Buckler's Hard Museum** tells the story of the inlet's shipbuilding history, with immaculately preserved 18th-century labourers' cottages and workshops. The bar at the Master Builder's Hotel makes a lovely stop for a drink by the fire or in the riverside garden, depending on the time of year.

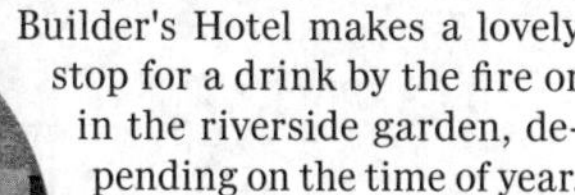

Bucker's Hard

### BEST RESTAURANTS IN THE NEW FOREST

**Beaulieu Bakehouse**
Freshly baked sourdough and pastries, locally roasted coffee, breakfasts and lunches. £

**Steff's Kitchen**
This cafe at Fairweather Garden Centre in Beaulieu serves breakfasts and lunches featuring homegrown ingredients. ££

**Verveine**
Innovative fish restaurant and fishmongers in Milford-on-Sea that serves surprise tasting menus. £££

**Elderflower**
British food is given a French twist at this fine-dining restaurant in Lymington. £££

**Haven**
Bistro-style meals and snacks served at indoor and outdoor tables with views of Lymington marina. £££

### GETTING AROUND

Getting to Surrey by public transport is easier from London than from Winchester. It's easiest to reach the beauty spots of the Surrey Hills by car or bike. Trains connect Winchester with Portsmouth, but to go as far as Chichester you'll have to change trains; both cities have direct connections to London. Arundel is a 30-minute train journey east of Chichester. In the New Forest, trains from London via Winchester arrive in Brockenhurst, where bikes can be hired.

# ISLE OF WIGHT

Ever since Queen Victoria chose Osborne as the location for her much-loved seaside palace, the Isle of Wight has been associated with old-fashioned English holidays. But the Isle of Wight's significance had been established years earlier: the island was an agricultural centre for the Romans, while the Normans built a castle at Carisbrooke. King Charles I was later imprisoned in Carisbrooke Castle before his execution in 1649.

Lined with beaches, dramatic white cliffs and tranquil sand dunes, the Isle of Wight's coastline is one of its biggest draws. For decades the island's sandy beaches have been a magnet for vacationing families, but these days the bucket-and-spade fun is surrounded by seafood shacks and yurt-filled camping sites. A mild climate and wide range of activities add to the Isle of Wight's appeal.

### TOP TIP

For the best prices, book ferries online in advance and check for mid-week offers. Travelling as a foot passenger is much cheaper than bringing a car, and foot passengers can bring a bicycle for no extra charge.

**Isle of Wight with the Needles (p177) in distance**

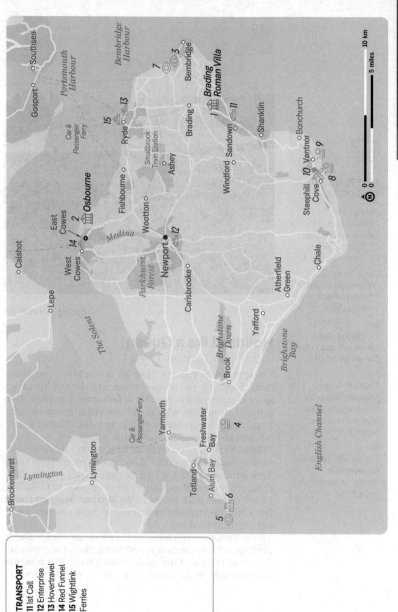

**HIGHLIGHTS**
**1** Brading Roman Villa
**2** Osbourne

**SIGHTS**
**3** Bembridge Harbour
**4** Compton Bay
**5** Needles
**6** Needles Battery
**7** St Helens Duver
**8** Steephill Cove
**9** Ventnor

**EATING**
**10** Crab Shed

**TRANSPORT**
**11** 1st Call
**12** Enterprise
**13** Hovertravel
**14** Red Funnel
**15** Wightlink Ferries

Brockenhurst
Calshot
Gosport
Southsea
Lymington
Lepe
West Cowes
East Cowes
Osbourne
Car & Passenger Ferry
Portsmouth Harbour
The Solent
Medina
Fishbourne
Ryde
Bembridge Harbour
Car & Passenger Ferry
Parkhurst Forest
Wootton
Smallbrook Train Station
Yarmouth
Newport
Ashey
Carisbrooke
Brading
Bembridge
Totland
Alum Bay
Freshwater Bay
Brading Roman Villa
Brighstone Down
Brook
Windford
Sandown
Yafford
Shanklin
Atherfield Green
Brighstone Bay
Bonchurch
Steephill Cove
Ventnor
English Channel
Chale
0 10 km
0 5 miles

### BEST PLACES TO EAT & DRINK

**Gossips Cafe**
At Yarmouth pier, this cafe serves breakfast and lunch as well as ice-cream sundaes. £

**Garlic Farm**
Try farm-grown garlic in foods like garlic ice cream and beer. ££

**Best Dressed Crab**
Try freshly caught lobster and crab at this Bembridge cafe. ££

**Salty's**
Yarmouth bar and restaurant known for its fish and chips and legendary summer nights. £££

**Hut**
Popular with yachties, this waterside restaurant is a place to linger. £££

DAVE SMITH 1965/SHUTTERSTOCK ©

Cycling, Isle of Wight

## Holiday Like a Queen

QUEEN VICTORIA'S HOLIDAY HOME

The spot Queen Victoria chose for her holiday home is certainly beautiful, and it's easy to see why she and her family spent as much time as possible at **Osborne**. The house itself is Italianate in style, with an opulent Victorian interior. The Royal Apartment rooms, which include the children's nursery, give an intimate glimpse into family life.

Queen Victoria's passion for India (a country she never visited) is reflected in a corridor of portraits of people from South Asia, painted at her request; modern viewers may balk at this celebration of the Queen's role as Empress of India. The palace reaches peak excess in the **Durbar banquet room**. Don't miss the intricate models of two Indian palaces, located beneath the balcony.

Away from the main house in the estate grounds is **Swiss Cottage**, a surprisingly low-key chalet where the royal children would play and the queen wrote letters. The **museum** here was built by the family to house their 'collections'. On

### WHERE TO STAY ON THE ISLE OF WIGHT

**Onefifty Cowes**
In a Victorian house, this B&B has the luxury touches of a boutique hotel. ££

**Tom's Eco Lodges**
Comfortably appointed eco pods, log cabins and safari tents sit on a spacious sea-view site. ££

**Hambrough**
Suites have balconies with wrap-around sea views at this luxurious Ventnor B&B. £££

display are gifts from all over the world, which serve as a reminder of the historical context of Queen Victoria's reign.

Follow the rhododendron walk to the beach, where you can eat an ice cream or swim in the sea.

## Cruise Around the Coast

BEACHES, CLIFFS & COVES

The nature reserve at **St Helens Duver** is an idyllic sand-and-shingle spit in the east of the island. Trails snake through the dunes and along the water's edge, from where there are views across to **Bembridge Harbour**. On the beach, limestone ledges create little rock pools, where you might spot crabs, sea anemones and brittle stars.

In the south of the isle, a 1-mile walk connects **Ventnor** with **Steephill Cove**, a tiny, sandy bay fringed by stone cottages, rickety looking shacks, and a clapboard lighthouse. At the beach, look for the **Crab Shed**, famous for its crab and mackerel pasties. The nearest car park is at the **Botanical Gardens**.

Perhaps the isle's most awesome coastal feature is the **Needles**, a row of three jagged white-chalk stacks extending out into the water from the cliffs at the Isle of Wight's most westerly tip. The Needles can be viewed from the Victorian fort complex **Needles Battery**; walk there along the cliff path from the car park at Alum Bay, or take the shuttle bus. South of the Needles is **Compton Bay**, a beautiful sandy beach.

## Meander over Roman Mosaics

UNCOVERING A ROMAN VILLA

The remains of **Brading Roman Villa** near Sandown contain some of England's most noteworthy and intact mosaics, housed within a well-designed museum. Wooden walkways lead over rubble walls, affording direct views of the coloured tiles and ruins below.

Two of the villa's most notable mosaics are of the snake-haired Medusa, believed to have been created to ward off evil and protect the home, and of a mysterious cockerel-headed man, whose significance is unknown. The centrepiece is a large, fractured mosaic of Bacchus, the god of wine.

### BEST ACTIVITIES ON THE ISLE OF WIGHT

**Watersports**
Kayaking is one of the few ways to access some of the island's hidden coves and caves. Windsurfing and kitsesurfing are popular in the isle's blustery southwest, especially around Compton Bay. Paddleboard hire and coasteering are also available. The island's sailing centre is Cowes, where the annual regatta (one of the world's biggest and longest running) is held.

**Cycling**
The hilly, 65-mile Round the Island route follows quiet lanes around the circumference of the isle. It's well waymarked, with signs in both clockwise and anticlockwise directions.

**Walking**
The Isle of Wight is one of the best spots in southern England for hiking, with 500 miles of walking paths, including 68 miles of coastal routes.

### GETTING AROUND

High-speed foot passenger ferry services operate between Portsmouth and Ryde and Southampton and West Cowes. Car and foot passenger ferries run between Southampton and Cowes, Portsmouth and Fishbourne, and Lymington and Yarmouth. Car hire is available on the island. Buses run between the island's major towns. A railway line runs from Ryde to Shanklin in the east of the Isle.

# OXFORD, THE COTSWOLDS & THE THAMES VALLEY

## HISTORY AND HONEY-HUED VILELAGES

From the lush Thames valley to the rolling hills of the Cotswolds, this bucolic region is full of stately homes, destination pubs and quaint villages.

Oxford is one of England's major travel destinations: home to hallowed Oxford University, historic streetscapes and a bunch of excellent museums from the Ashmolean to the Oxford University Museum of Natural History. As a place to stay, Oxford also has plenty of excellent restaurants and accommodation across every budget.

The Cotswolds bursts with charming villages of golden buildings, thatched roofs, and picturesque cottage gardens. Tour them all by car, bus or foot, on one of the many ancient footpaths along rivers and through farmers fields. These hills are also packed with beautifully decorated boutique hotels and gastropubs to enjoy a Sunday roast.

Gloucestershire has an eclectic clutch of towns to get acquainted with, whether you're into Roman history (Cirencester), Regency architecture (Cheltenham), or Victorian-era docklands (Gloucester), not to mention Gloucester Cathedral, considered one of the great medieval religious buildings of England. From there, head south into the wilds of the Forest of Dean, a lush pocket of forest and river and a base for outdoors adventures.

Finally, connected to Oxford by the mighty river Thames, Windsor is the other key must-see destination of this part of England. Beyond Windsor Castle, there's the gastronomic delights of Bray, wealthy riverside towns from Maidenhead to Henley to explore, and the glorious gardens and wooded hills of the Chilterns to ramble through.

ALEXEY FEDORENKO/SHUTTERSTOCK ©

### THE MAIN AREAS

**OXFORD**
Historic architecture, literature and learning.
p184

**BURFORD & THE COTSWOLDS**
Stone cottages, pubs and shops.
p194

**CIRENCESTER & AROUND**
Affluent town with Roman connections.
p199

TRAVELLIGHT/SHUTTERSTOCK ©

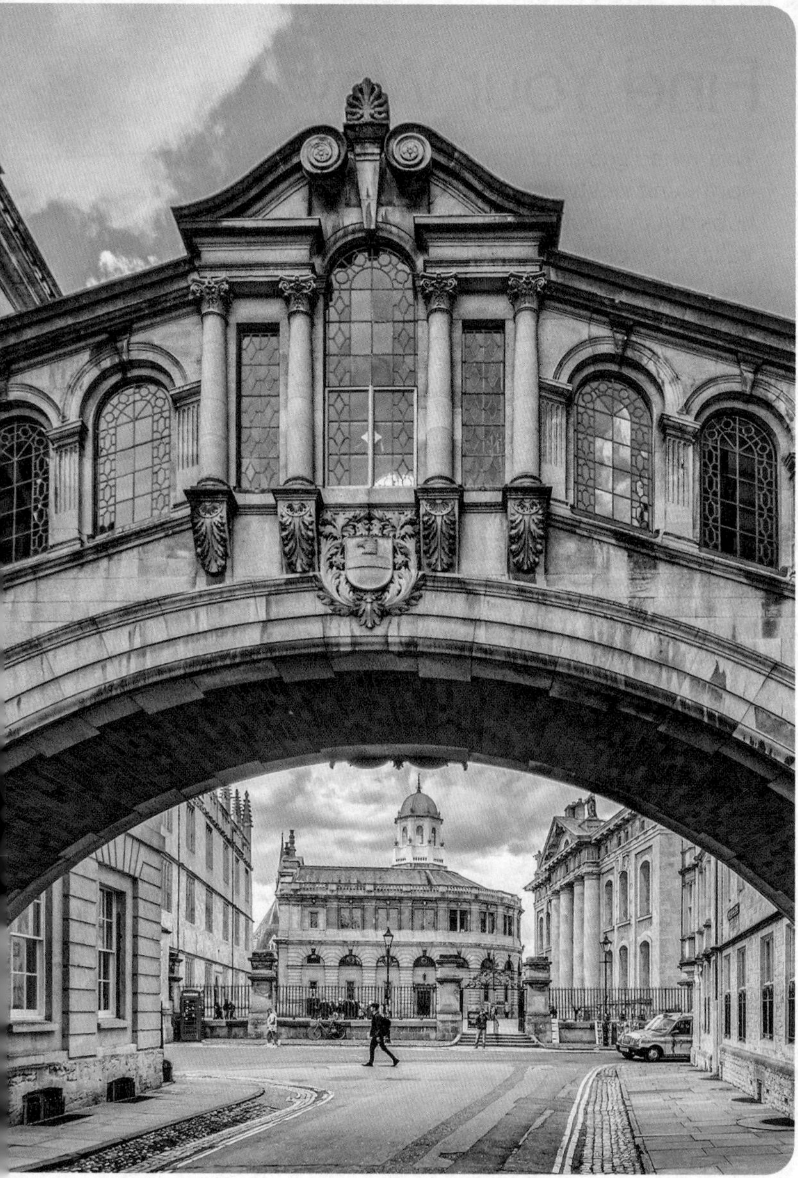

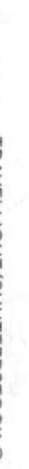

Above: Oxford (p184); left: Windsor Castle (p211)

**CHELTENHAM**
Regency buildings, horse-lovers and festivals.
p204

**WINDSOR & ETON**
Royal fanfare and the majestic Thames.
p210

**THE CHILTERN HILLS**
Sweeping valleys and stately houses.
p216

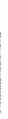

# Find Your Way

This varied geographic region spreads north- and westward from London. Key hubs dot the lowlands of the Thames Valley, the rolling hills of the Chilterns and the Cotswolds, as well as the industrial regions closer to Bristol and Wales.

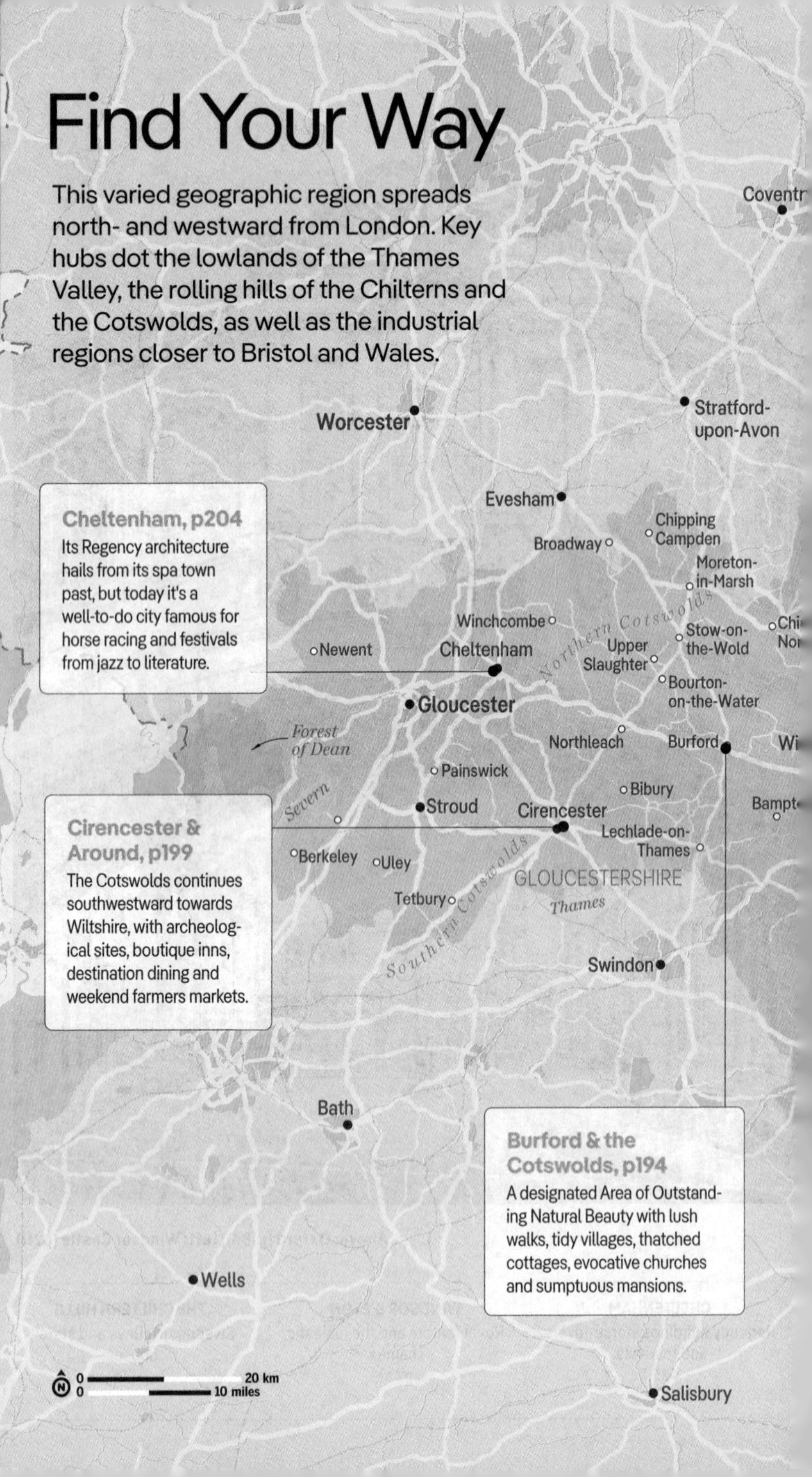

### Cheltenham, p204

Its Regency architecture hails from its spa town past, but today it's a well-to-do city famous for horse racing and festivals from jazz to literature.

### Cirencester & Around, p199

The Cotswolds continues southwestward towards Wiltshire, with archeological sites, boutique inns, destination dining and weekend farmers markets.

### Burford & the Cotswolds, p194

A designated Area of Outstanding Natural Beauty with lush walks, tidy villages, thatched cottages, evocative churches and sumptuous mansions.

Coventr
Worcester
Stratford-upon-Avon
Evesham
Broadway
Chipping Campden
Moreton-in-Marsh
Winchcombe
Northern Cotswolds
Chi
Nor
Newent
Cheltenham
Upper Slaughter
Stow-on-the-Wold
Bourton-on-the-Water
Gloucester
Forest of Dean
Northleach
Burford
Wi
Painswick
Bibury
Severn
Stroud
Cirencester
Bampt
Lechlade-on-Thames
Berkeley
Uley
GLOUCESTERSHIRE
Tetbury
Thames
Southern Cotswolds
Swindon
Bath
Wells
Salisbury

0 20 km
0 10 miles

### CAR

By far the easiest way to explore if you want to see as many villages, historic houses and grand gardens as possible. Parking is usually in designated areas on the outskirts of smaller villages, and parking and fuel costs will add up.

### TRAIN

Trains can get you to the major towns, but can be expensive. For smaller villages, bring your own bike or plan some long-distance walking (a popular local pasttime). You'll have to return to Reading or London to swap between different regions with different train operators.

### BUS

It's entirely possible to explore the region by bus plus you'll meet more locals, but you'll need plenty of time and excellent planning. Buses usually run by the hour, and some days not at all. Package deals on certain networks can cut costs.

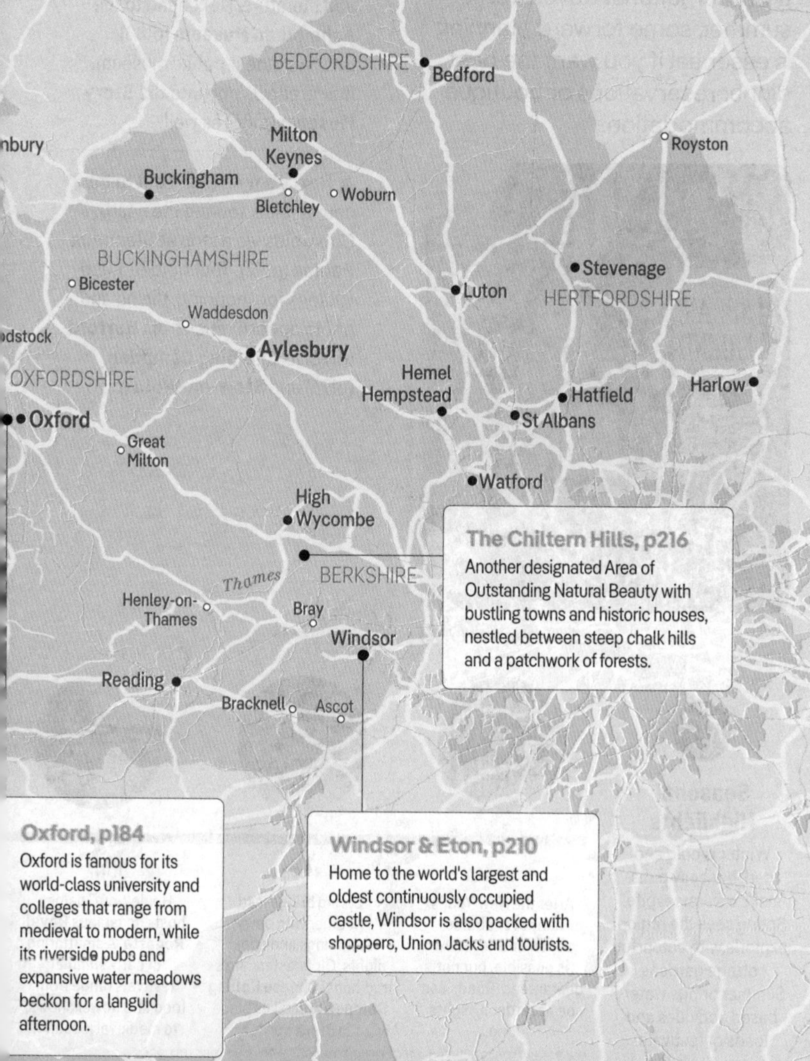

BEDFORDSHIRE
Bedford
nbury
Milton Keynes
Royston
Buckingham
Bletchley
Woburn
BUCKINGHAMSHIRE
Bicester
Stevenage
Luton
HERTFORDSHIRE
Waddesdon
dstock
Aylesbury
OXFORDSHIRE
Hemel Hempstead
Harlow
Hatfield
St Albans
Oxford
Great Milton
Watford
High Wycombe
Thames
BERKSHIRE
Henley-on-Thames
Bray
Windsor
Reading
Bracknell
Ascot

**The Chiltern Hills, p216**
Another designated Area of Outstanding Natural Beauty with bustling towns and historic houses, nestled between steep chalk hills and a patchwork of forests.

**Oxford, p184**
Oxford is famous for its world-class university and colleges that range from medieval to modern, while its riverside pubs and expansive water meadows beckon for a languid afternoon.

**Windsor & Eton, p210**
Home to the world's largest and oldest continuously occupied castle, Windsor is also packed with shoppers, Union Jacks and tourists.

# Plan Your Time

This is one of England's most popular regions for domestic and international travellers. In summer, some forward planning is essential if you want the best dinner reservations or boutique accommodation.

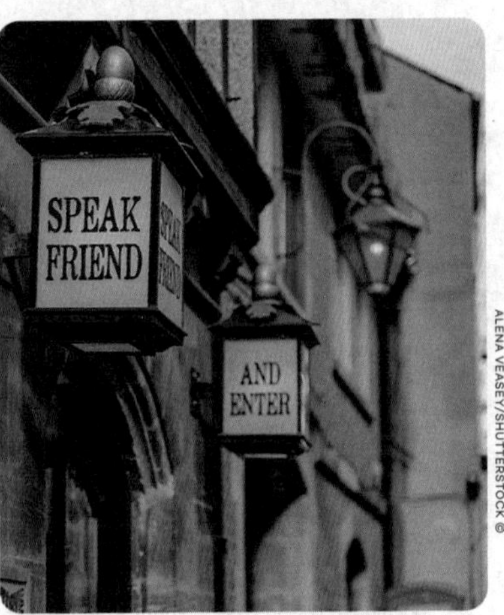


ALENA VEASEY/SHUTTERSTOCK ©

The Story Museum (p186)

## Just for a Weekend

- Head straight for **Oxford** (p184). Join a walking tour of the university and the city centre taking in the architectural beauty of this seat of learning and literature. Next head to the **Ashmolean Museum** (p188), Britain's oldest public museum. If time allows pop into the **Story Museum** (p186) as well.

- Next it's time to get out to the countryside, touring the nearby Cotswolds via a stop at **Blenheim Palace** (p192). Tour golden-hued villages for shopping, dining and photo opportunities from **Burford** (p196) to **Chipping Campden** (p196) and **Stow-on-Wold** (p198).

## Seasonal Highlights

Winter is cold and dark but cosy pubs make a warm respite. Spring sees the region explode with colourful cottage gardens. Summer brings water-based activities and loads of festivals.

### JANUARY

After the New Year's hangover abates, winter sets in. Snow is possible, but not guaranteed. Roads can be hazardous, nights long.

### MAY

Spring brings mild weather with dewy mornings and cool nights. Gloucestershire's traditional **Cheese Rolling Competition** takes place in Brockworth.

### JUNE

Henley-on-Thames hosts its famous **Royal Regatta**. A smattering of early summer festivals range from food and flower shows, to medieval jousting.

4KCLIPS/SHUTTERSTOCK ©, COMPOSEDPIX/SHUTTERSTOCK ©, NORDWAND/SHUTTERSTOCK ©

## 3 Days to Travel Around

- Stay overnight in a destination country hotel or inn and tour more of the Cotswolds. Explore village churches; farm shops; or historic houses with magnificent gardens like **Highclere Castle** (p193). Don't miss **Cirencester** (p199) with its Roman sites and excellent Corinium Museum.

- Next head west to visit **Cheltenham** (p204), **Gloucester** (p208) and the **Forest of Dean** (p209): each a very different experience from the other.

- Finally, return back to London via the Thames Valley stopping in **Marlow** or **Henley-on-Thames** (p215); **Bray** (p214) for lunch (restaurant bookings required); and a tour of **Windsor** and **Eton** (p210) to see how the other half live.

## With Plenty of Time...

- If you're here for more than a quick visit, slow right down. Plan walks in woods in the **Chiltern Hills** (p216), a cycle ride by the Thames to a pub in **Oxford** (p184), or an afternoon exploring its rivers by boat.

- Compare the architecture, art and atmosphere of a dozen historic houses as you tour through the centuries. Get tickets to a summer music festival. Browse the farmers' market in **Stroud** (p198) like a local.

- Book lunch at a Michelin-starred restaurant and dinner at a cosy country pub. Take the kids camping, stroll between **Cotswolds villages** (p196), or even enrol in a summer course at Oxford University.

**JULY**

Gardens are in full bloom, long days see beer gardens swell, and locals swim, SUP or kayak. Music festivals with bell tents abound.

**OCTOBER**

Enjoy **forest walks** with autumn colours. Stately homes run family-friendly Halloween events. **Cheltenham's Literature Festival** draws the crowds.

**NOVEMBER**

Families **forage** for late-season mushrooms in the forest. Almost every town hosts a November 5th **Bonfire Night**.

**DECEMBER**

The region is lit with twinkling lights, **Christmas-market** shopping experiences (mulled wine and mince pies) and pubs packed with merrymakers.

# OXFORD

A glorious ensemble of historic architecture and lush water meadows, Oxford is one of England's most beautiful cities. One of the main joys of visiting Oxford lies in the sense of intellectual history being forged in the centuries-old colleges, each with its own permutations of Gothic chapels, secluded cloisters and tranquil quadrangles.

Certain buildings stand out, from the domed and glowing Radcliffe Camera to the late Iraqi-British architect Zaha Hadid's modernist library in St Anthony's College. Irresistible old pubs dot Oxford's central alleyways, some doubling as literary landmarks, like the Lamb & Flag, a regular haunt of writers such as CS Lewis and JRR Tolkien.

And then there's the wide open water meadows that give Oxford its bucolic vibe despite its population density, fields that have not been touched since the Iron Age. In summer cows and horses graze down to the Thames, while in winter walkers in their designer Wellingtons pick paths through waterlogged fields.

### TOP TIP

Pavements are thick with tourists in the summer. If you've prebooked entry tickets, allow plenty of time to walk behind dawdling pedestrians.

**Radcliffe Camera, housing part of the Bodleian Library (p188)**

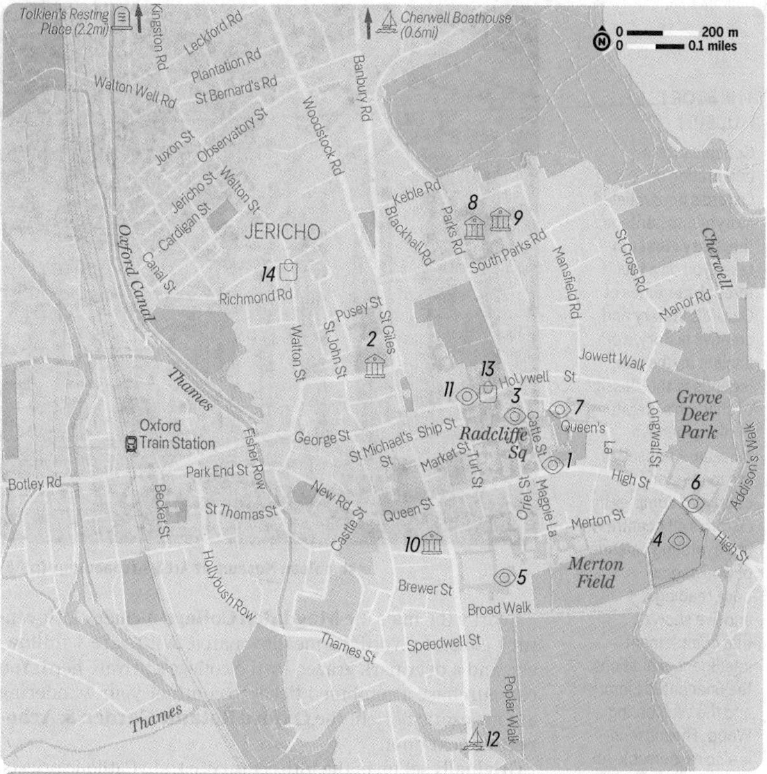

**SIGHTS**
1 All Souls College
2 Ashmolean Museum
3 Bodleian Library
4 Botanic Garden
5 Christ Church
6 Magdalen College
7 New College
8 Oxford University Museum of Natural History
9 Pitt Rivers Museum
10 Story Museum
11 Trinity College

**ACTIVITIES**
12 Salter's Steamers

**SHOPPING**
13 Blackwell's
14 Last Bookshop

## College Campuses

LEARNING STEEPED IN HISTORY

The university is very much this city's defining feature. Consistently ranked among the world's most prestigious academic institutions, Oxford University traces its history back to the 11th century. Over the next two centuries, a loose association of independent colleges developed and many of the original medieval buildings remain.

**Christ Church** is the quintessential Oxford college. The dramatic Great Hall once housed parliament under King Charles I. Hear the echo of footsteps strolling the quad. Then admire its gallery of Renaissance masterpieces and the 12th-century cathedral. If you only visit one college: make it Christ Church.

Christ Church

### THE STORY MUSEUM

Conceived as a celebration of Oxford's unparalleled storytelling heritage, the **Story Museum** takes you on a tour through centuries of Oxford's literary and creative history, from ancient myths and legends to the classics of children's literature.

This immersive museum – housed in a multi-storied courtyard complex in Oxford's city centre – has a rotating calendar of workshops, book readings, and live shows that complement intelligent exhibitions, the Enchanted Library and the Whispering Wood. The museum is also responsible for Oxford's annual **Alice Day** in July when the whole city celebrates of all things *Alice in Wonderland*.

**Ashmolean Museum of Art & Archaeology (p188)**

Nearby the majestic **Magdalen College** includes 15th-century cloisters, verdant meadows alive with rare wildflowers, and a deer park grazed by the college's private herd. You can purchase a combined ticket to continue your wandering among exotic flora in the **Oxford Botanic Garden & Arboretum** next door.

Originally set up in the 16th century to train Catholic priests, **Trinity College** is another popular college for its baroque chapel, dining hall and gardens. Due to current restoration work, you're advised to call ahead to ensure it's open to visitors.

**New College** (it's only 650 years old), with its walled gardens and five quadrangles including one that was inspired by the Palace of Versailles, also welcomes visitors, as does **All Souls College**.

## Oxford's Literary Life

STORYTELLERS, BOOKSHOPS & LIBRARIES

Oxford's most famous writers have an extraordinary record for producing epic works of fantasy, imbued with dreamy, otherworldly qualities, including Lewis Carroll, author of *Alice*

### WHERE TO EAT IN OXFORD

**Handle Bar Cafe & Kitchen**
A friendly bike-themed diner with health-focussed bites and outdoor seating where you can soak up the sunshine. £

**Arbequina**
Housed in two neighbouring shops, this buzzing tapas bar serves small mouthwateringly good small plates and cocktails. ££

**Magdalen Arms**
Top-quality cuisine, excellent hospitality and located in a picture-postcard building a short walk south of the city centre. ££

## TAKE ME TO THE RIVER

Step away from the bustle of Oxford's city streets to the bucolic green spaces of Port Meadow and the Thames. This 5.5-mile round-trip will take at least two hours (more if you plan to stop at the riverside beer gardens). Walking shoes are a must; there will be mud somewhere.

Head up 1 **Walton Well Rd**, over the Oxford Canal with its characterful narrowboats and on to the gate at the corner of 2 **Port Meadow**. Mentioned in the *Domesday Book* (1086), Port Meadow has been communal land for at least a thousand years. Head north on a paved path which then veers right over a small bridge and into the lightly wooded 3 **Burgess Field Nature Park** (alive with bluebells in spring).

Eventually you return to Port Meadow and follow one of the many paths past grazing ponies or cows, heading northwest to the crossing of 4 **Wolvercote Mill Stream** on the way to the Thames. Stop for a refreshment at the 400-year-old 5 **Trout** en route.

Now cross the Thames, and an island within it, via two bridges. On the far side, the Thames Path (a 183-mile long-distance walking route) heads left back towards Oxford. You'll spot the picturesque ruins of the 12th-century 6 **Godstow Abbey** on your way. Follow the Thames Path back past Port Meadow, now visible on the opposite bank. After a mile-long meander, you'll see a sign for an historic thatched-roofed pub the 7 **Perch**. Time for a pint?

Rejoin the Thames Path and continue south. Cross the river again on the red arched 8 **Medley Footbridge**. Then you'll find yourself back on the path to the Walton Well Rd gate of Port Meadow where your walk began.

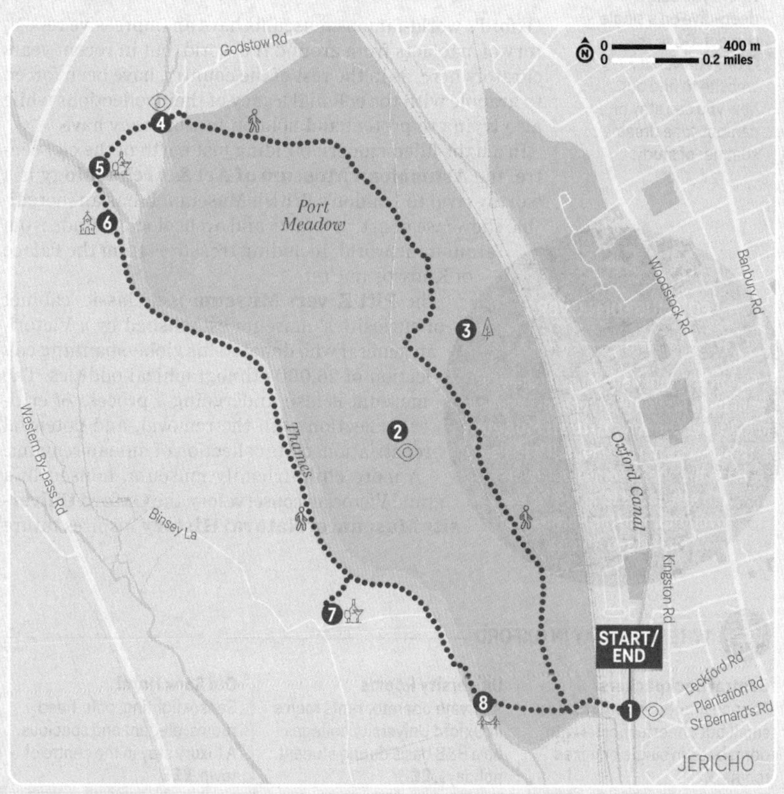

**WANT TO STUDY AT OXFORD?**

Have the 'dreaming spires of Oxford' inspired you to academic pursuit? Students come from across the globe to study in Oxford's world-class libraries, laboratories and museums. The rigorous application process demands intellectual achievement and top-notch references.

If you're more of a dilettante, Oxford's Department of Continuing Education offers introductory courses and specialist summer schools where you can deep-dive on a single subject. Go to the Oxford university website to find out how you can stay on campus for a dreamy summer of study.

*In Wonderland,* JRR Tolkien (of *The Lord of the Rings* fame) and CS Lewis who penned *The Chronicles of Narnia* here.

But the roll call of famous writers from Oxford does not end there. *Wind in the Willows* author Kenneth Grahame studied at Oxford, as did Graham Greene, Dr Seuss (aka Theodore Geisel), Jeanette Winterson, Iris Murdoch, Philip Pullman and Rachel Cusk, to name a few.

To get a sense of all this incredible brainpower, sign up for a guided tour of the beautiful domed reading rooms and underground tunnels of the **Bodleian Library**, one of the oldest libraries in Europe dating back to 1488. Then hit Oxford's bookshops (but book lovers beware, you may never escape). Floors of literary diversions greet you at **Blackwell's** while **Last Bookshop in Jericho** has an eclectic stock of secondhand and rare finds.

Fantasy fans will want to visit the **Oxford Botanic Garden & Arboretum** to see the chair where Will and Lyra from Phillip Pullman's Northern Lights meet up; head to the resting place of JRR Tolkien in **Wolvercote Cemetery** (a couple of miles north); or join an 'Inklings' tour.

## A City of Museums

HISTORY COLLIDES WITH MODERNITY

Oxford's world-famous museums have an impressive repository of artefacts from around the world, but in recent years curators here, as in the rest of the country, have been forced to grapple with the colonial legacy of their collections while also trying to protect and hold on to what they have.

In a light-filled modern building just north of the city centre, the **Ashmolean Museum of Art & Archaeology** is a worthy rival to London's British Museum. It has an incredible showcase of art, artefacts and archeological finds from around the world, including treasures from the Palace of Knossos in Crete.

The **Pitt Rivers Museum** is a classic 'cabinet of curiosities' museum established by a Victorian general who donated his globe-spanning collection of 26,000 ethnographical oddities. The museum is also undergoing a process of critical reflection with the removal, and potential repatriation, of its collection of human remains.

A more child-friendly museum, housed in a grand Victorian conservatory, the **Oxford University Museum of Natural History** inspires future

**FOR MUSEUM LOVERS**

Oxford's Ashmolean Museum may be England's first public museum, opening in 1683, but London's **British Museum** (p60) is its most famous. It has also been the site of some controversy, with a decades long tug-of-war over returning the Parthenon Marbles to Athens.

**WHERE TO STAY IN OXFORD**

**Central Backpackers**
Your best budget option is this small but cheerful hostel with dorm beds in single or mixed rooms. £

**University Rooms**
A private operator rents rooms in Oxford University colleges on a B&B basis during student holidays. ££

**Old Bank Hotel**
Sensor lighting, pale-hued rooms, elegant and spacious. A luxury stay in the centre of town. £££

River Cherwell

environmentalists. It's home to the dodo described in *Alice in Wonderland,* which has recently been 3D digitised along with other collections as part of a program of modernising and increasing access to this extraordinary collection for research.

## Oxford's Blue Spaces

ISIS, THE CHERWELL & THE THAMES

The mental health benefit of spending time in 'blue spaces' is not news to the residents of Oxford. The city has three main watercourses running through it: the **River Cherwell**, the **Thames**, and the **Oxford Canal** (completed in 1790) which terminates at Isis Lock. In Oxford, the Thames is called the Isis – when and how this came to be is open to debate – though in recent years a number of Oxford organisations have changed their names to avoid unwanted associations.

River Cherwell, begins its 40-mile journey to the Thames from Northamptonshire. One of Oxford's hidden gems is the **Mesopotamia Walk** passing university college grounds and **Parson's Pleasure** (once a men-only nude bathing area).

### HOPE FOR THE FUTURE

**Zoë Simmons**, Head of Life Collections at Oxford University Museum of Natural History, is a naturalist, entomologist and aspiring arachnologist. *@pselaphacus*

As part of the three-year HOPE for the Future project, more than one million British insects are being rehoused. Considered to be of international importance, the vast insect collection spans more than 200 years of British entomology including dozens of now-extinct species such as the large copper butterfly.

'This is an ambitious National Lottery Heritage-funded project creating a beautiful resource for researchers and visitors,' Simmons explains. 'The Westwood Room, which previously housed the collection, has also been restored to its original appearance from 1860.'

Experts will also travel across the country with insect collections to highlight the vital importance of insects in the natural world.

### SMALL MUSEUMS WORTH A VISIT

**Museum of Oxford**
The history of Oxford and its population told through local objects discovered or donated by the community.

**History of Science Museum**
Learn about scientific enquiry from instruments in the Islamic Golden Age to Einstein's famous blackboard.

**Modern Art Oxford**
Craving something modern? This contemporary art museum has fresh exhibitions, with activities for children too.

## BEST WATERSIDE PUBS IN OXFORD

**Perch**
An ancient village pub with a thatched roof that's tucked down a magical footpath just off the Thames.

**Head of the River**
Right next to Folly Bridge, and originally a waterfront warehouse, this popular pub is now part of the Fullers chain.

**Isis River Farmhouse**
The long stroll, or bike ride, to this atmospheric riverside pub with a large beer garden is worth the effort.

**King's Arms**
A 4-mile walk or cycle south of Oxford, this traditional English pub overlooks Sanford Lock.

**Trout Inn**
A 400-year-old pub, near the Godstow Abbey ruin, where you can drink or dine by a Thames weir.

CHRISDORNEY/SHUTTERSTOCK ©

Head of the River

Whiling away languid days on the river – or, as Oxford-educated writer Kenneth Grahame put it in *The Wind in the Willows*, 'messing about in boats' – is what an Oxford summer is all about. **Salter's Steamers** runs trip boats on the Thames, and rents punts, rowboats and motorboats. The Victorian-era **Cherwell Boathouse** also hires punts, or you can watch them head off from the deck of the award-winning restaurant. For something more energetic, **Oxford Kayak Tours** does half-day guided tours of Oxford starting in Cutteslowe – apparently the most challenging part is dodging inebriated punters.

## GETTING AROUND

If you arrive by car for the day, it's best to park and ride (catch a shuttle from a car park on the outskirts of town). Pay attention to which one you've parked at. If you're staying in Oxford make sure your accommodation comes with parking options.

Central Oxford is easy to explore by foot. You can also download the Stagecoach app to purchase a DayRider ticket for unlimited bus travel within Oxford (handy if you're travelling with kids as the Jericho museum is a bit of a trek).

Cycling is an excellent way to get around. Use Donkey Republic's app to find dockless bikes. Oxbikes is a local outfit that allows you to prebook a rental bike online.

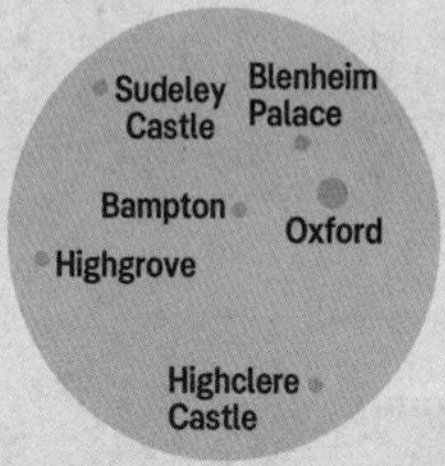

Sudeley Castle
Blenheim Palace
Bampton
Oxford
Highgrove
Highclere Castle

# Beyond Oxford

## There's more to Oxfordshire than the globally recognised university city. Film locations, prehistoric sites and stately homes are calling.

The villages in the countryside surrounding Oxford city ooze rustic charm. Witney has attractive stone houses, its wealth built on blanket production (an industry which began in the Iron Age). Mills, wealthy merchants' homes and blanket factories are still in evidence today.

*Downton Abbey* fans will recognise Bampton: it starred as the fictional village of Downton. Spot the filming locations for Isobel Crawley's home, the post office and the Grantham Arms. Downton Abbey itself, that is Highclere Castle, is closer to Newbury.

Then there's the magnificent Blenheim Palace adjoining the township of Woodstock, known for its antique shops. Southwest of Oxford, the Vale of the White Horse offers intriguing prehistoric attractions.

**TOP TIP**

Spring and summer are ideal touring times with country gardens blooming with colour, but Oxfordshires villages also light up with Christmas festivities in winter.

**Blenheim Palace (p192)**

### WHO PAID FOR ALL THIS?

'Many of the places we care for have direct or indirect links to slavery, including objects made from materials obtained by forced labour,' tweeted the National Trust in 2020, unleashing a storm of controversy.

The National Trust had just published a 115-page report on the 'Connections between Colonialism and Properties now in the Care of the National Trust', detailing 93 places with links to colonialism, slavery and the East India Company.

It certainly challenged some of the Trust's traditional supporters. Members accused the organisation of 'wokeism' and unduly veering into politics, others threatened to cancel their direct debits. However, despite the backlash, the head of the National Trust, Hilary McGrady, has vowed to continue 'decolonising' its country homes, one by one.

DAVID HUGHES/SHUTTERSTOCK ©

Sudeley Castle

## Stately Homes & Grand Gardens

STROLL VAST ESTATES

This affluent part of the world is home to some of Britain's most spectacular houses and gardens, many of them packed with exotic species gathered from far-flung countries on the behest of immensely wealthy owners.

How did these landowners acquire all that wealth? That's something more people are asking as they stroll England's vast estates today. One legacy of England's fortuned past is a countryside dotted with magnificent, centuries-old manors. These prestigious properties, with their inspiring architecture and craftsmanship, are now lovingly maintained by heritage preservation societies – or private owners – at considerable contemporary expense.

Unesco World Heritage Site–listed **Blenheim Palace** (not actually part of the royal family's property portfolio) is a monumental baroque fantasy designed by Sir John Vanbrugh and Nicholas Hawksmoor, and built between 1705 and 1722 by the Duke of Marlborough. Its majestic parklands and pleasure

### WHERE TO STAY BEYOND OXFORD

**Killingworth Castle, Woodstock**
Roadside inn built during KCI's reign, now a rustic dog-friendly, family-run pub with elegant rooms. **££**

**Artist Residence Oxfordshire, Witney**
A 16th-century thatched-roofed inn with comfy, quirky rooms and characterful converted farm buildings. **£££**

**Thyme, Lechlade**
This 60-hectare estate's luxury accommodation has an on-site restaurant, meadow spa and cooking school. **£££**

gardens, designed by the infamous landscape architect Lancelot 'Capability' Brown, sprawl around one of Britain's greatest stately homes.

This is also the birthplace of Sir Winston Churchill. After touring the grand halls, head down to an exhibition on Churchill history to admire his skill with a paintbrush. After wandering the estate like you're starring in a Regency period drama, take afternoon tea in **The Orangery**.

Next, **Highclere Castle**, with its 18th-century follies, is another grand estate landscaped by Lancelot 'Capability' Brown. Highclere is on the bucket list of every *Downton Abbey* fan, and its rooms are decked with images from the show. Never watched Downton? You might be more interested in the Egyptian Exhibition, narrating the search for and discovery of the Tomb of Tutankhamun in 1922 by George Herbert, 5th Earl of Carnarvon, Howard Carter and Evelyn, Lord Carnarvon's daughter. If neither piques your interest, this is a castle that's still very much a private home. The family photos of the Earl and Countess of Carnarvon, bedside novels, and their website blog all give you an insight into aristocratic life in the 21st century.

**Sudeley Castle** is another private castle but this one has Queen Katherine Parr, the last and surviving wife of King Henry VIII, buried in its grounds. The opulent gardens in the surrounding estate include spectacular avenues, an intricate knot garden (inspired by the pattern of one of Elizabeth I's gowns) and aviaries containing colourful birds.

Finally, **Highgrove** was the primary residence of King Charles III from the 1980s until his ascension to the throne in 2022. Built between 1796 and 1798 in a Georgian neoclassical style, the house itself is not open to the public. Come instead to see Charles' exquisite organic gardens, which include rows of sculpted yews and a 'carpet garden' modelled on an oriental rug.

**FOR MORE ON CHURCHILL**

Britain's obsession with its wartime prime minister Sir Winston Churchill makes even more sense after a visit to the **Churchill's War Rooms** (p64) and **Dover Castle** (p152).

### THE DESTRUCTION OF THE COUNTRY HOUSE

Neglect saw the ruin of many of England's historic houses until a pivotal 1974 exhibition at the V&A in London entitled 'The Destruction of the Country House' sparked a change in public opinion. No longer just for the elites, the historic house became a part of the fabric of England's national heritage, shared by everyone.

The income generated by opening up these houses (whether they're still inhabited or not) to the public has become a necessity for most. Some have rebranded as accommodation, others host weddings, sports carnivals, music festivals and seasonal events like Christmas lights and Easter trails. Of course all that foot traffic comes at a cost – but without it more houses would have slid into a state of irreversible disrepair.

### GETTING AROUND

Driving is really the only way to get from stately home to stately home with any expediency. Public transport really isn't an option unless you're bussing between towns only.

Parking is usually included with entrance fees. In the height of summer except to get a spot some distance from venue entrances when additional fields are opened to take overflow vehicles. Wear comfortable shoes that you don't mind getting dusty or muddy depending on the weather.

# BURFORD & THE COTSWOLDS



On the River Windrush, Burford is an historic market town and Cotswolds gateway – well residents insist it's a town, not a village, it received its charter back in 1090. The main road runs down a steep hill to a single-lane mediaeval bridge. Lanes of honey-coloured stone cottages meander east and west. Ditch the car as soon as you can: these roads are not designed for motor vehicles.

The historic high street is flanked with independent shops, cosy inns, and antiques stores. And as befits an agricultural centre, delis sell local produce from chutneys to cheeses. Burford's prosperity means there's plenty of accommodation from coaching inns to B&Bs and self-catering cottages nearby. A half-mile walk north in Fulbrook is the family-friendly family-run Carpenters Arms, while the Swan Inn by the river in Swinbrook is another much-loved traditional pub with an award-winning menu.

### TOP TIP

Summer is the peak Cotswolds touring season. It's ideal weather for walking and cycling in the countryside, beer gardens fill up with revellers enjoying a pint in the sunshine, and photographers make a beeline for the purple fields of the Cotswolds Lavender Farm.

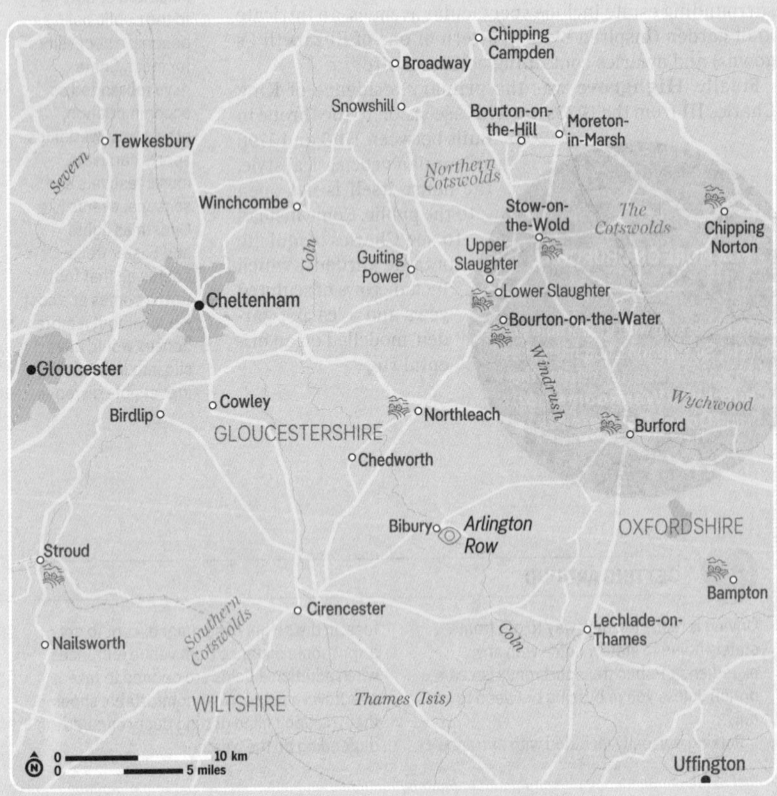

I WEI HUANG/SHUTTERSTOCK ©

Arlington Row, Bilbury

## Picture-Perfect Cotswolds

GET THAT QUINTESSENTIAL ENGLAND SHOT

Many of the most loved places for snapping that classic Cotswolds photo have fallen victim to over-tourism and social media madness. If you want to avoid the crowds, go early in the morning or late in the day – which is often when you'll get the best lighting anyway.

Starting in Burford, **Sheep St** has vine-covered stone houses set back from the road.

Looking very much like it did when it was built in the 14th century, the cottages of **Arlington Row** are the subject of the occasional visitor controversy. Want to know what it's like to live in a tourism hot spot? No 9 is available to rent through the National Trust website.

In summer you'll have trouble getting a shot of the bridges over the River Windrush in **Bourton-on-the-Water** without dozens of people. In winter you may snap that elusive snow shot for your Christmas cards.

Other notable places to visit include the cobblestone **Chipping Steps** in Tetbury; the Old Mill at Lower Slaughter; Grade I–heritage listed **Grevel's House** in Chipping Norton;

### BEST MICHELIN-STARRED EXPERIENCES

The Michelin star has been consistently awarded to these Cotswolds establishments. If you have the coin in your account, prebook a meal that doubles as a life experience.

**Nut Tree Inn, Murcott**
A traditional village pub that serves exceptional British dishes.

**Le Champignon Sauvage, Cheltenham**
Sophisticated French bistro run by a husband-and-wife team for over three decades.

**Le Manoir aux Quat'Saisons, Great Milton**
Globally recognised temple to haute cuisine but with a relaxed vibe.

### WHERE TO STAY

**Volunteer Inn**
A great value coaching inn with an Indian restaurant in Chipping Campden. Ask which rooms to avoid if you want a quiet night. £

**Wild Rabbit**
Bed and breakfast in simple yet stylishly furnished rooms in this traditional inn in Chipping Norton. £££

**Burleigh Court Hotel**
A boutique manor house hotel in Stroud with an on-site restaurant, an Art Deco plunge pool and cosy rooms. £££

ROAD TRIP

# A Cotswolds Jaunt

Given the Cotswolds' intricate spider's web of winding country lanes that connect its ancient market towns, time-warped villages and majestic stately homes, it's impossible to cover every highlight in a single day. This tour takes in some of the most picturesque spots.

### 1 Burford

Begin in the picturesque market town of Burford where there are antique shops, chintzy tearooms and specialist boutiques as well as the wonderfully preserved, centuries-old St John the Baptist's Church. The church's star attraction is the macabre 1625 Tanfield tomb, depicting local nobleman Sir Lawrence Tanfield and his wife lying in finery above a pair of carved skeletons. To stretch your legs, walk the 5-mile loop along the River Windrush to 12th-century St Mary's Church in the chocolate-box village of Swinbrook.

**The Drive:** Head 10 miles west on the A40 to Northleach with its wonderful melange of architectural styles. The ruins at Chedworth Roman Villa are a worthy detour from here. From Northleach take the A429 to Lower Slaughter via Burton-on-the Water.

### 2 The Slaughters

The picture-postcard villages of Upper and Lower Slaughter, roughly a mile apart, have somehow managed to maintain their unhurried medieval charm, despite receiving a multitude of visitors. If time allows, stroll a mile northwest along the river from the Old Mill in Lower Slaughter to Upper Slaughter, in an idyllic setting between a small ford and the hills. Book ahead if you want to eat at an exquisite Jacobean mansion: Lords of the Manor.

**The Drive:** Return to your car and drive 3 miles north on the A429 to Stow-on-the-Wold to visit photogenic St Edward's Church. Then continue on another 4.5 miles to Moreton-in-Marsh.

### 3 Moreton-in-Marsh

A top spot for independent shops (antiques, gifts and cheeses), better still if you're here

**Burford**

MALGOSIA JANICKA/SHUTTERSTOCK ©

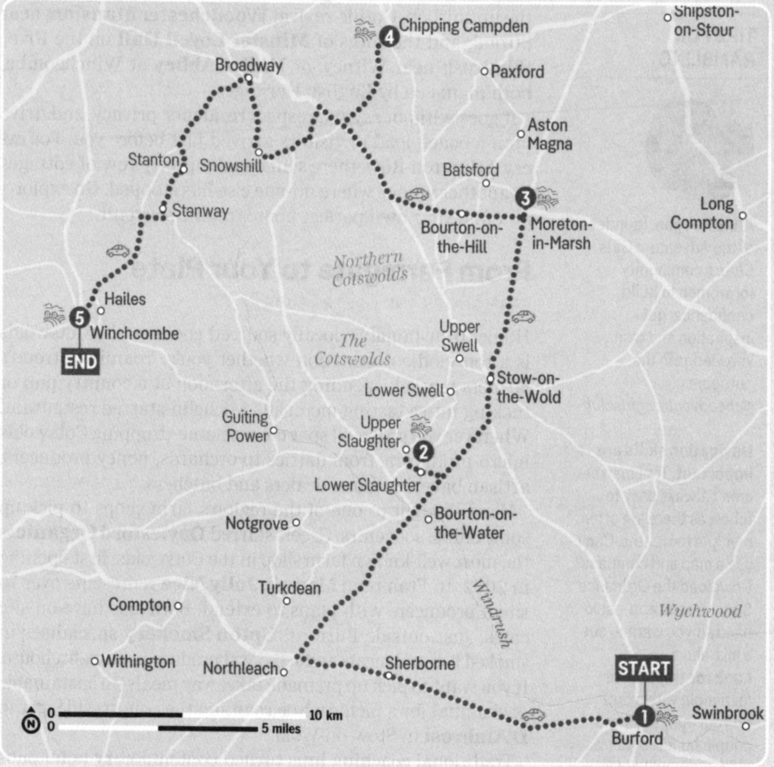


on market day: Tuesday. Wander around and you'll find plenty of tearooms, cafes and pubs. Just outside of town is the gorgeous Batsford Arboretum and Gardens with 1600 species of labelled trees from Japanese cherry trees to American redwoods, plus the Cotswold Falconry Centre where you can learn about local birds of prey and the ancient practice of falconry.

**The Drive:** Head next to Chipping Campden via the tiny Bourton-on-the-Hill. Slow down and take in the views. And if views are your thing, swing by Broadway Tower, too.

## 4 Chipping Campden

A standout, even for an area of such pretty towns, Chipping Campden is a glorious reminder of Cotswolds life in medieval times. Its gracefully curving main street is flanked by a picturesque array of stone cottages, fine terraced houses, ancient inns and historic homes, most made of that beautiful honey-coloured Cotswolds stone. While you're here, don't miss the 15th-century St James' Church. With extra time, consider a detour to the National Trust's Hidcote manor for its intricate Arts and Crafts movement–inspired garden.

**The Drive:** Head to Winchcombe via the tiny hamlets of Snowhill, Stanton and Stanway, where houses are crafted from gold-tinged Cotswolds stone and cottages have thatched roofs.

## 5 Winchcombe

Winchcombe is an ancient Anglo-Saxon town with dramatic stone and half-timbered buildings and excellent sleeping and eating options, including 5 North St where chef Marcus Ashenford's cooking is rooted in traditional seasonal ingredients. Stay overnight so you can explore wonderful Sudeley Castle, most famous as the home and final resting place of Catherine Parr (Henry VIII's widow), or walk 2.5 miles along the Cotswolds Way to the Neolithic Belas Knap Long Barrow burial chamber in the morning..

## TIPS FOR RAMBLING

**Alice Keegan**, founder of the Adventure Girls Club, a community for women to build confidence, get inspiration and gain knowledge in the outdoors. *@theadventuregirlsclub*

**Navigation skills are important**. Trail markers aren't always easy to follow as there are often multiple footpaths. Can't use a map and compass? Download the Ordnance Survey maps app – also handy if you want to cut a hike short.

**Look for trig points** (a triangle with a dot) on your map. At only a couple hundred metres elevation you'll get views of beautiful countryside.

**Wear proper hiking boots** especially in forests and fields. Trainers are not going to cut it in the mud.

Finally, **walk confidently through a field of cows – never run**. Don't come between a mother and her calf, even if you're following a footpath.

the unfinished, Gothic-revival **Woodchester Mansion**, near Stroud; and the ruins of **Minster Lovell Hall** on the River Windrush near Witney, or **Hailes Abbey** at Winchcombe, both managed by English Heritage.

It goes without saying, respect residents' privacy, and drive on if a coach-load of visitors arrived just before you. For every Arlington Row, there's an equally pretty row of cottages in another village where no-one else has stopped. Go explore, and find your own perfect photographic souvenir.

## From Farmgate to Your Plate

FARM SHOPS AND GASTROPUBS

Home to sustainable, locally sourced cooking, the Cotswolds is a top foodie destination whether you're roaming Stroud's farmers market, spending the afternoon at a country pub or tucking into a tasting menu at a Michelin-starred restaurant. Wherever you go, you'll spot menus name-dropping Cotswolds micro-producers, from dairies to orchards, honey producers, artisan bakeries, game dealers and butchers.

Head straight to one of the region's farm shops to pick up some edible souvenirs. Green-starred **Daylesford Organic** is the most well-known farm shop in the Cotswolds, first opening in 2002. In Frampton Mansell, **Jolly Nice** represents over 70 small producers with plans to extend. Both also have on-site cafes. Just outside Burford, **Upton Smokery** specialises in smoked fish and meats and sells local produce in an ex-firehouse. If you want to pick up premade takeaway meals (in sustainable packaging) for a picnic while roaming the countryside, get to **D'Ambrosi** in Stow-on-Wold.

Traditional coaching inns turned contemporary hotel pubs are worth planning your day around. The **Double Red Duke** in Bampton takes classic pub grub – steak, fish and chips, cheeseburgers – to a new level. Stroud's Woolpack Inn is loved by many for its views as much as the food. The ivy-covered Wheatsheaf-in Northleach serves British cuisine in an elegant dining room and in the garden. These are but a few of the exceptional destination dining spots in the Cotswolds.

### GETTING AROUND

Public transport in the Cotswolds requires planning and patience. Trains skirt the east and west regions, while buses connect towns from Oxford to Cheltenham via Burford (making this a great mid-way hub town to base yourself).

The Cotswolds Discoverer is a good-value car-free one-day transport pass that gives unlimited travel on trains and most bus routes throughout the region. See nationalrail.co.uk for more.

For the greatest flexibility, and the potential to get off the beaten track, having your own car is unbeatable (you just need to find a spot to park).

# CIRENCESTER & AROUND

Cirencester & Around

London

Cirencester – known then as Corinium Dobunnorum – ranked second only to London in Roman Britannia. Today the 'capital of the Cotswolds' is an elegant town with boutiques, an excellent museum, the cathedral-like St John the Baptist Church, with its perpendicular Gothic tower and fan vaulting, and a broad range of accommodation and dining options.

A medley of historic buildings flank the central square and surrounding streets, telling the story of Cirencester's growth and prosperity from a medieval centre for wool trade to the home of the Royal Agricultural College (now University) since the Romans wound up their occupation.

Cirencester's Charter Markets (Mondays and Fridays) are among the oldest in England (and were even mentioned in William the Conqueror's *Domesday Book*). Here you can grab a bite to eat plus arts, crafts and vintage souvenirs. And on the second and fourth Saturday of the month, there's also an excellent farmers market in the town square.

**TOP TIP**

From the ruins of the Cirencester's Roman amphitheatre (free entry) it is a 15-minute (half-mile) walk to the award-winning Corinium Museum in town.

**Cirencester**

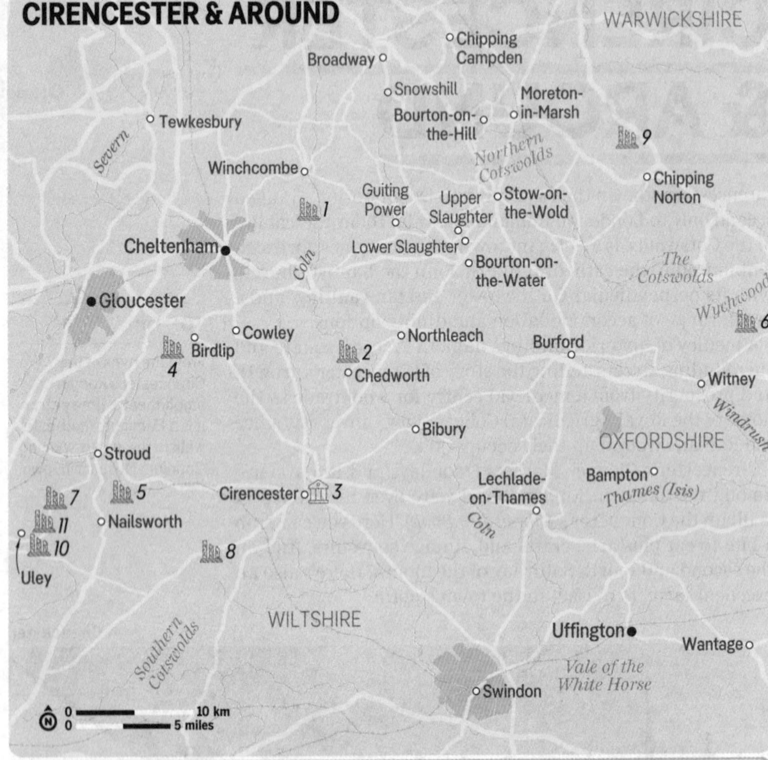


**SIGHTS**
**1** Belas Knap Long Barrow
**2** Chedworth Roman Villa
**3** Corinium Museum
**4** Great Whitcombe Roman Villa
**5** Minchinhampton and Rodborough Commons
**6** North Leigh Roman Villa
**7** Nympsfield Long Barrow
**8** Rodmarton Long Barrow
**9** Rollright Stones
**10** Ulley Bury
**11** Ulley Long Barrow

## The Rollright Stones & Other Ancient Sites

FROM ROCKS TO ROMANS

These gentle, fertile hills have been peopled for millennia. Neolithic, Bronze and Iron Age and Roman traces are quietly folded into the landscape, if you know where to look. Head 27 miles north of Cirencester for the **Rollright Stones**. Over 2000 years of prehistoric activity are quietly weathering away here: the Neolithic Whispering Knights 'portal dolmen' burial chamber (c 3800 BCE); King's Men stone circle (c 2500 BCE); and Bronze-Age King Stone (c 1500 BCE).

More Neolithic sites that grip the imagination include the 200-odd long barrows (burial chambers) of the **Cotswold Severn Group**. Belas Knap (c 3000 BCE) is probably the finest. Over 54m long, 18m wide and 4.3m high, it retains four

**Chedworth Roman Villa** **(p202)**

Rollright Stones

chambers, dry-stone retaining walls, massive limestone lintels and jambs, and a false entrance (alongside two genuine portals). The last of 37 burials excavated here dates to the Bronze Age. **Rodmarton Long Barrow** (c 3800 BCE), aka Windmill Tump, has three chambers from which 13 burials, arrowheads and even Roman coins were excavated.

Where the Cotswold Way mounts the Cotswold Escarpment, you'll find perfect Severn Valley views from **Nympsfield Long Barrow** and **Uley Long Barrow** (aka Hetty Pegler's Tump). Both dated to c 3800 BCE, they're some of Britain's earliest multi-chambered barrows. Human remains, ceramics, flint arrowheads and Roman coins were also found here.

Nearby Uley Bury (c 300 BCE) is an Iron Age hillfort with traces of Neolithic prehistory. **Minchinhampton** and **Rodborough Commons** are National Trust–managed hilltop commons with commanding views, manmade banks and ditches, and archaeology indicating that they, too, were Iron Age hillforts.

### BRITANNIA

Roman 'Britannia' lasted from the 1st to the 5th centuries CE. While Julius Caesar invaded in 55 and 54 BCE, it wasnt until 43 CE that his successor, Claudius, first invaded with intent. Landing in Kent, three armies under General Aulus Plautius defeated the disunited Celtic tribes.

By 87 CE, the suppression of Boudica's Celtics fused Rome's control of the south. Hadrian's Wall marked its northern limit, above which the Picts, and other tribes, remained free. Romano-British culture flourished, importing Christianity in the 4th century. Strife in the imperial heartlands saw the eventual withdrawal of the Romans.

### FOR ROMAN HISTORY

Love a Roman ruin? A visit to wind-whipped **Hadrian's Wall** (p565) is as dramatic as it gets. In London, head to the free-to-enter underground Mithreum.

### WHERE TO EAT IN CIRENCESTER

**Glaze Café & Kitchen**
A light-filled cafe with a simple menu but excellent homemade cakes in the New Brewery Arts Centre. **£**

**Tierra & Mar**
Authentic, exceptional Spanish tapas created with the best local ingredients. **££**

**Bathurst Arms**
Adorable historic pub with outdoor seating by the River Churn serving organic British cuisine. **£££**

## ENJOY THE COUNTRYSIDE

**Adam Henson** is a farmer and TV presenter from the Cotswolds. He's also the author of *Two for Joy: The Untold Ways to Enjoy the Countryside* (2022). *@adamhenson_ & @cotswoldfarmpark*

**Check in to nature**
Put your phone away and use all your senses. Walking should be a joyful, fun experience. I try to get that across in *Two for Joy*. The evidence is there, getting into nature is great for your mental health and wellbeing.

**Look out for flora and fauna**
The Cotswolds are famous for its iconic dry-stone walls but they're also a haven for wildlife. Slow down and look for coloured lichens, mosses and fungi, plus wrens, mice and voles. You'll also spot fieldfares and mistle thrushes feasting on berries from the hedgerows.

**Walk around the park**
I was born and bred at the Cotswold Farm Park. As well as sharing the best of British farming with visitors, it has a beautiful 2-mile wildlife walk.

LEFT: TASMIN WABY/LONELY PLANET ©; RIGHT: PJ PHOTOGRAPHY/SHUTTERSTOCK ©

**Oxfordshire walking path**

Artefacts from these strategic sites suggest the Romans commandeered them from the Britons, following the Claudian invasion of 43 CE.

This temperate corner of Roman 'Britannia' inevitably enticed heavy settlement, as abundant remains prove. Corinium Dobunnorum – Cirencester – was the province's second-largest walled city by the 2nd century CE. Its well-planned streets included a forum, basilica and amphitheatre. Built to hold around 8000, the contours of the now-overgrown amphitheatre can still be seen today. To best appreciate the city's Roman heyday visit **Corinium Museum**, where locally excavated mosaics highlight a well-curated collection.

The remains of numerous Roman villas have been uncovered in the surrounding countryside. Two of the finest lie just outside Cirencester: at **Chedworth**, you'll see three buildings, mosaics, a bath house and a heating system, while **Great Whitcombe** retains a bath house, shrine and mosaic floors. Closer to Oxford, the two remaining buildings at **North Leigh** also include a fine mosaic.

### WHERE TO STAY IN CIRENCESTER

**The Barrel Store**
A clean, modern and environmentally committed YHA with furnishings sourced from local artisans. **£**

**Kings Head Hotel**
A coaching inn since the 14th century, this central plush spot offers slick boudoirs and polished service. **££**

**Barnsley House**
A luxury country house hotel with outstanding gardens, restaurant, private cinema and on-site spa. **£££**

## Wildlife & Bird-Watching

BYO BINOCULARS

In the mosaic landscape of the Cotswolds, centuries-old farms intersperse with pockets of woodland and wildflower meadows and wildlife roams the corridors of grasslands, hedgerows and wetlands. Keep your eyes (and ears) open for chance encounters everywhere.

Birds like robins, wrens and skylarks are common in the farmlands and urban gardens in the Cotswolds, while barn owls can be spotted near Stow-on-Wold and in the Severn Valley at dawn or dusk. Once close to extinction, buzzards and red kites have made a comeback after a successful breeding program in the Chiltern Hills. And the restoration of limestone grasslands has revived populations of Adonis blue and fritillary butterflies.

In woodland areas, listen out for the song of willow warblers and chiffchaffs. You might spot foxes, badgers, bats or deer – although you're more likely to see these elegant white-spotted beauties on a Cotswolds estate than skipping across your path in the wild.

Water meadows and rivers are home to the elusive otter, plus water voles, dragonflies and magnificent kingfishers, as well as brown trout and freshwater crayfish. Hedgerows support thousands of insects, mice, shrews and other small mammals – and why you'll see birds of prey hovering overhead.

You won't have any trouble spotting rabbits, but also lookout for the larger (and rarer) brown hare which also calls the Cotswolds home.

**Robin**

### BEST PLACES TO COOL OFF

Following in the footsteps of the Romans, you can get into some healing waters in the Cotswolds. Rivers, including the Thames, may entice wild swimmers. Ask locals for their favourite locations, but don't forget to check on current conditions, from underwater obstructions to pollution. Alternatively, head to a public lido or swimming spot.

**Sandford Park, Cheltenham**
A broad 50m outdoor lido open year-round with a dedicated children's paddling pool.

**Cirencester Open Air Swimming Pool**
Spring and summer only spring-fed heated swimming pool in an historic setting.

**Cotswold Country Park & Beach**
A large recreational lake with a beach for swimmers plus kayaks, rowboats and SUPs for hire.

### GETTING AROUND

Cirencester is not on the train line. The closest station is at Kemble, 4.5 miles south, which connects to London Paddington. The Stagecoach West bus 882 takes you the final 20 minutes into town.

If driving, there's metered street parking on Market Place and Castle St. Free parking is easier to come by at night (including in designated car parks) and on weekends.

# CHELTENHAM

Perhaps best known for horse racing and its literature festival, Cheltenham owes its air of refinement to its heyday as an 18th-century spa resort. At that time, it rivalled Bath as the place for ailing aristocrats to recuperate, which is why it still boasts many graceful Regency buildings and manicured squares to wander in today.

Cheltenham is an excellent base for accommodation, drinking and dining, with a Michelin-garlanded restaurant, Le Champignon Sauvage, and plenty of worthy contenders like Lumiere. Accommodation runs the gamut from modern hotels if you're on a budget to luxurious boutique B&Bs, often in Georgian townhouses, that mix antiques with contemporary styling in what is known as 'Cotswolds chic'. The shopping scene is also alive and well here; browse boutiques, vintage stores and galleries in the Suffolks and Montpellier neighbourhoods nearby.

**TOP TIP**

If you arrive by train, or even if you're getting around town by foot (or bike), the Honeybourne Line is a walking track that runs from Cheltenham railway station to Pittville Park, with a branch off towards the town centre along the River Chelt.

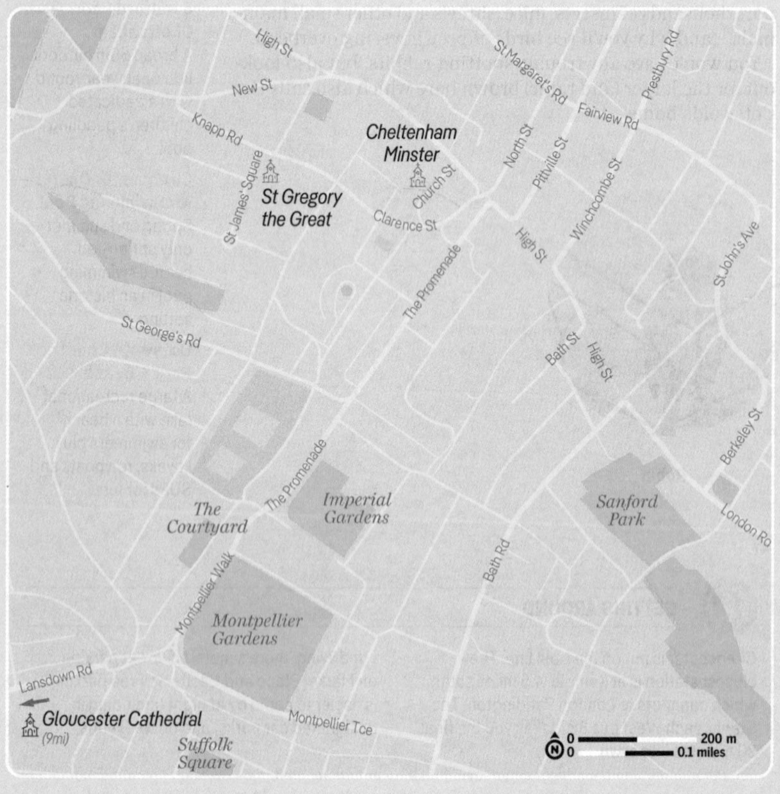

MICK ATKINS/SHUTTERSTOCK ©

Cheltenham Racecourse

## Festivals to Plan For

ALWAYS A GOOD TIME

Cheltenham knows how to host a festival. In March, 40,000 racegoers converge on Cheltenham Racecourse for England's premier steeplechase event, the **Cheltenham Gold Cup**. You can rub shoulders with Britain's aristocracy or soak up the atmosphere at more modestly priced enclosures.

Late April and early May is jazz season. The **Cheltenham Jazz Festival**, a six-day program of international stars and local jazz musicians, many for free, is staged in Montpellier Gardens and venues around town.

June brings the **Science Festival** to town, exploring the wonders of the natural world, the complexities of human psychology and the mysteries of space. The line-up typically includes household names like Sir Brian Cox, plus broadcasters like Kate Humble or Bryony Gordon.

In July, Cheltenham gets busy with **classical music gigs** programmed over 10 days in gorgeous historic venues like the Cheltenham Town Hall, Pittville Pump Room and nearby Gloucester Cathedral. You'll also stumble across free pop-up performances along the High St or in Imperial Gardens.

### BEST LUXURY SPAS IN CHELTENHAM

**Cowley Manor**
An Italianate mansion with a lavish modern spa, Cowley Manor has both an indoor and outdoor pool, gym, sauna and steam room. A two-course lunch on the terrace is part of the 'signature' experience.

**Ellenborough Park**
At this 15th-century mansion, choose from a range of treatments before unwinding in the Jacuzzi, sauna or steam room.

**Calcot Manor & Spa**
A family-friendly hotel with heated indoor and outdoor pools, plus a fireside hot tub and treatment rooms. Note: kids are allowed in the spa areas during selected times.

### WHERE TO GO FOR INDIAN IN CHELTENHAM

**Bhoomi Kitchen**
Good-value lunchtime *thali* at this top-rated South Indian restaurant. **££**

**The Mahal**
Pre-dinner cocktails and seven-dish tasting menu in an opulent pan-Indian restaurant. **£££**

**Prithvi**
Sumptuous contemporary interior with fine-dining Indian. Special mention for the desserts. **£££**

The month ends with relative-newcomer, the **Cheltenham Paint Festival**: a weekend of mural painting around the city that began in 2017. The legacy of previous festivals is visible all over town. Hop online for a **street-art walking tour** route, by artist and year.

Finally, and most famously, the **Cheltenham Literature Festival**. The world's longest-running literature festival draws a stellar line-up of writers, performers and speakers every October.

### BEST BOOKSHOPS IN CHELTENHAM

Of course the hosts of the world's first literature festival has a thriving bookstore scene.

**Hatchards**
This London-based retailer and official bookseller to the royal household opened their first regional store here in 2022.

**Waterstones**
Also on the Promenade, the high street chain with an independent bookstore feel; it has an in-house Costa on the 1st floor.

**Rossiter Books**
A family-run indie bookstore that locals love.

**Moss Books**
Has been selling secondhand books, specialising in art and history, since 1992.

**Cheltenham Rare Books**
Sells quirky, beautiful and rare books in excellent condition on Imperial Sq. It's one for bonafide book lovers and collectors.

## Two Churches & a Cathedral

BUILT TO LAST

Central Cheltenham has a few notable churches. **Cheltenham Minster** is the town's oldest surviving building, dating from the mid-11th century. Religious architecture lovers will admire the lierne vaulting in the baptistery and the large rose window. A couple of minutes walk to the east you'll find a 19th-century Roman Catholic church, **St Gregory the Great**. This Grade II–listed building is another one for architecture buffs. Designed by Charles Hansom, the English architect famous for revolutionising horse-drawn carriage design. You can still take a ride around New York's Central Park in a Hansom Cab today.

It is in neighbouring Gloucester – a mere 10 miles down the road – that you'll find the 1000-year-old blockbuster **Gloucester Cathedral**, a place of pilgrimage for centuries. Combining Norman Romanesque and Gothic design, its soaring columns and fan vaulting are surpassed only by Westminster Abbey for inspiring sighs of awe. You can't miss the cloisters; the tomb of King Edward II, who was murdered at nearby Berkeley Castle in 1327; or the the imposing 22m-high Great East Window. Also make time to see the illuminated manuscripts in the 15th-century library; climb the 69m tower; and visit the Norman crypt on a guided tour.

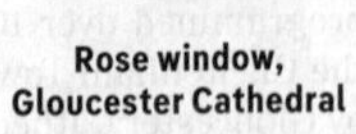

Rose window, Gloucester Cathedral

### GETTING AROUND

Cheltenham is easily visited by train with direct services from London and Bristol, plus connections to Gloucester and Stroud from Cheltenham Spa station.

Stagecoach and National Express buses will get you to Gloucester and the Forest of Dean.

If driving, be aware that Cheltenham has a peak-hour traffic problem and free parking is limited. In the centre there are several dedicated car parks and street parking is metered.

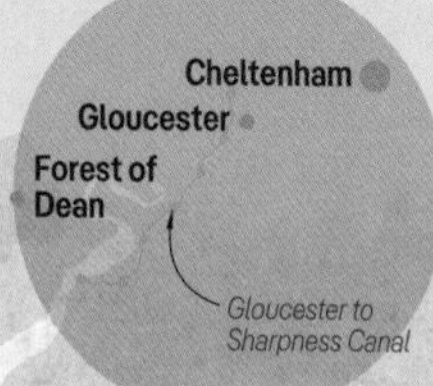

# Beyond Cheltenham

## A region of considerable contrasts from post-industrial Gloucester to the ancient woodlands in the Forest of Dean.

The city of Gloucester, home to a soaring medieval cathedral and soaring industrial-era dockland warehouses, is a short drive downhill from Cheltenham. Pop into the Beatrix Potter museum where you'll discover what happened after the city tailor was immortalised in her best-selling children's book. To the south, you'll find river valleys and lush hills, plus the picturesque 'bobo' village of Stroud. It was once connected to Gloucester by canal, something locals hope to bring back to life.

Venturing further southwest, the Forest of Dean houses England's oldest oak forest and is a hotspot for outdoor adventurers. Designated England's first National Forest Park in 1938, the 42-sq-mile woodland was once a royal hunting ground and then an iron and coal mining region. Today, its forests spill into neighbouring Herefordshire, and the River Wye skirts its western edge. Beyond it: Wales.

**TOP TIP**

Some business, particularly those running water-based activities, close over the winter months, as do most campsites and more remote YHAs.

**Gloucester docks (p208)**

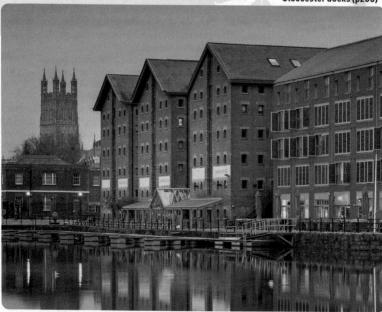

### A TALE OF TWO CANALS

England's canals have been undergoing a revival in recent years as people recognise their value for 'slow travel' activities from boating to fishing, walking and cycling, as well as corridors for England's unique wildlife.

Opening in 1779, Stroudwater Navigation once inked the village of Stroud to the River Severn to carry coal to inland villages, until it was abandoned in 1954. Also left to fall into dereliction, the 30-mile Thames & Severn Canal once flowed from Stroud to Lechlade on the Thames.

Today the Cotswold Canals Trust is gradually restoring the canal infrastructures, from its tunnels to locks, with the ultimate goal of reopening the link between the River Thames and the River Severn. All that was old is new again.

DAVID JC/SHUTTERSTOCK ©

Dean Forest Rail

## Gloucester's Docklands

MARVEL AT VICTORIAN INDUSTRY

Walking around the huge Victorian-era warehouses of Gloucester's docklands, it's easy to conjure the heyday of the 19th century with tall ships offloading cargo while workers shouted over the clamour of horses carts and trams. Timber, sugar and other raw materials came in and Cotswolds wool and Worcestershire salt went out.

Today the dockland basins are a lot more tranquil. You'll spy narrowboats bobbing at their moorings, wooden yachts being repaired in the dry docks, and the occasional tall ship stopping by.

Before the early 1800s, the trip up the River Severn from the sea was a hazardous journey so a bunch of industrialists got together to build a canal from Gloucester to Berkeley (although the course changed to Sharpness) to create a safe shortcut inland. As the canal was completed and this inland port grew in importance, so did the warehouses.

Losing to the advent of the railways, some canals were abandoned. But canal boating for leisure rather than commercial

### WHERE TO STAY IN THE FOREST OF DEAN

**YHA St Briavels Castle**
Book the family into this 800-year-old medieval castle with a haunted oubliette. **£**

**YHA Wye Valley**
Bunks, private rooms and pre-pitched bell tents are available in a beautiful riverside setting. **£**

**Tudor Farmhouse Hotel**
Award-winning foodie hotel. Plus bespoke experiences from foraging to stargazing. **£££**

transport continues, and is growing in popularity today. For visitors, the broad **Gloucester to Sharpness Canal** remains a fascinating piece of engineering. To learn more about its history, visit the refurbished **National Waterways Museum Gloucester** in the old Llanthony Warehouse. It also has a cafe and does 45-minute boat trips on the Gloucester and Sharpness Canal.

## The Magical Forest of Dean

LOST IN A FOREST

On the borderland between England and Wales, lies a region of ancient woodlands with mossy paths that once inspired JRR Tolkien's Middle Earth. The Forest of Dean is a centre for outdoors adventurers: from walking, cycling and mountain biking, to abseiling, gorge scrambling and paddling on the River Wye, this is the place to get into the great outdoors and test your limits.

For a leisurely family walk (or cycle), spotting peregrines and goshawks overhead, follow the scenic 8-mile **Peregrine Path** along the Wye riverbank.

Rock climbers and abseilers can enjoy epic views over the valley from the 504m-high **Symonds Yat Rock**. Cave explorers head to **Clearwell Caves**.

Off-road cyclists will love the **Forest of Dean Cycle Centre**. On the site of a former colliery (this was once free mining country), it has gentle rides for families as well as blue- and red-graded MBT trails. Bikes can be prebooked with Pedalabikeaway.

A popular filming location, the ancient forest at **Puzzlewood** has an otherworldly quality where children's imaginations can run wild.

In spring and summer, the River Wye is the big draw here. Canoes, kayaks and stand-up paddleboards are available for hire from outfits based in Symonds Yat.

A more sedate day outdoors can be had at the volunteer-run **Dean Forest Rail**, where classic steam engines ply a 4.5-mile rail line.

### RIVER SURFING

The Bristol Channel has the second-highest tidal range in the world, dropping by around 15m. When this happens, its tributary, the River Severn, experiences a remarkable natural phenomenon called the Severn Bore. A rolling surge of water from the highest tides funnels into the narrowing river, forcing a 3m wave upstream. Although the official advice is not to attempt to ride the wave, hundreds of kayakers and surfers do just that. Prime places to see the phenomenon are Stonebench and Minsterworth just outside Gloucester. Check the tide charts and just you might catch it.

### FOR TOLKIEN FANS

Visit the university that shaped **JRR Tolkien** (p186) and the fantasy writer's final resting place at **Wolvercote Cemetery** (p188) nearby.

### GETTING AROUND

Cheltenham and Gloucester have good train connections including to London and Bristol. To get to the Forest of Dean by public transport, take Stagecoach or National Express buses from Cheltenham and Gloucester. Then hire bikes to get between sights and activities.

A car gives you freedom and more time in destinations, and in these less-touristed parts of the region, finding parking is less of a worry.

# WINDSOR & ETON

Windsor & Eton
London

Facing across the Thames are the twin towns of Windsor and Eton, with Windsor Castle looming over them. According to Forbes, Windsor is the richest town in the UK with 250 multi-millionaires calling the place home, although you probably won't see many milling around the shops and diners squarely aimed at the visitor economy.

The town's beautiful Grade II–listed Victorian railway station and historic streetscapes sit in contrast with some less attractive modern additions to the town centre. During the Changing of the Guard (check online for dates) the high street is momentarily overrun by pomp, and travellers lapping up the fanfare.

On the north side of the Thames, Eton has a single historic commercial street and the sprawling campus of Eton College. The school, where pupils still wear bowties and morning coats, has famously educated 19 prime ministers (so far), and is the birthplace of the British dessert, the Eton Mess.

**TOP TIP**

Windsor is closer to Heathrow Airport than central London. It's a short (10-mile) car trip, but the local Green Line bus still takes around an hour, stopping at towns along the way.

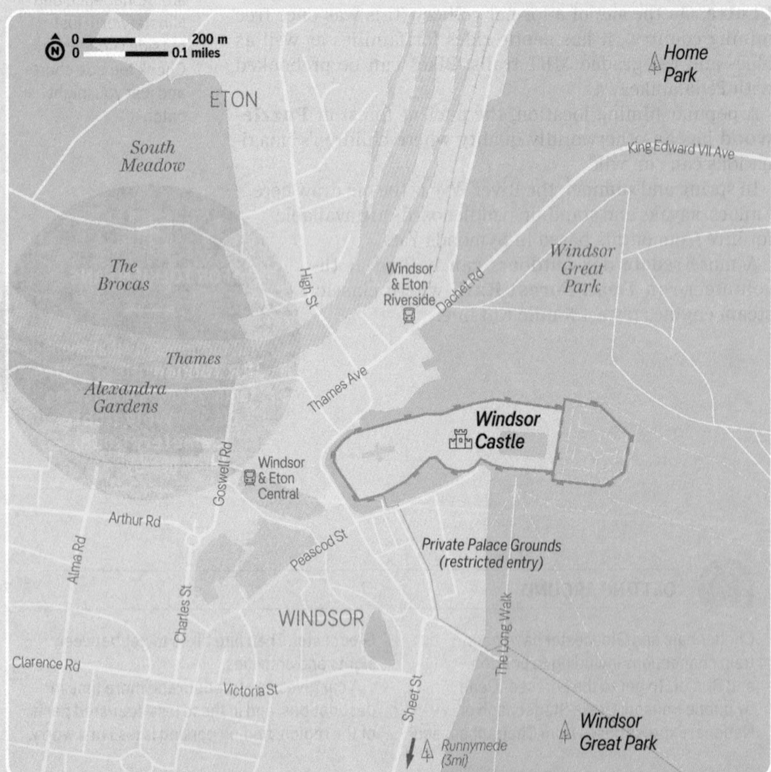

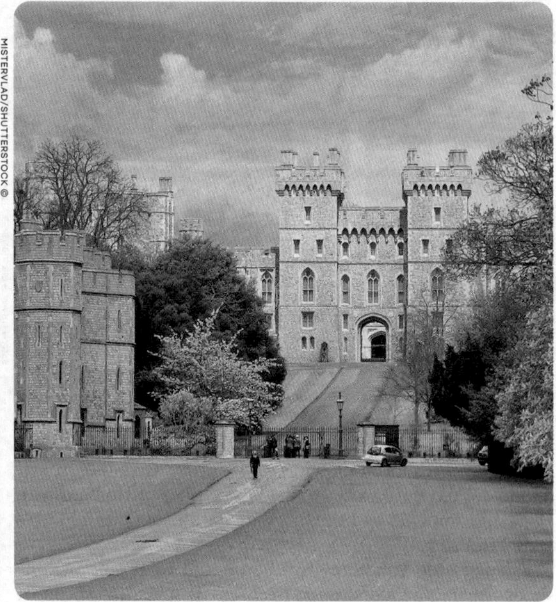
MISTERVLAD/SHUTTERSTOCK ©

Windsor Castle

## We'll Never Be Royals

SEE HOW THEY LIVE

The reason we're here. The imposing fortress that is **Windsor Castle** is the world's largest continually occupied castle. It has been home to 40 monarchs since it was founded by William the Conqueror in the 11th century.

Successive monarchs made their own marks, with Edward III's Gothic additions and Charles II's baroque flourishes to emulate Louis XIV's Versailles. George IV swept in with his team of artisans to establish what remains Windsor's identity as a palace within a medieval castle.

Thanks to all this rebuilding, the castle now holds almost 1000 rooms, in architectural styles that range from half-timbered fired brick to Gothic stone. In 1992, the favoured residence of Queen Elizabeth II was devastated by a blaze that destroyed 115 rooms, including nine State Rooms. The restoration work took five years.

### THE DEATH OF THE QUEEN

After the death of Queen Elizabeth II at Balmoral Castle in September 2022, the UK entered a period of official (and genuine) mourning. While lying in state at Westminster Hall, thousands of Brits queued to farewell their monarch.

On 19 September, after a funeral service at Westminster Abbey, the Queen's coffin was transferred to Windsor for a final procession to St George's Chapel.

Queen Elizabeth II's final resting place is in the King George VI Memorial chapel at Windsor Castle, where she is buried with her beloved Prince Philip and her parents.

The ledger stone, in Belgian black marble inscribed with brass lettering, reads George VI 1895–1952, Elizabeth 1900–2002, Elizabeth II 1926–2022, Philip 1921–2021.

### WHERE TO STAY IN WINDSOR

**76 Duke Street**
Charming B&B with a welcoming owner on a quiet residential street near the Thames. ££

**Macdonald Windsor Hotel**
Rich, deep reds and purples add a plush feel to this contemporary townhouse in central Windsor. ££

**Coworth Park**
Super-luxe Dorchester country house hotel with stables, a Michelen-starred restaurant and modern spa. £££

**Memorial to Magna Carta, Runnymede**

### A VERY ROYAL WEDDING

On 19 May 2018, Prince Harry and Hollywood actor Meghan Markle tied the knot at St George's Chapel in Windsor Castle. The £32 million event had a guest list that included film and TV stars, while a further 2000 members of the public were invited to watch from the grounds of Windsor Castle.

After the ceremony, the newlyweds paraded through Windsor in an open-top Ascot Landau carriage to the joy of the 10,000 fans who came to see them, before they held a black-tie reception at Frogmore House next door.

Harry's father Charles, then the Prince of Wales, was also married in Windsor in 2005, but in a somewhat controversial civil ceremony with Camilla Parker Bowles at the Windsor Guildhall. Queen Elizabeth II and Prince Phillip did not attend the ceremony.

Windsor Castle tour highlights include the Grand Reception room, with its chandeliers and gilding; the State Apartments decked with works of art by the likes of Holbein, Van Dyck and Rubens; and the intricate details of Queen Mary's Dolls' House.

It's suggested you allow two hours and wear comfortable shoes – there's a lot of ground to cover when visiting the most popular Royal estate in the UK.

A few miles downstream you can visit the open meadows of **Runnymede**, the 'birthplace of modern democracy'. Here in 1215, King John sealed the Magna Carta after hammering out a basic charter of rights that guaranteed the liberties of the king's subjects and restricted the monarch's absolute power.

The field remains much as it was, bar a few memorials. The American Bar Association erected the Memorial to Magna Carta styled to resemble a Greek temple. A short uphill path leads to an understated President John F Kennedy Memorial, sitting on an acre of land gifted to the US so that the memorial would stand on American soil. The main field also holds *The Jurors,* 12 bronze chairs commemorating the Magna Carta's 800th anniversary in 2015.

Next on your royal tour of Windsor, the spectacular **Windsor Great Park**, which is adjacent to the private 265-hectare Home Park at Windsor Castle. These 8 sq miles of carefully managed gardens are open to the public to stroll and admire the lake, woods and a deer park where red deer roam free. In 2022, King Charles III took over as Ranger of Windsor Great Park on his 74th birthday.

### GETTING AROUND

Trains run from London to Windsor direct from Waterloo, or from Paddington changing at Slough. National Express buses go direct from London Victoria.

There is metered street parking in Windsor and Eton, plus carparks both in town and on the outskirts with 'park and ride' shuttle buses. A car will give you flexibility to visit nearby attractions like Legoland, Great Windsor Park and the Thames Valley.

Marlow
Maidenhead
Henley-on-Thames
Bray
Windsor & Eton
Ascot

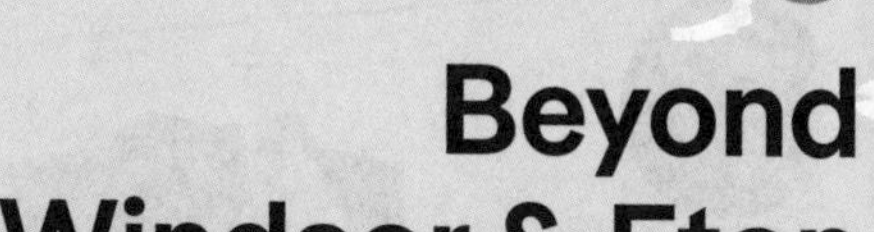

# Beyond Windsor & Eton

## The prosperous Thames Valley has historically served as a country getaway for the English elite.

This pastoral landscape within easy reach of London is peppered with picturesque villages, historic houses and world-class places to dine.

The riverside village of Bray is the country's undisputed gastronomic capital. Heading upstream, the Thames Valley is home to a cluster of well-heeled commuter towns – Taplow, Maidenhead, Marlow and Henley-on-Thames – notable for historic streets, lush river frontages with photo-worthy bridges, plus good shopping and dining. Picturesque Marlow and Henley put on a proper rowing regatta, while Taplow reportedly has 30 resident multi-millionaires. Maidenhead is a little sprawling, but a beautiful spot to wander by the Thames to the lock by Ray Mill Island. Beyond Windsor, Ascot royal race-meet in June draws an international crowd.

### TOP TIP

London's Elizabeth Line will drop you in Taplow or Maidenhead on its way to Reading, making this region all the more accessible from the capital.

**Maidenhead and the River Thames**

## WHY I LOVE THE THAMES VALLEY

**Tasmin Waby**, Lonely Planet writer

I've travelled to a few famous rivers – the Danube, Hudson, Neva, Mekong and Murray – but the Thames is one I got to know more intimately, living on my narrowboat.

The waterfront mansions and grand stone bridges along the river tell a story of wealth that you don't see from the motorway. Constantly changing as it winds its way from Lechlade to London, near here we pass wide water meadows and forested cliffs alive with bird song.

For a lover of local history (statues, unusual street names, graveyards) the riverside villages of the Thames Valley are fascinating to explore. And I love that this is also a gastronomic hot spot.

DIMPLEPATEL/SHUTTERSTOCK ©

Bray

## Berkshire's Michelin Dining Hot Spot

LOOSEN YOUR BELT IN BRAY

For an otherwise quiet riverside village of just over 9000, Bray has some serious gastronomic clout. Just 5 miles upstream from Windsor, Bray is home to three Michelin-starred restaurants. Two of them – of a total of eight in England – have three stars. Beyond these internationally renowned dining destinations, at which meals come with an accompanying price tag, you'll find a clutch of other outstanding restaurants and gastropubs to dine at in Bray.

Head of the table here is, of course, Heston Blumenthal's revered **Fat Duck**, long recognised as one of the world's most innovative restaurants. You'll need to book ahead if you want to dine here.

Bray's other triple-starred treat, **The Waterside Inn**, is run by Alain Roux, son of iconic French gastronome Michel (of London's legendary La Gavroche fame). It was first awarded three stars in 1985 and has held on to the accolade ever since. And as the name suggests, its dining room makes the most of the view of the Thames.

### WHERE TO EAT BEYOND BRAY

**Fego**
Popular neighbourhood cafe in Marlow doing breakfast and lunch including vegan and low-GI menus. £

**The Hand & Flowers**
Rustic two-Michelin starred pub in Marlow run by a husband-and-wife team. £££

**Seasonality**
Small produce store in Maidenhead doing exceptional take-away boxes plus in-house dining. ££

Also boasting a star from the Guide Rouge is another Blumenthal establishment, the **Hind's Head**. Heston's other Bray outfit, the **Crown at Bray**, does excellent British pub food in an atmospheric 16th-century inn.

Finally, lovers of Italian food (is that everyone?) will revel in the regional cooking and local produce at celebrity chef Giancarlo Caldesi's **Caldesi in Campagna.**

## Experiences on the Thames

A RIVER RUNS THROUGH IT

Along the Thames' 185-mile journey from a field in the Cotswolds to the North Sea, one of its most dramatic sites is the unmistakable towers, turrets and battlements of Windsor Castle. Did you know the Thames also powers the royal household? Almost half its energy comes from hydroelectric turbines at Romney Weir.

If you want to get out on the Thames to say hello to the swans and their fluffy grey cygnets, head to **John Logie** on the Windsor riverfront to hire a rowboat for an hour or three. Looking for something more relaxing? Cruise upstream on a skippered **Thames Charters'** motorboat, taking lunch overlooking the water at **Boulters Lock at the Boathouse**. For a scenic cruise downstream to the Runnymede, book a **French Brothers** river trip.

Anglers fish the Thames for perch, pike, barbel, chub and carp. To join them you'll need an English rod-fishing licence, plus a day ticket from a local fishing club because these river banks are all privately owned. However, you can fish anywhere between Staines Bridge and Teddington for free.

This is the only river in Europe to have a walking trail along its entire length. Stretch your legs, and get to know the Thames a little better, tackling the two-day, 22-mile section of the Thames Path from Windsory to Henley-on-Thames, overnighting in Marlow. Trains run direct back to London from both.

### BEST PLACES TO STAY NEAR THE THAMES

In a region rich with incredible luxury accommodation, you might find some of the most memorable places to stay are the quirky B&Bs or family-friendly campsites you discover.

**Embers, Henley**
In a riverside field, this summer-months-only campsite is perfect for free-range parents. Book tent pitch or a basic bell tent with air beds and a fire basket. £

**River Arts Club**
A quirky, art-filled homestead on the banks of the Thames in Maidenhead, this popular B&B-style hotel oozes with character. ££

**Shillingridge**
Is this even camping? Stay in one of two luxury safari lodges in Marlow, each sleeping six people. You get freestanding bathtubs, a wood-burning stove and options to carbon offset. £££

### GETTING AROUND

Driving is the most time efficient way to get from A to B in the Thames Valley even if roads can sometimes get congested and parking can be a challenge.

All of these towns are well connected with direct routes to London by train and bus. However, moving between riverside towns requires a patchwork of trains, buses and walking.

The Thames Path makes long-distance walks (or cycling) an attractive transport plan, if you have the time. Unsurprisingly the best way to visit these villages beyond Windsor is via a boat, although that's not entirely practical for many visitors.

# THE CHILTERN HILLS

The Chiltern Hills is a 324-sq-mile Area of Outstanding Natural Beauty dotted with historic houses, often on large well-maintained estates. Many of these are open to the public to meander in woodlands carpeted with bluebells in the spring. Spy red kites flying above.

Its townships range from small hamlets with a village green, local pub and red postbox, to larger centres ringed with identikit houses. Flintstone is a feature of these hills: you'll see it in historic churches, cottages and garden walls.

This is a popular cycling region, with groups of lycra-clad cyclists training on country roads (drivers: be warned). The 87-mile Ridgeway walking and mountain-biking route, considered Britain's oldest road, runs along the spine of the Chilterns.

### TOP TIP

Trains service Oxfordshire, Buckinghamshire and Hertfordshire on five different train lines fanning out from London, mostly circumnavigating the wooded hills of the Chilterns.

**Chiltern Hills**

PAUL MAGUIRE/SHUTTERSTOCK ©

**HIGHLIGHTS**
**1** Stowe Gardens

**SIGHTS**
**2** Bekonscot Model Village
**3** Bletchley Park
**4** Cliveden House
**5** Hellfire Caves
**6** Hughenden Manor
**7** Roald Dahl Museum
**8** Stonor House
**9** Waddesdon Manor

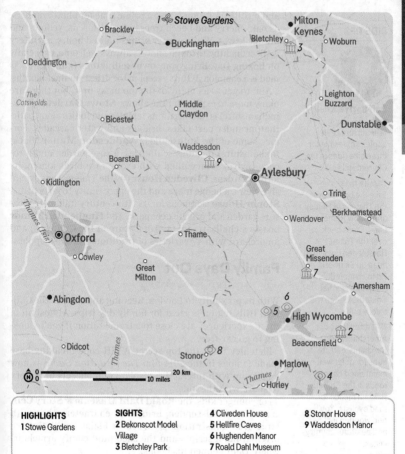

## The Gardens of England

HEDGEROWS, WOODLANDS & VIBRANT FLOWERS

Spending a day wandering the large estates of grand houses (some of which remain in private hands; others are managed by charities like the National Trust or English Heritage) is a popular local past time. In late spring and summer these vast gardens are awash with colourful flowers, butterflies

### WHERE TO EAT IN THE CHILTERNS

**The Chequers, Fingest**
Low-beamed pub with a large beer garden, serving quality British fare including a Sunday roast. **££**

**Bistro at The Boathouse, Henley**
Enjoy familiar dishes with sweeping Thames views from the deck. **££**

**Artichoke**
Award-winning restaurant in Amersham known for its innovative cuisine. **£££**

## RIDE TIPS

**Duff Battye**, a heavy metal PR, local fireman and keen angler, shares his top three bike rides in the Chiltern Hills.

**Family ride**
Take the bridge over the Thames at Henley and follow Remenham Lane. Cross back over the Thames at Hambleden Lock then head up Skirmett Rd to Hambleden – a quintessential Chilterns village with a cosy pub.

**Head for the hills**
Amersham and Berkhamstead are hubs for quiet well-maintained country roads in the Chiltern Hills – a mecca for road cyclists. You'll find wooded inclines and beautiful country vistas.

**A long-distance cycle**
The Chilterns Cycleway is a well-signposted 170-mile circular ride almost exclusively on roads. Wallingford is a good base to set off.

and birdlife. Autumn is also a prime time for photographers, as oak, cherry and beech trees blaze with reds, yellows and orange leaves. While winter brings limited hours, a wintery walk crunching through snow is always welcome, especially on Boxing Day. Bring your own wellingtons (gum boots) as mud is a common fixture, except in the driest summer months.

Aim to get to as many of the top picks first, but there are many more to explore if time allows. **Stowe Gardens** (Buckinghamshire) is famous for its temples and follies along paths that meander past lakes, bridges and water cascades. Former home of the Rothschilds, **Waddesdon Manor** (Buckinghamshire) includes sculptures, a rose garden and a rococo-revival aviary filled with exotic rare birds among its formal gardens. **Cliveden House** (by the Thames) has expansive views, a hedge maze and the opportunity to go boating. **Stonor House** is famous for its 17th-century Italianate pleasure garden and private deer park. And **Hughenden Manor** boasts a chalk stream (a rare feature of the Chilterns) and an orchard with 47 varieties of traditional English apples.

## Family Days Out

HOW TO ENTERTAIN YOUR KIDS

With its proximity to London, Reading and Oxford, the Chiltern Hills region is great for family day trips. Almost all of these experiences are close to a train station if you're looking to go car-free.

Bletchley Park, the top-secret WWII code-breaking base made famous in the 2014 film *The Imitation Game*, is now a museum with interactive displays and buckets of history to share with the kids.

For younger kids, the **Roald Dahl Museum & Story Centre** in Great Missenden, brings his characters alive with large-scale illustrations by Quentin Blake. You'll also see original manuscripts and the shed (and comfy armchair) where Dahl penned his books.

Another hit with kids of all ages, **Bekonscot Model Village** in Beaconsfield depicts seven different worlds from England in the 1930s. See castles, docklands, coal mines, villages and even a cricket green plus loads of humorous details like escaped convicts and punny shop names.

Fans of Stranger Things might be inspired to visit the **Hellfire Caves**, an underground labyrinth and home to the original Hellfire Club otherwise known as Francis Dashwood's Order of the Friars of St Francis of Wycombe. Here the a

### WHERE TO STAY IN THE CHILTERNS

**Stag & Huntsman**
Dog-friendly country pub in Hambleden with cosy rooms and self-catering cottages in a picture-perfect village. **££**

**Bel & the Dragon**
Comfy beds and stylish interiors in this 16th-century Tudor inn in Wendover's town centre. **££**

**St Michael's Manor Hotel**
A 500-year-old manor in St Albans, with hushed carpeted corridors and 30 elegant rooms of varying sizes. **£££**

secret society of wealthy English gentlemen (with powerful connections including US founding father, Benjamin Franklin) regularly met up.

## Walking & Cycling in the Chilterns

OVER HILLS & THROUGH WOODS

There are dozens of walks and bike rides to tackle in the Chilterns, from short 1.5-mile strolls to multiday trails through historic market towns, large country estates and tracts of ancient woodlands.

Most established walks are waymarked, or you'll see well-trodden paths over styles and across farmers' fields. Blogs with walk notes are plentiful, but nothing beats a reputable guidebook with maps. It's also worth noting, the controversial HS2 (High Speed Rail) project is under construction so some long-established walking routes have been 'temporarily' closed (ie, for many years) with unavoidable detours, which makes local advice and up-to-date maps essential. The Ordnance Survey Maps app is excellent, although a phone is obviously not ideal as your *only* navigation device.

The most famous walk – or bike ride – in the Chiltern Hills is **The Ridgeway**, which can be tackled in smaller sections (there are 22 miles that are not yet open to cyclists). Shorter walks range from easy to moderately challenging, so take your pick depending on the season.

The **Coombe Hill & Chequers Trail** near Ellesborough gives walkers a glimpse of the Prime Minister's country pile, Chequers. In spring, **Hughenden estate** (p219) is a top spot to walk in woods carpeted with bluebells.

**FOR ORGANIC GARDENERS**

o you love touring beautiful gardens and want to know more about sustainable garden management? Book a tour of **Highgrove** (p193), the pride and joy of His Majesty the King.

**CHALK STREAMS**

The world has fewer than 300 chalk streams – beautiful nutrient-rich environments that support rare species like brown trout, grayling, water voles and kingfishers – and most are in England.

The Chilterns, standing atop a chalk escarpment northwest of London, is home to nine chalk streams but these clear-water babbling brooks are threatened by the effects of climate change.

From lower rainfall to invasive species and pollution, there are serious challenges to face. That's where the Chilterns Streams Project has stepped into the breach. As well as conservation and education, they run guided walks along the Chess River and publish further walks near Berkhamstead and in the Misbourne Valley.

### GETTING AROUND

Travelling around the region really is easiest by car. However, if you're walking or cycling between towns, ditching the car means you don't need to circle back to your starting point.

One thing to note about the Chilterns: different private railway operators run each service, which may mean catching one line out and another back. Check which companies you're travelling with before buying a return ticket.

Similarly, buses that run between villages, and around larger towns, are also run by different coach companies. To plan a journey around the Chiltern Hills by train and bus, check out a transport website like www.traveline.info which includes all the different operators.

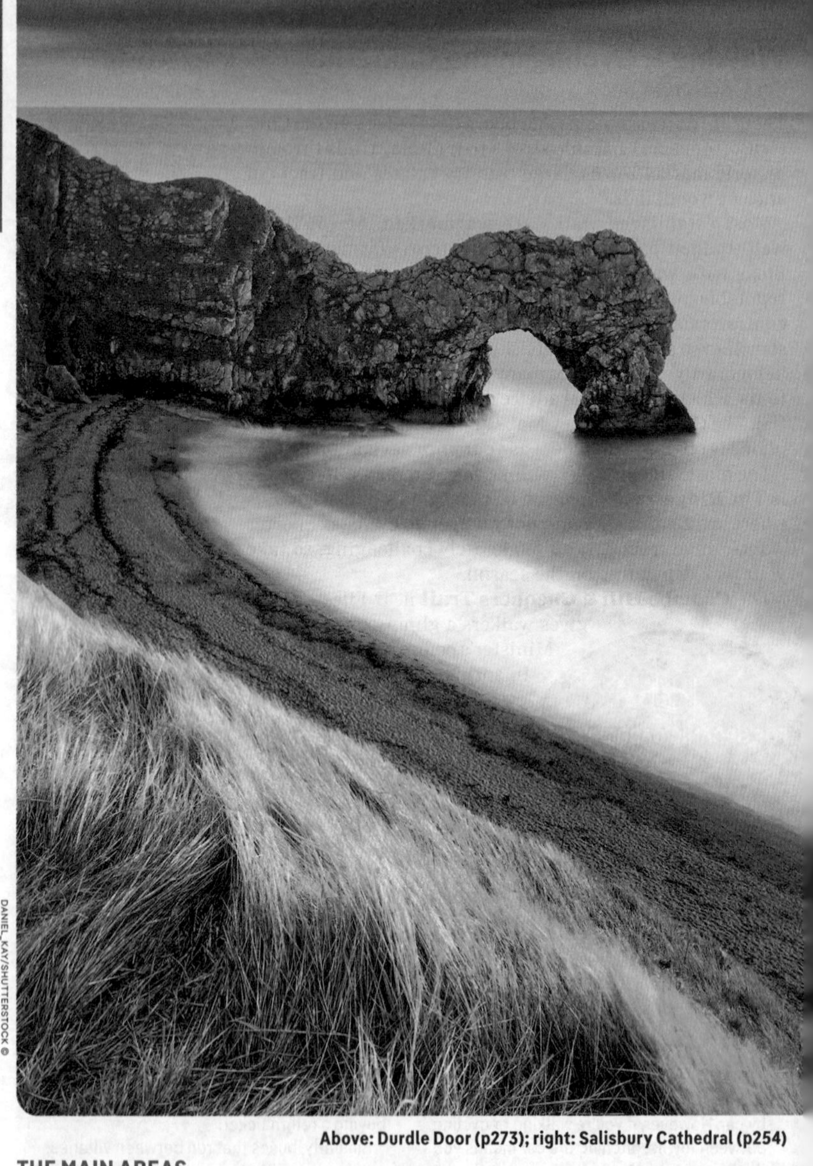

DANIEL_KAY/SHUTTERSTOCK ©

**Above: Durdle Door (p273); right: Salisbury Cathedral (p254)**

## THE MAIN AREAS

# BRISTOL, BATH & SOUTHWEST ENGLAND

## THE HEART OF THE WEST COUNTRY

Contemporary cities rub shoulders with the ancient past in this region of pastoral landscapes and wild coastlines.

The ancient and the urbane come together in this region more markedly than anywhere else in the country. Seismic shifts in the earth's history can be read in the rocks all along Dorset's coast, where fossilised sea creatures regularly crumble out of the cliffs. Some of the earliest monuments in Britain were built on the flat fields of Wiltshire, while the nation's oldest skeleton was found in a cave in the Mendip Hills (the Mendips). And in between all this is the finesse of Bath and the flurry of Bristol, and the historic cities and towns of Salisbury, Wells, Glastonbury and Sherborne, all ecclesiastical powerhouses at one time or another.

Just 12 miles separate Bath from Bristol, but they are like chalk and Cheddar cheese. Harmonious Bath prospered due to its thermal springs, which attracted the Romans and then the Georgians. Now, people come to admire their legacies: a well-preserved spa complex and terraces of beautiful Palladian buildings. Vibrant, innovative Bristol, the much more cosmopolitan of the two, grew wealthy from the trade that funnelled through its harbour. Once rundown and neglected, the Harbourside has been revitalised, epitomising the city's ambitious development of recent years.

Beyond the cities, the landscape varies widely, from the hedgerows and hummocked hills of sleepy rural Somerset to Dorset's dramatic coastline, battered by the sea and ravaged by the wind and rain.



**EXMOOR** Hiking and wildlife. **p248**

**SALISBURY** A superlative cathedral. **p253**

**BOURNEMOUTH** Seaside resort. **p261**

**DORCHESTER** Historic sights and Thomas Hardy. **p267**

**JURASSIC COAST** A 185-million-year-old coastline. **p270**

# Find Your Way

This region combines the best of the big-hitting cities of Bristol and Bath with the windswept moors, rolling plains, rugged coastlines and ancient landscapes that make the counties of Somerset, Dorset and Wiltshire famous.

### CAR

Driving is the best way of properly exploring the area. Indeed, with the exception of Stonehenge, you'll need your own vehicle if you want to visit the array of archaeological sights and stately homes, or venture into the wilder parts of Exmoor.

### BUS

Buses offer a decent alternative way of exploring main towns. First Bus, Morebus, Stagecoach and Salisbury Reds cover most of Somerset, Dorset and, to a lesser extent, Wiltshire. First Bus run some of its services onto Exmoor and along the Jurassic Coast in open-top buses.

### TRAIN

It's straightforward enough to reach the region's main hubs by train from London and the Midlands, including Bristol, Bath, Salisbury and Dorchester. You can also chug between them – and many local stations – fairly easily, although not always on direct services.

**Bristol, p226**

The southwest's capital of cool, Bristol blends thought-provoking museums with the best street art in the country, and it has an innovative food scene to boot.

**Exmoor, p248**

From moody moors to clifftop trails, thatched-cottage villages to its eponymous ponies, Exmoor is a wild and enchanting region.

**Jurassic Coast, p270**

Millions of years of history in the making, with fossil-filled cliffs, hauntingly beautiful shingle beaches and the chance to kayak among strangely shaped rock formations.

**ath, p233**
s golden terraces look ‹e they've been plucked raight out of a Jane usten novel, although ath's superbly preserved oman baths almost steal e show.

**The Mendips, p242**
Journey from one extreme to the other in bucolic rolling hills, where a craggy gorge snakes high above show caves glistening with stalagmites and stalactites.

**Wells, p239**
The Bishops of Bath and Wells have left a lasting legacy in the smallest city in England, which draws visitors for its sensational cathedral.

**Glastonbury, p245**
A ruined abbey, a mystical hill, plenty of folklore and witchcraft, and a rather famous music festival.

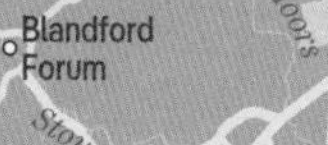


**Salisbury, p253**
England's finest cathedral? You decide. And while you're here, there's also stately homes and standing stones – Stonehenge lies just north of the city.

**Dorchester, p267**
Dorset's county town, best known for its many Thomas Hardy associations, is also home to a superlative Iron Age fort and a unique Roman townhouse.

**Bournemouth, p261**
With miles of sandy beach, a traditional pier and buoyant nightlife, Bournemouth has all the ingredients for a fun-filled break beside the seaside.

# Plan Your Time

Split your time between the historic cities of Bath, Bristol and Salisbury and the rest of rural Somerset, Dorset and Wiltshire. Admire Georgian architecture and 21st-century street art, Neolithic landscapes and two beautifully rugged coastlines.

FUKEZ84/SHUTTERSTOCK ©

Roman Baths, Bath (p236)

## A Tale of Two Cities

- Immerse yourself in **Bath** (p233), England's most beautiful Georgian city. Start at the superbly presented **Roman Baths** (p236), then follow in Jane Austen's footsteps on a **walking tour** (p235) around its set-piece architecture. Relax with a soak in **Thermae Bath Spa** (p236) or a drink in one of Bath's **olde-worlde pubs** (p237).

- Make the short hop to **Bristol** (p226) to admire the groundbreaking work of Isambard Kingdom Brunel: **Brunel's SS Great Britain** (p228) in the city's regenerated Harbourside charts the ship's story. Then hop between the cafes of chic **Clifton** (p232) or take a **street-art tour** (p230) of grittier Stokes Croft.

## SEASONAL HIGHLIGHTS

Spring is the ideal time to explore this rural region, with wildflowers in bloom, and foals and fawns on Exmoor. Coastal hikes are a good way to lose the crowds in summer.

**JANUARY**

The upcoming cider season is celebrated at **Wassail**, a Twelfth Night ceremony held across Somerset.

**MAY**

Some of the best street artists in the world descend on Bristol for **Upfest**, adding new murals throughout the month.

**JUNE**

Thousands of festivalgoers descend on **Glastonbury** for the country's biggest music festival.



GORDON HULMES TRAVEL/ALAMY STOCK PHOTO ©, MATT CARDY/STRINGER/GETTY IMAGES ©, AMY LAUGHINGHOUSE/SHUTTERSTOCK ©

## Four Days to Travel Around

- Start in the historic city of **Salisbury** (p253), best known for its towering **cathedral** (p254), where you can see one of the last remaining copies of Magna Carta.

- Visit nearby **Stonehenge** (p257) for an enigmatic introduction to ancient England, then head west for more stories from the past in **Glastonbury** (p245), where King Arthur was allegedly buried. Glastonbury's ruined **abbey** (p246) once looked like **Wells Cathedral** (p238); there's only 7 miles between the two to make your own comparisons.

- Continue on to **Exmoor** (p248), where windswept walks and rare wildlife await.

## If You Have More Time

- Visit **Salisbury** (p253) and **Stonehenge** (p257) before heading south to the Victorian seaside resort of **Bournemouth** (p261), with its unbroken stretch of golden beach. Head out into Poole Habour to spot squirrels on **Brownsea Island** (p265) en route to the **Jurassic Coast** (p270), England's only natural World Heritage Site, where you can climb to the top of **Portland Bill lighthouse** (p273) and join a **fossil walk** (p274) in Lyme Regis.

- Drive north to **Bristol** (p226) and **Bath** (p233), stopping off in **Wells** (p239) to visit its cathedral and to take a walk along the clifftops of nearby **Cheddar Gorge** (p243).

**AUGUST**

**Bournemouth Beach** beckons during the height of summer. There are quieter stretches either side of town.

**SEPTEMBER**

People dress up in their Regency finest and parade through Bath as part of the city's **Jane Austen Festival**.

**OCTOBER**

**Exmoor** is awash with the russet colours of autumn. Hear the calls of rutting stags on a red-deer safari.

**NOVEMBER**

Winter storms wash fossils out of the cliffs at **Lyme Regis** and **Charmouth**. See if you discover an ancient ammonite.

IAN WOOLCOCK/SHUTTERSTOCK ©, CHIPPICS/SHUTTERSTOCK ©, PHIL WOOLLEY/SHUTTERSTOCK ©, GOLDSITHNEY/SHUTTERSTOCK ©

Bristol

# BRISTOL

Bristol is a city that's well and truly on the rise. Disused warehouses have been reimagined as art galleries and museums, old cargo containers now host restaurants serving Modern British dishes with a West Country lilt, and a world-class street-art scene adds colour and spice.

The city's harbour has always dictated its fortunes. In the 18th century, Bristol was the busiest port outside of London, fuelled by the Transatlantic Slave Trade, in which Africans were enslaved, shipped to the New World and bartered for sugar, tobacco and rum. Today, the revitalised Harbourside is home to the M Shed museum, which takes an honest look at this tragic story, as well as Isambard Kingdom Brunel's crowd-drawing *SS Great Britain*.

Brunel's legacy lives on in Clifton too, where his suspension bridge spans the River Avon. Georgian and gentrified, Clifton provides a counterbalance to Stokes Croft, the fiercely independent neighbourhood where you'll find some of the city's best murals.

## TOP TIP

There are several walking tours that zoom in on a specific aspect of Bristol's history or way of thinking: learn about the city's dark past on a Transatlantic Slavery Walk with Bristol Walks and Tours or find out more about its contemporary culture on a street-art tour with Where the Wall.

**Clifton Suspension Bridge (p232)**

**HIGHLIGHTS**
**1** Bristol Lido
**2** Brunel's SS Great Britain
**3** M Shed

**SIGHTS**
**4** Clifton Arcade
**5** Clifton Observatory & Camera Obscura
**6** Clifton Suspension Bridge
**7** Clifton Suspension Bridge Visitor Centre
**8** Royal York Crescent
**9** Underfall Yard
**10** We the Curious

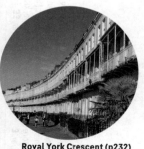

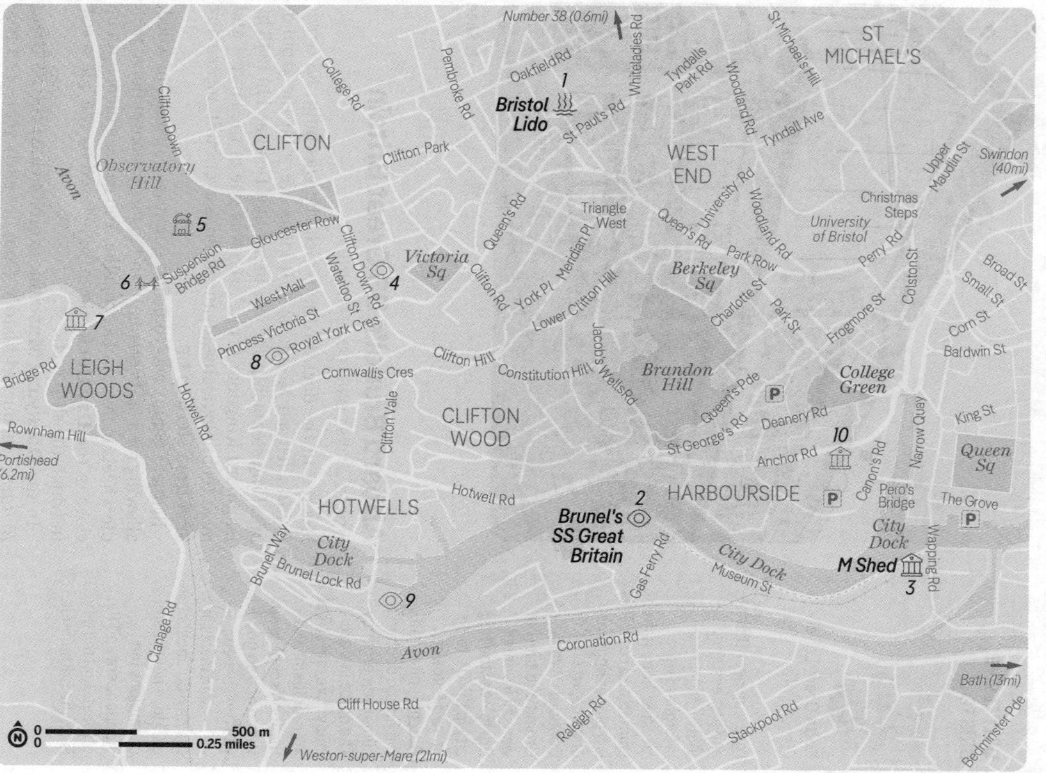


**Royal York Crescent (p232)**

**WHY I LOVE BRISTOL**

**Keith Drew**, Lonely Planet writer

I grew up near Bristol and just assumed that all big cities in England were creative, honest, free-spirited and cool. This is a pioneering kind of place, where the Concorde, Wallace & Gromit and trip-hop were all invented. Bristol was the first city in the UK to be named European Green Capital and the first to declare a climate emergency. The museums are innovative, the street art is brilliant, and the food scene is so varied and so good you'll wish there were more meals in the day. But most of all, I love how Bristol champions the independent and the offbeat. And the city is all the better for it.

JOALACERDA/SHUTTERSTOCK ©

M Shed

## Aboard Brunel's SS Great Britain

WORLD'S FIRST GREAT OCEAN LINER

Moored in the dockyard in which she was built, *SS Great Britain* (closed Mondays) still looks every bit the ground-breaking steamship she was in her day. Designed in 1843 by Isambard Kingdom Brunel, she was one of the largest and most technologically-advanced ships ever built, measuring 98m from stern to tip.

Brunel's genius was to use wrought iron instead of wood, allowing for a far bigger hull, and to forego conventional paddle wheels in favour of a propeller. You can see them both up close in the **Dry Dock**, cleverly enclosed by the 'glass sea' in which the ship rests.

In the **Dockyard Museum**, exhibits chart the *SS Great Britain*'s chequered history, from her early years as a passenger liner to her later, less glorious service as a quarantine ship and coal hulk. She was finally scuttled in the Falkland

### WHERE TO STAY IN BRISTOL

**YHA Bristol**
Riverside in the centre of town, this converted red-brick grain store has an excellent cafe-bar. **£**

**Artists Residence**
Georgian townhouse with a range of industrial-chic rooms, a cafe, kitchen and lounge bar. **££**

**Number 38**
Upmarket B&B with sweeping city views from contemporary rooms on the edge of the Downs. **£££**

Islands, where she lay rusting for nearly 40 years before being towed back to Bristol in 1970.

Following her immaculate restoration, you can really feel what life was like on board: the sound of babies crying fills the crowded steerage accommodation, while the smell of shaving cream wafts from the barber's in the plusher first-class cabins. Up on deck, **Go Aloft!** (over 9s only) to climb 25m up the rigging.

On the harbourside, **Being Brunel** presents a wealth of artefacts in a balanced look at the great engineer's life – as an innovator, artist and workaholic – and his lasting legacy.

## Discover the Essence of Bristol at M Shed

BRISTOL'S PAST, PRESENT, PEOPLE & PLACES

In many ways, the absorbing M Shed museum (closed most Mondays) epitomises Bristol. It has brought life to an old transit shed in the regenerated Harbourside area, and its creatively assembled memorabilia celebrates not just the city's famous people and places but also its unsung quarters and the everyday folk who have helped make Bristol what it is today.

**Bristol Places** focuses on the city's communities and includes mosaics from a Roman villa discovered in Brislington and an old Anderson shelter from Sea Mills – Bristol was heavily bombed during WWII. **Bristol People** champions household names, such as Aardman Animations (responsible for Wallace & Gromit) and trip-hop collective Massive Attack, alongside local graffiti artists, social workers and disability activists, while **Bristol Life** looks at what it means to be Bristolian.

The city's integral role in the Transatlantic Slave Trade is recognised in a searing display that also shows just how much the profits helped shape Bristol's landscape. While its reputation as the capital of street art is highlighted with works from Andy Council and Banksy; the latter's *Grim Reaper* stencil was controversially removed from the side of a nightclub boat in order to hang at the M Shed.

The cranes, steam train and boats that were used for work on the docks form part of M Shed's outdoor exhibitions and are occasionally open for rides.

### BEST LIVE MUSIC VENUES IN BRISTOL

**Louisiana**
This Grade II-listed pub has an impressive track record of breaking the next big indie band.

**Fleece**
A former sheep-trading market, Bristol's largest independent venue runs daily gigs and club nights.

**Thekla**
The hull of a converted German cargo ship makes an unusual venue for club brands and DJs.

**St George's Bristol**
This former church provides outstanding acoustics for classical concerts, folk bands and jazz sets.

**Bristol Beacon**
This charity-run concert venue, the largest in the southwest, regularly hosts big-name acts.

### WHERE TO EAT IN BRISTOL

**St Nicholas Markets**
St Nick's' food stalls offer everything from pie and mash to Japanese dumplings. £

**Pasta Ripiena**
Stellar stuffed-pasta dishes: handmade, wrapped in front of you and all deeply flavoured and delicious. ££

**Riverstation**
Light-filled waterfront locale serving rich Modern European cuisine in its restaurant and less-formal bar. ££

## STREET ART WALKING TOUR

Bristol has pioneered the street-art scene in Britain since the 1980s. This walk begins on Park St with one of the most famous pieces by Banksy, the anonymous Bristolian artist whose distinctive stencilled style and provocative works have earned him worldwide notoriety: **1 Well Hung Lover**, satirically painted on the side of a sexual-health clinic in 2006, is a rare surviving example of his early work in Bristol. Head down Park St and across the centre onto Quay St, where Nick Walker's bowler-hatted **2 Vanda**l pours paint down the side of a 10-storey building; the adjoining **3 Untitled mural of cranes** is part of Mariusz Waras' M-City project. Continuing onto Nelson St, you can't miss **4 See No Evil**, displaying Bristol artist Inkie's swirling style, or the huge, lumberjack-shirted **5 WolfBoy** by Aryz. Turn left onto Bridewell St, then right, and walk along the Haymarket to St James Barton roundabout, known locally as the Bearpit. Heading under the 51°02 apartment block leads to countercultural Stokes Croft and the **6 Full Moon pub**, its exterior covered with an astrological mural by Bristol artist Cheba. Carry on up to the junction with City Rd, where **7 Yellow Face Lady** looks more colourful than ever after a repaint by Stinkfish in 2021. Backtrack slightly and head up Hillgrove St to find Phlegm's **8 Tsunami of Roses** breaking across the house on the corner with Jamaica St. Turning right here takes you past the **9 PRSC Outdoor Gallery**, which belongs to a local community-action group, and back on to Stokes Croft and Banksy's iconic **10 Mild Mild West**. The mural, which adorns the wall of the Canteen, was voted by residents as the city's favourite alternative landmark.

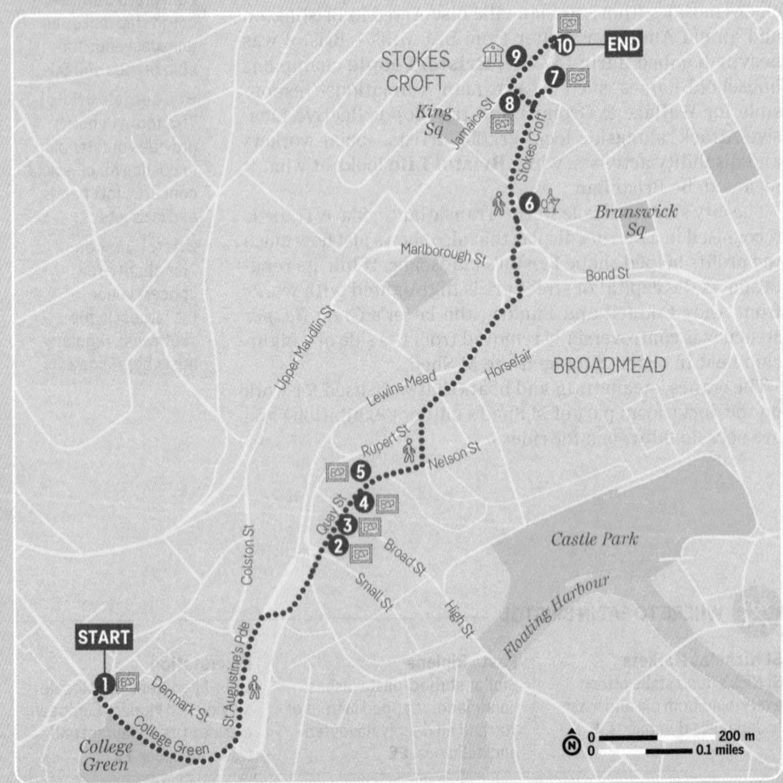

**Bristol Harbour Festival**

## Underfall Yard: Powering the Floating Harbour

HISTORIC WORKING BOATYARD

In its heyday, Bristol's docks were the second largest in the country. Low tide stranded the ships on the quayside, though, so a system of lock gates and sluices was designed to keep them afloat when the River Avon receded. The so-called Floating Harbour opened in 1809, and by the 1880s it was being operated entirely out of Underfall Yard.

The yard is home to some of the last surviving Victorian dock workshops in the world. You can nose around the boatbuilders and rigging companies still working here, and learn more about the Floating Harbour's workings in the **visitor centre** and adjoining **Pump Room**, which was still helping to power the whole network as recently as 2010.

### BRISTOL'S BEST FESTIVALS

**Bristol Harbour Festival**
July celebration of the city's music and arts, with hundreds of boats filling the harbour.

**Bristol International Balloon Fiesta**
Over 100 hot air balloons above Ashton Court in August, with spectacular musical event Nightglow.

**Upfest**
The largest festival of urban art in Europe redecorates the buildings of Bedminster each May.

**Love Saves the Day**
Music festival hosting a suitably eclectic range of bands at Ashton Court in early June.

### BRUNEL'S OTHER LANDMARKS

Isambard Kingdom Brunel's effect on Bristol was immense. He helped design the **Floating Harbour** and also built the **Great Western Railway** (which connected the city with London), **Temple Meads** train station, and the renowned **Clifton Suspension Bridge** (p232).

### WHERE TO EAT IN BRISTOL

**BOX-E**
Beautifully-cooked seasonal British dishes in a pair of old shipping containers on Wapping Wharf. **££**

**Canteen**
Community-run venue sums up Bristol's alternative character: sustainable vegetarian food, local suppliers and fair prices. **£**

**Primrose Café**
A Clifton institution, spilling out onto Boyce's Ave. Belt-busting brunches, imaginative lunches and towering cakes. **£**

**I LIVE HERE: WHERE TO DRINK IN BRISTOL**

**Michael Wiper**, one of the founders of Bristol-based craft brewery Wiper and True, shares his recommendations for the best places to drink in Bristol.

**Plough**
Easton's finest. It's so easy to accidentally spend five hours in this joy-filled pub.

**KASK**
Excellent wines in an impossibly chic but unfussy setting. Great cheese selection, too.

**Miners Arms**
A proper old-school boozer in St Werburghs, with cask ale galore.

**Old Market Assembly**
Right around the corner from our brewery and taproom, this is a go-to spot for late nights, live music and dancing.

## Hands-on Science Centre

Echoing Bristol's creative character, the interactive exhibits at **We The Curious** (closed at the time of research following a fire, but re-opening was imminent) let you walk through a tornado, produce your own animated film and explore intriguing questions such as why do rainbows make people happy. It is also home to an excellent 3D Planetarium. We The Curious is due to reopen in 2023; in the meantime, look out for staff staging scientific activities across the city.

## Exploring Clifton

The well-heeled suburb of Clifton is like a little enclave of Bath in Bristol, with terraces of fine Georgian townhouses that were in part built thanks to the area's brief spell as a summer spa.

Start with a few laps of **Bristol Lido**, a beautifully restored public bath that dates back to 1849, followed by breakfast at its poolside restaurant. Then head west to **Royal York Crescent**, one of the longest in Europe, which has fine views down towards Harbourside. Work your way through the quirky shops on neighbouring Princess Victoria St and the Mall, and in the Victorian **Clifton Arcade** across the main road, before settling down for a flat white or a bite to eat on Boyce's Ave.

On the open expanse of the nearby Downs, **Clifton Observatory** is home to a **camera obscura** and the **Giant's Cave**, a viewpoint at the end of a tunnel that enjoys a dizzying outlook over Avon Gorge from halfway down the cliff face.

Spanning the river below you is Isambard Kingdom Brunel's awe-inspiring **Clifton Suspension Bridge**, which took 33 years to build and wasn't finished until 1864, several years after Brunel's death. Walk across the bridge to the visitor centre on the other side to discover the story behind this remarkable feat of engineering. The free summer Weekend Bridge Tours are excellent, as are the Hard Hat Tours, which explore the cleverly designed vaults inside one of the massive supporting towers.

**GETTING AROUND**

If you're driving to Bristol, it's best to use one of the four Park & Rides on the city fringes. Traffic should improve with the introduction of Bristol's Clean Air Zone, which covers the city centre and part of Clifton, although parking is still expensive and it can be difficult to find a space. With the possible exception of hilly Clifton, it is easy to get around on foot and by bike – Bristol is the UK's first Cycling City, and there is a good network of cycling lanes and routes, plus several bike-rental companies in the city centre. Ferries provide a fun, and often quicker way of moving around the harbour.

# BATH

Bath is beautiful. Its rows of harmonious townhouses and famous crescents still exude the elegance that helped make this the most fashionable city in Georgian Britain.

But Bath wouldn't be Bath if it weren't for its thermal springs. Legend has it that King Bladud founded the city some 2800 years ago when his pigs were cured of leprosy by wallowing in its mineral-rich mud. The springs were revered by the local Celtic population, the Romans turned them into a social sanctuary, and the great and the good of Georgian high society flocked here to take in the city's restorative waters.

It was during this 18th-century heyday that Bath acquired its most celebrated buildings, all of them made from golden Bath stone. Over 5000 of the city's buildings are now listed by Historic England, part of the reason why Bath is the only city in Britain that's a Unesco World Heritage site in its entirety.

## TOP TIP

Bath's main sights are split between the centre, at the bottom of town, where you'll find the Roman Baths and Bath Abbey, and the Georgian showstoppers are an uphill walk away in the northern part of the city. It can make sense to split your sightseeing itinerary in the same way.

**Pulteney Bridge (p235)**

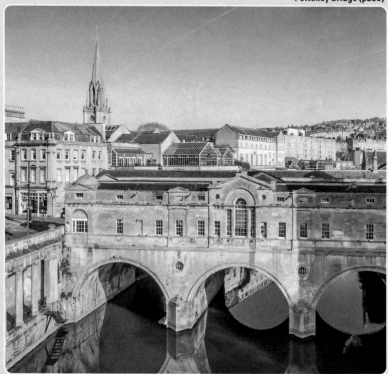

**HIGHLIGHTS**
**1** Bath Abbey
**2** Roman Baths

**SIGHTS**
**3** Jane Austen Centre
**4** Mary Shelley's House of Frankenstein
**5** Pump Room
**6** Sydney Gardens

**ACTIVITIES & TOURS**
**7** Bath Abbey Tower Tours
**8** Walk to the View

**SHOPPING**
**9** Mr B's Emporium
**10** Topping & Company

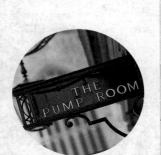

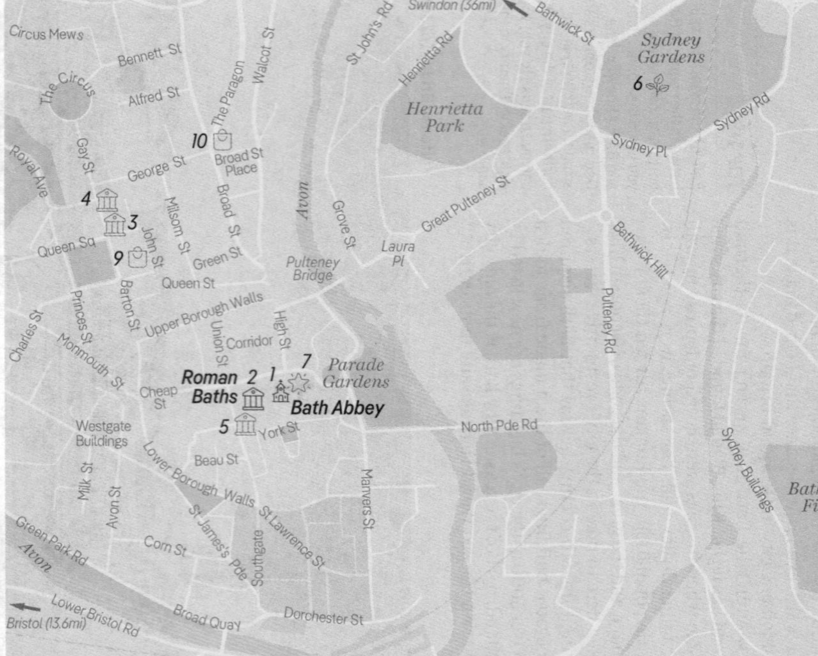


Pump Room (p238)

## WALKING TOUR OF GEORGIAN BATH

Bath owes much of its architectural harmony to the work of two men: John Wood the Elder and his son, John Wood the Younger, who between them designed many of the city's signature buildings. This walk starts with Bath's Georgian glory: the **1 Royal Crescent**. Completed in 1775, this grand sweep of townhouses was designed by John Wood the Younger; **2 No 1 Royal Crescent** (closed Mondays) offers an intriguing insight into what 18th-century life was like in one of the grandest homes in Bath.

Walking east along Brock St leads to **3 the Circus**, considered to be John Wood the Elder's finest work. This ring of elegant townhouses is full of symbology – its diameter is the same as Stonehenge (see p255) and the frieze that curves around its facades is decorated with Masonic emblems. Just around the corner, off Bennett St, John Wood the Younger's **4 Assembly Rooms** were the hub of Georgian Bath's social scene; the Upper Rooms, as they were known, regularly appear in Jane Austen's novels (see p235).

Retrace your steps and walk down Gay St to **5 Queen Square**, built in 1728 to demonstrate the talents of its architect, John Wood the Elder. From here, head east along New Bond St to **6 Pulteney Bridge**, a Palladian beauty designed by Robert Adams in 1773 and one of only four bridges in the world to have shops lining both sides.

Cross the bridge and continue along **7 Great Pulteney Street**, Bath's longest and widest Georgian street, to the **8 Holburne Museum**. You'll find works here by the 18th-century painter Thomas Gainsborough, who lived on the Circus. The impressive exterior of this Grade I–listed building starred as Lady Danbury's residence in the Netflix Regency romp Bridgerton.

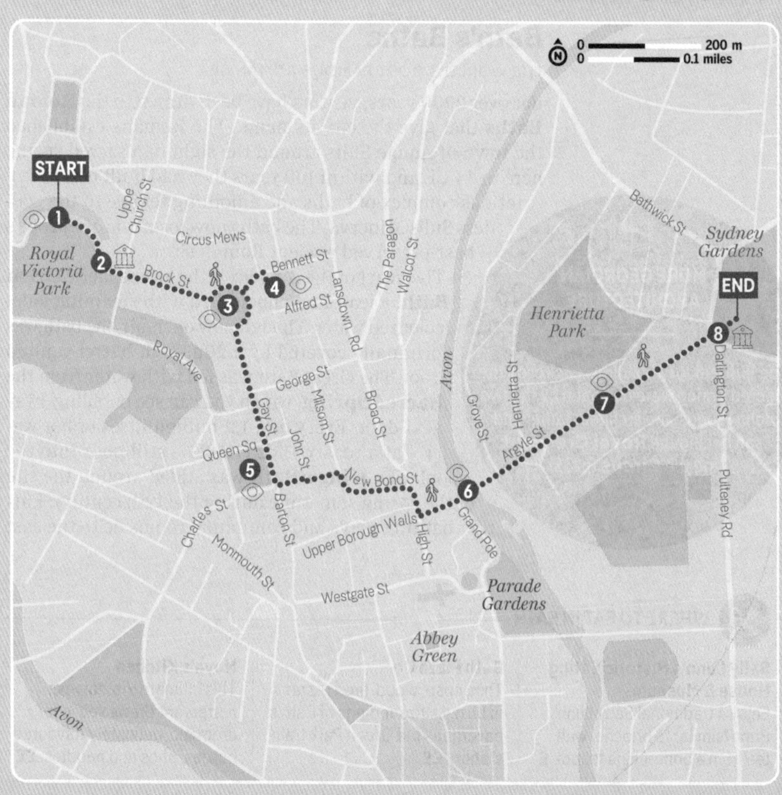

**TAKING THE WATERS**

You can put the healing powers of Bath's thermal waters to the test at the cutting-edge **Thermae Bath Spa**, the only one of its kind in the UK. The complex is split into the New Royal Bath (no under-16s) and, in a separate building across the aptly named Hot Bath St, the more intimate Cross Bath (no under-12s). The highlight is the rooftop pool in the main building, with its superb views over the city.

AROUNDWORLD/SHUTTERSTOCK ©

**Roman Baths**

## Bath's Baths

THE WORLD'S MOST FAMOUS ROMAN SPA

For over 2000 years, visitors have been drawn to the **Roman Baths** that give the city its name. The Romans established the town of Aquae Sulis around the sight of a sacred spring here in 44 CE and within 100 years they had built this ostentatious complex of baths and adjoining temple to the goddess Sulis Minerva. The baths now form one of Europe's best-preserved ancient Roman sites.

The heart of the complex is the atmospheric **Great Bath**, a lead-lined pool filled with steaming jade-coloured water. Though now open-air, the bath was originally covered by a 20m-high barrel-vaulted roof. The Great Bath was fed with water from the **Sacred Spring**, which you can see bubbling away next door. Every day, 1.2 million litres of hot water – at a toasty 46°C (115°F) – still pour into the pool. The **King's Bath** was added around the site of the spring sometime during the 12th century. Further bathing pools and communal rooms lie to the east

**MORE GEORGIAN ARCHITECTURE**

The 18th-century buildings encircling the Sacred Spring were designed by the two John Woods, the architect father and son behind the **Royal Crescent** and the **Circus** (p235).

**WHERE TO EAT IN BATH**

**Sally Lunn's Historic Eating House & Museum**
Enjoy a traditional Sally Lunn Bunn (similar to brioche) with tea from a bone-china teapot. £

**Bath Pizza Co**
Thin, crisp, wood-fired pizzas in buzzy surroundings of Bath's cavernous old Green Park train station. ££

**Noya's Kitchen**
This intimate Vietnamese restaurant draws you in for aromatic, delicately flavoured curries, phos and noodles. ££

and west of the Great Bath, with excavated sections revealing the hypocaust system that heated the spa.

An engaging **museum** connects the baths, displaying artefacts discovered on the site, while clever digital reconstructions instil the complex with the social atmosphere of Roman times. Look out for the intriguing 'curse tablets', and the gilded bronze head among the remains of the **Temple of Sulis Minerva**.

You can try a sip of the mineral-rich waters – believed to have curative powers – at the fountain on your way out.

## Medieval Masterpiece

MEMORIAL-FILLED ABBEY WITH TOWER VIEWS

Looming above the city centre, **Bath Abbey** was built between 1499 and 1616, making it the last great medieval church raised in England. The abbey's walls are filled with memorials, but its most striking feature is the west facade, where angels climb up and down stone ladders, commemorating a dream of the founder, Bishop Oliver King. The abbey is one of the few places in Bath where you can get a bird's-eye view of the city: on the **Tower Tour**, you'll climb up through the bell chamber and above the vaulted ceiling to gaze across the rooftops and down into the Roman Baths.

## Make a Beeline for the Skyline

A WALK WITH GLORIOUS VIEWS

One of the (many) great things about Bath is its natural setting, enclosed on three sides by the River Avon and with wooded hills rising up from the city's southern edge. You can get a taste of this countryside, and great views of Bath's honeyed houses, on the short walk up to Bathwick Fields; from the centre, it's a mile along North Pde, over the Kennet & Avon Canal and up into open meadows for grandstand views back over the historic skyline. The route is signposted as the latter half of the National Trust's scenic **Walk to the View** trail.

## Literary Bath

REVISITING AUSTEN AND SHELLEY

Bath's most famous resident, Jane Austen lived in the city from 1801 to 1806. Two of her novels, *Northanger Abbey* and *Persuasion*, are set here, providing a sharply observed insight into Regency Bath and its busy social calendar of public break-

### BEST PLACES TO DRINK IN BATH

**Colonna & Small's**
The champion baristas at this stripped-back, pioneering coffeehouse serve their own roasts alongside rare blends.

**Bell Inn**
The community-owned Bell is a real-ale pub known for its strong schedule of live music.

**Star Inn**
This labyrinthine pub of oak-panelled cubbyholes has been serving locals since 1759.

**Bath Distillery Gin Bar**
Cosy bar with 230 gins. Try a Gin Austen, or share a teapot of gin among friends.

**Opium**
Hunt out this quirky boudoir bar, which is tucked into the vaults below Grove St.

**Circus**
This bistro has a mouthwatering menu of seasonal Modern European dishes in a charming setting. **££**

**OAK**
Imaginative vegetarian restaurant bringing vegetables and grains to a whole new level of deliciousness. **£**

**Menu Gordon Jones**
Surprise dining (you get what you're given) showcasing experimental ingredients and eye-catching presentation. **£££**

## BEST PLACES TO STAY IN BATH

**Bath YHA**
Split across an Italianate mansion and modern annexes, this impressive hostel has huge rooms. **£**

**Brooks**
A scattering of antiques meet plush modern furnishings at this smoothly comfy, fairly central bolthole. **££**

**Grays**
A beautiful blend of modern, pared-down design and family treasures. All boutique rooms are individual. **££**

**Queensberry**
Stylish Queensberry is Bath's luxury choice. Heritage roots meet snazzy furnishings in these Georgian townhouses. **£££**

JIM MONK/ALAMY STOCK PHOTO ©

Sydney Gardens

fasts and lavish costumed balls. Austen was a regular visitor to the Grade I-listed **Pump Room**, built in 1795, and was particularly fond of the expansive **Sydney Gardens**, a popular place for Bath's high society to promenade; the Austen family lived at nearby 4 Sydney Pl (which can now be rented through Airbnb). Austen aficionados should visit the **Jane Austen Centre** on Gay St, where costumed actors guide you round exhibits covering the author's life and works.

A few doors further up Gay St, **Mary Shelley's House of Frankenstein** is a nod to the fact that Shelley wrote what is widely regarded as the world's first science fiction novel in Bath, in a house at 5 Abbey Churchyard, where the Pump Room now stands. This immersive museum blends history and horror in a chilling look at the author's tragic life and the culture that's grown up around her creation.

You can pick up a copy of *Frankenstein* or a Jane Austen novel at one of Bath's excellent bookshops. There's a vast collection of titles at **Topping & Company** on York St, and personable book-buying advice at **Mr B's Emporium** on nearby St John St.

## GETTING AROUND

If you're driving into Bath, it's best to use one of the main car parks on the southern edge of the city, on Corn St, Manvers St or Dorchester St, where the bus station and Bath Spa train station are both located. Bath is a compact and very walkable city, with most of its sights lying in the centre or a just few hundred yards to the north, although it's a bit of an uphill climb to reach the Circus and the Royal Crescent. The Mayor of Bath's Corps of Honorary Guides run free two-hour walking tours of the city and, in summer, the Pulteney Estate.

# WELLS

Wells is England's smallest city, and only qualifies for the title thanks to a magnificent medieval cathedral, an early Gothic masterpiece that sits plumb in the centre of the city.

Ancient Britons worshipped the springs that give Wells its name, as did the Romans, and the remains of a Saxon church founded by Ine, King of Wessex, lie within the cathedral grounds. A town grew up around the church, much in the same way that the cathedral has become the focal point for modern-day Wells, drawing visitors for its unusual architecture and world-class choir. The city's other great ecclesiastical sight, the grand Bishop's Palace, is just a few minutes' walk away.

You could easily spend a couple of days in Wells, taking in the cathedral and the palace and using the city, with its medieval buildings and cobbled streets, as an atmospheric base for exploring the limestone caves and gorges around nearby Cheddar (p243).

## TOP TIP

Time your visit to coincide with Wells' popular market (Wednesday and Saturday) located, unsurprisingly, on Market Place, the heart of the city for nine centuries. There's a great selection of stalls selling goodies such as regional cider and Somerset charcuterie; look out, too, for the quirky paintings of Wells by local artist Mike Jackson.

**Wells and its cathedral (p240)**

NIGEL JARVIS/SHUTTERSTOCK ©

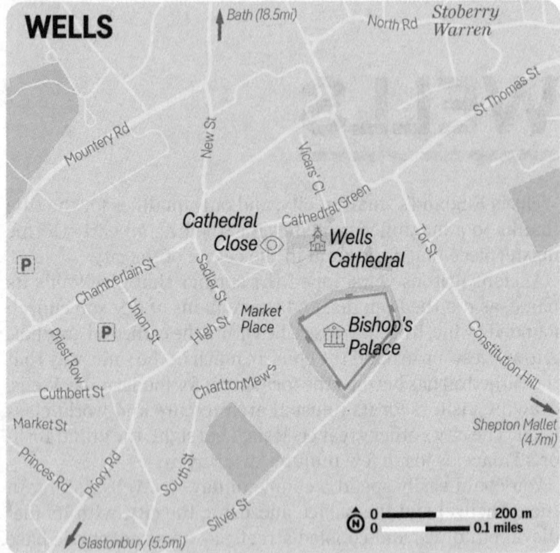

## BEST PLACES TO EAT IN WELLS

**Good Earth**
Long-running veggie cafe and wholefood stalls serving towering quiches, colourful salads and filling-packed jacket potatoes. £

**BDW's Bar & Grill**
Enjoy tasty burgers, hot dogs, chicken wings and dirty fries at this amiable grill. £

**Greek Taverna at The Sun**
This pub gets packed for its authentic, well-seasoned Greek dishes. The *loukanika* (sausages) are excellent. ££

**Nosh-stalgia**
Cafe-restaurant with quirky decor and beautifully-cooked Modern British dishes. Good value, given the quality. ££

## Stained Glass & Scissor Arches

ARCHITECTURALLY INTERESTING CATHEDRAL

Wells may be tiny, but the **cathedral** that makes this a city is gargantuan. To fully grasp its size and setting, surrounded by one of the largest **cathedral closes** in England, duck through medieval Brown's Gatehouse on Sadler St. As first impressions go, it's a corker: the cathedral standing proud across its green, its theatrical west front a riot of 300 or so carved figures.

The cathedral was built in stages between 1175 and 1508, and was the first example in the country of the early English Gothic style. It is the seat of the Bishop of Bath and Wells, who still live and work in the nearby Bishop's Palace.

Highlights inside include the famous **scissor arches**, an ingenious architectural solution to counter the subsidence of the central tower; the splendid 14th-century stained-glass **Jesse Window**; and the octagonal **Chapter House**, where the clergy used to meet to discuss the issues of the day. Time your wanderings so that you're in the north transept to see the astronomical clock in action – every 15 minutes, two little knights rush out to joust in a routine they've been diligently performing since 1392.

Try to catch evensong, when the cathedral's highly regarded choir are in full voice.

## WHERE TO STAY IN WELLS

**Ancient Gatehouse Hotel**
Old hostelry built right into the cathedral's west gate; has its own well-respected Italian restaurant. ££

**No 23**
Sweet, redbrick Victorian B&B run by affable owner. Smart, contemporary rooms with home comforts. ££

**Beryl Country House**
Grand gabled mansion with beautiful blast of English eccentricity. Every inch has an antique atmosphere. £££

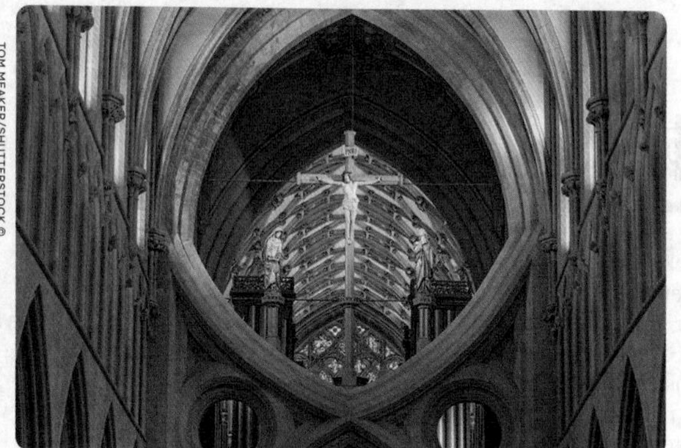

Wells Cathedral

# Bishops & Vicars

HOW BISHOPS SHAPED THE CITY

The bishops of Bath and Wells were a powerful lot. They once held great sway with national events in England and had a significant effect on life in Wells.

Bishop Jocelin effectively ran the country during Henry III's minority (Henry was only nine when he came to power) and had the moat-ringed **Bishop's Palace** built, just behind the cathedral, in 1206. It's purportedly the oldest inhabited building in England. You can look inside the palace's state rooms and the bishop's private chapel, and wander among the ruins of the great hall, but it's the shady gardens that are the real draw. The natural springs, after which Wells is named, bubble up in the palace's grounds in a series of tranquil pools.

Heading through the archway near the palace, known as the **Bishop's Eye**, leads into **Market Place**. Around 1350 Bishop Bekynton built the conduit here and ran pipes to it from the wells in the palace gardens so the town folk could have access to clean water. He also built **Penniless Porch**, in the northern corner of the square, as a shelter for beggars asking for alms.

If you pass through the porch, walk in front of the cathedral and turn right, you'll come to picturesque **Vicars' Close**. These two symmetrical rows of chimney-topped houses were built by Bishop Ralph in the mid-1300s to house the Vicars' Choral (the men of the cathedral choir) and are still inhabited by their successors today.

### ALL ABOARD THE STRAWBERRY LINE

Wells is located on the route of the Strawberry Line Path, a cycleway and footpath that traces the track beds of an old disused railway for 30 miles across the middle of Somerset. The path will eventually link Shepton Mallet with Clevedon, passing over the Mendip Hills and through Cheddar.

The path follows the route of the Cheddar Valley Line, better known as the 'Strawberry Line', thanks to vast amounts of locally grown strawberries its trains carried from villages outside of Wells to Yatton for transporting to London.

So far, small sections from Wells to Dulcote (towards Shepton Mallet) and Haybridge (towards Clevedon) are completed, as well as the cycleway section from Cheddar to Yatton.

### GETTING AROUND

The main central car parks in Wells – on Union St and next to the Bus & Coach Station – are just a few minutes' walk up the High St from Wells Cathedral and the Bishop's Palace.

All the chief sights are closely gathered together at the eastern end of the city – by far the best way to get around is on foot.

The Mendips

# THE MENDIPS

A limestone ridge of rocky slopes, deep gorges and spectacular caves, the windswept Mendip Hills, commonly called The Mendips, extend for 22 miles northwest of Wells. Cheddar Gorge is the natural draw, in more ways than one, and is home not only to the most famous karst feature in the country but also the region's most spectacular show caves.

The Mendips were formed around 280 million years ago, and remains from their caves show they sheltered woolly mammoths and prehistoric hunter-gatherers. A Mesolithic skeleton found in the entrance to Gough's Cave – known as Cheddar Man and now on display in the Natural History Museum in London – dates from around 10,000 years ago, when Britain was attached to continental Europe.

The plateau is a great place to spot wildlife. At Cheddar Gorge alone, you've got a good chance of seeing feral goats, Soay sheep, peregrine falcons and horseshoe bats, which roost in the far reaches of the caves.

## TOP TIP

At Cheddar Gorge, it's not possible to pay to only see Gough's Cave; the entry fee also includes smaller Cox's Cave, a museum of prehistory, the so-called Jacob's Ladder and a lookout tower. So try to give yourself at least half a day to make the most of your money.

Cheddar Gorge

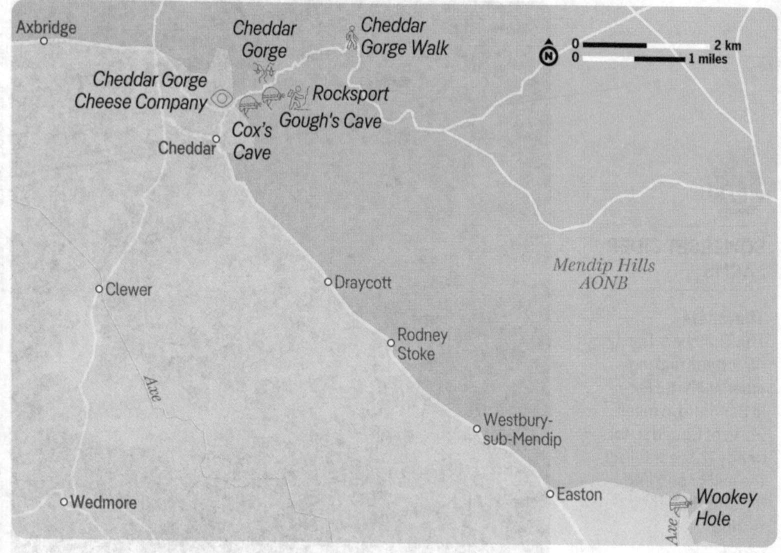


## Gorges, Caves & Clifftop Paths

ABOVE AND BELOW CHEDDAR GORGE

Carved out by glacial meltwater during the last Ice Age, **Cheddar Gorge** is England's deepest natural canyon, in places towering nearly 140m above the narrow, twisting road. It is riddled with subterranean caverns, most impressively at **Gough's Cave**, where toffee-coloured calcite has drip-drip-dripped into spectacular displays of stalactites and stalagmites. Further down the road, **Cox's Cave** has been given a multimedia 'Dreamhunters' exhibit to try and pep up its much smaller and simpler caverns in comparison.

Above ground, the undoubted highlight is the National Trust's **Cheddar Gorge Walk**, which loops around the clifftops for 3 miles. There are great views down into the gorge and across craggy formations, such as The Pinnacles and Wind Rock. Adventurous types can try rock-climbing with **Rocksport** (it also runs caving expeditions further into Gough's Cave).

Cheddar is also home to one of the nation's favourite cheeses, produced here since the 12th century. At the **Cheddar Gorge Cheese Company** watch the cheese-making process and buy some souvenirs, including Cheddar that's been aged in Gough's Cave.

Rock-climbing, Cheddar Gorge

Wookey Hole

**SOMERSET CIDER FARMS**

**Thatchers**
The Thatchers family have been making cider at Myrtle Farm in Sandford, 6 miles north of Cheddar, for nearly 120 years. Tour the mill or pop into its farm shop for a tasting.

**Wilkins**
Venture up to Roger Wilkins' rustic cider barn in Mudgley, 7 miles south of Cheddar, for traditional farmhouse cider straight from the barrel.

**Burrow Hill**
Famous for its cider brandy, Burrow Hill, 17.5 miles south of Glastonbury, specialises in single-variety sparkling ciders made from Kingston Black and Stoke Red apples.

## Meet the Witch of Wookey Hole

ODD-SHAPED CAVE FORMATIONS

The River Axe has gouged out a network of deep limestone caverns at Wookey Hole. Guided tours detail their striking stalagmites and stalactites, one of which is the legendary Witch of Wookey Hole who, it's said, was turned to stone by a local priest. Some of the magic is tarnished by the additional beyond-kitsch attractions, ranging from animatronic dinosaurs to pirate adventure golf.

**GETTING AROUND**

The lay-bys at the lower end of Cheddar Gorge are useful for admiring its towering cliffs close-up, but visiting the caves from here requires walking along the pavementless road; you're better off parking in the car parks just beyond the caves, or in the cheaper council car park on nearby Cliff St. Cyclists can reach Wookey Hole on National Cycle Network Route 3 from Wells.

London

Glastonbury

# GLASTONBURY

Glastonbury is unlike anywhere else in the South West – or in England, for that matter. Famous for the musical mud-fest that is Glastonbury Festival, the town has a much more ancient history. Its focal abbey, now lying in dramatic ruins, was allegedly the site of the first church in Britain, while Glastonbury Tor, rising above town to the southeast, has a long and mysterious pagan past. Both are linked to the legends of the Holy Grail and King Arthur.

This potent mix has attracted a blend of New Age mystics, spiritual healers, white witches and heathens, who over the last few decades, have settled in alongside the open-minded long-term residents. The upshot is an easy-going, accommodating community – and one of the most curious High Streets in the country, tinkling with crystals and thick with the smell of smouldering incense.

## TOP TIP

Unless you're actually going to Glastonbury Festival (early June), it's best to visit the town itself at another time of the year, as accommodation gets booked up months in advance (and at much higher prices than usual), and the area can get clogged with traffic heading to or from the event.

**Glastonbury Abbey (p246)**

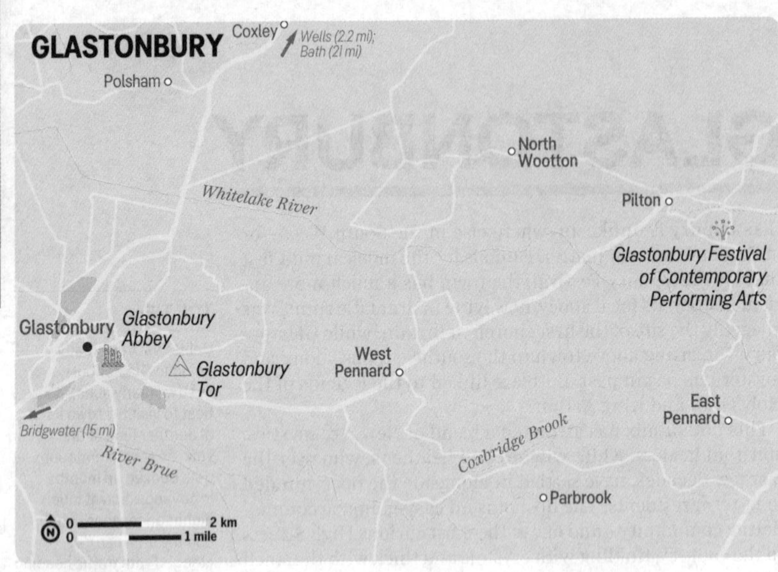


## BEST PLACES TO EAT IN GLASTONBURY

**Rainbow's End**
Psychedelic cafe with all-veggie food (homity pies, bountiful salads), potted plants and a laid-back vibe. £

**Old Tannery**
Buzzy, informal restaurant doing fine burgers and grilled mains. Good selection of locally-brewed beers. ££

**Queen of Cups**
West Country produce gets Middle Eastern makeover at this imaginative restaurant serving tasty small plates. ££

## The Cradle of English Christianity

ABBEY RUINS AND ARTHURIAN LEGENDS

The scattered ruins of **Glastonbury Abbey** give little hint that this was once one of England's great seats of ecclesiastical power. It was torn down following Henry VIII's dissolution of the monasteries in 1539, and the last abbot, Richard Whiting, was hung, drawn and quartered on the tor.

Like everything in Glastonbury, the abbey's history is wrapped up in myth and conjecture. Today's striking ruins include the shell of the **Lady Chapel**, which was built on the supposed site of the first church in England, a wattle construction allegedly founded by Joseph of Arimathea in 63 CE. The abbey's famous holy thorn tree is also said to have sprung from Joseph's staff.

In the 12th century monks uncovered a cross in the abbey's grounds inscribed *Hic iacet sepultus inclitus rex arturius in insula avalonia*, or 'Here lies buried the renowned King Arthur in the Isle of Avalon'. Inside the tomb below were two skeletons, purportedly those of Arthur and his wife Guinevere. The ensuing influx of pilgrims enabled the building of

## WHERE TO STAY IN GLASTONBURY

**Covenstead**
Wacky, wonderful B&B. Themed bedrooms and a riot of oddities – mock skeletons, draped python skins – downstairs. ££

**Glastonbury Townhouse**
Red-brick Edwardian townhouse with a clutch of quiet rooms, comfy beds and a contemporary vibe. ££

**Magdalene House**
Artfully decorated B&B, previously a school run by nuns. Tall, light rooms in soft tones. ££

the **Great Church**; enough of it remains, including the signature transept piers, to appreciate its immense size. Arthur and Guinevere's bones were reburied in a grand marble tomb inside the new church in 1278, but were lost following the abbey's destruction.

## Tall Tales & Fine Views

MYSTERIOUS TOWER-TOPPED HILL

Topped by the ruined tower of 15th-century St Michael's Church, the famed hump of **Glastonbury Tor** is visible for miles around.

In ancient times, when the area around Glastonbury was under water for much of the year, the tor would have appeared as an island, wreathed in mist and cut off by marshes. No wonder, then, that it's become the focal point for a wealth of local lore. According to legend, the tor is both the home of Gwyn ap Nudd, Lord of the Underworld and King of the Faeries; and Avalon, the place where King Arthur was taken after being mortally wounded in battle and now lies sleeping until his country calls again.

Invisible ley lines are said to converge here as well, and whether you can feel their energy on the half-hour climb up here or not, it is well worth it for the extensive views, which reach down into Dorset on a clear day.

## Festival Fever

MAJESTICAL MUSIC EXTRAVAGANZA

Glastonbury is synonymous with the enormous, alternative, frequently mud-soaked festival that sprawls across Worthy Farm in nearby Pilton each June. If you can bag a ticket to the Glastonbury Festival of Contemporary Performing Arts, then you're in for a wild ride of music, theatre, cabaret and carnival. Watching high-profile acts headlining the Pyramid Stage is just part of the Glastonbury experience. This is a mini city of arenas and ideas. Pop into eco-conscious Green Fields, visit Unfairground's late-night music and art mash-up or catch big-name DJs at steampunk Arcadia.

### BEST TYPICAL GLASTONBURY EXPERIENCES

**Chalice Well**
Healing pools and sacred springs, located where Joseph of Arimathea supposedly buried the Holy Grail.

**Goddess Temple**
Dedicated to the Lady of Avalon, this temple offers elemental blessings, priestess training and retreats.

**Elestial**
The most eye-catching of several stores in town that specialise in crystals and spiritual stones.

**Star Child**
Dark, pungent one-stop shop for sacred herbs, peace candles and magical space aromas.

**Wonky Broomstick**
Purveyors of all things magical, this witchcraft shop stocks items from the wiccan world.

### GETTING AROUND

Parking is easy to find in Glastonbury, and everything of interest in the compact town is within a few minutes' walk of each other. The Tor Bus runs every half-hour from the car park next to Glastonbury Abbey to the trailhead for Glastonbury Tor, a mile or so to the east, stopping off at the Chalice Well along the way.

# EXMOOR

Exmoor is one of England's smallest national parks, but it packs a surprising diversity into its 267 sq miles: wild and windswept moors, wooded combes, scattered villages and rolling farmland – not to mention the highest sea cliffs in England.

The busy little towns of Dulverton, Dunster, Lynton and Lynmouth are great places to base yourself, offering easy access to Exmoor's wilder realms. Over two-thirds of the park lies within Somerset, with the rest in Devon (p277), although no such distinctions are made on the ground.

Exmoor was a Royal Forest until industrialist John Knight bought it in 1820, establishing a series of farms and dramatically changing the landscapes and economy of the area in the process. Designated a National Park in 1954, today's Exmoor is a largely unspoilt region, where native ponies graze on open moorland, night skies are dazzling affairs, and the 600-plus miles of footpaths and bridleways invite exploration and adventure.

### TOP TIP

Phone signal can be a rarity on the moors (you can check the likelihood of mobile coverage ahead of time at signalchecker.co.uk). Make sure you download offline maps to your phone or satnav before setting out, in case you lose service while driving to your destination.

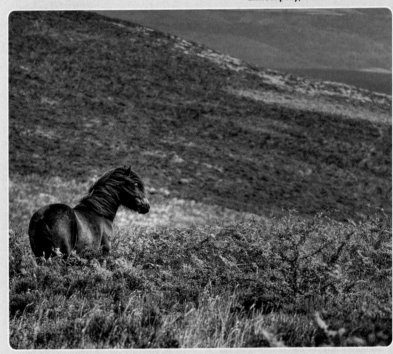

**Exmoor pony, Exmoor National Park**

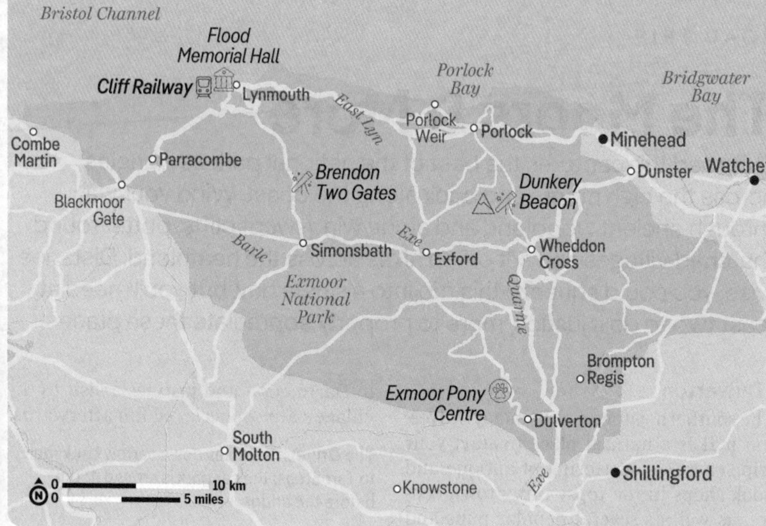


## Wild Encounters

MEET EXMOOR'S EXTRAORDINARY WILDLIFE

The varied landscapes of Exmoor are home to an abundance of wildlife. The Exmoor pony is the park's most famous species: a hardy breed of semi-feral ponies that roam freely across the moors. They're a common sight, particularly around Simonsbath, where you can often see them nibbling by the side of the road. Late spring is a good time to visit if you want to see newly born foals, while the **Exmoor Pony Festival** holds various shows, rides and pony-finding walks throughout August. A visit to the charity-run **Exmoor Pony Centre** near Dulverton offers the chance to meet these shaggy-maned animals up close.

England's only wild herd of red deer lives on Exmoor, numbering several thousand. Visit the more remote areas of the park in autumn and you'll hear the hills echoing to the bellows of rutting stags, or maybe even the crashing of antlers as two males come to blows. You can sometimes see red deer around Webbers Post, but the best chance of spotting one is on a wildlife safari, where an expert guide will take you off-road along forest tracks and over the open moors for close-up views. **Red Stag Safari** and **Exmoor Wildlife Safaris** offer half-day safaris – just remember to bring your binoculars.

### BEST PUBS ON EXMOOR

**Woods, Dulverton**
A happy marriage of characterful boozer and informal restaurant serving five-star food.

**Royal Oak, Withypool**
Traditional 18th-century pub with beamed ceilings, log fires and a selection of local gins.

**The Ship Inn (Bottom Ship), Porlock Weir**
This flagstone-floored, whitewashed pub with a harbourside beer garden.

**Tarr Farm Inn, Tarr Steps**
Lovely 17th-century inn known for its superb food, made with quality locally sourced ingredients.

### WHERE TO STAY ON EXMOOR

**Exmoor Forest Inn**
Chic, country-manor vibes at this foodie hotel, run by local farmers; tranquil setting in Simonsbath. ££

**Dunkery Beacon Country House Hotel**
Countryside vistas and an award-winning restaurant set this country hotel apart. £££

**Exmoor House**
Comfy rooms and considerate hosts lend this superior B&B in Dunster a home-away-from-home feel. ££

ROAD TRIP

# The Moors & More

This road trip captures the best of the national park as it angles across the high moors and back along the coast. Wind your way through ancient woodland and along windswept cliffs, potter round thatched villages and set off on hikes across the heathland. Distance-wise, you could squeeze this trip into a single day, but you'll need at least two to do it justice, more to properly appreciate these places.

### 1 Dulverton

The southern gateway to Exmoor, Dulverton makes a natural place to start your trip. There's a scattering of antique and book shops in the topsy-turvy town centre, as well as several popular pubs and restaurants.

**The Drive:** The shaded A396 traces the River Exe north for 8 miles to Winsford. It's a longer but quicker route than Northmoor Rd, which has some very sharp bends.

### 2 Winsford

With its thatched cottages and picturesque packhorse bridges, Winsford is the quintessential Exmoor village. A walk up nearby Winsford Hill is rewarded with views down to Dartmoor – and justifies a visit to the village's atmospheric old inn afterwards.

**The Drive:** It's 3 miles down narrow back roads to Tarr Steps; the car park is around 460m before the bridge.

### 3 Tarr Steps

Medieval Tarr Steps is the longest clapper bridge in Britain – a 55m-long string of gritstone slabs that spans the River Barle. The surrounding nature reserve is a lovely place for a walk; take your choice from a number of signposted trails.

**The Drive:** Backtrack to the B3223 and follow it for 20 miles to Lynton. The section beyond Simonsbath is one of the best drives in Exmoor, crossing open moorland dotted with wild ponies.

Lynmouth

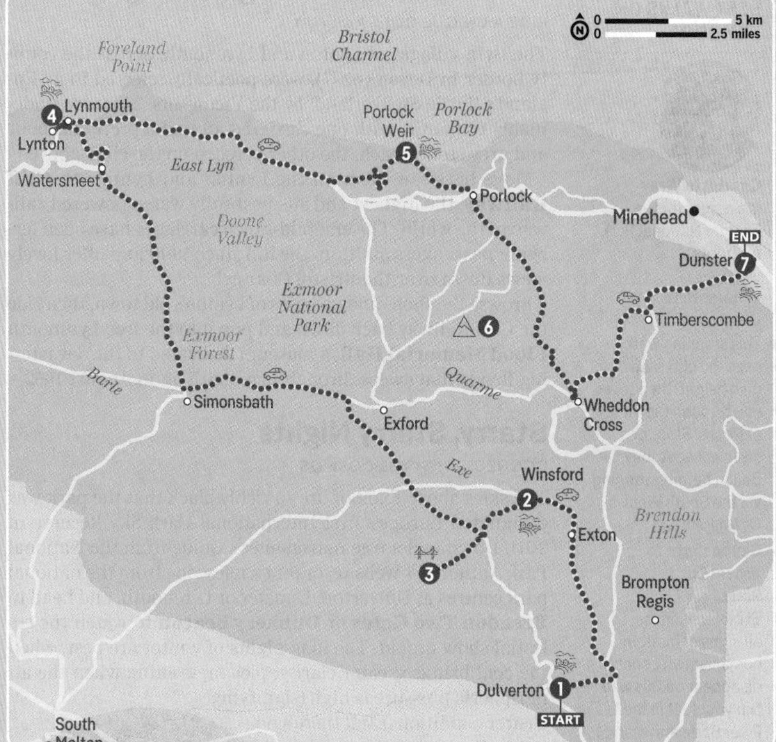


### 4 Lynton & Lynmouth

You could easily while away the day in this Victorian seaside stop, catching the funicular from harbourside Lymouth up to clifftop Lynton and soaking up the far-reaching views.

**The Drive:** Follow the A39 east, then take the cliff-hugging toll road down to Porlock for sea views glimpsed between pines.

### 5 Porlock Weir

The coastal village of Porlock Weir is centred around its tiny, tidal harbour, backed by pretty stone cottages and fronting a long, lonely foreshore.

**The Drive:** Leave the A39 just east of Porlock and climb up through wooded Crook Horn Hill to the open heathland atop Exmoor.

### 6 Dunkery Beacon

Hike up to the highest point in Somerset (519m) for sweeping, windswept views across the heather-clad moors to South Wales. The easy triangular route takes about an hour from the car park at the bottom of Dunkery Hill.

**The Drive:** To avoid backtracking, carry on driving towards Wheddon Cross and pick up the A396 down to Dunster.

### 7 Dunster

Medieval Dunster is one of Exmoor's most attractive villages, with its octagonal Yarn Market and red-stone Dunster Castle, the turreted country home of the Luttrell family for nearly 600 years.

**BEST WALKS ON EXMOOR**

**Charlotte Wray** is a ranger for the Exmoor National Park Authority.

**Lynmouth to Lee Abbey**
This stunning walk uses the cliff railway to gain height, then takes you through the Valley of Rocks. Stop for a swim at Lee Abbey Beach before returning via the South West Coast Path.

**Simonsbath to Wheal Eliza**
Part of our Exmoor Explorers series, all signs of modern human activity soon disappear on this walk. Dip your feet in the River Barle and marvel at the Iron Age hill fort Cow Castle.

**Dark Sky Discovery Trail**
Glow-in-the-dark fingerposts mark the way on this self-guided walk into the dark core of Exmoor. View constellations, planets and our own Milky Way.

## Victorian Seaside Engineering

RIDE A UNIQUE CLIFF RAILWAY

The twin villages of Lynton and Lynmouth, across the county border in Devon (p277), were poetically referred to as England's 'Little Switzerland' by the Victorians. They are undeniably romantic, with one clustered around a pretty harbour and grey stone beach, the other perched on the cliffs above.

Move between them on the Lynton and Lynmouth **Cliff Railway**, the highest and steepest fully water-powered railway in the world. The emerald-green carriages have been ferrying passengers 500ft up the hill since 1890 and offer lovely views down over the Bristol Channel.

Browse the shops and galleries of Lynton's old town, then ride the Cliff Railway back down and pop into the free Lynmouth **Flood Memorial Hall**, a museum dedicated to the devastating floods that swept through Lynmouth on 16 August 1952.

## Starry, Starry Nights

CONNECT WITH THE COSMOS

The skies above Exmoor are so richly black that the park was designated Europe's first International Dark Sky Reserve in 2011. Download a free Astronomer's Guide from the National Park Authority's website, or rent a telescope from the national park centres at Dulverton, Dunster or Lynmouth, and head to **Brendon Two Gates** or **Dunkery Beacon** to watch the celestial show unfold. The long nights of winter are best, when the cold brings greater clarity; pick an evening when the atmospheric pressure is high (signifying clearer conditions) and there's no moon. For more guidance, join one of the Dark Sky Discovery Hub's presentations or guided stargazing walks, which are held in Exford throughout the year.

**MORE ARTHURIAN TALES?**

Clifftop **Tintagel Castle** (p305) in Cornwall has been entwined with the legend of King Arthur since the 12th century, when Geoffrey of Monmouth claimed it was the place where the king was conceived.

**GETTING AROUND**

Car is by far the easiest way to explore Exmoor, but it's not the only option. The open-top Exmoor Coaster is the most useful bus service, stopping at Dunster and Porlock on its way from Minehead to Lynton. Buses connecting other areas of the park tend to be much less reliable. The best way to get around is on foot, across the bridleways of inland Exmoor (a great option for cyclists, too) or along the spectacular coastal path that runs all the way from Minehead to Lynmouth – and beyond.

# SALISBURY

Salisbury has been an important provincial city for nearly a thousand years. Its streets form an architectural timeline ranging from medieval walls and half-timbered Tudor townhouses to Georgian mansions and Victorian villas. Majestic Salisbury Cathedral takes top billing, though, bounded by the largest cathedral close in the country and capped by the tallest spire in Britain.

Nestled at the convergence of the Avon and Nadder valleys, Salisbury is a leafy city, dotted with parks and gardens and run through by five different rivers. There are plenty of artisan bakeries and art cafes to pop into while wandering its historic streets, or to pick up provisions for a walk through the city's water meadows, from where landscape artist John Constable captured the cathedral in a series of compelling paintings during the 1800s.

Within a few minutes' drive of Salisbury lie Old Sarum, the city's predecessor, and the flamboyantly decorated stately home of Wilton House.

## TOP TIP

With its flat, compact layout, riverside footpaths and easy access to the surrounding countryside, Salisbury is a great place for walking. Download a copy of the *Salisbury and Wilton Walking Map* from the Visit Wiltshire website (visitwiltshire.co.uk) for routes around the city and out to Old Sarum and Wilton House.

**Salisbury**

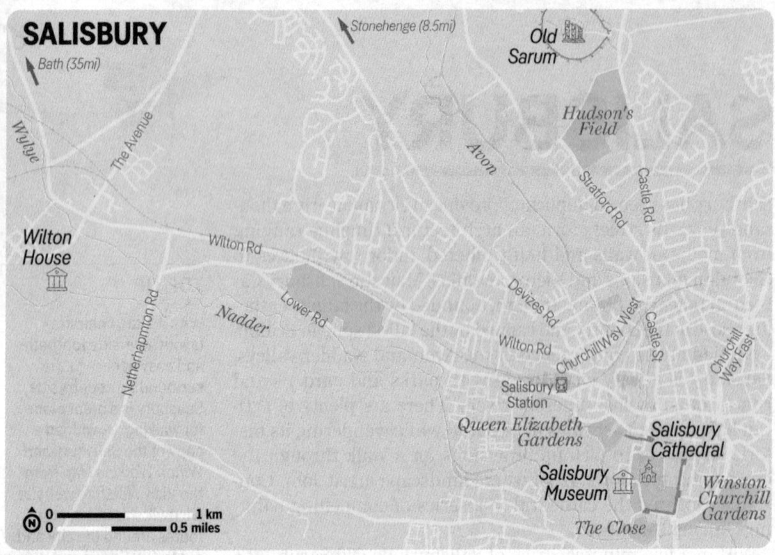


### BEST PLACES TO EAT IN SALISBURY

**Yard Café**
Coffee shop and vintage store with a trendy mishmash of benches, seats and sofas. £

**Fisherton Mill**
Art and craft gallery forms the backdrop to this laid-back cafe with a refined lunch menu. ££

**Anokaa**
Contemporary take on high-class Indian cuisine. Spices and flavours make the meat-free menu sing. ££

**Allium**
Impeccable richly flavoured dishes (pork belly, guinea fowl, cod cheeks) overlooking Market Sq. £££

## A Higher Spire & Important Parchments

ENGLAND'S TALLEST CATHEDRAL

Few of England's churches can hold a candle to the grandeur and sheer spectacle of 13th-century **Salisbury Cathedral**. This elaborate structure has pointed arches, flying buttresses and a renowned spire, and is home to one of the most important documents in the English language.

The cathedral was built between 1220 and 1258, in the early English Gothic style. In the north aisle, look out for a fascinating medieval clock, probably the oldest working timepiece in the world, dating from 1386. Outstanding statuary and tombs line the sides of the tall, narrow nave, including that of William Longespée, son of Henry II and half-brother of King John. When his tomb was excavated, a well-preserved rat was found inside Longespée's skull; intriguingly, it had died of arsenic poisoning.

Salisbury cathedral's 123m-high crowning glory, its spire, was added in the mid-14th century, and is the tallest in Britain. It weighs around 6500 tonnes and required an elaborate system of cross-bracing, scissor arches and supporting buttresses to keep it upright; look closely and you'll see the weight has buckled the four central piers of the nave.

### WHERE TO STAY IN SALISBURY

**Merchant's House Hotel**
Fifteenth-century inn where Lord Nelson stayed. Best rooms have high ceilings and exposed beams. Unlimited breakfast. ££

**Cathedral View**
Attention to detail defines this Georgian townhouse; flower displays and home-baked biscuits in elegant rooms. ££

**Chapter House**
This 800-year-old boutique beauty, with wildly wonky stairs and duck-your-head beams, has stunning rooms. £££

Head through to the **Chapter House** to see the cathedral's 1215 Magna Carta, the best preserved of just four original surviving parchments in the world. The document is part of a thought-provoking exhibition that explores its relevance today, referencing COVID-19 lockdowns and Black Lives Matter protests.

## Exhibitions of the Ancient Past

WEIGHTY FINDS FROM WILTSHIRE'S SITES

**Salisbury Museum** covers every major period in the region's history, but it's the hugely important archaeological finds in the **Wessex Gallery** that make this a must-visit, especially if you're going on to visit nearby Old Sarum and Stonehenge. Look out for the Stonehenge Archer, the bones of a man found in the ditch near the stone circle, and the similarly curled-up skeleton of the Amesbury Archer, considered the most significant Late Neolithic burial ever found in the UK.

## Step back in time at Old Sarum

THE REMNANTS OF ORIGINAL SALISBURY

The vast ramparts of Old Sarum sit on a turf-covered hill 2 miles north of the city. You can wander the grassy Iron Age defences and see the original cathedral's stone foundations. It was abandoned after just 50 years, when the monks decided to up sticks and start a new cathedral in nearby New Sarum (as Salisbury is still officially known).

## Admire Inigo Jones' Wilton House

SENSATIONAL STATELY HOME

Stately Wilton House (closed in winter), 3 miles west of Salisbury, provides an insight into the rarefied world of the British aristocracy. The home of the Earls of Pembroke since 1542, it has been expanded, improved and embellished by successive generations. Wilton was rebuilt after a fire in the mid-1600s by Inigo Jones, whose best work was done in the striking Single and Double Cube rooms, constructed in Palladian style and stuffed with the earls' superb collection of paintings (Van Dyck, Rembrandt, Tintoretto, et al).

### BEST PLACES TO DRINK IN SALISBURY

**Haunch of Venison**
Featuring wood-panelled snugs and crooked ceilings, this creaky 14th-century drinking den is packed with atmosphere.

**Craft Bar at the Salisbury Arms**
Craft beer and cider, creative cocktails, and sustenance via towering burgers and hand-cut fries.

**Tinga**
The colourful bar at this authentic Mexican restaurant does great cocktails and tequila tastings.

**Caboose**
Art Deco, speakeasy vibes at an inspired Parlour bar, a 1920s watering hole for railway engineers.

### SMELL A RAT?

The rat found in William Longespée's tomb is on display in **Salisbury Museum**, along with Bronze Age jewellery, the oldest gold coins in Britain and other notable finds from Wiltshire's prehistory.

### GETTING AROUND

The cathedral and the museum face each other within the sheltered confines of the Close, and Market Sq is less than a five-minute walk away through the North Gate. Buses run to Wilton from the city centre and the train station, most stopping right outside Wilton House. Stonehenge Tour buses call in at Old Sarum on their way back from the stone circle to Salisbury.

Lacock
Avebury
Longleat
Stonehenge
Stourhead
Salisbury

# Beyond Salisbury

## Take a trip back into England's prehistoric past, where two of the most significant stone circles in Europe stand just 25 miles apart.

Nowhere does Britain's ancient past feel so present than in the countryside that extends north of Salisbury. The rolling plains here have more mysterious stone circles and burial mounds than anywhere else in the UK.

Neolithic man was carving ceremonial banks and ditches into the Wiltshire landscape over 5500 years ago, a practice that culminated in the building of Stonehenge, England's most famous archaeological site. Mystical and ethereal, this is a place that teases and tantalises the imagination, leaving more questions than answers.

Although it lacks the dramatic trilithons, the massive stone circle across Salisbury Plain at Avebury is just as rewarding to visit. It's bigger than Stonehenge and easier to access up close.

**TOP TIP**

National Trust members get free entry to Stonehenge, Stourhead, Lacock Abbey and Avebury Manor, plus free parking in Lacock village and Avebury.

**Avebury Stone Circle (p260)**

DENIS CRAPHAN/SHUTTERSTOCK ©

**PRACTICALITIES**

adult/concession/child £20/£18/£12

Summer season: Mon-Sun 9:30-19:00
Winter season: Mon-Sun 9:30-17:00

**english-heritage.org.uk/visit/places/stonehenge**

TOP SIGHT

# Stonehenge

Stonehenge is the most famous prehistoric monument in Europe. This compelling ring of monolithic stones has attracted a steady stream of pilgrims, tourists and New Age travellers for the last 5000 years. But despite countless theories about the site's purpose, from a sacrificial centre to an astronomical clock, no one knows exactly why Ancient Britons expended so much time and effort on its construction.

### Visitor Centre

To make some sense of what you're about to see, it pays to start at the visitor centre. Engaging audiovisual displays plot the site's development and show where and how Stonehenge fits in within the landscape – and, most importantly, the movement of the sun.

The exhibition includes finds such as antler picks and arrowheads, and the strikingly lifelike model of the face of a Neolithic man who was buried in a long barrow nearby. The highlight, however, is a 360-degree projection of Stonehenge, allowing you to experience the changing seasons (including the midsummer sunrise) from 'inside' the circle.

### Stone Circle

The building of Stonehenge as we know it today was a process that lasted over 1000 years. The first phase started around 3000 BCE, when the outer circular bank and ditch were

**DID YOU KNOW?**

Stonehenge isn't a henge, which is formed when a bank encloses a ditch; at Stonehenge, it is the other way around.

Significant finds in the landscape around Stonehenge include the Amesbury Archer (see p253), whose grave contained the oldest gold objects ever found in Britain.

**STONE CIRCLE EXPERIENCE**

To really appreciate Stonehenge, join the Stone Circle Experience (book three months in advance), an hour-long hosted visit where you can wander around inside the circle, getting up close to the stones. Visits are held out of hours, in the early morning/evening, when the quietness adds to the ambience.

**TOP TIPS**

- The best time to visit Stonehenge is on weekdays, before 11am or after 2pm.
- Download English Heritage's free audio tour for comprehensive guides to the exhibition, stone circle and surrounding landscape.
- Regular shuttle buses make the 1.5-mile trip from the visitor centre to the stones (5 minutes), although it's more atmospheric to walk; ask the driver to drop you off at Fargo Woods then follow the trail, past the Cursus and Cursus Barrows, from there.
- You're allowed (free) access inside the stone circle during the summer and winter solstices (around 21 June and 20 December, respectively).
- See **nationaltrust.org.uk** for downloadable walks in the Stonehenge Landscape.

created. Within this were 56 pits – known as Aubrey Holes after John Aubrey, the antiquarian who discovered them in the 1600s – in which cremated remains were buried. These are now marked by concrete plaques.

About 500 years later, Stonehenge's main sarsen (a boulder of silicified sandstone) stones were hewn from the Marlborough Downs, 20 miles away, and dragged to the site. The largest were erected in a horseshoe and crowned by massive lintels to make the trilithons (two vertical stones topped by a horizontal one). The huge slabs of the Great Trilithon were worked carefully to ensure its uprights perfectly framed the setting sun on midwinter's day.

Surrounding this horseshoe was a ring of 30 sarsens (17 of which are still standing), each one linked to the next by a similar lintel. Four Station Stones were arranged around the edge of the enclosure in a layout that, again, was governed by the movement of the sun. Two curving rows of smaller bluestones – hauled here from the Preseli Mountains in South Wales, an incredible 250 miles away – were also added.

The entrance to the circle is marked by the Heel Stone and, slightly further in, the Slaughter Stone. These stones were aligned to coincide with sunrise at the midsummer solstice, which some claim supports the theory that the site was some kind of celestial calendar – although, as with everything at Stonehenge, the exact purpose is unknown.

### Stonehenge Landscape

Although few visitors venture beyond the circle, Stonehenge actually forms part of a huge complex of ancient monuments that you are free to wander round.

North of the circle lie the Cursus Barrows, a humped cemetery of Bronze Age burial mounds. From these, you can make out the ridge of the nearby Cursus itself, an elongated embanked oval built around 1000 years before Stonehenge was raised. More burial mounds, the Old and New King Barrows, sit beside the Avenue, a ceremonial pathway that linked Stonehenge with the River Avon, 1.5 miles away.

The only visible remains of the Neolithic settlement at Durrington Walls, further up the Avon and connected to the river by its own smaller avenue, is the massive henge that was built around it. Durrington was believed to have housed the builders of Stonehenge, who also erected nearby Woodhenge.

Scan this QR code for prices and opening hours.

KEVIN STANDAGE/SHUTTERSTOCK ©

Stourhead

## Stately Homes

TEMPLES AND TIGERS

Overflowing with temples and exotic trees, **Stourhead**, 45 minutes' drive west of Salisbury, is landscape gardening at its finest. The magnificent 18th-century gardens spread across the valley, with a picturesque two-mile circuit taking you past ornate follies, around a centrepiece lake and to the Georgian Temple of Apollo.

A 20-minute drive to the north lies Elizabethan **Longleat**, the ancestral home of the Marquess of Bath. The estate was transformed into Britain's first safari park in 1966, turning Capability Brown's landscaped grounds into a drive-through zoo.

## A Country House on Cloisters

THE BIRTHPLACE OF PHOTOGRAPHY

An hour's drive northwest of Salisbury, **Lacock** is interesting not just for its abbey, an unusual melding of medieval cloisters and Victorian family home, but also the village itself, which has been in the hands of the National Trust since 1944

### ON LOCATION IN LACOCK

Lacock's pristine appearance has unsurprisingly made it a favourite location for costume dramas and period feature films. The village and its abbey pop up in *The Other Boleyn Girl*, *Downton Abbey* and BBC adaptations of *Wolf Hall*, *Moll Flanders* and *Pride & Prejudice*. Several scenes from the *Harry Potter* films were also shot here – the abbey's cloisters were used variously as Professor Snape's classroom and the corridors at Hogwarts, while the cottage next to the village's 15th-century church stood in for James and Lily Potter's house in *Harry Potter and the Philosopher's Stone*.

### WHERE TO STAY BEYOND SALISBURY

**Sign of the Angel, Lacock**
Fifteenth-century restaurant rich in pizzazz. Burnished beams and duck-down duvets deliver a warm, rustic feel. **££**

**Pear Tree Inn, Whitley**
Charming farmhouse conversion with skilfully furnished rooms, a cosy bar, and airy sunroom dining. **££**

**Avebury Lodge, Avebury**
Within the stone circle, rooms at this lovely veggie B&B are plastered in antiquarian knick-knacks. **£££**

### A WALK TO WEST KENNET

The landscape beyond Avebury Stone Circle is rich in prehistoric sites. This easy walk (three miles return) takes in two of the most impressive. From the National Trust car park in Avebury village, cross the main road, then pick up the footpath just to the west that cuts south to Silbury Hill, rising from the fields ahead. Over 30m high, the chalk mound is the largest artificial earthwork in Europe. It was built in stages from around 2500 BCE, at the confluence of the River Kennet and several streams and springs, although no-one knows exactly why.

Continue on, cross the road and then follow the path for half a mile up to West Kennet long barrow, England's finest burial mound. Dating from around 3650 BCE, its entrance is guarded by huge sarsens. You can actually walk inside the chamber, where about 50 skeletons were found when the long barrow was excavated.

and seems to have been preserved in mid-19th-century aspic – there are no telephone poles or electric street lights here.

**Lacock Abbey** was founded in 1232 by Ela, Countess of Salisbury, and some of the original structure is evident in the atmospheric cloisters. The converted country-house rooms include a stunning Gothic entrance hall with bizarre terracotta figures. It was through the latticed window in the abbey's South Gallery that William Henry Fox Talbot captured the world's first photographic negative in 1835. This tiny image is on display in the **Fox Talbot Museum** (included in admission), which details his groundbreaking process.

## Wander Among the Sarsens at Avebury

A STONE-CIRCLE SUPERLATIVE

Avebury is the largest **stone circle** in the world. At nearly 350m wide, it is four times the size of Stonehenge. It was erected at around the same time, from 2500 to 2200 BCE, and originally consisted of 98 standing stones surrounding two inner circles. Unlike Stonehenge, you can wander freely around Avebury; visiting at dawn or dusk is particularly evocative.

The village, just under an hour's drive from Salisbury, has grown up within and around the henge – you can have a drink at the only pub in the world inside a stone circle here – and the main road to Swindon cuts right through its centre, providing the bizarre spectacle of cars whizzing past.

Start on the High St and walk round the stone circle in an anticlockwise direction. When Avebury was first built the bank was four times higher than it is today, the ditch much deeper, and together they would have gleamed sharp white with chalk.

The standing stones in the southwest sector include the **Barber Surgeon Stone**, named after the skeleton of a man found beneath it – find out more about him in the **Alexander Keiller Museum**, named after the archaeologist who supervised the re-erection of many of the stones in 1934. The northwest sector has the most complete collection of standing stones, including the massive 65-tonne **Swindon Stone**, one of the few never to have been toppled.

### GETTING AROUND

You can reach Stonehenge from Salisbury on the Stonehenge Tour bus (which is actually a simple shuttle service rather than a proper tour), although these can quickly get full on busy days. Wiltshire's public transport coverage is sparse, so you'll need your own car for sites beyond Stonehenge. Parking at Lacock and Avebury is in National Trust car parks, which are free to members.

# BOURNEMOUTH

London
Bournemouth

Bournemouth's beach has been drawing holidaymakers to this corner of the east Dorset coast since the Victorian days. Hints of this halcyon era survive in the landmark pier and several regal villas ranged along the clifftops, but this is very much a modern seaside resort.

The beach still takes centre stage: miles of golden sand, running from Southbourne round to Alum Chine, backed by a promenade and opening out onto calm, clean, clear waters. Take your pick from the student hangouts around the pier or quieter stretches further west. Thanks in part to Bournemouth University, the town's nightlife scene is strong, attracting people from the surrounding region into the centre and the rejuvenated LGBTIQ+ hub of the Triangle. Cool, colourful Flirt Café & Bar serves as a laid-back focus for the local gay community; DYMK Bar is a good choice for early evening drinks before heading upstairs to the livelier DYMK Club, famous for its oversized cocktails.

## TOP TIP

The cliffs behind Bournemouth Beach are precipitous in parts, but you can save yourself the strenuous climb back up the steeper sections by catching one of the historic funicular 'cliff lifts' at West Cliff, East Cliff (out of action at the time of research) and Fisherman's Walk. The lifts run from Easter to October.

**Bournemouth**

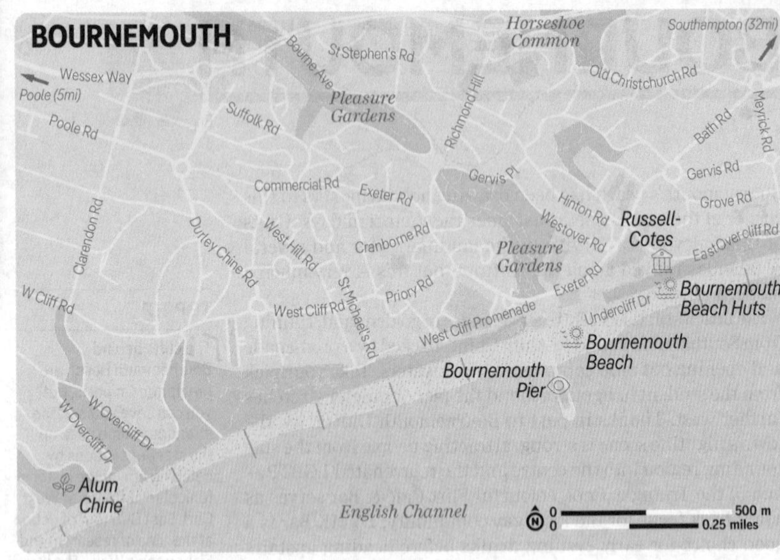


## Once More unto the Beach

SANDY SHORES & TROPICAL GARDENS

If one thing has shaped Bournemouth, it's the **beach**. This glorious strip of soft sand is backed by ornamental gardens, kids' playgrounds, cafes, several hundred beach huts and several thousand deckchairs. Check the BCP CouncilBeach Check app to avoid congested areas.

Roughly marking the middle of the town beach, **Bournemouth Pier** mixes a nostalgic slice of old-time seaside resort with indoor climbing walls and a zip-wire that links the pier to the beach. Even if you're not tempted by the amusement arcade, the coastal views from the end of the pier are worth the walk.

A notable feature along Bournemouth's coastline are its chines, steep river valleys worn into the cliffs. They were planted during the town's 1920s heyday, most beautifully so at **Alum Chine**, a subtropical enclave containing species from the Canary Islands, New Zealand, Mexico and the Himalayas.

**MORE BEACHES?**

Bournemouth Beach is the most celebrated part of a wonderful 10-mile sandy stretch that runs from **Sandbanks to Hengistbury Head** (264).

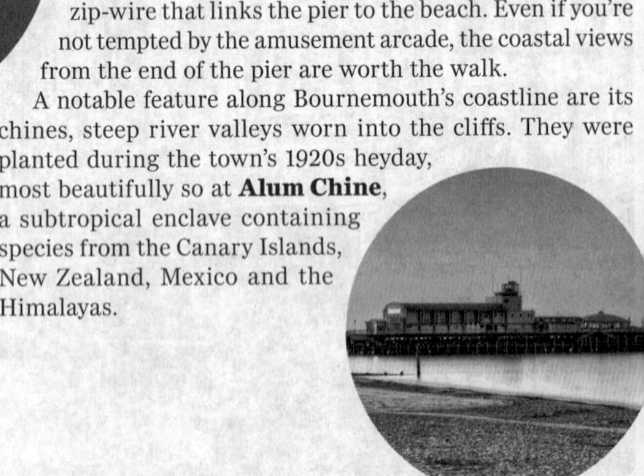

**Bournemouth Beach and Pier**

Russell-Cotes Art Gallery & Museum

## Souvenir-Stuffed Seaside Villa

FASCINATING PRIVATE COLLECTION OF ART

Ostentation oozes from the arresting **Russell-Cotes Art Gallery & Museum**, a mash-up of Italianate villa and Scottish baronial pile overlooking Bournemouth Beach. It was built at the end of the 1800s for Merton and Annie Russell-Cotes as somewhere to showcase the remarkable range of souvenirs gathered on their world travels. You can spend a good hour or two taking them all in, especially the beautifully presented Japanese trinkets in the Mikado Room and the paintings that line the walls of the richly flamboyant Main Hall.

### BEST PLACES TO STAY & EAT IN BOURNEMOUTH

**Mory House**
Serene, pristine Edwardian B&B, mixing contemporary bedrooms with elegant stairwells and stained glass. Two-night minimum stay. £££

**Amarillo**
Jazzy, great-value B&B. Comfortable rooms in a peaceful, leafy residential setting. Bike hire, too. ££

**Urban Reef**
Sea views, wide-ranging menu and a laid-back vibe draw a cool crowd to this cafe-bistro. ££

**Sobo Fish**
Locally caught seafood cooked to perfection in this unassuming little restaurant in Southbourne. ££

**Sixty Million Postcards**
Quirky pub–American diner. Settle in a booth or the beer garden with a towering burger. £

### GETTING AROUND

Bournemouth is very walkable, although the chines down to the beach are fairly steep. The flat seafront promenade is a joy for cyclists; it's also covered by a couple of cute land trains, which link Alum Chine (in the west) with Boscombe (in the east) via Bournemouth Pier.

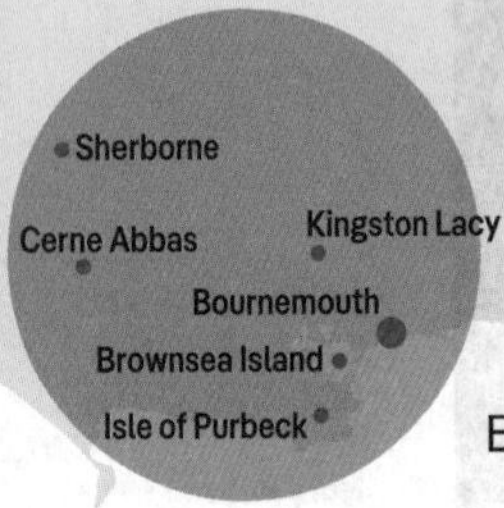

Sherborne
Cerne Abbas
Kingston Lacy
Bournemouth
Brownsea Island
Isle of Purbeck

# Beyond Bournemouth

## Bournemouth sits at the centre of a long stretch of glorious beaches, with a variety of historic properties lying only slightly further afield.

From Bournemouth, the sandy shoreline extends in both directions. Head east for colourful beach huts and windy walks, or west if you want to rub shoulders with the hoi polloi on Sandbanks.

This finger of land forms one side of expansive Poole Harbour, plonked in the centre of which is Brownsea Island. Spiritual home of the Scouting Movement, this wooded islet is well worth a day trip for its myriad wildlife.

Inland from Bournemouth, visit Kingston Lacy's exquisite rooms en route to the refined town of Sherborne. This is a great place to enjoy a long lunch before looping back via the giant chalk figure that the Saxons carved into the hill at Cerne Abbas.

### TOP TIP

The Sandbanks Ferry (four-minute trip from Sandbanks to Studland) is a handy shortcut from Poole to Corfe Castle and the Jurassic Coast.

**Cerne Giant (p266)**

ROBERTO LA ROSA/SHUTTERSTOCK ©

IAN_SHERRIFFS/SHUTTERSTOCK ©

Red Squirrel

## Red Squirrels & Boy Scouts

DECAMP TO BROWNSEA ISLAND

There's a wealth of wildlife on **Brownsea Island**, in the middle of Poole Harbour, but most people are here for the red squirrels: Brownsea is a stronghold for these bushy tailed, tufty eared, beguiling little mammals. Trails weave through heath and woods and along the windswept cliffs on the south coast, with stunning views to the **Isle of Purbeck**.

Brownsea's other claim to fame is as the home of the Scouting Movement, after Robert (later Lord) Baden-Powell set up an experimental scouting skills camp here in 1907.

Catching a ferry to Brownsea Island from busy Poole Quay, a 6.5-mile drive from Bournemouth, gives you the chance to take in Europe's largest natural harbour on the way.

### CAMPING AT THE HOME OF THE SCOUTS

It's easy to see why Robert Baden-Powell chose Brownsea for the site of his first camping expedition. Evenings here – when the boats have left and the sun starts dipping behind Studland and the shy sika deer come out to graze – are magical. Half of the site is reserved for international scout groups; the other half is open to the public. It's a wild, natural site, where tents spread out organically by the shoreline; bring your own or book one of the pre-pitched ones – the Tree Tents, suspended from the hardwoods, are the most fun.

## Art, Antiques & Ancient Egypt

COUNTRY HOUSE MEETS PRIVATE MUSEUM

Dorset's must-see stately home, **Kingston Lacy** (entry by timed ticket), half an hour or so by car from Bournemouth, looks every inch the setting for a period drama. The Bankes family moved

### WHERE TO EAT BEYOND BOURNEMOUTH

**Poole Arms**
Ancient, green-tiled pub on Poole Quay is strong on locally landed seafood. ££

**Elms**
Well-presented comfort dishes in a beautiful lunchtime setting just outside Sherborne. ££

**Green**
Pure West Country élan at this affable, elegant spot: enjoy Dorset crab and chargrilled hake. £££

**BEST BEACHES NEAR BOURNEMOUTH**

**Sandbanks**
Wafer-thin peninsula, curling around Poole Harbour, fringed by white-sand beaches and expensive real estate.

**Hengistbury Head & Mudeford Sandbank**
Unspoilt Hengistbury for tussock-topped dune walks; Mudeford for swimming on one side, watersports on the other.

**Avon Beach**
Sand and shingle; a brilliant place for paddleboarding, with views of the Isle of Wight.

here after their home in Corfe Castle (see p270) fell to Parliamentarians during the Civil War. Highlights include the elegant marble staircase and the unusual guestrooms that were designed to resemble military campaign tents. But what really sets Kingston Lacy apart is its extravagant collection of art and antiques. In the gilt-smothered Spanish Room alone, there are paintings by Diego Velàzquez, Bartolomé Esteban Murillo and Francisco de Zurbarán. Kingston Lacy is also home to an unrivalled assortment of Egyptian artefacts, gathered during William John Bankes' expeditions to Upper Egypt in the early 1800s.

## Tour Sir Walter Raleigh's Sherborne

CASTLES & A GLORIOUS ABBEY CEILING

Wealthy Sherborne, an hour and a quarter's drive northwest of Bournemouth, gleams with a mellow, orangey-yellow stone, most magnificently in **Sherborne Abbey**. Established in the early 8th century, it is one of the most beautiful parish churches in England, with a mesmerising fan-vault ceiling that's the oldest in the country.

On the hill overlooking Sherborne to the east lie two castles, both connected to Sir Walter Raleigh but now in very differing states. Elizabeth I gave **Sherborne Old Castle** to Raleigh, her onetime favourite, in the late 16th century. Oliver Cromwell reduced it to rubble in 1645, leaving today's picturesque ruin of fractured gatehouses and towers. Raleigh began building impressive **Sherborne New Castle** in 1594, but only got as far as the central block before being imprisoned by James I. It has been in the hands of the Digby family ever since. In the mid-1700s, landscape-gardener extraordinaire Capability Brown added a massive lake and splendid waterside gardens.

## A Giant in Every Sense

ANCIENT FIGURE CARVED IN CHALK

Nude, full frontal and notoriously well endowed, the 60m-high **Cerne Giant** chalk figure, on the hillside above the village of **Cerne Abbas**, is outlined in all his glory.

In 2021, archaeologists were finally able to date the giant to the late Saxon period, ruling out theories that he was prehistoric or Roman. You can walk up to his feet, but the best views are from the car park; it's an hour's drive from Bournemouth.

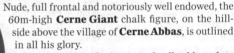

**MORE ART-FILLED HOMES?**

Merton and Annie Russell-Cotes filled their house in Bournemouth with so many paintings and trinkets from their travels that it has been turned into the **Russell-Cotes Art Gallery & Museum** (p263).

**GETTING AROUND**

Places along the coast east and west of Bournemouth, including Poole Harbour (for Brownsea Island), Sandbanks and Avon Beach, are served by Morebus. A car is more convenient, though, and you'll need your own wheels to get to Kingston Lacy and the Cerne Giant. In summer, a land train runs from Hengistbury Head to Mudeford Sandbank.

# DORCHESTER

In many people's eyes, Dorchester is Thomas Hardy's fictional Casterbridge. The Victorian writer was born nearby and spent most of his life in a house on the edge of town, and his literary locations can still be found among Dorchester's Georgian terraces: a grey-brick building on South St (now a bank) provided inspiration for the house of the Mayor of Casterbridge, while the Corn Exchange on the High St appears in *Far from the Madding Crowd*.

But the history of this vibrant county town goes much further back than that. The local tribe constructed a huge hilltop fort here in the Iron Age, and under the Romans Dorchester prospered into a tidy administrative capital, evidenced by the wonderful mosaics on display in the Roman Town House and on the walls of the Dorset Museum. The cracking exhibitions here progress the story through to modern-day Dorchester, an attractive town where you won't go short of great places to eat.

### TOP TIP

Start exploring at Thomas Hardy's birthplace and Max Gate, and then visit the Dorset Museum to see the world's largest collection of Hardy memorabilia. The museum also displays finds from Maiden Castle and Roman Dorchester, which sets the scene for trips out to the Iron Age fort and to Dorchester's well-preserved Roman Town House.

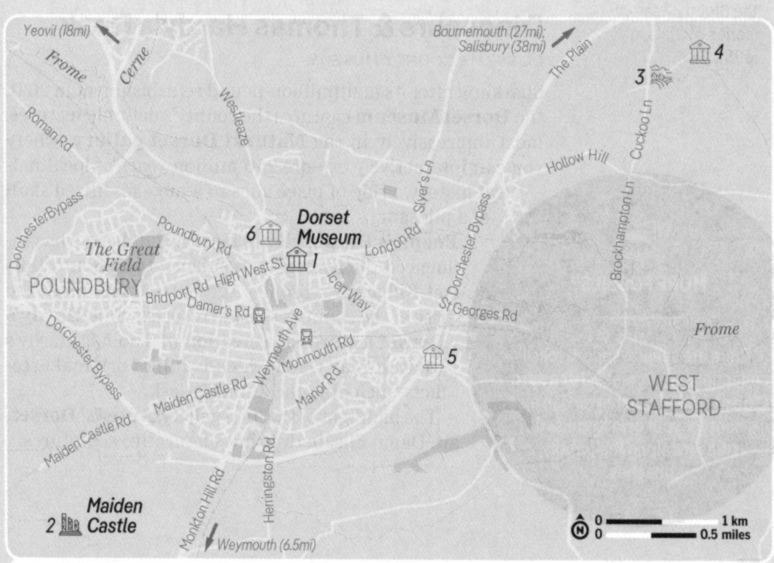


**HIGHLIGHTS**
**1** Dorset Museum
**2** Maiden Castle

**SIGHTS**
**3** Hardy's Birthplace Visitor Centre
**4** Hardy's Cottage
**5** Max Gate
**6** Roman Town House

## BEST PLACES TO EAT IN DORCHESTER

**Posh Partridge**
Salads, toasted sandwiches, local specials (Dorset faggot [meatballs], Portland crab) are mainstays at this farmhouse-kitchen-style cafe. £

**La Caverna**
Book ahead for intimate dining (seven tables) at this cellar-restaurant serving quality Italian food. ££

**Al Molo**
Stylish upmarket fish restaurant in the building where Judge Jeffries stayed during the Bloody Assizes (series of trials in 1685). ££

BJOERN WYLEZICH/SHUTTERSTOCK ©

Fossil from Charmouth (p273)

# Dinosaurs & Thomas Hardy's Desk

DORSET'S COUNTY MUSEUM

Sparkling after its multimillion-pound refurbishment in 2021, the **Dorset Museum** captures the county's defining features, most impressively in the **Natural Dorset gallery**, where you can interactively explore 250 million years of local natural history. Pride of place goes to a huge fossilised skull of a pliosaur.

**People's Dorset** charts how the landscape has influenced the lives of its residents, from South Dorset Ridgeway's Bronze Age burial mounds to the rise of the county's seaside resorts, while **Hardy's Dorset** features a recreation of Thomas Hardy's study at Max Gate, which is full of original artefacts, including the author's desk.

The highlight of the final gallery, **Artists' Dorset**, are Dame Elisabeth Frink's figurative sculptures.

**MORE FOSSILS?**

There are several superb fossil collections on Dorset's **Jurassic Coast** (p270), where you can also hunt for your own fossilised treasure along the pebbly beaches.

## WHERE TO STAY IN DORCHESTER

**Beggars Knap**
Fabulous guesthouse with opulent rooms and beds ranging from French sleigh to four-poster. Excellent value. ££

**Westwood House**
Contemporary meets Georgian in this 18th-century townhouse of subtle checks, cosy throws, brass lamps and mini-sofas. ££

**Yalbury Cottage**
Gently rustic bedrooms at this archetypal thatched English cottage overlooking the fields of Lower Bockhampton. ££

## The Durotriges & Durnovaria

ANCIENT AND ROMAN DORCHESTER

Occupying a massive slab of horizon on the southern fringes of Dorchester, **Maiden Castle** is one of the largest Iron Age hill forts in Europe. It was capital of the local Durotriges tribe and densely populated with clusters of roundhouses. The Romans captured Maiden Castle in 43 BCE – a skeleton with the remains of what might be a Roman crossbow bolt in his spine was discovered at the fort (now on display in the Dorset Museum).

Within 20 years the Romans had founded Durnovaria (modern-day Dorchester), an era powerfully evoked by the **Roman Town House**, the only one of its kind in the country, in Colliton Park. Peer through the glass panels to see the beautiful mosaics in the owner's study and the ingenious underfloor heating system (hypocaust) in the winter dining room.

## On the Hardy Trail

FOLLOW IN THE AUTHOR'S FOOTSTEPS

Dorset's most famous author and poet, Thomas Hardy spent most of his life in and around Dorchester. Start your pilgrimage at **Hardy's Birthplace Visitor Centre** in Higher Bockhampton, three miles northwest of town. You can park your car here and walk through Thorncombe Wood to **Hardy's Cottage** (entry by pre-booked ticket only), where the author was born in 1840. The thatched cottage is stone floored and simply furnished, much as it would have been when Hardy was growing up here. He wrote *Far from the Madding Crowd* (1874) in one of the upstairs bedrooms.

Thanks to the novel's financial success, in 1885 Hardy moved to **Max Gate** (entry by pre-booked ticket only), the villa he built for himself and his first wife on the outskirts of Dorchester. In the downstairs rooms, Hardy entertained visitors like JM Barrie and Rudyard Kipling over afternoon tea. In the studies he wrote *The Mayor of Casterbridge* (1886) and the controversial *Tess of the d'Urbervilles* (1891) and *Jude the Obscure* (1895). Hardy lived at Max Gate for over 40 years until his death in 1928.

Most of the author's personal possessions are now on display in the Dorset Museum.

### HARDY'S HALLMARKS

Thomas Hardy's novels are renowned for their evocative descriptions of the Wessex landscape in which they're set, a 'partly real, partly dream country' he based on Dorchester and the wider county.

Hardy grew up amid the poverty of rural Dorset, and his books often depicted a bleak and tireless life of working in the fields or struggling to survive in the workhouses and slums of Dorchester. Social injustice was a key theme throughout his novels, alongside the hypocrisy of Victorian society's attitude towards women. His female characters are generally strong, independent women who struggle against the social mores of the day – a frustrating and, in Tess d'Urberville's case, ultimately tragic plight.

### GETTING AROUND

Trains drop passengers off at Dorchester West (from Bath and Bristol) or Dorchester South (London Waterloo and Bournemouth), which are just 450m apart on the southwestern edge of town. There are several car parks in the roads south of the High St. You can cover the centre of Dorchester on foot in a matter of minutes; Max Gate is walkable, too – it's 20 minutes or so from the town centre – but you'll need a car to visit Hardy's Cottage and Maiden Castle.

# JURASSIC COAST

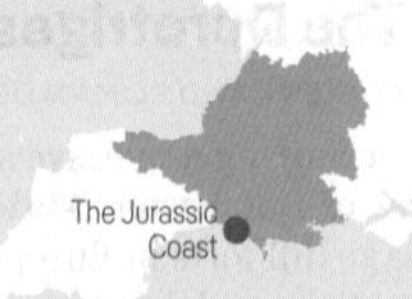


England's first natural World Heritage site, the Jurassic Coast is a striking shoreline of compacted cliffs, shingle beaches and eroded landforms. Stretching from the chalk stacks of Dorset's Old Harry Rocks to Exmouth in East Devon, it encompasses 185 million years of the earth's history in just 95 miles.

The great environmental change that took place here – deserts usurped by deep oceans, tropical seas retreating to leave swamps and forests – reveals itself through its layer cake of cliffs, and the prehistoric creatures that are regularly washed out of them.

Massive earth movements tilted the region's rocks, forcing most of the oldest formations to the west, and the youngest to the east, so working your way along the coast is like taking a continual trip through time. Pockets of creamy-coloured Cretaceous rocks pop up around Lulworth Cove, working back through the millennia to the fossil-rich, dark-clay Jurassic cliffs at Lyme Regis.

### TOP TIP

If you're using First Bus's Jurassic Coaster service to get around, try to catch the X52 – an open-top bus that runs between Lulworth Cove and West Bay via Durdle Door and Abbotsbury – so you can make the most of the gorgeous views of Chesil Beach along the way.

**Lulworth Cove (p272)**

SHAUN JACOBS/SHUTTERSTOCK ©

**HIGHLIGHTS**
**1** Corfe Castle
**2** Durdle Door
**3** Portland Lighthouse

**SIGHTS**
**4** Charmouth Heritage Coast Centre
**5** Chesil Beach
**see 8** Donosaurland
**6** Fleet Lagoon
**7** Lulworth Cove
**see 7** Lulworth Cove Visitor Centre
**8** Lyme Regis Museum
**9** Monmouth Beach
**see 7** Stair Hole Bay
**10** Tout Quarry Sculpture Park & Nature Reserve
**11** West Bay
**see 5** Wild Chesil Centre

**ACTIVITIES**
**12** Abbotsbury Swannery

**Corfe Castle village (p272)**

PATRYCK KOSMIDER/SHUTTERSTOCK ©

Moors
Farnham
Chettle
Sturminster Newtown
Stalbridge
Sherborne
Yeovil
Barwick
Stoke-sub-Hamdon
South Petherton
Illminster
Chard
Crewkerne
Drimpton
Corscombe
Evershot
Beaminster
Marshwood
Axminster
Lyme Regis
Charmouth
Bridport
Simene
Brit
Asker
Litton Cheney
Burton Bradstock
Long Bredy
Abbotsbury
South West Coast Path
Fleet Lagoon
Lyme Bay
Frome
Wey
Cerne Abbas
Blandford Forum
Stour
Wimborne Minster
Dorchester
Puddletown
Moreton
Clouds Hill
Bere Regis
Piddle
Bovington
Wool
Sherford
Poole
Wareham
Corfe Castle
Lulworth Cove
Durdle Door
Weymouth
Wyke Regis
Chiswell
Isle of Portland
Portland Lighthouse
Swanage
English Channel
10 km
6 miles

**BEST PLACES TO STAY ON THE JURASSIC COAST**

**Lulworth YHA**
Comfy, shiny-bright hostel, small and simple, but enjoys a great location above Lulworth Cove. £

**Lulworth Cove Inn**
A veritable vision of driftwood-chic, with whitewashed floorboards, wicker chairs and roll-top baths. £££

**Crabbers' Wharf**
A range of smart self-catering apartments right on Portland Harbour with wonderful waterside views. ££

**Lyme Townhouse**
Lovely little rooms and a central setting make this a good-value guesthouse with luxury flourishes. ££

**Alexandra**
Hotel and restaurant with Lyme Bay views from the best bedrooms; back-facing ones are charming, too. ££

STERLING IMAGES/SHUTTERSTOCK ©

**Lulworth Cove Inn**

## Get the Keys to Corfe Castle

PICTURESQUE RUINED FORTRESS

The fractured battlements of Corfe Castle are a startling sight, crowning the hill above the village of the same name. Once home to Sir John Bankes, Charles I's chief assistant, the castle was destroyed by Cromwellian forces during the English Civil War. Wander around the gap-toothed keep and among the turrets and soaring walls that still sheer off at precarious angles.

## Eroded Coves & Sculpted Sea Arches

WITNESS NATURE'S EFFECT ON LANDSCAPES

The stretch of coast between Lulworth Cove and Durdle Door is a lesson in geology. For millions of years, the elements have been creating an intricate shoreline of curved bays, caves, stacks and weirdly wonderful rock formations.

The relentless power of the sea is on show at **Lulworth Cove**, a scallop-shaped natural harbour, and nearby **Stair Hole Bay**, where waves have gorged out a series of caves and tiny arches, and the rock face has been twisted into

**WHERE TO EAT ON THE JURASSIC COAST**

**Lulworth Lodge**
Laid-back bistro in Lulworth focuses on locally caught seafood and elevated pub classics. ££

**Cove House Inn**
History-rich fishers' inn with Chesil Beach-side beer terrace, great pub food and memorable sunsets. £

**Crab House Café**
Beach-shack chic at the head of Portland, serving fresh fish, crab and oysters. £££

dramatically zigzagging folds. Learn more about how this shoreline has been shaped at the **Lulworth Cove Visitor Centre**.

Following the South West Coast Path west from Lulworth (2.5 miles return) leads to the 150-million-year-old arch of **Durdle Door**. Created by a combination of massive earth movements and erosion, the immense arch is framed by shimmering bays – a magnificent place for a swim.

The beach and car parks (you can also drive direct to Durdle Door) can get very busy in summer, so try to visit early and on a weekday. And avoid peak season if you can.

## Tour the Isle of Portland

DORSET'S WINDSWEPT EXTENSION

The **Isle of Portland** is a hard comma of rock fused to the rest of Dorset by the ridge of Chesil Beach. It is starkly beautiful, at times bleak, a little rough around the edges – and all the more compelling because of it.

On the Isle's central plateau, a laborious quarrying past is evident in the chiseled works at **Tout Quarry Sculpture Park & Nature Reserve**, more than 50 sculptures carved into Portland Stone in situ.

For a real sense of Portland's remote nature, head to its wild southern tip, Portland Bill, where waves lash against the craggy rocks. Its candy-striped **lighthouse** offers breathtaking views; on regular guided tours, you can make out the choppy waters of the Portland Race, a surging vortex of tides that swirl around the treacherous ledges just offshore.

## Shingle, Sandstone Cliffs & Swans

ATMOSPHERIC PEBBLE BEACH

Stretching for 18 miles from Portland to West Bay, **Chesil Beach** is a mesmerising barrier comprising billions of pebbles of flint, chert and quartzite washed up in winter storms over the last 10,000 years.

At the **Wild Chesil Centre**, an energy-sapping hike up sliding pebbles – the ridge is at its 15m highest here – leads to the constant surge and rattle of waves on stones. The centre lies alongside the eastern tip of expansive **Fleet Lagoon**, which throngs with birdlife.

**Abbotsbury Swannery** is home to a 600-strong colony of nesting mute swans (mass feedings twice daily), while **West Bay** sees a steady stream of visitors, thanks to its shingle beach and handsome sandstone cliffs, which featured in the hit TV series *Broadchurch*.

### WATERSPORTS ON THE JURASSIC COAST

**Kayaking**
Kayak out to the chalk stacks of Old Harry Rocks with Fore / Adventure, or paddle among the rock arches at Lulworth Cove with Lulworth Outdoors.

**Sailing**
The sailing events at the London 2012 Olympics were held in Portland and Weymouth. Try sea sailing in the enclosed environment of Portland Harbour with the Andrew Simpson Watersports Centre.

**Windsurfing & kitesurfing**
Take advantage of the best wind conditions on the south coast with a windsurfing or kitesurfing lesson at the Isle of Portland's Official Test Centre.

**Watch House Café**
Wood fired pizzas and pasta at this rustic cafe in the fine shingle of West Bay beach. ££

**Oyster & Fish House**
Expect dazzling food and sweeping views of Lyme Bay at Mark Hix's super-stylish, open-plan cabin. £££

**Lilac**
Sensational seasonal dishes and top-notch wines in an intimate cellar-restaurant in central Lyme Regis. ££

## FOSSIL-HUNTING TIPS

**Dr Paul Davis**, Geology Curator at Lyme Regis Museum, is a world expert on the fossils of the early Jurassic.

**What to look for**
The best fossils are found among patches of fool's gold (pyrite), where the sand and shingle is dark. Look for regular symmetrical shapes – round coils are ammonites, stars are crinoids, bullet shapes are belemnites. Most fossils are smaller than a £2 coin.

**When to go**
October to Easter, when the storms wash fossils from the cliffs. Start around two to three hours after high tide. And keep away from the cliffs and muddy landslips.

**Get more info**
Visit the Lyme Regis Museum for help and advice and to report any significant finds.

# There Be (Sea) Dragons!

ROCK-HARD RELICS OF THE PAST

The stretch of coast between Lyme Regis and Charmouth is prime fossil-hunting territory. This is one of the most unstable sections of Britain's shore, and regular landslips mean nuggets of prehistory keep tumbling from the cliffs.

In 1812 local teenager Mary Anning found the first near-complete ichthyosaur skeleton near Lyme Regis, propelling the town onto the world stage and turning it into a centre for pioneering palaeontologists. **Lyme Regis Museum**, located on the site of Anning's former home, tells her story and exhibits some spectacular and rare local fossils. There are more fossilised remains at the joyful **Dinosaurland**, higher up the hill in Lyme, and in **Charmouth Heritage Coast Centre,** three miles to the east, which has a fossil 'touch table' and is home to the locally discovered ichthyosaurus that featured in the BBC documentary *Attenborough and the Sea Dragon*.

For your own piece of prehistoric treasure, there are easy finds at **Monmouth Beach** – at low tide, the receding sea exposes a rocky ledge containing hundreds of ammonite fossils. Sign up for one of the informative **fossil walks** run by Lyme Regis Museum or Charmouth Heritage Coast Centre.

**MORE GEOLOGY IN ACTION**

The crumbling golden cliffs at **West Bay** (p273) are the result of falling sea levels some 175 million years ago.

## GETTING AROUND

Connecting the dots along the Jurassic Coast is easiest with your own car. The most useful bus route is the Jurassic Coaster, which stops in Lulworth Cove, Durdle Door, Portland Bill, West Bay and Lyme Regis. Other buses serving Lulworth Cove and Portland Bill require changing in Weymouth. The best way to make the short hop between Lulworth and Durdle Door is by foot along the beautiful coast path.

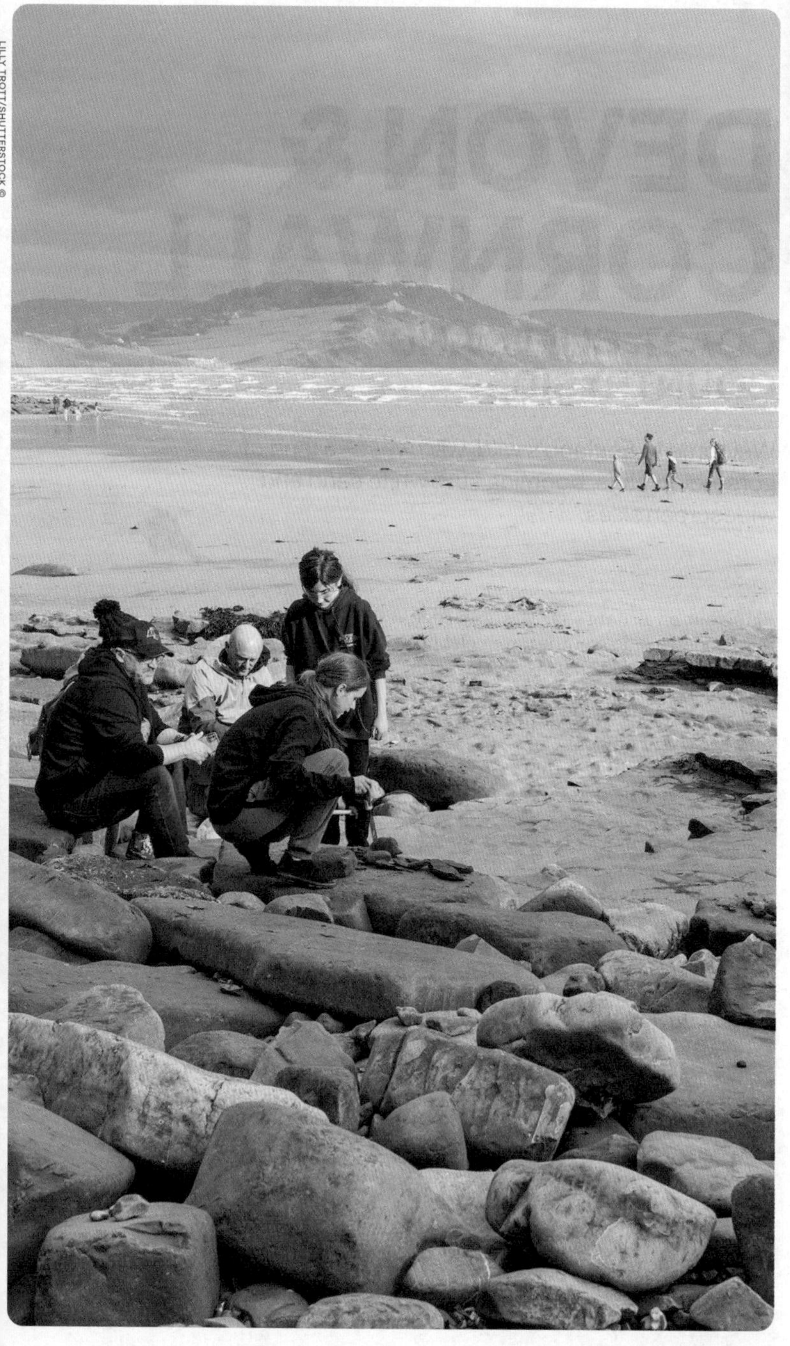

LILLY TROTT/SHUTTERSTOCK ©

Charmouth beach

# DEVON & CORNWALL

## COAST, CLIFFS AND COUNTRYSIDE

Welcome to England's wild, wild west – a land of gorse-clad cliffs, booming surf, white sand and widescreen skies.

Flung out on Britain's far westerly edge, these side-by-side counties are celebrated for their natural charms: craggy cliffs cloaked in gorse, rocky tors on empty moors, golden beaches washed by surf. Every year millions of visitors flock here to feel the sand between their toes and paddle in the briny blue, and with miles of coastline, countryside and clifftops to explore, it's really no wonder.

If you want to experience the region's landscapes at their best, you'll need to ditch the car and get active. Hiking trails and cycling paths criss-cross the countryside, and the South West Coast Path winds its way through a stunning coastal kaleidoscope. Kayak the rivers, hike the moors, bike the back lanes, paddleboard the beaches or coasteer the cliffs – the adventures just never seem to end here.

And while the West Country's popularity inevitably means crowds, with the help of a decent map and an adventurous spirit, chances are you'll nearly always be able to find a patch of sand to call your own.

Just don't make the mistake of thinking they're the same place. Devon and Cornwall have proud, independent spirits of their own, and there's a gentle sense of rivalry between these two lands either side of the River Tamar. Think close cousins, not identical twins.

SAVO ILIC/SHUTTERSTOCK ©

### THE MAIN AREAS

**Above: Mousehole (p314); left: Ilfracombe (p299)**

**ST IVES**
West Cornwall's artistic hub.
**p309**

**FALMOUTH**
Hip harbour town.
**p317**

**FOWEY**
Beaches, coast and coves.
**p323**

# Find Your Way

Devon and Cornwall have frequent train connections to London and stations in between, as well as to the north of England via Bristol. The A30 and A38 (via the Tamar Bridge) are the main road routes.

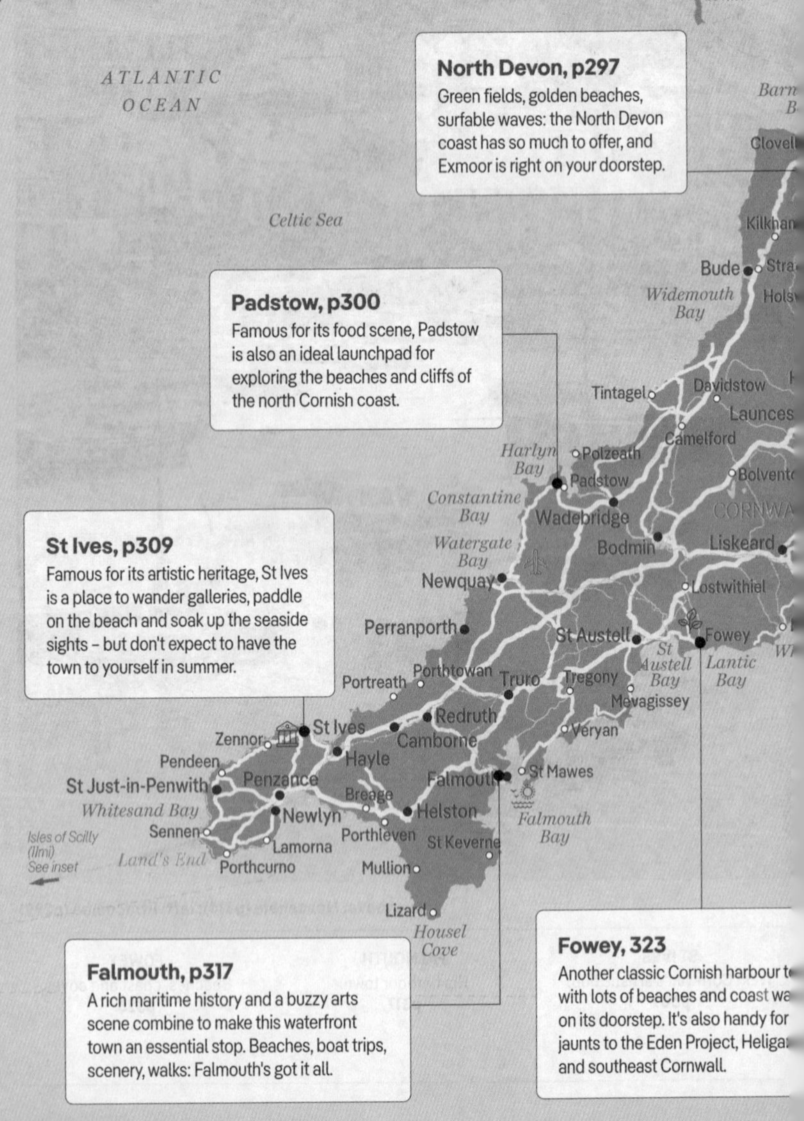

**North Devon, p297**
Green fields, golden beaches, surfable waves: the North Devon coast has so much to offer, and Exmoor is right on your doorstep.

**Padstow, p300**
Famous for its food scene, Padstow is also an ideal launchpad for exploring the beaches and cliffs of the north Cornish coast.

**St Ives, p309**
Famous for its artistic heritage, St Ives is a place to wander galleries, paddle on the beach and soak up the seaside sights – but don't expect to have the town to yourself in summer.

**Falmouth, p317**
A rich maritime history and a buzzy arts scene combine to make this waterfront town an essential stop. Beaches, boat trips, scenery, walks: Falmouth's got it all.

**Fowey, 323**
Another classic Cornish harbour t with lots of beaches and coast wa on its doorstep. It's also handy for jaunts to the Eden Project, Heliga and southeast Cornwall.

## CAR

There's no doubt that a car brings maximum freedom in this part of Cornwall, but parking can be tricky (and often pricey) in larger towns, and summer traffic can be a real headache. Petrol costs can be high in rural areas.

## BUS

Travelling by bus around the southwest is cheap and usually reliable, but nearly always takes longer than the train. Rural services are less frequent, and in the case of some remote villages, non-existent.

## TRAIN

The main train line between London and Penzance stops at all the main cities (including Exeter, Plymouth and Truro), with branch lines to Exmouth, Barnstaple, Paignton, Looe, Newquay, Falmouth and St Ives.

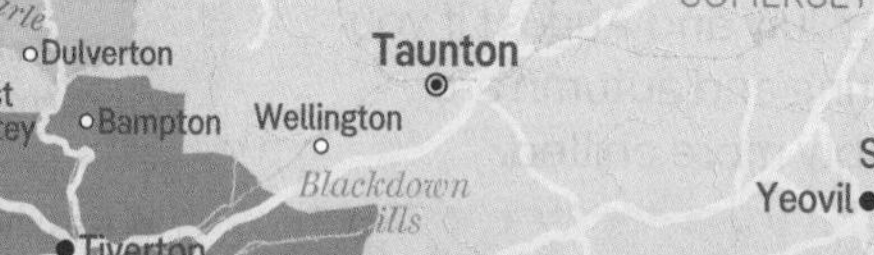
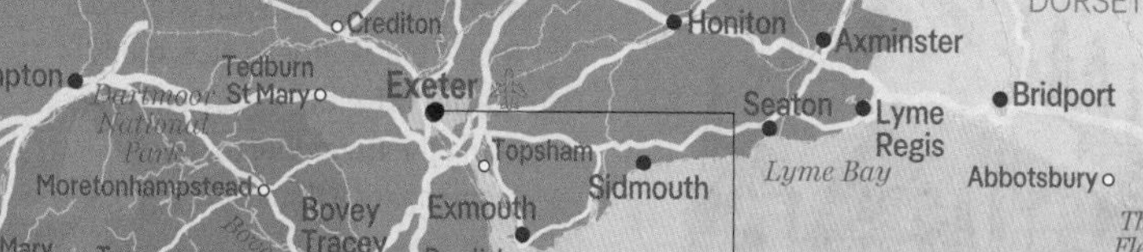

### Exeter, p282

Devon's capital is home to Roman city walls, a Norman cathedral and a vibrant contemporary culture.

### ymouth, p290

scover a history of seafarers in tain's 'Ocean City', where an citing cultural regeneration is eathing new life into the area.

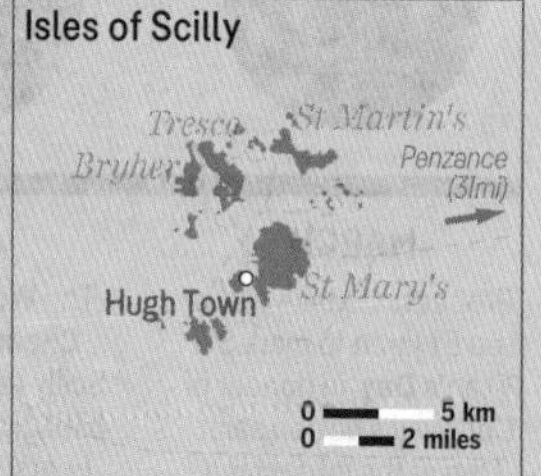

# Plan Your Time

The one big drawback about the West Country is that it takes a while to get there – and an even longer time to get around, especially during heavy summer traffic. It's definitely worth avoiding July and August if you can; spring and autumn are noticeably more chilled.

CRISTINA NIXAU/SHUTTERSTOCK ©

Exeter Cathedral (p283)

## A Capital Day Trip

- Head straight for **Exeter** (p282), where Roman, Tudor and Georgian buildings jostle for space beneath the shadow of a towering Norman cathedral. Start with a walking tour with **Redcoat Tours** (p283), taking in the 2000-year-old **Roman city walls** (p284) and the **medieval passages** (p284) beneath the city's streets.

- Next head to **Exeter Cathedral** (p283), one of Devon's most impressive ecclesiastical sights, and climb the tower for a rooftop tour. If the weather's nice, round the day off with a cruise or cycle along the **River Exe** (p284), stopping for a drink at Exeter Quay.

## Seasonal Highlights

No matter when you visit, there's likely to something happening in the southwest – be it a music festival, food fair, folk tradition or, er, flaming tar barrel run.

### MARCH

Processions take place on 5 March to mark **St Piran's Day**, in honour of Cornwall's patron saint. One of the largest is a mass march across the sands of Perranporth.

### APRIL

The **World Pilot Gig Chamionships** on Scilly revolves around pilot gigs (long rowing boats). Teams come from across the world, and accommodation is booked out.

### MAY

Padstow's chaotic **May Day Festival** involves two colourful 'osses' (blue and red) twirling around the town's streets, while Helston celebrates the coming of spring on **Flora Day**.



MATT CARDY/STRINGER/GETTY IMAGES ©, GLENMORE/SHUTTERSTOCK ©, SCORSBY/SHUTTERSTOCK ©

## 5 Devon Days

● From the big city, you could easily while away a few days circling round the South Hams. Essential stops here include the eco-friendly, alternative town of **Totnes** (p287) and the historic harbour of **Dartmouth** (p287), combined with a day of kayaking and sightseeing along the **River Dart** (288) and some laid-back beach time, perhaps around **Start Bay** (289) or **Bigbury-on-Sea** (p289).

● Devote another day to **Plymouth** (p290) to wander around the cobbled Barbican, visit the Box and marvel at the National Marine Aquarium, then round things off with a day or two hiking among the otherworldly tors and cycling the trails on wild **Dartmoor** (p296).

## A Week in the West

● A week should be just enough to tackle a whistle-stop tour around Cornwall's classic sights. Begin in the harbour town of **Fowey** (p323), Daphne du Maurier's adopted home, with adventures to the amazing **Eden Project** (p325) and the **Lost Gardens of Heligan** (p326).

● Cross to the north coast for some surfing in **Newquay** (p306), a day in foodie **Padstow** (p300) and a cycle-ride on the Camel Trail, and another exploring the cliffs and beaches around **St Agnes** (p306) and **Perranporth** (p307).

● Venture west to **St Ives** (p309), then circle round the headland via **Land's End** (p314), **Penzance** (p314) and **St Michael's Mount** (p316). You should just have time for a final day in **Falmouth** (p317).

**JUNE**

Hooray, and up she rises... Sea-themed songs fill the air during the **Falmouth International Sea Shanty Festival**. Bottles of rum and pieces of eight optional.

**JULY**

Major music acts play against the backdrop of the biomes across several weekends during the **Eden Sessions**.

**AUGUST**

Plymouth's skies are filled with colour in mid-August for the **British Fireworks Championships**, and Watergate Bay hosts the **Boardmasters music festival**.

**SEPTEMBER**

Fiction fans descend on Torquay for the **International Agatha Christie Festival**, and with kids back at school, resorts quieten.

# EXETER

Founded 2000 years ago by the Romans as Isca Dumnoniorum, Exeter is a city where history awaits around every corner. Traces of the town's Roman walls still stand, alongside a Norman castle, a monumental twin-towered cathedral, a medieval guildhall and plenty of Tudor gabled architecture. This is a city that has lived many historical lives, leaving behind an attractive, eclectic centre where history comes alive on every street. Today it's a lively university town with a buzzy nightlife, vibrant arts scene and plethora of independent businesses, while Exeter Quay has been reinvented as a riverside leisure destination.

### TOP TIP

From local live music to large-scale festivals, there's always something going on in Exeter. Check the calendar of events at visitexeter.com to find out what's happening when you visit. Foodies shouldn't miss the weekly farmers' market, held every Thursday on the junction of South and Fore Sts.

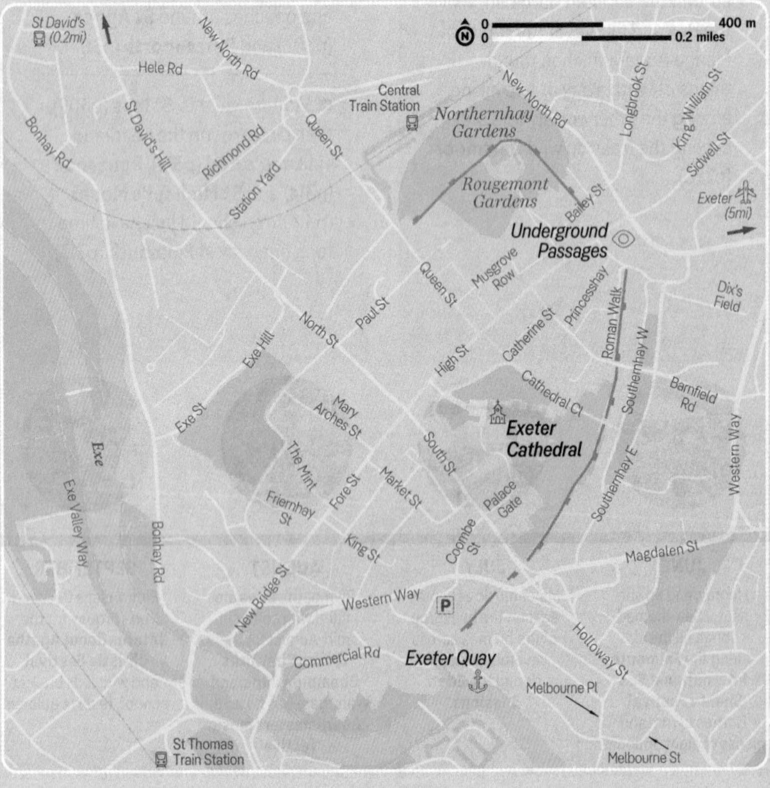

Exeter Cathedral

## A Medieval Masterwork

CLIMB THE TOWERS OF EXETER CATHEDRAL

Built by the Normans on the site of a Saxon Abbey in 1114 and rebuilt throughout the 13th and 14th centuries, the **Cathedral Church of St Peter**'s blend of architectural styles showcases Exeter's long history, deserving lengthy exploration. The dazzling jewel in the cathedral's crown is its elaborate West Front Image Screen, covered with scores of carved figures depicting angels, kings, lords and saints. Carved in the 14th century, this masterpiece of medieval creativity would have once been entirely coloured: you can still see traces of red behind some of the figures. Inside, don't miss the exquisite fan-vaulted ceiling. A programme of special tours, including rooftop tower tours, runs throughout the year.

## Step into History

EXPLORE EXETER WITH THE EXPERTS

Dive into Exeter's many past lives with a local expert. Run by Exeter City Council, **Redcoat Tours** offers a diverse, year-

### BEST EATS IN EXETER

**Red Panda**
Southeast Asian street food from a colourful independent takeaway. **£**

**Cork & Tile**
Authentic Portuguese tapas and wine bar on Exeter's historic Gandy St. **££**

**Old Firehouse**
Popular student hangout loved for its square pizzas, Sunday roasts and live music. **££**

**Harry's**
Family-run restaurant in a 19th-century Gothic building, with a diverse menu full of local produce. **££**

**On the Waterfront**
Cool quayside restaurant and bar known for its tapas, pizzas and cocktails. **££**

### WHERE TO STAY IN EXETER

**Globe Backpackers**
Dorms and private rooms in a converted 18th-century townhouse just outside the city centre. **£**

**Townhouse**
Cosy and seriously stylish B&B with friendly vibes, gorgeous decor and breakfast hampers in bed. **££**

**Southernhay House**
Contemporary luxury, quirky decor and quality food in a beautiful Georgian townhouse. **£££**

round programme of free, funny and fascinating tours led by passionate locals clad in bright red blazers. Tours range from the city's Roman origins and historic architecture to ghosts and legends. For a solid overview of local history start with the 'Heart of Exeter' or 'Introducing Exeter' tours. Occasionally, the Redcoat team run a specialist tour to tie in with a specific event, including Halloween ghost tours. Most tours depart from the Cathedral Green, with no booking required.

**JURASSIC PARK**

Across a 95-mile stretch of coastline in Devon and Dorset, the **Jurassic Coast** (p270) is England's only natural Unesco World Heritage Site. East Devon's section is the oldest, formed during the Triassic period 252 to 200 million years ago.

There's no better way to see it than from the water: from Exmouth, **Stuart Line Cruises** offers a range of sea trips. How far you'll go depends on tides and conditions: usually Ladram Bay or Sidmouth. Highlights along the way include the **Orcombe Point Geoneedle** – the official start of Jurassic Coast – and **Straight Point**, a low headland home to a huge colony of kittiwakes, as well as shags and other gulls. There's a chance of dolphin sightings in warmer months.

## Underground Exeter

GOING DEEP BENEATH THE CITY

Don a hard hat and get ready to duck on a tour of Exeter's **Underground Passages**, a system of 14th-century vaulted tunnels built to bring clean drinking water into the city through lead pipes. Squeeze through claustrophobia-inducing narrow passageways, with the unnerving rumble of traffic overhead, to learn about this clever piece of medieval engineering. It's a unique experience; there's no similar publicly accessible system in Britain.

## An Exe-ellent Adventure

CRUISING THE RIVER EXE

Once the lifeblood of industry and trade in the city, today the **River Exe** lends Exeter a gentle, countryside atmosphere. The Quayside area is buzzing on sunny days, with plenty of options for alfresco dining and drinks. A short walk or cycle south, though, will have you in the tranquil surroundings of the parks and meadows that line the river and the **Exeter Ship Canal**, which runs alongside the Exe to Topsham. **Exeter Cruises** run seasonal trips along the canal through this greenery as far as the Double Locks pub.

To slow down and escape the city, rent a kayak, canoe or paddleboard and set off on a leisurely journey downriver. With a full day, you can paddle to the birdlife-rich **Exminster Marshes RSPB Reserve**, the only place in Devon where lapwings still breed. Several companies around the quay offer equipment rentals; **Saddles and Paddles** also rent bikes to hit the Exe Estuary Trail.

**GETTING AROUND**

Exeter's centre is compact and fairly walkable, with plenty of footpaths, but expect a few hills and cobbles on some older streets. It's also a very bike-friendly city with numerous cycle routes. Day trippers coming by car should use one of the three Park & Ride services to avoid driving in the city centre, which can get very congested.

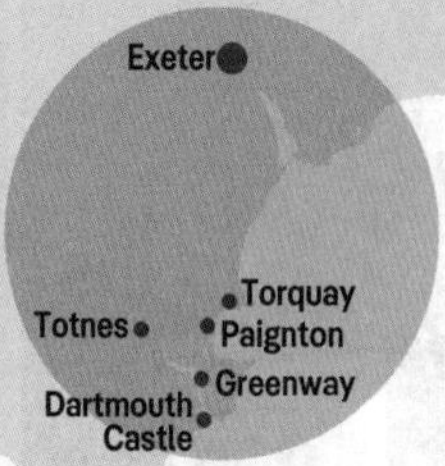

# Beyond Exeter

## Holiday heaven Devon: hop between classic seaside towns, historic harbours, tranquil estuaries and big sandy beaches

After spending a few days exploring Devon's big city, it's time to set out for the bucolic countryside of South Devon. This is one of the county's most scenic areas: a chocolate-box contrast of fields, coast, beaches and seaside towns which have been attracting holidaymakers since the great Victorian tourism boom of the late 19th century. The centrepiece is the optimistically named English Riviera, a breezy stretch of coast that incorporates the resort towns of Torquay and Paignton. Further along the coast brings you to the South Hams, an area renowned for its beaches, country houses and pretty towns like Dartmouth, Salcombe and Totnes.

**TOP TIP**

Regatta season brings a party atmosphere to Torquay and Dartmouth, and major music and literature festivals to Dartington, near Totnes.

Torquay

**BRIXHAM**

At the western end of Tor Bay, **Brixham** is the smallest town on the English Riviera, and has a very different feel to Torquay and Paignton. Life here still revolves (as it has for centuries) around fishing: Brixham is home to one of the UK's biggest fishing fleets, and a slew of restaurants make creative use of the catch. There's also a life-sized replica of the *Golden Hind*, the ship on which Devon-born explorer Sir Francis Drake circumnavigated the globe in the late 1500s.

For the full fishy experience, book a tour of the historic **Fish Market** (including a fish breakfast) through Rockfish restaurant, with all proceeds supporting the Fishermen's Mission charity.

**Princess Gardens**

## Exploring the English Riviera

RETRO BRITISH BEACH VIBES

With 22 miles of coastline and over 20 beaches to explore, there's no better way to spend a sunny day on the English Riviera. Start with a walk along the Victorian seafront in **Torquay** (25 miles south of Exeter), with its wide, palm-lined promenade and numerous gardens. The historic **Princess Pier**, built in 1890, and neighbouring **Princess Gardens** are perhaps the most iconic sights, named for Queen Victoria's fourth daughter Princess Louise. Torquay's most popular beach is **Torre Abbey Sands**, a sandy, tidal beach overlooked by one of Torbay's most historic buildings, **Torre Abbey**, built in 1196. Rent a kayak or paddleboard from **Wesup Abbey Sands** to make the most of the bay's calm waters, or lose yourself amid the abbey's attractive gardens above.

The long, pink-hued beach at **Paignton**, 3 miles further south, also boasts a grand Victorian pier, but this one is steeped in seaside nostalgia, home to an amusement arcade and funfair rides. Despite a slightly tired feel, the retro vibes

**WHERE TO EAT BEYOND EXETER**

**Anchorstone Cafe**
Tuck into succulent Dartmouth crab, lobster or hand-dived scallops at this creekside cafe in Dittisham. **£**

**Riverford Field Kitchen**
An eco-friendly, farm-to-table dining experience near Totnes with veg-centric seasonal menus. **££**

**The Angel, Dartmouth**
Relaxed fine-dining and special tasting menus at a multi-award-winning riverside restaurant. **£££**

and sandy beaches continue to appeal to families, especially the golden sands of **Goodrington Beach** and **Broadsands**.

For a vintage seaside day out, head for the **Babbacombe Cliff Railway**, a 1920s funicular that will transport you from the upper station on Cliffside Rd down to the rust-red shingle sand at **Oddicombe Beach**. Pause in the clifftop gardens at **Babbacombe Downs** before descending for views along the coast as far as Dorset.

## Historic Buildings & Hippie Vibes

ETHICAL, ALTERNATIVE TOTNES

At the top of the Dart Estuary, 30 minutes by train south of Exeter, **Totnes** is a charming market town packed with historic buildings and incredible Tudor architecture. It's also one of the most ethical places in Britain: in 2006, Totnes was one of the first towns in the UK to declare itself a Transition Town, and in 2011 it became a Fairtrade Town. **Riverford Farm**, birthplace of the organic veggie-box subscription service, lies nearby, and Totnes' high street is one of the most independent in England, crammed with zero-waste shops, local crafts boutiques and vegan cafes. Historic highlights include **Totnes Castle** (a Norman motte and bailey castle with 13th-century stone keep) the colonnaded **Tudor buildings** near the top of High St, **Totnes Museum** with its Elizabethan Garden, and the ancient **Guildhall** tucked away down a leafy side street behind the church.

## Fortress Views

DISCOVER DARTMOUTH CASTLE

From its vantage point at the entrance to the Dart estuary, 45 miles south of Exeter, the imposing limestone artillery fort of **Dartmouth Castle** has been watching over Dartmouth and the River Dart for over 600 years. The oldest parts of the fort date from 1388, built during the Hundred Years' War to protect from potential French invasion. A booming sound-and-light show inside the Victorian-era point battery brings history to life. Don't miss the estuary views from the top of the gun tower, which is one of the oldest gun forts in England, built in the 1490s. You can walk to the castle, but the **Dartmouth Castle Ferry** is much more romantic.

**DAWLISH WARREN**

Every autumn, up to 23,000 birds arrive in the Exe Estuary to overwinter. Many of them flock to the grasslands, salt marshes and mudflats of **Dawlish Warren National Nature Reserve**, one of the south west's best birdwatching locations, centred on a 1½ mile long spit of white sand dunes. In spring and summer, visit for the tranquil beach and abundant wildflowers. For a day trip, walk the 6-mile coast path there from Teignmouth, returning by train.

**MORE CASTLES?**

If you're a castle fan, don't miss the fortresses in **Pendennis** (p320), **St Mawes** (p320), **Restormel** (p327) and **Totnes**, as well as myth-shrouded **Tintagel** (p305)

**WHERE TO FIND ESTATES & GARDENS IN SOUTH DEVON**

**Overbeck's Garden**
Clinging to the cliffs above Salcombe, a hidden paradise of layered subtropical gardens.

**Coleton Fishacre**
An evocative country house with Art Deco 1920s interiors and a tropical garden overlooking the sea.

**Dartington Estate**
Visit this 1200-acre charity-owned country estate for walks in the Grade II–listed gardens or the Deer Park.

## PADDLEBOARDING IN DARTMOUTH

**Alana Bonnick**, marine biologist and founder of The Paddle Shack, shares her favourite SUP spots. *@thepaddle shackdevon*

Heading upriver, you can explore a multitude of beautiful creeks and hidden beaches. The higher reaches of the Dart are nontidal, offering calm meandering stretches of water. Along the coast, you'll find **Castle Cove**, **Sugary Cove** and **Compass Cove** to the right, or turning left you'll reach **Mill Bay**.

Good trip planning is important: the Dart is very tidal, and winds can affect you, while coastal paddles are more advanced due to sea chop and changing weather. Alternatively, book a guided paddle with us – we have a local seal colony on our doorstep and see them on most paddles!

## A Day on the Dart

WILDLIFE, CRUISES AND VINEYARDS

Flowing serenely through a deep wooded valley, the Dart Estuary is the final, tidal stretch of the **River Dart**. Rich in wildlife and dotted with waterside villages like idyllic Dittisham, the estuary is best explored from the water.

One of the best ways to explore is on a kayak or paddleboard. Rent a kayak or board from **Totnes Kayaks**, in Stoke Gabriel, and follow the tide up- or downriver, keeping your eyes peeled for otters, seals, kingfishers and more. **Canoe Adventures** run year-round voyages in their 12-seater wooden canoes.

If you'd prefer someone else to do the work, catch the 90-minute cruise from Dartmouth to Totnes with **Dartmouth Steam Railway and Riverboat Company**, which provides an amusing, insightful commentary and unparalleled views from the top deck. Alternatively, you can rent your own self-drive motorboat from **Dartmouth Boat Hire**: keep your eyes peeled for kingfishers, cormorants, grey herons, little egrets and even seals.

On dry land, you can also follow the **Dart Valley Trail**, a 16-mile footpath from Dartmouth to Totnes through ancient woodlands, passing within reach of Sandridge Barton Winery, home of **Sharpham Wines**. Pop in for a tour and tasting – it would be rude not to!

## The Mystery Maestro

VISIT AGATHA CHRISTIE'S HOLIDAY HOME

**Greenway**, Agatha Christie's secluded riverside getaway, lies in a remote spot above the River Dart, surrounded by beautiful gardens. Christie called the Georgian manor 'the loveliest place in the world', and it's still filled with the author's collections and treasures. The best way to arrive is to take the small, twin-decked **Greenway & Dittisham Ferry**, or to walk to the house from Dartmouth via the **Dart Valley Trail**, a delightful, easy riverside stroll of about 4 miles.

Slapton Sands

### WHERE TO FIND TOP PUBS IN SOUTH DEVON

**The Cove, Hope Cove**
Beach views, local spirits and ever-changing taps featuring the UK's best craft beers.

**The Bull Inn, Totnes**
Organic wines, local beers and seasonal special cocktails at this ethical, organic pub.

**The Kings Arms, Strete**
Devon-brewed ales and cider and epic sea views at a community-owned clifftop pub.

Beach near Hallsands

## Start Me Up

HIKE TO START POINT

The grand sweep of **Start Bay** offers fantastic walks and coastal views. Follow the meandering A379 coast road west from Dartmouth to **Slapton Sands**: a narrow strip of shingle beach with the sea on one side and the broad sweep of **Slapton Ley**, the south west's largest freshwater lake, on the other (look out for a WWII Sherman Tank left-over from D-Day rehearsals). From here, the coast path strikes out to the historic **Start Point Lighthouse**, built in 1836. There are many little coves and beaches to discover nearby, as well as the ruined village of **South Hallsands**, a 'lost village' swept away by a storm in 1917.

**MORE RIVER ADVENTURES**

Cornwall's three great tidal rivers – the **Fal**, the **Helford** (p322) and the **Fowey** (p324) – all offer boat trips, paddleboarding, cruises and much more.

### ISLAND WALKS & SEA TRACTORS

Just off the coast from the family-favourite beach of **Bigbury-on-Sea** lies an iconic South Devon landmark, the wild and windswept **Burgh Island**. With its rocky coastline and tiny hidden coves, this tidal island makes an adventurous day out.

At low tide, you can walk there across a spit of sand stretching out from Bigbury, or at high tide hitch a ride on the Sea Tractor – a true one-off, designed in 1969 and the only one of its kind in the world. It's operated by **Burgh Island Hotel**, a striking Art Deco hotel that's almost as famous as the island itself.

End with a pint at the island's landmark tavern (and one of England's oldest), the 14th-century **Pilchard Inn** – supposedly haunted by a smuggler's ghost.

### GETTING AROUND

The London Paddington to Penzance main line cuts through South Devon, calling at Totnes and Newton Abbot; some services also stop at Dawlish and Teignmouth. A branch line takes in the coastal stations en route from Exeter St David's to Paignton.

Bus links are good between South Devon's main towns; inevitably they're less frequent between smaller towns and villages. **Traveline South West** (travelinesw.com) has timetables.

# PLYMOUTH

Britain's 'Ocean City', Plymouth has long been a city of seafarers. A string of voyagers set out from here, among them the Mayflower Pilgrims, Captain James Cook and Sir Francis Drake, who began his circumnavigation of the globe here.

Home to Europe's largest naval base and the second biggest fresh fish market in England, Plymouth is still intrinsically linked to the sea. Badly bombed during WWII, and hastily rebuilt, Plymouth's city centre is defined by functionality, rather than beauty. But pockets of historic architecture remain, while an ongoing waterfront regeneration and exciting new Cultural Quarter are creating a city that deserves a second look.

## TOP TIP

The city lies on Plymouth Sound, a deep, sheltered inlet in the English Channel where the Rivers Plym and Tamar meet the sea. With the city centre spread along the waterfront, sometimes the most direct route from one side to the other is by ferry, rather than car or bus.

**Plymouth**

## PLYMOUTH'S MARITIME HISTORY WALKING TOUR

Discover Plymouth's sights and delve into its maritime history with this city centre walking tour, setting out from the striking **1 Victorian Guildhall** at the heart of the city. Follow Armada Way down to reach **2 The Hoe**, a clifftop park with unbeatable views of Plymouth Sound and several notable sights. Front and centre, the towering **3 Plymouth Naval Memorial** commemorates over 23,000 sailors of WWI and WWII who have no known grave. Nearby stands a statue of **4 Sir Francis Drake**: explorer, privateer and mayor of Plymouth, who, according to popular legend, played bowls in the Hoe while awaiting the Spanish Armada in 1588. Sir Francis Drake was also an early slave trader. At the eastern end, heavy stone walls enclose the **5 Royal Citadel**, a 17th-century fortress still in use by the military today, and overlooking the sea is the iconic red and white **6 Smeaton's Tower lighthouse**. Originally built on Eddystone Reef in 1759, it was moved to the Hoe in the 1880s.

Pause for views from the top of the **7 Belvedere 'Wedding Cake'**, a grandiose Victorian structure with three tiers of colonnaded terraces, then take the steps down to follow the coast road around to **8 Sutton Harbour**. Here the **9 Mayflower Steps** memorial marks the approximate site from which the Pilgrims set sail for North America in 1620. Follow Southside St into **10 The Barbican**, an area of cobbled streets, historic architecture and quirky shops. Return via the picturesque New Ln, passing the timber-clad **11 Elizabethan House** – dating from 1599 – to end at the **12 Mayflower Museum**. Allow a little time for a visit to learn more about the story of the Pilgrim Fathers, as well as the history – and impact – of English colonisation.

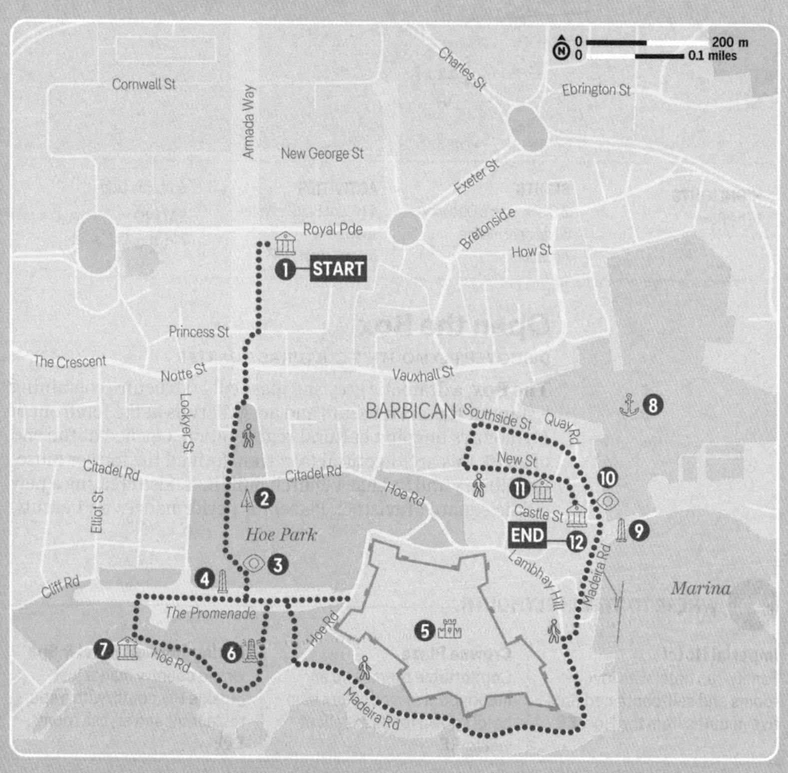

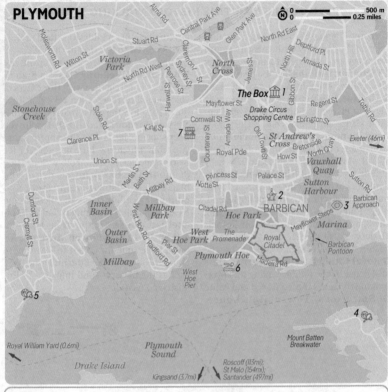

## PLYMOUTH

**HIGHLIGHTS**
1 The Box

**SIGHTS**
2 Black Friar's Distillery
3 National Marine Aquarium

**ACTIVITIES**
4 Mount Batten Watersports
5 Southwest SUP
6 Tinside Lido

**EATING**
7 Plymouth Market

# Open the Box

DISCOVER PLYMOUTH'S CULTURAL QUARTER

**The Box**, a dramatic grey and glass cubic structure containing a state-of-the-art museum and art gallery, is at the forefront of Plymouth's ongoing cultural regeneration. Opened at the end of 2020, this architectural icon transformed the former museum, library and St Luke's church buildings, also creating a new public square (Tavistock Place) for performances and events.

### WHERE TO STAY IN PLYMOUTH

**Imperial Hotel**
Family-run hotel with lovely rooms and self-contained flats, five minutes from the Hoe. **££**

**Crowne Plaza**
Comfortable rooms and an indoor pool at a popular chain hotel known for its excellent views. **££**

**Boringdon Hall Hotel & Spa**
Grand country manor just outside Plymouth, with a spa, restaurant and stylish rooms. **£££**

Alongside Plymouth Art University's Arts Institute, this exciting redevelopment forms the heart of Plymouth's new Cultural Quarter. Inside, permanent exhibits tell the story of England's Ocean City, from vast ship figureheads in the lobby to the excellent 100 Journeys exhibit showcasing the momentous voyages that have set out from Plymouth over the centuries.

## Ocean City

WATERY ADVENTURES, INDOORS AND OUT

Wherever you go in Plymouth, the salty tang of the sea is never too far away, so it's fitting that the city is home to the **National Marine Aquarium**, the UK's largest aquarium, with vast tanks showcasing marine life both local and exotic: sand tiger sharks, lemon sharks, barracuda, rays and loads more.

For a very different view of the Ocean City, head for a dip at the lovely **Tinside Lido**, a striking art deco lido built in 1935 overlooking Plymouth Sound. Or book a session with **Mount Batten Watersports** or **Southwest SUP**, who can help you explore the dramatic sights of Plymouth Sound on the water.

## Naval Strength

THE ROYAL NAVY'S GIN HISTORY

At the heart of the historic Barbican district, **Black Friar's Distillery** has been the home of Plymouth Gin since 1793, making it the oldest working gin distillery in England. Their naval-strength gin was supplied to the Royal Navy for nearly 200 years; officers made it into a 'medicinal' drink with lime juice, inventing the Gimlet cocktail. The building itself, a former monastery, dates from the early 1400s. It's worth a visit for the Refectory Bar's stunning beamed ceiling alone. Take one of the tours which run throughout the day for a glimpse of the Victorian still, an insight into the production process and a tasting.

**Black Friar's Distillery**

### PLYMOUTH'S SECRET FOOD SPOT

**Jodie Pierre**, local chef and owner of Maurish *@areyoufeeling maurish.*

The market is undergoing a transformation at the moment, turning into more of a food court. There are some great places to eat in the market now and it's bringing different clientele in. **Maurish** serves home-cooked Mauritian food, inspired by my dad who came from Port Louis.

Other must-visit food stalls here are **Taste of Thailand** for authentic Thai food, **Everest Flavours** for Nepalese street-food snacks (don't miss their Everest Spicy Special), and **At Kitchen** or **Tea & Bun** for Asian cuisine. For dessert, try a bubble waffle from **Kawaffle**.

### GETTING AROUND

Plymouth is a mainline stop on the London–Penzance rail route. The city centre is quite sprawling and can be hilly. You can get between the waterfront areas by ferry or water taxi; the tourist office can provide a leaflet outlining all available water links. For longer distances, Plymouth Citybus is the main bus provider. Be aware that the Barbican district has some cobbled and uneven streets.

# Beyond Plymouth

**Devon's biggest city lies within surprisingly easy reach of nature, from quiet beaches to tranquil river valleys.**

Location is one of Plymouth's biggest selling points. Perched on the coast at Devon's western border, this waterside city is within day-tripping distance of some of the southwest's top attractions. It's less than a 20-minute drive to the edge of Dartmoor, Cornwall is just a ferry ride across the Tamar, and South Devon's coastal highlights are all less than an hour away.

Moving eastwards from the city leads to some of the most underrated beaches in Devon, as well as some of the best views on the South West Coast Path. And tucked along the Devon–Cornwall border, the Tamar Valley AONB is a rich landscape where heritage and nature collide.

**TOP TIP**

The Tamar Valley railway line from Plymouth to Gunnislake is known for its views: grab a window seat and enjoy.

River Tamar

Combestone Tor

## Tour the Tors

TAKE A HIKE ON DARTMOOR

Dartmoor's tors are legendary. Though they look like they were dropped upon the landscape by a giant hand, these freestanding hilltop outcrops of granite were formed from molten rock some 280 million years ago and left exposed by millennia of erosion. The bizarre shapes of these stacks and monoliths have inspired humankind for centuries. Some were used as places of worship by Dartmoor's ancient inhabitants, others have inspired folklore and legends that persist to this day.

There are over 160 tors in all. Some, like the face-shaped **Combestone Tor**, can be seen from the road, while others require a walk. For the best views, try **High Willhays** (the highest point in the park), **Leather Tor** or **Black Tor**.

## England's Last Castle

ARCHITECTURAL ICON – OR FOOLISH FOLLY?

It may look the part of a medieval fortress, with its portcullis and arrow slits, but there's an oddly unweathered quality to **Castle Drogo**, 33 miles northeast of Plymouth. This was, in fact, the last castle built in England, constructed between 1911–31 for self-made millionaire Julius Drewe and designed by the renowned architect Edwin Lutyens. Drogo was

### GREAT DARTMOOR WALKS

**Lydford Gorge**
The deepest gorge in the south west, home to a 30m waterfall and a magical whirlpool.

**Wistman's Wood**
Easy stroll from a pub to a mossy oak woodland straight from a fairytale.

**Bellever Forest**
Several waymarked trails in a dense pine forest: climb Bellever Tor and explore Kraps Ring Bronze Age village.

**Princetown Railway Track**
Follow the old railway to King's Tor, passing two abandoned quarries, Swelltor and Foggintor.

**Yes Tor and High Willhays**
The two highest points on Dartmoor; 619m and 621m above sea level respectively.

### WHERE TO FIND CLASSIC DARTMOOR PUBS

**Warren House Inn**
Legendary pub along the B3212 in Postbridge where the fire has remained lit since 1845. ££

**Three Crowns**
Part-thatched inn with 13th-century features and a modern atrium dining room in Chagford. ££

**Rugglestone Inn**
Log fires and home-cooked food in a beautiful, wisteria-clad stone property beside the moors in Widecombe. ££

surprisingly state of the art for its time, with electric lights, a switchboard, even a lift – all powered by renewable energy from a hydro turbine on the River Teign.

From the castle, you can set out on one of Dartmoor's most atmospheric walks around and into the plummeting **Teign Gorge**, crossing the river at Fingle Bridge.

### STARGAZING ON DARTMOOR

Dartmoor's vast, sparsely populated landscapes provide prime stargazing conditions. On clear nights, head for remote, hilltop car parks like the ones at **Haytor** or **Holming Beam**; gostargazing.co.uk has a full list and light pollution map. Castle Drogo's **Piddledown Common** is good spot for both stargazing and nocturnal wildlife, coming alive with badgers, bats and tawny owls.

## On Your Bike

TIME FOR TWO-WHEELED FUN

Dartmoor's cinematic landscapes are a joy to explore on two wheels. There's an extensive network of routes, bridleways and byways, covering everything from challenging mountain trails to gentler paved paths.

One of the best is the 11-mile **Granite Way**, running along an old railway line from Okehampton to Lydford. Paved, traffic-free and mostly flat, this popular route crosses the 165m-long Meldon Viaduct, affording spectacular views of Meldon Reservoir's dam. Or for moorland views and majestic tors, try the ride from **Princetown** to **Burrator Reservoir**. There are two route options: one follows the old Princetown Railway past granite quarries, the other crosses open moorland on permitted bridleways via Ditsworthy Warren. Downloadable maps for all three routes and many others are available at visitdartmoor.co.uk.

**Dartmoor Bike Park** provides a different kind of biking experience. Located within the woodlands at River Dart Country Park, near Ashburton, the bike park has a range of mountain bike trails and terrains to suit riders of all abilities.

### MORE BIKE RIDING

Cornwall has some excellent bike trails to try too, including the famous **Camel Trail** (p302) near Padstow and the **Coast to Coast Cycle Trail** (p307) between Portreath and Bissoe.

## Adventures on Horseback

BRIDLEWAYS AND HORSE TREKKING

With miles of bridleways to explore, Dartmoor is an excellent horse-riding destination. For new visitors, the southeast has several easy rides and gentle slopes, while for experienced riders southwest Dartmoor's remote high moors are an unbeatable adventure. Several stables offer guided horse trekking; family-run **Cholwell Riding Stables**, between Tavistock and Lydford, caters for riders of all levels.

### GETTING AROUND

Dartmoor's public transport network is sadly less than comprehensive. Bus services exist between most towns and villages, although often only a few times a day, so a little planning is required to explore without a car. Two additional bus services run seasonally, the Dartmoor Explorer and the Haytor Hoppa. If driving, be prepared for single-lane roads, tight bends, narrow bridges and animals on the road. The speed limit on the moors is 40mph.

# NORTH DEVON

Intensely rugged and in places utterly remote, north Devon has a coast to inspire. In the 1970s the South West Coast Path officially opened here – the epic long-distance trail that begins in Minehead and marches along the coast of North Devon before skirting round the entire southwestern corner of England. It's wonderful for hiking, and you'll also find plenty of fine beaches and coves to explore here, from the eminently surfable sands of Croyde to the dune-backed Braunton Burrows. And if you're a wildlife lover, don't miss a boat trip out to Lundy, North Devon's very own island nature reserve.

### TOP TIP

The Bristol Channel's tides are the second most variable in the world after Canada's Fundy Bay. Whole beaches can disappear at high tide, leaving walkers and rock-poolers cut off – always check tide times before setting out. Stick to lifeguarded beaches and learn your beach flags.

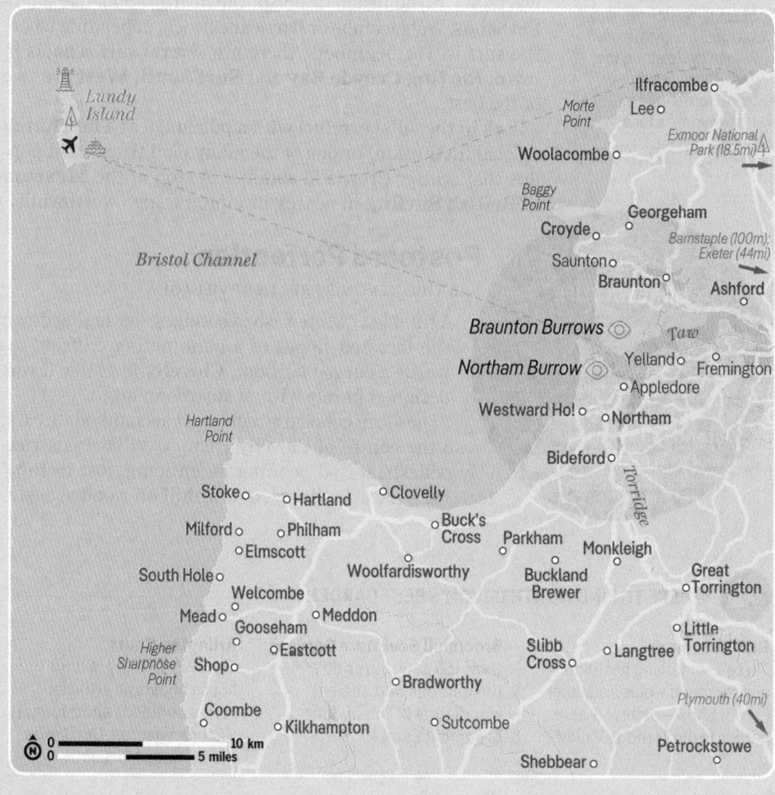

### THE TARKA TRAIL

Exmoor, North Devon and Dartmoor are linked by the **Tarka Trail**: a 180-mile figure-of-eight walking and cycling loop inspired by the route taken by the title character in Henry Williamson's 1927 novel *Tarka the Otter*. Starting in Barnstaple, the trail heads up through Exmouth, along the north coast, then down to Okehampton on the northern edge of Dartmoor, ending with a ride on the scenic Tarka Line railway.

The cycling section starts in Braunton and follows a disused Victorian railway path 30 miles south to Meeth. Traffic-free and tarmacked, the gentle 6-mile cycle along the Taw-Torridge Estuary from Barnstaple to Instow makes for a lovely day out.

## Island Escape

CATCH A BOAT TO LUNDY

Tiny **Lundy Island** in the Bristol Channel is home to a population of around 180 Atlantic grey seals, plus puffins, Lundy Ponies and feral goats. From March to November, visitors can hop aboard MS *Oldenburg*, a 1950s ferry whose timetable and departure point (Ilfracombe or Bideford) varies with the tides. The crossing takes around two hours. In winter months, this is replaced by an infrequent helicopter service.

The island wardens run seasonal guided walks, Rockpool Rambles and Snorkel Safaris, timed with ferry arrivals. Climb the narrow spiral staircase of **Old Light** – a historic lighthouse built in 1820 – for views of the entire island.

Lundy's facilities are sparse: there's just one pub (the Marisco Tavern) and a village shop. For an overnight adventure, there are several accommodation options for an off-grid escape, all managed by the Landmark Trust.

## Wave Function

DEVON'S TOP SURF TOWN

The crescent of sandy beach in **Croyde** has been drawing surfers here since the 1920s. Experienced surfers can hit the waves at Croyde Beach or one of the nearby spots like Saunton Sands, Woolacombe or Barricane Beach, depending where the surf is. For beginners, there are several surf schools in town: **Surfing Croyde Bay** and **Surf South West** are two of the best.

Back in the village, refuel with a pub lunch at **The Thatch** (a local institution) or one of the many food trucks and pop-ups that scatter Croyde in summer. A stop at the **Museum of British Surfing** in nearby Braunton is also worthwhile.

### MORE WILDLIFE

If you loved Lundy's wildlife, you'll definitely want to take a ranger-guided tour of **St George's Island** (p325), or take a trip out to **Tresco** (p316) on the Isles of Scilly.

## Postcard Perfection

IS THIS DEVON'S PRETTIEST VILLAGE?

A tumble of whitewashed cottages zigzagging down the forested slopes of a plummeting cliffside towards a curved harbour, **Clovelly** feels like it was designed purely with postcards in mind.

The steep cobbled streets can't accommodate cars, so the centre of Clovelly Historic Village is strictly pedestrianised, lending an enticing 'lost in time' feel. Deliveries are dragged downhill on wooden sledg-

### WHERE TO FIND NORTH DEVON'S BEST GARDENS

**RHS Rosemoor**
There's something beautiful all year round – plus a summer Flower Show – at this 65-acre garden in the Torridge Valley.

**Broomhill Sculpture Gardens**
Over 150 sculptures dot the gardens and ancient woodlands of the historic Broomhill Estate.

**Arlington Court**
This 19th-century manor house boasts an artificial lake, woodlands and a formal Victorian garden. Don't miss the Carriage Museum.

HELEN HOTSON/SHUTTERSTOCK ©

Clovelly

es; the Clovelly Donkeys, who once carried supplies in and fisher's hauls out, now spend their days posing for photos at the historic stables.

Make your way downhill past craft workshops and quaint shops to reach **Clovelly Quay**, where the sea wall affords the best views of the hill-hugging town. Clovelly's two museums are worth a short visit: the **Kingsley Museum** – former home of *The Water Babies* author Charles Kingsley – and the cramped and atmospheric **Fisherman's Cottage Museum**.

### ILFRACOMBE'S ART SCENE

In 2012 Damien Hirst gave the seaside town of **Ilfracombe** a gift that many of the town's inhabitants would rather return. Hirst's 20m tall bronze statue **Verity** stands on the harbourside: naked, pregnant, holding aloft a huge sword and flayed on her sea-facing side to reveal sinew, fat and an unborn foetus. Whether you think it's an eyesore, or an allegory for truth as the artist affirms, Hirst's divisive statue feels like the herald of Ilfracombe's vibrant art scene.

A slew of galleries and studios have popped up in the last few years: **Fore St** is emerging as a hub for indie shops and art galleries, while elsewhere in town the **Aluna Collective** and **Fleek** art galleries sell works by local artists.

## North Devon Nature

EXPLORE A SPRAWLING DUNE SYSTEM

Backing the popular Saunton Sands beach, **Braunton Burrows** is one of the largest dune systems in the British Isles at approximately 1000 hectares. These are home to a rich diversity of wildlife, including rare orchids, butterflies and reptiles. **Northam Burrows** are smaller but equally scenic, grazed by free-roaming sheep and home to England's oldest golf course. Both are beloved by birdwatchers: look out for curlews, oystercatchers and lapwings in winter.

### GETTING AROUND

Car is the easiest way to explore, but in peak season congested roads and packed car parks can be an issue. In some areas, especially around the Hartland Peninsula, expect narrow country lanes which may prove a challenge for those not used to them. Stagecoach operates regular bus services connecting most towns and beaches on the coastline, including a seasonal open-top bus.

# PADSTOW

If anywhere symbolises Cornwall's increasingly chic cachet, it's Padstow. This old fishing port has become one of the county's most cosmopolitan corners thanks largely to the influence of celeb chef Rick Stein and others who have followed in his wake. Glitzy restaurants and posh boutiques now sit a little incongruously alongside the town's old pubs and pasty shops, making it quite hard to know where the real Padstow and the postcard version of it begins.

Whether the town's managed to hold on to its soul during the gentrification process is debatable, but it's hard not to be charmed by the seaside setting. Padstow's main asset is its location beside the lovely Camel Estuary, a lifelong favourite of poet John Betjeman, who holidayed here for many years. The sandy sweep of Daymer Bay and the treacherous sandbank known as the Doom Bar unfurls along the estuary, and the town of Rock, a small fishing village turned fancy resort town, can be reached by ferry.

## TOP TIP

Padstow and the surrounding area is packed in July and August: it's much more pleasant to visit in spring or autumn, when the big crowds have left and you can appreciate the scenery in (relative) peace and quiet. Book accommodation well ahead, or base yourself in the nearby town of Wadebridge.

**Camel Estuary (p302)**

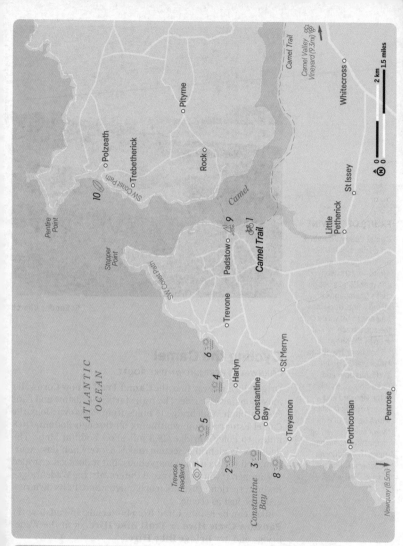

**HIGHLIGHTS**
1 Camel Trail

**SIGHTS**
2 Booby's Bay
3 Constantine Bay
4 Harlyn Eay
5 Mother Ivey's Bay
6 Trevone
7 Trevose Head
8 Treyarnon

**ACTIVITIES, COURSES & TOURS**
9 Jubilee Queen
10 Polzeath

ATLANTIC OCEAN
Pentire Point
Stepper Point
Trevose Headland
Constantine Bay
SW Coast Path
Polzeath
Trebetherick
Pityme
Rock
Padstow
Camel
Camel Trail
Trevone
Harlyn
Constantine Bay
St Merryn
Treyarnon
Porthcothan
Penrose
Newquay (8.5mi)
Little Petherick
St Issey
Whitecross
Camel Valley Vineyard (9.3mi)
0 2 km
0 1.5 miles

Constantine Bay

St Enodoc Church

### FRUITS OF THE VINE

**Camel Valley Vineyard**, producing since 1989, has a range including award-winning whites and rosés, and a bubbly that's Champagne in all but name. Book for a tour and to sip wines on the sun terrace, or just drop by the shop.

The newer **Trevibban Mill**, established in 2008, has one- and three-hour tours taking in the vineyard and winery before finishing with a tasting of either five or seven wines. Sit on the bewitching patio framed by wildflower meadows and sip a crisp, chilled white.

## Cycling the Camel

CORNWALL'S BEST-KNOWN BIKE ROUTE

Originally a railway line, the **Camel Trail** is now Cornwall's most popular bike ride. The trail starts in Padstow and runs east through Wadebridge (5 miles from Padstow) along the Camel Estuary before continuing on through Bodmin (10.8 miles) to Poley's Bridge (18.3 miles) on Bodmin Moor. The Padstow–Wadebridge section makes a lovely half-day excursion, and the scenery is marvellous, but it does get crowded in summer. If you want to avoid the crowds, the Wadebridge–Bodmin section is usually much quieter and, in its own rugged way, just as scenic.

Bikes can be readily hired from both ends: in Padstow, try **Padstow Cycle Hire** or **Trail Bike Hire**, or at the Wadebridge end, try **Bridge Bike Hire**.

For sustenance en route, try the **Camel Trail Tea Garden** just outside Wadebridge, or if you're pedalling all the way to Bodmin Moor, the homely **Snails Pace Cafe** near St Breward.

### WHERE TO STAY AROUND PADSTOW

**Treyarnon Bay YHA**
A 1930s-era beach hostel on the bluffs above Treyarnon Bay. Pleasant rooms, plus camping space and bell tents. £

**Padstow Harbour Hotel**
Formerly the Metropole, this period beauty commands a panoramic view over the estuary. £££

**The Pig at Harlyn Bay**
A new addition to the litter of these rustic-chic hotels, with inventive rooms and a super bistro. £££

## Boat Trips Up the Camel

UP THE ESTUARY

In the middle of the Camel runs the treacherous sandbank known as the **Doom Bar**, which has claimed many ships over the years (and also gave its name to a popular local ale). It's a unique habitat, with important bird and sea life populations. Between Easter and October, the Jubilee Queen runs scenic trips along the coastline, while **Padstow Sealife Safaris** offers visits to local seal and seabird colonies.

## Rock On

LIVE THE MILLIONAIRE'S HIGH LIFE

The exclusive enclave of **Rock**, across the Camel Estuary from Padstow, is now one of Cornwall's priciest postcodes – earning the area a whole bevy of disparaging nicknames (Cornwall's St-Tropez, Kensington-on-Sea etc). While it's certainly a far cry from the sleepy seaside backwater recalled fondly by John Betjeman, the dune-backed white sands of **Daymer Bay** remain as glorious as ever, and if you're a poetry fan, you'll want to stroll up to **St Enodoc Church**, where the poet was buried on a typically drizzly Cornish day in May 1984. It doesn't take long to find his ornate headstone.

Along the coast is **Polzeath**, the area's main surfing beach: contact **Surf's Up** or **Era Adventures** if you want some watery action.

The **Black Rock Ferry** runs across to Rock regularly (taking just 10 minutes); otherwise it's about half an hour by bus or car.

## Beaches & Beacons

HIKE OR BIKE TO TREVOSE HEAD

Four miles west of Padstow town looms the distinctive outcrop of Trevose Headland, topped by a lighthouse since the mid-19th century. It's accessed via a private toll road; the wonderful coastal views are just about worth it, but even better, hike or bike here to drink in the scenery for free.

En route to the headland, you'll pass four of Padstow's so-called **Seven Bays**: Trevone, Harlyn, Mother Ivey's and Booby's Bay. On the opposite side are the more dramatic sands of Constantine and Treyarnon, backed by rugged rocks and a fine tidal pool. Furthest of all is Porthcothan, a 5-mile drive from Padstow.

### PADSTOW ON A PLATE

**The Seafood Restaurant**
The restaurant that started the Stein saga, and still one of Cornwall's top places to eat. It's now managed by his middle son, Jack. **£££**

**Paul Ainsworth at No 6**
TV chef Ainsworth is often called the heir to the Stein crown, and his food thoroughly deserves the plaudits. **£££**

**Prawn on the Lawn**
An offshoot of a London original, this tiny seafood bar is a fresh addition to Padstow's dining line-up. **££**

**The Mariners**
Paul Ainsworth took over this country pub in 2019, and it's become Rock's go-to spot for gastronomes. **££**

**St Kew Inn**
A rustic, character-filled pub with plenty of flagstones and beams, and a sweet beer garden. **££**

### GETTING AROUND

There are a couple of car parks beside the harbour in Padstow, but they fill up quickly, so it's usually better to park at one of the large car parks at the top of town and walk down. First Kernow buses connect Newquay and Padstow. The **Black Tor Ferry** runs to Rock year-round (the crossing only takes around 10 minutes), or you can book a late-night trip via the **Rock Water Taxi**.

# Beyond Padstow

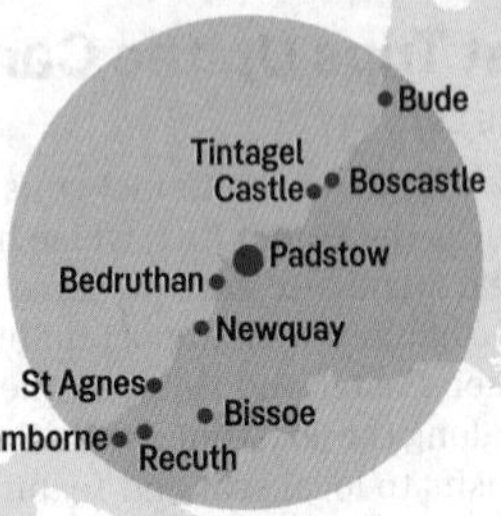

Bude
Tintagel Castle
Boscastle
Padstow
Bedruthan
Newquay
St Agnes
Bissoe
Camborne
Recuth

**If it's the quintessential Cornish combination of crags, bays and white-horse surf you're after, then the north coast delivers – and then some.**

Battered by breakers and scoured by the tides, north Cornwall is where you feel the full force of Mother Nature's handiwork. With its cliffs, tidal pools, sea caves and golden beaches, the north coast presents the image of Cornwall most people hold in their imaginations, and this is where you'll find many of the county's most popular beaches. It gets hectic in season, so if you're looking for somewhere a little quieter, the stretch of shoreline around Bude is often a good bet. And don't overlook the seam of granite that runs down the county's middle: from wild Bodmin Moor to the old mining country around Camborne and Redruth, Cornwall's spine offers a compelling insight into its rugged, elemental past.

### TOP TIP

The distances between towns aren't huge along the north coast, but the winding, twisting coast road means that you're best off taking things easy and not trying to pack in too much in one day. Buses are a feasible way of getting around, and you won't have to worry about car parking.

**Bude shoreline**

GARY PERKIN/SHUTTERSTOCK ©

***Gallos* (known as the King Arthur statue) by Rubin Eynon, Tintagel**

## Idylls of the King

KING ARTHUR'S FABLED BIRTHPLACE

The spectre of King Arthur looms large over **Tintagel** and its clifftop **castle**, 22 miles northeast of Padstow. Local legend claims the legendary king was born, or possibly conceived, here. In fact, it's largely the 13th-century work of Richard, Earl of Cornwall.

Arthurian links aside, it's a soul-stirring spot for a stronghold. The castle's most striking modern feature is the controversial new footbridge which has been constructed between the two sides of the medieval castle, re-creating a land bridge that existed 500 years ago. It's a hair-raising feeling as you walk across and see the rocks far below your feet (although the alternative, a dizzyingly steep staircase cut into the rocks, is almost worse).

### BUDE SEA POOL

Thirty-five miles from Padstow along the so-called Atlantic Highway, **Bude** is a blustery beach town which has been reeling in day-trippers and beachgoers since the great Victorian tourist boom in the late 19th century. Like Newquay, it's not the prettiest town, and is mainly visited for its beaches. Summerleaze is the closest beach to town; its main attraction is the **Bude Sea Pool**, a saltwater lido built in the 1930s, which warms up fast on sunny days and is perfect for kids.

### WHERE TO EAT ON THE NORTH COAST

**Outlaw's New Road, Port Isaac**
Classy seafood in Cornwall by Nathan Outlaw – with a price tag to match. There's a smaller seafood bar too. **£££**

**The Fish House, Newquay**
Newquay's top place for seafood, bar none, with a lovely location right beside Fistral's sands. **££**

**Emily Scott, near Newquay**
Top chef Emily Scott has a cracking new restaurant on the seafront at Watergate Bay. **£££**

## SURFING THE NORTH COAST

**Andy Cameron**, Managing Director of Wavehunters at the Extreme Academy on Watergate Bay, names his favourite North Coast surf spots. *watergatebay.co.uk/extreme-academy*

**Polzeath**
My all-time favourite spot which works on all stages of the tide. The paddle can be tough on a big swell, but that keeps the crowds down.

**Watergate Bay**
A huge, friendly surfers' beach. Even on a summer's day you can find a wave to yourself. At the far end, you can find a super-fun right hander. Mid to high tide and back is best.

**Lundy Bay**
A proper winter spot. It's not for beginners, but when everywhere else is blown out, Lundy is the spot: catch the right peak and you could be in for a head tuck or even get barrelled.

# Witch's Brew

PICNIC ON BOSCASTLE'S CLIFFTOPS

Cornwall's north shore has its share of pretty harbours, but none can hold a candle to **Boscastle**, 25 miles northeast of Padstow. Nestled in the crook of a river valley, it's the perfect Cornish harbour: slate-roofed cottages, a stout granite harbour, headlands dusted with thrift, sea campion and gorse. Hard to believe the whole place was almost washed away during a freak flood in 2004. The cliffs provide the perfect backdrop for a blustery picnic: you can pick up supplies at the excellent **Boscastle Farm Shop**.

The village's endearingly weird **Museum of Witchcraft & Magic** is a must-see, with exhibits including witch's poppets (a kind of voodoo doll), divination pans, enchanted skulls, pickled beasts and a horrific 'witch's bridle' designed to extract confessions from suspected hags.

# Surf's Up

CATCH A NEWQUAY WAVE

Fifteen miles southwest of Padstow, **Newquay** is Cornwall's surf central. There are scores of schools here to choose from: **Escape Surf School**, **Fistral Surf School** and **SSS Surf School** all have good reputations.

**Fistral Beach** is legendary for its waves. Other options within easy reach of Newquay include Crantock, Holywell Bay and Watergate Bay, where another of the area's best surf schools is based: **Wavehunters at the Extreme Academy**. For coasteering, SUP and kayaking, try **Newquay Watersports Centre**.

# Geological Jenga

WATCH THE SUNSET OVER BEDRUTHAN STEPS

The stately rock towers of **Bedruthan** (properly known as Carnewas) loom out of the sea like giant stone sentinels between Newquay and Padstow (20 minutes by car). The area is owned by the National Trust, which runs the car park and cafe; clifftop paths radiate out along the coast. Bedruthan is a sunset spot par excellence: pack a picnic and a blanket, and settle down to watch the show.

# Cliffs & Chimney Stacks

STALK THE ST AGNES COAST

Abandoned engine houses litter the hilltops around **St Agnes**, one of Cornwall's great tin-mining boom towns,

## WHERE TO SLEEP ON THE NORTH COAST

**Treago Farm Campsite**
Few campsites have such a swish setting as this one, in the valley just behind Porth (Polly) Joke beach. **£**

**Watergate Bay Hotel**
This laid-back hotel is a family favourite that's firmly focused on getting you into the great outdoors. **£££**

**The Scarlet**
Cornwall's chic adults-only eco-hotel features sea-view rooms, alfresco hot tubs and a belter of an infinity pool. **£££**

Surfer, Fistral Beach

about 30 miles from Padstow. For many people, this is the quintessential part of the coast path. A popular target is **Wheal Coates**, a much-photographed clifftop engine house which still boasts its original brick chimney, and the nearby cove of **Chapel Porth**, an improbably photogenic beach (with a very popular cafe) at the bottom of a dramatic, rock-strewn valley. If you're feeling energetic, you can combine the walk with a loop over the top of the **Beacon**, from where the views stretch across most of Cornwall on a clear day.

## Pedal Power

BIKE THROUGH A MINING VALLEY

An old mineral tramway runs between Portreath and the inland village of Bissoe, which has been resurrected as the **Coast to Coast Cycle Trail**, and explores the rugged mining country around the Poldice Valley. It's mostly flat and easy, although there are a few uphill and off-road sections, and at several points the trail crosses a minor road. Bikes and maps can be hired at the Devoran end from **Bissoe Bike Hire**, which also has a good cafe. There are car parks at both ends if you want to bring your own bike.

### ST PIRAN'S BEACH

East of Newquay, the coast road tracks craggy scenery to **Perranporth**, another breezy beach town blessed with a fabulous 3-mile stretch of sand. Its name derives from Cornwall's patron saint, St Piran, who supposedly brought Christianity to the county. The remains of an ancient chapel dedicated to him are hidden in the dunes, marking the start of a processional march on St Piran's Day (5 March).

The beach is a stunner, and a brilliant spot for a sunset walk, especially once you get away from the crowds and head up towards the dunes.

### NORTH COAST CAFES

**Chapel Porth Cafe**
Baguettes, butties and the house special: hedgehog ice cream (vanilla, clotted cream and hazelnuts). £

**Strong Adolfo's**
On the road to Wadebridge, this sleek Scandi-style cafe serves delicious lunches and lavish cakes: hygge-tastic. ££

**Pavilion Bakery**
Newquay's boutique bakery: stunning sourdoughs, artisan breads and melt-in-your-mouth croissants. £

**BODMIN MOOR**

Hugging the edge of the Devon border, the stark, barren expanse of **Bodmin Moor** is the county's wildest and weirdest landscape. Pockmarked by bogs and treeless heaths, Cornwall's 'roof' is well worth taking the time to explore: lofty peaks, stone circles, ancient churches and Cornwall's highest hill, the 419m-high **Brown Willy** (in case you're wondering, the name comes from the Cornish *bronn wennili*, or 'hill of swallows').

While you're here exploring the moor, you could also factor in a visit to the pretty cascade of **Golitha Falls**, the spooky underground caves of **Carnglaze Caverns**, the forest trails of **Cardinham Woods** and perhaps a visit to the notorious **Bodmin Jail** (part of which is now...a boutique hotel).

Carn Brea Castle

## King of the Carn

THE HIGHEST POINT OF CENTRAL CORNWALL

Standing at 736ft, **Carn Brea** is the distinctive rocky hill that broods over the rough, gorse-thatched landscape between Redruth and Camborne. It's now topped by the Bassett Monument, a Celtic cross dedicated to mine-owner Frances Bassett, who owned many of the richest mines hereabouts. At the top, you'll find the forbidding bulk of **Carn Brea Castle**, where the Bassetts once hosted lavish feasts (it's now, rather bizarrely, a Middle Eastern restaurant). The view is really something, with both of Cornwall's coasts visible, as well as distant Penwith and Bodmin Moor. Come for sunset, and bring a picnic.

## Hard Rock Country

DELVE INTO CORNWALL'S MINING HERITAGE

In many ways the gritty twin towns of **Redruth** and **Camborne** represent the essence of Cornwall's tin-seamed soul. A century-and-a-half ago, these towns were the beating, booming heart of the county's mining industry. Since 2006 they've formed a Unesco World Heritage Site: the Cornwall & West Devon Mining Landscape, a huge area encompassing everything from open moors and clifftops to historic mine workings and engine houses like **East Pool Mine** and **King Edward Mine**, both near Camborne. A brilliant way to explore is along the **Great Flat Lode** – a 7.5km bike trail that runs along a famously rich seam of tin ore. It forms part of the wider **Mineral Tramways** network.

**GETTING AROUND**

Bus services are fairly good along the north coast, with most major towns served by at least one regular bus route, most of which are provided by First Kernow. The open-top Atlantic Coaster between Newquay and Padstow is a fine ride, via Watergate Bay, Mawgan Porth and Harlyn Bay. Newquay is also on the branch railway line from Par, which connects up with the main Paddington–Penzance line.

# ST IVES

If there was a prize for the prettiest of Cornish ports, St Ives would surely take the top spot. It's a dazzling sight: a tightly packed cluster of slate roofs, old fishers' cottages and church towers spread out around a brilliant turquoise bay. Once a busy pilchard harbour, St Ives became the centre of Cornwall's arts scene in the 1920s and '30s, when luminary figures such as Barbara Hepworth, Terry Frost, Ben Nicholson and Naum Gabo migrated here in search of artistic freedom and escape.

St Ives remains an artistic centre, with numerous galleries lining its cobbled streets, including the renowned Tate St Ives, a westerly outpost of the London original. But it's also one of the Cornish towns that's been most changed by Cornwall's tourism boom: an infamous hot spot for second homes and sky-high house prices, it's packed to the gunwales in summer. Visit in early spring or autumn if you can.

## TOP TIP

Parking in St Ives is hellish for much of the year but, thankfully, there's an alternative. A scenic branch line trundles along the coast to St Ives from the mainline station of St Erth, enabling you to let the train take the strain. There's plenty of parking next to St Erth station.

**St Ives**

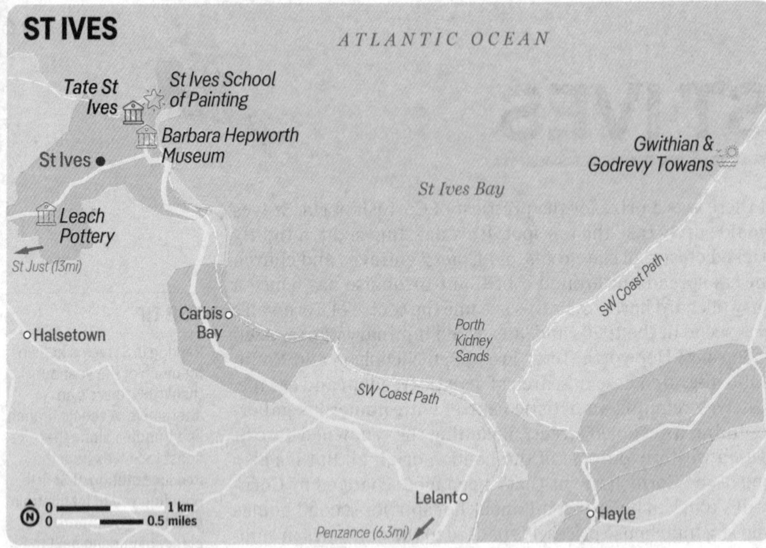


### THE ROAD TO ZENNOR

The twisting B3306 coast road makes for a rollercoaster road trip. Between St Ives and Sennen is a panorama of craggy tors, auburn heaths and booming surf. It also offers access to a wealth of spectacular walks like **Gurnard's Head**, **Pendour Cove** and **Porthmeor Cove.**

In the quaint **Zennor**, visit the Church of St Senara; inside, look out for a carved bench end which depicts a mermaid holding a mirror and comb – a reference to the folk tale of the Mermaid of Zennor. Don't miss lunch at the **Gurnard's Head** pub.

## Art on the Beach

TOUR KEY ART SPACES IN ST IVES

**Tate St Ives** is the town's artistic centrepiece. Focusing on the coterie of experimental artists who congregated at St Ives after WWII and turned the little seaside town into a magnet for modern artists, the museum showcases work by many of the key artists of the St Ives scene in luminous, white-walled surroundings. It offers a compelling insight into the St Ives story, and a new exhibition space hosts a seasonal exhibition devoted to a contemporary artist, providing a contextual counterpoint to the main collection. Don't miss a coffee or a bite to eat at the rooftop cafe, which offers widescreen views over Porthmeor Beach.

Barbara Hepworth's former studio is now a moving museum, the **Barbara Hepworth Museum & Sculpture Garden**. The studio has remained practically untouched since her death in a fire in 1975, and the adjoining garden contains some of her most famous sculptures, many of which were inspired by the elemental forces she discovered in her adopted Cornish home: rock, sea, sand, wind, sky.

### WHERE TO STAY IN ST IVES

**Saltwater**
It's driftwood-chic all the way at Saltwater, where bright blue and yellow bedrooms echo the landscape. **££**

**27 The Terrace**
This three-storey B&B has been given a stylish refit, and also has two apartments and private parking (hallelujah!). **££**

**Primrose House**
Scandi chic and proximity to Porthminster are the USPs here – and it has parking too. **£££**

If St Ives has inspired you to pick up a brush, then why not book a course at the **St Ives School of Painting**? You can choose from short two-hour workshops, or longer courses covering everything from mark making to experimental landscapes.

## Pot Luck

LEARN TO THROW FROM THE PROS

While other St Ives artists broke new ground in sculpture and abstract art, potter Bernard Leach was hard at work reinventing British ceramics in his studio in Higher Stennack. Drawing inspiration from Japanese and oriental sculpture, and using a unique hand-built 'climbing' kiln based on ones he had seen in Japan, Leach's pottery created a unique fusion of Western and Eastern ideas. His former studio, **Leach Pottery**, displays examples of his work, and has been enhanced by a new museum and working pottery studio, as well as a shop selling Leach ceramics alongside other contemporary potters. If you'd like to learn how to throw a pot or perfect a glaze, you can also book one of the excellent pottery courses.

## Out on the Towans

GOLDEN SAND, GRASSY DUNES

On the east side of St Ives Bay, the dune-backed flats of **Gwithian** and **Godrevy** unfurl in a glimmering sea-fringed curve between the Hayle Estuary and Godrevy Point, and join together at low tide to form Hayle's much-lauded '3 miles of golden sand.' Godrevy Lighthouse perches on a rocky island and famously inspired Virginia Woolf's stream-of-consciousness classic *To the Lighthouse* (1927).

The twin beaches are brilliant for a blustery walk, whatever the weather. You can also usually see a colony of resident seals at **Mutton Cove**, a pebbly beach at the base of a steep cliff to the east of Godrevy Point. The cliffs are also good for watching seabirds including cormorants, guillemots and several gull species, and the grassy dunes (towans in Cornish) provide an important coastal habitat.

### WHERE TO EAT AROUND ST IVES

**Porthminster Beach Cafe**
Cracking beach bistro with a sun-trap terrace and superb Mediterranean-influenced menu. ££

**Porthminster Kitchen**
The beach cafe's in-town sister restaurant, showcasing the same Med-inspired cooking but with a harbour view. ££

**One Fish St**
Seafood-themed tasting menus that change depending on what's been landed on the quay. £££

**Searoom**
Run by the St Ives Liquor Company (makers of the town's premium craft gin), this wharf-side restaurant specialises in Cornish-tinged small plates. ££

**Blas Burgerworks**
St Ives' boutique burger joint with a great choice of buns for carnivores, veggies and vegans alike. ££

**Halsetown Inn**
Prime pub grub a mile from St Ives in tiny Halsetown. It's part village boozer, part premium gastropub. ££

### GETTING AROUND

Attempting to drive through the town centre is a recipe for holiday nightmares. If you're driving, the largest car park by far is Trenwith, a brisk uphill walk from town, and it's usually the most likely to have spaces. Otherwise, consider leaving your car at St Erth or Lelant stations and catching the scenic St Ives train line into town. First Kernow runs buses to Penzance, Marazion and along the Zennor coast road via Sennen and Land's End.

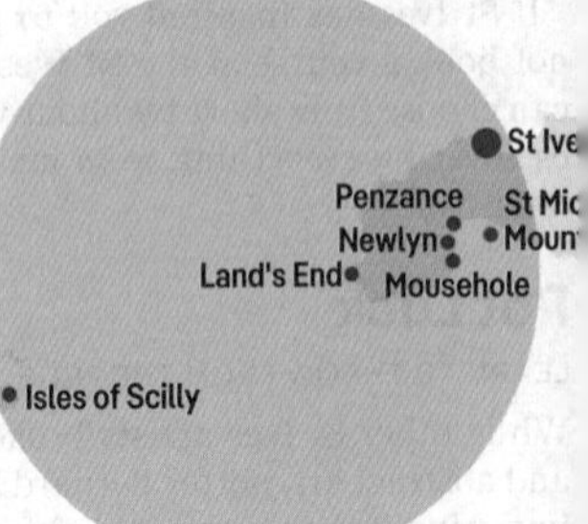


# Beyond St Ives

West and south of St Ives sprawl the wild expanses of the Penwith peninsula, a crooked finger of land edging out into the Atlantic like a toe testing the water.

Stark and remote, spotted with mine stacks, ancient farmland and windswept moor, this is an untamed corner of Cornwall, a long way from the county's cosy harbour towns and neatly kept beaches. The salty old town of Penzance lies on the south side of the peninsula, about 10 miles from Land's End and Cornwall's famous clifftop theatre, the Minack. But the real beauty of this corner lies off the beaten track: it's a land where stone monuments rise up from the hilltops, ancient moorland butts up against gorse-topped cliffs, and forgotten settlements stand out in relief against the skyline. And for a real escape, the lesser-visited islands of Scilly feel like a whole different world.

### TOP TIP

Get a good map if you're searching for the ancient sites, especially more out-of-the-way ones: the *Ordnance Survey Explorer Map 102: Land's End, Penzance & St Ives* is the one to go for.

**Minack Theatre (p314)**

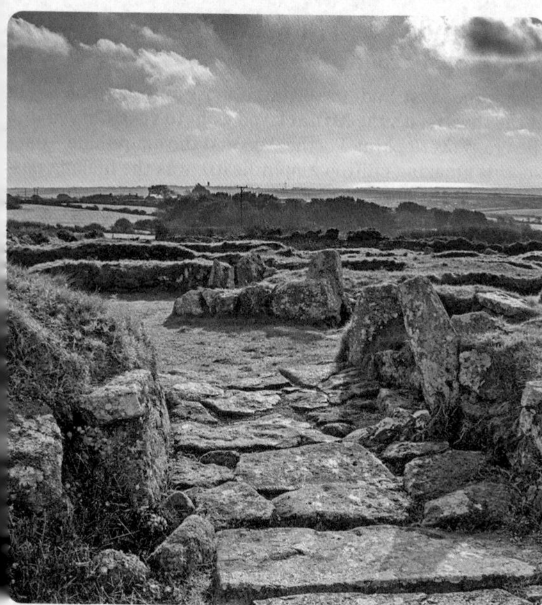

Carn Euny

## PENWITH'S PREHISTORY

Penwith is littered with strange archaeological remains, dating from Neolithic times right through to the Bronze Age. Among them are the ring-shaped **Mên-an-tol** (holed stone), numerous menhirs, impressive stone circles including the **Merry Maidens** and **Boscawen-un**, and distinctive dolmens (Neolithic burial chambers), which in Cornwall are known as quoits – **Lanyon Quoit** and **Chûn Quoit** are among the best-preserved examples. You can also visit the remains of Bronze Age settlements at **Chysauster** and **Carn Euny**.

## Into the Dark

TOUR A REAL-LIFE TIN MINE

Tin mining was the staple industry in west Cornwall throughout much of the 18th and 19th centuries. To experience what life was like for Cornwall's 'hard rock men' and 'bal maidens', you can venture underground at **Geevor Tin Mine**; the last working mine in west Cornwall, it closed in 1990. It's a maze of dank shafts and tunnels where miners once worked for hours at a stretch – and today an unforgettable experience for visitors.

It's also worth swinging by the National Trust–owned **Levant Mine & Beam Engine**, a pioneering steam-powered engine used to pump floodwater from the deep underground shafts, and one of the only working examples in the world. Photographers won't want to miss the atmospheric mine ruins around **Botallack**, teetering spectacularly over the Atlantic.

## PENWITH PIT STOPS

**Argoe**
Local boy Rich Adams is making waves with his stylish Newlyn seafooderie, specialising in local fish and shellfish. £££

**Shore**
Penzance's best bistro, big on local seafood and Cornish produce, overseen by top chef Bruce Rennie. £££

**Tolcarne Inn**
Ben Tunnicliffe's much-lauded gastropub in Newlyn consistently wins awards for its superior seafood. £££

## The Play's the Thing

THEATRE ON THE EDGE

Forget the West End: for Britain's most unforgettable night at the theatre, it's the **Minack** you want to visit. Carved into the crags overlooking Porthcurno and the azure-blue Atlantic, this amazing clifftop amphitheatre was the lifelong passion of theatre lover Rowena Cade, who dreamt up the idea in the 1930s. Experienced theatre-goers bring wine, picnic supplies, wet-weather gear and – most importantly, considering the seats are carved out of granite – a comfy cushion.

Beneath the Minack lies the sandy wedge of **Porthcurno**, a hugely popular beach that offers excellent swimming and sunbathing (it gets very busy in season). Nearby is **PK Porthcurno**, an imaginative museum that explores the area's unlikely role as a hub for global telecommunications.

## Last Stop Kernow

MAINLAND BRITAIN'S WESTERNMOST POINT

The clue's in the name. **Land's End** is where Cornwall (and mainland Britain) comes to a screeching halt: a panorama of black granite cliffs falling away into a maelstrom of white surf and sea spray. Famous as the last port of call for charity walkers on the 874-mile slog from John O'Groats in Scotland, the views here are epic. The photo-op beside the Land's End signpost ('New York 3147; John O' Groats 874) is a cliché, but essential nonetheless.

Unfortunately, the site has been blighted by a spectacularly tacky theme park, built in the 1980s. Thankfully, you can bypass the tat entirely and just pay for the car park instead. The coast path south of Land's End remains as wild and beautiful as any in Cornwall; the rocky beach at **Nanjizal Bay** is an excellent target, with impressive sea caves to explore.

## Fine Art & Fishmongers

TOUR GALLERIES AND PICK UP A FISH SUPPER

Overlooking Mount's Bay, the old port town of **Penzance** marks the last stop on the Great Western Railway, and is a pretty place for an afternoon wander. A visit to admire the art collection at **Penlee House Museum & Gallery** is well worth the time, with a collection of paintings from the Newlyn School and other local luminaries.

For something more contemporary, swing by **The Exchange** and its sister space, the **Newlyn Art Gallery**, which can be reached along Penzance's grand seafront promenade.

### MOUSEHOLE

A muddle of cottages and alleyways gathered behind a granite breakwater, **Mousehole** (pronounced *mowzle*) looks like something from a children's storybook (a fact not unnoticed by author Antonia Barber, who set her much-loved fairy tale *The Mousehole Cat* here). In centuries past this was Cornwall's busiest pilchard port, but the fish dried up in the late 19th century, and the village now survives mostly on tourist traffic.

Packed in summer and all but deserted in winter, it's ripe for a wander, especially at Christmas, when the village puts on its famous Christmas lights. Don't miss a pint at the hugger-mugger **Ship Inn**: on 23rd December, it serves stargazey pie, a pilchard pie baked in honour of local hero Tom Bawcock, who braved stormy seas to save the village from famine.

### PENWITH PIT STOPS

**Gurnard's Head**
This is one of west Cornwall's top dining pubs: best of British dishes, inspired by Cornish produce. **£££**

**Tinner's Arms**
Zennor's pub may well be Cornwall's most venerable boozer; it's believed to have been built around 1271. **££**

**Trevaskis Farm**
Farm-grown produce, trails, pick-your-own fruit and a legendary Sunday roast (reservations essential). **££**

Jubilee Pool

**Newlyn** is Cornwall's last commercial fishing port of scale, and it's a great place to pick up fresh crab, lobster and fish fresh off the boats, or from the quayside fishmongers like **W Harvey & Sons**. If you prefer to let someone else handle the cooking, book a meal at **Argoe** or **Mackerel Sky Cafe**.

## Getting into Hot Water

SWIM IN A LISTED LIDO

The glorious **Jubilee Pool** is Penzance's most beautiful landmark. Built in the 1930s on the seafront at Battery Rocks, during Britain's great lido-building boom, this Art Deco marvel has had a chequered history: it lay derelict for many years, but has been beautifully restored and now makes for one of Cornwall's most memorable swims. A £1.8 million investment has also brought a very 21st-century addition: one section of the pool is now geothermally heated to a toasty 35°C, powered by hot rocks deep underground. It's without a doubt Cornwall's most stylish swimming pool – but demand for the geothermal section is high, so book well in advance. The cafe is excellent, too.

**BACK TO SCHOOL**

Experimental landscapes? Screen printing? Life drawing? You'll find courses for all of these and much more at the **Newlyn School of Art** – the innovative art centre run by local artist and curator Henry Garfitt.

Housed in the stately Victorian surroundings of Newlyn's former village school, it offers a huge range of classes and courses for all abilities, many of which are taught by prominent local painters (the roster of tutors reads like a Who's Who of the Cornish art scene). Classes are kept small (maximum of 10 people) and are open to artists of all levels of experience.

### WHERE TO STAY AROUND PENWITH

**Venton Vean**
A modern B&B, finished in stylish greys and blues, wood floors, bay windows and an eye for design. **££**

**Old Coastguard Hotel**
This coastal beauty ranks as one of Cornwall's top shoreside hotels, offering gardens and sea views. **£££**

**Artist Residence Penzance**
Penzance's most entertaining hotel, this townhouse combines period architecture with quirky style. **£££**

## Holy Island

WALK TO AN ISLAND ABBEY

Looming in the middle of Mount's Bay, **St Michael's Mount** is Cornwall's very own fairytale castle. There's been a monastery here since at least the 5th century, but the present abbey was mostly built by Benedictine monks (the same religious order that also constructed the island's sister abbey at Mont St-Michel in France) during the 12th century. Highlights of the main house include the rococo drawing room, the armoury and the 14th-century church, but it's the amazing clifftop gardens that really steal the show.

The most atmospheric way to reach the Mount is via the cobbled causeway from Marazion, which can be crossed for around four hours around low tide. From April to October, ferry boats run when the causeway is covered.

### EXPLORING SCILLY

There are two ways to get to Scilly: by sea and by air. The *Scillonian III* ferry runs from Penzance to St Mary's between April and October and takes about three hours. Much faster (just over 20 minutes), but prone to bad weather cancellation, is a flight from Land's End Airport, near Zennor. Summer flights also operate from Newquay Airport or Exeter.

To explore the other islands, including St Agnes, Bryher and St Martin's, the **St Mary's Boatmen Association** (scillyboating.co.uk) provides boat transfers year-round, with a reduced service in winter. Wildlife-watching trips and cruises out to many of the uninhabited islands, such as Annet, Teän and the Eastern Isles ,are also offered.

## Scilly Time

ISLAND HOP FROM ST MARY'S

While only 28 miles west of the mainland, in many ways the **Isles of Scilly** feels like a different world altogether. Life on this little archipelago seems to have hardly changed in decades: there are no traffic jams, no supermarkets, no multinational hotels, and the only noise pollution comes from breaking waves and cawing gulls.

Only five of the islands are inhabited: **St Mary's** is the largest and busiest of the islands – but at just over 3 miles at its widest point and covering an area of roughly 6 sq miles, it's hardly huge. It's a pleasure to explore by bike, with many prehistoric remains to discover, best seen around **Halangy Down**, and loads of lovely beaches like **Porthcressa**, **Pelistry Bay** and **Porthmellon**. Bikes can be hired from **St Mary's Bike Hire** in Hugh Town, the island's main settlement and the docking point for the Scillonian ferry. Alternatively, motorised buggies are available from **Scilly Carts**.

A short boat trip across the channel from St Mary's brings you to **Tresco**, the second-largest island. The islands' key attraction is **Tresco Abbey Gardens**, laid out in 1834 on the site of a 12th-century Benedictine priory by the horticultural visionary Augustus Smith. The 7-hectare gardens are now home to more than 20,000 exotic species, from towering palms to desert cacti and crimson flame trees, all nurtured by the temperate Gulf Stream. Admission also covers the Valhalla Collection, an outdoor museum made up of figureheads and nameplates salvaged from the many ships wrecked off Tresco.

### GETTING AROUND

Penzance is the last stop on the railway line from London Paddington. It's a handy bus hub, with regular services to St Ives and Land's End, including open-top double deckers in summer. Penzance is also the home dock for the *Scillonian III*, which sails to the Isles of Scilly between April and September.

# FALMOUTH

Few seaside towns in Cornwall boast such an arresting location as Falmouth, overlooking the broad River Fal as it empties into the English Channel. Surrounded by sea, Falmouth is an appealing jumble of lanes, old pubs, slate roofs and trendy cafes – and with its clifftop castle, sandy beaches and excellent maritime museum, it's an ideal base for exploring Cornwall's south coast.

Historically, the town made its fortune during the 18th and 19th centuries. Between 1689 and 1851, this was the home port for the Packet Service – the vital communications link that underpinned the smooth running of the British Empire. The days of the tea clippers, trading vessels and privateers has long passed, and these days the town is supported by a lively tourist trade and student crowd from nearby Falmouth University. Nevertheless, the docks remain an important centre for ship repairs – spot the cranes as you walk to Pendennis Point.

### TOP TIP

Falmouth gets busy in summer and parking can be tricky, but the Ponsharden Park & Float allows you to park your car on the outskirts and catch a boat into town. Handy buses shuttle from the main square, The Moor, to locations around town, including the beaches.

**Falmouth**

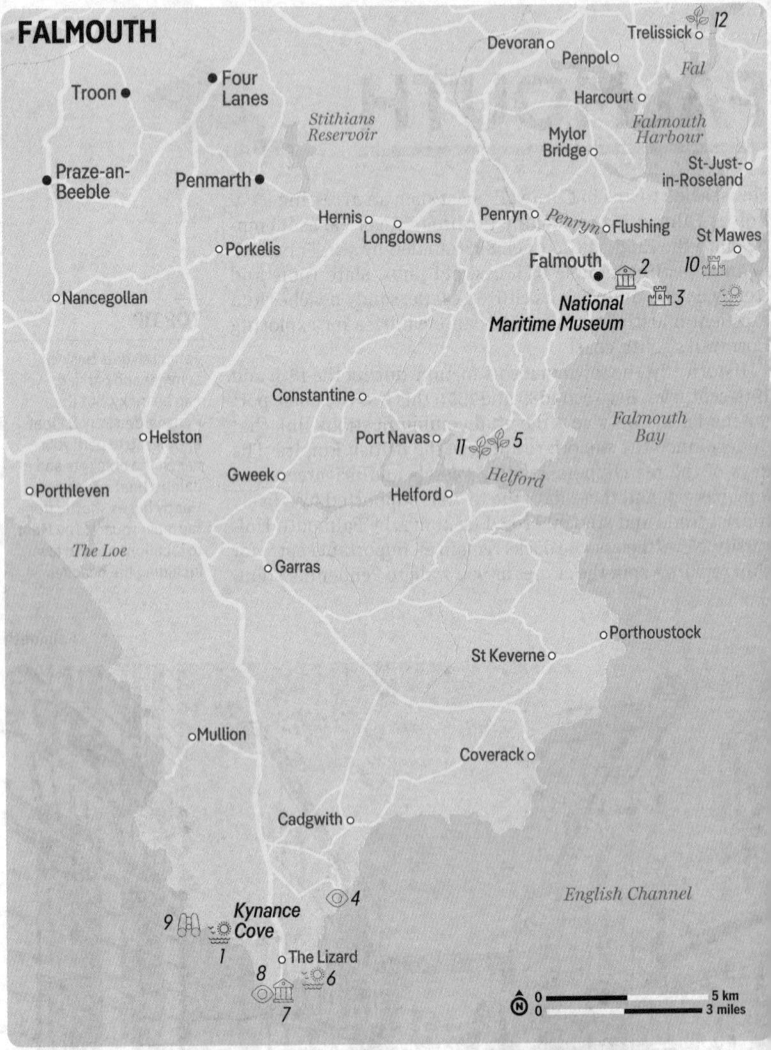

# FALMOUTH

**HIGHLIGHTS**
**1** Kynance Cove
**2** National Maritime Museum
**3** Pendennis Castle
**7** Lizard Lighthouse
**8** Lizard Point
**9** Predannack Wollas
**10** St Mawes Castle
**11** Trebah Garden
**12** Trelissick

**SIGHTS**
**4** Devil's Frying Pan
**5** Glendurgan
**6** Housel Bay

Kynance Cove (p321)

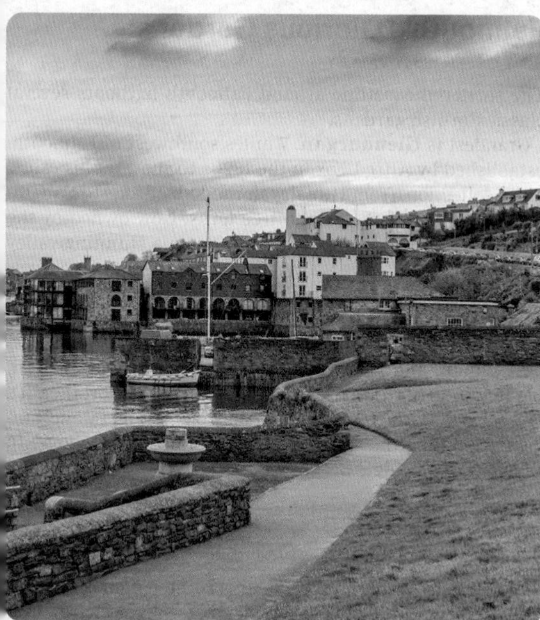

Falmouth Harbour

## The Queen of Cornish Rivers

MESSING ABOUT ON THE RIVER

The **River Fal** is one of Cornwall's great tidal river systems. Lined with overhanging oaks, inlets and creeks, it's a fascinating place to explore by boat, either self-piloted or on a guided tour. **Enterprise Boats** offer various routes to Trelissick gardens, Truro and St Mawes. Alternatively, you can rent your own motorboat from **Falmouth Boat Hire** on Custom House Quay.

The river and coastline are also fantastic for spotting wildlife. Depending on the season, there's birdlife galore, from cormorants and curlews to snowy egrets. Further out to sea, you may be in with a chance of spotting dolphins, porpoises, basking sharks, seals and even minke whales. **AK Wildlife Cruises**, run by the unflinchingly enthusiastic Captain Keith, is the best operator.

### BEST PLACES TO EAT IN FALMOUTH

**Harbour Lights**
The one and only place for fish and chips in Falmouth. Accept no alternative. £

**Meat Counter**
Burger joint that turns out the best patties in town, including veggie and vegan options. £

**Star & Garter**
Gourmet gastropub focusing on nose-to-tail dining. The menu is meat-heavy, so veggies might struggle. Lovely water views, too. £££

**Verdant Seafood Bar / Verdant Taproom**
This trendy craft brewery has a tiny seafood spot in town. You can also visit the industrial-style taproom near Penryn for top pizzas. ££

**Pizza Please**
Hipster pizza in a quaint Penryn courtyard. ££

**Hooked on the Rocks**
Seafood restaurant in a grand spot beside Swanpool Beach. ££

### WHERE TO FIND A PINT IN FALMOUTH

**Beerwolf Books**
A brilliant boozer and bookshop rolled into one: sounds like heaven. You can even bring your own grub.

**The Chain Locker**
A classic Falmouth drinking hole. Not as ramshackle as it once was, but still nautically fun. Plenty harbourside tables.

**The Working Boat**
A good sundowner spot under the Greenbank Hotel, with plenty of tables out on the quayside.

## Falmouth's Glorious Gardens

HOW GREEN IS MY VALLEY

The sheltered coastline around Falmouth harbours several classic Cornish gardens.

Grandest is **Glendurgan**, 7 miles southwest of Falmouth, established by Alfred Fox in the 1820s to show off his exotic plant collection, from Himalayan rhododendrons to Canadian maples and New Zealand tree ferns. Now owned by the National Trust, the gardens tumble down a stunning valley and offer breathtaking views of the Helford; they have their own ornamental maze, too. The walk along the river from the Ferryboat Inn via Durgan village is delightful, and passes several secluded beaches that offer super swimming.

Next door, and accessible via the coast path, is **Trebah**, planted in 1840 by Charles Fox, Alfred's younger brother. It's less formal, with riotous rhododendrons, gunnera and jungle ferns lining the sides of a steep ravine leading down to the quay and shingle beach.

### FALMOUTH'S BEACHES

Falmouth's trio of beaches – **Gyllyngvase**, **Swanpool** and **Maenporth** – are the town's main summer draw. All three can be reached on foot via the coast path, or by bike. Hiring a kayak or SUP is also a great way of exploring the coast. There are places to hire SUPs and kayaks at all three beaches, and each has its own cafe nearby. **WeSup**, based at Gylly, offers a memorable sunrise tour, plus yoga sessions and SUP retreats. The beaches also offer good snorkelling at high tide.

## Ships & Castles

DEEP DIVE INTO FALMOUTH'S PAST

Standing formidably atop Pendennis Point, Falmouth's Tudor fortress, **Pendennis Castle**, commands a widescreen view over the whole of Falmouth Bay. It was built as part of Henry VIII's massive 16th-century castle-building programme, and designed to work in tandem with its sister fortress across the river at St Mawes: any vessel entering the Carrick Roads without permission would have been shredded by cannon fire, although ironically the fortress only saw real action during the Civil War. The circular walk up to the castle from town is lovely, and takes you past Gyllyngvase Beach, Castle Beach and Falmouth Docks: take a picnic for when you reach the point. If you want to visit the sister fortress over in St Mawes, regular ferries shuttle across the harbour from Prince of Wales Pier.

The town's other historical must-see is the **National Maritime Museum**, a sister outpost of the original in Greenwich, London. Imaginative displays focus on Falmouth's history as a port, and on the broader impact of the sea on history and culture. The centrepiece is the five-storey Flotilla Gallery, where an array of small vessels, ranging from rowing boats to rescue craft, are suspended from the ceiling. Don't miss the view from the top floor of the lookout tower, offering a 360-degree panorama across the entirety of Falmouth Bay.

### BOATING SIDE TRIPS

In summer, Enterprise Boats stop off at the riverside pontoon next to **Trelissick** (p322), allowing you to hop off, have a hike and catch a return boat back.

### WHERE TO STAY IN FALMOUTH

**Merchants Manor**
A venerable town hotel turned boutique beauty: expect bold fabrics, indulgent colour schemes and fun prints. **£££**

**Highcliffe B&B**
Vintage furniture and upcycled design pieces give each room here its own bespoke feel. **££**

**Greenbank Hotel**
The queen of Falmouth's hotels, with a knockout position beside the boat-filled estuary. **£££**

Pendennis Castle

## Cliffs, Coves & Choughs

MAINLAND BRITAIN'S SOUTHERNMOST POINT

Twenty-three miles south of Falmouth, the British mainland reaches its southernmost tip at **Lizard Point**, historically one of Britain's deadliest headlands. Hundreds of ships have come to grief around here over the centuries, from Spanish treasure galleons to naval frigates, which explains the looming presence of the **Lizard Lighthouse**, built in 1751 and now an interesting heritage centre. It's the only lighthouse in Cornwall you can actually climb; book a guided tour to ascend into the tower to see the lamp room and foghorn.

Trails lead out to the point from the village, where a steep track winds down to the long-disused lifeboat station and shingly cove. It's one of the most dramatic patches of coast in Cornwall. Numerous other paths lead around the headland: popular targets include **Housel Bay**, the **Devil's Frying Pan** and **Predannack Wollas**, whose blustery clifftops memorably featured in the BBC's big-budget adaptation of *Poldark* starring Aiden Turner.

A mile north of Lizard Point, the National Trust–owned inlet of **Kynance Cove** is a showstopper, studded with craggy

**SEAL SOS**

At any given time, there are hundreds – often thousands – of common and grey seals to be found around the Cornish coast, but sadly not all of them have the happy life they deserve. The **Cornish Seal Sanctuary** rescues sick and orphaned seals, nursing them carefully back to health before re-releasing them into the wild.

There are some fun exclusive experiences on offer, including the chance to be a keeper for the day, feed the residents their breakfast and take a behind-the-scenes tour of the rehabilitation centre. Excitingly, there are also guided walks to a secret creek nearby to spot wild Cornish beavers, reintroduced here as part of an important conservation study.

### WHERE TO FIND WATERFRONT PUBS

**Pandora Inn**
On the banks of Restronguet Creek, this thatched inn is one of Cornwall's landmark pubs, in situ since the mid-1600s.

**The Ferryboat**
Lovely beachside pub with picnic tables that have dreamy river views; you can grab a ferry over to the Lizard-side bank.

**Shipwright's Arms**
Once a quaint pub, this is now a posh gastropub. The food is great, and there's nowhere better for a River Helford vista.

### WHY I LOVE THE LIZARD

**Olly Berry**, Lonely Planet writer

The Lizard still feels untamed and raw in a way very few corners of Cornwall do these days. Mother Nature still holds all the trump cards here: savage cliffs, wild waves, stormy skies, all the good stuff.

Some parts get busy, but happily the gentrification bandwagon hasn't rolled in here just yet – and if you're prepared to hike, it's pretty easy to find secret, scramble-down coves that most people never take the time to find. My tip? Come in the middle of winter, on a stormy day – that's when the Lizard will really show you what it's about.

offshore islands rising out of searingly blue seas that seem almost tropical in colour. The cliffs around the cove are rich in serpentine, a red-green rock popular with Victorian trinket makers. They're also a great place for spotting choughs; look out for their distinctive red bills and feet. When the seas aren't too rough, the cove offers an exhilarating swim; in summer it gets busy, so aim to arrive before 10am. The beach cafe offers pasties, drinks, ice creams and an absolutely cracking crab sandwich.

## A Smuggler's Creek

EXPLORE THE HELFORD

The oak-lined banks of the River Helford seem steeped in mystery, so it's little wonder that Daphne du Maurier decided to use it as the setting for her famous smuggling tale, *Frenchman's Creek* (1941). **Koru Kayaking** offers excellent two-hour trips from the Budock Vean Hotel as well as riverboat cruises. Or you can hire your own vessel from **Helford River Boats** at Helford Passage.

Alternatively, you can park on the edge of Helford Village and walk; a pleasant circular walk through the woodland circles round to the creek; an OS map comes in handy. Lunch at the waterfront **Shipwright's Arms** makes a pleasant way to end the walk.

## Walk the Trelissick Trails

GRAND GARDENS

Grandly located at the head of the Fal estuary, 4 miles south of Truro, **Trelissick** is one of the most impressive of all of Cornwall's aristocratic estates – and in a county that's awash with them, that's saying something. A sprawling expanse of fields and parkland, it's criss-crossed by walking trails. The best way to reach the gardens is with **Enterprise Boats**, which runs trips from Truro and Falmouth. **Canoe Cornwall** offers half-day trips in Canadian canoes, along with archery sessions, axe-throwing and bushcraft.

### GETTING AROUND

Falmouth sits at the end of the railway branch line from Truro. Local buses shuttle round town and the surrounding area, including to the beaches; check out OTS Falmouth (otsfalmouth.co.uk) for details and timetables.

You really need a car to get the most out of exploring the Lizard, although there are local buses from Helston and Falmouth to Mullion and Lizard village; consult the First Kernow (firstbus.co.uk/adventures-bus/services/lizard) website for details.

# FOWEY

In many ways, Fowey feels a little bit like Padstow's south-coast sister – an old working port turned well-heeled holiday town, with a tumble of pastel-coloured houses, portside pubs and tiered terraces overlooking the wooded banks of the River Fowey. The town's wealth was founded on the export of china clay from the St Austell pits, but it's been an important port since Elizabethan times, and later became the adopted home of the writer Daphne du Maurier, who lived at the grand house at Menabilly for many years and used it as the model for Manderley in *Rebecca*. Today it's an attractive and increasingly upmarket town, handy for exploring Cornwall's southeastern corner. There are some fine beaches nearby, too.

**TOP TIP**

To avoid the inevitable summer queues, it's an excellent idea to book tickets for big attractions like the Eden Project and the Lost Gardens of Heligan online in advance.

**Fowey**

## FOWEY

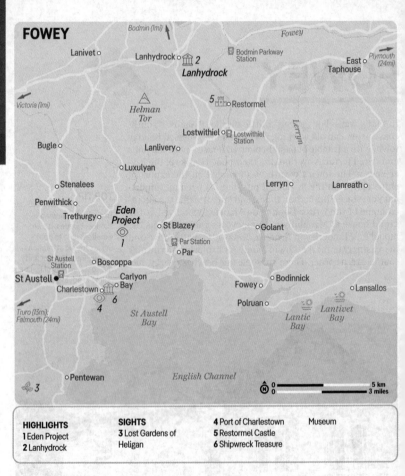

Bodmin (1mi)
Fowey
Lanivet
Lanhydrock 2
Lanhydrock
Bodmin Parkway Station
East Taphouse
Plymouth (24mi)
Victoria (1mi)
Helman Tor
5 Restormel
Lerryn
Lostwithiel
Lostwithiel Station
Bugle
Lanlivery
Luxulyan
Stenalees
Lerryn
Lanreath
Penwithick
Trethurgy
Eden Project 1
St Blazey
Golant
Par Station
Par
St Austell Station
Boscoppa
St Austell
Carlyon Bay
Charlestown 6
4
Bodinnick
Fowey
Lansallos
Polruan
Truro (13mi); Falmouth (24mi)
St Austell Bay
Lantic Bay
Lantivet Bay
Pentewan
English Channel
3
0 5 km
0 3 miles

**HIGHLIGHTS**
**1** Eden Project
**2** Lanhydrock

**SIGHTS**
**3** Lost Gardens of Heligan
**4** Port of Charlestown
**5** Restormel Castle
**6** Shipwreck Treasure Museum

## Fowey River Life

KAYAKING, KINGFISHERS AND HERONS

It's said Kenneth Grahame got the inspiration for his children's classic, *The Wind in the Willows,* while wandering around the quiet creeks of the River Fowey. Like the Fal and the Helford, it's ideal for exploring by kayak, with lots of quiet inlets and plentiful birdlife; several operators run trips and offer kayak hire, including **Encounter Cornwall** and **Fowey River Expeditions**.

A few miles north along the creek, the riverside hamlet of **Golant** makes a pleasant detour, with a waterfront pub (the Fisherman's Arms) for lunch and excellent kayaking opportunities, while **Lerryn** has a picturesque riverside church.

River Fowey

Charlestown Harbour

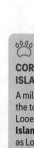

**CORNWALL'S ISLAND EDEN**

A mile offshore from the touristy town of Looe is **St George's Island** (known to most as Looe Island). In 1965 it was occupied by Surrey sisters Babs and Evelyn Atkins, who established a nature reserve here, and lived there peacefully for most of their lives, restoring habitats and monitoring wildlife populations.

Guided walks are run by the island ranger, who can help you spot grey seals, cormorants, shags and oystercatchers. It's managed by the Cornwall Wildlife Trust, which also arranges boat transfers.

## Avast Me Hearties

EXPLORE A TIME-TRAVEL PORT

Set around its massive granite quay and backed by Georgian buildings, the port of **Charlestown** looks like Long John Silver might stumble out from a pub at any moment. In previous centuries most of the china clay from the St Austell quarries was shipped out from here, but it's now a favourite location for film crews. You can wander round the Georgian quays, and with a bit of luck, see some tall ships docked alongside the harbour.

While you're here, don't miss a visit to the endearingly quirky **Shipwreck Treasure Museum**, which houses a massive collection of objects and ephemera recovered from more than 100 shipwrecks, ranging from telescopes, muskets, scrimshaw and coins to howitzer cannons.

## Gardens – Past & Future

FROM VICTORIAN GREENHOUSES TO SPACE-AGE BIOMES

If Cornwall has a must-not-miss attraction, it's surely the amazing **Eden Project**. Built at the bottom of a china clay pit, Eden's giant biomes here have become both an iconic

### WHERE TO STAY AROUND FOWEY

**Fowey Hall**
This hilltop Victorian manor supposedly inspired Toad Hall, and is well geared for families. ££

**Coriander Cottages**
Rural cottage complex on the outskirts of Fowey, with ecofriendly, open-plan barns. ££

**Fowey Harbour Hotel**
Boutique-style sleeps with dreamy views over the river. £££

**UPSTAIRS DOWNSTAIRS**

**Lanhydrock**, 2.5 miles southeast of Bodmin, offers a fascinating insight into life in Victorian England. The house was rebuilt after a devastating fire in 1881 as a home for the Agar-Robartes family, who made their fortune from mineral mining, particularly tin and china clay.

No expense was spared in the refurbishment: the house was equipped with mod cons such as radiators, roasting ovens, warming cupboards and flushing loos, as well as a pioneering cold room beside the vast kitchens.

The ornate Long Gallery, famous for its plaster ceiling, somehow survived the fire. The house was gifted to the National Trust in 1951 along with 160 hectares of parkland, offering a wealth of walks.

**Lost Gardens of Heligan**

landmark and a beacon of Cornish regeneration. Looking rather like a lunar landing station, or perhaps a Bond villain's lair, Eden's bubble-shaped domes recreate a variety of habitats around the globe, from dry savannah to steamy rainforest. It's quite an amazing experience: as you walk through the biomes, you'll see everything from tropical palms to banana trees, coffee plants and stinking rafflesia flowers, and learn loads about Eden's ecological mission. But it's not all education: Eden also offers adrenaline-driven activities, including England's longest zip line, a giant gravity swing, a 12m-high bungee drop and a heart-stopping 25m 'free fall' jump on to an airbag. The easiest way to get here is by bus from St Austell, but a bike trail also runs close by.

Entrepreneur Tim Smit is the brains behind Eden, but his first Cornish labour of love was the restoration of the **Lost Gardens of Heligan**, Cornwall's real-life secret garden. Formerly the family estate of the Tremaynes, Heligan's magnificent 19th-century gardens fell into disrepair following WWI, when many of its gardeners were killed. Since then, the gardens have been splendidly restored by a huge army of garden-

**WHERE TO EAT AROUND FOWEY**

**Appletons**
Previously at Fifteen and Trevibban Mill near Padstow, chef Andy Appleton now has a classy bistro on Fore St. ££

**North Street Kitchen**
Shack-style dining with a chalkboard menu filled with oysters and fresh fish dishes. Also check out Fitzroys. ££

**Sam's**
A Fowey stalwart for years: good fish, burgers, salads and steaks. There's a second branch on Polkerris. £

ers and volunteers. It's a horticultural wonderland: as you explore the maze of trails, you'll see working kitchen gardens, fruit-filled greenhouses, a secret grotto and a lost-world Jungle Valley of ferns, palms and tropical blooms – complete with its own rope bridge.

## 100% Adrenaline

JUMPING OFF CLIFFS FOR FUN

With the frankly genius tag line 'Throwing people off clifftops since 2009', **Adrenaline Quarry** offers a whole host of heart-in-your-mouth fun. If you love the idea of hurtling down a zip line at 40mph, or struggling not to lose your lunch on a giant swing that simulates free fall, then this place will be right up your street. If that's not enough, you can also coasteer round the quarry, then chuck axes at tree stumps. Or you're welcome to just hang out by the lake, have a picnic and go for a wild swim, for free.

Handily, it's right next to Menheniot train station, which has direct connections to Liskeard and Plymouth.

## King (or Queen) for the Day

TOUR A CLASSIC NORMAN KEEP

High on a hilltop above Lostwithiel, 9 miles from St Austell, the ruined castle of **Restormel** was built by Edward the Black Prince (the first Duke of Cornwall), although he only stayed there twice during his life. It's one of the best-preserved circular keeps in the country, but almost nothing remains of the interior, apart from some side rooms and a medieval garderobe (storage room). Still, the view from the top of the battlements is a stunner: you'll see clear to the coast on a good day.

**Restormel**

### THE RIVER TAMAR

The mighty River Tamar has marked the age-old dividing line between Devon and Cornwall for over a thousand years (it was officially declared as Cornwall's eastern edge in 936 by King Athelstan, the first king of a unified England).

Since 1859, the two rival counties have been linked by the great span of the **Royal Albert Bridge**, a masterpiece of Victorian engineering designed by the great railway engineer Isambard Kingdom Brunel; a second crossing (rather unimaginatively named the Tamar Bridge) was built to carry cars, and opened in 1962.

Tourists seldom take the time to explore the Tamar, and that's a massive oversight. Paddle pioneer-style in a Canadian canoe with **Canoe Tamar**, or hit the **Tamar Trails**, a network of 25km of hiking and biking trails between Gunnislake and Tavistock.

### GETTING AROUND

Bus services to Fowey are limited: the only really useful service runs to St Austell, Heligan and Mevagissey via Par train station, where you can catch trains on the main London–Penzance line.

A branch line spurs off from the main railway line at Liskeard and chugs down to Looe. Local buses connect the main towns and villages along the coast, including Mevagissey, Looe and Polperro.

Most visitors cross the Tamar into Cornwall via the Tamar Bridge, which is open 24 hours: you only pay the toll when heading back to Devon.

SPIROVIEW INC/SHUTTERSTOCK ©

Above: Pepys Library (p338); right: Norwich (p3

# CAMBRIDGE & EAST ANGLIA

## QUINTESSENTIALLY ENGLISH SCENES

Historic cities, timeless backwaters, coastal nature reserves and beautiful beaches await in this under-explored corner of the country.

East Anglia was once a vital hub for England's wealth and power, but attention shifted north during the Industrial Revolution and the bulge on the east coast of England slipped into gentle obscurity. Today towns such as Cambridge and Norwich are popular tourist stops, but the main appeal of East Anglia is the chance to step out of the modern age into a gentler, calmer vision of England.

Which vision you choose is up to you. It could be drifting through the grounds of the Cambridge colleges by punt (a pole-propelled long, narrow boat) or hiring a day boat to explore the Norfolk Broads. It could be wandering through coastal marshes in search of bitterns (a type of water bird), basking on dune-backed beaches or roaming the parterre gardens of decadent stately homes. It could be fine dining on Norwich's glam St Benedict's St, stopping for lunch in a half-timbered medieval pub, or seeking out some of the country's best seafood on the Norfolk coast.

Many tourist experiences here are slightly informal – don't be surprised to find yourself buying seafood straight from fisherfolk, hiking to the beach through whispering reed beds or clambering up a steep ladder to the top of a church spire. Along the way, you'll discover the rich history and fascinating culture of one of the most relaxed corners of the country.

### THE MAIN AREAS

**CAMBRIDGE**
The quintessential English university town. p334

**NORWICH**
History, fine dining and culture. p346

**THE SUFFOLK COAST**
A calmer vision of the seaside. p355

**THE WOOL TOWNS**
Half-timbered history. p358

# Find Your Way

East Anglia fills the bump to the north of the River Thames. Fast train lines and highways run as far as Cambridge and Norwich but travelling elsewhere involves navigating minor roads through flat farmland and sprawling wetlands.

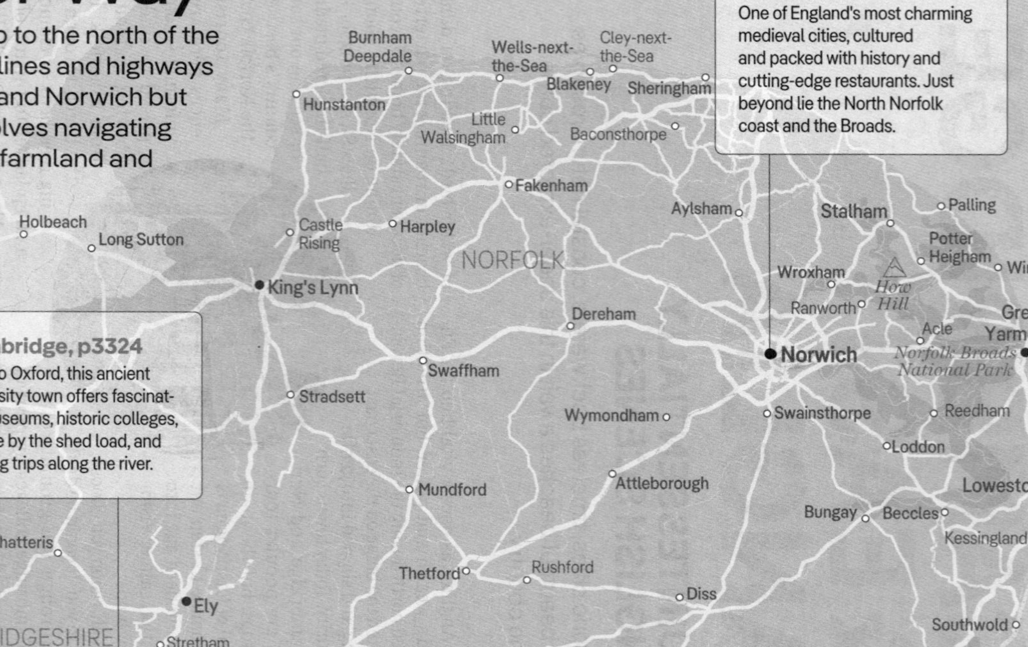

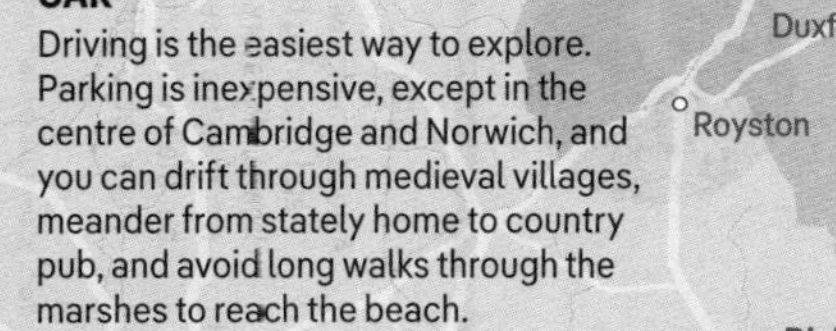

**CAR**

Driving is the easiest way to explore. Parking is inexpensive, except in the centre of Cambridge and Norwich, and you can drift through medieval villages, meander from stately home to country pub, and avoid long walks through the marshes to reach the beach.

**TRAIN**

Trains are better for getting to East Anglia than getting around East Anglia. Fast services run from London to Cambridge, Colchester, Ipswich and Norwich, with connections to Cromer, Ely and King's Lynn, but you'll have to swap to a bus to reach the rest of the coast.

**BUS**

National Express buses buzz to major towns and inexpensive local buses connect smaller towns and villages, though not always quickly or frequently (and there are few Sunday services). The Coastliner/Coasthopper bus routes between Cromer and King's Lynn are perfect for exploring the North Norfolk coast.

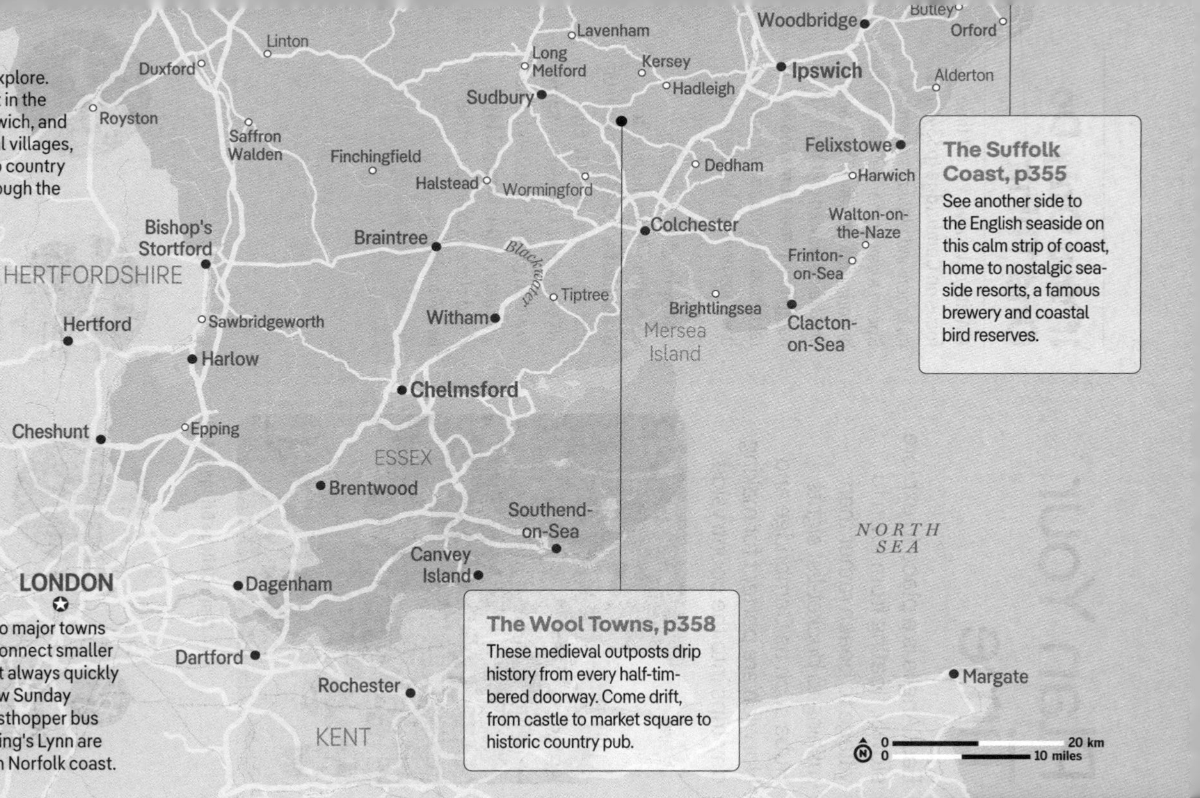

**The Wool Towns, p358**

These medieval outposts drip history from every half-timbered doorway. Come drift, from castle to market square to historic country pub.

**The Suffolk Coast, p355**

See another side to the English seaside on this calm strip of coast, home to nostalgic seaside resorts, a famous brewery and coastal bird reserves.

# Plan Your Time

East Anglia is a place to explore slowly, floating from town to village to beach rather than rushing to bucket-list sights. Hubs such as Cambridge and Norwich are perfect for making day trips into the countryside.

CHRISDORNEY/SHUTTERSTOCK ©

Clare College Bridge (p340)

## If You Only Do One Thing

- With only have a short time, focus on **Cambridge** (p334) and its green and pleasant environs. Spend a day or more exploring the historic colleges and The Backs and being wowed by the city's magnificent **museums** (p338), and take in some culture – on stage, in the pubs or in the lecture halls.

- Stay local for a day trip. Go punting down the river to **Granchester** (p344) for maximum nostalgia, or drive out to **Ely** (p345) for civil war history, **Saffron Walden** (p344) for stately home grandeur, or **Duxford** (p344) to stand close to planes that flew in two World Wars.

## Seasonal Highlights

East Anglia is busy in summer, calmer in spring and autumn and quiet in the winter. Visiting out of season means cheaper accommodation but the best time for seafood is the summer.

### JANUARY

A quiet time for tourism, but ducks and birds of prey are still easily spotted in the coastal reserves.

### MARCH

Come to Cambridge for the **Lent Bumps** boat races and the **Footlights Revue**, and enjoy quiet sights as the first signs of spring emerge.

### APRIL

A good time for walking and exploring the Broads. Migratory birds return to the reserves but the tourist crowds have yet to gather.

CARMINA_PHOTOGRAPHY/SHUTTERSTOCK ©, PHIL PHOENIX/SHUTTERSTOCK ©, ERNIE JANES/SHUTTERSTOCK ©

## 5 Days to Travel Around

● With more time to spare, zip up to **Norwich** (p346), with its cathedral, museums and gourmet restaurants, and devote a day to boating on the **Norfolk Broads** (p351). Pop over to **Southwold** (p357) for a fun-filled day on the beach and an Adnams ale, or go birding at **Minsmere and Dunwich Heads** (p356).

● On day four, visit the nostalgic seaside resorts of **Cromer** (p352) and **Wells-next-the-Sea** (p353), stop in on dainty brick-and-flint villages, and be wowed by elegant **Holkham Hall** (p353). To close, whoosh on to **Cambridge** (p334) for a day punting on the Granta.

## 10 Days for Deeper Exploring

● On a longer trip, soak up medieval (and older) history in **Colchester** (p360), **Bury St Edmunds** (p360) and the half-timbered villages of **Lavenham** (p360) and **Long Melford** (p360). Spend a seaside day in **Aldeburgh** (p357) then go on a culinary safari through **Norwich** (p346) and the fishing villages of the **North Norfolk coast** (p354).

● Take a day walk on the pilgrim trail to **Walsingham** (p354), and whip out your binoculars to spot seals at **Blakeney** (p353) or bitterns at **Cley Marshes** (p353). Stay in **King's Lynn** (p352) to visit the royal residence at **Sandringham** (p352), then finish with colleges and museums in **Cambridge** (p334).

**JUNE**

More Bumps draw crowds to Cambridge, while classical music fans head to Aldeburgh and birders hit the Suffolk and Norfolk coasts.

**JULY**

The summer peak. Come for activities and events in all the big towns and perfect weather on the busy beaches.

**OCTOBER**

The crowds diminish as the weather cools, meaning quieter sights, with flocks of migrating birds flying overhead and rutting red deer at Minsmere.

**DECEMBER**

Temperatures plummet and tourism slows to a trickle, but Christmas markets bring seasonal sparkle to Cambridge, Norwich and other towns.

# CAMBRIDGE

If East Anglia has one superstar city, it's Cambridge. A celebrated seat of learning since 1209, this appealing jumble of historic streets and cultured colleges is the archetypal English university town – an East Anglian mirror to Oxford, its closest competitor and archrival during the annual boat races on the River Thames.

At first glimpse, Cambridge can seem rather antiquated, with its Hogwarts-style colleges, pedalling academics and gliding punts. But the city has an edge too, best experienced in its agreeable pubs and hip restaurants as well as on stage, particularly during the annual Cambridge Footlights comedy revue.

With Cambridge being a lodestone for knowledge, there are some fascinating museums attached to the university, covering everything from archaeology to polar exploration. And while the colleges exude a definite air of wealth and privilege, there's much to see for free, from historic churches to the world-class Fitzwilliam Museum.

Cambridge
London

### TOP TIP

Be careful of bikes and e-scooters when walking around the streets – some of the students whizzing around town have their minds on higher things than pedestrians. If you prefer to join the pedalling throngs, bikes can be rented in the town centre and at the train station.

Punting, King's College

TOMASDARGUZIS/SHUTTERSTOCK ©

King College Chapel

## Be Humbled by King's College Chapel

MEDIEVAL MAGNIFICENCE

Every Cambridge college is an architectural wonder, but the grandiose 16th-century chapel at King's College is a vision of heaven on earth. To get the measure of this extraordinary Gothic monument, come during a service to hear the sound of the chapel's famous choir and organ reverberating off the walls beneath the world's largest fan-vaulted ceiling.

The majesty of the chapel is in the detail. Look at dogs and dragons on the walls, symbolising the Beaufort family and the Tudors, respectively – all are different. More heraldic motifs dot the walls, including the Tudor rose of Henry VIII, who completed the chapel in around 1544, and the portcullis symbol of Margaret Beaufort, mother of Henry VII. Examine the wooden screen dividing the antechapel and choir to see the initials of Henry VIII entwined with those of Anne Boleyn.

Every great chapel needs a signature painting, and at King's it's Peter Paul Rubens' *Adoration of the Magi* (1634) behind the high altar. An interesting exhibition in the side chapels charts the construction of this landmark monument. Visit during Evensong – the timetable is posted on the chapel website – to appreciate the full glory of the acoustics.

### VISITING THE COLLEGES

Post Covid-19 pandemic, Cambridge's colleges are more circumspect about admitting visitors than in the past. While most allow visitors to explore the college courts, gardens and specific buildings (including chapels and libraries), this is at the discretion of the college porters – a cohort of efficient administrators who straddle the line between helpful stand-in parents for students and iron-rod rule-keepers.

Entry is often dependant on whether porters are available to open the doors – call ahead to confirm. Some colleges charge a fee, some have defined entry times, some only admit current students and alumni, and all close to visitors over the two-week Christmas break and during the annual exams between early April and mid-June.

### WHERE TO FIND TOP-END ACCOMMODATION IN CAMBRIDGE

**University Arms Hotel**
This lavish reconstruction of Cambridge's original grand dame hotel oozes elegance and vintage charm. **£££**

**Varsity Hotel**
The modern take on Cambridge luxury, with designer furnishings and huge windows taking in the views. **£££**

**Duke House**
Elegant boutique B&B accommodation in the former student house of the Duke of Gloucester. **£££**

**HIGHLIGHTS**
**1** Fitzwilliam Museum
**2** King's College Chapel

**SIGHTS**
**3** Bridge of Sighs
**4** Cambridge University Botanic Garden
**5** Clare College Bridge
**6** Corpus Christi College
**7** Corpus Clock
**8** Great St Mary's Church
**9** Kettle's Yard
**10** Kitchen Bridge
**11** Little St Mary's Church
**12** Magdalene College
**13** Mathematical Bridge
**14** Museum of Archaeology & Anthropology
**15** Museum of Zoology
**16** Pepys Library
**17** Polar Museum
**18** Round Church
**19** Sedgwick Museum of Earth Sciences
**20** Trinity College
**21** Trinity Hall College
**22** Whipple Museum of the History of Science
**23** Wren Library

**ACTIVITIES & TOURS**
**24** Cambridge Chauffeur Punts
**25** Scudamore's Punting

**SHOPPING**

# CAMBRIDGE

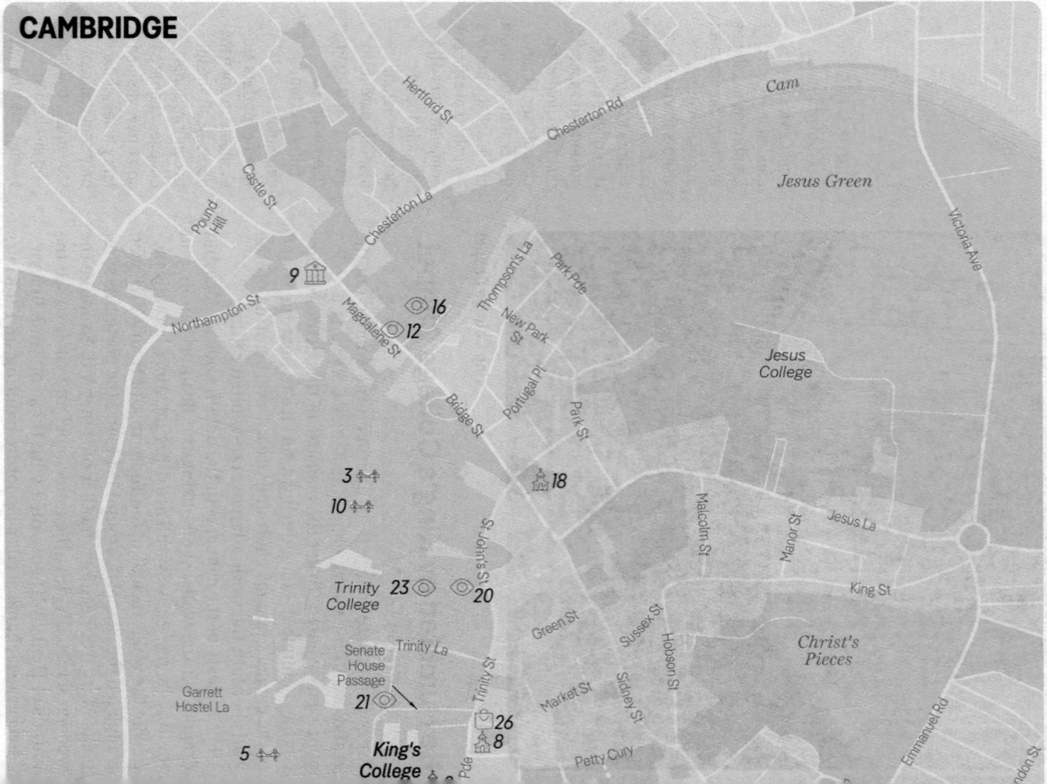

Parker's Piece
Park Tce
Regent Tce
Regent St
Gonville Pl
Hills Rd
Andrew's St
Downing Pl
Downing St
Tennis Court Rd
Lensfield Rd
Bateman St
Trumpington Rd
Trumpington St
Fitzwilliam Museum
Little St Mary's La
Mill La
King's Pde
Queen's La
Granta Pl
Fen Causeway
Silver St
Newnham Rd
Queen's Rd
1
4
6
11
13
14
15
17
19
22
24
25
0 200 m
0 0.1 miles

Corpus clock (p338)

## Be a College Library Bookworm

SEE ENGLAND'S GREAT COLLECTIONS

Entry to the venerable libraries at the Cambridge colleges is granted erratically, but if you can gain access, the collections of tomes are like something from *The Name of the Rose*.

The most famous library of all is the **Pepys Library** at riverside **Magdalene College** – pronounced 'Maud-lyn' – with some 3000 books bequeathed by the 17th-century diarist to his old college, from illuminated manuscripts to a 1540s tally of Royal Navy's ships.

Over at elegant **Corpus Christi College**, alma mater of Christopher Marlowe, the legendary **Parker Library** holds the world's finest collection of Anglo-Saxon manuscripts, but it's only open to visitors on tours led by badge-accredited guides.

The third great library stands within the hallowed grounds of Isaac Newton's old university, **Trinity College**, easily identified by its gateway statue of Henry VIII (holding a table leg not a sceptre after a famous student prank). The **Wren Library** preserves more than 55,000 books published before 1820, including works by Shakespeare, Newton and Jonathan Swift, and an original *Winnie the Pooh* (A A Milne and his son Christopher Robin were both graduates). The college was only admitting students and alumni in 2022, but access may be restored.

### EXPLORING OTHER COLLEGES

The colleges we've highlighted are just the beginning. Swing by **St John's College** to see the vast Gothic chapel designed by Sir George Gilbert Scott and the ecclesiastical-looking Bridge of Sighs, a masterpiece of stone tracery and a common focus for student pranks.

Other seats of learning worth visiting include **Christ's College**, with its gilded heraldic gate; **Pembroke**, home to Wren's first chapel; Hampton Court-like **Queens'**; graceful, Georgian-fronted **Peterhouse**; and **Emmanuel**, with its elegant Wren chapel and plaque for former student, John Harvard, founder of Harvard University.

Also make time to visit **Gonville & Caius** – so good they founded it twice (hence the double name) and famed for its baroque Senate House and three gates known as Virtue, Humility and Honour, symbolising the progress of the good student.

## Set Your Watch by the Corpus Clock

SEE TIME STUTTER AND STOP

Outside graceful Corpus Christi College on King's Parade, you can set your watch – or at least try to – at the 24-carat gold **Corpus Clock**, first unveiled in 2008. This fantastical timepiece is operated by a hideous clockwork insect 'time-eater' that turns the cogs with its legs. The clock is only accurate once every five minutes; at other times it slows, stops or speeds up – a tribute, according to its creator JC Taylor, to life's irregularity.

## The Country's Best College Museum

ABSORB HISTORY THROUGH YOUR PORES

Fondly dubbed 'the Fitz' by locals, the colossal neoclassical treasure house known as the **Fitzwilliam Museum** is actually just the grandest of the University of Cambridge's many student museums. Imagine being a student and having not only the best libraries in the country to browse, but also one of Britain's finest collections of artworks and classical treasures!

### WHERE TO STAY ON A BUDGET IN CAMBRIDGE

**Cambridge YHA**
A short stroll from the train station, with spotless dorms and rooms, and a cafe and bar. **£**

**University Rooms**
To sleep in the heart of history, book empty student rooms in the Cambridge colleges during university holidays. **£**

**Worth House**
A charming Cambridge B&B, bringing great breakfasts and design style to a location north of Midsummer Common. **££**

Cambridge Botanic Garden

As you wander, you'll spot plenty of students swotting up on Mediterranean history by examining the exquisite classical ceramics, old master paintings, and Roman, Egyptian and Cypriot grave goods, part of a collection bequeathed by the 7th Viscount Fitzwilliam to his old university.

## Relax in the Botanic Garden

FIND SERENITY IN GREENERY

The city's botanic garden was created as a teaching tool for students in 1846, before being thrown open to the general public. Founded by Charles Darwin's mentor, Professor John Henslow, this green expanse is full of hidden corners and secret spaces, making a great space for a game of hide-and-seek with the kids. If you're more botanically minded, there are more than 8000 plant species to admire, from mature deciduous trees to an army of pitcher plants and palms in the Victorian-era greenhouses. Free guided tours run from May to September.

### SEEING THE CAMBRIDGE COLLEGES

The Society of Cambridge Tour Guides chair **Gerald Smith** shares his tips for getting the best from the Cambridge colleges.

Cambridge's riverside colleges are rightly legendary – particularly Queens' (highly photogenic), King's (with its spectacular, perpendicular Gothic chapel) and St John's (best for river views). My favourite, though, is Pembroke College, founded in 1347. You can enter without charge into a haven of tranquillity. Take a seat in the chapel and admire the elegant architecture of Christopher Wren's earliest building, or explore the grounds with its huge banana tree!

My top tip? The public are welcome to attend Evensong at any college chapel. Note that colleges may close at certain times so check their websites or visit with an accredited blue or green badge guide.

### WHERE TO EAT IN CAMBRIDGE

**Midsummer House**
Cutting-edge cuisine from double Michelin-starred chef Daniel Clifford, in an unexpected setting. £££

**Smokeworks**
It's all about ribs, wings and loaded fries at this beloved hipster grill by St Bene't's Church. ££

**Cambridge Chop House**
Meaty mains (plus fish, fowl and more) in a location to die for, overlooking King's College Chapel. ££

**VISITING STEPHEN HAWKING**

Easily missed among the more famous colleges (and unconnected to better-known Trinity), diminutive **Trinity Hall College** has a graceful, wood-lined chapel, but it's most famous as the alma mater of the great astrophysicist Stephen Hawking. It was here that Hawking became a doctor despite the onset of motor neurone disease, before moving on to a fellowship at Gonville & Caius College (p338), where he worked until his death in 2018. A stone memorial engraved with the words, 'Remember to look up at the stars and not down at your feet,' stands outside the late scientist's room in Caius Court.

Bridge of Sighs

## Explore the College Backs and Bridges

GO BEHIND THE SCENES

To get a better understanding of life at the Cambridge colleges, pop behind the college's street-facing facades to **The Backs** – a peaceful sprawl of formal gardens, neatly trimmed lawns and meadows that are still occasionally grazed by livestock, set within the college grounds.

Whether you're exploring on foot or by punt, the bridges linking the colleges precincts on both sides of the river are the focus of attention. Most famous is the fanciful Rialto-style **Bridge of Sighs** in the grounds of St John's College. Nearby is the more restrained **Kitchen Bridge**, built following designs by Christopher Wren in 1709.

The oldest river crossing is the **Clare College Bridge** from 1639 (note the decorative balls, one allegedly vandalised by the architect in protest at his fee). Further south is Queens' College's flimsy-looking wooden **Mathematical Bridge** – despite what some guides say, it was not designed by Isaac Newton or assembled without nuts and bolts.

### WHERE TO DRINK IN CAMBRIDGE

**The Eagle**
Sink a pint in the pub frequented by WWII air aces as well as Crick and Watson, discoverers of DNA.

**Cambridge Brew House**
Real ales and IPAs fill the taps at this fun microbrewery pub near the historic centre.

**The Maypole**
What you lose in history, you make up for in atmosphere at this friendly student watering hole.

## A Personally Curated Collection

HOW ART CURATORS LIVE

If you've ever wondered what art gallery curators do at home, pop into **Kettle's Yard**, a living art gallery created by HS 'Jim' Ede (1895–1990), former curator at the Tate Gallery in London. Free guided tours explore a lifetime's collection of artworks and found objects, displayed in a row of imaginatively converted cottages. Look out for works by Joan Miró, Henry Moore and lesser-known artists such as primitive nautical artist Alfred Wallis. Don't be tempted to move anything – it's a condition of the museum's bequeathment that everything is preserved exactly as Ede left it!

### WHY I LOVE CAMBRIDGE

**Joe Bindloss**, Lonely Planet writer.

I've been coming to Cambridge since my school days for gigs, meals and days out on the river, and I'm consistently charmed by the way the city manages to resist the pressures of the 21st century. Cows still graze in the middle of Cambridge, academics totter around on sit-up-and-beg bicycles and picnics on Jesus Green are still the preferred social activity. Take a walk at first light and you may feel like you've been teleported back in time to somewhere between WWII and the reign of Henry VIII.

## Punting on the Granta

DRIFT ALONG A FAMOUS WATERWAY

Navigating the river that runs through town (known variously as the Cam and Granta) on a pole-propelled punt is the most Cambridge experience imaginable.

At the Bridge St and Silver St bridges, you can join punt tours led by current and former students through the college Backs or south to Grantchester, or rent a self-poled punt to explore. Guides certainly cram their tours with facts, but the central section of the river can feel as crowded as Venice on Everyone Ride a Gondola Day.

With stations at both bridges, **Scudamore's** has been poling travellers up and down the Cam since 1910. **Cambridge Chauffeur Punts** at Silver St is another reliable operator. For faster navigation, you can also rent canoes and kayaks.

During Lent and in May, the river is taken over by college rowers for the energetic Bumps races.

## The University Museums

GET A MUSEUM EDUCATION

Get off the tourist trail at the University of Cambridge's charming student museums. Start south of the centre at the **Polar Museum**, stuffed with explorer's gear, photographs, maps, journals and tragic last messages.

At the university's Downing St campus, the **Sedgwick Museum of Earth Sciences** contains a stellar collection of fossils, including items from Darwin's voyages. Close by, the **Museum of Archaeology & Anthropology** displays cultural objects from as far afield as the South Pacific and British Columbia, Canada.

### GET YOURSELF TO GRANTCHESTER

Whether you come by bus, bike or punt, **Grantchester** (p344) is one of the most rewarding day trips from Cambridge – indeed, you could fit it into half a day if you pole your punt efficiently.

### WHERE TO SNACK IN CAMBRIDGE

**Aromi**
A local institution serving stacked Sicilian-style pizza slices, plus good gelato, round the corner on Peas Hill.

**Locker**
A sociable student cafe, serving salmon, avocados and other things smashed on toast.

**Fitzbillies**
This Cambridge institution serves the city's stickiest, sweetest Chelsea buns.

A short walk west, the excellent **Museum of Zoology** has stuffed animals, myriad bones and beaks, and a two-horned narwhal. Around the corner is the **Whipple Museum of the History of Science**, with an intriguing collection of telescopes, astrolabes and sextants.

**BEST CAMBRIDGE EVENTS**

**Cambridge Beer Festival**
A real ale and IPA extravaganza in May, featuring lots of high-spirited beer drinking on Jesus Green.

**The Bumps**
Rowing races on the Granta river in February/March and May, where college crews try to 'bump' their rivals' boats.

**Cambridge Shakespeare Festival**
Performances of the Bard's work in the evocative settings of the college courts in July and August.

**The Footlights Revue**
Top comedy in April and May from the Cambridge Arts Theatre (which launched almost every British comic you know).

## Go to Church

HISTORY OUTSIDE THE COLLEGES

Cambridge's ancient churches are jammed full of history. Start the ecclesiastical journey at **Great St Mary's**, where a modest fee gains you access to the top of the tower and epic views over a sea of dreaming college spires.

Further south near Peterhouse College is dainty **Little St Mary's**, containing a memorial to student Godfrey Washington, great-uncle of George, whose family coat of arms was reputedly the inspiration for the American flag.

North of Great St Mary's is the curious **Round Church**, an arcane-looking chapel constructed in 1130 by the Knights Templar, remodelled from a Gothic design after the tower collapsed in 1841.

## Educate Yourself

GAIN SOME COLLEGE KNOWLEDGE

For a brainiac tourist experience, public lectures on wide-ranging topics are held at Cambridge colleges throughout the year (see https://talks.cam.ac.uk for a schedule).

Another intellectual stop is the legendary **Cambridge University Press** bookstore on Trinity St, the oldest bookseller in Britain, founded in 1534. Here you'll find the latest publications on everything from climate change to quantum mechanics.

If you just want some in-depth knowledge while exploring Cambridge, arrange a city tour with a blue-badge or green-badge guide from the **Society of Cambridge Tourist Guides** (sctg.org.uk/tours).

Cambride Beer Festival

**GETTING AROUND**

Cambridge is best explored on foot, but bicycles can be hired from Rutland Cycling, with branches by the train station and under the Grand Arcade in the centre, or there are rideshare e-scooters and e-bikes from Voi. Licensed taxis are pricey; save with Uber or take local buses (most stop in or near the Drummer St bus station). Park centrally under the Grand Arcade mall, or use the five Park & Ride car parks on the outskirts, which have regular bus transfers to the centre.

Ely
Cambridge
Grantchester
Duxford
Saffron Walden

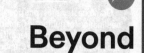

# Beyond Cambridge

## Exploring the Fenland countryside around Cambridge will take you away from the crowds into a quieter East Anglia.

Easy day trips from Cambridge by bus, train, car or punt will take you away from the refined colleges and into the calmer world of Fenland or the Fens. In this airfield-flat landscape, you'll find pretty villages of half-timbered houses, grand stately homes and – bucking the trend – Britain's best aviation museum.

Ely was the home turf of Oliver Cromwell, who set the country on the path to democracy but unleashed havoc in the process. Inside the cathedral known as the 'Ship of the Fens', you can view the aftermath of iconoclastic purges by several members of the Cromwell clan.

Beyond the Cromwell connection, the big lure of visiting is to see the contrast between urbane, highbrow Cambridge and laid-back Fenland life.

**TOP TIP**

Leave the car at home – the villages around Cambridge are easily accessible by bus, train or punt.

**Audley End House (p344)**

**PUNTING IN CAMBRIDGE**

Grantchester is just one possible destination for punters in Cambridge. For a shorter trip, consider drifting around the Backs of the Cambridge colleges (p340) with a sparky, former student guide. If you visit King's College Chapel in Cambridge (p335)

## Punt Your Way to Grantchester

CAMBRIDGE'S FAVOURITE PUNTING TRIP

With its thatched cottages, flower-filled gardens and classic cream teas, **Grantchester** (of TV drama fame) is the picture postcard image of England. Rupert Brooke, Virginia Woolf, John Maynard Keynes, EM Forster and Bertrand Russell put the place on the map with their intellectual afternoons in the **Orchard Tea Garden**. You can still follow their example today. Pick up a self-poled punt from Scudamore's (p341) in Cambridge and pole for an hour past meadows and English gardens to take tea under the apple trees.

**THE TOWN THAT ORCHIDS MADE**

If you visit Audley End, be sure to swing into nearby **Saffron Walden** – the medieval hub for saffron production in England. Here you can wander tidy streets lined with half-timbered houses, paid for by the medieval trade in saffron orchids, used as a vivid yellow dye for cloth until the 1700s. While you're here, visit the ornamental **Bridge End Gardens** and the surprisingly cosmopolitan **town museum**, packed with tribal objects from the Americas and Oceania. Come on Tuesday or Saturday for the excellent town **market** (a stop at the Saffron Walden Fishmonger's seafood bar comes highly recommended).

## Indulge your Inner Aerophile

WHERE HISTORY TAKES FLIGHT

Plane spotters go weak at the knees at the **Imperial War Museum** in Duxford. This cathedral to aviation features 200 vintage aircraft, many veterans of service in WWI and WWII. You can run your fingers over the fuselage of everything from a WWII Spitfire to a Lockheed Blackbird.

There's more than militaria on display here – iconic civilian aircraft include the de Havilland Comet, the first commercial jetliner, and a decommissioned Concorde. Duxford is 9 miles south of Cambridge, accessible by bus on Sunday or by car on other days (allow 30 minutes for the drive).

## See How the Other Half Live

ROAM LAVISH ROOMS AND GARDENS

Accessible via its own train station, palatial, English Heritage-managed **Audley End House** near Saffron Walden (45 minutes south of Cambridge) is a masterclass in elegant living. If you've recently snagged a lottery win, seek interior design inspiration in rooms dripping with priceless furniture, moulded Jacobean plaster, heirloom paintings, woodcarvings and taxidermy.

The house was designed to place its creator, the first Earl of Suffolk, at the top table of the English gentry, and it certainly worked – Charles II was so impressed that he purchased Audley End for the princely sum of £50,000 (about £9 million today) in 1668. The elegant gardens were designed by master gardener Lancelot 'Capability' Brown.

**WHERE TO STAY AND EAT IN ELY**

**Peacock's Tearoom**
A dainty tearoom in Ely's arty, antique-y riverside area, with tasteful, cosy B&B rooms. **££**

**Riverside Inn**
Surprisingly lush rooms await at this friendly riverside guesthouse, next to the narrow boat marina. **££**

**Old Fire Engine House**
Ely's poshest plates draw on a rich palette of seasonal and local Cambridgeshire produce. **££**

## Meet the Cromwells in Ely

THE MOST NOTORIOUS ENGLISHMAN

King-killer and instigator of the English Civil War, Oliver Cromwell (1599–1658) lived in relative obscurity in the town of **Ely** – 30 minutes from Cambridge by bus or train – before finding his great calling to tear down the monarchy.

Cromwell didn't go about it by asking politely. Dominated by a striking octagonal tower, Ely's soaring Gothic **cathedral** – known locally as the 'Ship of the Fens' – only narrowly escaped destruction as Cromwell silenced the choir and took over the nave to stable his horses.

Cromwell, also known as The Lord Protector, wasn't the first Cromwell to cause mayhem in Ely – during the Reformation, his great, great grand-uncle Thomas Cromwell was responsible for the destruction of the cathedral's medieval windows and every statue in the Lady Chapel.

The cathedral's windows were later refitted with some of Britain's most striking modern stained glass. Look out for depictions of Noah's Ark and the Tower of Babel, as well as panels salvaged from across Europe in the attached **Stained Glass Museum**.

While Cromwell is a rather ambiguous figure in his home country, he is an unequivocal villain across the water in Ireland. During his invasion of 1649, he purportedly ordered the Irish Catholic population to go either "to hell or to Connaught" after the confiscation of their lands.

To get under the skin of the Lord Protector, visit the **Cromwell House Museum** in his former home on St Mary's St, where interactive displays examine his tumultuous and bloody life and encourage you to answer the question: 'Oliver Cromwell, hero or villain?'

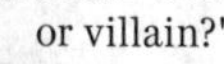

### KING COLLEGE CHAPEL'S GLASS

If you visit King's College Chapel in Cambridge (p344, admire the 16th-century stained glass and consider how close it came to being shattered by Cromwell's armies, who scrawled graffiti on the walls and used the chapel for military exercises during the English Civil War.

### CROMWELL & CAMBRIDGE

Despite being the scourge of the monarchy, Oliver Cromwell was no humble tiller of the soil. Born into a landed family, the future king-killer studied at Cambridge's Sidney Sussex College, and it's said the stained-glass windows in nearby King's College Chapel were spared on Cromwell's orders out of nostalgia for his student days.

At 29, Cromwell was elected as an MP, representing Huntingdon and later Cambridge – where draining the Fens to stop flooding was one of his great achievements – before taking the head of Charles I and adopting the title of Lord Protector, a king in all but name. After the Restoration, Cromwell's body was exhumed and his own head was plonked on a spike at the Tower of London, before being reburied inside Sidney Sussex College.

### GETTING AROUND

Coming from Cambridge, you can reach Grantchester by punt or on the number 18 bus, and Saffron Walden on the number 7. For Ely, take your pick from the slow number 12 bus or the fast train. Bus services stop running on Sunday, except for the Sunday-only 132 bus to Duxford.

Norwich
London

# NORWICH

If your experience of Norwich is limited to Steve Coogan's Alan Partridge, prepare to be pleasantly surprised. The Norfolk capital may be a little stuck in its ways, but it's also historic, cultured and fun.

This was one of the most important cities in England before the wool trade fell on hard times in the 16th century, and fluffy gold filled the streets with grand flint churches and imposing townhouses, and paid for the elegant cathedral that towers over the city centre.

Local enterprise has kept the city proudly independent to this day – you'll see far fewer chain stores and far more family-owned businesses than in most towns of this size.

The castle and cathedral are obvious drawcards, but it's worth staying on to haggle for antiques in eclectic emporiums, soak up Norwich history in the town museums and feast at some of East Anglia's finest restaurants.

### TOP TIP

Norwich may be a laid-back country town at heart, but be ready to make reservations for dinner, particularly at weekends.

Norwich

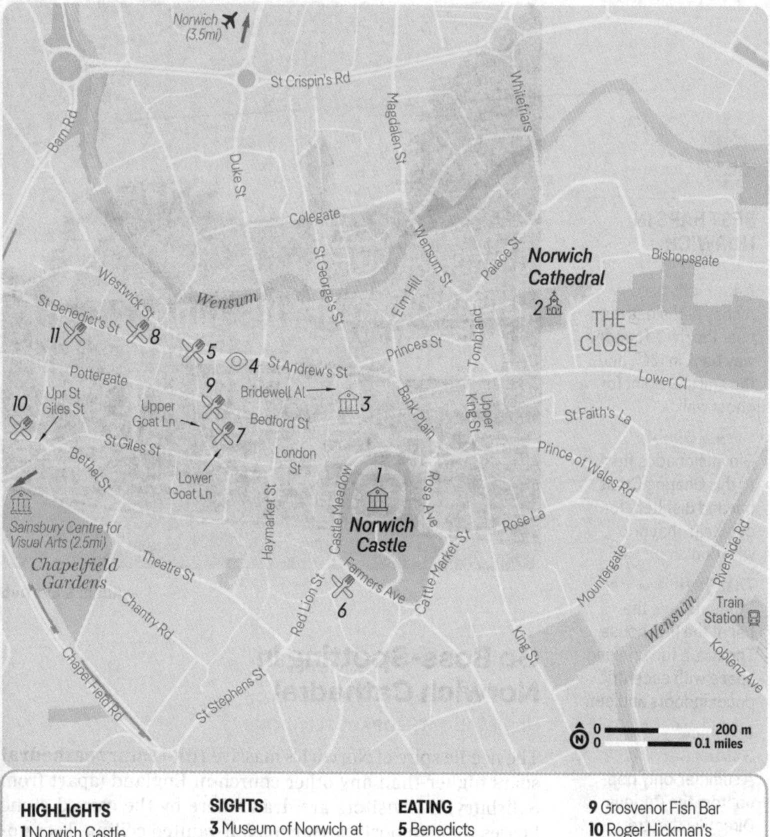

**HIGHLIGHTS**
**1** Norwich Castle
**2** Norwich Cathedral

**SIGHTS**
**3** Museum of Norwich at the Bridewell
**4** Strangers' Hall

**EATING**
**5** Benedicts
**6** Benoli
**7** Biddy's Tearoom
**8** Farmyard
**9** Grosvenor Fish Bar
**10** Roger Hickman's
**11** Tipsy Vegan

## Discover Supermarket Art

NORWICH'S ART POWERHOUSE

Housed in a Norman Foster–designed pavilion at the University of East Anglia, Norwich's most impressive art collection was amassed not by fine art experts but by supermarket mogul Sir Robert Sainsbury. The superstore's orange colour scheme is notably absent; instead, the **Sainsbury Centre for Visual Arts** displays paintings by David Hockney and Francis Bacon, sculptures by Edgar Degas, Henry Moore and Alberto Giacometti; and objects from myriad cultures, from the Arctic to the Aztecs, in calming grey spaces. The university is about 3 miles west of the centre; you can get here on bus 22, 25 or 26 in about 25 minutes.

**Grosvenor Fish Bar**

**BEST BARS IN NORWICH**

**Adam & Eve**
A cosy real ale tavern near the river, founded way back in 1249, and the starting point for ghost walks.

**Gyre & Gimble**
Gin aficionados flock to this Charing Cross bar and distillery for cocktails that drip with cool.

**The Playhouse Bar**
Students love the bar at the Playhouse Theatre, a fun drinking space with eccentric decor indoors and out.

**Botanical Garden Bar**
A summer-only pop-up from the Curious Directive theatre company, open Thursday to Saturday at Saint Simon & Saint Jude Church.

Adam & Eve pub

## Go Boss-Spotting in Norwich Cathedral

MEDIEVAL CATHEDRAL SPLENDOUR

The needle spire of Norwich's massive 11th-century **cathedral** soars higher than any other church in England (apart from Salisbury) but visitors are drawn here by the carved stone bosses that support its soaring, fan-vaulted ceiling. Peer upwards and you'll spot fire-breathing dragons, besieged castles, choirs of angels and paganistic green men among the spidery stonework.

Head to the remarkable cloisters to see bosses up close – a menagerie of monsters, saints and knights writhes just overhead. Right outside the cathedral is the chapel of Norwich School (formerly King Edward VI School) where Admiral Nelson was educated.

**WHERE TO STAY IN NORWICH**

**38 St Giles**
Hailed for top-class breakfasts and boutique B&B rooms overflowing with period furniture. £££

**Gothic House**
There's a Tim Burton feel to this atmospheric Regency-era B&B on antiques-lined Magdalen St. ££

**3 Princes**
Handsome accommodation in a historic townhouse with a shaded courtyard garden. £££

## Uncover East Anglian History

TRIPLE THE HISTORY

Between them, the three museums run by Norfolk Museums – the imposing **Norwich Castle** on the hilltop, the **Museum of Norwich at the Bridewell,** and **Strangers' Hall** at Charing Cross – tell the founding story of Norwich, Norfolk and East Anglia.

Start the journey through time at the castle – currently under renovation but still stuffed with, well, stuffed animals, art and displays on the Romans, Egyptians and Boudica (the Iceni queen who led the resistance against the Roman occupation).

The Bridewell museum focuses on city history, from wool and shoe-making to Colman's Mustard, with a fine mock-up of a vintage shop, while Strangers' Hall recreates the elegant life of Norwich's wealthy medieval wool merchants.

## Fine-Dine Your Way Around Norwich

THE BEST FOOD OUT EAST

The Norwich dining scene could hold its own in any city in the land, but you'll need a booking for weekend evenings at posher places. Start the foodie tour on St Benedicts St, home to such legends as **Benedicts**, where Modern British chef Richard Bainbridge cooks up a storm using quality Norfolk ingredients.

Nearby is **Farmyard**, a hip, green space where gourmands gather for meals of 'bistronomy' – coley with agretti, pork belly with blackberries and the like. Nearby, the **Tipsy Vegan** brings vegan cooking with a sense of fun (vegan chorizo, seitan burgers and mushroom Wellington for Sunday brunch).

Across town near the castle, **Benoli** gives Italian cooking the care it deserves, while **Roger Hickman's** on Upper St Giles St offers refined set menus that draw on a broad palette of European and Asian flavours.

For snacks on the hoof, detour south to Lower Goat Lane where **Biddy's Tearoom** has sticky buns as big as your head, and **Grosvenor Fish Bar** serves calamari, cod cheeks and soft-shell crabs and chips.

### ANTIQUE NORWICH

Norwich is a bit of a museum piece, so it shouldn't be a big surprise that there's great antique shopping in town. Start the hunt on antique-tastic Magdalen St, where every second shop is piled high with heirlooms and bric-a-brac. Pick of the crop is **Looses Emporium**, an Aladdin's cave of treasures and trinkets, from period furniture and vintage glad rags to reclaimed shop signs and plastic Daleks.

Several of Norwich's historic churches have found new life as hubs for the antiques trade. Browse ceramics, clothes, furniture, collectable toys, old vinyl and more at **St Gregory's Antiques & Collectables** off St Benedicts St and **All Saints Antiques Centre** in Westlegate.

### GETTING AROUND

Central Norwich is easily walkable, but plenty of local buses zip around town and out to the university. Central Norwich isn't particularly car-friendly – park under the castle, or use the Park & Ride car parks on the outskirts.

Travelling further afield, buses roll from the main bus station off Surrey St to Cromer, King's Lynn and Wroxham (for the Broads). All three towns are also served by train, but Norwich station is a hike from the centre on Thorpe Rd.

Wells-next the-Sea
Cley-next-the-Sea
Cromer
Sandringham
King's Lynn
Norwich
Wroxham
The Broads

# Beyond Norwich

## Roam north from Norwich for sand, seals, seabirds, stately homes and boat trips on the Broads.

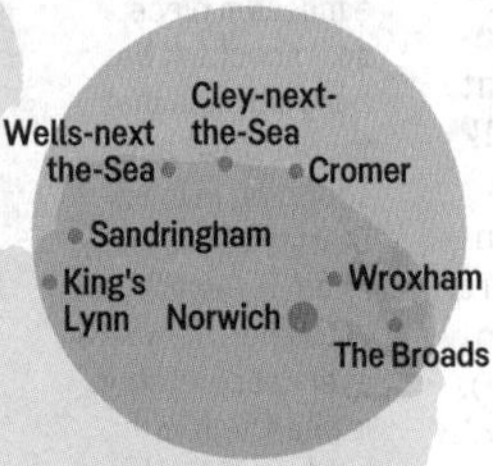

Norwich is the gateway to one of the most beguiling parts of the country. Scattered around Norwich are extravagant stately homes, the beach-fringed resorts of Norfolk's seafood coast, and the waterlogged marshes of the Norfolk Broads.

Families flock here in summer for relaxing days on the sand and boating on the Broads, while birders and walkers gather year-round in the marshes along the foreshore. Wherever you go, you'll get a sense of stepping outside time into a lost summer from the 1950s.

Handy bus services make it particularly easy to explore the North Norfolk coast, buzzing from beach town to fishing port to nature reserve to grand house. En route you can feast on some of the country's best seafood, from Cromer crabs to brown shrimp hauled from the Wash bay.

### TOP TIP

If you plan to explore the North Norfolk coast, first jump on the train to Cromer. From here, the daily Coasthopper bus runs hourly to Wells, connecting with the Coastliner to King's Lynn.

**Wells-next-the-Sea (p353)**

Hotel de Paris, Cromer

**CROMER'S VINTAGE SEASIDE**

The agreeably old-fashioned seaside resort of **Cromer** (45 minutes from Norwich by train) is the end of the line...well, the end of the railway line. Legions of Victorian holidaymakers once trundled into town by steam train to enjoy the sea air, seafood and pier shows. The Cromer pier show is still running, as is the nostalgic **Hotel de Paris** on the clifftop above the beach.

Waves break dramatically on the pebbles and hardy souls brave the breakers for surfing lessons at the **Glide Surf School** on the seafront. The same waters provide a home for Cromer's famous brown crabs, which are hauled in by the small boats parked up on the foreshore. Nearby, the **Henry Blogg Museum** pays tribute to Henry Blogg, the most decorated lifeboatman in Royal National Lifeboat Institution (RNLI) history.

## Float Around the Norfolk Broads

A MAZE OF WATERWAYS

About 9 miles northeast of Norwich, Wroxham is the easiest gateway for the Norfolk Broads, a vast area of wetlands created when the rivers Wensum, Bure, Waveney and Yare flooded gaping holes created by 12th-century crofters digging for peat. In the process, a vast wetland ecosystem and playground for leisure boating was created.

Numerous companies will rent you a day boat, overnight boat, canoe or kayak to explore 125 miles of winding waterways. In Wroxham, **Barnes Brinkcraft** and **Broads Tours** are the big operators for organised trips and day boat rentals, while **Mark the Canoe Man** offers guided paddles and kayak and canoe rentals.

Back on land, the **Museum of the Broads** in Stalham (8 miles beyond Wroxham) is a jumble of vintage boats and displays on the lives of local marsh-dwellers, with its own vintage steam launch. In the grounds of How Hill House, teeny **Toad Hole Cottage** has recreated eel-catchers' rooms and a nature trail whispering through the reeds.

### WHERE TO STAY IN NORTH NORFOLK

**Cley Windmill**
North Norfolk's most charming stop is in Cley-next-the-Sea, set in a historic windmill gazing out over the swishing reeds. £££

**Blakeney Hotel**
An elegant boutique hotel beside the marshes in Blakeney, blending design chic with top-notch facilities. £££

**Bank House**
Georgian elegance on the banks of the River Great Ouse in King's Lynn, with superior on-site brasserie dining. ££

### ROYAL SANDRINGHAM

Plenty of stately homes are fit for a king, but in the case of **Sandringham** near King's Lynn, we mean that literally. Both Queen Elizabeth II and her son King Charles III grew up in this lavish Victorian manor, constructed as a home for King Edward VII and Queen Alexandra.

The sumptuous reception rooms – still regularly used by the royals and open on selected summer dates – contain their original Edwardian fixtures and fittings and a wealth of glinting gifts from European royal families.

It's surreal to imagine generations of royals treating this grand house as just a family home. The stables house a flag-waving museum filled with royal memorabilia, while the garage contains the very first royal motor car, a Daimler Mail Phaeton from 1900.

Norfolk wetlands

Inside 14th-century **St Helen's Church** – the 'Cathedral of the Broads' – you can see a magnificent painted medieval rood screen, and climb steep ladders to the tower for panoramic views. For family fun, head to **BeWILDerwood** – a fantasy forest playground with aerial mazes, cycle routes and more to trigger young imaginations.

## See Norfolk's Big Houses

MANSIONS ON AN EPIC SCALE

Norfolk may feel a little forgotten today, but this was once the epicentre of extravagant living. Discover just how extravagant at gorgeous **Blickling Hall** (14 miles north of Norwich), one time home of the Boleyn family, where the flamboyant interiors feature every imaginable luxury, including some of the finest Jacobean moulded plaster ceilings in existence.

Ten miles further north and closer to Cromer, **Felbrigg Hall** is topped by a curious parapet spelling out the family motto. This historic pile is less ostentatious from the outside, but just as extravagant within. Note the hand-painted wallpaper in the Chinese Bedroom, fitted in 1752 but facing a constant threat from insect pests.

### WHERE TO STAY ON THE NORFOLK COAST

**Deepdale Backpackers & Camping, Burnham Deepdale**
Farmyard camping, glamping and budget rooms, with a good shared kitchen. £

**Red Lion, Cromer**
A cosy stop above the seafront, with snug, sea-facing rooms and good pub grub. ££

**The Quay**
A prime location for Wells town and the beach, with creek and harbour views from the upper floors. ££

After an overnight stop at Cromer or Wells-next-the-Sea, head to palatial **Holkham Hall**, the home of the Earl of Leicester. This perfectly symmetrical Palladian villa was constructed as a display case for the first earl's astonishing art collection, assembled on a grand tour of Europe from 1712 to 1718. Guided tours take in guest rooms dripping with tapestries and a warren of hidden passageways used by servants.

Closer to King's Lynn is **Houghton Hall**, built for Britain's first prime minister, Sir Robert Walpole, in 1730. This grand, Palladian-style pile overflows with gilt, tapestries and murals, and the gardens are dotted with contemporary sculptures by Rachel Whiteread, Henry Moore, Anish Kapoor and others.

## Bask on Norfolk's Beaches

SUBLIME SANDS

Norfolk's best beaches lie hidden behind a baffle of whispering reeds, but they're there alright, and you can reach the coast from Norwich in less than an hour. Bring your bucket and spade to beach hut-backed **Wells Beach**, reached by a long stroll (or an easy bus ride) from the fishing village of Wells-next-the-Sea.

Sand gives way to pebbles at **Cley-next-the-Sea** – a fine beach for walking, with uplifting views all the way to the end of the Blakeney National Nature Reserve.

A short hop west, sublime **Holkham National Nature Reserve** faces Holkham Hall across the A149. This stunning sweep of dune-backed, seashell-sprinkled sand is accessed via a hike across a wide buffer of salt marshes and pine forest.

There's more sugary sand at **Brancaster Beach**, a wonderfully windswept stretch of shoreline that melts into the horizon at low tide. Pick up a seafood picnic in nearby Brancaster Staithe.

## Meet the Norfolk Wildlife

SEABIRDS, SEALS AND SCENERY

Wildlife fans are richly rewarded in Norfolk. If feathered friends are your fancy, make for **Cley Marshes**, Holkham National Nature Reserve, **Royal Society for the Protection of Birds (RSPB) Titchwell Marsh** or **RSPB Snettisham** to spot marsh harriers, bitterns and more.

It's not just birds. The dune-backed curls of sand at **Scolt Head** and **Blakeney Point** are haul-out points for thousands of common and grey seals, with some 3000 seal pups born every winter. Both headlands can be reached on foot along the shore, but it's easier to come by boat. Beans Boat Trips,

### HANSEATIC HISTORY IN KING'S LYNN

Laid-back King's Lynn, 45 miles northwest of Norwich, was a major port for the medieval wool trade and an important depot for German traders from the Hanseatic League. Discover the history of the fisherfolk who hauled brown shrimp and shellfish from The Wash at the charming **True's Yard** museum, then drop into the 15th-century **Guildhall** (where Shakespeare performed as a young actor) on King St.

Follow a line of Hanseatic merchants' warehouses to Queen St to reach the chequerboard-patterned town hall – now home to the **Stories of Lynn** museum – facing the often-flooded **Lynn Minster** across a medieval market square. Further back from the River Great Ouse, the **Lynn Museum** has delightful displays on local industries and Seahenge, a Bronze Age timber circle that lay submerged for 4000 years.

### WHERE TO FIND THE BEST SEASIDE CAFES

**Wells Beach Cafe**
An inviting weatherboard cafe just back from the sand in Wells-next-the-Sea, run by the team from Holkham Hall.

**Rocket House**
An Art Deco charmer in the same building as the Henry Blogg Museum, with sweeping sea views from the balcony.

**Two Magpies Bakery**
Part of a cute East Anglian chain, serving coffees, cookies and oversized sausage rolls by Blakeney quay.

**NORFOLK'S BEST SEAFOOD**

**Sarah Knight** and **Thomas Large**, proprietors of Brancaster Bay Shellfish and the Mussel Pod in Brancaster Staithe, share their Norfolk seafood tips.

Some of the best seafood in Norfolk can be caught in the **White Horse** right in our village of Brancaster Staithe. They offer fresh Brancaster oysters, locally caught lobsters and an amazingly varied seafood platter of the freshest seafood around, including smoked salmon from the **Staithe Smokehouse**. From late September through March, the spread includes our own Brancaster mussels. For cooking seafood at home, you can't beat **Gurneys** in Burnham Market, with a huge selection of fresh fish and shellfish. They also make their own fishcakes, pâtés and curries – a real treat!

Bishop's Boats and other operators have regular departures from the tiny quays in Blakeney and Morston.

Afterwards, swing by Blakeney's mustard-yellow **Moorings** restaurant for a fine menu of seafood with saffron and samphire.

## Feast on Norfolk seafood

CRABS, SMOKED SALMON AND MORE

The Norfolk Coast serves up a feast! From Cromer's famous, fat brown crabs to local brown shrimp, mussels and oysters, the entire coast is one big seafood buffet.

Start the banquet in Cromer, where fisher-owned **Davies Fish Shop** sells Cromer crabs, dressed the old-fashioned way. Brick and flint Cley-next-the-Sea has bonfire-scented kippers, mackerel and fish pâtés from the **Cley Smokehouse** and picnic-ready seafood at **Picnic Fayre**.

At Wells-next-the-Sea, you'll need a booking to sample crabs served every which way at highly regarded **Wells Crab House**. The ocean's bounty spills over to Brancaster Staithe, where the **White Horse** serves legendary seafood platters indoors or outside under canvas, and the **Mussel Pod**, **Crab Hut** and **Staithe Smokehouse** make an art form of their respective catches.

## The Norfolk Walk

TRACE A PILGRIM TRAIL

Buses trundle along the North Norfolk coast, but the shoreline can also be explored on foot along the serene **Norfolk Coast Path**, which threads between the creeks, marshes and beaches for 84 miles between Hunstanton and Hopton-on-Sea. The 21-mile section from Cley-next-the-Sea to Burnham Deepdale is particularly rewarding.

Consider a side trip to historic **Walsingham**, a destination for Catholic pilgrims since medieval times, with its abbey ruins and candle-filled pilgrim complex (complete with ready-to-sprinkle holy water). Walk here from Norwich on the **Walsingham Way** (37 miles; three days), then continue on to Wells on the pint-sized **Wells & Walsingham Light Railway**.

**GETTING AROUND**

A car is helpful for exploring the Broads (and accessing the marinas for day-boat rentals), but you can also reach most places by bus or train.

Greater Anglia trains run to Cromer and King's Lynn, where you can pick up the Coastliner/Coasthopper bus to pretty much anywhere on the coast. For the Broads, take the bus or train from Norwich to Wroxham.

Railway fans can ride the miniature Bure Valley Steam Railway along 9 miles of narrow-gauge tracks between Aylsham and Wroxham. Larger locos steam along the old North Norfolk Railway between Sheringham and Holt, while the dainty Wells & Walsingham Light Railway links Wells-next-the-Sea to Walsingham.

# THE SUFFOLK COAST

North of the River Orwell, the Suffolk Coast breaks down into a series of coastal marshes and windswept beaches that offer some of the best birdwatching in the country. Nature reserves such as RSPB Minsmere and Dunwich Heath keep birders in feathered heaven, within sight of the looming Sizewell nuclear power station.

Tucked away between the reed beds are two of East Anglia's most lovely seaside resorts – cultured Aldeburgh and elegant Southwold – reached via winding backroads that take you off the mainstream tourist circuit. Further south is Orford Ness, a shingle island with a surreal atomic heritage, and Sutton Hoo, the final resting place of an Anglo-Saxon king.

The area is best explored with a hire car, staying in country pubs or Airbnb rooms in the tiny villages inland from the coast. Allow extra time to get here – north of Ipswich, the A12 shrinks to a back lane.

## TOP TIP

Summer and winter opening hours operate on the Suffolk Coast. Attractions that open daily from April to September may only open at weekends in winter, and bird reserves close by 4pm from November to January.

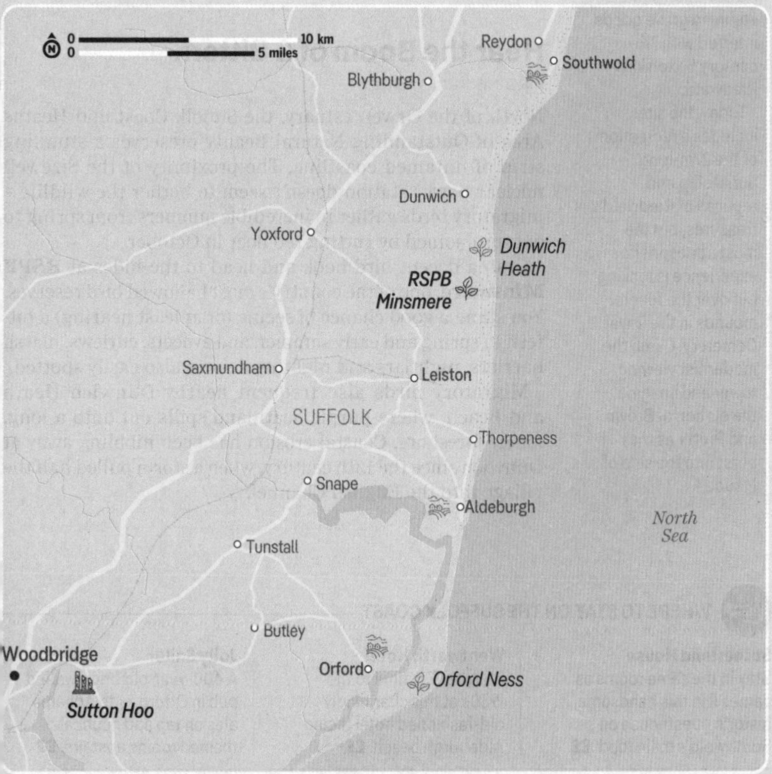

0 10 km
0 5 miles
Reydon
Southwold
Blythburgh
Dunwich
Yoxford
Dunwich Heath
RSPB Minsmere
Saxmundham
Leiston
SUFFOLK
Thorpeness
Snape
Aldeburgh
North Sea
Tunstall
Butley
Woodbridge
Orford
Orford Ness
Sutton Hoo

### ENGLAND'S MOST FAMOUS ROYAL FUNERAL

You'll need to use your imagination to get the best from **Sutton Hoo**, the site of England's best-known ship burial. Uncovered by widowed landowner Edith Pretty and amateur archaeologist Basil Brown in 1938 – a story evocatively told in the Netflix drama *The Dig* – the site was assumed to be Viking, until closer examination of the stunning grave goods interred with 7th-century Saxon king Rædwald.

Today, the site includes a recreation of the 27m-long burial ship and replicas of Rædwald's treasures, but the most atmospheric experience is looking out over the funeral mounds in the Royal Cemetery. Climb the modernist viewing tower and imagine the elation of Brown and Pretty as they burst into the side of Mound 1.

Aldeburgh

## Hear the Boom of a Bittern

BIRDING BRILLIANCE

North of the Orwell estuary, the Suffolk Coast and Heaths Area of Outstanding Natural Beauty preserves a stunning strip of untamed coastline. The proximity of the Sizewell nuclear power station doesn't seem to bother the wildlife – migratory birds gather in incredible numbers from spring to autumn, joined by rutting red deer in October.

Grab a decent bird book and head to the hides at **RSPB Minsmere**, one of the country's most hallowed bird reserves. You stand a good chance of seeing (or at least hearing) a bittern in spring and early summer, and avocets, curlews, marsh harriers, nightjars and nightingales are also easily spotted.

Migratory birds also frequent nearby Dunwich Heath and Beach, where purple heathland spills out onto a long, lonely foreshore. Coastal erosion has been nibbling away at Dunwich since the 13th century, when a storm pulled half the village into the English Channel.

### WHERE TO STAY ON THE SUFFOLK COAST

**Sutherland House**
Stay in the same rooms as James II in this handsome, historic guesthouse on Southwold's main road. **££**

**Wentworth Hotel**
Step back in time to the 1930s at this charmingly old-fashioned hotel facing Aldeburgh beach. **££**

**Jolly Sailor**
A 400-year-old brick-walled pub in Orford, with Adnams ales on tap and nautical-themed rooms upstairs. **££**

Further south, the Orford Ness nature reserve fills the longest shingle spit in Europe. Owls, falcons, hares and Chinese water deer are the top spots here, with the looming 'pagodas' that were used to test the triggers for Britain's nuclear bomb in the 1950s forming an eerie backdrop.

Climb to the roof of 12th-century **Orford Castle** for sweeping views along the coast, and swing in for lunch at the **Butley Orford Oysterage**, run by Pinney's of Orford smokehouse and oyster farm.

## Another Side to the Seaside

A SOPHISTICATED SEASIDE SCENE

With their screeching amusement arcades and drunken hen and stag parties, English seaside resorts aren't for everyone, but the Suffolk Coast offers a more genteel version.

Follow Victorian sunseekers to **Southwold** for sea and surf with hardly a gambling machine in sight. The best sand spills out of the dunes at **Denes Beach**, but it was **Adnams Brewery** that put the town on the map. The smell of yeast still drifts from the historic brewery buildings, which are open for tastings and tours.

You can quaff Adnams ales all over town, including in the elegant **Swan** on the main road. For a light feed, **Two Magpies Bakery** serves fat sausage rolls and sweet buns, plus sourdough pizzas on Saturday evenings.

North of the town's whitewashed lighthouse, Southwold Pier is famed for the satirical slot machines in Tim Hunkin's Under the Pier Show (see sidebar). In the town's tiny **museum**, look out for a flint arrowhead embedded in a prehistoric human vertebra.

Around 18 miles south, **Aldeburgh** trades the sand for endless miles of shingle. It's a place for long, contemplative walks, passing Maggi Hambling's **Scallop** sculpture, commemorating composer and Aldeburgh resident Benjamin Britten.

There's a quirky museum in the half-timbered **Moot Hall**, and you can buy spray-fresh seafood from fisher-owned shacks along the foreshore. Alternatively, drop into the **Lighthouse** restaurant for inventive takes on Modern British cuisine.

### TIM HUNKIN'S ECCENTRIC SOUTHWOLD

The Suffolk Coast has long attracted eccentrics, but engineer and inventor Tim Hunkin has elevated eccentricity to an art form. Starting out as an on-tour special effects man for prog rockers Pink Floyd, Hunkin presented the '80s TV show *The Secret Life of Machines* before devoting his energies to creating the most surreal slot machines in existence.

At the **Under the Pier Show** on Southwold Pier, Hunkin's coin-operated inventions explore everything, from town planning to ageing and wealth redistribution, with a constant flow of new creations targeting the issues of the day (the 'Whack a Banker' machine was a big hit in 2022). Don't miss his cheeky water clock at the end of the pier, which bares all every half hour.

### GETTING AROUND

Public transport is limited on the Suffolk Coast. From Monday to Saturday, local buses run from Southwold to Lowestoft and Norwich, and from Aldeburgh to Ipswich.

To reach Aldeburgh from Southwold, take the 99A bus to Halesworth and change to the 521. There are train stations at Darsham and Halesworth, connecting with local buses.

# THE WOOL TOWNS

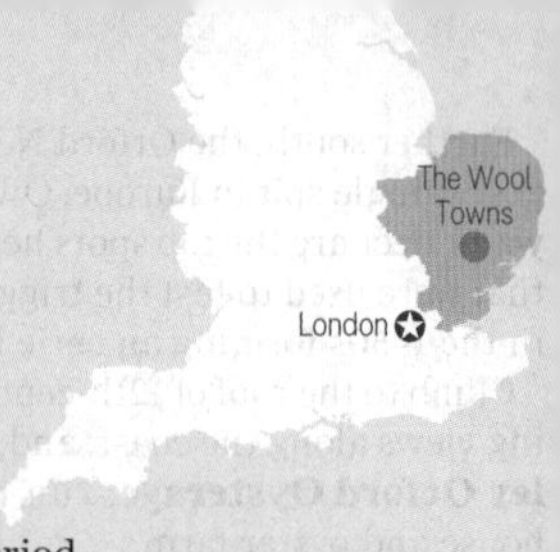

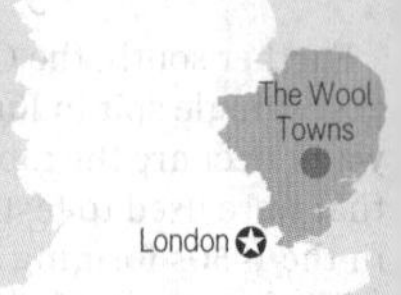


It might be surprising today, but during the medieval period, East Anglia was one of the richest places on the planet thanks to broadcloth – a warm, dense woollen fabric, dyed with the same vivid blue woad that the ancient Celts used as war paint.

The fabulous wealth earned from the production and sale of broadcloth allowed the residents of 'wool towns' such as Colchester, Bury St Edmunds and Lavenham to stuff their streets with cathedral-sized churches and half-timbered mansions, many of which are still in use today.

If you're looking for the chocolate box vision of England, you'll find it here, in the rambling farmland that inspired great master painters from John Constable to Thomas Gainsborough. But this is a quiet corner of the country – shops close early, buses stop running on Sundays, and nightlife is often limited to the village pub.

### TOP TIP

If you make it to Bury St Edmunds, book in for a tour of the elegant Theatre Royal, England's only working Regency theatre, which welcomed its first audience in 1819. Tours run on Wednesday and Saturday – call ahead to book.

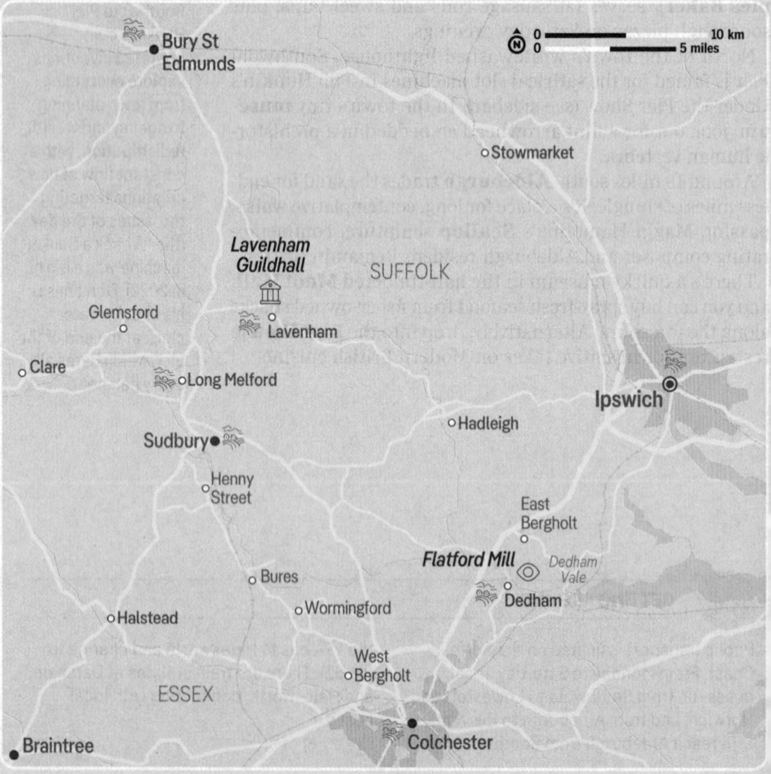

Lavenham

## Wander Wonky Lavenham

HALF-TIMBERED HEAVEN

Medieval architecture pops up all over East Anglia, but for half-timbered perfection, it's hard to beat lovely **Lavenham** in Suffolk. In this magical museum-piece, exposed beams and pargeting (moulded plaster) are the norm, and some houses lean so precariously that they seem held up only by the weight of history.

The wool trade made Lavenham one of the richest villages in England from the 14th to the 16th century. Take a turn around the behemoth **St Peter & St Paul Church**, the 16th-century **Lavenham Guildhall** and the charming **Little Hall**, with its curious medieval-meets–Middle East interiors.

To get the best from the architecture, stay overnight to explore before the day-trippers arrive. The rambling **Swan at Lavenham**, with its swish spa and latticework of ancient beams, or the agreeable **Angel** pub are solid options. Book in for wine and tasty Modern European nosh at **Number 10** in a half-timbered beauty on Lady St.

### BEST DINING IN THE WOOL TOWNS

**Le Tolbooth**
An East Anglian legend. Spectacular locally-sourced British dishes are served in a half-timbered house beside the River Stour in Dedham. **£££**

**Scutcher's**
Traditional recipes get a Modern British makeover at this cheerleader for farm-fresh produce in Long Melford. **£££**

**Maison Bleue**
Candles, starched linen and intimacy are the offering at this elegant French establishment in Bury St Edmunds' historic heart. **£££**

**Pea Porridge**
Michelin-starred and agreeably unpretentious. Expect Southwold sea bass, venison moussaka and other Suffolk-meets-the-Med treats in Bury St Edmunds. **£££**

### THE SUTTON HOO TREASURES

If you want to see the Sutton Hoo treasures in the flesh, head to Room 41 in the **British Museum** (p60) in London, where you can view Rædwald's sword, shield and helmet alongside modern reproductions.

### WHERE TO STAY IN THE WOOL TOWNS

**Swan at Lavenham**
Marvellously medieval rooms full of exposed timbers, fine fabrics and unusual angles. **£££**

**Chantry**
Stay surrounded by period details in a graceful Georgian townhouse from 1780 in Bury St Edmunds. **£££**

**Dedham Hall**
An air of old England infuses this delightful 15th-century farmhouse set in a gorgeous garden in Dedham. **££**

**ENGLAND'S OLDEST TOWN**

To see beyond the Essex stereotypes, head to **Colchester**, England's oldest town – founded as Camulodunum, the capital of Roman Britain in 49 CE. The backstreets of this prosperous country town are full of half-timbered houses built by medieval wool weavers, and a timeworn Roman wall snakes through the town centre – a memento of the siege by Iceni queen Boudica in 60–61 CE.

The most famous sight in town is Colchester's massive **castle** – the largest Norman keep in Britain – built over the ruins of a temple honouring the Roman Emperor Claudius. Also worth a peek are the charming **Hollytrees Museum**, with its Victorian toys and doll's houses, and the wave-like **Firstsite** gallery, one of the most dynamic art spaces outside London.

## The Towns that Wool Built

DISCOVER EAST ANGLIA'S WOOL WEALTH

Lavenham was just one of the villages made fabulously wealthy by wool. Up the road at **Long Melford**, more half-timbered houses and the cathedral-sized **Holy Trinity Church** stand testament to the area's fortunes. Wool money also paid for the construction of Elizabethan **Melford Hall** (which once hosted Queen Elizabeth I) and early-Tudor **Kentwell Hall**, almost facing each other across Long Melford's main road.

Much medieval money gravitated to nearby **Bury St Edmunds**, bankrolling the 16th-century **St Edmundsbury Cathedral** and one of England's richest Benedictine monasteries – now a jumble of picturesque ruins in the **Abbey Gardens**. To learn more about the towns that wool built, head to **Moyse's Hall**, with its macabre displays on the witch trials led by Witch-Finder general Matthew Hopkins and the infamous Red Barn murder.

## Step into an Old Master Painting

SEE CONSTABLE AND GAINSBOROUGH COUNTRY

The Wool Towns gave England two of its greatest painters – John Constable and Thomas Gainsborough. Between them, these two masters created some of the most enduring images of Georgian England.

To learn more about Gainsborough, drop by the **Gainsborough's House** museum in Sudbury, where the great portrait and landscape painter was born in 1727. A few miles down the road in Ipswich, the Tudor-era **Christchurch Mansion** is dotted with works by both Gainsborough and Constable.

To step into an old master painting in real life, follow the River Stour from Dedham to **Flatford Mill**, where Constable painted his famous *The Hay Wain* and a string of other masterpieces in the 1820s. Managed today by the National Trust, Flatford Mill has hardly changed – indeed, **Willy Lott's House** looks *exactly* the same.

The walk past tortured willows from Dedham (or the train station in Manningtree) to Flatford Mill is delightful, but families also gather to travel along the River Stour by rented rowboat, canoe or stand-up paddleboard.

**GETTING AROUND**

Trains run to Colchester, Bury St Edmunds and Manningtree (within walking distance of Dedham), connecting with local buses to Lavenham, Long Melford and Sudbury.

Alternatively, pop your bike on the train and pedal along sleepy, flat backroads, from historic village to country church to medieval coaching inn at your leisure.

Willy Lott's House

# BIRMINGHAM & THE MIDLANDS

## HEARTLANDS, HILLS AND HISTORY

The Midlands' rolling hills and gentle farmlands are pockmarked by lively cities and the ruins of a pioneering past. Welcome to the heart of England.

'Black by day and red by night,' was how American writer and US Consul in Birmingham Elihu Burritt once described the neighbouring Black Country during a visit in 1868. Watching the thick smoke and raging fires rise from the region's cacophonous iron foundries, Burritt was astounded by the power and extent of production across this humming industrial landscape. Not for nothing did Birmingham gain the nickname the 'city of 1000 trades'.

But while the UK's second-largest city and the surrounding areas are rightfully proud of their roles in Britain's rise to global prominence, things have changed much since then. Culturally diverse and a hub of gastronomic innovation, Birmingham is now a bright dynamic metropolis pierced by charming canals and offering easy transport links to every corner of the Midlands.

And though the Midlands may still sometimes be associated with the smog of the Industrial Revolution, this is a region that stretches far and wide to the greenest pastures, where the air is crisp and the silence ecstatic. From the ragged widescreen hills of the Peak District down to Herefordshire's languid apple orchards, the scenery outside of the Midland's gregarious towns and cities is as diverse as the people who populate them.

Fanning out from Birmingham, this underrated region is a beguiling cocktail of crumbling castles, global cuisine, literary legend and soaring scenery.

### THE MAIN AREAS

**BIRMINGHAM**
The region's busy urban centre.
p368

**STRATFORD-UPON-AVON**
Shakespeare and castle ruins.
p380

**THE SHROPSHIRE HILLS**
Rolling country walks and stargazing.
p389

**HEREFORD**
Cider, orchards and medieval history.
p397

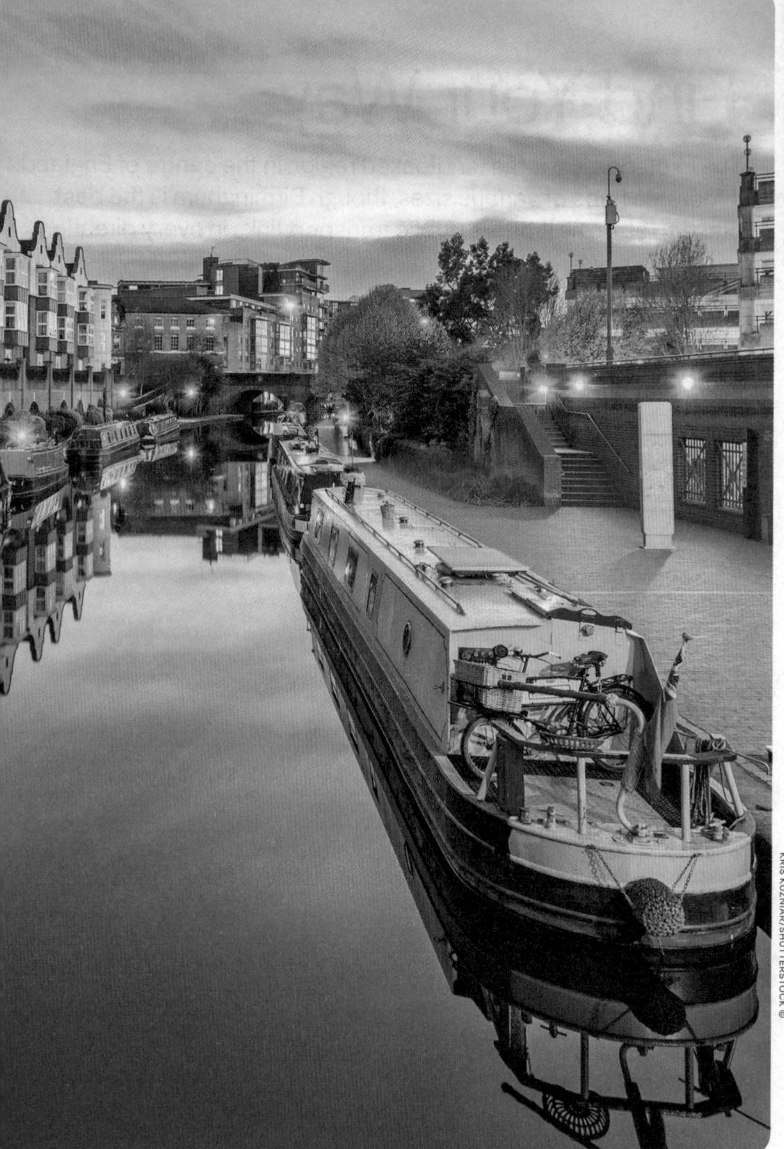

KRIS KUZNIAR/SHUTTERSTOCK ©

Above: Birmingham (p368); left: Shrewsbury (p395)

**THE PEAK DISTRICT**
Hiking, cycling and mountain views.
**p407**

**NOTTINGHAM**
Pubs, caves and Robin Hood.
**p416**

**LINCOLN**
Soaring spires and old-fashioned coastal towns.
**p425**

# Find Your Way

The Midlands is a large landlocked region in the centre of England. It features hubs of various sizes, though Birmingham is the best place to start, as it offers public transport links in every direction.

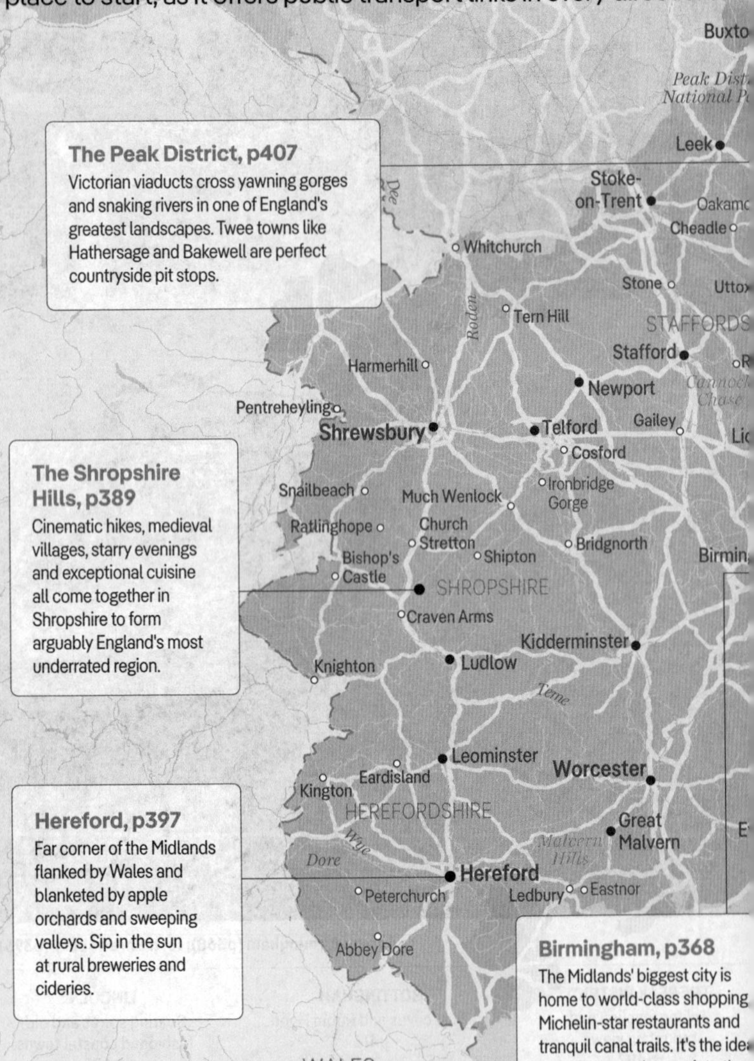


**The Peak District, p407**
Victorian viaducts cross yawning gorges and snaking rivers in one of England's greatest landscapes. Twee towns like Hathersage and Bakewell are perfect countryside pit stops.

**The Shropshire Hills, p389**
Cinematic hikes, medieval villages, starry evenings and exceptional cuisine all come together in Shropshire to form arguably England's most underrated region.

**Hereford, p397**
Far corner of the Midlands flanked by Wales and blanketed by apple orchards and sweeping valleys. Sip in the sun at rural breweries and cideries.

**Birmingham, p368**
The Midlands' biggest city is home to world-class shopping Michelin-star restaurants and tranquil canal trails. It's the ide base for venturing out into the region.

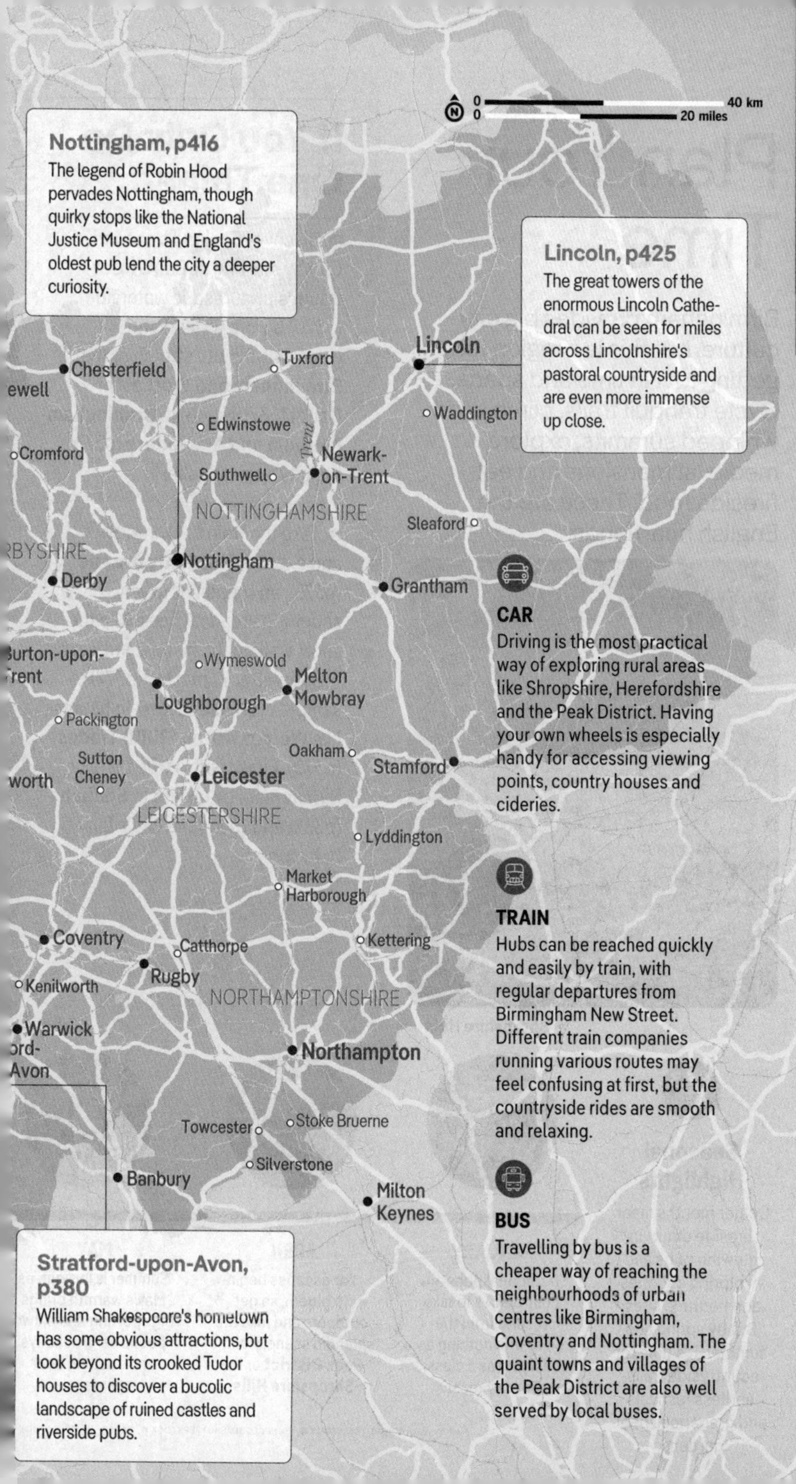

## Nottingham, p416

The legend of Robin Hood pervades Nottingham, though quirky stops like the National Justice Museum and England's oldest pub lend the city a deeper curiosity.

## Lincoln, p425

The great towers of the enormous Lincoln Cathedral can be seen for miles across Lincolnshire's pastoral countryside and are even more immense up close.

Chesterfield
ewell
Tuxford
Lincoln
Edwinstowe
Waddington
Cromford
Trent
Newark-on-Trent
Southwell
NOTTINGHAMSHIRE
Sleaford
RBYSHIRE
Nottingham
Derby
Grantham
Burton-upon-Trent
Wymeswold
Melton Mowbray
Loughborough
Packington
Oakham
Sutton Cheney
Stamford
worth
Leicester
LEICESTERSHIRE
Lyddington
Market Harborough
Coventry
Catthorpe
Kettering
Rugby
Kenilworth
NORTHAMPTONSHIRE
Warwick
ord-Avon
Northampton
Towcester
Stoke Bruerne
Silverstone
Banbury
Milton Keynes
0 40 km
0 20 miles

### CAR

Driving is the most practical way of exploring rural areas like Shropshire, Herefordshire and the Peak District. Having your own wheels is especially handy for accessing viewing points, country houses and cideries.

### TRAIN

Hubs can be reached quickly and easily by train, with regular departures from Birmingham New Street. Different train companies running various routes may feel confusing at first, but the countryside rides are smooth and relaxing.

### BUS

Travelling by bus is a cheaper way of reaching the neighbourhoods of urban centres like Birmingham, Coventry and Nottingham. The quaint towns and villages of the Peak District are also well served by local buses.

## Stratford-upon-Avon, p380

William Shakespeare's hometown has some obvious attractions, but look beyond its crooked Tudor houses to discover a bucolic landscape of ruined castles and riverside pubs.

# Plan Your Time

Birmingham provides big city culture, but this is a region for getting lost in time and space. Cycle tranquil trails, climb wind-whipped summits, explore medieval mansions and eat fireside food. These are the English heartlands.

EDDIECLOUD/SHUTTERSTOCK ©

Shropshire Hills

## If You Only Do One Thing

- Discover England's second City by starting at **Gas Street Basin's** picturesque waterside (p370) before walking the gentle 45-minute stretch of the **Birmingham and Worcester Canal** (p370) south to **Birmingham Museum and Art Gallery** (p371), the city's finest gallery.

- Take the train back into town and explore **Piccadilly Arcade** (p375), an ornate Victorian shopping arcade. Then make the short walk to the historic streets of the **Jewellery Quarter** (p372) to sample craft beer at low-lit haunts like **Wolf** (p370) and **1000 Trades** (p370). Finish with a true taste of Birmingham by taxiing to **Shababs** (p372) and trying the city's famed balti curry.

## Seasonal Highlights

Colder months mean fireside drinks in glowing pubs and exploring galleries and heritage sites. But by spring and summer, it's time for countryside trails, endless festivals and gregarious beer gardens.

### JANUARY

Traditional pubs are cosy places to take respite from the cold, with nothing as satisfying as a classic Sunday roast.

### APRIL

Landscapes begin to bloom, so get outdoors and hike the splendid scenery of the **Peak District** or the **Shropshire Hills**.

### MAY

Summer is in sight, as May's warmth brings big sporting finals, two public bank holidays and swelling beer gardens.

MARON_STUDIO/SHUTTERSTOCK ©, EDDIECLOUD/SHUTTERSTOCK ©, MARSO/SHUTTERSTOCK ©

## Three Days to Travel Around

- Start in the spectacular **Malvern Hills** (p404) by hiking up to the panoramic summit of **Worcestershire Beacon** (p404), before taking the short train to Hereford and enjoying thirst-quenching ciders at **Beer in Hand** (p398) and Barrels.

- Begin with a train to historic Ludlow to see quintessentially English scenes at **Ludlow Castle** (p393) and **Dinham Bridge** (p393). It's also a foodie epicentre, so don't miss **Vaughans'** famous pork, crackling and stuffing baps (p391).

- Hire a car on day three and visit heritage sites **Wenlock Priory** (p392) and the pioneering **Ironbridge Gorge** (p396). Finish with a night under the stars in Shropshire's **Carding Mill Valley** (p390).

## If Your Time Isn't Limited

- Start with the bright lights and exceptional restaurants of **Birmingham** (p368), before heading north to the **Peak District** (p407). Spend a couple of days hiking, climbing and cycling through the cinematic landscapes of the Hope Valley: **Mam Tor** (p409), **Stanage Edge** (p410) and the vast **Derwent Reservoir** (p409).

- Head south to historic Buxton and unwind at thermal spas at the **Buxton Crescent Hotel** (p411). Check out the unique **Devonshire Dome** (p410) before hiring a car to see opulent homes like **Chatsworth House** (p410) and the sampling the renowned **Bakewell Puddings** (p410) of charming Bakewell. Travel back to Birmingham via **Derwent Valley Mills** (p415), a Unesco World Heritage site.

**JULY**

Birmingham's live music festivals are in full swing. Look out for **Supersonic**, **Wireless** and the magnificent **Mostly Jazz, Funk & Soul**.

**AUGUST**

Head north of Nottingham to Sherwood Forest for a celebration of England's most famous outlaw at the **Robin Hood Festival**.

**SEPTEMBER**

Foodie capital Ludlow hosts three gastronomic events throughout the year, but the original and best is the **Ludlow Food Festival**.

**DECEMBER**

Christmas markets pop up across the region, so wrap up and enjoy a toasty mug of gluhwein or mulled cider.

# BIRMINGHAM

With over one million people residing within its boundaries, Birmingham is England's second-largest city and easily the biggest city in the Midlands. Romans skirted around its borders almost 2000 years ago, though the city didn't achieve real prominence until the dawn of the industrial age. Factories, funnels and foundries turned Birmingham into a smoky thriving metropolis, while its canals and eventually its railways presented the city with myriad trade routes around the country and the world.

A combination of Luftwaffe air raids and questionable town planning gave Birmingham a somewhat dismal image during the late 20th century, but fresh new architecture, gleaming trams and the arrival of some fabulous restaurants have helped make it the Midlands' renaissance city. World-class shopping and unique museums bring the smart centre plenty of buzz, but make time for neighbourhoods like Harborne and Moseley, where creative locals put their hearts into some fine artisan shops, bars and cafes.

## TOP TIP

Birmingham city centre is very walkable and most places can be reached within 15 minutes on foot. Neighbourhoods such as Stirchley can be reached by train, though bus or taxi is a better option for Moseley and Harborne. Cycling is best enjoyed on canal towpaths (particularly towards the university).

**Gas Street Basin (p370)**

**HIGHLIGHTS**
**1** Barber Institute of Fine Arts
**2** Birmingham & Worcester Canal
**3** Gas Street Basin

**SIGHTS**
**4** Birmingham Back to Backs
**5** Birmingham Museum & Art Gallery
**6** Coffin Works
**7** Curzon Street station
**see 22** Custard Factory
**8** Museum of the Jewellery Quarter
**9** Roundhouse Birmingham
**10** Sarehole Mill
**11** St Andrew's
**12** St Philip's Cathedral

**ACTIVITIES, COURSES & TOURS**
**13** GoBoat

**EATING**
**14** Balti Triangle
**15** Blow Water Cafe
**16** Chakana
**17** Eat Vietnam
**see 6** Opheem
**18** Orelle
**19** Shababs
**20** Shahi Nan Kebab House

**DRINKING & NIGHTLIFE**
**21** Attic Brew Co
**22** Floodgate Street
**see 22** Gibb St
**23** GlassHouse
**24** Lower Trinity St
**25** Rea St
**26** Vyse St
**27** Wildcat

**SHOPPING**
**28** Bullring
**29** ENKI
**30** Grand Central Birmingham
**31** Great Western Arcade
**32** Kings Heath High St
**33** Mailbox
**34** Piccadilly Arcade
**35** Polar Bear Records
**36** Punks and Chancers

## BEST CRAFT BEER IN BIRMINGHAM

**Attic Brew Co**
Creative Stirchley brewers with plenty of space outdoors. Flagship pale Intuition is an easy-drinking introduction.

**Digbrew**
Converted industrial warehouse offering a range of beers to go with generously sized pizza slices.

**Wolf**
Revolving beers alongside delectable toasted sandwiches and indulgent pies that pair perfectly with the drinks.

**Tilt**
Sip on several beer styles while slapping metal balls around vintage pinball machines.

**1000 Trades**
Low-lit Jewellery Quarter bar with monthly menu changes and live music each week.

Brimingham Museum and Art Gallery

## Canal City

EXPLORE BIRMINGHAM'S HISTORIC WATERWAYS

'More canals than Venice' is the dramatic – if rather tongue-in-cheek – phrase that locals in Birmingham invariably return to when discussing the city's famous waterways. And while Birmingham's canal network might not be as storied as its counterpart on the Adriatic, there's plenty to see and do here. Once used as fume-ridden trade routes in the 18th and 19th centuries, the city's canals are clean, pleasant and pass by some of Birmingham's prettiest scenery.

With its jaunty waterside pubs, bars and bistros, **Gas Street Basin** is the lively epicentre of Birmingham's canals. Enjoy the atmosphere here before walking the 45-minute stretch of the **Birmingham and Worcester Canal** south to the University of Birmingham's grounds. This tranquil trail finishes amid some fine Edwardian architecture and it's just a short walk to the Barber Institute of Fine Arts, a quiet Art-Deco gallery containing a splendid collection of little-known works from the likes of Monet, Turner and Degas.

### WHERE TO STAY IN BIRMINGHAM

**Grand Hotel**
Plush Art Deco hotel in the heart of town, where Winston Churchill once stayed. **£££**

**Bloc**
Smart Japanese pod-style rooms alongside golden design touches nodding to the historic Jewellery Quarter's past. **£**

**Staying Cool**
Penthouse apartments in the remarkable Rotunda, with retro furniture imbued by bold blasts of colour. **££**

There are also multiple ways of getting on the water itself, the most active of which is by climbing inside a kayak for a guided tour starting from the historic **Roundhouse Birmingham**. For a less strenuous experience, **GoBoat** offers self-drive ecofriendly electric boats from its spot in Brindley Pl. Route 2 – which heads down the Old Line towards the University of Birmingham – is particularly picturesque.

## Industrial Relics

BUILDING A PRODUCTION POWERHOUSE

Once known as the 'city of 1000 trades', Birmingham may have sleek new tramlines and gleaming glass skyscrapers but they mask a city built on belching black chimneys and howling factories. And if you look closely enough, relics of that industrial past can still be found dotted across town.

For a window into Birmingham's pre-industrial past, head out to Hall Green's **Sarehole Mill**. Dating back to 1771, the old watermill next to the River Cole was originally used to grind wheat and years later fascinated a young JRR Tolkien, who used the bucolic surroundings in his writings.

Back in the city centre, the **Birmingham Back to Backs** are the last surviving 19th-century back-to-back houses, and show how working people lived as the industrial age dawned and took over British society. On a more macabre note, the quirky **Coffin Works** is a beautifully preserved factory where accoutrements to coffins were once made – funerals were big business in Victorian Birmingham.

Abandoned in 1981, the Museum of the Jewellery Quarter is a unique time capsule in virtually the same condition as it was at the turn of the 20th century. The story of one of the country's biggest manufacturing hubs during the Industrial Revolution, the Jewellery Quarter is told in visceral detail here.

Forming part of both past and future, Roman-esque **Curzon Street station** was Birmingham's original railway terminus and will be part of the upcoming HS2 developments, a high-speed railway linking London with Birmingham due for completion between 2029 and 2033.

## A Splash of Colour

AN UNDERRATED ART SCENE

While **Birmingham Museum and Art Gallery** offers 40 traditional galleries in a grand old Victorian building, the museum's strength is consistently showcasing some of the region's most innovative pop-up exhibitions, displaying the creativity and local passion of its curators. The museum is

### BEST PIZZA IN BIRMINGHAM

**Otto**
Laid-back Jewellery Quarter pizza joint serving regular signature combinations and a revolving cast of specials. ££

**Peacer**
Relaxed Moseley restaurant offering New-York-style 20in pizzas by the slice that are all vegetarian. £

**POLI**
Colourful York Rd favourite with outdoor seating. Birmingham's best pizza in the summer months. ££

**Alicia's Micro Bakehouse**
Exceptionally soft dough bases are perfect for soaking up beer from Stirchley's many nearby taprooms. ££

**Park Regis**
Stylish spa hotel located between Broad St's jaunty bars and Edgbaston Village's sophisticated bistros. ££

**Hotel Indigo**
The Tetris-meets-Lego exterior appears odd, but this modern spot offers some spectacular views across the city. ££

**Genting Hotel**
Slick option for time-strapped travellers, located just a few minutes' walk from Birmingham International Airport. ££

**WHY I LOVE BIRMINGHAM**

**James March**, Lonely Planet author

There's a stunning mural of the four members of Black Sabbath in a small unremarkable car park on the industrial outskirts of the city centre. Sometimes I walk past and wonder why it was painted there. Arguably the inventors of what we now know as metal, Sabbath are one of Birmingham's greatest musical exports but this mural is nowhere near the heart of the city.

But maybe that's why I love my home town. We don't like to show off in Birmingham, but peel back the layers and there's gold to be found. A jocular city with incredible food, a pioneering heritage and the most green space in Europe. The journey is half the fun.

also home to the world's largest public Pre-Raphaelite collection, though the stunning Pre-Raphaelite stained glass windows by Edward Burne-Jones in nearby **St Philip's Cathedral** feel almost hidden in plain sight.

The pleasant grounds of the University of Birmingham make for an enjoyable afternoon stroll, and tucked away behind the School of Mathematics is arguably the city's best art gallery. Within the **Barber Institute of Fine Art's** quiet Art Deco corridors is a splendid collection of lesser-heralded works from the likes of Van Gogh, Manet and Renoir.

For a more visceral experience, the high walls flanking Digbeth's **Custard Factory** form a perfect industrial canvas for Birmingham's most talented graffiti artists. Some of the city's boldest work is found on **Floodgate St**, **Gibb St** and **Lower Trinity St**, but look out for the small car park on nearby **Rea St** hiding a magnificent mural of local heroes Black Sabbath.

Across the city centre in the historic Jewellery Quarter lies another notable piece of street art. Just above a bench next to the train station on **Vyse St** is Banksy's festive work highlighting the issue of homelessness, with two reindeer riding into a starry sky.

## Foodie Fireworks

A WILDLY CREATIVE FOOD SCENE

One of the biggest factors in Birmingham's 21st-century renaissance has been the quality and consistency of its food scene. No British city outside of London has more Michelin-star restaurants than Birmingham. For a window into the city's gastronomic heritage you'll need to head out to the **Balti Triangle** neighbourhood.

Developed by Birmingham's fledgling Pakistani community in the early 1970s, the balti is a fiery one-pot curry that's still popular today and is a symbol of the city's diversity. The Balti Triangle is the dish's spiritual home, with **Shababs** and **Shahi Nan Kebab House** particularly good options.

From the Americas to Asia, Birmingham's lively neighbourhoods offer a variety of global cuisine, with the chefs themselves often leaving their home countries to set up in the second city. Moseley's **Chakana** is the city's first Peruvian restaurant, **Eat Vietnam** in Stirchley is an aromatic open-kitchen delight, and **Blow Water Cafe** in Kings Heath brings a sublime taste of Hong Kong to Birmingham.

Back in the centre is where the city's reputation began to soar, however, and local chefs are the ones making it happen, with Aktar Islam's progressive Indian cooking at **Opheem** the latest to receive a Michelin star in 2019,

**BEST BRUNCH IN BIRMINGHAM**

**Ju Ju's**
Hearty homemade food served all day in a quiet canalside corner of Birmingham city centre. ££

**Cherry Reds**
Friendly bistro with an outdoor terrace and a spacious upstairs. Serves excellent full English breakfasts. £

**Urban**
Consistently great food made with quality ingredients at both city centre and Jewellery Quarter locations. £

Villa Park

arguably symbolising Birmingham's gastronomic evolution. With widescreen panoramic views and fine French cuisine, eating from the 24th-floor perch of **Orelle** is Birmingham's newest pièce de résistance.

## Pioneering the Beautiful Game

SEE WHERE FOOTBALL BEGAN

On 22 March 1888, William McGregor, the Scottish director of Birmingham football club Aston Villa, wrote to a handful of other clubs proposing the foundation of a league competition, eventually becoming the Football League. Over 130 years later, the glitz and glamour of the global phenomenon Premier League (p608) can be traced back to Birmingham.

The breathless excitement of Premier League football still takes place at Villa's stadium, **Villa Park**, in the neighbourhood of Aston and a bronze statue of McGregor can be seen outside the Directors' Entrance of the Trinity Rd Stand. Local rivals Birmingham City also play regular football matches at their stadium, **St Andrew's**, which is walkable from the vibrant pubs of Digbeth.

### BEST SUNDAY ROASTS IN BIRMINGHAM

**Baked in Brick**
Digbeth pizza joint offering a surprisingly excellent roast every Sunday featuring Birmingham's best Yorkshire pudding. ££

**Clifden**
Hockley pub with several rooms, a large beer garden and roast beef piled up high. ££

**Plough**
Spacious Harborne pub that's always busy for good reason. Great food along with Sunday roasts. ££

**Red Lion**
Homely Jewellery Quarter spot with a heated beer garden for winter Sundays. ££

### BEST COFFEE IN BIRMINGHAM

**Damascena**
Middle Eastern institution with five branches across the city. Its rich Turkish coffee is sublime.

**Faculty Coffee**
Quality brews and home-baked cakes just a stone's throw from New St station.

**Pause**
Specialty coffees, 'cinnabuffins' and brunches hidden away in Kings Heath's charming Kings Court alley.

## BEST SINGLE-SPIRIT HIDEAWAYS

**Amy Seton** is a Birmingham-based whisky specialist and entrepreneur, and the owner of Jewellery Quarter whisky bar and tasting room, Grain & Glass.

**Tierra** – Mezcal
Legendary taco restaurant Tierra doubles as a tequilaria. Knowledgeable staff, tequila-influenced cocktails, a small bar with rotating expressions, plus tasting flights.

**40 St Pauls** – Gin
Voted best gin bar in the world, this is the city's worst-kept secret! Lots of emphasis on unusual finds, all underpinned with a cracking gin-forward cocktail menu.

**Jungle Bird** – Rum
A relative newcomer but with a pedigree of staff that makes Jungle Bird a 'must visit'. Alumni from Island Bar have joined forces to create a cocktail-focused bar with rum at its core.

TRAVELLIGHT/SHUTTERSTOCK ©

Great Western Arcade

## The Stirchley Stroll

SAMPLE BIRMINGHAM'S TASTIEST PUB CRAWL

With its lively modern taprooms, Stirchley is the focal point of Birmingham's ever-expanding craft-beer scene. So much so, that the neighbourhood even has its own dedicated 'beer mile' for intrepid ale aficionados to merrily enjoy as they amble down the understated Pershore Rd and its various tributaries.

Bright and airy **Attic Brew Co** is conveniently situated across Mary Vale Rd from Bournville station, while **Glass-House**'s canalside location is secluded and offers plenty of room for drinking at its outdoor tables during the summer. In the winter months the cosy confines of **Cork & Cage** and **Wildcat** are ideal spots for sampling their myriad sours, stouts, and hazy pales.

### BEST COCKTAILS IN BIRMINGHAM

**Atelier**
Scandi-style space offering great multicourse tasting menus explained by creative mastermind Robert Wood.

**Couch**
Laid-back cocktail bar in Stirchley with a thematic menu, comfy sofas and a friendly atmosphere.

**Ikigai**
Low-lit Japanese bar with specialty sakes and Japanese whisky. Sample its 'Tour of Tokyo' menu.

# Arcades & Bullrings

MARQUEE MALLS TO VICTORIAN BOUTIQUES

The bulbous **Bullring** is Birmingham's busiest, most renowned shopping centre and its 15,000 gleaming aluminium discs are a bizarre sight on first viewing, though inside it's fairly conventional and contains one of only four Selfridges stores in the UK. The new building was constructed in 2003, though the original brutalist Bullring Centre still holds a lot of affection in the memories of locals.

**Grand Central**, above New Street station and **Mailbox** also bring a smorgasbord of marquee brands and boutiques, though a more evocative shopping experience can be found inside the city's historic arcades.

Located across from Snow Hill station, the **Great Western Arcade** is an ornate Victorian delight filled with independent sellers, while the **Piccadilly Arcade**, across from New Street station, has an even more interesting story. Dating back to 1925 and containing a lavishly painted ceiling fresco, it was once an Edwardian cinema – which explains the sloping floor.

Outside of the city centre, **Kings Heath High St** has long operated as a welcoming neighbourhood platform for independent businesses and boutiques, from institutions like legendary record shop **Polar Bear Records** on York Rd to modern favourites, such as handmade gift shop **ENKI**.

Keep an eye out for **Punks and Chancers**' ubiquitous 'YES BAB' T-shirts. The ethical clothing brand is often found at artisanal markets and is wildly popular for using the local term of affection 'bab'.

### THAT ODD CYLINDRICAL BUILDING

The 1960s were not kind to Birmingham, as the city reshaped itself in an increasingly brutalist fashion. Of all of the unloved relics of that time period, however, one has managed to reinvent itself time and time again and remains one of the city's most eye-catching landmarks.

**The Rotunda** is the 82m (266ft) cylindrical tower designed by architect James Roberts and opened in 1965 as an office block alongside a bank (with vaults) and various shops and leisure outlets.

After an IRA bombing in 1974 and the threat of demolition in 1993, it was given Grade-II-listed status in 2000. These days it houses residential apartments and 35 serviced apartments at the top with spectacular panoramic views across Birmingham.

### GETTING AROUND

Birmingham's city centre is compact, flat and walkable, with even the cool neighbourhoods of Digbeth and the Jewellery Quarter at either end having less than 30 minutes' walking time between them. West Midlands Trains are regular, and the Cross City Line from Birmingham New Street offers services out to trendy Stirchley every 10 minutes (make sure to get off at Bournville, however). Trams have also been servicing the city since 2016, and are a smooth and stress-free way of travelling to Centenary Sq and especially up to the burgeoning Edgbaston Village.

Driving can be a slow process in the city centre, though there are three large NCP car parks and plentiful parking at the Bullring and Grand Central. As Birmingham is a constant work in progress, be wary that certain road closures don't always pop up on navigational devices. And despite its relatively flat terrain, Birmingham is car-centric. Cycling is still a challenge and best saved for exploring large green spaces, such as Sutton Park and Cannon Hill Park.

Lichfield
Wolverhampton
Dudley
Birmingham
Stourbridge

# Beyond Birmingham

Warm and welcoming, the historic Black Country borders Birmingham, with leafy Staffordshire further north.

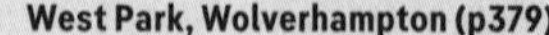

Flowing west from Birmingham towards the city of Wolverhampton some 13 miles away, the once heavily industrial area known as the Black Country is one of the Midlands' most distinct areas. Its unique name dates from the 1840s, when this was a smoky soot-ridden landscape packed with coal mines, iron foundries and steel mills.

These days the area is friendly and welcoming, with some of the finest pubs in the Midlands. First-time visitors may only detect a subtle change in accent after leaving Birmingham, but the people here are a fiercely proud lot who feel very separate from the second city. Further north, the rolling meadows and lonely church spires of Staffordshire are watched over by Lichfield's momentous three-spired cathedral.

**TOP TIP**

The area's top attractions, such as the Black Country Living Museum, is most efficiently reached by car.

**West Park, Wolverhampton (p379)**

Black Country Living Museum

### ORANGE CHIPS

While the Black Country does a fine line in real ale and hearty pies, the region's one true delicacy emanates a bright glow from a paper bag. Instead of the classic chips you would expect to find at British fish and chip shops, what you might receive here are often served in a thin and crispy paprika-and-salt batter. And it's the batter's vivid orange colour that sets these chips apart from the rest of the Midlands. It's believed the chips first gained popularity during the war years as chefs and families were looking for a way to break up the monotony of wartime fare. But whatever the origin, they're proper Black Country.

## History Comes Alive

STEP INTO A LOST WORLD

Despite its evocative history of smoking chimneys and roaring foundries, a cursory glance at the Black Country's houses, roads, shops and parks resembles a scene of fairly typical suburban life in the UK. But there's one unique corner of this region just a 25-minute taxi ride from Birmingham that provides an authentic snapshot of what life was like at the very heart of the Industrial Revolution.

A painstakingly recreated industrial landscape, the **Black Country Living Museum** is a vast open-air museum allowing visitors to step back in time and immerse themselves in local life at the turn of the 20th century. Spanning 26 acres, its streets are lined with faithfully recreated shops and houses complete with heritage vehicles and quirky local characters in period dress who'll explain their distant lives.

In fact, so realistic is the environment here that its rustic waterway docks were used to film the canal scenes for the popular 1920s TV crime drama *Peaky Blinders*. But it's the interactive element that really sets this museum apart. Enjoy

### WHERE TO STAY IN THE BLACK COUNTRY

**Domo, Oldbury**
Stylish boutique rooms in a Georgian house on a quiet square in Oldbury. £

**Village Hotel, Dudley**
Laid-back hotel within walking distance of Dudley Zoo and the Black Country Living Museum. £

**Premier Inn, Wolverhampton**
Smart budget option in the Black Country's largest city, well-located next to the train station. £

fish and chips for lunch at a turn-of-the-century chip shop, step inside a dusty 1930s garage with vintage cars and sip on an ale at a spit and sawdust public house.

If nearby Ironbridge Gorge tells the story of how the Industrial Revolution started, a day trip here shows what it became.

**BEST PUBS IN LICHFIELD**

**Beerbohm**
Cosy bar featuring 10 keg taps specialising in quality Belgian beer, with a lounge upstairs.

**Brewhouse & Kitchen**
Spacious brewpub serving hearty food that pairs well with beer. Also offers tasting experiences.

**Whippet Inn**
Laid-back street-corner micropub offering six cask beer taps and homemade flavoured scratchings.

**King's Head**
Lichfield's oldest pub, dating back to the 15th century, with timber beams and red-brick facade.

**George IV**
Good selection of local real ale and regular live music, comedy shows and film nights.

## A Visionary Home

DISCOVER A SURPRISINGLY INFLUENTIAL CITY

Approaching Lichfield on the 40-minute train ride from Birmingham, visitors are met with the unusual sight of three brooding spires on the horizon. Constructed in the 14th century and soaring over 250ft above the town's skyline, the majestic **Lichfield Cathedral** is one of only three triple-spired cathedrals in the UK and is the only one that dates back to the Middle Ages.

For a small city of less than 40,000, Lichfield has long punched above its weight, and its unique cathedral is just the beginning. The quiet medieval grounds surrounding the cathedral were once home to Erasmus Darwin, grandfather to Charles and one of 18th-century Britain's most important thinkers. **Erasmus Darwin House** is where he spent much of his life, and a walk upstairs to the breezy Lunar Room explains why his radical ideas about science and evolution frightened the establishment of the time.

But Darwin wasn't the only intellectual giant who called Lichfield home. Native Samuel Johnson's pioneering *A Dictionary of the English Language* is one of the most influential books ever written and the **Samuel Johnson Birthplace Museum** houses an original copy, as well as several of his more jocular quotes dotted around on the walls.

For something a little more macabre head back out to the busy **Market Square**, the execution site of the last person in England to be burned at the stake for heresy.

## Real Ale Country

SIP ON THE REGION'S FINEST

Real ale runs deep in the Black Country, and the region is home to some of the Midlands' most historic cask-beer pubs. Whether it's a quiet afternoon pint of mild or a few beers around the bar with a gaggle of gregarious raconteurs, the Black Country pub is still an institution here, despite the region's loss of its traditional industries throughout the later 20th century.

Well into their sixth generation of brewers, Bathams are arguably the most famous Black Country brewer, and its pub

**WHERE TO STAY IN LICHFIELD**

**George**
Elegant Georgian hotel in the centre of town that's a five-minute walk from everywhere. ££

**St Johns House**
Restored 17th-century Regency house turned hotel, with 12 rooms individually decorated with Egyptian cotton. ££

**Cathedral Hotel**
Contemporary budget-friendly spot just a few minutes' walk from the imposing spires of Lichfield Cathedral. £

Lichfield Cathedral

the **Vine** (35-minute taxi from Birmingham) in Brierley Hill is the place to sample its famous dark milds – especially the flagship Batham's Bitter.

Almost 200 years old and unique for its white-and-pistachio-green ceiling above a majestic Victorian mahogany bar, the **Old Swan Inn** (30-minute taxi from Birmingham) in Netherton is a survivor of numerous changes in ownership. It's still here to tell the tale and this brewpub's Original – a slightly sweet 3.5% light mild – is the perfect beer to sup while you pull up a chair and read the pub's story.

On the southern flanks of the Black Country, Stourbridge's burgeoning brewing tradition grows ever stronger, with Craddock's Brewery operating out of the Edwardian **Duke William** pub and **Green Duck Beer Co**'s friendly taproom, ideal for a few low-key Saturday afternoon pints (both pubs a 25-minute train from Birmingham Snow Hill).

## BEST GREEN SPACES IN THE BLACK COUNTRY

**Priory Park, Dudley**
Serene park featuring the 900-year-old ruins of St James's Priory, founded by Cluniac Monks.

**Sandwell Valley Country Park, West Bromwich**
Vast 660-acre park good for children, with its rope bridge, swings and zip wire.

**Warley Woods, Smethwick**
Tranquil woodland spanning 100 acres on the edge of Sandwell with several tree-covered trails.

**West Park, Wolverhampton**
One of the most unspoiled examples of a landscaped Victorian park left in England.

**Willenhall Memorial Park, Willenhall**
Created out of the spoil heaps of a 1920s colliery and now a lush woodland.

## GETTING AROUND

The Black Country is well served by regular West Midlands Trains between Birmingham and Wolverhampton leaving from New Street station, and between Birmingham and Stourbridge leaving from both Snow Hill and Moor Street stations. However, once in the region, the wide-ranging bus network may be a better option for travelling between towns.

There's also the ever-extending West Midlands Metro, a tram running between Birmingham and Wolverhampton that was the first of its kind in the Midlands for almost 50 years and covers towns that the trains bypass. It also famously has its own unique pub crawl, for those in the mood for a tram-based ale trail.

# STRATFORD-UPON-AVON

If William Shakespeare had been born anywhere else, then Stratford-upon-Avon, with its meandering river and crooked Tudor houses, would still be a lovely place to visit. The fact is, however, that arguably the most famous English person to have ever existed called this small Warwickshire town his home, and thus, it's difficult to stroll a couple of minutes without spotting a reference to the Bard.

But you don't need to be a fan of Shakespeare's work to appreciate his legacy in the town and the number of evocative historic sites here, still standing half a millennia later. And while modern Stratford uses Shakespeare to draw in millions of visitors each year, quirky attractions bring a lighter side to the town. So dive into the history, but remember there's much more to Stratford than its famous playwright son.

### TOP TIP

With a population of just 30,000, Stratford-upon-Avon is small and eminently walkable. The town centre is only a five-minute walk from the train station and is well signposted. Just remember to alight at Stratford-upon-Avon and not Stratford-upon-Avon Parkway (essentially a large car park on the edge of town).

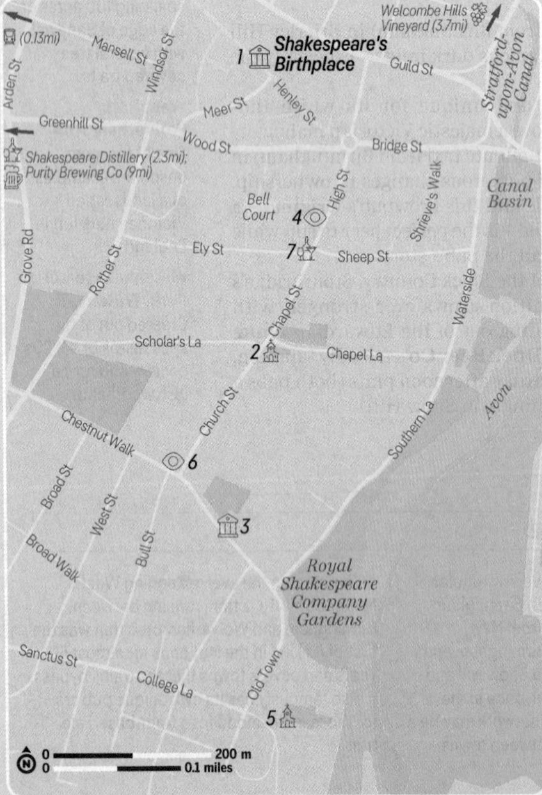


**HIGHLIGHTS**
1 Shakespeare's Birthplace

**SIGHTS**
2 Guild Chapel
3 Hall's Croft
4 Harvard House
5 Holy Trinity Church
6 Trinity College

**DRINKING & NIGHTLIFE**
7 Garrick Inn

Harvard House

## A Walk Through Time

STROLL DOWN STRATFORD'S HISTORIC SPINE

While a walk down Stratford-upon-Avon's historic spine starts and ends with significant Shakespeare sites, the trail is also a fascinating journey through medieval, Elizabethan, Georgian and Victorian architecture.

Start at **Shakespeare's Birthplace** but quickly weave through the crowds down to No 1 High St, a white stucco-coated street corner building dating back to 1616 and now home to the **Shakespeare Distillery**. Further down lies the black-and-white timber frame of **Harvard House**, dating back to 1596 and built by Thomas Rogers, grandfather to the benefactor of Harvard University, John Harvard. Next door is the similar-looking **Garrick Inn**, Stratford's oldest public house and named after the influential 18th-century actor David Garrick.

Head past the Victorian Gothic **HSBC bank** on the corner of Chapel St to the late-medieval **Guild Chapel**, famous for its uncovered wall paintings by 15th-century artist Hugh

### BEST PUBS IN STRATFORD

**Ya Bard**
Friendly and compact five-tap craft beer bar that feels like someone's living room.

**Dirty Duck**
Classic actors' post-show haunt opposite the Royal Shakespeare Company, with bucolic views onto the waterfront.

**One Elm**
Relaxed pub with a tranquil courtyard, offering some exceptional food from a seasonal produce menu.

**Stratford Alehouse**
The finest spot for real ale and cider, with walls covered in colourful beer mats.

**Garrick Inn**
Timber-framed and supposedly haunted, this 15th-century pub is the town's oldest watering hole.

### WHERE TO STAY IN STRATFORD

**Arden**
Rustic rooms and a magnificent brasserie, perfectly located across the street for RSC Gorvey Garden Theatre. ££

**Hotel du Vin**
Smart Georgian boutique hotel with a French bistro, a wine cellar and 46 cosy rooms. ££

**Welcombe Hotel, BW Premier Collection**
Opulent neo-Jacobean mansion on the outskirts, with a spa and steam room. ££

Clopton. Further down the road the imposing sight of the former **Trinity College** looms into view, a Grade-II-listed building dating back to around 1700.

Turning left down onto the quieter Old Town, **Hall's Croft** is a handsome Elizabethan building once owned by William Shakespeare's daughter, Susanna Hall, and her husband Dr John Hall, whom she married in 1607. Finish the walk amid the serene leafy surroundings of **Holy Trinity Church**, the scene of William Shakespeare's baptism, marriage and burial.

**BEST CAFES IN STRATFORD**

**Yorks**
Artisanal coffee roasters centrally located beneath a 17th-century townhouse, serving fine brunch food and pastries.

**HR Coffee Bar**
Hidden behind a car park and serving unusual lunches, such as homity pie and Reuben sandwiches.

**Box Brownie Coffee**
Using locally roasted Monsoon Estate beans, this might be the best coffee in Stratford.

**Bensons**
Rustic cafe opposite Shakespeare's Birthplace. Serves up great breakfasts and a lovely afternoon tea.

**Bardia's**
Wooden bar adorned by flowers hanging from the ceiling making this a unique space.

## Distilleries, Vineyards & Breweries

GET INTO THE STRATFORD SPIRIT

While chances are slim that Stratford's famous Bard ever sampled a refreshing gin and tonic in his lifetime, he probably wouldn't mind his name being used at **Shakespeare Distillery** after a taste of its flagship Stratford Dry. Though it has a shop in town inside the historic No 1 High Stt building, jump in a taxi and head out to the actual distillery on the outskirts of town and take a tour.

Lighthearted and informative, the tour is lead by various jocular personalities explaining the history of gin and the distilling processes, before ending with a tasting session and a chance to sample the elderflower and quince gin.

It's possible Shakespeare may have drunk wine in his day, but it certainly wouldn't have been this local. Surrounded by apple orchards and strawberry fields on a hilltop terroir, **Welcombe Hills Vineyard** is just north of Stratford and offers vineyard tours and wine tastings between May and September.

It's almost certain that Shakespeare enjoyed a drop of ale while penning his plays. In the 21st-century **Purity Brewing Co** supplies delightful cask beers to Stratford and the surrounding areas. The brewery is located 10 miles from Stratford in the Warwickshire countryside, and its Mad Goose pale ale has been ubiquitous in the Midlands beer scene since 2008. Tours every Saturday showcase how it has sustained its excellence for so long.

**GETTING AROUND**

There are regular trains between Stratford and Birmingham New Str, though be aware that they run just once an hour on Sundays and can get quite crowded. Once in town, most attractions are within a 10-minute walk of each other and won't require any form of transport. The only exception is Anne Hathaway's Cottage, which is around a 20-to-25 minute walk, though the number 19 bus service stops nearby and the City Sightseeing Open Top bus goes directly there.

Coventry
Leamington Spa
Warwick
Stratford-upon-Avon

# Beyond Stratford-upon-Avon

Idyllic rolling countryside showcasing some of the Midlands' most unique historic sights. Let your imagination run wild.

The languid green countryside fanning out from Stratford-upon-Avon in all directions is pierced by winding canals and sleepy villages, though larger towns, such as Warwick, feature just as much history as Shakespeare's storied hometown. Warwick's imposing 1000-year-old castle is visible for miles, while the skeletal remains of Coventry's WWII bomb-devastated cathedral is one of the region's most macabre and fascinating sights.

And though on first impression this rolling farmland and its lonely spires evoke an old-fashioned Middle England romanticism (that only continues for those venturing south to the Cotswolds, p194), the likes of Coventry's FarGo Village offer an exciting future. With its jaunty graffiti, vegan food joints and myriad independent boutiques, it's a 21st-century creative haven.

**TOP TIP**

Try to pair up a visit to Warwick and Leamington Spa as the two are separated by only 3 miles.

**Coventry Cathedral ruins (p385)**

### BEST RESTAURANTS IN WARWICK

**La Mesa**
Charming townhouse with dishes crafted on the spot, depending on the available fresh produce. ££

**Art Kitchen**
Well-presented Thai cuisine with a strong emphasis on fresh, high-quality ingredients that give exceptional taste. ££

**Dough & Brew**
Laid-back pizza and pasta joint, pairing its food with a great selection of craft beers. £

**Tailors**
Classic modern British recipes with a contemporary twist, forming a well-crafted tasting menu. £££

Great Hall, Warwick Castle

## Grand Castles & Spectacular Ruins

FEEL THE REMNANTS OF HISTORY

With its rising turrets, formidable walls and regular reenactment events, **Warwick Castle** (15-minute taxi from Stratford) resembles the sort of monolithic fortress typically seen in movies or adventure books. Its oldest parts date back to the 11th century and the entire structure is still in remarkably good condition. The same can't be said of **Kenilworth Castle** (25-minute taxi from Stratford), though its ruins offer a ghostly evocative quality unlike anywhere else in the region. Partially destroyed during the English Civil War, its ragged red sandstone towers can still be climbed, and a walk through the small door on Great Hall's southern wall reveals cinematic views across Warwickshire's pastoral landscape.

Despite the grandeur of both castles, neither of them possesses the security of a moat. Head over to the relatively humbly sized **Baddesley Clinton** (30-minute taxi from Stratford) to see one of the region's more curious sights. Surrounded by water and at least 600 years old, this moated manor house is something of an architectural oddity, as if half-mansion half-castle.

### WHERE TO STAY IN WARWICK

**Rose & Crown**
Relaxed 17th-century pub with 13 en-suite rooms and easy access to the breezy downstairs lounge. £

**Globe**
Well-located inn with 18 stylish en-suite rooms that include cosy handmade Hypnos mattresses. £

**Old Fourpenny Shop**
Quirky hotel a few minutes' walk from town, with rustic rooms, a pub and restaurant. ££

However, it's the fragmented walls and soaring spire of **Coventry Cathedral** (30-minute taxi from Stratford) that provokes a reaction more than anywhere else here. Devastated by a ferocious German bombing blitz on the night of 14 November 1940, its nave suffered a direct hit and was left a smoking ruined shell. But its survival was an inspiring sight and the stained glass windows in the modernist **New Cathedral** next door reflect a gaudy kaleidoscope of colours.

## Two-Tone City

DISCOVER A MUSIC GENRE

When The Specials' haunting single 'Ghost Town' reached number 1 on the UK singles chart in July 1981, **Coventry** announced itself on the British music landscape. But more than that, the style of two-tone – a genre fusing traditional Jamaican ska music with elements of punk rock and new wave music – had now hit the mainstream.

After a 30-minute taxi up from Stratford, step through an unassuming doorway on Walsgrave Rd to enter the **2-Tone Village** – a colourful hodgepodge of cafes, shops AND bars, and home to the **Coventry Music Museum**. A passion project founded by local Pete Chambers, the small museum's walls are crammed with musical memorabilia celebrating the city's achievements, and even contains half of the car used in the famous 'Ghost Town' video. It's interactive too, with a musical instrument room downstairs and the chance to try on a classic two-tone porkpie hat.

Sample authentic Caribbean and English food at the black-and-white chequered **2Tone Cafe** and **Simmerdown Restaurant** across from the museum, where the fiery jerk sausage is an institution and ska beats boom through the speakers. A couple of doors down lies the **2Tone Corner Shop**, full of memorabilia and with shelves selling the distinct clothing of the era – polo shirts, braces, trilby hats and Harrington bomber jackets.

When evening falls, the **Knights Bar** showcases regular live music with an unsurprisingly heavy dose of ska.

## Sit Back & Relax

UNWIND IN A SPA TOWN

Despite a population hovering around the 50,000 mark, **Leamington Spa** enjoys a grandstanding history an an elegant 19th-century spa town for the rich and famous (indeed, its

### FAVOURITE LIVE MUSIC SPOTS

**Pete Chambers** is Director Curator at The Coventry Music Museum.

**Tin, Canal Basin Coventry**
Presenting an inspiring selection of bands that are mooted nationally and locally, plus those that still demand a healthy following, like The Monochrome Set.

**HMV Empire Coventry**
Coventry has waited a long time for such a well-designed venue. If it's good enough for Mr Sheeran, it's probably good enough for you.

**Knights Venue, 2-Tone Village**
Tiny venue, huge ambition, and a temple to ska and reggae, hosting The Heptones, Dandy Livingstone, Dave & Ansell Collins, and many more.

### WHERE TO STAY IN COVENTRY

**Telegraph Hotel**
Sleek mid-century modernism, with brass panels and smooth varnished timber in a former newspaper office. ££

**Britannia**
Imposing brutalist hotel near Coventry Cathedral. Located five minutes from the city's commercial centre. ££

**Hotel Ibis**
Budget option with smart rooms just a short walk from the main train station. £

## CYCLE THROUGH CANAL COUNTRY

The unhurried pace of life in rural Warwickshire is perhaps best appreciated along its tranquil canal towpaths. Passing through docile countryside and quiet villages interspersed by the occasional market town, this is the English heartlands at its finest. But taking a narrow boat along these waters and operating lock after lock can be a time-consuming process, so cycling makes for a fine alternative.

The Warwickshire Ring is a connected series of canals forming a 100-mile circuit around the West Midlands, and one of its most historic stretches is the one- to two-day journey (depending on pace) between Warwick and Rugby.

Start in the shadows of the formidable 1 **Warwick Castle**, though make time to explore the town's medieval streets and hidden 2 **Hill Close Gardens**. Make the short 3-mile ride east to Leamington Spa, home to some fine white stucco Regency architecture and famous 3 **Royal Pump Rooms**, popular with the well-heeled upper classes of the 19th-century.

From here there's a relatively flat landscape of leafy green countryside as the towpath meanders east through rural Warwickshire. Canalside pubs form a significant part of life in this bucolic part of England, especially in the summer months when the golden evening sun forms long shadows across the water. Stop off for a beer or two at sublime watering holes 4 **Two Boats Inn** in Long Itchington or 5 **Boat in Stockton**.

Continue to 6 **Braunston Marina**, the busiest canal junction in the country, where there's plenty of opportunity for refreshments in its charming village centre.

Finish the journey by riding into vibrant Rugby, birthplace of rugby football and home to the ornate 7 **Rugby School** where William Webb Ellis allegedly picked up a football, and the rest IS history.

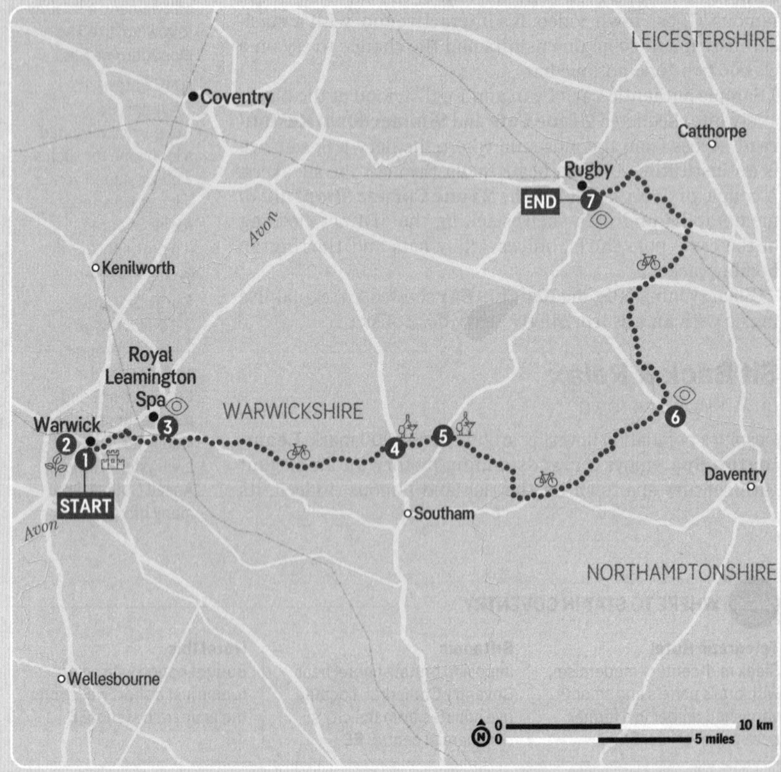

Royal Pump Rooms

full title is Royal Leamington Spa), a status immediately revealed by the grandeur of the town's Regency architecture. After a 30-minute train ride from Stratford, a short hop across the arched stone Victoria Bridge to the 200-year-old **Royal Pump Rooms** marks the site of Leamington's spa-town epicentre. With the town's healing treatments and medicinal water qualities big business in Victorian England, the building housed 17 hot baths and THREE cold baths.

While the 'water cure' craze was a short-lived thing, unwinding in style in Leamington is still an idyllic way of paying homage to the town's glamorous past. The **Spa** is situated on the northern flanks of the city centre on a row of Georgian townhouses, and treatments include time in a steam chamber or a hydrotherapy room, a hot stone massage and a thai compress massage.

Floatation-therApy spas certainly weren't a thing during the height of Victorian hydrotherapy, but they are becoming more popular these days. The first of its kind in Warwickshire, **Spa Float** on Newbold St uses floating science as a new way of relaxing body and mind.

For something a little more extravagant head to the outskirts of the town where the opulent **Elan Spa** feels like the spiritual successor to Leamington's original spa craze.

## BEST RESTAURANTS IN LEAMINGTON

**Oscar's**
Laid-back French restaurant on Chandos St offering classic fare, including moules marinière and steak frites. ££

**Carisma Tapas & Wine Bar**
Colourful Spanish tapas in the heart of town with a charming leafy courtyard out back. ££

**Kayal**
Authentic seafood from India's Kerala region in a stylish wooden-and-stone interior. ££

**Moorings**
High-quality gastropub on Leamington's canalside, just outside the town centre, serving a fine Sunday roast. ££

**La Coppola Ristorante & Oyster Bar**
Jaunty local Italian in the town centre with ostentatious decor but excellent cuisine. ££

## WHERE TO STAY IN LEAMINGTON SPA

**Mallory Court Country House & Spa**
Stylish luxury country hotel on the edge of town featuring a 3 AA Rosette restaurant. £££

**Angel Hotel**
Former coaching inn with 50 contemporary-styled rooms and the award-winning Counting House restaurant. ££

**Thomas James Hotel**
Easy-going budget option with smart rooms located just a short hop from the train station. £

Midland Air Museum (MAM)

## Take to the Skies

GO ABOVE THE CLOUDS

From the inventor of the jet engine to the creation of the legendary Spitfire WWII fighter plane, the Midlands has a long and deep aviation heritage, and **Coventry Airport** – a 25-minute taxi ride from Stratford – is a cornucopia of experiences.

The **Midland Air Museum (MAM)** is adjacent to the airport and features 60 historic aircraft as part of its impressive collection, including the large Avro Vulcan strategic bomber and the Mil Mi-24 helicopter gunship. And with jet engine inventor Sir Frank Whittle as one of Coventry's most famous sons, the **Sir Frank Whittle Jet Heritage Centre** is a fascinating exhibition illustrating the story of the jet age.

For a more visceral experience, book in with **Almat Aviation** and get behind the yoke of a real aircraft on a 30- or 60-minute flight. Taking off in a single-engine Cessna with an experienced instructor on hand at all times, the exhilarating ride takes would-be pilots over the gentle Warwickshire landscape and gives a unique perspective to the county. Bear in mind that these aircraft are small, and gusts of wind can bring on air sickness, even in perfect flying conditions.

If that's your reality, **Flight Simulator Midlands** is the ideal alternative; the thrill of flying a giant 747 anywhere in the world is a pretty good replacement for riding in a Cessna.

### GO TO FARGO

Once a miserable industrial estate, Coventry's cultural hub of FarGo Village, which first opened in 2014, is now a vibrant canvas for surreal street art, vintage boutique stores and busy craft beer taprooms. Whether it's sifting through classic vinyl records at **Just Dropped In** or chewing on spiced Indian wraps at the **Paneer Wrap Street Food Company**, FarGo is one of the Midlands' coolest hangouts. The addition of a live music venue and an indoor street-food space has only added to FarGo's allure.

### GETTING AROUND

There are regular West Midlands Railway trains linking Coventry and Leamington Spa, from which there are then easy links to Warwick and Stratford-upon-Avon. Driving around these last three towns is relatively easy, as they're all quite small and simple to navigate, although larger Coventry means dealing with a sometimes gridlocked ring road. All town centres in this region are walkable, with nowhere more than a 10-minute stroll.

Hiring a car is really only necessary for driving out to rural National Trust houses and the occasional historic site.

# THE SHROPSHIRE HILLS







Flanked by the Welsh border on one side and the urban sprawl of the West Midlands on the other, Shropshire is a largely rural but at times spectacular corner of England, and its hills are home to some magnificent hiking and cycling trails, pockmarked by quaint villages and ancient forts.

Surrounded by yawning green valleys and imposing heather-blanketed hills, Church Stretton is a small market town in the heart of the Shropshire Hills that was once described by Victorian visitors as 'Little Switzerland.' Despite its lofty moniker and quick train links to larger towns, Church Stretton never became a busy tourist destination and that's a good thing, as this cinematic region is one of England's prettiest yet least understood.

Time stands still here, and the lingering silence of Shropshire's rolling pastoral scenes should be savoured. Unwind, explore and enjoy the gentle escapism of England's most underrated region.

## TOP TIP

While the train line that splits the hills between Shrewsbury and Ludlow is handy, hiring a car is a good idea for exploring beyond that narrow route. Bus links are scarce in a rural place like this, so driving to its various trailheads and historic sites is a no-brainer.

**Shropshire Hills**

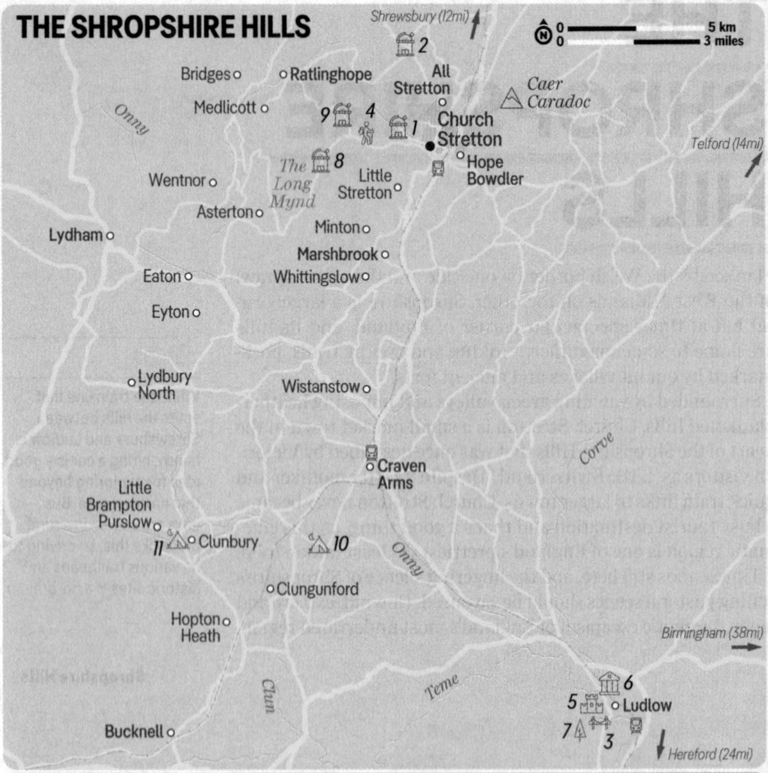

## THE SHROPSHIRE HILLS

| SIGHTS | | ACTIVITIES, COURSES & TOURS | SLEEPING |
|---|---|---|---|
| **1** Carding Mill Valley Car Park | **4** Long Mynd | **8** Pole Cottage Car Park | **10** Shropshire Hills Glamping |
| **2** Cross Dyke Car Park at Boiling Well | **5** Ludlow Castle | **9** Shooting Box Car Park | **11** Shropshire Luxury Glamping |
| **3** Dinham Bridge | **6** Ludlow Museum | | |
| | **7** Whitcliffe Common Nature Reserve | | |

# An Untamed & Unspoiled Landscape

SEE 'LITTLE SWITZERLAND' UP CLOSE

Taking its name from the Welsh *mynydd*, the **Long Mynd** (Long Mountain) is a vast stretch of moorland covered in thick heather and wandering sheep. This wind-whipped plateau is one of many fine walking sites within the **Carding Mill Valley**, and all the trails begin from the village of **Church Stretton**.

## WHERE TO STAY & EAT IN CHURCH STRETTON

**Old Coppers Malt House**
Hearty pub food in a historic building with a surprisingly large vegan and vegetarian menu. £

**Larches Lodge**
Norwegian log cabin set among a canopy of larch trees, featuring an indulgent hot tub. ££

**Victoria House**
Ostentatious rooms decorated with antique furniture and original artwork. Includes homemade breakfast. £

For the most widescreen views of the Shropshire Hills and beyond, take on the **Burway Loop**. This 5-mile hike is the most challenging but also the most rewarding as it passes by Pole Bank – the Long Mynd's 500m-high summit. It gives spectacular views of the western slopes, where a patchwork of earthy green fields unfurl beneath, with the leaden outline of Wales' rolling hills in the hazy distance.

For something a little different, try the **Lightspout Waterfall Walk**. This moderately difficult trail follows the same route as the Burway Loop before bending left down Lightspout Hollow, where the 4m-high waterfall gently cascades down a rocky hillside.

Carding Mill Valley is also home to a shimmering reservoir, which is reached by following the **New Pool Hollow Walk**. One of the region's simplest walks, this 30-minute stroll is an easy-going introduction to the valley, while the rising hills around the reservoir give the small pool an evocative appearance, helped further by the curious old Victorian water tower emerging from the middle.

## Dark Sky Discoveries

SEE A BLANKET OF STARS

Shropshire is one of the few regions on this densely populated island without a city, and its unsullied countryside provides ample opportunities to see a full canvas of stars in the night sky. There are four designated Dark Sky Discovery Sites in the Shropshire Hills and all are at National Trust car parks: **Carding Mill Valley**, **Cross Dyke Car Park at Boiling Well**, **Pole Cottage** and **Shooting Box Car Parks**.

With minimal light pollution making visibility crisp and clear, it's possible to see the Milky Way, and you don't need special equipment either, although binoculars and telescopes bring new dimensions to the experience. It's magical enough with the naked eye.

## Under the Stars in Style

SLEEP IN GLAMOROUS OUTDOOR SURROUNDINGS

With a mass of glittering stars coating the night sky throughout the year, spending the evening in the great outdoors makes sense in the Shropshire Hills. Glamping is a comfy way of doing this and there are plenty of sites where you can observe the majesty of the solar system in lush green surroundings accompanied only by the sound of silence.

### I LIVE HERE: FAVOURITE LUDLOW GASTRONOMY SPOTS

**Rory Bunting** is an award-winning chef and founder of Forage Britain.

**Vaughans**
It is almost impossible for any carnivore to walk past Vaughan's sandwich shop, with its roasted pork shoulders in the window. But for vegetarians, there's also a huge selection of salads and jacket potato fillings.

**Globe**
The Globe and its secret garden are a great place to unwind in the sun with a glass of something tasty. Superb sister restaurant Chang Thai is conveniently located right next door.

**Charlton Arms**
Facing up historic Broad St with outstanding views of the River Teme, the award-winning gastro delights and well-stocked cellar of the Charlton Arms make it a worthy place to stop.

### WHERE TO STAY IN MUCH WENLOCK

**Raven**
Historic 17th-century coaching inn with an excellent AA Rosette restaurant focusing on local produce. ££

**Manor House**
Quaint black-and-white timbered 16th-century B&B with cosy rooms and a garden. ££

**Gaskell Arms**
Rustic 17th-century pub offering old-fashioned rooms and a vast beer garden for the summer sun. ££

## RUINS & PIONEERS DRIVING TOUR

Although this is a largely pastoral landscape, the Shropshire Hills have a long history and are dotted by a number of unique heritage sites. Few are in easy locations to reach, however, so it's a good idea to rent a car first. Though it's located just outside of the official Shropshire Hills area, the **1 Ironbridge Gorge** Unesco World Heritage Site is so significant that it would be foolish to start anywhere else. Not only is this charming little town home to the pioneering Iron Bridge, but there are also several fascinating museums in the area that bring some context to the bridge's importance.

A five-minute drive west into the Shropshire Hills proper lies **2 Buildwas Abbey**, next to the banks of the River Severn. A Cistercian monastery dating back to the 12th-century, the surviving parts of the abbey are still in surprisingly good condition, most notably the stunning vaulted ceiling and tiled floors of the chapterhouse.

A short journey south is **3 Wenlock Priory**, a spectacular ruined 12th-century monastery in a picturesque setting on the outskirts of Much Wenlock. Though Henry VIII's dissolution of the monasteries brought along the skeletal state it finds itself in today, sections like the south transept still stand at their full height and form majestic silhouettes on bright days.

Head 30 minutes south to explore arguably the best-preserved medieval manor house in England. Situated just outside the small market town of Craven Arms, **4 Stokesay Castle** is over 700 years old, and its black-and-yellow timber exterior is striking, while the wooden-beamed Great Hall is a window into another world. Finish at the imposing **5 Ludlow Castle**, where the highest towers offer some of the finest panoramas in Shropshire.

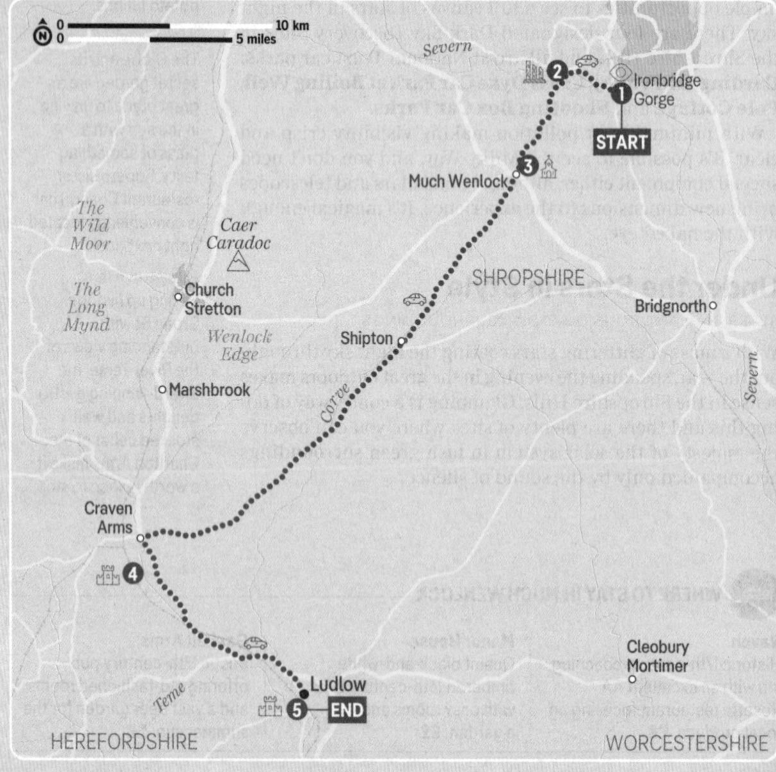

The southern hills are particularly fruitful and **Shropshire Luxury Glamping** at Purslow Hall Farm has smart industrial-style pods alongside a soothing hot tub. Further east lies **Shropshire Hills Glamping**, and its rustic hilltop cabin offering panoramic views of the surrounding landscape. Both are within 30 minutes of Ludlow and pair perfectly with a nearby weekend break.

## Poetry in Motion

WHERE TO FIND LUDLOW'S BEAUTY

Once described by poet laureate John Betjeman as 'the loveliest town in England', **Ludlow** certainly has some stiff competition for that lofty title, but its crooked medieval streets, 11th-century castle and grandiose surroundings certainly help.

Circle around behind the castle and down to the elegant 200-year-old **Dinham Bridge**, under which runs the flowing River Teme. From this valley, the castle ruins peek above lush treetops while the forested hillside of **Whitcliffe Common** rises to the west.

And it's from a short 10-minute walk up through that hillside that Ludlow's most spectacular vista emerges. Dense green trees on either side of Whitcliffe Common perfectly frame an achingly English vignette of rolling hills, a majestic church tower, rust-brown chocolate-box rooftops and stocky grey castle turrets. Choose one of the many benches and sit for a while, taking it all in.

In fact, Ludlow Castle itself was purposely built on a hilltop and its ruined towers offer some beautiful panoramas deep into Herefordshire's apple orchards to the south and towards Shropshire's highest hills to the north.

A more unique view is found from **Ludlow Museum**, so head upstairs and find the window pointing south down Broad St. With its timber Tudor houses to the left and the old road softly arcing away in the distance, it's a scene that will have changed little over 500 years.

Wenlock Priory

### OLYMPIC INSPIRATION

It's difficult to imagine the idyllic chocolate-box village of Much Wenlock claiming to be a forerunner to the pomp of the modern Olympic Games, but the link is very real.

The story goes back to 1850, when Dr William Penny Brookes created the annual Wenlock Olympian Games to 'promote the moral, physical and intellectual improvement' of locals. The first Games were a mixture of athletics and traditional country sports, then held every year, and eventually inspired Baron Pierre de Coubertin to visit in 1890.

Coubertin went on to establish the International Olympic Committee, and the first modern Olympics were held six years later in Athens in 1896. Maybe, just maybe, thanks to Much Wenlock.

### GETTING AROUND

The hills aren't an easy place to navigate by public transport alone, so hiring a car is recommended. This is especially true if your itinerary includes rural areas to the west. Shrewsbury is the largest town in Shropshire and will have the most car-hire options.

The train running between Shrewsbury and Ludlow is very useful, however, for the many activities available at Carding Mill Valley. It calls at Church Stretton roughly once an hour and the village serves as an ideal base for exploration.

There are local buses serving the region, but they are slow and will eat into your all-important time.

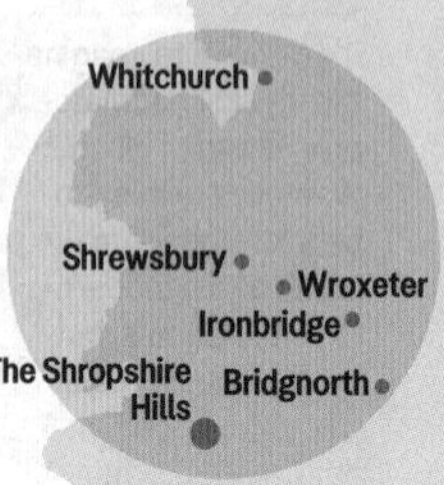

Whitchurch
Shrewsbury
Wroxeter
Ironbridge
The Shropshire Hills
Bridgnorth

# Beyond the Shropshire Hills

## Explore undisturbed scenery dotted by ancient heritage sites and foodie hot spots. Slow down and savour it.

While the remainder of Shropshire's landscape flattens out a little, the region is no less intriguing. From tiny Whitchurch's burgeoning food scene down to the momentous Ironbridge UNESCO World Heritage Site, there are plenty of unique places to discover. Ancient history enthusiasts will be delighted too, as the ruins of Wroxeter Roman City display the stony remains of what was once the fourth-largest city in Roman Britain.

Shrewsbury – the largest town in the region and hometown of Charles Darwin – works well as a great from which to navigate out in different directions. Take your time and enjoy an easy-going journey amid gently rolling countryside with some fascinating stops along the way.

### TOP TIP

Whitchurch is easily reachable by train, but for the attractions east of Shrewsbury, it's best to hire a car.

Iron Bridge (p396)

Shrewsbury

**BEST BOUTIQUES IN WHITCHURCH**

**Homefolk**
Quirky boho-inspired interior accessories made by 30+ artisans, from porcelain animal heads to velvet cushions.

**Lornashouse**
Stylish family-run lifestyle gift shop offering clothes, jewellery, homeware and even pet accessories.

**Doodle Alley**
Relaxed painting haven that doubles as a gift store offering personalised plates, mugs and gnomes.

**MOOand BOOM**
Ethical shop offering a range of sustainable homeware, clothing and gifts. Also has a cafe.

## The Foodie Capital up North

DISCOVER WHITCHURCH'S UNEXPECTED FOOD SCENE

With its Michelin-star restaurants and quality produce, Ludlow was for many years the place to go in Shropshire for fine food. But it now has an unlikely competitor far up in the county's northern extremities. Just a 30-minute train ride north from Shrewsbury on the edge of the Shropshire Hills, **Whitchurch** is a small town of less than 10,000 that is home to a couple of the Midlands' hottest restaurants, alongside a few lovely local institutions.

Opened in 2017 **Docket No.33** is the vision of chef Stuart Collins and restaurant manager Frances Collins. Their sublime nine-course tasting menu comes with a perfectly chosen wine pairing and the menu changes every six weeks, with only their famous chickpea chips starter staying put. At the time of writing, the restaurant plans to relocate across the road under the new name of Docket Restaurant by Stuart Collins.

Down the High St and around the bend lies **Wild Shropshire**, chef James Sherwin's terroir-led micro-seasonal restaurant focusing on local produce. Opened in 2020, it started

**WHERE TO STAY IN SHREWSBURY**

**Darwin's Townhouse**
18th-century Georgian townhouse with cosy rooms and a secluded private garden perfect for summer days. ££

**Hencote**
Luxury lodgings just on the outskirts of town at a vineyard with sweeping countryside views. £££

**Drapers Hall**
Independent boutique hotel of just six individually designed rooms set inside a timber Tudor building. ££

originally as a pop-up and stocks intriguing sake cocktail flights alongside its fabulous food.

Moving away from restaurants, historic street Watergate offers a masterclass in the humble pie. **Powell's Pies** is a small family-run business that 'hand-raises' its pork pies according to a 19th-century recipe, while across the street is the **Pie Hole**, a friendly joint offering a variety of different handmade pies and pastries (and – bizarrely – a Welsh rum).

Italian **Etzio** is a longstanding favourite too, but remember to book ahead, as this is a town that will only become more popular in time.

### BEST BARS IN SHREWSBURY

**Tap & Can**
Craft beer next to the train station featuring regular tap takeovers and a huge fridge.

**Glou Glou**
Relaxed and unpretentious wine bar with a revolving wine board; hosts regular events.

**Admiral Benbow**
Traditional pub with Shrewsbury's best selection of local cask ales on a quiet secluded street.

**Oil**
Low-lit bar offering craft beer, outdoor seating and its own pizza joint across the street.

**Libertine Cocktail Bar**
Colourful cocktail bar featuring a menu of classics and more left-field creations with amusing descriptions.

## A World First

CROSS A PIONEERING BRIDGE

Compared to the Brooklyn Bridge in New York, Tower Bridge in London or any other significant bridge one cares to mention, the old **Iron Bridge** just outside of Telford will seem small in stature. But this pioneering structure – built in 1779 as the world's first cast-iron bridge and a 30-minute taxi ride from Shrewsbury – marked a turning point in design and engineering and is rightly celebrated as a symbol of the burgeoning Industrial Revolution.

Following its construction, cast iron came to be widely used in the construction of bridges, aqueducts and buildings. So influential is the bridge that it gave its name to the majestic forested valley surrounding it and became recognised as a Unesco World Heritage Site.

But admiring the famous bridge isn't the only reason to visit **Ironbridge Gorge**. Not only is this charming town home to quaint cafes and picturesque pubs, there are several museums that give true context to the significance of what happened here.

The **Museum of the Gorge** tells the story and works as an ideal overview, while the **Coalbrookdale Museum of Iron** delves further into the material that gave birth to the bridge. **Blists Hill Victorian Town** is an open-air interactive museum bringing this small region to life and is a quirky option for families.

So while the old bridge might not be hundreds of metres high, its beauty and importance are unparalleled.

### GETTING AROUND

As with the Shropshire Hills, trains are limited in scope, so it's a better idea to hire a car if you're planning to spend a few days here. The hourly train service between Shrewsbury and Whitchurch is useful, however, and some services continue down to Ludlow too.

Buses are available, but there are a number of interesting attractions and destinations to the east of Shrewsbury that are far more efficiently reached by car. Ironbridge Gorge, Much Wenlock, among others can be reached in under 40 minutes by car, but will take hours by bus.

# HEREFORD

Surrounded by the densely forested hills and romantic stone cottages of the Wye Valley, as well as the languid apple and pear orchards of the Herefordshire countryside, Hereford is a compact medieval city with an easy-going nature on the rolling River Wye. Famous for its abundance of cider and the remarkable Mappa Mundi hidden inside Hereford Cathedral, the city of 60,000 lies around 20 miles from the Welsh border and was once described as 'Hereford in Wales' in an early town charter dating from 1189.

Though modern Hereford is firmly rooted in England, it can feel as much part of the south-west as it does the Midlands, thanks to that passionate cider culture and its starry, largely pollution-free evening skies. But that mix of identities only adds to the intrigue of this handsome and historic corner of the country. Welcome to Hereford.

## TOP TIP

Hereford has more than 20 miles of traffic-free paths and it's a lovely place to explore on two wheels. There are over 200 Beryl Bikes available at 69 different bays dotted around the city in their distinctive mint-green colour. E-bikes are available too, if you prefer an electronic push.

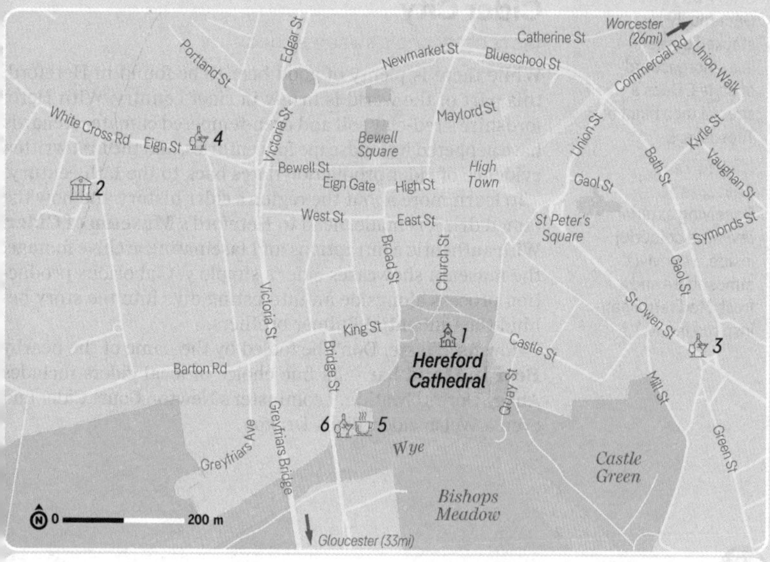


**HIGHLIGHTS**
1 Hereford Cathedral

**SIGHTS**
2 Museum of Cider

**DRINKING & NIGHTLIFE**
3 Barrels
4 Beer in Hand
5 De Koffie Pot
6 Left Bank Village

## BEST RESTAURANTS IN HEREFORD

**Bookshop**
Modern British restaurant serving beautifully presented brunch, rustic evening mains and an award-winning Sunday roast. ££

**Cotto**
Authentic Italian cooking with a modern twist. Includes a cocktail bar serving finely crafted Neapolitan classics. ££

**Beefy Boys**
Generously stacked burgers in a smorgasbord of styles. Does a special taco night on Tuesdays. £

**Mediterrané Restaurant**
Deceiving exterior reveals a colourful inside, a convivial atmosphere and a fresh Mediterranean-inspired menu. ££

Hereford Cathedral

## Cider City

TASTE HEREFORD'S SWEETEST DROP

While there is plenty of good beer to be found in Hereford, this part of the world is firmly in cider country. With Herefordshire's red-clay soil and even-tempered climate, orchards have peppered its landscape for centuries, and the first written evidence of cider production dates back to the 15th century.

To learn more about the region's cider history and how the famed drink is made, head to Hereford's **Museum of Cider**. With authentic contraptions and fascinating archive footage, the museum showcases cider's simple yet laborious production process alongside an interesting dive into the story behind the influential Bulmer brothers.

Now for a taste. Don't be fooled by the name of the nearby **Beer in Hand** bar – its fine choice of local ciders includes Abbey Dore's Gwatkin, Leominster's Newton Court Cider and even a Welsh cider, Black Dragon.

## BEST HOTELS IN HEREFORD

**Green Dragon Hotel**
Centrally located 17th-century coaching inn with a hint of Art Deco glamour and several stylish bars. ££

**Castle House Hotel**
Grade-II-listed Georgian villa on a quiet street near the cathedral, with a waterside terrace. £££

**Charades**
Friendly family-run guesthouse in a stylish Victorian building conveniently located near the train station. ££

Local favourite **Barrels** is a gregarious 18th-century coaching inn serving up the cloudy and refreshing Rosie's Pig, alongside craft cider from Bishops Frome's Celtic Marches cidery.

End this apple adventure at **De Koffie Pot** in the lively **Left Bank Village**. While its selection isn't as impressive as some of the others mentioned, its vast outdoor seating area and romantic location on the banks of the Wye bring an unmatched allure, especially when the sun sinks behind the 15th-century Wye Bridge on a warm summer's evening.

**BEST CAFES IN HEREFORD**

**Rocket Kitchen Cafe**
Delectable cakes and well-brewed coffee. Outdoor seating offers a romantic framed view of the cathedral. £

**Cafe Miro**
Suntrap garden is great for summer. Its beef and blue cheese sandwich is wonderfully indulgent. £

**Sabores de Portugal**
Quality coffee that goes perfectly with its exceptional *pastéis de nata* (Portuguese egg-custard tarts). £

**Cafe Ascari**
Family-run institution going for 60 years, with a handwritten menu and friendly service. £

**Sensory & Rye**
Stylish airy joint serving artisan coffee with a lunch menu that changes with the seasons. £

## Mapping the Medieval World

HOW OUR ANCESTORS SAW EARTH

What did the medieval world look like to those with such primitive methods of travel? Centuries before the Industrial Revolution would pave the way for powered transport, there was a fine line between fact and conjecture. And there's fascinating evidence of this at **Hereford Cathedral**, where the remarkable Mappa Mundi still resides.

The largest medieval map still in existence and dating from around 1300, it was drawn on a single sheet of vellum, and the low-lit room where the map is located inside the cathedral only adds to its mystique. Despite being quite difficult to read (especially at first), the map is astounding to view, and on closer insepction the detail is extraordinary.

With Jerusalem at its centre, reflecting how religious society was at the time, the Mappa Mundi depicts 420 towns, 15 Biblical events, 33 animals and plants, 32 people and five scenes from classical mythology. Behind is the original board it was mounted on (with visible nail holes) and where it hung, with little regard, for many years on a wall of a choir aisle in the cathedral.

This is a window into a forgotten and, at times, fantastical world via one of England's most unique and enduring artefacts, and it perhaps deserves a grander platform. But the map's home is here in Hereford and a chance to observe its distant world shouldn't be missed.

**GETTING AROUND**

Hereford's town centre is small and easily navigable on foot, so travelling by car, taxi or bus won't be necessary. Cycling is also a pleasant option and there are plenty of Beryl Bike stations around the city with bikes for hire for a small fee.

The train station is near to the city centre and has good links to Ludlow, the Malvern Hills, Birmingham, and even direct services to London Paddington.

# Beyond Hereford

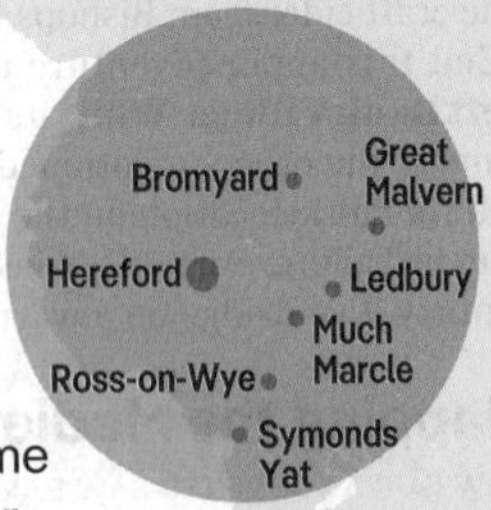

## The evocative green landscapes beyond Hereford are easygoing, packed with good-time festivals and unfurling views, little changed for centuries.

Sun-kissed apple orchards and rolling bucolic hills blanket this lush green corner of the Midlands' southern reaches, while the River Wye bobs and weaves alongside romantic stone villages. The land surrounding Hereford is fertile ground for slow-paced exploration, and no adventure here should ever feel rushed. Whether it's cycling between charming medieval black-and-white towns or kicking back in a breezy apple orchard sipping freshly poured cider, Herefordshire demands that you take life a little less seriously.

Hereford is a great city to explore for a couple of days, but make time to get outdoors, visit the festivals and enjoy the scenes of a pastoral landscape that has stayed largely tourist-free for many years.

### TOP TIP

Travel by train between Hereford and the Malvern Hills is quick and easy, but a car will be required to explore beyond these areas.

**Malvern Hills**

Saracen's Head

## A Feast of Festivals

DIVE INTO A PACKED CALENDAR

The people living in this dreamy corner of the Midlands are a gregarious bunch and they like nothing more than seeing a packed festival calendar where they can indulge in their passions and generally have a good time socialising in an oh-so-pretty landscape.

The **Herefordshire Walking Festival** has been running for over 20 years and takes place each June with a wide variety of walks to take on. As well as the famous Herefordshire Trail, the festival also features WWI memorial walks, dog-friendly walks and countless others.

A little less taxing but no less interesting is the **Ledbury Poetry Festival**. With its lively readings, thought-provoking discussions and expert writing workshops, it's a unique celebration of the written word in one of Herefordshire's most picturesque towns (20-minute train from Hereford).

Taking place every September, the laid-back **Bromyard Folk Festival** has been running since 1968 and attracts a plethora of local and award-winning national acts and

### BEST CIDERIES IN HEREFORDSHIRE

**Westons Cider**
Guided tours, a well-stocked shop, and the Scrumpy House serves a fine Sunday roast.

**Gwatkin Cider Co Ltd**
Farm-shop and collection of antique cider-making equipment open daily. Holds a three-day summer music festival.

**Pips Cider**
Beautiful Golden Valley orchard; can be visited by appointment and its award-winning ciders tasted on-site.

**Oliver's Cider & Perry**
Progressive cider producers only open on Saturdays, but tours and tasting can be booked ahead.

### WHERE TO STAY IN THE WYE VALLEY

**Saracen's Head**
Riverside B&B in a charming half-timbered inn offering 10 airy whitewashed rooms. ££

**Orles Barn Hotel**
Seventeenth-century barn with an excellent restaurant and an old-fashioned lounge perfect for cosy winter comfort. ££

**Glewstone Court**
Stately home turned boutique hotel with spacious and luxurious rooms and an award-winning restaurant. £££

international folk institutions (30-minute taxi from Hereford).

For a sweet dive into local culture, **Big Apple** is a quaint countryside trail around Much Marcle's rural cider orchards (30-minute taxi from Hereford). Tractor trailers transport folks and families between various orchards where strong local cider and perry can be merrily sampled at will.

And back in Hereford, beer canopies and food tents line the riverside for **Beer on the Wye** and its 135 different ales of every conceivable style, hue and strength.

### BEST PLACES FOR LUNCH IN LEDBURY

**Ledberry**
Tranquil walled garden decked in plants and fairy lights; a perfect summer sun trap. ££

**Malthouse Cafe**
Relaxed brunch spot with a pleasant courtyard. American-style pancakes drizzled with maple syrup are sublime. £

**Pot & Page**
Charming vegan brasserie with a smorgasbord of loose-leaf teas. Also doubles as a bookshop. ££

**Prince of Wales**
Home-cooked food and a generous helping of pies served on Ledbury's most picturesque street. £

## Ledbury Market House's Legs

WITNESS A FINELY BALANCED LANDMARK

Sitting near the foothills of the Malvern Hills and just a 20-minute train ride from Hereford, **Ledbury** is a quirky and laid-back medieval market town, though at first glance one building immediately captures the attention ahead of all others.

Started in 1617 and completed decades later in 1668, the black-and-white timbered **Ledbury Market House** gives the impression of levitation but it's actually balancing on 16 oak pillars. Despite its odd appearance, that was actually the custom of the day in many market towns, with the markets themselves taking place below and the upper rooms often used for the transaction of business or as a town hall.

A charter market is still held below to this day, on Tuesdays and Saturdays.

## Boutique Heaven

BROWSE THROUGH SMALL-TOWN TREASURES

For a town with a population of less than 10,000, Ledbury's medieval streets and hidden alleys are bulging at the seams with eclectic boutiques and friendly artisan stores.

Inspired by the owner's former life in Bali, **Tinsmiths** is a haven for creative independent homeware, ceramics and artist prints. Squeeze down the narrow **Design Quarter alley** and find a cornucopia of smart Nordic delights at **HUS & HEM**. Further down, **Ledbury Books & Maps** is unique for – as its name implies – having a corner of the shop dedicated entirely to maps.

The **Homend Mews** is another blink-and-you'll-miss-it alley and it conceals the seductive **Choccotastic** chocolate shop and its alluring gold-sprinkled bars.

### WHERE TO STAY IN LEDBURY

**Talbot**
Sixteenth-century black-and-white coaching inn hosts both Old-World and contemporary rooms in the heart of town. ££

**Feathers**
Striking black-and-white Tudor building with 22 individually decorated rooms; original beams and cosy fireplaces downstairs. ££

**Harlequin BnB**
Two spacious and luxurious rooms on a quiet street a few minutes' walk from town. £

## BLACK & WHITE VILLAGES CYCLING TRAIL

While most of modern England is a busy and dynamic place with ever-expanding cities humming to the mantra of 'work hard, play hard', there are still pockets of rural life where it feels as if time has stood still for centuries.

With their timber-framed ever-enchanting architecture and the high streets filled with cosy pubs and tea rooms, north Herefordshire's black-and-white villages are an alluring window into a simpler time. And there's no better way to view them than during a slow summer bike ride.

Beginning from charming 1 **Leominster**, the full route is 42 miles long and lasts from two to three days, though there are shorter versions available. Roll north through the quaint villages of 2 **Eyton** and 3 **Kingsland** before stopping at picturesque 4 **Eardisland**. Refuel at Rita's Tearooms and stroll the banks of the River Arrow, admiring the thatched houses and the 14th-century yeoman's hall known as Staick House.

Continue west to the picture-postcard village of 5 **Pembridge** and its timber-framed buildings lining the main street, including the 17th-century New Inn pub. Climb west beyond 6 **Luntley Court** and 7 **Almeley**, while enjoying the sweeping vistas and rolling farmland to the north. It's then downhill into pretty 8 **Eardisley**, where the quirky cafe-bookshop New Strand is a fine spot to take a break.

Head back east towards gorgeous 9 **Weobley**, arguably the best-preserved of all the black-and-white villages, while the 185ft spire of the church of St Peter & St Paul's only adds to the dreamy scene. The bike-friendly Ye Olde Salutation Inn is a perfect spot to spend the night before finishing back at 10 **Leominster** the next day.

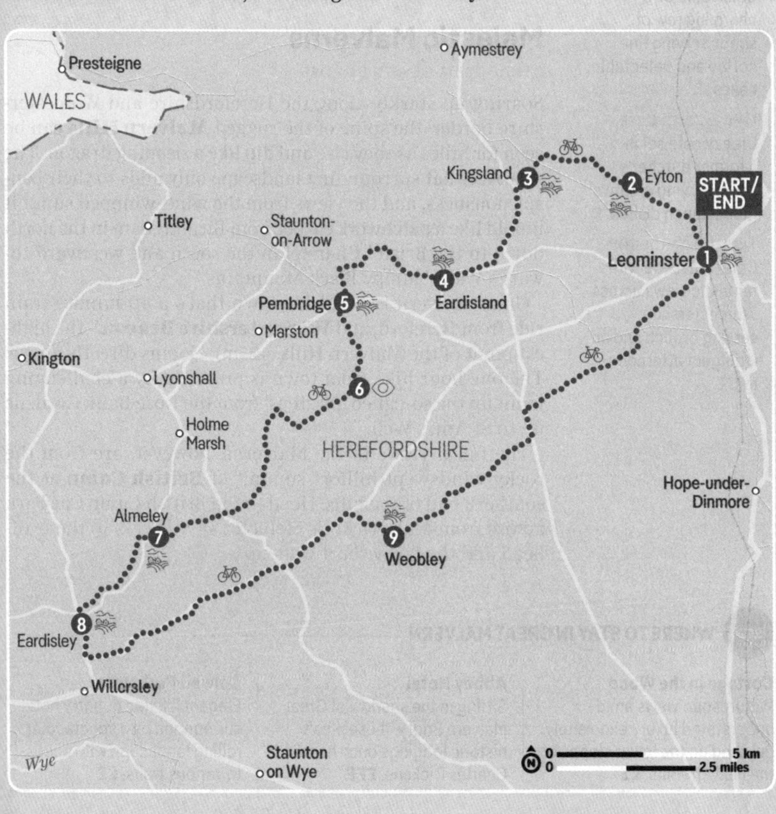

**BEST CAFES IN GREAT MALVERN**

**FAUN**
Rustic cafe serving award-winning roast coffee and freshly baked sourdough bread with exceptionally friendly service. £

**Abbey Road Coffee**
Small cafe on a charming row of shops serving fine coffee and delectable cakes. £

**Mac & Jac's Cafe**
Breezy cafe set in a former butcher's shop, serving creative global lunch dishes. £

**Terrace on the Hill**
Cafe/brasserie with fantastic views across Worcestershire, serving brunch and an indulgent afternoon tea. £

Goodrich Castle

## Majestic Malverns

STRADDLE A GRAND BORDER

Soaring up starkly along the Herefordshire and Worcestershire border, the spine of the rugged **Malvern Hills** can be seen for miles as they rise and dip like a sleeping dragon. The relatively flat surrounding landscape only adds to their conspicuousness, and the views from the wind-whipped summit unfold like a patchwork carpet from Birmingham in the north down to the Bristol Channel in the south and westward towards Wales' lumpy Black Mountains.

Great Malvern is a hillside town that's a 40-minute train ride from Hereford, and **Worcestershire Beacon** – the highest point of the Malvern Hills (425m) – looms directly above. The one-hour hike from town is preceded by a challenging jaunt up the so-called '99 steps' from the Rose Bank Gardens up to St Ann's Well.

The finest views in the Malverns, however, are from the rocky windswept hillfort summit of **British Camp** at the southern end of the hills. Head to the British Camp Car Park across from Malvern Hills Hotel for easy access to the trailhead and the fairly short walk up.

**WHERE TO STAY IN GREAT MALVERN**

**Cottage in the Wood**
Picturesque views amid understated luxury exquisitely perched on the lower slopes of the Malvern Hills. ££

**Abbey Hotel**
Sitting in the shadow of Great Malvern Priory, these plush historic lodgings once hosted Charles Dickens. £££

**Colwall Park Hotel**
Elegant hillside country hotel surrounded by a spectacular rolling landscape with access to various trails. ££

The 9.3-mile **End to End Walk** along the hills' spine is the most strenuous of all the Malvern Hills hikes, though it can be divided into sections, rather than taken in one go.

An easier walk is the two-hour circular walk around **North Hill**, which gives some magnificent views towards the hazy Shropshire Hills to the northwest.

## On the Water

ADVENTURE DOWN A GREAT RIVER

The **River Wye** begins high up in the Cambrian Mountains in Wales and ends by flowing into the Severn estuary, but it also forms a huge part of Herefordshire's identity as it weaves its way through the county's quiet hills and gentle meadows.

Pay homage to the great river and feel closer to nature by getting on the water itself and choosing a paddleboarding or canoeing adventure.

Ross-on-Wye is a 30-minute taxi ride south of Hereford and it's from here that **Paddlingboarding Adventures** runs a range of different courses, covering everything from 2½-hour stand-up paddleboarding beginner's sessions to the sensory relaxation of paddleboard yoga. The most popular route is the half-day paddle from Kerne Bridge to Symonds Yat, but more experienced paddleboarders should try the full-day section from Symonds Yat to Redbrook, paddling past Biblins Bridge and down the valley, looking out for kingfishers, peregrine falcons, herons, swans and otters.

Canoeing is perhaps a more conventional mode of traversing the water, but it's no less thrilling or engaging. The nearby **Canoe the Wye** offers a number of hire options, running from half days to a full two-day rental. Get on the water and glide by forested hillsides, the elegant Pencraig Court and the spectacular Norman ruins of Goodrich Castle.

While these activities are available year-round, try to save them until the summer sun's golden rays can blanket Herefordshire's landscapes as you begin a languid journey downstream.

## Crumbling Castles

EXPLORE EPIC RURAL FORTRESSES

This corner of the Midlands is dotted with ghostly castle ruins , built as defensive barriers against Welsh raiders or defending against attacks in their own country during the English Civil War , that hark back to a more dangerous and unpredictable time.

The best-preserved castle – and by some distance, the most photogenic – is **Goodrich Castle** (30-minute taxi from

### I LIVE HERE: FAVOURITE RIVERSIDE PICNIC SHOPS

**Rich Edwards** runs White House Glamping, a tipi glamping site on the river, near Ross-on-Wye.

**Pengethley Farm Shop, Ross-on-Wye**
A friendly stop for picking up a chunk of Hereford Hop Cheese, Two Farmers Herefordshire crisps, local fruit and cider for a riverside picnic.

**Oakchurch Farm Shop, Staunton on Wye**
This is the place to stock up on supplies like Peter Cooks bread, sausage rolls and chutneys, local cheese, before hitting the nearby river beach at Bredwardine.

**Number 25, Kington**
Provides ample treats for a picnic atop nearby Hergest Ridge, straddling the English–Welsh border. For far-reaching views and wild ponies for company, this is the spot to enjoy alfresco charcuterie and local apple juice.

### WHERE TO STAY IN ROSS-ON-WYE

**Kings Head**
Historic 14th-century coaching inn with cosy open fireplaces, rustic oak beams and a secluded courtyard. ££

**Old Court House**
B&B in a restored 17th-century house located right in the heart of town. £

**Bridge House**
Elegant whitewashed Georgian house near the banks of the Wye, offering some gorgeous views. ££

**WHAT IS PERRY?**

Herefordshire's neat orchards might bring apples and cider to mind, but look closely and you'll see rows of trees bearing small green pears. These are perry pears and they are the base of a drink similar to cider in production, but with its own distinct taste.

Perry is made by fermenting the juice of freshly squeezed pears with the help of natural yeasts. The flavours can be remarkably varied, depending on the pear type, the degree of sweetness and whether the perry is sparkling or still.

But remember, perry is not a 'pear cider' because cider is made from apples. So avoid anything with those misleading labels, and try to seek out the real thing.

Snodhill Castle

Hereford). Perched on a rocky sandstone outcrop overlooking the River Wye around 4 miles south of Ross-on-Wye, its high stone towers date back to at least the early 12th-century, but historians speculate it could be even older. On display inside is 'Roaring Meg', one of the most powerful cannons constructed during the civil war, while the various lookout points offer panoramic views of the rolling Wye Valley.

Sitting only a mile or so from the Welsh border in the elegant Olchon Valley, **Longtown Castle** (35-minute taxi from Hereford) dates from shortly after the Norman invasion and was built to control newly conquered Welsh territory. While it was of strategic importance back then, these days its ruined stone husk provides stunning vistas towards Wales' Black Mountains and is free to enter all year round.

**Snodhill Castle** (30-minute taxi from Hereford) is unusual in that it was forgotten for over 350 years and essentially abandoned after the civil war. It was rescued from collapse and loss in 2017; piecing together its mysterious past is all part of Snodhill's intrigue.

**GETTING AROUND**

For the most part, a car is essential for exploring this picturesque corner of the Midlands, and it makes travelling around the Wye Valley and the rural lands flanking the Welsh border far easier. Buses are available but infrequent, and eat into precious time.

The Malvern Hills are perhaps the one exception, thanks to the good West Midlands Trains service between Hereford and Great Malvern, which also calls at Ledbury. The service also goes all the way back to Birmingham, though note that it's an hour-and-a-half journey.

# THE PEAK DISTRICT

The Peak District

London





A romantic collection of yawning valleys, stone villages, soaring hills and historic homes, the Peak District is the majestic northernmost point of the Midlands. From the wind-whipped hills of the Hope Valley down to charming chocolate-box towns like Bakewell and Buxton, this is England at its most alluring.

The Peak District was England's first national park when it opened in 1951, and over 70 years later the region still delights with its wide array of activities and adventures. And because of the mixture of outdoor pursuits and seductive village life, it's a place to be taken at any pace, whether on an activity-packed day trip or a week-long meander.

Flanked to the south by Derby, to the west by Manchester and to the east by Sheffield, the Peak District is one of the country's most accessible landscapes and has everything a traveller could need for exploring the great English outdoors.

### TOP TIP

Some of the finest hiking, cycling and climbing is found in the beautiful Hope Valley, yet there's no need to hire a car. Catch a Northern Rail train on the Hope Valley Line between Sheffield and Manchester and alight at one of the many outdoor hot spots, such as Edale and Hathersage.

**Bakewell (p410)**

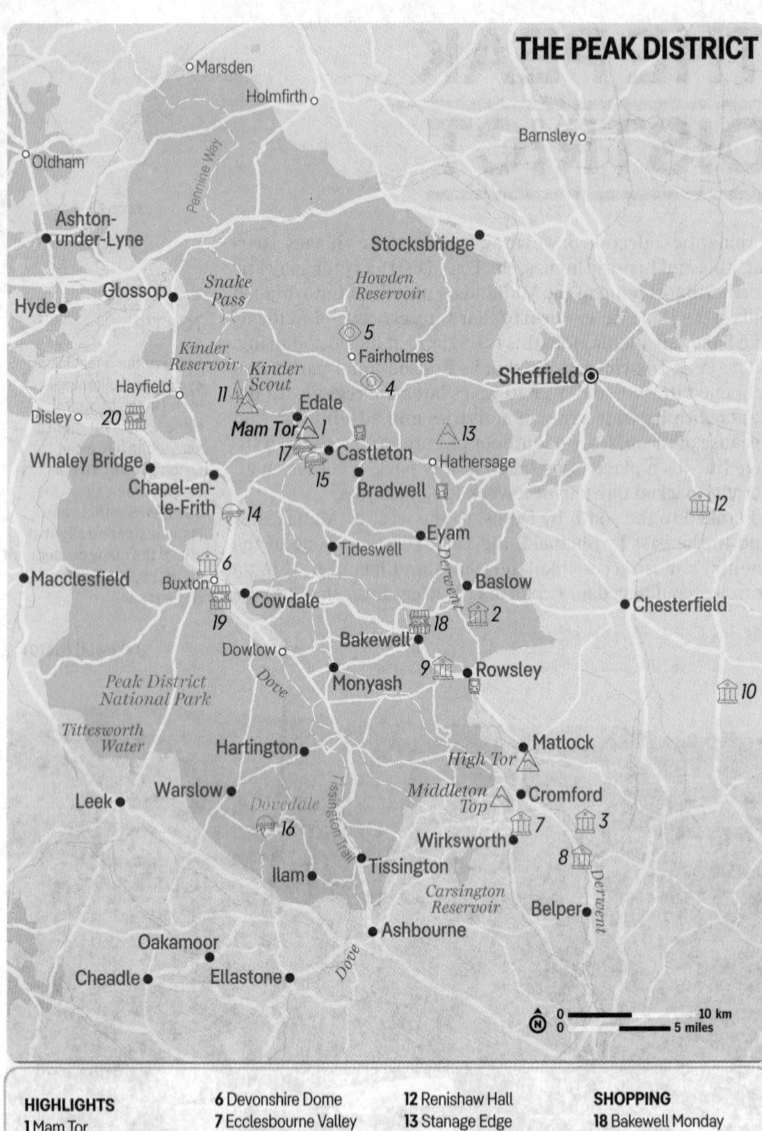


**HIGHLIGHTS**
**1** Mam Tor

**SIGHTS**
**2** Chatsworth House
**3** Critch Tramway Village
**4** Ladybower Reservoir
**5** Derwent Reservoir
**6** Devonshire Dome
**7** Ecclesbourne Valley Railway
**8** Great British Car Journey
**9** Haddon Hall
**10** Hardwick Hall
**11** Kinder Scout
**12** Renishaw Hall
**13** Stanage Edge

**ACTIVITIES, COURSES & TOURS**
**14** Dove Holes Cave
**15** Speedwell Cavern
**16** Thor's Cave
**17** Treak Cliff Cavern

**SHOPPING**
**18** Bakewell Monday Market
**19** Buxton Market
**20** New Mills Indoor Market

Mam Tor

### BEST CAFES IN HATHERSAGE

**Coleman's Deli**
Beautifully prepared lunches made with fresh ingredients. Try the roast beef, Emmenthal and sauerkraut sandwich. £

**Cintra's Tea Room**
Quaint tearoom with a hidden garden serving hearty breakfasts and a classic afternoon tea. £

**Nineteen Ten**
Quality roasted coffee at a relaxed fire-heated space outside the Bank House pub. £

**Riverside Kitchen at David Mellor**
Bright and airy family-run cafe offering homecooked lunches using locally sourced ingredients and produce. ££

## Grand Adventures

EXPERIENCES ON THE BIGGEST SCALE

With its snaking mountain trails, ragged limestone edges and tranquil lakes, the Peak District provides a glorious windswept canvas on which to taste the great outdoors.

The Peak District's hiking epicentre is the tiny village of Edale, where several of the region's best walks begin. The panoramic views from the 510 m-high summit of **Mam Tor** are remarkable and the 7km hike is moderately challenging, while the difficult **Kinder Scout Loop** climbs the Peak District's highest point. And don't miss the fascinatingly macabre trail from **myGuidedWalks** exploring the mangled wreckage of the area's many aviation crash sites.

One of the most evocative cycling trails flanks the edges of **Ladybower Reservoir** and **Derwent Reservoir** – the site where the Dambusters practiced their famous Operation Chastise (a legendary WWII attack on German dams using 'bouncing bombs'). Learn more while enjoying a traditional Yorkshire pudding at the rustic Yorkshire Bridge pub with cycling tour operator **Glory Days** on its **Pudding and Ale Tour**. Further south, the Monsal Trail is a meandering 8-mile

### WHERE TO STAY IN HATHERSAGE

**George**
Rustic 600-year-old building that inspired *Jane Eyre*, with cool contemporary rooms and a fine restaurant. £££

**Little John Hotel**
Twelve cosy en-suite bedrooms alongside a specialist craft beer pub serving an excellent Sunday roast. ££

**Millstone Country Inn**
Historic inn perched up in a secluded location with sweeping views over the Hope Valley. ££

delight on a disused rail line taking in dense forest, historic lime kilns and soaring Victorian viaducts.

**Stanage Edge** is a rugged gritstone escarpment that's a beautiful setting for climbing, but first-timers will need a helping hand. **Pure Outdoor** in Bamford are well-experienced and run a number of courses to help beginners embark on a thrilling experience.

**THE BAKEWELL PUDDING**

In between exploring grand mansions and hiking epic hills, any visit to the Peak District should always be tempered by an indulgent break in proceedings to enjoy a Bakewell Pudding.

According to legend, the Derbyshire dessert was created by accident following a misunderstanding at a local Bakewell inn. Since then, it's been a fixture on any trip to Bakewell. The pudding is made using puff pastry and a layer of sweet strawberry jam, topped with a thick egg and almond custard, and isn't to be confused with the smaller and (arguably even sweeter) Bakewell Tart.

Sit upstairs at The Old Original Bakewell Pudding Shop restaurant, order a pudding and enjoy a true local favourite.

## Extravagant Homes

ENTER A GRANDIOSE WORLD

With such handsome scenery on their doorstep, it's perhaps no surprise that some of England's wealthiest people once chose to build their opulent homes here in the Peak District. Now largely open to the public, they're a window into a luxurious world and a wellspring of stories and personalities.

**Chatsworth House** is a lavish 16th-century mansion near Bakewell and is recognisible for its appearances in various adaptations of Jane Austen's *Pride & Prejudice*. The grand estate contains over 30 rooms, the famous Devonshire art collection and a majestic 105-acre garden.

Nearby **Haddon Hall** is a grand manor house and one of the most complete of its kind. With the origins of the hall dating back to the 11th-century, its handsome 16th-century Long Gallery is a marvel, and there's also a medieval chapel on site.

The 400-year-old **Renishaw Hall** is probably as elegant as anywhere in the region, but it's the house's beautiful Italianate gardens featuring marble statues, clipped yew hedges and a tranquil fountain that keep visitors returning.

Notable for its exceptionally large windows, **Hardwick Hall** is an Elizabethan architectural masterpiece and an early example of an English interpretation of European Renaissance architecture. One remarkable feature of the house is that much of the present furniture and other contents are listed in an inventory dating back to 1601.

## A Cavernous Wonder

SEE AND HEAR A MARVEL

There are some buildings to which photographs simply don't do justice. Rising above Buxton's quaint chocolate-box rooftops in 1789, the **Devonshire Dome.** Once the largest unsupported dome of its type in the world, it is an extraordinary piece of architecture that really needs to be visited to be appreciated.

Not only is the dome's cavernous size breathtaking to witness from within, but the remarkable acoustics provide

### WHERE TO STAY IN BAKEWELL

**Rutland Arms**
Nineteenth-century coaching inn with refurbished bedrooms, an excellent restaurant and an extensive wine menu. ££

**H Hotel**
Luxury boutique hotel with 10 stylish suites, each telling a local story beginning with 'H'. ££

**Melbourne House**
Cosy B&B in a rustic 300-year-old house, a short walk from central Bakewell. ££

Devonshire Dome

one of the Peak District's most visceral experiences. Stand in the centre of the dome, speak a few words and listen to them echo around this yawning great structure. It's surreal, yet somewhat awe-inspiring too.

Be aware, however, that this is an active college campus, so photographs are not allowed inside.

## I LIVE HERE: TOP PLACES TO EAT & DRINK NEAR MATLOCK

**Caroline Povey** is Marketing Director of Landal Darwin Forest holiday resort, just outside Matlock.

**Bentley Brook Brewery, Lumsdale**
After visiting the nearby waterfalls, cosy up in the taproom and enjoy one of their real ales, a delicious coffee and cake, or a warming pie straight from the oven.

**Mad Hatter, Matlock**
Located in the centre of town, Mad Hatter is renowned for its incredible cakes and 'freakshakes', as well as its cocktails after dark.

**Parkys Eatery, Cromford**
A friendly little bistro near the Derwent Valley Mills World Heritage Site, serving homemade breakfasts and lunches and the most incredible sweet and savoury afternoon teas.

## Transport Tales

RIDE BACK IN TIME

Good transport has been essential over the years for anyone who wants to see the Peak District's grand landscapes, and that history is still being kept alive today.

Ride beautiful vintage trams at **Critch Tramway Village** along its meticulously recreated period street, featuring a restored pub, ornate tearooms and a traditional sweet shop.

On a larger scale, **Ecclesbourne Valley Railway**'s 9-mile route is the longest heritage railway in the Peak District and uses a mixture of heritage steam and diesel locomotives.

Located in Ambergate, the **Great British Car Journey** displays a curated selection of forgotten classic British cars, such as the Morris Marina and Hillman Avenger.

### WHERE TO STAY IN BUXTON

**Buxton Crescent Hotel**
Historic 18th-century hotel with a luxury spa and 81 renovated rooms and suites. £££

**Palace Hotel**
Victorian hotel in the style of a French château, with an opulent restaurant and spa. ££

**Old Hall Hotel**
England's oldest hotel, dating to 1573. Features 35 elegant bedrooms in the heart of Buxton. ££

### BEST PUBS IN BUXTON

**Buxton Brewery Tap House & Cellar**
Stone-walled taproom with a huge keg selection, serving cocktails and a wine of the month.

**Cheshire Cheese**
Cosy old pub with wood-beamed ceilings, multiple rooms and at least 10 ales on tap.

**Red Willow**
Quality ale house conveniently located near the train station, pouring everything from sours to porters.

**Queen's Head Hotel**
Great beers in a pub that gets busy at night and often features live bands.

## Going Underground

DELVE INTO CAVES AND CANYONS

Climbing rocks in this part of the world is popular (and challenging) enough, but exploring inside them is also an option.

A formerly flooded lead mine, **Speedwell Cavern** is possible to explore via an underground boat ride culminating in the huge Bottomless Pit lake. **Treak Cliff Cavern** is notable for its hanging stalactites and stalagmites, as well as its vast deposits of the rare Blue John Stone.

The evocatively titled **Thor's Cave** is the largest cave that you can visit for free, but you'll need a torch to explore all the way to the back. **Dove Holes Cave** near Dovedale offers perhaps the most spectacular view (and is perfectly framed for photographers).

## Market Matters

ENJOY A TIMELESS ENGLISH SCENE

There are moments in the Peak District that seem to capture a different age. Markets have been part of the fabric of life here for centuries and their charm and aromas still form lively focal points throughout the week.

Running since 1330, the **Bakewell Monday Market** has around 80 stalls, selling clothes, shoes, freshly baked bread, flowers, wool and hot food.

At 1032ft above sea level, **Buxton Market** is England's highest market and runs every Tuesday and Saturday, while the first Saturday of each month sees a range of quirky craft and vintage stalls.

**New Mills Indoor Market**. in a town already supplied with plenty of boutique shops, is abundant with oddities.

### GETTING AROUND

For an area that's incredibly rural in places, the public transport in the Peak District is pretty good, and some of the most popular towns and villages have railway lines either passing through or terminating. In the south the Derwent Valley Line runs from Derby to Matlock, where buses then branch off towards the likes of Bakewell, while further north the Hope Valley Line calls at popular outdoor adventure stops, such as Edale and Hathersage. Buxton is also reachable by train, and travelling this way is a good sustainable choice for protecting the region's nature for future generations.

It's still wise, however, to consider hiring a car, as some villages and heritage sites can be time-consuming to reach any other way. And if your visit is limited, then driving will be by far the most efficient way to maximise your stay in this sublime slice of England.

# Beyond the Peak District

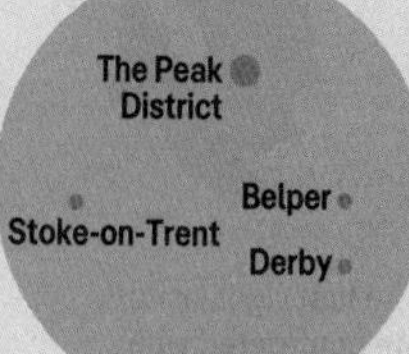




## Gain a new admiration for the remnants of English industrial life dotting the land flanking the Peak District's southern hills.

As the high hills of the Peak District gently flatten towards rolling pastoral scenes further south, signs of industrial heritage appear. The area known as The Potteries is built on one of England's most uniquely local industries and its contribution to the Midlands' creative past shouldn't be missed.

Further east, the winding Derwent Valley between Derby and the Peak District contains a pioneering series of 18th- and 19th-century mill complexes – essentially the world's first 'modern' factories. Now a Unesco World Heritage Site, this is where water power was first successfully harnessed for textile production and contributed to Britain becoming a global superpower. Foodie hot spot Belper only adds to the intrigue of this historic region.

### TOP TIP

Stoke-on-Trent's multiple town centres can be quite confusing at first, so be prepared – it's the UK's only polycentric city.

River Derwent (p415)

**WHO WAS WEDGWOOD?**

The first sight visitors are confronted with after stepping out of Stoke-on-Trent train station is a bronze statue of a man holding a vase. As inscribed underneath, that man is Josiah Wedgwood and his influence is felt all over the region.

An immensely successful pottery designer and manufacturer, he's most famous for his blue-and-white jasperware products, though his tireless work ethic and scientific approach were important factors in building his empire. Eminent patrons included Empress Catherine II of Russia, who ordered 952 pieces in 1774.

Wedgwood was also a prominent slavery abolitionist and his *Am I Not a Man And a Brother?* medallion is still an emotive piece of art today.

Wedgwood porcelain

## Inside Josiah Wedgwood's World

GET CRAFTY WITH STOKE'S TALISMAN

Thanks to the local availability of clay, salt, lead and coal, the Staffordshire Potteries became a centre of ceramic production in the early 17th century, and that heritage is showcased at the 240-acre **World of Wedgwood** on Stoke-on-Trent's southern edges, around a 45-minute drive south of the Peak District. For a full appreciation of the craft, book a one-hour session upstairs in the Clay Studio with its friendly and patient tutors.

Sitting at the potter's wheel for the first time can feel a little daunting, as you sculpt your spinning pot, but it's also a visceral window into this region's heritage and comes with a satisfying sense of achievement.

Head back downstairs afterwards and tour the wonderfully curated **V&A Wedgwood Collection** to admire just how skilled the potters were who turned this part of England into a world leader in ceramics. Around 3500 objects are on display, including Wedgwood's renowned jasperware and black basalt vases and ornaments.

**WHERE TO STAY IN STOKE-ON-TRENT**

**DoubleTree by Hilton**
Has 147 smart contemporary rooms with an air-conditioned gym, heated indoor swimming pool and sauna. ££

**Premier Inn Trentham**
Easy-going hotel with restaurants nearby and simple access to the spectacular Trentham Gardens. £

**North Stafford Hotel**
Cosy rooms inside an exceptional Grade-II-listed Jacobean building across from Stoke-on-Trent train station. ££

For something a little more modern, on-site boutique **Josiah & Co** sells the products of over 50 local artisans from across Stoke-on-Trent and Staffordshire. Unsurprisingly, afternoon tea is a big draw, and the ostentatious **Wedgwood Tea Room** serves up delicate sandwiches and cakes on some spectacular crockery.

For further culinary adventures, two-Michelin-star chef Niall Keating serves up a 12-course tasting menu as fine as the china it's presented on at nearby restaurant **Lunar.**

## Water Tours Through Time

GLIDE THROUGH A PIONEERING VALLEY

Pierced by the snaking River Derwent, the **Derwent Valley Mills** Unesco World Heritage Site is a majestic unfurling landscape of forested woodlands and quaint waterside villages. The reason Unesco were interested in it, however, is because the valley is home to several 18th- and 19-century mill complexes that were the blueprint for the world's future factory systems.

With its years of industry long in the past, the river now operates as a peaceful way of seeing one of the most influential corners of England. Start at the fantastic **Museum of Making** for an introduction to the region. Set inside a former silk mill, the upstairs section features an interactive map that lights up each of the mills along the valley.

Departing from the nearby Phoenix Green riverboat station, the electric zero-emission **Derby Riverboat** *Outram* makes a gentle 45-minute journey north to the spectacular **Darley Abbey Mills** and back, accompanied by full audio commentary by actor David Suchet.

Further north towards Matlock, **Birdswood** runs two-hour cruises departing from historic **Cromford Wharf**, with full commentary detailing the history of the Cromford Canal and the local heritage sites. And when the boat stops to turn around, there's the option to take a short 300m stroll to take in views of the **Victorian Leawood Pumphouse** and the stone aqueduct over the River Derwent.

### BEST RESTAURANTS IN BELPER

**Arthur's**
Five- and 10-course tasting menus that change every month, showcasing Belper's finest local produce. £££

**Vegan Revelation**
Bright cafe in a former antique shop serving delightful plant-based food. Sample the homemade quiche. ££

**Black Swan**
Presents a range of affordable tapas dishes, including plentiful vegan and vegetarian options. ££

**Olive Moroccan**
Colourful Moroccan restaurant with a fine mezze selection and sumptuously cooked lamb tagine. ££

### GETTING AROUND

The Derwent Valley Line running from Derby to Matlock runs along the beautiful Derwent Valley and calls at foodie hot-spots like Belper, too.

Stoke-on-Trent's scattered geography, however, makes train travel redundant so it's better to take a bus or taxi. The 100, 101 and 21 buses go to Trentham Gardens, while the 100 bus is the only one to drop near World of Wedgwood, so splitting a taxi fare is recommended (for groups).

For longer trips, hiring a car may be a more efficient option for exploring both The Potteries and the Derwent Valley in one visit.

# NOTTINGHAM

Nottingham

London

While local source of mischief Robin Hood and his hometown of Nottingham will always be intertwined in the minds of wide-eyed newcomers, it's important to know there's far more to the city than its famous tights-wearing outlaw.

With one of the largest student populations in the UK, the visceral energy of youth is immediately visible when walking past enthusiastic skateboarders zipping around Old Market Sq, and even more so down towards the vibrant bars and bistros of Hockley. But this is a city built on a past both glamorous and macabre.

Nottingham's Lace Market was once a busy epicentre for majestic lace and embroidery production, while a couple of streets over the steps of the National Justice Museum was once the scene of public hangings in front of vociferous mobs.

These days, the crowds come to Nottingham for its bumping music scene, creative restaurants and an infectious youthful dynamism.

## TOP TIP

Nottingham city centre is easily navigable and compact enough to walk. However, it's also one of the few Midlands cities with a modern tram system, and if your hotel is near the Royal Centre then it's a quick and affordable way to travel from Nottingham train station with luggage.

Lace Market

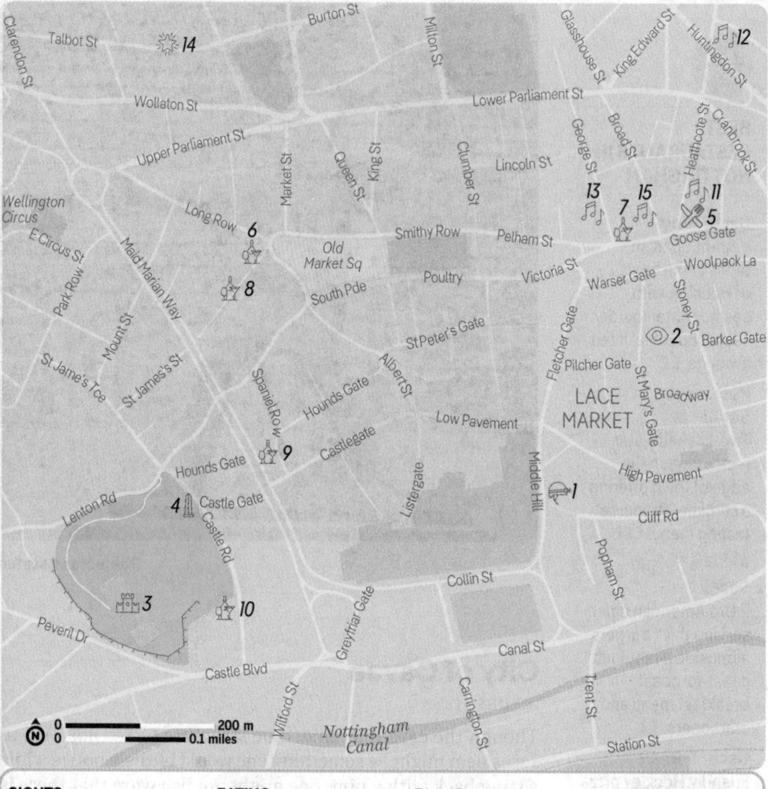


| SIGHTS | EATING | | ENTERTAINMENT |
|---|---|---|---|
| 1 City of Caves | 5 Sexy Mamma Love Spaghetti | 7 Lost Property | 11 Jamcafé |
| 2 Lace Market | **DRINKING & NIGHTLIFE** | 8 Malt Cross | 12 Metronome |
| 3 Nottingham Castle | 6 Bell Inn | 9 Ye Olde Salutation Inn | 13 Peggy's Skylight |
| 4 Robin Hood Statue | | 10 Ye Olde Trip to Jerusalem | 14 Rock City |
| | | | 15 Rough Trade |

## Ancient Inns

TASTE HISTORY AT THESE PUBS

The modern craft beer taprooms that adorn the lanes and side streets of Hockley are all well and good, but it's a point of pride that Nottingham's centre is home to not one, but three of England's oldest pubs.

Residing beneath the cliff of Nottingham Castle's lofty hilltop site, **Ye Olde Trip to Jerusale**m claims to be the oldest of Nottingham's historic watering holes. Dating back to – allegedly – 1189, the pub offers an alluring combination of low-sloping sandstone ceilings, silver suit of armour and spectacular Rock Lounge.

**Ye Olde Salutation Inn** has parts dating back to 1240, yet has somehow found a new life as a lively rock and metal pub, whereas the **Bell Inn** has been looking onto Old Market Sq for almost 600 years.

## BEST RESTAURANTS IN NOTTINGHAM

**Bar Iberico**
Vibrant Spanish tapas in the heart of Hockley, with cosmopolitan outdoor seats underneath red awnings. ££

**Restaurant Sat Bains**
Two-Michelin-star restaurant on the edge of town offering a sublime 10-course tasting menu. £££

**Annie's Burger Shack**
Retro American diner serving thick burgers alongside a fabulous coast-to-coast breakfast menu and craft beers. ££

**Oscar & Rosie's**
Friendly Hockley pizza and beer joint famous for its delicious and photo-friendly 'metre of pizza'. ££

**Cod's Scallops**
A new standard for fish and chips, especially when served alongside oysters, cockles and whelks. ££

Robin Hood statue

## City of Caves

GO DEEP DOWN

Though the cave-like sandstone structure of Ye Olde Trip to Jerusalem might be something one would blithely notice while sitting back with a pint, one might not be aware that there is actually a vast network of over 800 caves beneath Nottingham. Since the city sits upon a soft sandstone ridge, it means that artificial cave dwellings can be crafted relatively easily using rudimentary tools.

Fully open to the public, **City of Caves** is a fascinating network that's been used variously over the years as a medieval tannery, public house cellars, 19th-century slums and a WWII air-raid shelter.

## WHERE TO STAY IN NOTTINGHAM

**St James Hotel**
Stylish hotel with contemporary rooms, an art gallery and a fine location near Nottingham Castle. ££

**Lace Market Hotel**
Georgian townhouse in the Lace Market area with 51 individual bedrooms, suites and feature rooms. ££

**Roomzzz Aparthotel**
Has 106 modern budget-friendly rooms perfectly situated for gigs at the famous Rock City nearby. £

## Nottingham's Mysterious Outlaw

DELVE INTO A LEGEND

Star of both film and imagination, Robin Hood is the unavoidable reference point when starting with all things Nottingham. Whether he really existed or not, his noble intentions and life outside the law (hence 'outlaw') are both exciting and inspiring and perhaps that's why the legend still endures today.

The best place to learn more is a tour with the man himself. Starting from the Cross Keys pub, the multi-award-winning **Robin Hood Town Tour** is far more than just a regular walking tour. Wearing full period dress, Ezekiel Bone leads a 2½-hour tour twinning the history of Nottingham with the legend of Robin Hood across 1000 years. A charismatic raconteur, Bone explores the myth while pondering some interesting philosophical questions as the tour journeys from the **Lace Market** through to its satisfying conclusion at **Ye Olde Trip to Jerusalem**.

Along the way, the tour passes the bronze **Robin Hood Statue**, with Robin posed to fire an arrow. Interestingly, the statue's headgear isn't the typical peaked cap found in Hollywood movies, but a rounder skullcap more akin to what he may have worn in medieval England. The statue is located just outside Nottingham Castle, which has an interactive **Robin Hood exhibition** in which visitors can fire virtual arrows, among other things.

So don't just tour with Robin, be him too (briefly).

## Magical Music Venues

BLAST THE SOUND OF NOTTINGHAM

What Nottingham lacks in legendary music acts, it more than makes up for with its range of exuberant and renowned venues.

'THE UK'S BEST LIVE MUSIC VENUE & CLUB' reads the bombastic and brightly lit slogan above the entrance to **Rock City**, Nottingham's famous gig venue on Talbot St. With its no-frills charm, sticky floors and blistering atmosphere, it's no surprise that Rock City has attracted the likes of Nirvana, Oasis, David Bowie and Guns N' Roses over the years.

The Malt Cross is a Grade-II-listed Victorian music hall with a unique elevated stage, while **Peggy's Skylight** is a laid-back haven for jazz lovers. More recently, **Metronome** has delighted with its diverse live music, moving image and spoken-word performances.

### BEST CRAFT BEER IN NOTTINGHAM

**Neon Raptor**
On-site brewery taproom offering eight fresh kegs in a light and airy building near Hockley.

**Liquid Light**
Classic industrial-estate dog-friendly taproom with wooden tables and bright whitewashed walls splashed with art.

**Hop Merchant**
Historic city pub that's a good spot to watch sport with a decent cask beer.

**Junkyard**
Relaxed bar hidden down a Lace Market alleyway, with 15 taps and two stacked fridges.

### BEST MUSEUMS IN NOTTINGHAM

**National Justice Museum**
Crime museum in a former Victorian courtroom, prison and police station with costumed character performances.

**Nottingham Contemporary**
Eye-catching arts centre with revolving exhibitions, an events programme, and a breezy downstairs cafe.

**Nottingham Industrial Museum**
Industrial heritage museum with working steam engines, a Victorian kitchen and a blacksmith's forge.

### BEST CAFES IN NOTTINGHAM

**Doughnotts**
Creatively designed premium doughnuts are a delicate sweet delight. Has upstairs seating with coffee. £

**Yolk**
Laid-back street-corner brunch spot with bold yellow decor, excellent hot chocolates and continental-style outdoor space. £

**200 Degrees**
Nottingham institution with several cafes around the city, thanks to consistently good coffee. £

**Beeston**
Bright, airy and spacious neighbourhood joint with ceiling plants, comfy sofas and board games. £

200 Degrees

## After Dark

EXPLORE NOTTINGHAM'S BREEZY NIGHTLIFE CORE

With its gaudy street art, breezy bistros and community spirit, **Hockley** is Nottingham's vibrant epicentre when evening falls.

Spinning funky and choppy beats since 2008, **Jamcafé** is the coolest spot in the neighbourhood and serves up a selection of local craft beers and natural wines. A low-lit speakeasy with a penny-top bar and sister bar **Lost Caves** below, **Lost Property** is home to some delectable cocktails.

Obscure vinyl records and a smorgasbord of beers are the order of the day at **Rough Trade**, while **Sexy Mamma Love Spaghetti** is an easy-going Italian with a chalkboard menu serving rustic classics like risotto and gnocchi.

### GETTING AROUND

The east Midlands' largest city is still compact and walkable, from the Royal Centre on the north side down to Nottingham train station in the south. Driving can be laborious, especially at weekends, although there are plenty of car parks flanking the city centre on all sides. The Lace Market Car Park is handy for the bars and restaurants of Hockley, though most hotels are towards the Royal Centre and Nottingham Castle.

The Nottingham Express Transit (NET) tram system pierces the city from north to south and stops conveniently close to the train station. East Midlands Airport can be reached by the regular blue Skylink buses.

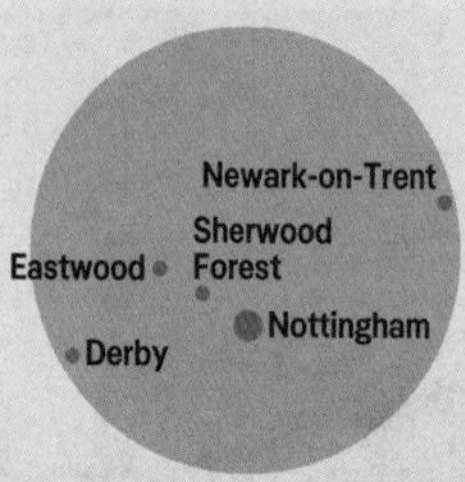

# Beyond Nottingham

A humble green landscape becomes a wide canvas for centuries of stories. Settle in and enjoy.

The scenery surrounding Nottingham is largely flat, and made up of quiet green meadows and ancient oak forest, particularly to the north, where further Robin Hood adventures can be had within the famous foliage of Sherwood Forest.

To the west lies Derby, a city with many industrial tales to tell and a fine gateway to the Peak District, as the nearby hills of the Derwent Valley begin to rise. The River Trent – the UK's third-longest river – meanders in a northeasterly fashion, brushing past Nottingham and up to Newark-on-Trent, a pivotal place in the bloody English Civil War.

There are fascinating stories here, some brutal and some fantastical, but all are worth exploring.

**TOP TIP**

The East Midlands is well served by train, though driving is a far more efficient method of reaching Sherwood Forest.

**Nottingham Castle (p423)**

Museum of Making

### BEST RESTAURANTS IN DERBY

**Darley's**
Multi-award-winning restaurant set in a 200-year-old mill with a riverside terrace serving modern English cuisine. £££

**BEAR**
Rustic stripped-back spot for coffees and delectable lunch fare in an old banking building. ££

**Fill-in Kitchen**
Laid-back street food joint hosting a rotating cast of pop-up kitchens every three months. ££

**ANOKI**
Indian fine dining beneath the majestic gilded vaulted ceiling of a former movie theatre. ££

## Local Pride & Power

HOW TO MAKE AN ENTRANCE

Opened in 2021 and just a 20-minute train trip from Nottingham, Derby's **Museum of Making** has one of the most arresting entrance halls of any UK museum.

Suspended in air above the glass entrance is the skeletal frame of a Toyota Corolla, while further towards the back is the unmistakable sight of a silver aircraft engine, also hanging from wires. The Toyota and the Rolls-Royce Trent 1000 jet engine are symbolic of Derby's industrial heritage, and yet also its presen; uniquely in the modern world, those industries are still in Derby to this day.

The museum is housed in a 300-year-old former silk mill, and it explores Derby's effect on Britain through quirky artefacts and stimulating interactive displays.

### WHERE TO STAY IN DERBY

**Cathedral Quarter Hotel**
Thirty-eight stylish rooms inside a Grade-II-listed former police station on a beautiful Georgian street. ££

**Aston Court Hotel**
Contemporary rooms in a relaxed hotel opposite Derby train station, perfectly located for travellers. £

**Stuart Hotel**
Stylish hotel with an on-site restaurant near both the train station and Derby's commercial heart. ££

## Awesome Ales

SAMPLE THE CASK ALE CAPITAL

Served from a cask via hand pump in traditional pubs, the floral taste of real ale is as popular as ever, and Derby's pubs are some of England's finest purveyors.

The charming stone interior of the **Exeter Arms** is seductive enough, but its selection of local breweries, including Derby's Dancing Duck, makes one want to spend all day here. The **Brunswick Inn** is a majestic old railway pub and has a long list of quality real ales for under £4.

The **Old Silk Mill** is recognisable for its colourful political mural, and inside it offers a fine selection of cask ales. And don't forget to pair up great real ale with live music at the **Flowerpot.**

## A Brutal Conflict

TRACE CIVIL WAR GHOSTS

The English Civil War was a bloody series of wars and battles that ended with the famous beheading of King Charles I in 1649. Nottinghamshire was a Royalist stronghold for several years, with Charles even raising the royal standard at **Nottingham Castle** in 1642 in one of the earliest statements of his power.

His most fervent supporters, however, were 20 miles east in the strategically important town of **Newark-on-Trent**, with the imposing (though now ruined) **Newark Castle** watching over the River Trent crossings. Jump on a 40-minute train ride from Nottingham to explore its unique history.

Start by getting an overview at the **National Civil War Centre** on Appleton Gate, the UK's only museum dedicated to telling the story of the event that shaped England as we know it today. A short walk from here is the timber frame of the **Old White Hart**, the oldest pub in Newark and once used as a billet (living quarters) for Royalist soldiers.

Stroll down Stodman St, flanking the vast market square, where the leaning black-and-white frame above the Gregg's shop was used as the **Governor's House**. It almost directly faces **St Mary Magdalene Church**, which, at 71m high, was a useful military lookout point.

The town came under siege from the Parliamentarians in 1643, 1644 and 1645–46, before Charles gave Newark the order to surrender in May 1646, as he slipped away for nearby Southwell disguised as a member of the clergy.

### THE LOST KING UNDER A CAR PARK

Richard II last English king to die in battle, perishing at the Battle of Bosworth in 1485. For centuries his grave and body was presumed lost for centuries. The chances of ever recovering his remains (and identifying them, too) seemed slim to none.

Yet in August 2012 the University of Leicester, in collaboration with the Richard III Society and Leicester City Council, began one of the most ambitious archaeological projects ever attempted – to find those lost remains. And, amazingly, they succeeded.

One month later, underneath a car park in the city of Leicester, archaeologists discovered not only what was once the friary of Grey Friars, but also the skeletal remains of the lost king.

### WHERE TO STAY IN NEWARK

**Riverside Rooms**
Picturesque waterside location in an old lock-keeper's cottage, with four rustic luxurious rooms. **£££**

**Millgate House**
Nineteenth-century red-brick former miller's house, with smart rooms and a pleasant outside courtyard. **££**

**Travelodge**
No-frills budget option for an easy night's rest near the centre of town. **£**

### FAVOURITE COUNTRYSIDE CAFES

**Paul Baker** is Executive Director at Creswell Crags archaeological park.

**All Mine Cakes (By the Lake), Southwell**
Renowned for their amazing cakes and treats, they also cater for gluten-free and other dietary needs. Excellent spot for exploring rural footpaths or the local Minster.

**Harley Café, Welbeck**
Delicious cakes with ingredients from their award-winning farm shop. Ideal for exploring the beauty of the Welbeck Estate or the historic museum collections.

**Idle Valley Nature Reserve Cafe, Retford**
With beautiful views across the lake, this is one of the sites where beavers are being reintroduced to the UK.

## Legendary Trails

RAMBLE THROUGH NOTTINGHAMSHIRE'S FAMOUS FOREST

Whether or not Robin Hood and his merry band of outlaws actually hid out in this corner of northern Nottinghamshire is part of the legend, but the dense woodland of **Sherwood Forest** is a very real place and lies a 55-minute bus ride from Nottingham on the Sherwood Arrow.

The **Sherwood Forest Visitor Centre** is found at the park's southeastern corner just off Swinecote Rd and is the starting point for a number of tranquil trails. With over 1000 acres to explore, the 1.5-mile **Major Oak Trail** shouldn't be missed, and its leafy path weaves a way to the twisted branches and vast canopy of the ancient **Major Oak** tree. Regular events are held here too, including the always lively **Robin Hood Festival**.

## Inspiring Classics

SEE WHERE GREAT NOVELS BEGAN

The novelist David Herbert Lawrence – better known as DH Lawrence – was a well-travelled writer whose wanderlust took him as far as Australia, Italy, Ceylon (Sri Lanka), the US, Mexico and the south of France. Yet it was the stark coalfields of his native Nottinghamshire that were the setting for some of his greatest (and most controversial) works, including *Lady Chatterley's Lover* and *Women in Love*.

The **Blue Line Trail** in Lawrence's hometown of Eastwood takes in many significant sites of Lawrence's early life, including his local pub the **Three Tuns**, the **Mechanics Institute** where Lawrence spent much time reading and the **DH Lawrence Birthplace Museum**, an authentically recreated miner's cottage.

### GETTING AROUND

East Midlands Railway and CrossCountry serve the East Midlands very well by train from Nottingham, and the likes of Derby, Leicester and Newark-on-Trent can all be reached in under an hour. Nottingham is also only just over an hour from Birmingham by train too.

Sherwood Forest is the main attraction that isn't well-served by train, though there is the Sherwood Arrow bus service running hourly from Victoria bus station in Nottingham and stopping right outside the Sherwood Forest Visitor Centre. The journey takes one hour, though through the short days of winter it might be more efficient to hire a car, which will halve the travel time.

# LINCOLN

With its skyscraping medieval cathedral and imposing Norman castle, Lincoln is by far the most conspicuous city in what is a relatively flat surrounding landscape (anyone who has made the taxing walk up the appropriately named Steep Hill will attest to the strategic ingenuity of building a castle at its summit). In fact, so attractive is the site that this far-flung corner of the Midlands has been inhabited for almost 2000 years, going back to its old Roman name of Lindum Colonia.

But while the artefacts and architecture of yesteryear are still alluring, modern Lincoln is a dynamic vibrant place. Allurements from the lively waterside bars and bistros of Brayford Waterfront to the eye-catching street art of the Sincil Bank Art Project mean you don't need to be a history buff to have a great time in Lincoln.

This is a city dominated by a grand cathedral, but not defined by it. Welcome to Lincoln.

## TOP TIP

As the UK's fourth-steepest street, Steep Hill is a real challenge and virtually impossible to climb for anyone with accessibility requirements. Thankfully the Walk and Ride bus (sometimes called the 'Steep Hill Shuttle') is a regular service straight to the top departing from Stonebow on the High St.

**Lincoln Castle (p427)**

## LINCOLN

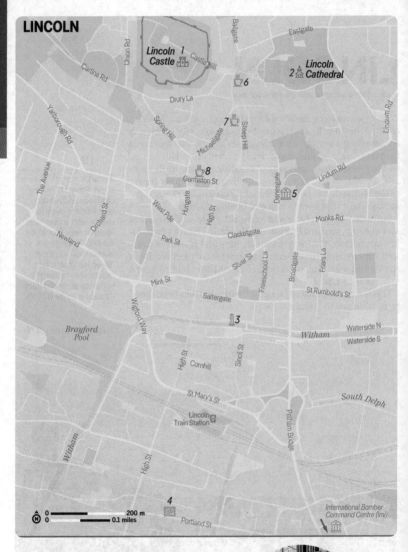

Lincoln Castle 1
Lincoln Cathedral 2
Bailgate
Eastgate
Union Rd
Castle Hill
Carline Rd
Drury La
Yarborough Rd
Spring Hill
Michaelgate
Steep Hill
Lindum Rd
The Avenue
Garmston St
Danesgate
West Pde
Hungate
High St
Orchard St
Newland
Monks Rd
Clasketgate
Park St
Silver St
Freeschool La
Broadgate
Friars La
Mint St
Saltergate
St Rumbold's St
Wigford Way
Brayford Pool
Witham
Waterside N
Waterside S
Cornhill
Sincil St
St Mary's St
South Delph
Lincoln Train Station
Pelham Bridge
International Bomber Command Centre (Imi)
Portland St
0 200 m
0 0.1 miles

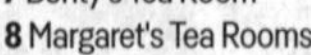

**HIGHLIGHTS**
**1** Lincoln Castle
**2** Lincoln Cathedral

**SIGHTS**
**3** Empowerment sculpture
**4** Sincil Bank Art Project
**5** Usher Gallery

**EATING**
**6** Bells Tea Shop
**7** Bunty's Tea Room
**8** Margaret's Tea Rooms

**Bunty's Tea Room (p428)**

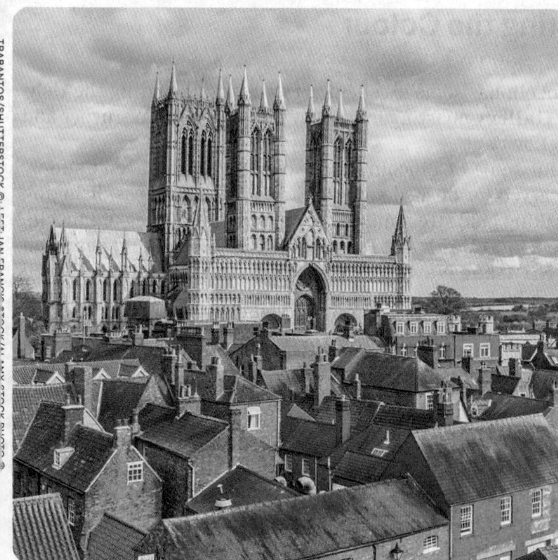

Lincoln Cathedral



## Hilltop Treasures

DISCOVER THE SPECTACULAR CATHEDRAL QUARTER

From The Straight's mix of traditional sweet shops and eclectic fashion boutiques to Steep Hill's cobblestones and tea rooms, the Cathedral Quarter gets more dramatic the higher it rises.

And the crowning glory is **Lincoln Cathedral**, the hilltop perch only adding to its gargantuan size. With its three Gothic towers soaring high above the city, the cathedral was the tallest building on Earth when completed in 1311 and it held that title for 237 years until a storm blew its spire down in 1548.

Nearby **Lincoln Castle** is even older, built in the 11th century by William the Conquerer, and now holds one of only four surviving copies of the Magna Carta.

### FAVOURITE FAMILY-FRIENDLY LINCOLN ATTRACTIONS

**Danielle Crozier** is Operations Manager at the International Bomber Command Centre.

**Lincoln Cathedral**
The new coffee shop and exhibition space are fantastic, and the newly landscaped Dean's Green, which re-opened after 40 years, provides a glimpse of the cathedral not previously visible. Children love to find the famous, mischievous Lincoln Imp.

**Museum of Lincolnshire Life**
This is a great family friendly, free, social history museum with a cafe and play area. Set within the original barrack buildings of the Lincolnshire Militia, exhibits tell of the daily local lives since 1750.

**International Bomber Command Centre**
Military history is in my blood and has been brought to life in the most extraordinary and moving way, thanks to digital technology.

### WHERE TO STAY IN LINCOLN

**Cathedral View Guest House**
Twelfth-century cottage with nine rustic timber-framed rooms offing fine views of Lincoln Cathedral. ££

**Castle Hotel**
Smart boutique hotel with 18 rooms and three serviced apartments facing Lincoln Castle's imposing walls. ££

**Doubletree by Hilton Lincoln Hotel**
Luxury option overlooking Brayford Waterfront, with fabulous views of the cathedral from its higher floors. £££

## Bring the Colour

FIND LINCOLN'S UNUSUAL ART

Lincoln has some excellent art galleries, including the **Usher Gallery** boasting fine art by the likes of JMW Turner and LS Lowry at.

But some of Lincoln's most original works aren't simply reserved for hushed galleries and abstract spaces. Bringing striking bold street murals to an underloved area of Lincoln, the **Sincil Bank Art Project** includes a stunning depiction of **Sir Isaac Newton** on the corner of Kirby St and Sincil Bank by French artist Zabou.

Also look out for the angular **Empowerment sculpture** over the River Witham and the now-annual **Imp Trail** and its colourful sculptures dispersed across the city.

### BEST TRADITIONAL PUBS IN LINCOLN

**Birdcage**
Fine real ales, a friendly atmosphere and hearty home-cooked food, just outside the city centre.

**Cardinal's Hat**
Lively pub with great beers in a historic timber Tudor building named after Cardinal Wolsey.

**Strugglers Inn**
Award-winning pub near the castle with a vibrant beer garden and excellent revolving cask ales.

**Treaty of Commerce**
Compact-looking old High St pub near the train station reveals a surprisingly large beer garden.

## Tasty Tearooms

SIP A TRUE LINCOLN TRADITION

While the selectively sourced coffee and minimalist decor of modern cafes has become ubiquitous across the country, Lincoln's traditional English tea rooms are a cosy throwback to a simpler time.

And none more so than **Bunty's Tea Room** on Steep Hill. With its 1940s wartime-era music, floral table covers and afternoon tea served in delicate china, it's like stepping back in time. Further up is **Bells Tea Shop**, a quaint yet hugely popular affair set in an old Grade-II-listed timber cottage.

**Margaret's Tea Rooms** is a relative newcomer, having opened in 2017, offering an extensive selection of 18 different teas of all styles and aromas.

The Cardinal's Hat

### GETTING AROUND

Lincoln is a compact and walkable city but the Steep Hill is no joke, and anyone not in a position to walk it should consider the Steep Hill Shuttle bus. There are also other bus services that stop near the cathedral, such as the 7, 8, 17 and 18.

Lincoln's main train station is situated on flat ground near the Cornhill shopping district and also within a short distance of the bars and restaurants around Brayford Pool.

The multistory Lincoln Central Car Park is spacious, located near the Cornhill shopping district and conveniently next to Melville St, one of the main arteries passing through the city.

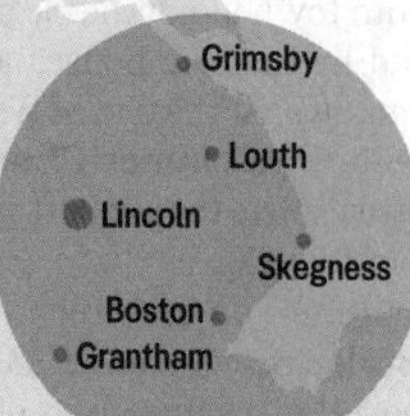

# Beyond Lincoln

## Tranquil trails, lively summertime seasides and charming market towns. Lincolnshire is a peaceful treat.

Though Lincoln and its monstrous cathedral – visible for miles – may give the impression that this land is as flat as a pancake, one only has to take a journey through the rolling chalk hills and gently swaying barley fields of the Lincolnshire Wolds to know that this isn't the case.

This is also the only region of the Midlands with a coast, from the old fishing centre of Grimsby down to Skegness; the original British package-holiday capital. It's pockmarked by quaint market towns, such as Louth and Stamford too, the latter once described by Sir Walter Scott as 'the finest stone town in England'.

Rural retreats don't come much better, or as underrated, as Lincolnshire.

**TOP TIP**

A car is essential here. It's about an hour's drive to both Stamford and Skegness.

**Stamford**

## LOUTH HERITAGE TRAIL WALKING TOUR

A Georgian market town in the heart of the Lincolnshire Wolds 45 minutes from Lincoln by car, Louth is home to a well-regarded food scene, and its historic centre makes for a charming heritage trail.

Start at the old Market Place, where the four-face Italianate 1 **clock tower** dates back to the mid-19th century. Head west along Cornmarket, where the ornate 2 **Masons Arms** is said to date back to the 17th century. Stroll down the narrow Little Butcher Ln to Mercer Row, where the even narrower Pawnshop Passage is home, on the right-hand side, to a 3 **bulbous Regency bow window**, probably the oldest shop window in town.

Continue west to Gospelgate, home to some delightful 4 **Georgian homes**, and then onto Crowtree Ln, where the town seems to turn into an idyllic country lane with the 5 **old grammar school** on the left-hand side.

Turn right up Irish Hill and right again to head east back into town along the elegant Westgate, flanked by historic houses and dense green hedgerows. At the end of Westgate is the 15th-century 6 **St James' Church** and its soaring grey spire, the highest parish church spire in the UK.

Walk by the sculpture on the green and head north up Bridge St, where the 7 **Old Cemetery** on the left gives fine views of St James' in a peaceful setting. Turn right on Cistern Gate and right again down Broadbank to emerge on Cannon St and the stylish 1930s facade of the 8 **Playhouse Cinema**.

Turn left down Eastgate to the solemn 9 **War Memorial**, erected in 1921 following WWI. Head back to the 10 **Market Place** to finish.

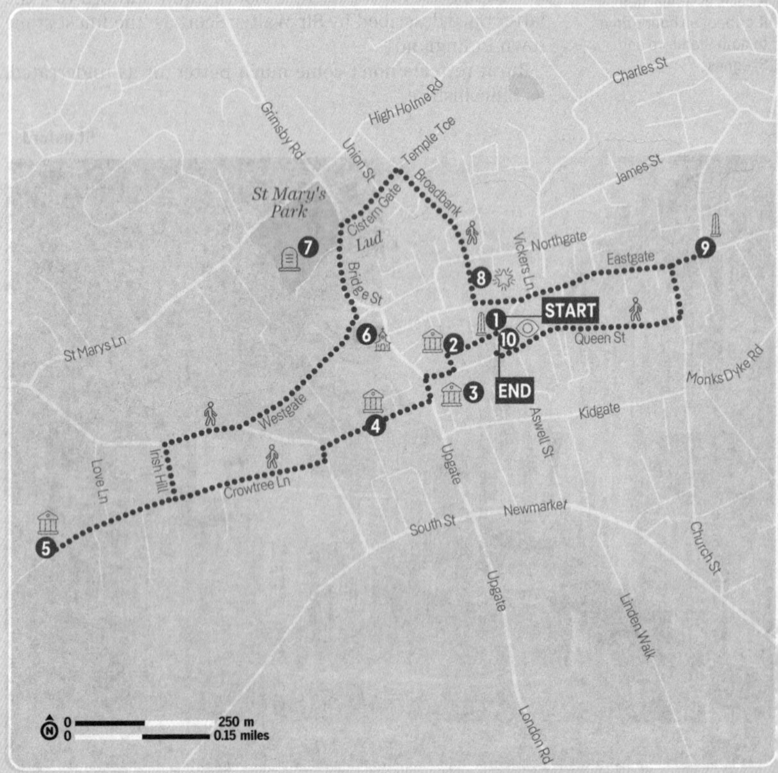

## By the Seaside

SEE THE ORIGINAL HOLIDAY TOWN

During the British seaside's interwar golden age, **Skegness** became one of England's best-loved holiday destinations, it sits around a one-hour drive from Lincoln. Though its star has faded with cheap flights to sunnier climes, 'Skeg Vegas' is now a happy-go-lucky spot that doesn't try to be anything else (don't miss the tongue-in-cheek 'Welcome to fabulous Skeg Vegas' sign).

Stroll to **Skegness Pier** for panoramic coastal views and kitsch arcades, before grabbing classic fish and chips at **Trawler's Catch** and then hitting the soft sands of **Skegness Beach** if the sun's out.

If the skies are grey, however, book in with the **Spirit of Skegness Distillery**, which has a variety of quality gins and rums made using a copper still named Dora.

## Tall Towers & Soaring Spires

LOOK UP TO MAJESTIC LANDMARKS

One of the quintessential images of England, the lonely church spire still forms romantic pastoral scenes across the country, and Lincolnshire is home to some of the finest.

At 295ft high **St James' Church** in Louth (45-minute drive from Lincoln) possesses the highest church steeple in England, a title once held further south in Grantham, where the steeple of **St Wulfram's** reached 281ft in the 13th century.

The tower of **St Botolph's** in Boston (one-hour drive from Lincoln) is Britain's tallest medieval church tower at 272ft and was once a prominent landmark for sailors approaching land.

The most curious tower is found further north in Grimsby (one-hour train from Lincoln), where the 200ft-high **Grimsby Dock Tower** closely resembles the Torre del Mangia in Siena, Italy.

### BEST RESTAURANTS IN LOUTH

**Auction House**
Husband-and-wife team serving contemporary modern British food and cocktails in a rustic setting. ££

**Greyhound Inn**
Stylish pub with cowsheds and gazebos outside, serving everything from bao buns to wood-fired pizza. £

**Bar Castilléjar**
Tapas joint with daily revolving menus. Named after the small Spanish town of Castilléjar. ££

St James' Church

### GETTING AROUND

Driving is by far the most efficient way of navigating this part of the world, especially if you're looking to travel directly to the coast or to the Lincolnshire Wolds from Lincoln. Cars can be hired from Lincoln city centre easily enough.

Rural buses are quite a novel way of seeing the countryside, though these should only be taken if not pressed for time. Grimsby is really the only place of note reachable directly by train from Lincoln.

CALLY ROBIN/SHUTTERSTOCK ©

**Above: Whitby (p460); right: Wensleydale (p45**

# YORKSHIRE

## GRIT, GLAMOUR AND WILD PLACES

Yorkshire's strong regional identity is rolled into its scenic, storied landscapes, historical attractions and diverse communities.

Yorkshire is a region of staggering historical wealth and opulence, with castles, abbey ruins and country house estates seemingly hidden in every valley. But it's also an industrial heartland, tarred with soot and grime from more than 200 years of manufacturing and mining.

The beautiful walled city of York, once a Roman stronghold, then a Viking settlement, and later a medieval seat of huge political power, is the region's poster pin-up. Wealth seeped from its deep, complex foundations into the surrounding area, and today North Yorkshire is home to many of the region's biggest tourist attractions. Beyond the city, the Yorkshire Dales and North York Moors national parks unfurl like a pastoral idyll, with secluded waterfalls, distinctive peaks, remote stone farmhouses and excellent windswept hiking and biking trails. Heading east, the Yorkshire coastline is bounded by large tracts of sandy beach, plunging cliffs and storied 18th-century fishing communities such as Whitby, a haunt of Bram Stoker's *Dracula*. Further south, the hills collapse into the pancake-flat Yorkshire Wolds; puffins and other important birdlife throng the cliffs; and the maritime city of Hull is in the throes of regeneration. Revival is a theme in West and South Yorkshire, too, where the once industrial centres of Leeds, Bradford and Sheffield are repurposing old mills, warehouses and factories into bars, shops, restaurants, museums and cultural spaces. Welcome to Yorkshire, where life is endlessly fascinating and good fun.

### THE MAIN AREAS

# Find Your Way

Covering an area half the size of Belgium, Yorkshire is huge. We've picked the places that have helped define this history-packed region, from literary villages to brooding national parks and evolving coastal communities.

### CAR

Driving is the best way to fully explore all of this region's beautiful rural pockets – especially if you're short on time and want to stitch together a longer itinerary. All of the big gateway cities (Leeds, York, Hull, Sheffield) have car rental agencies.

### BUS

If you don't want to drive Yorkshire's narrow country roads, there are several bus routes cutting through the Yorkshire Dales, North York Moors and along the Yorkshire coast. Services can be infrequent, or sometimes only run in summer. Pay close attention to online schedules.

### TRAIN

A good option for travelling between the bigger cities and towns, such as Leeds, Bradford, Sheffield, York and Harrogate. Services are reliable and stations are central. On the North York Moors Railway and Keighley & Worth Valley Railway, the journeys themselves are also the attraction.

**Haworth & Brontë Country,** **p468**

The Georgian hometown of the famous Brontë sister novelists has made this pretty, lively village and its moody moorlands a beacon for literary fans.

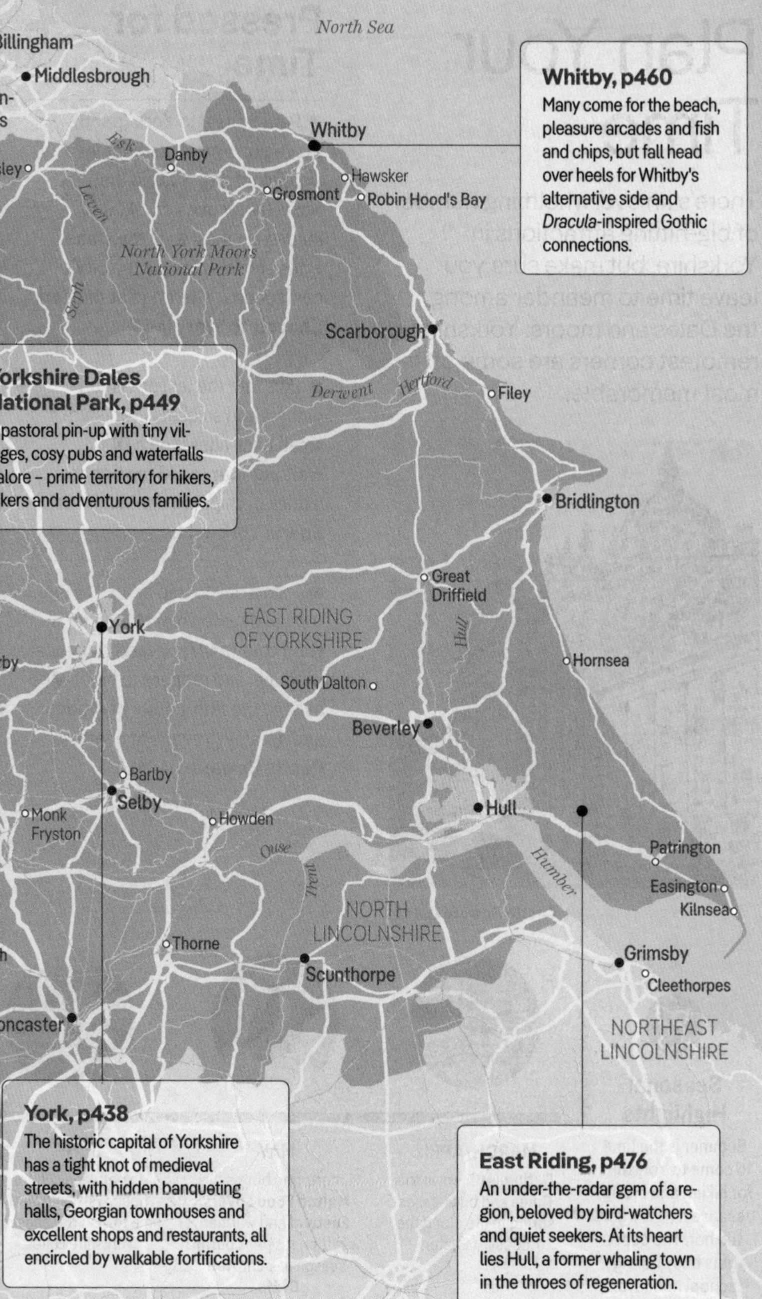


**Whitby, p460**

Many come for the beach, pleasure arcades and fish and chips, but fall head over heels for Whitby's alternative side and *Dracula*-inspired Gothic connections.

**Yorkshire Dales National Park, p449**

A pastoral pin-up with tiny villages, cosy pubs and waterfalls galore – prime territory for hikers, bikers and adventurous families.

**York, p438**

The historic capital of Yorkshire has a tight knot of medieval streets, with hidden banqueting halls, Georgian townhouses and excellent shops and restaurants, all encircled by walkable fortifications.

**East Riding, p476**

An under-the-radar gem of a region, beloved by bird-watchers and quiet seekers. At its heart lies Hull, a former whaling town in the throes of regeneration.

# Plan Your Time

There's an overwhelming number of big-hitting attractions in Yorkshire, but make sure you leave time to meander among the Dales and moors. Yorkshire's remotest corners are some of its most memorable.

LEONID ANDRONOV/SHUTTERSTOCK ©

Castle Howard (p446)

## Pressed for Time

- Parachute into **York** (p438), the region's most historically significant city. Soak in the 'wow' factor of its crooked medieval lanes, walk the stone walls and learn about the city's confectionary heritage at the **York Chocolate Story** (p441).

- Dive into the lesser-visited ginnels and snickets (Yorkshire's small back alleys) on a **DIY walking tour** (p443) and go for a drink in shipping containers at **Spark: York** (p441.

- Take a day to hop across to the rural market town of Malton for a **food tour** (p447) packed with local produce, and prepare to be bowled over by the 18th-century grandeur and dreamy grounds at nearby **Castle Howard** (p446).

## Seasonal Highlights

Summer is the time to come to Yorkshire for hiking and biking, because it rarely gets too hot. The coast gets busy during school holidays.

**MARCH/APRIL**

Daffodils bloom in the Dales and businesses spring to life along the coast at Easter.

**MAY**

Late spring brings the **Malton Food Lovers Festival** and warmer weather; it's peak puffin season at **Bempton Cliffs**.

**JUNE**

In between school holidays, it's a great time to visit the coast o Yorkshire Dales.

ANDY WASLEY/SHUTTERSTOCK ©, MARK CAUNT/SHUTTERSTOCK ©, COLIN WARD/SHUTTERSTOCK ©

## If You Have a Week

- From York, spread your wings west to the **Yorkshire Dales National Park** (p449) or east to the **North York Moors National Park** (p454) – preferably, do both. Starting in the west, cut straight to the heart of the Dales with a stop in **Hawes** (p458) to visit the Wensleydale Creamery and taste test the region's most famous cheese.

- Go glamping, or get lost on the moors with a night at England's highest pub, the **Tan Hill Inn** (p452). Or head south to **Malham Cove** (p450) for one of England's best day hikes. With a couple of days left to spare, make a beeline for **Whitby** (p460) and its beaches and Gothic delights on the Yorkshire coast.

## With Time to Linger

- Explore more of the **North York Moors National Park** (p454) and the coastline. Go stargazing at **Dalby Forest** (p467), try fossil hunting or rock pooling in picturesque **Robin Hood's Bay** (p467), or taste inventive British cooking at a rural Michelin-starred pub with rooms, such as the **Black Swan at Oldstead** (p446).

- Take a wildlife and World War Two safari right down to **Spurn Point** (p480), and drop by **Hull** (p478) for its maritime heritage. Head to West Yorkshire to visit **Brontë country** (p468) and indulge in craft beer with a **Leeds** (p473) night out.

- Tour world-class art at the **Yorkshire Sculpture Park** (p474) and learn about Yorkshire's industrial past at the excellent **National Coal Mining Museum** (p475).

**JULY**
**Camping** and glamping season is in full swing; go **hiking** or take a waterfall swim.

**AUGUST**
Events and festivals flourish with the warmest weather and school holidays; Whitby gets swamped.

**OCTOBER**
Pub fires are lit, the **Yorkshire Dales Cheese Festival** descends, and Whitby goes big for Halloween with its **Goth Weekend.**

**DECEMBER**
**Castle Howard** gets dressed for Christmas, and well-heeled visitors descend on York for **Christmas shopping** and festivities.

# YORK

The layers of history in York run unfathomably deep. The Roman city of Eboracum was founded here around 71 CE. Relics of this past remain, but only around 3% of Roman York has been excavated – you can't dig anywhere in this city without finding another archaeological site. By the 9th century, York had become the capital of the Anglo-Saxon kingdom of Northumbria. At that point it was captured by the Vikings, who claimed it as Jorvik. Yet it's the later medieval period that defines the cityscape today. Encircled by 2.5 miles of 13th–14th century defensive walls, York still retains many of its medieval features – hidden banqueting halls, crooked half-timbered houses and exquisite mansions are just some of the treasures attracting visitors. It's one of the best museum cities in the UK, but there's also a living, breathing modern community here – the shopping, dining and pubs are all top-notch, too.

## TOP TIP

Ticket fees to York attractions can quickly up. The Visit York Pass ( yorkpass.com) provides a discount, giving acces to more than 40 of York' key sights (including Yo Minster and the Jorvik Viking Centre) with a sin digital ticket; three- anc six-day passes also incl sights around the North York Moors.

York

**HIGHLIGHTS**
**1** Merchant Adventurers' Hall
**2** National Railway Museum
**3** York Minster

**SIGHTS**
**4** Barley Hall
**5** Bootham Bar
**6** Dig
**7** Hospitium
**8** Jorvik Viking Centre
**9** Monk Bar
**10** Museum Gardens
**11** St Mary's Abbey
**12** The Shambles
**13** York Chocolate Story

**SLEEPING**
**14** Grays Court

**EATING**
**see 14** The Bow Room at Grays Court
**15** York Cocoa House

**DRINKING & NIGHTLIFE**
**16** Perky Peacock

**Merchant Adventurer's Hall (p441)**

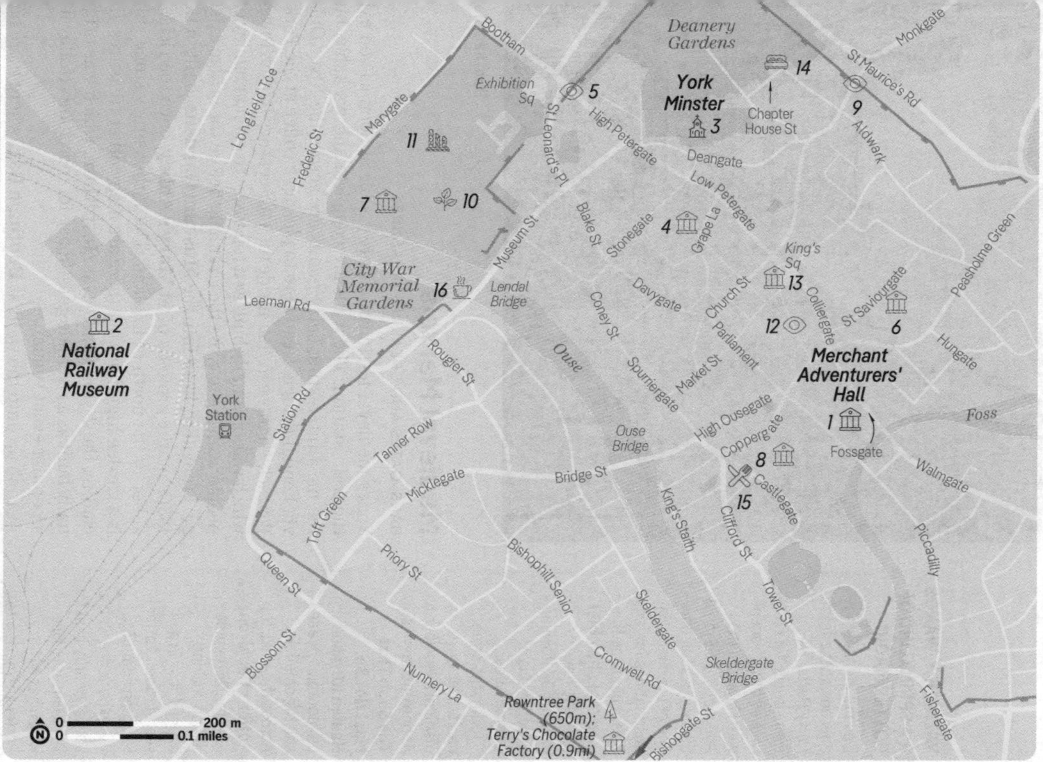

### WIZARDRY, WANDS & A SPRINKLING OF POTTER MAGIC

Despite the fact that only one scene from *Harry Potter* was ever shot in York (the railway bridge scene with Hagrid in the *Philosopher's Stone*), the city has become one of the must-visit destinations for fans. This is because the medieval **Shambles** is said to have inspired JK Rowling's descriptions of Diagon Alley.

Today, the street capitalises on its magical associations. At one end there's **The Shop That Must Not Be Named** for quidditch memorabilia, wands and broomsticks. Across the road, the **Potions Cauldron** runs fun 25-minute potion-making experiences in a secret room. Potter fans can complete the experience with a stay at nearby Minster Walk Guest House, which has a Harry Potter-themed suite – room 8¾.

Bootham Ba

## Medieval Marvels

BARS, GATES AND CREAKING TREASURES

York's medieval fortifications are visible as soon as you exi the train station. The walls are complete and walkable, bu the most interesting entry points are across the River Ous via Lendal Bridge. Head here to pick up a coffee at the Perk Peacock – a tiny cafe/bar inside the 14th-century Barker Towe which was originally built as a toll tower to syphon money o people wanting to cross the river long before the bridge exist ed. From here, head into the **Museum Gardens**, built in th 1830s on the grounds of **St Mary's Abbey**, once the riches abbey in the north of England. The 13th-century stone rui is a garden highlight, but there are many other treasures, in cluding the 2-storey medieval **Hospitium**, which was origi nally built as a riverside guesthouse for merchants (today it' a popular event venue).

Climb up onto the walls at **Bootham Bar,** where there ha been a city gateway for almost 2000 years. From here, th northern wall walk to **Monk Bar** is arguably the pretties section. It takes you past the Gothic hulk of York Minster an its soaring arches, constructed between 1220 and 1480. Pee

### WHERE TO STAY IN YORK

**Safestay York**
Lively Micklegate hostel with Georgian features, a bar and regular events for guests. **£**

**Goodramgate Apartments**
Studio, one-bed and two-bed apartments in Grade-II-listed buildings around the medieval centre. **££**

**Clementine's Townhouse Hotel**
Colourful rooms are inspired by York's confectionary past. Free Kit-Kats a bonus. **££**

into the gardens of the elegant 17th- and 18th-century houses along the elevated walkway. At Monk Bar, take the stairs down and follow the Ogleforth backstreet to Grays Court, the oldest continuously inhabited house in York, with gardens that back directly onto the city walls. It dates to the 11th century and has hosted kings and knights over the years. Today it's a wonderful boutique hotel and home to the Michelin-recommended Bow Room restaurant.

Diving into the tangle of medieval streets south of the minster, there's Barley Hall in Coffee Yard. This medieval townhouse was only rediscovered in the 1980s when the site was bought for redevelopment. It was saved by the York Archaeological Trust, which painstakingly restored it to its original plans. Inside, the double-height banqueting hall is the highlight but there's also annual exhibitions. From here, head south onto The Shambles, a picture-perfect street of medieval half-timbered houses. The name comes from the Saxon word *shamel*, meaning 'slaughterhouse' – a reference to the fact that in 1862 there were 26 butchers shops on this street.

A little further south, the **Merchant Adventurers' Hall** is York's greatest medieval building, still owned by the same guild who founded it in the 14th century. These entrepreneurial Tudor founders were merchants who made their fortunes by 'adventuring' money in overseas markets at a time when York was an important international port. Today the hall includes a small cafe and exhibits about the guild. In the Great Hall, a forest of timber beams, it's still possible to see signs of when it was used as a hospital between the 14th and 20th centuries.

### BEST LOCAL BITES

**Spark: York**
Local street food, bars and music in a 2-storey shipping-container complex. £

**Mannion & Co**
A York institution, always busy – come for fat sandwiches, Yorkshire rarebits and fancy brunches. £

**Fish & Forest**
Delicate plates of game and seafood with contemporary British creativity. ££

**Star Inn The City**
Plum riverside setting and locally inspired menu from Michelin-starred Yorkshire chef Andrew Pern. ££

**Los Moros**
Shambles street food stall turned contemporary North African restaurant with delicious sharing plates. ££

## Chocolate City

TOURS, TASTINGS AND CONFECTIONARY HERITAGE

Two of the world's biggest confectionary giants were founded in York. Both family businesses, Rowntree's (creator of Kit Kat, Smarties, Rolos, Aero and Quality Street) was established here in 1862, while Terry's (creator of the Chocolate Orange and All Gold – the world's first chocolate box) emerged in 1767. Neither business exists in its original form anymore, but visitors can learn all about their history at **York Chocolate Story**. The attraction is part museum, part interactive experience, covering 4000 years of chocolate history. Old packaging and adverts are among the exhibits, and the tour ends with

### A TASTE OF YORKSHIRE

North of York, the lovely market town of **Malton** (p447) has been dubbed the food capital of Yorkshire. Tasting tours have been developed, and Georgian stables have been converted into an artisanal food court with Yorkshire gelato, macarons, craft gin and the Bluebird Bakery.

**Guy Fawkes Inn**
Bed down with history in the creaking inn where Guy Fawkes was born in 1570. ££

**No 1 by GuestHouse**
Stylish and sophisticated digs with a petite spa, in-house bar and restaurant. £££

**Vices**
Gorgeous, Italian-designed private-house hotel with three suites and personalised tech. £££

## YORK'S BEST PUBS

**Angus McArthur** runs the York Ghost Merchants shop on the Shambles.

When I'm craving a good old pub, I head to the backroom of **The Black Swan**, upstairs in **The Shambles Tavern**, or the famously haunted **Golden Fleece**. Try the **Minster Inn** if you want somewhere quiet. It's a short walk for me through the grounds of the deserted Victorian asylum at Bootham Park. There's always a warm welcome and it's a bit of a haven.

For a great Sunday lunch, I travel to the countryside. The **Dawnay Arms** at Newton-on-Ouse is about 7 miles beyond the city walls. Go for a walk along the river, then inside for the log fire. The food is consistently good.

**York Chocolate Story (p44**

visitors getting to decorate their own lollipop. There's also chocolate-focused on-site cafe.

For a more artisanal experience, head to **York Coco Works**. This independent, contemporary factory brough chocolate-making back inside the medieval city walls in 201 Its focus is on sustainable supply chains, and tours cover pro duction processes as well as tastings by strength and geograph ical regions. It's housed in a glass box, so you can see insid even if you don't want the tour, and there's a shop and cafe

You can also stroll in the 30-acre **Rowntree Park**, create by the family in 1921 as a memorial to its Cocoa Works sta who died in World War Two. Across the road from the south ern end of the park, the Art Deco **Terry's chocolate facto ry** still stands. Both sites are about a 30-minute walk fror the medieval centre, and on the route of the hop-on, hop-o City Sightseeing York bus.

## York Museum Hop

FAMILY-FRIENDLY AND EDUCATIONAL ATTRACTIONS

There are dozens of quality museums in York, many of the with engaging activities for families. A good place to start

### WHERE TO DRINK IN YORK

**Bettys**
Yorkshire's premier tea room has a grand base on St Helen's Sq – prepare to queue.

**Brew York**
Sip wittily named, award-winning craft beers in this brewery's warehouse taproom off Walmgate.

**Guy Fawkes Inn**
Creaking medieval pub, with hidden courtyard out back, is the birthplace of Guy Fawkes (1570).

## HIDDEN YORK: A SNICKETS & GINNELS WALKING TOUR

)iscover a quieter side to York by taking the :ity's small back alleys known in Yorkshire ιs snickets and ginnels. From Bootham Bar, ιead down High Petergate to the **1 Hole n the Wall pub**; in 1816 excavations here ound a hole that led to dungeon with chains .nd manacles. Pop through the unmarked nicket beside the pub for one of the best iews of York Minster, framed by Georgian ιouses.

Backtracking, head down to Stone- ;ate and grab a beer at the **2 House of Trembling Madness**. Opposite this pub, valk through **3 Coffee Yard**. You'll pass , blocked-up doorway elaborately deco- ated with carved Tudor roses (the York- hire rose) before the ginnel opens onto a ourtyard and the entrance to **4 Barley Iall**. Continuing straight down the al- ;yway, glimpse the medieval banqueting :all through glass windows cut into the brick. Beyond that, note the wrought-iron 'Swinegate' gate and its pig design. You'll have to duck to exit the ginnel. Turn slightly right and then head down **5 Finkle St**, which in medieval times was used to drive cows and pigs to Swinegate market. At the end of Finkle St, take the door to the right of the Roman Baths pub down to the **6 Roman Baths Museum** – a subterranean exhibition around excavations of a 3rd-to-4th century Roman military bathhouse.

Follow Church St into Goodramgate and take the inconspicuous gate on the left to 15th-century **7 Holy Trinity Church**, which still has no electricity or running water. Continuing north again on Goodramgate, take the ginnel next to the Mind charity shop, which leads to **8 Bedern Hall** – a medieval refectory that fell off the map in the 19th century when slums took over the area. Pause at its little courtyard cafe.

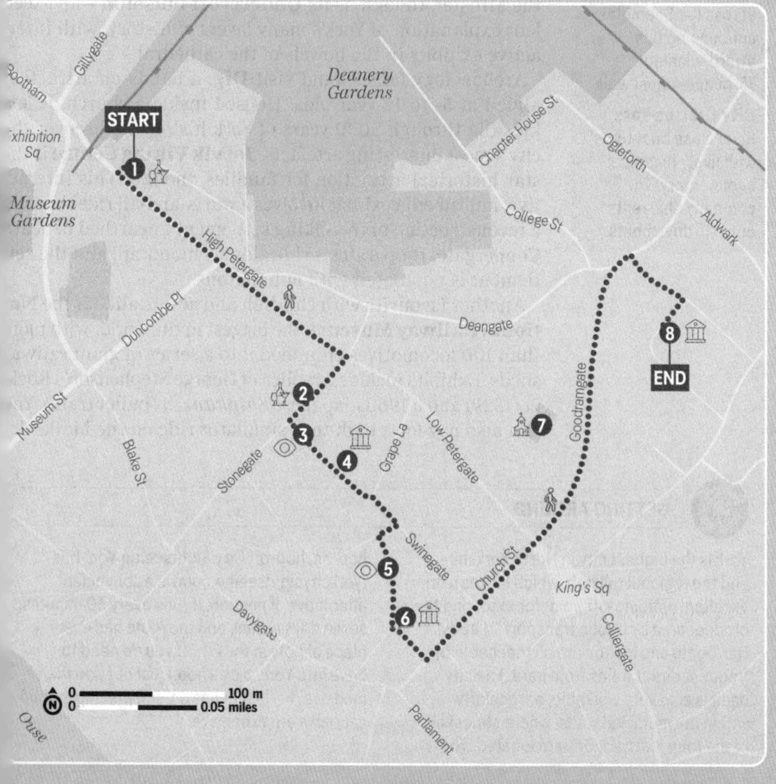

## BEST ACTIVITIES IN YORK

**Brewtown**
Entertaining minivan day tours behind the scenes at some of North Yorkshire's smallest distilleries and breweries.

**Ghost Hunt of York**
Every evening a 'death bell' rings across the Shambles, announcing this award-winning 75-minute ghost walk.

**City Cruises York**
River Ouse boat tours with lively historical commentary. The company also rents out self-drive boats.

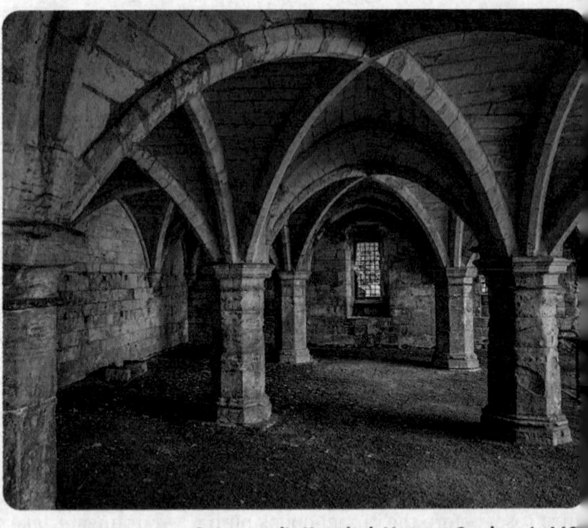

St Leonard's Hospital, Museum Gardens (p440

York Minster, where you can scale the 275 steps up the towe to the highest point in York for unbeatable views. The star o the Minster, though, is its **Undercroft museum** – an excellent explanation of York's many layers of history, with inter active exhibits in the bowels of the cathedral.

Archaeology fans should visit **Dig**, a hands-on attractio aimed at 5- to 12-year-olds. Housed inside a church, it let kids dig through 2000 years of York history to discover th city's most interesting artefacts. **Jorvik Viking Centre** is th star historical attraction for families, though. This interac tive, multimedia exhibit involves a warts-and-all ride throug a reconstruction of the Viking settlement unearthed beneat Coppergate. It operates a ride along a monorail, and the settlement is populated with automatons.

Another favourite with children and adults alike is the **National Railway Museum**, the biggest in the world, with mor than 100 locomotives crammed into a series of giant railwa sheds. Exhibits include a replica of George Stephenson's Rocket (1829) and a 1960s Japanese *Shinkansen* (bullet train). Yo can also pay for a high-tech simulator ride on the Mallard.

## GETTING AROUND

York is the biggest city in North Yorkshire and the regional rail hub, which makes it an excellent jumping-off point for exploring the broader area by public transport – Leeds, Harrogate and Malton are all reachable by frequent direct trains from here. The city itself is also very walkable, particularly within the medieval walls, where almost all of the tourist attractions are located. The hop-on, hop-off City Sightseeing York bus (yorkcitysightseeing.com) is a convenient alternative, if needed. It runs every 30 minutes, seven days a week and the route hits every place of note in the city. If you do need to drive into York, pick a hotel just outside the medieval walls that has on-site parking; public car parks are expensive.

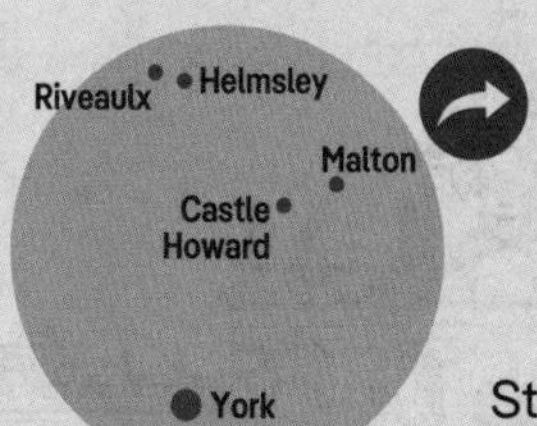


# Beyond York

## Storied ruins, vibrant market towns and one of England's best stately homes frame the road north.

The route between York and the North York Moors National Park is far more than just a stretch of motorway. Ruined abbeys are being reclaimed by nature, and the shells of alluring castles peek from behind smart Georgian houses in the market towns of Helmsley and Pickering. Among the Howardian Hills – designated an Area of Outstanding Natural Beauty (AONB) – and surrounding areas, there lie many treasures. One of the greatest attractions is Castle Howard, the opulent stately home used as a filming location for productions including *Brideshead Revisited* and *Bridgerton*. Food, too, is a highlight of this area, which is home to local butchers and bakers, passionate chefs and makers, and some of the UK's best quality farms.

**TOP TIP**

Book a night at one of the region's atmospheric village gastropubs, which offer dinner and B&B packages.

**North York Moors National Park**

**YORKSHIRE ON SCREEN**

Castle Howard is one of England's most prized on-location film sets, partly thanks to the 1940 fire that gutted some of the rooms, making them perfect canvasses for set designers. In 1981, it became famous for its role as the home of *Brideshead Revisited* in the seminal TV series. Since then, it's featured in dozens of films and TV series including the movie adaptation of *Brideshead Revisited*, *Death comes to Pemberley*, *Victoria* and *Bridgerton*.

Other famous North Yorkshire filming locations you can visit include Goathland and the North York Moors Railway (p465), Whitby (p460), and the walled garden and Duncombe Park estate in Helmsley (p448). The website filmedinyorkshire.co.uk has more information on filming locations across the region.

Castle Howard

## Dramatic Design at Castle Howard

A ROMP THROUGH ARCHITECTURAL ROYALTY

This grande dame of Yorkshire, an hour northeast of York by bus, was the first domestic house in England built with a domed roof, in the style of St Paul's Cathedral in London. Incredibly, with no prior architectural experience, dramatist John Vanbrugh was commissioned to build Castle Howard, working with the much-lauded architect Nicholas Hawksmoor (of St Paul's and Blenheim Palace fame). Today, the **East Wing** of the house is still inhabited by descendants of the original owner, the 3rd Earl of Carlisle.

Construction started in 1699 but the house we see today took more than 100 years to complete. Tours start in the **West Wing**, which was the last part of the house to be completed in the early 1800s by the 3rd Earl's grandson, long after Vanburgh's death. While the West Wing was built in restrained Palladian style, the rest of the house is flamboyantly baroque. The large **antiquities collection** was compiled by the 4th Earl. Other highlights include the **Chapel**, decorated

**BEST COUNTRY GASTROPUBS WITH ROOMS**

**Black Swan at Oldstead**
Country inn vibes, Michelin-starred food – the pride and joy of Yorkshire chef Tommy Banks. £££

**Owl at Hawnby**
Classic British comfort food and house-made charcuterie in a tiny moorland hikers' village. ££

**Hare at Scawton**
Four rooms in a 12th-century village inn with 3 AA Rosette tasting menus. £££

in 1870s Arts and Crafts style, with Burne-Jones stained glass windows; and the **Long Gallery**, still occasionally used for balls and dinners, with its 1770s Rome paintings by Panini.

Castle Howard is built on a natural ridgeline, and the gardens are a rare example of an early **18th-century English estate landscape** – most were destroyed in the late 1800s when the overly manicured landscaping of Capability Brown became the height of fashion.

Take the walk from the East Wing along the temple terrace backed by the **Ray Wood**, to reach the hilltop, colonnaded **Temple of the Four Winds**. Then walk around the **South Lake** for the best view of the giant **Mausoleum**. Walk back via the **Atlas Fountain**. Families should also make a point of visiting the **Skelf Island adventure playground**, beside the Great Lake and its waterside cafe.

## Craft Beer & Local Food in Malton

GRAZING IN YORKSHIRE'S FOOD CAPITAL

It was the legendary late Italian chef Antonio Carluccio who first gave this well-heeled Georgian market town, a half-hour train ride from York, the moniker of 'Yorkshire's food capital', thanks to its high concentration of quality delis, butchers and local producers. The town also has its own craft gin distillery, **Rare Bird**; its own award-winning craft brewery and taphouse, **Brass Castle**; and its own coffee roastery, **Roost**. There's also a cooking school, the **Cook's Place**, offering butchery classes and a cookbook club, and the town even runs its own **food tours** (see visitmalton.com/malton-food-tour for dates).

Start at **Talbot Yard**, a courtyard of 19th-century stables converted into tiny food shops. Try Yorkshire gelato made with local dairy at **Groovy Moo**, and come early for the Bengali five-spice roll at **Bluebird Bakery**. Elsewhere in town, **Malton Relish** is a superior eat-in deli serving treacle tarts, Yorkshire curd tarts, lavish sandwiches and breakfasts. And don't miss **McMillans of Malton**, a specialist whisky shop with a candlelit, three-floor whisky bar, the **Library**, behind a fake wall.

Every second Saturday of the month (March to November), the **Malton Monthly Food Market** is held in its Market Place. And twice a year (late May and August bank holidays) the **Malton Food Lovers Festival** attracts thousands of people, with chef demonstrations and tastings.

### TO HUNT OR NOT TO HUNT?

British hunting traditions remain a key aspect of local life in North Yorkshire, despite huge controversy over some activities. Shooting game birds – grouse, partridge and pheasant – is such a popular pastime on the large country estates that the birds appear in local fashions and homewares decor.

The season runs September to February (depending on the bird), when they're strung up outside butchers and appear on local restaurant menus. Fox-hunting is most controversial, where packs of horseback shooters use dogs to flush out foxes for sport.

Though it's been banned in England since 2005, several Yorkshire towns still hold dog-led, simulated 'trail hunts'. However, activists argue that such activities are sometimes a front for continuing animal-welfare abuses.

### WHERE TO STAY BEYOND YORK

**Pheasant Hotel**
Country chic rooms and 2 AA Rosette food in a handsome village outside Helmsley. £££

**Star Inn at Harome**
Sister hotel/restaurant to the Pheasant, but with a Michelin star and quirkier rooms. £££

**Alice Hawthorn**
Lovely old village pub championing low food miles, with timber-clad, contemporary garden rooms. ££

Helmsley Castle

## Ruins, Parks & Gardens Around Helmsley

GATEWAY TO NORTH YORK MOORS

This handsome market town, 1¼ hours north of York by bus, marks the start of the long-distance **Cleveland Way** hiking trail. The town's premier attraction is the ruin of the 12th-century **Helmsley Castle**, an English Civil War stronghold. Pay to enter and you get a free audio tour. The castle's tumultuous history is explained through an interactive exhibit in the site's mansion house.

Follow a path from the castle car park to find the regenerated 18th-century **Helmsley Walled Garden**. Its greenhouse **Vine Cafe** is one of the nicest spots in town for coffee, cake, or lunch. In Helmsley's **Market Square**, try **Bantam** for bistro-style local-produce plates, or **Hunters of Helmsley** for pork pies, sausage rolls, Scotch eggs, local hams and Wensleydale cheeses. Down the road, there's also a snug little fireside microbrewery taphouse at **Helmsley Brewing Co**.

On the edge of town, **Duncombe Park** encompasses 450 acres of classic country-strolls parkland and the **National Centre for Birds of Prey**, with around 40 aviaries, picnic areas and a tea room.

### A RAMBLE TO RIEVAULX

**Riveaulx** was chosen by Cistercian monks in 1132 as a base for their missionary activities in the north of England. More than a century after the dissolution of the monasteries left it to wrack and ruin, Thomas Dumcombe II built the temple-topped hillside **Riveaulx Terrace** above the abbey for visitors to admire its romantic reclamation by nature.

One of Helmsley's most popular walks is the 3-mile path between Helmsley Castle (look for the Cleveland Way trailhead marker just outside the car park entrance) and Rievaulx Abbey. The path crosses farming fields, dips into the woods of Duncombe Park and then ascends onto a hill with beautiful valley views, before joining the quiet, riverside country road to Riveaulx village.

### GETTING AROUND

Malton is easily accessible from York by direct train (25 minutes). From Station Ave in York, the 31X bus runs to Helmsley (1¼ hours), and the Castleline bus runs to Castle Howard (1 hour) before terminating at Malton.

# YORKSHIRE DALES NATIONAL PARK

Want to see rural England at its most bewitching? Come to the Dales, where glacial valleys tumble into babbling brooks and sheep outnumber people. Although less dramatic than the peaks and fells of the Lake District, the park's undulating humps are no less beautiful – and the remote country pubs are a delight. The national park stretches for 841 sq miles and although popular with hikers, cyclists and potholers, several of the Dales still feel little explored. The park's busiest areas are the limestone cove at Malham, in the south of the park; and the village of Hawes, where the Wensleydale Creamery is based, in the park's centre. But you could easily spend weeks here, pootling about on waterfalls trails, climbing to windswept hill plateaus, scrambling through castle and abbey ruins, or simply drinking pints of ale in beer gardens with spectacular views.

## TOP TIP

The Yorkshire Dales are popular with holidaying Britons and there are few large-scale accommodation options, which means beds can be scarce – especially in summer and over public holidays. There are some excellent small rural B&Bs, pretty glamping sites and family-run inns here, but most need to be booked well in advance.

Sheep on road to Tan Hill Inn (p450)

## YORKSHIRE DALES NATIONAL PARK

Richmond
Grinton
Reeth
Thwaite
Muker
Eden
Swaledale
Buttertubs Pass
Garsdale Head
Askrigg
Wensleydale
Wensley
Leyburn
Ure
Hawes
2
Dentdale
15
11
Raydale
Aysgarth
Middleham
Gawthrop
Cowgill
West Burton
7
Ellingstring
NORTH YORKSHIRE
Bishopdale
Coverdale
Leighton Reservoir
12
Ribblehead
Langstrothdale
10
17
Great Whernside (705m)
Buckden
Angram Reservoir
Roundhill Reservoir
Stean
Ribblesdale
Littondale
5
Ingleton
9
Kettlewell
3
Horton-in-Ribblesdale
Arncliffe
Wharfedale
13
8
Pateley Bridge
Stainforth
Greenhow Hill
16
14
1
Grassington
Nidd
Malham Cove
4
Settle
Malham
6
Malhamdale
Burnsall
Appletreewick
Long Preston
Barden Reservoirs
0 10 km
0 5 miles
Gargrave
Bolton Abbey

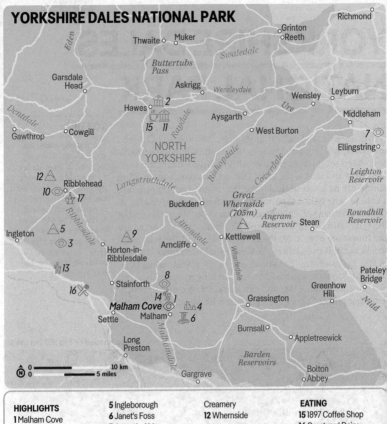

**HIGHLIGHTS**
**1** Malham Cove

**SIGHTS**
**2** Dales Countryside Museum
**3** Gaping Gill
**4** Gordale Scar
**5** Ingleborough
**6** Janet's Foss
**7** Jervaulx Abbey
**8** Malham Tarn
**9** Pen-y-ghent
**10** Ribblehead Viaduct
**11** Wensleydale Creamery
**12** Whernside

**ACTIVITIES & TOURS**
**13** Ingleborough Estate Nature Trail
**14** Malham Landscape Trail

**EATING**
**15** 1897 Coffee Shop
**16** Courtyard Dairy

**DRINKING**
**17** Station Inn

# Malham Cove & the Landscape Trail

ONE OF ENGLAND'S BEST HIKES

Whernside (p453)

Despite the slightly misleading name, Malham Cove is actually an 80m-high vertical limestone cliff, formed by a huge glacial waterfall that gushed only briefly some 12,000 years ago. Today, the 0.75-mile amble through fields from the village centre to the cliff is one of Yorkshire's most popular short walks. The Royal Society for the Protection of Birds (RSPB) sets up a birdwatching lookout at the base of the cliff in spring/summer to spot the peregrine falcons that nest in the cliff's nooks.

Many visitors take the stairs on the left-hand side of the cliff up to the vast limestone plateau above it, which

Malham Cove

has spectacular views and was a filming location in *Harry Potter and the Deathly Hallows*. However, only a fraction of hikers take on the 4.5 mile, circular **Malham Landscape Trail**, undoubtedly one of the best day hikes in England. From the top of the cove, the trail heads east to **Gordale Scar**, a narrow canyon with cascades and the remains of an Iron Age settlement. Walkers must then retrace their steps to head south to **Janet's Foss** waterfall, popular with wild swimmers, and back into Malham village.

Extending the trail to loop around the boardwalks of marshy **Malham Tarn** – an internationally important nature reserve, accessible on foot from Malham Cove – bumps the trail up to an 11-mile hike. Visit malhamdale.com for trail maps and further information.

### GRASSINGTON & THE DALES WAY

The Dales Way is a quiet, 80-mile hiking path from Ilkley on the southern edge of the Dales to Bowness-on-Windermere in the Lake District (p460). The section around Grassington is particularly pretty, and the market town itself featured in a recent adaptation of *All Creatures Great & Small*; its heritage streets transformed into Darrowby, the setting for James Herriot's rural veterinary tales.

Following the river south, the route passes **Burnsall**, a lovely stone village where picnickers launch dinghies and kayaks in summer. Beyond is the beautiful village of **Appletreewick**, home to the excellent Masons Campsite. About 6 miles south is **Bolton Abbey estate**, with stepping stones, a river beach and glorious walking trails framed by ruins.

## Farmhouse Cheese & the Wensleydale Trail

WALLACE & GROMIT'S FAVOURITE

What might French monks have to do with Yorkshire cheese, you ask? The answer can be found at **Jervaulx Abbey**, where Cistercian monks settled in 1156 CE. It was these monks – from

### RURAL STAYS IN THE DALES

**YHA Grinton Lodge**
Incredible views at this converted lodge, now a hostel with dorms, camping and glamping pods. £

**Low Mill Guest House**
Award-winning three-room rural B&B inside a sympathetically converted 18th-century riverside mill. ££

**Lister Barn**
Barn conversion of eight rooms with a communal living space, boot room and outdoor patio. ££

## TAN HILL INN & THE ROAD TO NOWHERE

The northeastern Dales above Reeth is a pocket of the park that's abjectly beautiful and almost completely devoid of people. Yet here in the midst of the fog-shrouded plains, a 45-minute drive from the nearest town, lies the lonely **Tan Hill Inn** – Britain's highest pub (with an elevation of 528m). Built to service the miners' community of which there is now no trace, the pub today is a surprisingly hopping live-music destination at weekends, attracting motley crews of hikers, beer-swilling musicians and good-time seekers who bunker down together while the wind howls outside. There's eight en-suite bedrooms, a bunkhouse, a summer camping space and a large car park popular with overnighting camper vans.

Tan Hill Inn

Roquefort – who brought the original recipe for Wensleydale cheese to England, according to historical records. Today, the privately owned abbey is an enchanting ruin (admission at the time of writing was by honesty-box donation).

The Wensleydale cheese that exists today – now globally renowned because of the cheese-obsessed character in Aardman animations' *Wallace & Gromit* productions – is largely still around thanks to the **Wensleydale Creamery**, now a cheese-making museum with live demonstrations, *Wallace and Gromit* photo ops, cheese tastings and a popular cheese-themed cafe in the lively little village of Hawes. Visit Monday to Friday and you can see the cheesemakers sifting the curds and whey through a glass viewing wall in the factory. In the **1897 Coffee Shop** (named after the year the creamery was founded), order the Wensleydale tea special, which comes with a wedge of fruit cake with Wensleydale cheese – a Yorkshire tradition.

Before leaving Hawes, drop by the **Dales Countryside Museum**, which takes a journey through the area's social history, including dairy farming, lead mining and the rise of the railways.

## PLACES FOR CYCLISTS IN THE DALES

**Dales Bike Centre**
Bike rentals (including e-bikes), plus a repair shop, cafe and bike-friendly accommodation in Fremington.

**Swale Trail**
Beautiful 12-mile, mountain-biking valley path from Reeth to Keld, suitable for families.

**Buttertubs Pass**
Running from Hawes to Thwaite, a popular cycling challenge, featured in the Tour de France.

Travelling further west across the Dales, visit the **Courtyard Dairy** near Settle, one of England's most-awarded cheese shops. Visitors can see inside the cheese maturing room, before tasting and buying local artisan cheeses at the deli. Or book ahead for cheesemaking classes.

## Daredevil Thrills around Yorkshire's Three Peaks

CAVING AND HIKING IN RIBBLESDALE

The national park's southwestern skyline is dominated by a triangle of distinctive hills known as the **Three Peaks**: **Pen-y-ghent** (694m), **Whernside** (735m) and **Ingleborough** (724m). Easily accessible via the Settle–Carlisle railway line, this is one of England's most popular areas for outdoor activities, attracting thousands of hikers, cyclists and cavers each weekend. The Pennine Way runs through here, but one of the biggest draws is the self-contained, 24-mile **Yorkshire Three Peaks Challenge** (threepeakschallenge.uk), which involves tackling all three peaks in under 12 hours (an ascent of 1585m).

The Settle–Carlisle line is also famous for the spectacular 30m-high **Ribblehead Viaduct**, a 10-minute walk from remote Ribblehead station. Completed in 1875, it spans 400m with 24 arches, and can be seen for miles. A wood-beamed pub with rooms' **Station Inn** is a prime spot for taking it in, with a beer garden looking onto it.

Some 10 miles south of Ribblehead, the **Ingleborough Estate Nature Trail** leads to a show cave (open year-round) and **Gaping Gill**, one of Britain's largest subterranean chambers. The latter is opened to the public twice a year (in late May and August) during Winch Meets run by Yorkshire potholing clubs. Daredevils are airlifted down the almost 100m-deep shaft to the chamber floor for a fee.

### BEST WATERFALL WANDERS

**Hardraw Force**
An easy 0.5-mile woodland walk (£4 entry) leads to England's highest single-drop waterfall.

**Aysgarth Falls**
This low, triple-tiered waterfall on the River Ure has multiple free viewing points.

**Ingleton Waterfalls Trail**
Five waterfalls, including the 14m-drop Thornton Force, along this spectacular 4.5-mile circular trail (£8 entry).

**Pen-y-ghent**

### GETTING AROUND

To get to the quietest places in the Dales, you'll need a car. Beware, though, that many of the national park's asphalt roads follow old farming tracks and in places they remain single track. Although the narrow lanes are fairly quiet, tractors, oncoming traffic, flocks of sheep and even occasional river crossings can pose significant hazards for nervous drivers: be careful. Those without a car can access some of the more remote areas (such as Ribblehead Viaduct) using the Leeds–Settle–Carlisle railway line. There's also a local bus network (see dalesbus.org), with extra services running on Sundays and bank holidays between mid April and mid October.

# Beyond Yorkshire Dales National Park

Masham
Yorkshire Dales National Park
Ripon
Nidderdale
Knaresborou
Harrogate

## Some of Yorkshire's best attractions lie between its two national parks. Take time to delve into the nooks and crannies.

The sliver of Yorkshire that runs between the Yorkshire Dales National Park and the North York Moors National Park is packed with regional highlights. On the eastern edge of the Dales, there's Nidderdale – classified as an Area of Outstanding Natural Beauty and a continuation of the rolling hills, stone villages, cave systems and skinny, sheep-filled lanes that characterise the Dales National Park. Beyond, visitors will find a succession of thriving Georgian market towns – Masham, Knaresborough, Ripon and Thirsk, to name a few – along with heritage breweries, vast country estates and Unesco-listed Studley Royal and Fountains Abbey. The biggest town is Harrogate, a genteel spa centre; its illustrious fans once included Agatha Christie and Queen Victoria.

**TOP TIP**

If you don't want to base yourself deep in the Dales, Masham is a good compromise between town and country.

**Fountains Abbey (p458**

Turkish Baths (p456)

## Taking the Waters in Harrogate

SPA QUEEN OF THE NORTH

For centuries, Harrogate (a 45-minute drive east from Grassington in the Yorkshire Dales National Park) has been synonymous with spa culture in the north of England. Natural thermal spring waters, laced with a therapeutic cocktail of minerals, were first discovered bubbling out of the ground here by William Slingsby in 1571. Within 100 years, the town developed a reputation for its medicinal waters, which were marketed as a cure for everything from digestive ailments to skin disease. Harrogate's latest boom trade is conferences, but the Georgian spa movement still defines the town, and its heritage draws thousands of visitors a year.

The 1841 octagonal **Royal Pump Room**, built to cover the Old Sulphur Well, is now an excellent small museum (Harrogate's only museum) dedicated to the town's spa and wellness industry, which flourished right up until the creation of the National Health Service (NHS), after World War Two saw the introduction of free healthcare. Exhibits include fascinating photos of visitors undertaking hydrotherapy

### TEA TIME AT BETTYS

Founded in 1919 by Swiss expat Frederick Belmont, it may look a little prim inside, but people queue around the block for a table in Harrogate's original **Bettys Tearoom** (there's several across Yorkshire; York's is busiest) because they know its cakes – and friendly service – are the best. Resist the temptation to order the afternoon tea and go DIY to create a plate of Bettys' signature bakes: fondant fancies; the Yorkshire curd tart (curd cheese, currants, nutmeg and a touch of lemon curd); and the Fat Rascal (an all-butter fruit scone with glacé cherries and almonds). The lunch menu is also a cracker, serving Yorkshire produce on dainty Wedgwood china.

### BEST PLACES TO STAY IN HARROGATE

**Lawrance**
Central and contemporary serviced apartments across three heritage buildings – perfect for families. **£**

**White Hart**
Classic hotel with smart rooms and a stylish pub, on the edge of Montpellier Quarter. **££**

**Rudding Park**
Award-winning spa-and-stay packages on a leafy country estate, 15 minutes' drive from central Harrogate. **£££**

### FORBIDDEN CORNER'S DARK THRILLS

Forbidden Corner is a modern walled garden furnished with Victorian-style follies, some veering into Gothic horror, others merely surreal fantasy. There's no map for this alternative mini theme park, five miles south of Leyburn on the eastern edge of Nidderdale, so it's a case of diving in to explore the many tunnels, twisted turns and dead ends – an experience that may make you feel like you've fallen into David Bowie's *Labyrinth*. It's popular with families, even though small children are guaranteed to feel scared witless at some turns; adults may leave feeling a little rattled, too. Tickets must be prebooked.

**Valley Gardens**

treatments, including peat baths, sulphur baths and aix douche massage. You can smell the potent, sulphuric waters at the museum but not try it. For that, you need to take a stroll around the circular pump house to the wall opposite Hales Bar, which still has a public tap. Note, though, that the council now deems it unsafe to drink.

Across the road from the museum, head into **Valley Gardens.** Of the 85 springs and wells within a two-mile radius of the Royal Pump Room, 35 are in this area, which the Victorians converted into a landscaped pleasure park for spa visitors in the 1850s. The concentration of the springs is in the central area once known as **Bog's Field**; many are labelled and still have their own small pump rooms or protective covers. Another renowned strolling space in Harrogate is the **Stray**, a 200-acre area of open grassland that's been preserved for the people of Harrogate ever since Slingsby first discovered Tewit Well here.

If you do one thing in Harrogate, make it a trip to the town's **Turkish Baths**, which is the only original spa still in operation. Built in 1897 at a cost of £10 million in today's money, it follows the design principles of a hammam, with

### BEST PLACES TO EAT IN HARROGATE

**Major Tom's Social**
Pleasingly grungy beer bar whipping up delicious slabs of pizza alongside local craft drinks. **£**

**Three's a Crowd**
Neighbourhood gastropub serving imaginatively designed British dishes, with a beer garden out back. **££**

**Drum & Monkey**
Popular seafood institution serving British lobsters, Nidderdale trout and oysters with Champagne. **£££**

a series of rooms that get gradually hotter. The decor is an exquisite profusion of arabesque arches, painted screens and mosaic terrazzo, which was sensitively restored in the 1990s to return the baths to their former glory. The baths offer guided history tours most Wednesdays, and both these and the three-hour spa sessions and treatments should be booked ahead.

## Caves & Gorge Scrambling Around Nidderdale

ADVENTURES IN NATURE

The Yorkshire Dales National Park and Nidderdale AONB combined offer one of the UK's greatest adventure playgrounds. While the west of the Dales is home to Gaping Gill and Ingleborough Cave, the east lays claim to another series of cave systems, gorges and geological oddities that have been formed over millions of years. All are within an hour's drive of the Yorkshire Dales National Park borders.

**Stump Cross Caverns** was discovered in 1860 by lead miners who opened up the caves for guided tours. This is very much a show cave aimed at families, with geology information boards, fairy doors, fossil quizzes and UV illuminations after 3pm. Above ground, there's a cafe and families can take part in gem dig sessions and meet the resident cavewoman. The underground afternoon tea is unique.

In upper Nidderdale, **How Stean Gorge** is a remote adventure centre built around a spectacular hidden canyon dripping with moss and ferns. There's a camping field and wooden lodges with wood-fired hot tubs. Both are in walking distance of the gorge's walkways and entry-level caves, suitable for children of all ages. The site also offers via ferrata climbing, kayaking at a nearby reservoir, and gorge scrambling, which involves slithering over the boulder-strewn riverbed at the base of the gorge, jumping into pools.

In Knaresborough, there's also **Mother Shipton's Cave**, a curious attraction named after a prophetess who was (supposedly) born in this cave on the banks of the River Nidd in 1488. The premise is a bit gimmicky, but the surrounding park is a lush riverside beauty with pathways and boardwalks through ancient royal woodlands. The cave itself features a natural petrifying well, where the waters (rich in calcium carbonate and calcium sulfate) magically turn objects to stone.

**SWINTON PARK: BIKING, GLAMPING & DRUIDS**

Less than two miles from Masham, Swinton Park is a beautiful 20,000-acre estate. Owned by the same family since the 1880s, the estate centrepiece is a turreted, Grade-II-listed luxury **castle hotel** with an excellent **spa**, two **restaurants**, a **cookery school**, on-site **cottage rentals**, and gardens with a **wild swimming lake**.

But the sustainably minded owners also operate **Swinton Bivouac**, a scattering of low-impact **glamping yurts** and **off-grid tree lodges** lit by candlelight at night, which makes the park affordable for all. There are **mountain-biking trails** from the bivouac barn cafe, which offers bike rentals (book ahead) and trail maps. The icing on the cake is a woodland **druid's temple**, built in the 19th century as a Victorian folly.

**BEST GLAMPING & HUTS**

**Swinton Bivouac**
Mongolian yurts with wood-burning stoves and woodland tree lodges on a beautiful country estate. ££

**House & Huts at Jervaulx**
Two large en-suite shepherds huts, one with stargazing roof, on the grounds of Jervaulx Abbey. £

**Yurtshire**
Kid-friendly meadow yurts one mile from Fountains Abbey; second luxury site and wellness spa nearby. £££

## A Tour of Yorkshire's Beer Heartland

HERITAGE TAPROOMS AND BREWERY TOURS

The cobbled streets of Masham on the eastern edge of the Dales, a 45-minute drive east of Hawes, have been permeated with the aromas of hops and malts for almost two centuries. The fact that there are two giant brewing companies in this one tiny town is down to a family feud. **Theakston Brewery** was founded here in 1827 and is still run by a descendent of the founder, Robert Theakston. Guided tours take visitors through the traditional, 4-storey brewing system, which still uses some of the original 19th-century equipment. Head five minutes down the road to **Black Sheep Brewery** and the guided tours there will show a more modern process, but also include an explanation of why Paul Theakston – the 'black sheep' of the family – ended up leaving Theakstons in 1992 to establish his own brewery. Book ahead for either tour.

Today, Theakstons most famous ale is still Old Peculier, which can be ordered on tap at the old stone **Black Bull in Paradise** bar, at the heart of the brewery. Black Sheep has a more contemporary bar and shop area, which also includes a **beer-themed restaurant**, in a lofty barn conversion. Alongside traditional ales, it produces rotating small-batch craft beers and a carbon-neutral session IPA called Respire.

## Rambles Through Fountains Abbey & Studley Royal

IN THE FOOTSTEPS OF MONKS

No matter what the weather, the riverside ruins of F**ountains Abbey**, an hour's drive east of Grassington in the national park, and the water gardens of **Studley Royal estate** that now surround them are utterly captivating. Now run by the National Trust, the complex is one of Yorkshire's two Unesco World Heritage Sites. Tours of the abbey and gardens run on weekends (free with admission ticket), and there are several different **walking trails** ranging from 2.5 miles to 8 miles. The grounds are vast and packed with treasures, including temple follies, a medieval flour mill, **St Mary's Church** and a **deer park**.

The abbey was established by a band of rebel Benedictine monks in 1132 and quickly adopted by the Cistercians, growing to become the most successful Cistercian venture

### A POTTED HISTORY OF RICHMOND

Some 40 miles north of Harrogate, sleepy Richmond was once one of the most important cities in England. Its first lord was Alan Rufus in 1086, cousin to William the Conquerer, who bequeathed Rufus a vast estate of 250,000 acres and built him a castle to control the north. The estate's income made Rufus one of the richest men to have ever lived in Britain. After many power shifts, **Richmond Castle** was eventually abandoned in the 16th century, then taken over by militia in the 1850s. Richmond remains a military town – the castle played an important role in WWI, when it became a prison for conscientious objectors. Tour the 1788 **Georgian Theatre Royal**, considered Britain's most complete Georgian playhouse.

### CHARMING FOOD STOPS

**Boar's Head**
Inn with rooms at the heart of beautiful Ripley village – order the local ploughman's lunch. ££

**Saddle Room**
Pub classics and warm service in a former racehorse stables next door to Forbidden Corner. ££

**Grantley Hall**
Opulent country house hotel with Michelin-starred Shaun Rankin restaurant, afternoon teas and bistro dining. £££

Fountains Abbey

in the country by the middle of the 13th century. Their story is told inside the **Porter's Lodge**, which hosts an intricate model of the abbey in its prime and an exhibition about its inhabitants' lives. The remains of the abbey itself, with a huge vaulted cellarium and Romanesque cloister, are especially picturesque because of their riverside valley setting.

Whereas the abbey ruins have great gravitas, the series of temple-fronted pools, cascades and bridges that constitute the **Studley Royal gardens** to their west are pure frivolity and fun.

There are large car parks at Fountains Abbey, as well as a year-round bus (no 139; 15 mins) from Ripon on Mondays, Thursdays and Saturdays.

## BEST GIN EXPERIENCES

**Harrogate Tipple**
Pick botanicals from Ripley Castle's gardens and make gin inside the castle walls using Harrogate springwater.

**Cooper King Distillery**
Taste England's first carbon-negative gin on a tour of the region's most sustainable distillery.

**Spirit of Masham**
Visit Corks & Cases wine store in Masham to taste Yorkshire rhubarb or chai gin.

**Spirit of Harrogate**
Sample developmental gins and gin liqueurs at this Montpellier Quarter shop, home of Slingsby gin.

## GETTING AROUND

There are a number of irregular or infrequent bus services (see dalesbus.org) travelling around the eastern Dales and to some of the market towns. Harrogate, Knaresborough, Thirsk and Northallerton also all have train stations, but none are connected directly to stations in the Yorkshire Dales. Instead, they run through York or Leeds, which means piecing together an extended trip through this area via public transport is hard work. Hiring a car is by far the easiest way to make the most of your time if you want to visit a handful of places.

Whitby

London

# WHITBY

Sea-lashed graves, ghoulish legends and the headland carcass of a giant abbey – there's no doubt Whitby has the bones of a good horror story. At least, that's how novelist Bram Stoker must have felt when his visits to this coastal fishing town inspired him to write *Dracula* in 1897. Ever since, Whitby has played up its alternative associations and today it's undoubtedly the Gothic capital of the UK. But this seafaring town is also where Captain Cook was apprenticed and later returned to build his expedition ships before circumnavigating Australia and New Zealand in the 18th century. Huddles of salt-bitten fisher cottages frame the cliffs on either side of the harbour, from where fishing trawlers, pleasure boats and rowers make daily pilgrimages out to sea. It's also a favourite with holidaying Brits, especially families, who come for the fish and chips, old-fashioned amusement arcades and the huge, sandy Blue Flag beach below West Cliff.

## TOP TIP

Getting cars in and out of Whitby's centre can be a nightmare. Most cottage rentals come with parking permits but spaces are har to come by. However, the North Yorkshire coast has one of the region's best bu networks – this is one area that's possible to travel around without a car.

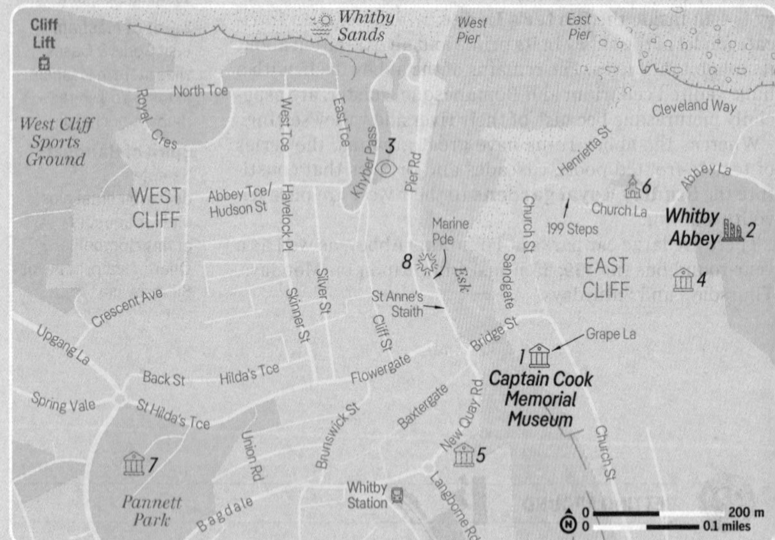


**HIGHLIGHTS**
**1** Captain Cook Memorial Museum
**2** Whitby Abbey

**SIGHTS**
**3** Bram Stoker Memorial Seat
**4** Chomley House
**5** Endeavour Experience Whitby
**6** St Mary's Church
**7** Whitby Museum

**ENTERTAINMENT**
**8** Dracula Experience

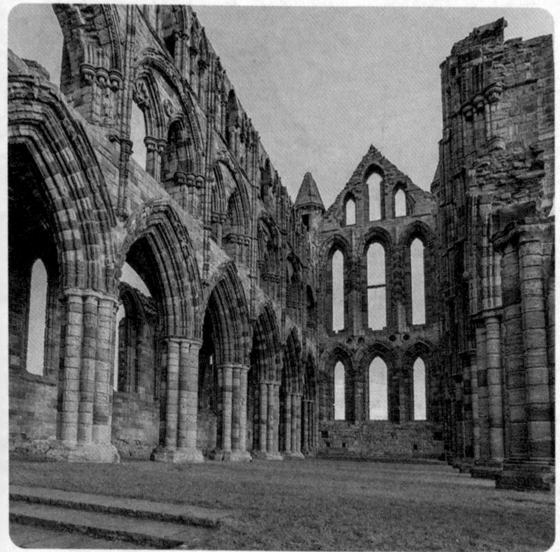

Whitby Abbey

### WHY I LOVE WHITBY

**Lorna Parkes**, Lonely Planet writer

Having visited the town for years with my Yorkshire family, Whitby has come to feel like a second home. I've always been drawn to myths and legends, and this historical harbour town has been peddling them convincingly for thousands of years.

There's an aura of magic here, and anything goes. Goths and steampunk fans can promenade around the harbour dressed in full cosplay finery and nobody bats an eyelid. My perfect day involves Magpie's fish and chips, rummaging through Whitby's vintage stores and bookshops, and watching sandcastles get washed away by the tides with my kids.

## Goths, Ghouls & Dracula: An Offbeat Pilgrimage

FINDING WHITBY'S DARK SIDE

Tales of witchery and ghostly folklore have dogged Whitby ever since Anglo-Saxon St Hilda landed here to found a monastic community in 657 CE. Any tour of the town should start with Hilda's home, **Whitby Abbey**, the haunting ruin that can be seen for miles on the headland of East Cliff. Next to the abbey is **Cholmley House**, a mansion built with some of the abbey stone in the 16th century after the land was sold off following the dissolution of the monasteries. Inside, there's an excellent museum about the headland and the people who have lived here for 3000 years.

Both the abbey and neighbouring **St Mary's Church** feature as Count Dracula haunts in Bram Stoker's 1897 novel, which has made the area a pilgrimage site for Goths, who come to tour the graveyard and have their photos taken here. The oldest parts of the church date to the 12th century, and inside the pews and boxes are all misaligned and skewed. Look for

### BEST PLACES TO STAY

**La Rosa**
Gothic-inspired hotel with lavish rooms decorated with old film props, and a music-filled cocktail lounge. ££

**Marine Hotel**
Centrally located, two of the three harbour-view rooms at this seafood-restaurant-with-rooms have balconies. £££

**Bagdale Hall**
Tudor mansion with six rooms (10 more in neighbouring house), quiet bar and ghost legends. £££

## BEST WATER ACTIVITIES

**Yorkshire Coast Nature**
Responsible operator running whale-watching, bird-spotting and wildlife photography tours along the coastline.

**Mackerel fishing trips**
Run by local fishers from Whitby harbour – check boards around Endeavour Experience (New Quay Rd) for times.

**Whitby Surf School**
Take a lesson (April–September), try stand-up paddleboarding or rent gear by the beach huts on Whitby Beach.

**Bark Endeavour Whitby**
Twenty-minute, pirate-themed harbour tour on a smaller replica of Cook's *HM Bark Endeavour* (embark at Fish Quay, Pier Rd).

Replica of HM Bark *Endeavour*

the sign on the door informing vampire hunters that Dracula is not, in fact, buried here. Before or after your trip to the top of the headland, be sure to take the **199 steps** to/from Church St – a rite of passage for Whitby visitors.

Locals called East Cliff's headland 'the hill of the dead' long before the Irish novelist set foot in town, because of the ghostly Barguest coach – a funeral wagon pulled by headless horses, that visits the graves of sailors. Whitby's most famous apparition, along with many others, can be explored on excellent **ghost tours**. There's one on either cliff side, but Dr Crank's 7.30pm tours (no booking required) from the whalebone arches on West Cliff are particularly good. He also runs a tour specifically centred around *Dracula*; check whitbywalks .com for dates of both.

One of Whitby's more macabre attractions is the **hand of glory** – a mummified human hand purportedly cut from a hanged man and used by local witches to ward off discovery in the 19th century. It now resides in **Whitby Museum**, along with other town relics, including locally found fossils.

Above the Kyber Pass is the hotel where Bram Stoker lodged during his holidays in Whitby. Across the road, look for the

## BEST SEAFOOD EXPERIENCES

**Fisherman's Wife**
No-bookings, 1950s restaurant that sources locally and has amazing sea views, plus a casual takeaway hatch/patio. **££**

**Magpie Cafe**
Takeaway fish and chips, and a superior fish restaurant (book ahead or prepare to queue). **££**

**White Horse & Griffin**
Modern British dishes are the focus at this underrated, old pub restaurant on East Cliff. **££**

battered bench furthest away from the whalebone arches, now known as **Bram Stoker Memorial Seat**. This is where the author sat to contemplate the ruins across the harbour, and the bench usually receives a steady stream of pilgrims (and flowers) around Halloween. Below Kyber Pass, on Marine Pde, hardcore fans (or scare seekers) can do the **Dracula Experience**, a deliberately kitsch, theatrical tour with special effects and live actors.

## In the Footsteps of Captain Cook

WHITBY'S SEAFARING HERITAGE

In the 17th and 18th centuries, Whitby's harbour was thronged with shipbuilding yards and the town was considered an important training hub for sailors, thanks to its position along a particularly treacherous stretch of the North Sea coastline. In 1746, this led to the arrival of Whitby's most famous inhabitant, James Cook, who was apprenticed here for nine years and later returned to build his Pacific voyage ships in Whitby's dockyards. The house where he lived is now the excellent Captain Cook Memorial Museum, with highlights including the attic where he lodged, Cook's own maps and letters, and etchings from his South Sea voyages.

Captain Cook's most famous ship – the HM Bark *Endeavour*, in which he completed his first voyage – has been reconstructed as a full-size replica and permanently moored in Whitby Harbour since 2018. Inside, the **Endeavour Experience** is a family friendly museum about Cook's 1768 voyage, including a sandpit, star navigation room, botanical art displays and audio effects with letter readings and cannon fire. The **Orlop Deck** is a lunch restaurant, and the upper deck has been turned into an alfresco bar area.

The **whalebone arch** (now a replica) above Khyber Pass is a small acknowledgement of the town's past as an 18th-century whaling centre. Whitby's most prolific whaler was William Scoresby, also an Arctic explorer, who is remembered in history as the inventor of the ship crow's nest. There's a blue plaque outside his former home on Bagdale.

### BEST DRINKING SPOTS

**Whitby Brewery**
Craft brewery with courtyard beer garden in the shadow of the abbey; summer live-music gigs.

**Green Dragon**
Tiny independent beer bar attached to a bottle shop inside a Georgian cottage.

**Duke of York**
Snag a harbour-view table in this cosy waterside pub, relax with comfort food and pints.

**Rusty Shears**
Vintage daytime coffee shop and gin parlour, serving cakes, lunches and Whitby's best breakfasts.

### GETTING AROUND

Whitby is small enough to explore on foot, but there's also a hop-on, hop-off bus (coastalandcountry.co.uk) that travels between the East and West Cliffs. Parking is difficult in Whitby; if arriving by car, park up and try to use the local bus services to explore further afield.

Saltburn-by-the-Sea
Staithes
Runswick Bay
Sandsend
Whitby
Boggle Hole
Beck Hole
Goathland
Mallyan Spout

# Beyond Whitby

## A string of photogenic coastal villages unfurl around Whitby, while the North York Moors harbour quiet country paths and pubs.

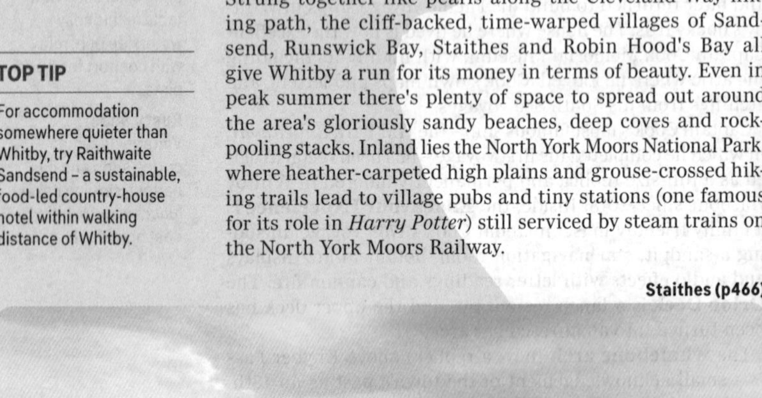

Incredibly pretty and incredibly popular, the coastline around Whitby is one of Yorkshire's most charming assets. Strung together like pearls along the Cleveland Way hiking path, the cliff-backed, time-warped villages of Sandsend, Runswick Bay, Staithes and Robin Hood's Bay all give Whitby a run for its money in terms of beauty. Even in peak summer there's plenty of space to spread out around the area's gloriously sandy beaches, deep coves and rock-pooling stacks. Inland lies the North York Moors National Park, where heather-carpeted high plains and grouse-crossed hiking trails lead to village pubs and tiny stations (one famous for its role in *Harry Potter*) still serviced by steam trains on the North York Moors Railway.

**TOP TIP**

For accommodation somewhere quieter than Whitby, try Raithwaite Sandsend – a sustainable, food-led country-house hotel within walking distance of Whitby.

**Staithes (p466)**

North York Moors Railway

## Day Trip to Goathland

A FOOD-FUELLED WATERFALL HIKE

The fact that some of the shops and tea rooms in Goathland, a 20-minute drive southwest of Whitby, still trade on its starring role in the British TV drama *Heartbeat* is a little weird for anybody unfamiliar with the hit 1990s show. Plenty of tourists still come to see Goathland as Aidensfield, but there are other reasons why this tiny moorland village deserves your time. **Goathland Station**, one of the stops on the North York Moors Railway, played Hogsmeade Station in the first three *Harry Potter* films. And in 2021 the village welcomed its first fine-dining restaurant, **Homestead**, serving North York Moors produce inside an 18th-century farmhouse.

Next door to the restaurant, there's a signposted path leading downhill to **Mallyan Spout**, a stuttering waterfall of sorts that helped put Goathland on the map for 19th-century tourists. The spout itself is not very impressive, but the **circular 3-mile walk** that starts here is a lovely amble. Heading north alongside the river, the wooded valley path leads

### RIDING THE RAILS

The 18-mile, volunteer-run North York Moors Railway (NYMR) is one of Yorkshire's most spectacular journeys – not least because it runs lovingly restored steam locomotives and vintage carriages. Services run daily between the end of March and beginning of November, but the standard ticket only allows travel from Whitby to Pickering, which has a well-preserved 1930s station. In between that, there's Grosmont (home to the NYMR engine shed), Goathland, Newtondale Halt and Levisham stations – all wonderfully remote and perfect jumping-off points for moorland walks. Ask specifically for a ticket that's valid on the hop-on, hop-off Moors Explorer trains. You can also book overnight stays in camping coaches at Levisham and Goathland (see nymr.co.uk).

### WHERE TO EAT & DRINK

**Cove**
The old chapel in Robin Hood's Bay houses this kid-friendly cafe with secret sea-view terrace. £

**Betsy & Bo**
Order fruit cake and Wensleydale cheese with Baytown coffee at this vintage Staithes deli cafe. £

**Fish Cottage**
Fresh, contemporary seafood dishes such as crab fritters and cod burgers, served in Sandsend. ££

to the beautiful village of **Beck Hole**. Stop for a pint at the unique **Birch Hall Inn**, a tiny retro pub with an open fire and 1970s wallpaper, and beers served through a hatch in the wall. The path continues back to Goathland through farms and orchards, following the track bed of the original Whitby–Pickering railway. Make a detour along the hilly path from Birch Hall Inn to the lesser-visited **Thomason Foss** – a much more impressive waterfall with a swimmable pool. It's around an extra mile to walk there and back.

**SCARBOROUGH FOR KIDS**

Holidaymakers have been coming to Scarborough, 20 miles south of Whitby, since the early 17th century, making it one of Britain's first seaside resorts. Today it's well past its prime and the centre feels quite run down, but it's still got two huge beaches separated by a headland castle ruin and a number of attractions for kids.

**Peasholm Park**, a Japanese-styled early 20th-century pleasure park, has cascades, dragon boat pedaloes and a famous naval warfare production on its lake each summer.

Across the road is **Scarborough North Bay Railway**, a large miniature train that drops riders close to the **Sea Life Centre**, where kids can explore a tropical ocean tunnel, rainforest zone and penguin island.

## Fishing Villages, Smuggler Coves & Fossil-Hunting

A COASTAL HOP AROUND WHITBY

You can either walk out of Whitby to explore its neighbouring coastal villages using the **Cleveland Way**, or catch one of the regular buses. Heading north from Whitby's whalebone arches, the clifftop promenade runs all the way to **Sandsend**, a pretty estuarine village an hour's walk from Whitby, with two seafront cafes (one selling bodyboards and wetsuits), stand-up paddleboards for hire, and a sandy beach. Five miles further north, **Runswick Bay** is another broad stretch of sand with tightly packed hillside cottages once occupied by herring fishers. There's a solitary pub, the **Royal Hotel**, with a small, elevated outdoor patio overlooking the sea. Hidden Horizons runs **fossil-hunting tours** here from spring to autumn (hiddenhorizons.co.uk).

Three miles north of Runswick Bay, **Staithes** is a much bigger, even more photogenic village with a steep walk down to reach the well-preserved heritage high street. In the 18th and 19th centuries, Staithes was a thriving fishing port. A small handful of boats still make a living off local crabs, lobster, mackerel and cod. The village has been home to an artists' colony since around the start of the 20th century and there are a handful of local galleries and studios here. Staithes also claims itself as 'Captain Cook's Village' but Cook lived here in 1745 only briefly, as an apprentice to a grocer. The **Staithes Story heritage centre** holds some Captain Cook memorabilia, as well as local art, history and fascinating sepia photos.For the best photo op of the village, head over the estuary bridge behind Cobbles cafe and up the hill on the northern cliff bank. Beyond Staithes, it's worth travelling the next 10 miles up to **Saltburn-by-the-Sea** for its old-fashioned **Victorian pier**, swathes of beach and excellent **Seaview** fish restaurant.

**WHERE TO WALK**

**Falling Foss**
Boardwalks meander off into the forest from this mill cafe beside a gushing waterfall.

**Hutton-le-Hole**
Collect the walking leaflet (£1) from Ryedale Folk Museum for trails around this picture-perfect village.

**Hole of Horcum**
Spectacular hike around 400ft-deep natural moorland amphitheatre; Follow with pints at Levisham's Horseshoe Inn.

Robin Hood's Bay

Picturesque **Robin Hood's Bay**, six miles south of Whitby, has a steep descent similar to Staithes' to get into the old town, where narrow cobbled streets with good pubs and cafes spill out onto a giant, popular rockpooling beach. The village's name has nothing to do with the hero of Sherwood Forest – the origin of its name is a mystery and the locals call it Bay Town. It was once a major centre for smuggling, which is a topic well explored, along with other local history, in the volunteer-run **Bay Museum**.

At low tide, it's an easy walk south along the beach from Robin Hood's Bay to **Boggle Hole**, a secluded cove in a deep coastal cleft. It's inaccessible by car (drivers can park at the clifftop and walk down); at the bottom of the cove there's a YHA hostel housed in an old mill, with a cafe and bar.

## LOOKING TO THE SKIES

In December 2020, the Yorkshire Dales and North York Moors national parks were jointly classified as **international dark sky reserves**. The North York Moors have a slightly more developed astrotourism scene, but both parks have designated 'dark sky friendly' accommodation, which will provide telescopes or binoculars, blankets and reclining seats for guests.

**Sutton Bank National Park Centre** has stargazing guides and a star hub with reclined outdoor seating for DIY stargazers. For a more guided experience, **Astro Dog** runs stargazing tours at **Dalby Forest** – the darkest spot in the North York Moors. February and October bring the Dark Skies Festivals, with organised night runs, wellness walks, astrophotography workshops and more.

## GETTING AROUND

There are regular, mostly reliable bus services running north and south along the coast from Whitby Bus Station. Take the X4 north for Sandsend, Runswick Bay, Staithes and Saltburn, or the X93/X94 south for Robin Hood's Bay and Scarborough. Goathland is on the North York Moors Railway line running from Whitby to Pickering, but it's not a cheap trip; car is the easiest way to reach the village.

# HAWORTH & BRONTË COUNTRY



The brooding moors, windswept valleys and gritty towns of the South Pennine hills proved a winning combination for the Brontë sisters – Emily, Anne and Charlotte – who were inspired by their homeland to pen some of England's greatest literary fiction. Today, thousands of visitors a year come to pay their respects at the handsome parsonage in Haworth where the sisters lived and worked. The village core surrounding it still bears a strong resemblance to the quaint country hub the Brontës would have found upon moving here in 1820. Steep, cobbled Main St – sometimes part of the race route for the Tour de France – is lined with independent shops, pubs and tearooms. But just a few steps off the drag and you're up onto the moors. And chugging softly through this landscape is the Keighley & Worth Valley Railway, which cuts through Haworth and its surrounding villages, passing abandoned mills and burbling river trails.

**TOP TIP**

If you can, book your trip [to] coincide with the Hawor[th] 1940s Weekend in May. One of the largest event[s] of its kind in the country, [it] involves dances, dress-u[p,] decorations and period military reenactments along Main St. Alternativ[ely,] the Brontë Parsonage organises the Brontë Festival of Women's Wri[ting] each September.

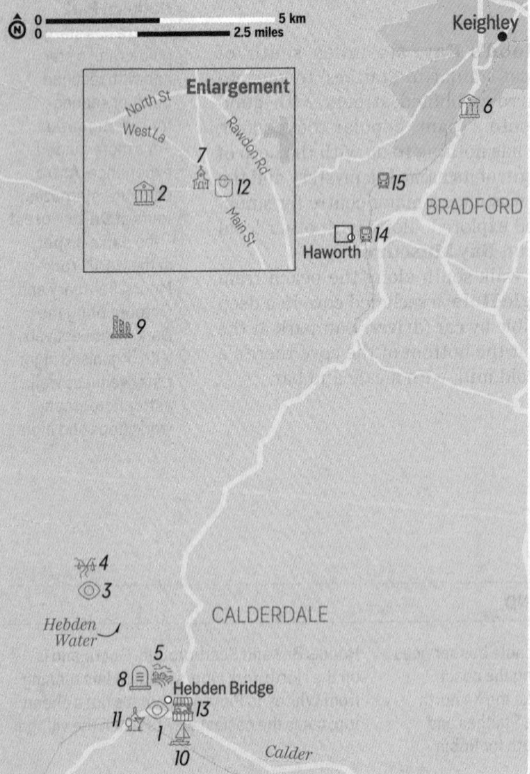


**SIGHTS**
1 Bridge Mill
2 Brontë Parsonage Museum
3 Gibson Mill
4 Hardcastle Crags
5 Heptonstall
6 Museum of Rail Travel
7 St Michael & All Angels Church
8 Sylvia Plath's Grave
9 Top Withens

**ACTIVITIES & TOURS**
10 Brontë Boats

**DRINKING & NIGHTLIFE**
11 Stubbing Wharf Pub

**SHOPPING**
12 Cabinet of Curiosities
13 Hebden Bridge Open Market

**TRANSPORT**
14 Keighley & Worth Valley Railway
15 Oakworth Station

Top Withens

## Step into Brontë World

A WANDER THROUGH HAWORTH

Tucked away behind the church at the top of Main St, the **Brontë Parsonage Museum** guides visitors through Georgian rooms where Emily, Anne and Charlotte wrote and lived, culminating in an exhibition that explores the social context behind why the sisters originally published novels such as *Wuthering Heights* and *Jane Eyre* under male pseudonyms. A highlight is Charlotte Brontë's miniature, handwritten books. Opposite the parsonage, duck into **St Michael & All Angels Church** to pay your respects at the Brontë Chapel, where Charlotte, Emily and other family members are interred.

There is a popular walk to **Top Withens**, the farmhouse (now a ruin) that is thought to have inspired Emily Brontë's imagining of Wuthering Heights, Catherine Earnshaw and Heathcliff's house in the novel of the same name. The easiest route is through the church graveyard, heading southwest past allotments and chicken coops until you hit the public footpath signs (in English and Japanese). The route mostly follows the **Pennine Way**, passing **Brontë Waterfall**.

### YORKSHIRE'S LESBIAN PIONEER

Anne Lister lived just 10 miles from the Brontës when they were growing up, but socialised in a far less-sheltered sphere. Lister became financially independent when she inherited **Shibden Hall** and estate, near Halifax, in 1836. She became a remarkable, social-climbing industrialist who dressed in men's clothing and conducted numerous lesbian affairs before marrying a woman.

The portion of the diaries detailing her lesbian affairs was written in code, but its content was uncovered by local historian Helena Whitbread in the 1980s. Lister's life is retold in the hit TV series *Gentleman Jack*, which was filmed at Shibden Hall. The house is open to the public and has become a pilgrimage site for LGBTIQ+ tourists.

### WHERE TO STAY AROUND HAWORTH

**Weavers Cottage & Loft**
Two sweet little apartments inside a Grade II-listed cottage right by Haworth's railway station. £

**Fleece Inn**
A dash of country chic above a traditional pub on Haworth's Main St. ££

**Hebden Townhouse**
Smart 12-room B&B in a great spot opposite Hebden Bridge's canal, 8 miles from Haworth. £££

**BEST PLACES TO SHOP IN HAWORTH**

**Hawksbys**
Gorgeous gallery selling British designers, with a large selection of studio pottery.

**Souk**
The go-to rummage fest for vintage gear, particularly 1940s dress-up.

**Mrs Beightons Sweet Shop**
Pick up some Yorkshire liquorice, including Pontefract cakes, at this wood-panelled Victorian-style sweet emporium.

**Cabinet of Curiosities**
Small-batch toiletries with a Gothic edge – try the mustard bath powder, made to traditional recipe.

**Sonia's Smile**
Haworth is a certified fair-trade town and this shop is packed with global fair-trade goodies.

**Mrs Beightons Sweet Shop**

It's 8 miles there and back to Haworth, or 10-miles one way if you continue on the trail to Hebden Bridge, a quirky mill town in the Calderdale Valley.

Back in Haworth, there are several shops selling beautifully bound copies of the Brontë sisters' novels, including the **Cabinet of Curiosities**, which has a bookshop tucked into a back corner.

## Ride the 'Iron Horse' Through Brontë Country

HOME OF THE RAILWAY CHILDREN

The journey to and from Haworth by heritage steam and diesel train is a wonderful day out. Book the Day Rover ticket on the **Keighley & Worth Valley Railway** (KWVR) and you can ride the line all day long, from Keighley to Oxenhope via Haworth, and visit the railway's two museums free of charge. This 5-mile line, built between 1864 and 1867, has been restored to its former glory by local volunteers. Each of the six stations is packed with original character, from booking halls with open fires to stationmasters dressed in period garb – and the line possesses so many exceptional vintage

**WHERE TO EAT & DRINK IN HAWORTH**

**Hunters of Haworth**
Tiny cafe specialising in puff pastry pies (including veggie options); take away or eat in. **£**

**Pavé**
Lovely French-themed bistro serving build-your-own charcuterie and cheeseboards with Yorkshire produce. **£**

**Haworth Steam Brewery**
A 1940s-themed brewpub with a steampunk edge, serving pub food alongside Haworth-made gin and ales. **££**

carriages that it's constantly used in period TV and film productions. The most famous is *The Railway Children*, which used KWVR's **Oakworth station** as its filming base for the 1970 Jenny Agutter film adaptation and more recently for *The Railway Children Return* (2022).

Ingrow West station is home to the worthwhile **Museum of Rail Travel**, where you can climb into heritage carriages to have your photo taken, and the **Carriage Works and Engine Shed**, which details the history of rail in Yorkshire and allows visitors to see engineers restoring rail parts. **Oxenhope station** has a platform buffet carriage for bacon sandwiches and hot drinks, and the steam trains have the Jubilee Bar for onboard pints. The smaller stations are all good jumping off points for walks in the Brontë moors.

**BEST ENTERTAINMENT IN HEBDEN BRIDGE**

**Trades Club**
One of the UK's coolest live music venues, still run by a socialist members cooperative.

**Nelsons Wine Bar**
Vegan wines and plant-based food, with regular vinyl DJs – a hub for Hebden's LGBTQ+ community.

**Hebden Bridge Picture House**
Gorgeous independent heritage cinema with an attached bar, the Nightjar.

**Vocation Brewery**
Hebden Bridge's own phenomenally successful craft brewery runs this taphouse down by the river.

## Mill Heritage & Art in Alternative Hebden Bridge

THE UK'S LESBIAN CAPITAL

Home to Yorkshire's largest LGBTIQ+ community, the canalside town of Hebden Bridge has a wonderfully alternative vibe and a leafy valley location in the midst of moorland walking trails, making it one of West Yorkshire's most interesting, picturesque towns. **Brontë Boats** offers day hire along the Rochdale Canal for visitors to explore the valley by water. A 15-minute walk south of the centre, **Stubbing Wharf Pub** – the subject of a famous Ted Hughes' poem – has seating along the canal towpath and is the base for Hebden Bridge canal cruises, which allow ticket-holders to board with pints from the pub.

The liveliest shopping areas are Market St and around St George's Sq, where the **Hebden Bridge Open Market** (open Thursday to Saturday) hawks food, retail and artisan wares. Check out the square's **Bridge Mill**, a repurposed cloth mill that now uses its original waterwheel to produce electricity for the cafe and shops that inhabit it.

Above town, **Hardcastle Crags** has 15 miles of footpaths through a steep-sided woodland valley leading to **Gibson Mill**, an 1800s riverside cotton mill surrounded by picnic tables. Inside, there's a small exhibition about the history of the mill, a cafe and secondhand bookshop. It's a steep 30-minute walk uphill to Hardcastle Crags car park from central Hebden Bridge. Higher on the valley plateau, you can also visit **Sylvia Plath's grave** in the churchyard of the photogenic village of **Heptonstall**.

**GETTING AROUND**

Haworth is small and easily walkable, though it's a steep slog from the train station to the top of Main St. The Keighley & Worth Valley Railway opens up the surrounding rural area to those without a car. If you don't want to pay for the KWVR, an alternative is the Brontëbus, which runs regular daily services connecting Keighley, Haworth, Hebden Bridge, Oakworth and Oxenhope.

# Beyond Haworth & Brontë Country

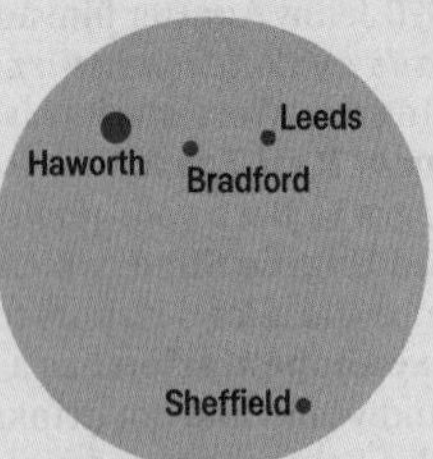


## The urban centres of Bradford, Leeds and Sheffield are packed with regenerated relics of industry – and bags of creativity.

There are dozens of interesting museums and attractions in West and South Yorkshire, many of them directly linked to the area's industrial past. From the 18th century onwards, Leeds and Bradford were driven by textile manufacturing, giving rise to mills, factories and an influx of South Asian immigrants whose continued presence forms a core part of the regional identity. Sheffield was a powerhouse of the British steel and iron industries and both West and South Yorkshire were synonymous with coal production. Today, these cities are buoyed by students, and regenerated mills and warehouses have become bars, restaurants and shopping centres. In 2025, Bradford will take on the mantle of UK City of Culture.

**TOP TIP**

If you prefer nightlife and top-quality food over country air, Leeds is a more logical base than Haworth.

**Winter Garden, Sheffield (p475)**

Kirkgate Market, Leeds

## Unpicking the Film Heritage of Leeds & Bradford

HOME OF THE MOVING IMAGE

French inventor Louis Le Prince (1841–90) made history in Leeds, a 50-minute drive east of Haworth, by becoming the first person to capture the moving image in 1888. Two years later he mysteriously disappeared, never to be seen again, but today he's widely considered the father of cinematography. And Le Prince's invention left a legacy – Bradford became an important centre for film-making in the early 20th century, and was designated the world's first Unesco City of Film in 2009. The city is home to the **National Media & Science Museum**, where visitors can learn about the birth of photography, cinema and TV, watch Le Prince's original Leeds film and see his single-lens camera on display. There's also a Bradford movie trail and film heritage app, which can be downloaded from bradford-city-of-film.com.

**Leeds International Film Festival**, which runs each February, is the largest film festival in England outside of

### BEST BARS IN LEEDS

**Whitelock's Ale House & Turk's Head**
Leeds' oldest pub (1715) and its contemporary sidekick occupy an atmospheric hidden alleyway off Briggate.

**Belgrave Music Hall & Canteen**
The best live-music venue in town carries local beers and has a brilliant roof terrace.

**Assembly**
Hebden Bridge's Vocation Brewery runs this underground beer hall, with tasty street food.

**Northern Monk**
Inside a heritage mill, Leeds' most famous craft brewery runs tours and pours creative beers.

**Viaduct Showbar**
Friendly, raucous drag shows on Leeds' LGBTQ+ strip.

### WHERE TO EAT IN LEEDS

**Kirkgate Market**
There's a huge street-food hall at the back of this lovely Victorian market. £

**Reliance**
Charming wood-floored gastropub with natural wines, platters of charcuterie and superior Sunday roasts. ££

**Ox Club**
Inventive, contemporary British cooking with a focus on local produce and grill techniques. £££

### A DAY OF CURRY IN BRADFORD

**Fatima Patel** was born and raised in Bradford, and is the founder of the annual Bradford Curry Awards and mela. *@BfdCurryAwards*

**Café Regal**
Try an authentic Kashmiri breakfast, including traditional channa puri (chickpea curry with fried flat breads), paya (trotters) or haleem (shredded chicken and mixed lentils). There's a breakfast buffet on weekends.

**MyLahore**
Popularly titled the 'British Asian Kitchen', its colourful menu has tantalising South Asian flavours, from curries to a blend of fused Indo-Chinese dishes. Good selection of vegetarian and vegan options, too.

**International Restaurant**
Dress up to go for dinner. It's been serving original South Asian flavours to Bradford locals since 1976. My personal favourite is the Garlic Chilli Chicken Karahi – yum.

London. Film fans can also visit the **Hyde Park Picture House** – a Grade-II-listed, gas-lit cinema that champions local filmmakers, and screens independent films from around the world. There's another heritage 1920s cinema at **Leeds Industrial Museum**, housed in Grade-II-listed Armley Mill. The museum tells the story of Louis Le Prince's life and work in Leeds, alongside exhibits about the city's manufacturing past. Complete your tour by searching for Le Prince's blue plaque on **Leeds Bridge**, where he shot his 1888 film in the city centre.

## Around the Yorkshire Sculpture Triangle

ART HUB OF THE NORTH

The Yorkshire Sculpture Triangle is a collaboration between four leading Yorkshire art venues that recognises the region's important contribution to British sculpture. Barbara Hepworth and Henry Moore were born here and Damien Hirst grew up here, and their works form an integral part of these internationally significant collections.

Of all the venues, the **Yorkshire Sculpture Park**, an hour's drive southeast of Haworth by car, is the largest and most impressive. Here, works from artists including Ai Weiwei, Andy Goldsworthy, Damien Hirst and Henry Moore are scattered across 500 acres of 18th-century landscaped parkland. Combine a stroll through the fields with lunch at the **Weston**, Yorkshire Sculpture Park's newest gallery space.

Housed in a striking concrete building, **Hepworth Wakefield** is much smaller but contains a significant swag of Hepworth's drawings, plaster casts and studio photos.

**Leeds Art Gallery** is a small repository for 19th- and 20th-century British art heavyweights, but also home to the quiet yet utterly spectacular **Tiled Hall Cafe**. Despite its name, the **Henry Moore Institute** next door doesn't display works by Moore; it's a sculpture research library, with small temporary sculpture exhibition spaces.

Another important Yorkshire artist, David Hockney, is on permanent display at **Salts Mill**, once the largest factory in the world, and the centrepiece of **Saltaire** – an industrial village 20 minutes east of Haworth by car, purpose-built in 1851 by philanthropic wool baron Titus Salt, and now a Unesco World Heritage Site.

### WHERE TO SHOP IN LEEDS

**Corn Exchange**
The dome of this 1863 trading hub is a city landmark, housing independent shops and cafes.

**Victoria Quarter**
Designer shops inhabit Leeds' loveliest Victorian shopping arcade; browse beneath the stained-glass ceiling.

**Thornton's Arcade**
Quiet heritage strip, famed for its giant automaton clock, is home to tiny independent shops.

## Touring South Yorkshire's Industrial Heritage

COAL AND STEEL LEGACY

In Sheffield's city centre, an hour and half south of Haworth by car, pride of place goes to the **Winter Gardens**, a wonderfully ambitious public space with a soaring glass roof. The **Millennium Gallery** hosts the Metalwork Collection, charting the transformation of Sheffield's steel industry into craft and design, namely through Sheffield plate manufacturing. **Kelham Island Museum** located in the city's oldest industrial district, now in the throes of regeneration, is an excellent museum dedicated to Sheffield's industrial heritage.

There are also several fascinating museums outside the city centre. Some four miles southwest, there's the **Abbeydale Industrial Hamlet**, exploring the cottage-industry era that preceded the industrial revolution. It includes 18th-century forges, workshops and machinery such as the original, working waterwheel that would have powered the hamlet's metalworking before the advent of mills and factories. Around four miles northwest of Sheffield there's **Magna** – an unashamed celebration of heavy industry housed at the Templeborough steelworks, which was the world's most productive steel smelter in its heyday.

But the star attraction of this region is the **National Coal Mining Museum**, about halfway between Sheffield and Leeds. Based at the former Caphouse Colliery, the highlight is the underground tour (departing every 10 to 15 minutes) led by former miners who give genuine, fascinating accounts of what it was like to work here. It involves descending almost 140m in a cage to explore the mine's subterranean passages at the coal seam with a helmet and head torch.

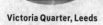

Victoria Quarter, Leeds

### THE UK'S FIRST ART HOSTEL

In 2022, Leeds' only hostel opened a permanent base on the edge of the city centre – and it's no ordinary hostel. Riding the wave of Leeds' self-declared 2023 Year of Culture, the Art Hostel is a social enterprise project designed to showcase the work of emerging creative talent from the UK and abroad.

Artists were given free rein to design the rooms as works of art, taking inspiration from local history and culture, politics and the environment, and leaning heavily on recycled materials. There's a mix of private rooms and dorms, and sleeping here is like wandering through a fantasy.

### GETTING AROUND

Leeds is the biggest rail hub in this area. it's an hour's train ride to Sheffield, with frequent departures. To get between Bradford and Sheffield, you'd need to change at Leeds. Leeds and Bradford are also both connected to Hebden Bridge on the Caldervale train line. The Yorkshire Sculpture Park and National Coal Mining Museum of England are difficult, though not impossible, to get to by bus (there's no local train) – driving is by far the easiest way to reach them and other outlying sights. It takes less than 20 minutes to reach Wakefield Kirkgate, the closest station to Hepworth Wakefield, from Leeds Train Station.

# EAST RIDING

Heading south from Scarborough and east from York, the historic maritime city of Hull and pancake-flat Yorkshire Wolds often get unfairly discounted by tourists because of their out-of-the-way location. Inland, this quiet county of rolling farmland has been preoccupied with agriculture for hundreds of years. Hull – often the butt of English jokes because of its grimy reputation – grew rich off whaling in the 18th and 19th centuries, and remains a major seaport. But its year as UK City of Culture in 2017 has given the city a new lease of life. Excellent pubs, good museums and a top-class aquarium make Hull worthy of your time. Nearby is Beverley, a sleepy Georgian market town with one of England's finest churches. Perhaps the region's biggest highlight is the coast, where puffins roost and birdwatchers congregate. At the very southern tip is Spurn Point – one of Yorkshire's most fascinating, underrated day trips.

East Riding

London

## TOP TIP

The puffin season at Bempton Cliffs runs from April to July and the best months to see them are May and June. During summer, the *Yorkshire Belle* runs puffin-viewing boat trips from Bridlington, with guides from the Royal Society for the Protection of Birds (RSPB).

**Hull Maritime Museum (p478)**

Hull
Hull
See Enlargement
Hedon
Humber
EAST RIDING OF YORKSHIRE
Withernsea
Patrington
Easington
6
Kilnsea
11
9
Grimsby
Cleethorpes
NORTHEAST LINCOLNSHIRE
0 5 km
0 2.5 miles
0 500 m
0 0.25 miles
8
Queens Gardens
George St
Low Gate
Alfred Gelder St
High St
7
Queen Victoria Square
Hanover Sq
12
3
Bowlalley La
2
Hull Old Town
Whitefriargate
13
Market Pl
Postrengate
Trinity Square
High St
Garrison Rd
Castle St
10
Castle St
Myton Bridge
Tower St
Hull Marina
Blanket Row
4
14
5
1
Hull
Deep
Humber
Nelson St

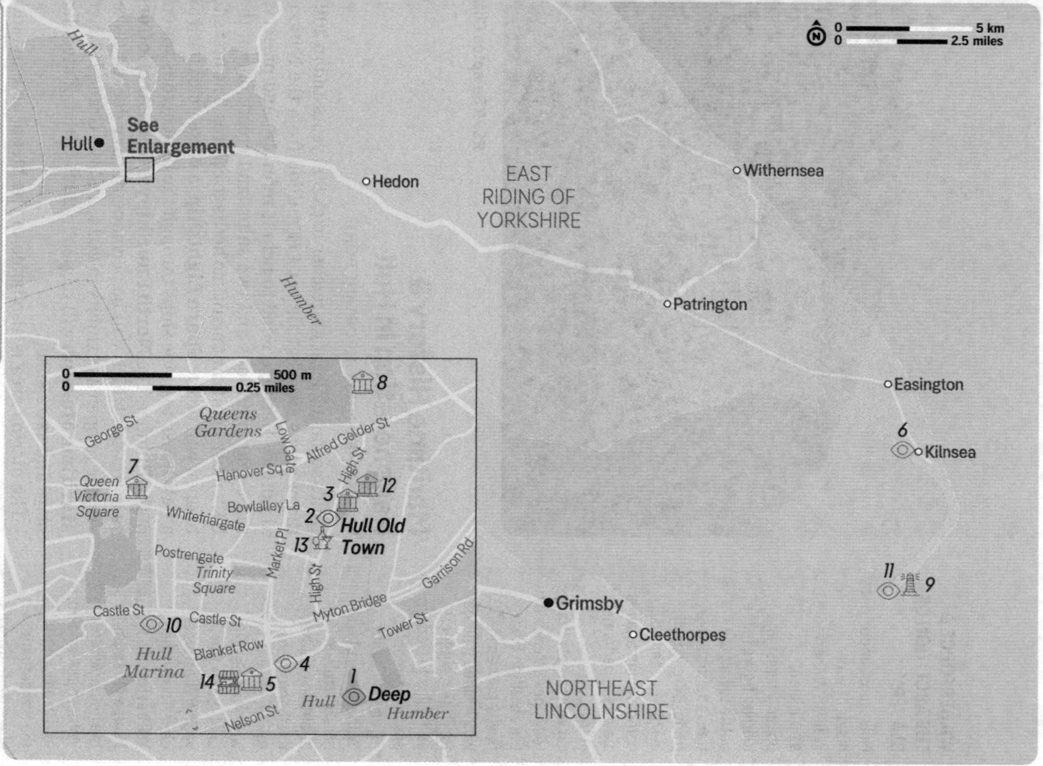

**HIGHLIGHTS**
**1** Deep
**2** Hull Old Town

**SIGHTS**
**3** Hull & East Riding Museum
**4** Humber St
**5** Humber St Gallery
**6** Kilnsea Wetlands
**7** Maritime Museum
**8** North End Shipyard/Arctic Corsair
**9** Spurn Lighthouse
**10** Spurn Lightship
**11** Spurn Point
**12** Streetlife Museum

**DRINKING & NIGHTLIFE**
**13** Ye Olde Black Boy

**SHOPPING**
**14** Fruit Market

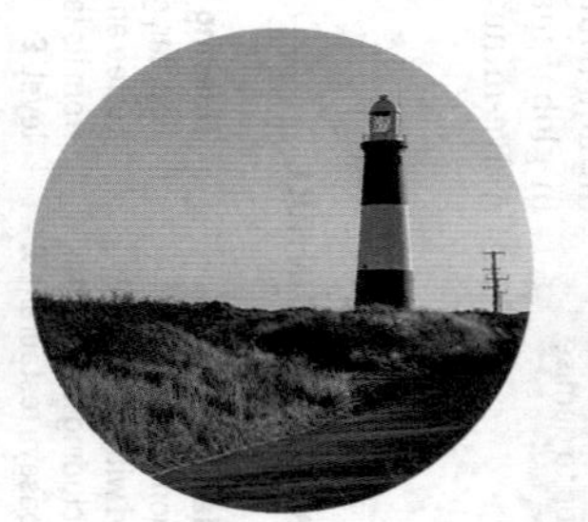

**Spurn Lighthouse (p480)**

### WILBERFORCE & THE ABOLITION OF SLAVERY

Hull's most important resident was William Wilberforce, a politician, philanthropist and leading figure in the battle to halt the transatlantic slave trade. Born in Hull in 1759, he started campaigning against slavery in parliament in 1789.

It was largely thanks to his persistence that the abolition bill was finally passed in 1807, which made it illegal for British subjects and ships to trade in enslaved people.

Due to ill health, Wilberforce played less of a role in the abolition of slavery itself across the British Empire, which wasn't achieved until 1833 – the year Wilberforce died. Today, the **Wilberforce House Museum** (in the house where Wilberforce was born and lived), charts the transatlantic slave trade from its inception to demise.

**RSPB Bempton Clif**

## Maritime History & Regeneration in Hull

YORKSHIRE'S MOST IMPORTANT PORT

Hull's seafaring legacy stretches back 800 years and in 2019 the city was awarded almost £14 million from the National Lottery Heritage Fund to help it refurbish and preserve three maritime sites and two ships, and create one of the UK's most significant maritime heritage centres. The first site to open will be the **Spurn Lightship**, a vessel once used as a lighthouse to guide ships through the treacherous waters of the Humber. The **North End Shipyard** and **Arctic Corsair** trawler, which will be permanently dry docked there are due to open as exhibits in 2024, and the Grade II-listed **Maritime Museum** will reopen in 2025 with updated displays and extra space.

The marina area is also home to **the Deep**, an outstanding aquarium and marine education centre heavily involved in global marine conversation and breeding programmes. A five-minute walk from the Deep there's the regenerated

### WHERE TO EAT IN HULL

**Trinity Market**
Old-fashioned market hall revamped with street food kiosks, including Indian from Hull's Tapasaya restaurant. **£**

**Thieving Harry's**
Popular, grungy cafe has good coffee and lovely marina views from its laid-back mezzanine level. **£**

**Butler Whites**
Well-polished warehouse conversion with soaring ceilings, chandeliers and a globally inspired menu. **£££**

## DRIVING TOUR: FROM THE COAST TO THE WOLDS

Heading south from Scarborough or Filey, follow the A165 until the turn off for **1 RSPB Bempton Cliff** nature reserve. Passing through sleepy Bempton village, you'll soon hit the broad headland and RSPB car park, from where trails lead off to the cliff edge. Shags, guillemots, gannets, kittiwakes, albatrosses and razorbills are some of the birds seen along this bone-white coastline. Puffins are the major draw from April to July.

From here, it's a 15-minute drive to **2 North Landing** at Flamborough Head– a beautiful deep cove. Burgers and Yorkshire Tea are now served from the old lifeboat station, and the boats marooned on the steep bank are Yorkshire cobles, still used for crab and lobster fishing. If you're lucky, you might spot a grey or common seal here. Rejoin the A165 and drive south to Beverley, a pretty market town that still retains some medieval features, not least **3 Beverley Minster**. Its foundations were laid in 1220 but it took 200 years to complete. Some 10 miles south of Beverley along the A164, you'll see **4 Skidby Mill** across the flat Wolds horizon before you reach it. This lovely 1821 windmill soars 75ft and houses the East Riding's Museum of Rural Life.

Scale the inside to see the giant mill stones, before stopping for refreshments at the Sails Cafe. Carry along the A164 until you reach **5 Humber Bridge Country Park**, a 48-acre local nature reserve based around an old chalk quarry that has been rewilded. Follow the Chalk Walk through the woods, checking out the quarry history info boards, until you reach **6 Humber Bridge** over the estuary. This marvel of engineering was the longest single-span suspension bridge in the world when it opened in 1981.

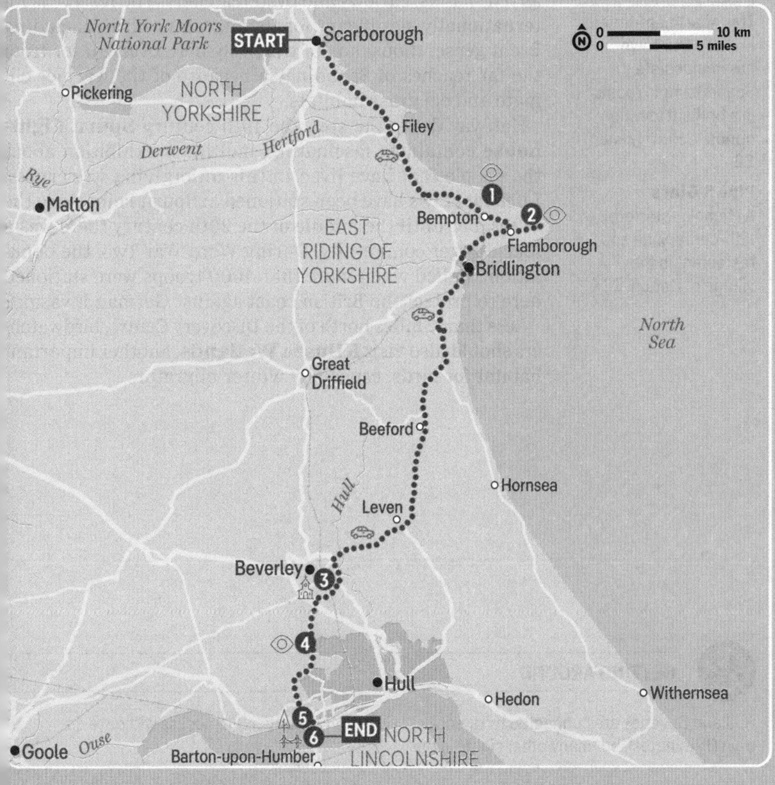

## BEST PLACES TO STAY IN EAST RIDING

**Hull Trinity Backpackers**
Dorms, private rooms and a coffee shop inhabit this Georgian house in Hull's Old Town. **£**

**Kingfisher Lakes Glamping**
Safari tents and log cabins (some with hot tubs; two-night minimum) around two lakes, with kayaks for paddling and a warm welcome. **££**

**Hideout**
This apartment-hotel in Hull's Old Town has immaculate, Scandi-simple rooms in a brilliant location opposite Hull Minster. **££**

**Pipe & Glass**
A Michelin-starred, 15th-century inn and restaurant in the village of Dalton. **£££**

**Fruit Market** and **Humber St** – Hull's epicentre of cool, crammed with warehouse restaurants, bars, galleries and independent shops. **Humber St Gallery** is the social nexus, with rotating exhibitions, a ground-floor cafe and summer roof terrace bar.

Heading north past **Hull Minster** into the centre of town, kids will love the **Museum Quarter**, with the **Streetlife Museum** and **Hull & East Riding Museum**, which includes the Ferriby boats – Bronze Age vessels discovered on the Humber foreshore. Backing onto the Museum Quarter is Hull's lovely **Georgian Old Town**. This section of High St has some wonderful old pubs, including **Fretwells**, the **Lion & Key**, and **Ye Old Black Boy** (a favourite of poet and former resident Philip Larkin).

## Safari down Spurn Point

WILDLIFE & WORLD WAR TWO HISTORY

Wild, erosive and bleakly beautiful, **Spurn Point Nature Reserve** is one of Yorkshire's most underappreciated protected areas. The return beach walk to the end of the point is around 7 miles, but the Yorkshire Wildlife Trust also runs three-hour **Spurn Safaris** most weekends. Guides point out local wildlife, including roe deer, owls and wading birds such as red shanks, curlews and oystercatchers. The reserve is internationally significant for its migratory birds, including Brent geese, thousands of which fly here over winter from the far reaches of Scandinavia because of the warmer climate and eel grass habitats.

Halfway down the spit, the 19th-century **Spurn Lighthouse** contains a fascinating, multifloor exhibition about the people that have lived in this unforgiving wilderness. Lifeboat crews have been stationed at Spurn Point since the 1820s, but until the middle of the 20th century there was a much larger community. During Word War Two, the population swelled when more than 1000 troops were stationed here to protect the British coast against German invasion.

Less than 2 miles north of the Discovery Centre, birdwatchers should also visit **Kilnsea Wetlands**, another important habitat for birds, especially winter migrators.

### GETTING AROUND

Hull and Beverley are connected by direct train (15 minutes), but many other sights in the region are difficult to access without a car.

Atlantic puffin

# MANCHESTER, LIVERPOOL & NORTHWEST ENGLAND

## REVOLUTION, SCIENCE AND MUSIC

Industrious cities, coastal towns, rolling landscapes, and a nature-filled isle welcome you to the northwest of England.

Built on the backbone of the Industrial Revolution, campaigning and community, the streets in the northwest are a timeline through the past and a future vision. The region produced some of the most enduring music and implemented some of the most important social changes in the modern world, from the vote for women and fair pay to the protection of birds. It also pioneered the football league as we know it. The region's heart is mighty Manchester, a city oozing with creativity, innovation and growth. Towards the water, we have perennial rival Liverpool, proud of its ability to hold its own when it comes to football, music and food. Nestled between the two is Chester, a city on the River Dee, Tudor in style and enveloped by the most complete Roman walls in Europe. In contrast to the skyscrapers and urban streets, there is leafy Lancashire to the north and Cheshire to the south, rich with rolling countryside and some surprising history. Offshore is the Isle of Man, a Unesco designated biosphere reserve for its natural beauty but also home to the fastest motorbike races.

### THE MAIN AREAS

TRABANTOS/SHUTTERSTOCK ©, SCULPTOR: ANDY EDWARDS

**Above: Beatles statue (p509), Liverpool; left: Eastgate clock, Chester (p499)**

# Find Your Way

The walkable cities are well-linked by trains and buses, meaning you can leave the car at home. Hop on the ferry across the Mersey or the Steam Packet boat to the Isle of Man.

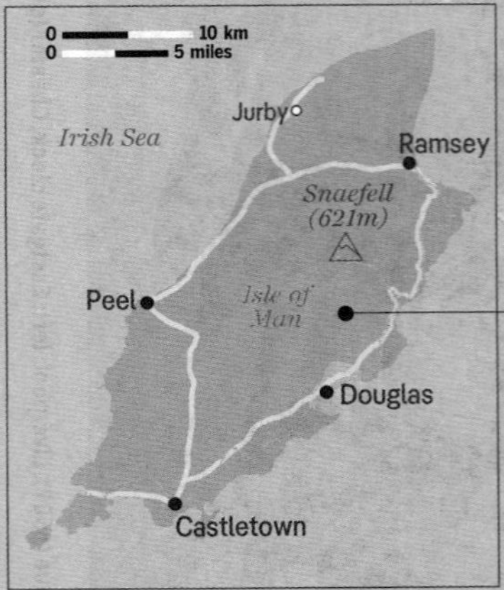


Isle of Man (38mi) (see inset)

**Isle of Man, p512**
Scenic coastlines, lush valleys and nature-rich hills punctuate this beautiful, motorbike race–loving island off the northwest coast.

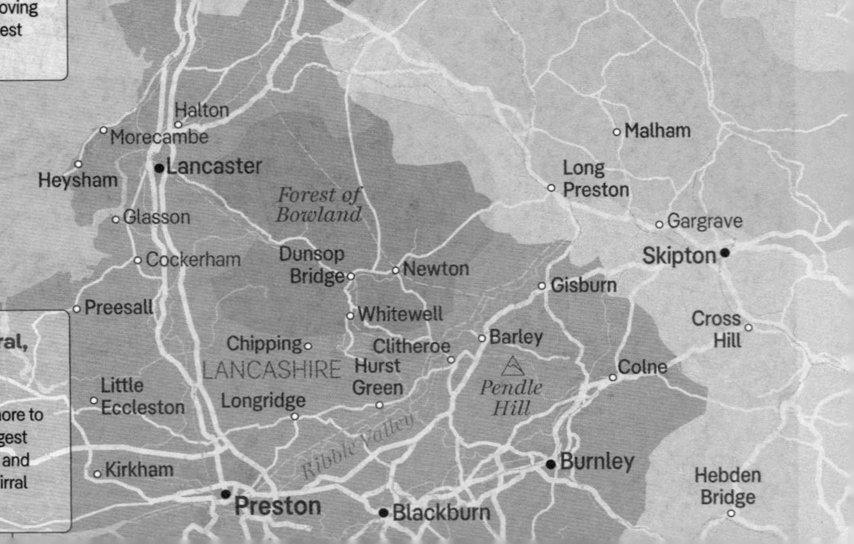


**Liverpool & the Wirral, p504**
Music and football attract visitors, but there's plenty more to entertain with England's largest church, fantastic museums, and the attractive nature-rich Wirral just a ferry ride away.

## CAR

While a car isn't necessary for exploring the northwest, it can help for visiting more remote parts of Lancashire and Cheshire. Rental cars are available at airports, stations and other local destinations.

**BUS**

Travelling by bus is great for local travel in and around cities. Check out the hop on hop off-tour buses to access some popular attractions. Each area has a journey planner, which will help you quickly get from A to B.

**TRAIN**

Use trainline.com to plan journeys and buy tickets. Many stations use e-tickets, making it a simple way to get around. Merseyrail covers Merseyside and will get you from the Wirral up to Southport.

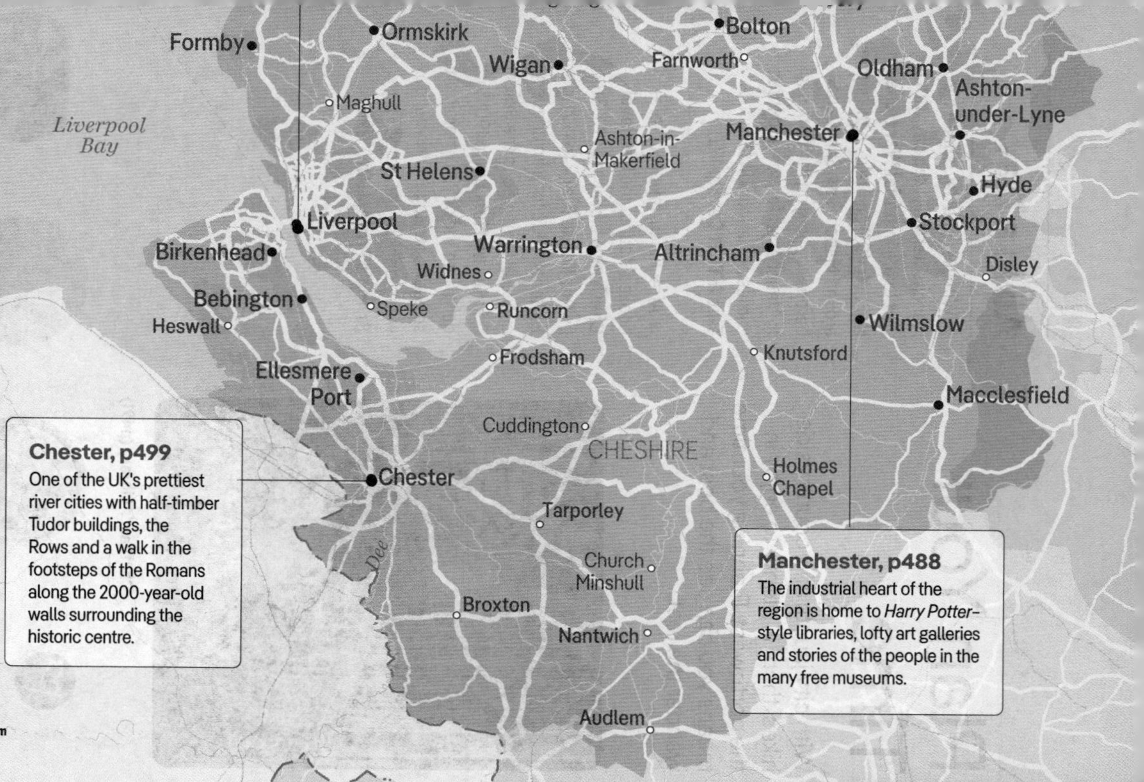

**Chester, p499**

One of the UK's prettiest river cities with half-timber Tudor buildings, the Rows and a walk in the footsteps of the Romans along the 2000-year-old walls surrounding the historic centre.

**Manchester, p488**

The industrial heart of the region is home to *Harry Potter*–style libraries, lofty art galleries and stories of the people in the many free museums.

# Plan Your Time

With city jaunts and countryside hikes, there is plenty to enjoy in the northwest. Planning your time means you can see the best and wander the rest.

ARNDALE/SHUTTERSTOCK ©

Chetham's Library (p491)

## All in a Day

- With just one day, spend it in Manchester. Start the day with a visit to the **Imperial War Museum North** (p493) and take in the sights around Manchester Ship Canal before hopping on the tram back to Manchester for rice and three curries at Mancunian favourite **This & That Cafe** (p492).

- After lunch, take your (pre-booked) tour of the **Medieval Chetham's Library** (p491). Stop by **Pot Kettle Black** (p492) in Barton Arcade for a luxurious hot chocolate, then go to the **Science & Industry Museum** (p490) to delve into the city's dynamic and scientific heritage. End your day with a drink by the fire at **The Briton's Protection** (p491).

## Seasonal Highlights

Autumn and winter can be rainy so enjoy comforting bowls of stew, toasty pub fires and welcoming museums. Spring and summer are great for beach days, hiking and enjoying nature.

### JANUARY

Colder months call for comforting bowls of hearty northern **scouse stew** and beers by the fire.

### MARCH

The birds start coming back from migration and nesting at **Parkgate** and the **Formby Dunes.**

### APRIL

Spring arrives, and the boating community assembles for the **Easter Boat Gathering** at the **National Waterways Museum** in Ellesmere Port.

SERGII KOVAL/SHUTTERSTOCK ©, MELANIE HOBSON/SHUTTERSTOCK ©, CHRISTOPHER FURLONG/GETTY IMAGES

## 3 Days to Travel Around

- After a day in Manchester, make your way to Liverpool. Start with the **Liver Building** (p506) for panoramic city views. Have a bowl of scouseat (stew) **Welsford Bistro** (p507) before visiting the **Anglican Cathedral** (p506. Make your way to the **Walker Art Gallery** (p507) and then have a night out in a **Beatles-themed bar** (p508)

- Enjoy browsing the shops on **the Rows** (p500) and walking along the **Roman Walls** (p500). Finally head off on a woodland walk at **Delamere Forest** (p502).

## If You Have More TIme

- For a longer stay, drive up to Blackpool for an experience up the **Blackpool Tower** (p497), then grab your boots for a hike in the **Forest of Bowland** (p498).

- After all that fresh air, enjoy some lunch in **Lancaster** (p497) before hunting out the modern landmarks, the **Panopticon** (p498)

- Next up, head back to Liverpool to take the Steam Packet Ferry over to the Isle of Man. On the island, enjoy the rich heritage on the route of the **steam railway** (p515), which brings you to the impressive **Laxey Wheel** (p514) and picturesque views from **Snaefel mountain peak** (p515).

**JULY**

Celebrate everything that is Manchester with the spectacular costumes for the **Manchester Day Parade** in the city centre.

**AUGUST**

Head to the Isle of Man for the fast and furious **Isle of Man TT** motorbike races.

**SEPTEMBER**

Celebrate autumn with culinary specialities at the **Isle of Man**, and **Manchester Food and Drink Festivals**, and visits to the parks for the amber leaves.

**DECEMBER**

Revel in the festivities as the northwest welcomes the **Christmas markets** and festive concerts.

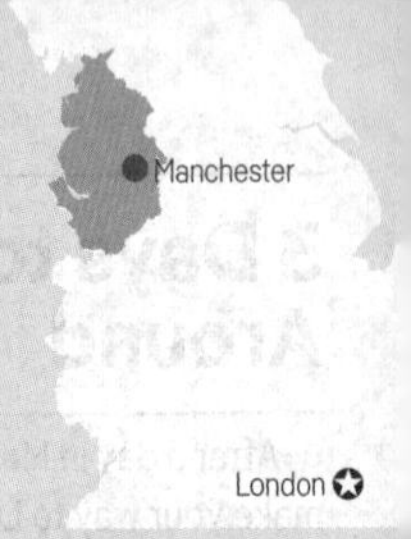

# MANCHESTER

Manchester constantly pushes boundaries. It was the world's first industrial city, with a working canal system and Britain's largest inland port, and campaigners here fought hard for women's right to vote and fair working hours, pioneering the cooperative movement.

In 1996 Manchester rose from the ashes of an IRA bomb, the biggest detonated in the UK since World War Two, blending the old with the new to create a fascinating patchwork city that tells a story at each street corner, as do the many free museums around the city centre and beyond.

Today the city retains the appeal of its history-rich past, even as it expands towards the sky; breathes new life into derelict corners, including with its first new public park in 100 years; and leads the digital revolution at MediaCity. Regularly voted one of the friendliest cities in the UK, you'll be hard-pushed to resist Manchester's charm.

### TOP TIP

Tucked between the Pennines and Peak Distr hills and surrounded by coastline, Manchester a the region around it are infamous for rainy weath expect some rain and w as well as sunshine! Brin your waterproofs, layers and sun cream to prepa for changeable weather

**MediaCity**

**HIGHLIGHTS**
**1** Chetham's Library
**2** Manchester Museum

**SIGHTS**
**3** Elizabeth Gaskell's House
**4** Greater Manchester Police Museum
**5** Imperial War Museum North
**6** Lancashire Mining Museum
**7** Manchester Art Gallery
**8** Manchester Jewish Museum
**9** National Football Museum
**10** People's History Museum
**11** Science & Industry Museum
**12** Tandle Hill
**13** The Lowry
**14** Whitworth Art Gallery

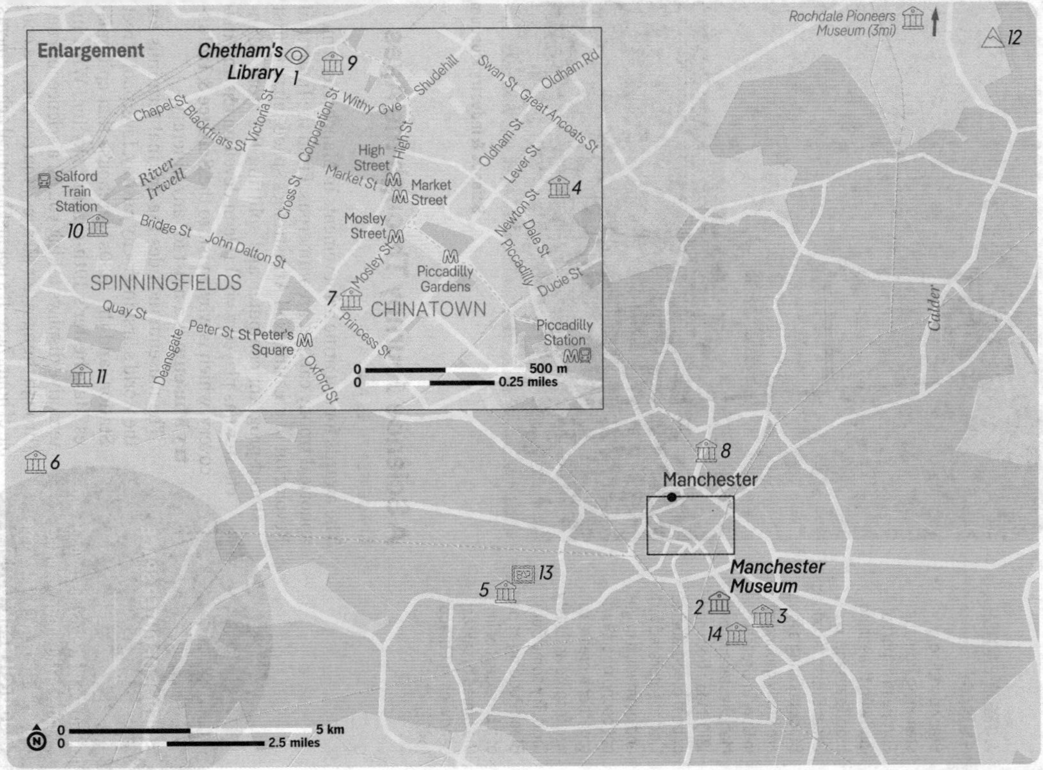

Enlargement
Chetham's Library 1
9
Chapel St
Blackfriars St
Victoria St
Corporation St
Withy Gve
Shudehill
Swan St
Oldham Rd
Great Ancoats St
Oldham St
Lever St
4
Salford Train Station
River Irwell
Cross St
High Street
High St
Market St
Market Street
Mosley Street
Newton St
Dale St
Piccadilly
Ducie St
10
Bridge St
John Dalton St
Mosley St
Piccadilly Gardens
SPINNINGFIELDS
7
CHINATOWN
Quay St
Peter St
St Peter's Square
Princess St
Piccadilly Station
Deansgate
Oxford St
11
0 500 m
0 0.25 miles

Rochdale Pioneers Museum (3mi)
12
Calder
6
8
Manchester
Manchester Museum
13
5
2
3
14
0 5 km
0 2.5 miles

National Football Museum (p492)

**A GREAT BRITISH SAUSAGE**

Black pudding, stemming from the European import of 'blatwurst' meaning blood sausage, is a Great British favourite. Black pudding's roots are firmly grounded in Bury in Greater Manchester since 1810. Made from pork or beef blood, suet (a kind of saturated fat) and oatmeal, it might not sound good, but together it creates a wholesome and tasty food. Try some Bury Black Pudding as part of a breakfast or in the famed breakfast sandwich at **Elnecot** (p492).

Science & Industry Museum

## A Science Journey Through the Ages

SPACE, TEXTILES AND ATOMS

The awards for scientific achievements in Manchester's metaphorical trophy cabinet are numerous. From the Industrial Revolution to creating Neil Armstrong's space suit, the first stored-program computer and splitting the atom, Manchester has played a vital role in development and discovery, which is why a visit to the **Science & Industry Museum** is a must for any itinerary.

The museum includes the original terminus for the world's first inter-city railway, Liverpool Street Station, and the 1830s warehouse that epitomises Manchester's 19th-century skyline. With interactive displays taking you on a science journey through the ages (for all ages), you can spend a couple of hours here. It's not just historical achievements celebrated, either. With a rich programme of temporary exhibitions including displays that explore the science of music, cancer and more, you can see how Manchester continues to strive in the field of scientific endeavour.

**SCIENCE OF OUTER SPACE**

Wonder at the planetary discoveries and wander in the shadows of the Grade I-listed Lovell Telescope at **Jodrell Bank** (p503), a Unesco World Heritage Site.

### WHERE TO STAY IN MANCHESTER

**Wilde Apart Hotel, St Peter's Square**
Centrally located contemporary accommodation with pod-style apartment rooms and huge comfortable beds. £

**The Cow Hollow, Newton Street**
An affordable, luxurious boutique hotel housed in a turn-of-the-century textile mill in the Northern Quarter. £

**Hilton, Deansgate**
An icon of the city with floor-to-ceiling windows in every room, giving you some of the best views of the city. ££

## Discovering Democracy

IDEAS WORTH FIGHTING FOR

The story of Britain's 200-year march to democracy – from the rights of people with disabilities to the radical mass meetings in Manchester that led to the 1819 Peterloo Massacre – is told in all its pain and pathos at the superb **People's History Museum**, housed in a refurbished Edwardian pumping station. The voices of those who took part in creating social change, whether on a local scale with the cooperative movement or campaigning for the vote for women, are heard here, Colourful and distinctive protest banners play a prominent role in telling each struggle's story, demonstrating a powerful tool in the battle for change.

## Medieval Time Capsule

A PUBLIC LIBRARY FOR OVER 350 YEARS

**Chetham's Library**, founded by wealthy textile businessman Humphrey Chetham to 'overcome poverty by curing ignorance', is the oldest public library in the English-speaking world. Opened in 1653 and housed in a medieval sandstone building from 1422 (one of the most complete complexes in the northwest), the book collection started life chained to the shelves with portable seats for the readers. The impressive collections include original works by Greek polymath and philosopher Aristotle and Richard Hollingworth's 1656 *Mancuniensis,* the oldest history of Manchester.

Soak up the atmosphere as you wander through the dark and imposing bookshelves. It's a unique and essential place of considerable significance in the history of learning. Here, Marx and Engel devoted many hours to research while forming the idea for their *Communist Manifesto.*

## Art of the City

CREATIVITY FOR EVERYONE

The Greek-style, columnated **Manchester Art Gallery** has stood at the corner of Mosley and Princess Sts for nearly 200 years and is home to some significant artworks. The first piece the gallery purchased, back in 1827, was a painting of renowned black actor Ira Aldridge by James Northcote. With three buildings to explore and work spanning the continent, you can step away from the bustle and immerse yourself in the ornate, high-ceiling rooms with some of the 25,000 pieces in the collection.

### BEST LITERARY CAFES

**Manchester Central Library Cafe**
An informal library cafe located between the Local History department and Tourist Information. A perfect place to stop on your library tour. £

**Portico Library Cafe**
Dine beneath the Portico's Regency domed-glass roof and enjoy locally sourced food in one of the oldest lunch spots in town. ££

**Chapter One Books**
Unfussy independent book shop and cafe with a passion for good coffee and cakes. £

### WHERE TO FIND TRADITIONAL PUBS

**The Old Wellington**
Manchester's only remaining Tudor building (1552) serves real ales and hearty meals. ££

**The Briton's Protection**
A firm favourite with local Mancunians, this comforting pub from 1806 has a roaring open fire. ££

**The Peveril of the Peak**
The cosy and unpretentious Peveril (1821) is Manchester's most photographed pub. Darts, pool and a jukebox. ££

## History of the Local Constabulary

INSIDE MANCHESTER'S VICTORIAN POLICE STATION

One of the city's best-kept secrets is the **Greater Manchester Police Museum**, housed within a former Victorian police station. Rest your head on wooden pillows in the original 1890s cells with mugshots staring down at you, and cringe at the gruesome improvised weapons used by the prisoners against the police during the Strangeways Prison riots in the 1990s. You'll also have the chance to step inside the rare Police Box and stand at the docks of the original 1895 Magistrate Courts.

### BEST INDIE EATERIES

**This & That Cafe**
A firm local favourite since 1984, secretly tucked down Soap St in the Northern Quarter. Home to 'rice and three curries,' it's perfect for a warming lunch in the city centre. £

**Mr Thomas' Chop House**
Traditional food with a modern twist is served in an old pub's original and decoratively tiled rooms. ££

**Elnecot**
Upmarket foods served in industrial elegance at the heart of Ancoats. Delicious breakfasts include Bury Black Pudding, a local delicacy. ££

## From Pogrom to Community

A TIMELINE OF MANCHESTER JUDAISM

Housed in a Grade II–listed Victorian Gothic building that once housed a synagogue, the **Manchester Jewish Museum** tells the story of Manchester's thriving Jewish community, which 100 years ago numbered more than 30,000 in Cheetham Hill alone. Take in the personal artefacts and recorded voices of those who attended the synagogue, the heart-wrenching accounts of those who escaped the Nazi German concentration camps as well as the uplifting tales of building community and businesses. Stepping into the Sephardi Synagogue, you will discover the grandeur and ceremony of the Torah scrolls, the traditions that took place, and the reason behind the unusual styles of the memorial stained glass.

## The Nation's Favourite Game

HUMBLE BEGINNINGS TO MULTI-BILLION-POUND INDUSTRY

The **National Football Museum** charts the evolution of the game, from when the Lancashire and Yorkshire Railway team was set up in 1878 in Newton Heath as a leisure activity between departments, to the worldwide phenomenon that it is today. Stories from the stand enrich the timeline with local spectators sharing their passion for the game; there's also the opportunity to unleash your inner Marcus Rashford in a penalty shootout.

## Gallery in the Park

A GALLERY BRINGING THE OUTSIDE IN

Among the first English art galleries to be built in a park, the ornate 1889 redbrick **Whitworth Art Gallery** is the place to explore contemporary and traditional art in a Royal Institute of British Architects award–winning gallery. Peeling back

### WHERE TO HAVE COFFEE AND CAKE

**Pollen**
Upmarket bakery next to the New Islington Marina serving fresh coffee, pastries and sourdough bread. ££

**Siop Shop, Tib Street**
Laid-back, cosy and colourful cafe with the best freshly made doughnuts in town and vegan options. ££

**Milk & Honey Cafe**
Inclusive community cafe in St Peter's House run by volunteers. Serves delicious cakes and hearty soups. £

Imperial War Museum North (p494)

the tradition of chintz wallpaper, the Whitworth celebrates a diverse collection of over 5000 works, including bold geometry and Arts and Crafts designs by William Morris. Explore art outside the bounds of a gallery by taking to **Whitworth park**, where you can get up close with some unusual and unlikely sculptures, including Cornelia Parker's *Meteor Fall* (2015).

## Manchester's Best Museums

THE CITY REGION'S HISTORY AND FUTURE

A wealth of free museums across Manchester and beyond delve into the history, industries and diverse cultures that make up the city.

Inspired by the spirit of collaboration, **Manchester Museum**, situated at the heart of Manchester University's neo-Gothic buildings on Oxford Rd, aims to create a more inclusive, imaginative and caring museum. In addition to the favourite Ancient Egypt and Sudan galleries, vivarium and Earth Science displays, new cultural galleries (opening in 2023) will look at ideas around identity, in particular stories of South Asian and Chinese culture.

### BEST HOT CHOCOLATE IN MANCHESTER

**Black Milk**
Vintage-style diner serving over-the-top hot chocolate and desserts that are stoo good to resist! Vegan options available. ££

**Cocoa Cabana Ancoats**
Award-winning northwest chocolatier, cocktail bar and tearoom selling decadent hot chocolate handcrafted with only the finest local ingredients. ££

**Pot Kettle Black**
Smooth and luxurious hot chocolate served from the beautifully designed cafe the under the glass-domed roof of Victorian-built Barton Arcade. ££

### WHERE TO FIND UNUSUAL SOUVENIRS

**Manchester Craft and Design Centre, Oak Street**
One-off pieces of jewellery, ceramics and needlecraft by talented independent designers and makers.

**Fred Aldous, Lever Street**
A city favourite since opening in 1886, selling arts and craft materials as well as unusual giftware.

**Paramount Books, Shudehill**
A quirky treasure trove of secondhand books, magazines and vinyl where you can pay in both pounds and euros.

## GREATER MANCHESTER WALKS

**Dr Andrew Read**, creator of the GM Ringway – Greater Manchester's 300km hiking trail – shares his recommendations for the best walks in the region.

**Marple**
This suburb offers countless hiking opportunities. Walk west from the station, turn right along the canal, and you'll soon cross England's tallest aqueduct with views over the Goyt Valley.

**Holcombe Hill**
Hop on the X41 express bus and 40 minutes later you'll arrive in Ramsbottom. Head west up Holcombe Hill. After a short but steep walk, you'll arrive at Peel Tower and enjoy stunning 360-degree views.

**Wigan Flashes**
For a watery walk, take the train to Wigan. Join the canal at Wigan Pier and head towards Leigh. You'll pass through peaceful wetlands renowned for their birdlife and biodiversity.

**Peel Tower, Holcombe Hill**

The purpose-built **Imperial War Museum North** (IWM North) transports you to life in the north during conflict using the help of projected voices and videos. Gunshots and sirens resonate through the expansive gallery where you can get up close with armoured vehicles, part of the rubble from the World Trade Centre, and the more personal artefacts of war in the form of letters and diaries.

Coal mining shaped Manchester's economic and physical landscape. **Lancashire Mining Museum** at Astley Colliery, a 45-minute drive from Manchester is home to the last remaining headgear on the Lancashire coalfields, and an engine house. Closed in 1970 and saved from demolition by dedicated volunteers, it has been restored and turned into a museum sharing a vital part of the region's heritage. Recent photographs and stories enrich the narrative of life at the pit.

In 1844 the Rochdale Society of Equitable Pioneers developed the model of the modern cooperative movement to support the mill and textile workers afflicted with deprivation and poverty to provide quality, affordable food. The **Rochdale Pioneers Museum**, 30 minutes by train and tram from Manchester, lets you step into a recreation of the first rudimentary shop and explore how the movement developed within local and national communities.

### WHERE TO FIND LIVE MUSIC

**Matt & Phreds**
Manchester's only dedicated jazz club, tucked away on Tib St, has a welcoming and eclectic atmosphere.

**Night & Day Cafe, Oldham Street**
You can hear various genres at the Mancunian favourite boldly coloured music venue.

**Band on the Wall, Swan Street**
Dance away into the early hours with a cocktail to live music from reggae to rock and folk.

## Home of a Novelist

A COMMENTARY ON 19TH-CENTURY MANCHESTER

Connect to the world of an English novelist by stepping into **Elizabeth Gaskell's House**, a beautifully restored Victorian Regency-style villa. Take a moment to relax in the space that was once familiar to Charles Dickens and Emily Brontë, who visited Gaskel at her home. Explore the writing and collections of the author who penned *Cranford* (1853) along with her social observations from the time.

## Painting the Industrial Landscape

THE STRANGE BEAUTY OF SMOG

Artist LS Lowry was renowned for painting the industrial landscapes of northwest England, capturing the essence of the people and places of the 20th century with his 'stick men' in everyday settings. **The Lowry** is an art gallery, theatre and event space celebrating creativity in the north with a beautiful selection of Lowry's work. These works offer a snapshot of Manchester's factories and smog-filled streets of the past, including the wonderful *Going to Work* at the Mather & Platt factory.

## Activists' Meeting Place

THE PRECURSOR TO PETERLOO

A park with plenty of history, **Tandle Hill** in the northwestern neighbourhood of Oldham was the meeting place for political activists in the days leading up to the Peterloo Massacre. The woodland was planted to stop these meetings and now provides a welcome break, along with the views over Oldham, Rochdale, Manchester and Cheshire, on a clear day.

### TOURS TO BOOK BEFORE YOU GO

**Coronation Street Tour**
Go behind the scenes on the working sets of the nation's favourite northern soap opera and walk the famous cobbled street to visit the Rovers Return pub.

**Manchester United Stadium Tour**
Experience life in the changing rooms, press room, tunnel and pitch side, then take in the impressive trophy cabinet of one of the world's most famous football teams.

**City River and Canal Tour**
Hop on a one-hour canal cruise to experience Salford Quays, Old Trafford and the disused dry docks from a different perspective.

### GETTING AROUND

Manchester is well linked by buses, trains and trams. Purchase a Wayfairer ticket to travel on all public transport in Greater Manchester as well as parts of Cheshire, Lancashire and more.

South Manchester is fairly flat with well-paved areas. The further norther you travel towards the Pennines the hillier it gets.

Travelling by bike can be a great way to explore the city, and there are some specific car-free cycle routes, such as the Fallowfield Loop.

It can be useful to have a car when visiting the outskirts of Greater Manchester, such Tandle Hill, but it's not worth driving and parking in the city centre.

# Beyond Manchester

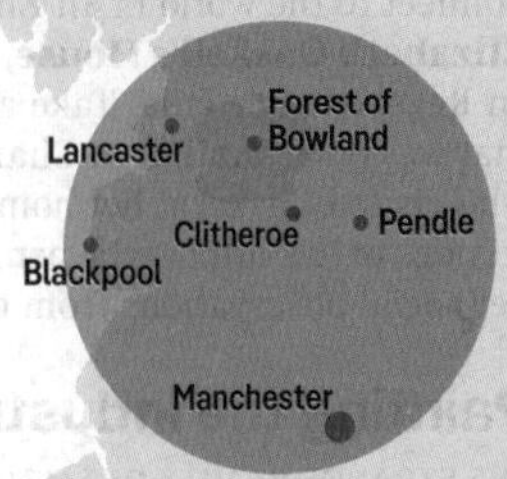


## Step away from the metropolis to savour countryside views, coastal walks and some northern comfort-food favourites

North of Manchester is Lancashire, where the inclement weather has inspired excellent comfort foods, including the deliciously syrupy and spiced slab cake parkin and the heart-warming hotpot. Here you'll also find the Ribble Valley, a rugged landscape that inspired *The Lord of the Rings* author JRR Tolkien. Then there's Lancaster, the Georgian jewel in the northwest crown with close links to the persecution of witches. Some fascinating tales echo in the hills around Pendle and the walls of Lancaster Castle prison, where the Pendle witches met a gruesome end. Heading coastwards, the seaside town of Blackpool brings a sweet nostalgic essence to the sea breeze with three piers and one of Britain's best-loved landmarks, an ode to the Eiffel Tower.

**TOP TIP**

Bring your sturdy shoes to hike the hills up to 20th-century landmarks and distant views across the Ribble Valley.

**Blackpool Tower and Central Pier Ferris Wheel**

Ashton Memorial (p498)

## Sky-High Coastal Views

EIFFEL TOWER OF THE NORTHWEST

When it opened in 1894, the **Blackpool Tower** was Britain's tallest manmade structure, standing at 154m. It has since reigned supreme as one of the most popular tourist destinations in the north. It can be seen from as far away as the Lake District or Wales on a clear day! Shooting skywards in the glass lift, you watch the ground and people below fade into the distance, and then look out to spectacular views along the entire coast. It take around 1.5 hours to get here by train from Manchester.

## Lancaster

ENGLAND'S DARK PAST

**Lancaster Castle**, one hour by train from Manchester, dominates the local skyline, perched on a hilltop in the middle of the town. Not simply a castle, it was the longest-serving prison in Europe, with the first gaoler mentioned in 1200 and the jail closing in 2011. It has seen some of the country's darkest

### BEST INDEPENDENT SHOPS IN LANCASTER

**Arteria with Gallery 23**
A thoughtfully curated stock of handmade, hand-picked and original gifts, from baby toys and clothes to luxury body products and hand-knitted scarves.

**Penny Street Collectables**
A treasure trove of eclectic vintage collectables, jewellery, homewares and tasteful modern home ideas, beautifully displayed in a compact shop.

**Atticus Books**
Packed to the brim book nook hosting regular events, from poetry readings and book groups to solo-musician gigs, art exhibitions and film screenings.

### WHERE TO GET LUNCH IN LANCASTER

**The Whale Tail**
Understated vegetarian cafe set in an old cheese warehouse. Great selection of vegetarian, vegan and gluten-free food. £

**The Old Bell**
Cute family-run cafe with a vibrant atmosphere set in a cobbled side street. Serves fresh food and drinks. ££

**Brew Lancaster**
Independently owned cafe with locally sourced food served by friendly staff in a light and airy setting with window seats. ££

**BEST SHOPS IN CLITHEROE**

**Valley Living**
Beautifully compact, owner-run, local gift shop selling a range of British-made homewares, gifts and cards on Clitheroe high street.

**Clitheroe Books**
Three-storey, floor-to-ceiling labyrinth of secondhand books with an opportunity to find a hidden treasure in the tranquillity of a traditional bookstore.

**Rue 5**
Small contemporary jewellers selling bracelet charms and modern designs using precious stones, and dealing with fine diamonds if you're looking for something extra special.

history play out – over 200 executions took place here, for anything from murder to stealing cattle, and it was here that the Pendle witches were sentenced to death in 1612.

Atop a hill in Lancaster's Williamson Park, a disused quarry, is the spectacle of **Ashton Memorial**, a folly nicknamed the 'Taj Mahal of the north', which was built by Lancaster Industrialist Lord Ashton in memorial to his second wife Jessy. Take the 235 steps up to the 1st-floor gallery (opening hours change seasonally), which offers views over Morecambe Bay and the Lakes. Here you can admire the splendour of Cornish granite and dome-top sculptures representing Commerce, Science, Industry and Art.

## Forest of Bowland

WITCHES, WIZARDS AND A CASTLE

Despite the name, the **Forest of Bowland** is made up of a sumptuous blend of rolling landscapes, moorland, forests, peaks and valleys, covering much of the Ribble Valley, which runs into neighbouring Yorkshire. An Area of Outstanding Natural Beauty, it offers respite from the industrial uniform of the region. Lace up your boots to walk part of the **Lancashire Witches Walk**, taking you along the likely route that the witches were taken from Colne to their trial, prosecution and hanging at Lancaster Castle.

Panoramic views over the forest's undulating landscape can be enjoyed at **Clitheroe Castle's Norman Keep and Museum**, built in 1186, where 350 million years of local history are unpacked. Here you can learn about the formation of the terrain you see and discover why the Ribble Valley is a favoured breeding ground for the impressive but rare sky-dancing birds of prey, Hen Harriers.

## Panopticon Views

TOUR 21ST-CENTURY LANDMARKS

An early morning hike to catch the golden hour is a magical way to start the day. High up on the peaks of the Lancashire hills, juxtaposed against the green, rolling backdrop, are four large modern sculptures, the **Panopticon**, symbolising the region's renaissance. From the tubular **Singing Ringing Tree** of Pendle Hill to the **Atom** in Colne, they offer a unique way to experience the landscape here.

**GETTING AROUND**

The main cities and towns of Lancashire can be reached by train, while the more remote parts of the Forest of Bowland are serviced by local buses that run seasonal and infrequent timetables. The Wayfairer ticker from Transport for Greater Manchester can get you to some of the main attractions.

Driving is sometimes the easiest option when visiting Lancashire as you're able to get between points of interest easily and at your own leisure.

# CHESTER

Chester
London

Half-timber shopping galleries, cobbled streets and the main river are hugged by an almost complete set of weatherworn Roman-era walls, making Chester justifiably one of England's prettiest city centres. The Roman walls circuit the entire city centre, taking in most of the main attractions along the way, including the Roodee (the world's oldest racecourse), Chester Cathedral and the River Dee. The Tudor- and Victorian-era centre flaunts the spectacular Rows emanating from Watergate St – the only covered timber shopping gallery in the world dating from the 13th century – and the eye-catching Eastgate Clock. A perfectly walkable city with waterside strolls, views from the walls, and shelter under the Rows from the rain.

### TOP TIP

Try to avoid visiting Chester during the races when more than 200,000 people descend on the city for 'a day at the races' at Chester Racecourse.

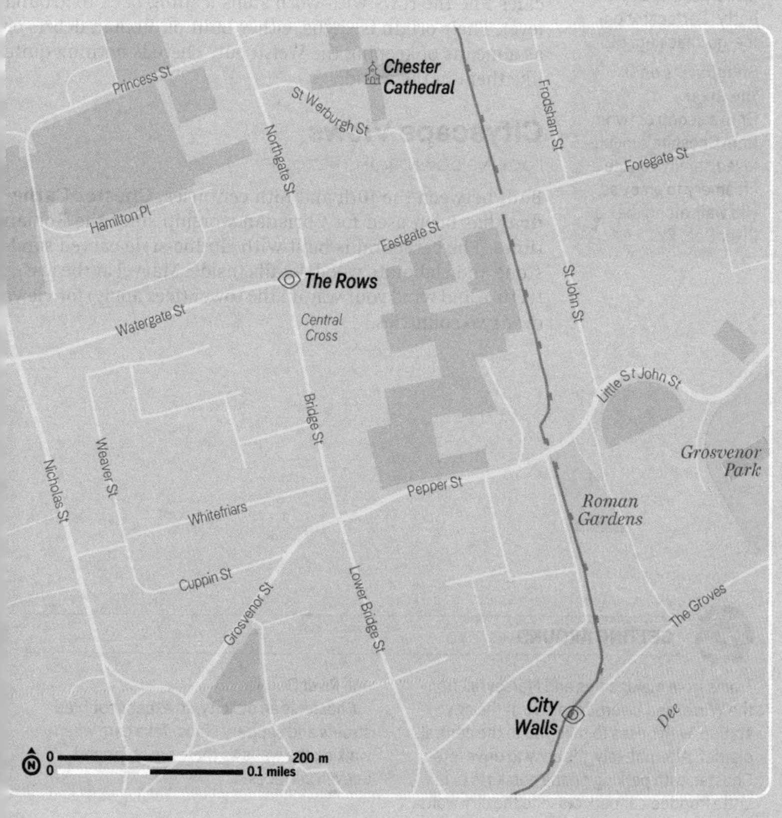

## The City Walls

A 2000-YEAR-OLD LANDMARK

As popular with locals as with visitors, **the Chester walls** are Britain's oldest, longest and most complete Roman walls, built as part of the fortress of Deva Victrix between 70 and 80 CE. The circuit takes you around the historic centre, incorporating the astonishing views of the city and river. It is a unique way to explore the city's heritage, from the medieval gatehouses to the towers at the corners of the walls. The **Tourist Office** has a leaflet outlining the approximately 2-mile walk, which takes around 1½ hours.

### BEST ON-THE-GO SNACKS

**Dinky Doughnuts**
A blink and you'll miss it stall in an arch under the Eastgate Clock serving freshly fried doughnuts and drinks. **£**

**Chip'd**
Transportable Dutch *friets* served in a cone with sauce, or in a roll for a traditional British favourite, the 'chip butty.' Perfect for on-the-go snacking. **££**

**Snugbury's on the River**
Grab a scoop or two from Cheshire's much-loved, family-run ice creamery to enjoy as you walk along the River Dee. **££**

## Medieval Shopping Galleries

A ONE-OF-A-KIND WALKWAY

A unique feature of the city is the medieval **Rows**, continuous half-timber galleried arcades providing a second row of shops above those on the main streets fanning out from the main Central Cross. Dark and imposing, the low ceilings and wooden beams form the main walkway of the Rows, with views out to the street from the open balustraded sides. Quaint shops and cafes line the rows with worn steps leading back to ground level. Their origin is vague, either built on Roman debris or as a means of keeping the Welsh out. There is nothing quite like them in the world.

## Cityscape Views

LOOKING DOWN FROM THE TOWER

Built between the 10th and 16th centuries, **Chester Cathedral** has been used for Christian worship since the Roman times. The cathedral is built with Gothic-style carved sandstone and elaborate wood details inside. Marvel at the architecture and wind your way up the tower (fees apply) for views over two countries.

### GETTING AROUND

Trains from major cities and Merseyrail from the Wirral and Liverpool arrive at the city station, with buses to take you to the central district. Alternatively, it's easy to drive into Chester, with parking on the outskirts or in Little Roodee car park close to the city walls and River Dee.

Chester is an old city, so expect cobbled streets and slippery slabs. Take care when walking the walls as there are steps and uneven surfaces.

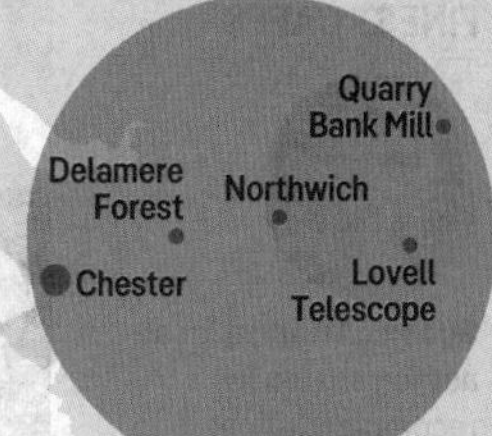


# Beyond Chester

Leafy suburbs punctuated with national landmarks, industrial heritage and sandy views over the plains.

One of England's smaller counties, Cheshire is a prize between Greater Manchester and Merseyside. With a surprisingly dynamic past, these lush green plains are home to the start of the Manchester Ship Canal and Northwich's very lucrative salt-mining industry. Cheshire's history, dating to the Triassic period is evidenced throughout the region in the ancient sandstone landscape, golden buildings and sandstone masterpieces such as the Cheshire Sandstone Trail. There are literary links to Lewis Carroll, who created the fantastical grinning Cheshire Cat in *Alice in Wonderland*, plus links to science at Jodrell Bank and aeronautics at Avro. The area packs a punch when looking for things to do.

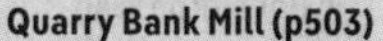

## TOP TIP

Try some of the delicious crumbly-yet-creamy, nutty-flavoured, locally produced Cheshire cheese and some decadently velvety Cheshire ice cream.

**Quarry Bank Mill (p503)**

## CHESHIRE'S FINEST CAFES

**Susan Earlam**, a local author, shares her recommendations for delicious cafes in Cheshire.

**Ethos Concept Store** When in Macclesfield, I am drawn to the delicious wholesome food and sweet treats here. If they were cooking for me every day, I'd have no problem switching to being a full-time vegan.

**The Green** Small but perfectly situated, The Green in Bollington is an ideal spot for walkers but is very popular during holidays and weekends (make sure to book!). The Miami is possibly the best avocado on toast I've ever had.

**Henry's Cafe** With its affordable and homely menu, this is a down-to-earth spot in the middle of highly affluent Prestbury. It is joyous and often works with charities.

**Lovell Telescope (right)**

## Woodland Wandering

FOREST OF THE LAKES

Various deciduous and evergreen trees and many lakes make up the 2400-acre **Delamere Forest**, just 5 miles west of Chester. A beautiful spot to visit in Cheshire, Delamere, meaning 'forest of the lakes', offers all kinds of activities, from walking, birding and mountain biking to tree-top and Segway adventures. If adrenaline-fuelled activities aren't for you, there are plenty of opportunities for forest bathing and woodland strolls, enjoying the sunlight twinkling through the canopy and taking in the sounds of the birds, including sandpipers, coots and the rare Mediterranean gull, and the gentle lapping of water of the many lakes.

## The Peaks of the Plains

A TRAIL THROUGH THE TRIASSIC SANDS

The 48-mile long-distance **Cheshire Sandstone Trail** route offers tantalising glimpses of the Cheshire plains through the trees; winding sandstone paths carved from the Triassic landscape; and copper-mine relics. For a short walk with views follow the Cheshire Sandstone Trail signs from the Ring 'O Bells pub in Frodsham to hike the three-quarter mile woodland trail upwards to the **Frodsham War Memorial** and be rewarded with a panorama over Ellesmere Port and to the Liver Building on a clear day.

### WHERE TO GLAMP IN CHESHIRE

**Welltrough Hall Farm Shepherd's Hut**
Cuddle up next to the log burner or soak in the hot tub in a charming shepherd's hut in picturesque surroundings. **££**

**Honeypot Hideaways**
Luxury wooden pods with double beds, kitchenette, toilet and shower. An adults-only site. **££**

**Lloyds Meadow Glamping**
Large opulent bell tents with comfy beds give you a comfortable stay under canvas. **££**

## A Spinning Tale

STEP INTO THE INDUSTRIAL REVOLUTION

At the National Trust **Quarry Bank Mill**, a 40-minute drive from Chester, you can immerse yourself in the noise and vibration of the machinery in a working 18th-century water mill, one of the world's best preserved. Take a tour of the Apprentice House and lay your head on the straw beds where these workers would have slept. Outside are the superbly landscaped gardens and renovated glass houses.

## A Salty Tale

INSIDE THE SALT WORKS

From the Roman times to the late 1980s, **Lion Salt Works** created salt at this site in Northwich. During this time, it was a significant industry that shaped the area's people, economy and landscape. Interactive displays in the on-site museum allow you to listen in on the conversations in which a young apprentice would have taken part and visit the warehouse to see the expansive salt pans heated to extract the salt from the water – this was a hot and dangerous workplace. To get here from Chester, it's a 20-minute drive.

## Beacon of the Countryside

THE GIANT SATELLITE DISH

Standing proud among the fields in Cheshire is the famous Unesco World Heritage Site–listed **Lovell Telescope** at Jodrell Bank. In the 1950s, it was the largest radio-controlled telescope in the world. Part of the University of Manchester, you can wander in the shadows of the telescope. In the on-site museum and planetarium, immerse yourself in projections and digital displays that take you into the archives of the science realm and demonstrate how immense space is.

## Experience a Lancaster Raid

NSIDE THE MANCHESTER FIGHTER PLANES

Between 1926 and 2011, Avro produced 20,000 aeroplanes at their production site in Woodford, Cheshire. Today the site houses the volunteer-run **Avro Heritage Museum**, where you can climb inside the cockpits of the Vulcan and Lancaster aeroplanes or try your hand at landing a plane with the flight simulator. The humbling and heart-pounding virtual-reality experience of going on a Lancaster air raid is made even more captivating with recordings taken in 1944.

### BEST COUNTRY PUBS

**Ring 'O' Bells**
Four-hundred-year-old traditional pub at the foot of the Cheshire Sandstone Trail serving real ales and hearty home-cooked meals. **££**

**The Churchill Tree**
Cosy and welcoming British pub on the grounds of Alderley Park serving upmarket food with an international influence. **££**

**The Salt Barge**
A stone's throw from the Lion Salt Works with a roaring open fire and outdoor seating, serving a sizeable Sunday lunch and British pub classics like steak and chips, pies and curry. **££**

### GETTING AROUND

You can get to most destinations in Cheshire by train, but accessing the main points of interest involves walking for around 20 minutes from the station, as they tend not to be centrally located to the towns and villages.

Walking and cycling are enjoyable in and around Cheshire with plenty of paved villages as well as signposted countryside footpaths and cycling routes.

Cars can be useful when in Cheshire as many sights are far apart, meaning you can see more on your visit if you have your own transport.

# LIVERPOOL & THE WIRRAL

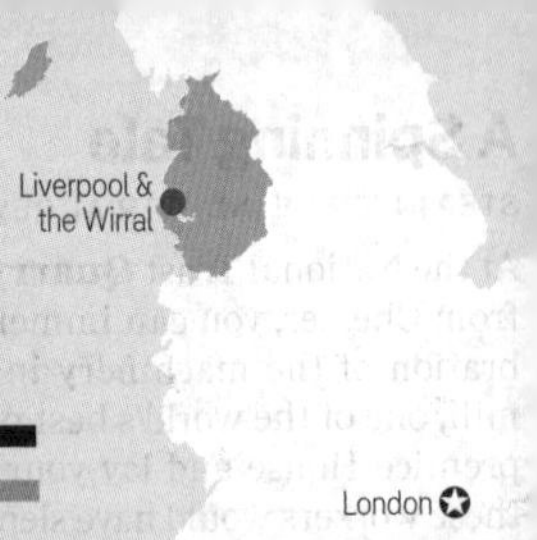

Liverpool & the Wirral

London

Where the River Mersey meets the Irish Sea, you have the dynamic maritime city of Liverpool, prominent on the world front for football, food and music; the Beatles formed here in 1960, setting the stage for all boy bands to come.

The city's riches were gained by wealthy merchants trading enslaved African people and purchasing land throughout America and Africa. This history is explored at the International Slavery Museum at the Royal Albert Dock. The legacy of the wealth can be seen in the architecture along the waterfront, with Pier Head and Three Graces taking central stage.

In the words of Gerry Marsden's famous song about the river, you can take a 'Ferry 'cross the Mersey' to reach the desirable peninsular of the Wirral. It's home to soap giant Lever and some of the best Victorian-era seaside resorts, and its marshes and wetlands are a haven for wildlife.

**TOP TIP**

Buy a Merseyrail Saveaway ticket to use when travelling around and between Liverpool and the Wirral. It's also valid on Mersey Ferries.

**Royal Liver Buildiing (p506)**

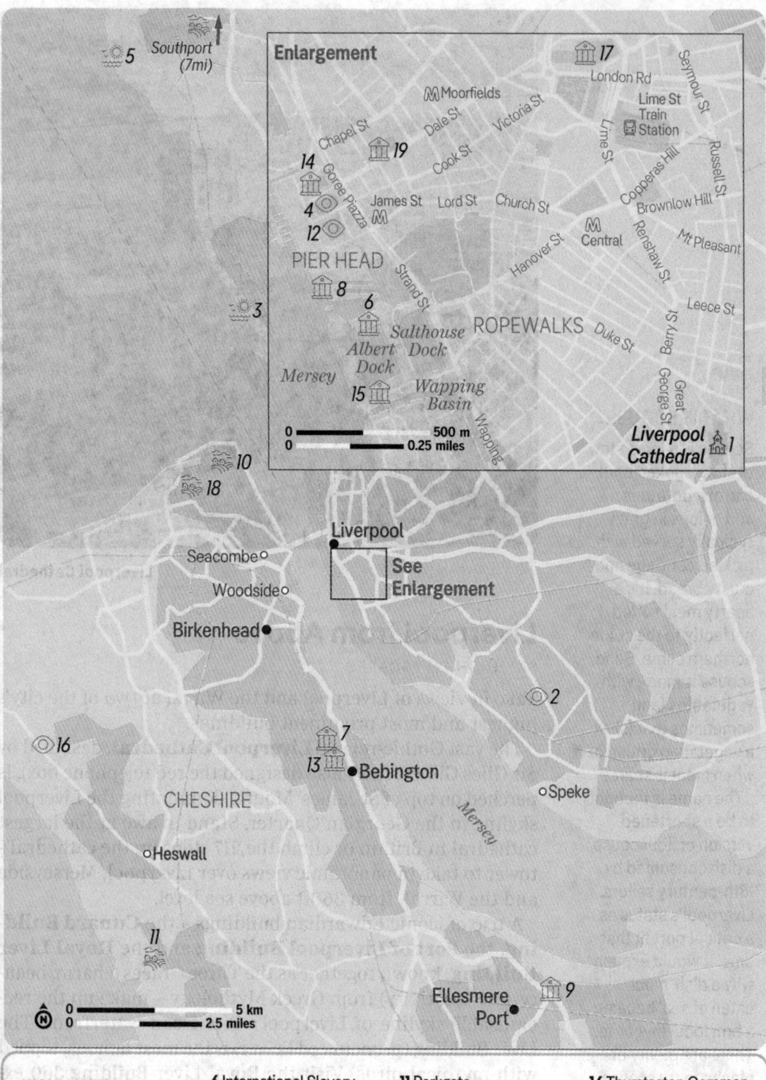


**HIGHLIGHTS**
**1** Liverpool Cathedral

**SIGHTS**
**2** 20 Forthlin Rd
**3** Crosby Beach
**4** Cunard Building
**5** Formby Beach
**6** International Slavery Museum
**7** Lady Lever Art Gallery
**see 6** Maritime Museum
**8 Museum of Liverpool**
**9** National Waterways Museum
**10** New Brighton
**11** Parkgate
**12** Port of Liverpool Building
**13** Port Sunlight Museum
**14** Royal Liver Building 360
**15** The Beatles Story
**16** Thurstaston Common
**17** Walker Art Gallery
**18** Wallasey
**19** Western Approaches Museum
**see 17** World Museum

**WHAT IS SCOUSE?**

Scouse is a local stew of slow-cooked beef, carrots, potatoes and onions in gravy, typically served with pickled cabbage and crusty bread. It's a hearty meal suited perfectly to the colder northern clime. Blind scouse is made with vegetables (and sometimes lentils) as a vegetarian option or when meat is scarce.

The name is thought to be a shortened version of 'lobscouse,' a dish consumed by 18th-century sailors. Liverpool's status as a critical port at that time, it would explain why a dish 'much eaten at sea' became a firm local favourite. There are plenty of places to try scouse while you're here.

Liverpool Cathedral

## Liverpool from Above

SKY-HIGH CITYSCAPES

Take in views of Liverpool and the Wirral at two of the city's highest and most prominent buildings.

The vast Gothic-revival **Liverpool Cathedral**, designed by Sir Giles Gilbert (who also designed the red telephone box), is perched on top of St James' Mount, dominating the Liverpool skyline in the Georgian Quarter. Stand in awe at the largest cathedral in Britain or climb the 217 steps up the cathedral's tower to take in panoramic views over Liverpool, Merseyside and the Wirral, from 360ft above sea level.

A trio of iconic Edwardian buildings – the **Cunard Building**, the **Port of Liverpool Building** and the **Royal Liver Building**, known together as the Three Graces (charm, beauty, and creativity) from Greek Mythology – make up the recognisable skyline of Liverpool's Pier Head waterfront. The Liver Building (pronounced lie-ver) is the most famous, topped with mythical birds. Visit the Royal Liver Building 360 experience to enjoy a 70-minute tour through some beautiful rooms and end with a 360-degree view of the city.

**WHERE TO STAY IN LIVERPOOL**

**The Resident**
This former 1800s warehouse close to the main railway stations has rooms with mini-kitchens. £

**Titanic Hotel**
Located in the historic docks in an iconic building. Large comfortable rooms and resident rum bar. ££

**The Baltic Hotel**
Stylish, quirky decor with comfortably compact rooms in the vibrant Baltic Triangle area. £

# Art & Nature of the World

TWO OF LIVERPOOL'S OLDEST MUSEUMS

The **World Museum** is like the British Museum of the north. This free museum is a must for rainy days, with an aquarium, planetarium and exhibits ranging from live bugs to human anthropology. A museum highlight is the exploration of world cultures, topical for a very diverse city, and a new approach to addressing Britain's colonial past.

The most extensive art collection in England outside of London can be found at the **Walker Art Gallery**, just a short walk from the World Museum. You can expect to find some of the finest European Renaissance paintings by Rembrandt and Turner, alongside classical white marble sculpture and iconic contemporary images of life.

# Liverpool's Seafaring Past

HORRIFIC HISTORY AND MARITIME STORIES

Discover Liverpool's seafaring history; the city's links to the barbaric transatlantic trade of enslaved people; and items that have been seized by border control in the museums at Royal Albert Dock.

The **International Slavery Museum** reveals the horrors of the transatlantic trade of enslaved people and Liverpool's role in this practice between 1700 and 1807. The uncensored exhibition includes an eslaver's log, which depicts a typical journey sailing to West Africa to capture as many people as possible before taking the 'middle passage', a voyage of one to six months, to the West Indies. Many enslaved people died on this harrowing journey in cramped and poor conditions, shackled to the decks to prevent rebellion or escape. Those who survived were sold for sugar, rum and raw cotton, which was brought back to England to be sold for profit.

Discover the history of one of the world's leading ports at the **Liverpool Maritime Museum**. A museum of all things nautical, its exhibits cover the story of famous cruise ship the *Titanic* plus the tactics of smugglers and the items seized from them by border control, including live birds, elephant's feet and kilos of cocaine.

# Top-Secret Underground Bunker

DIRECTING BRITISH WORLD WAR TWO WARSHIPS

The **Western Approaches Museum** opens the doors of a top-secret underground bunker to share a real-life game of Risk. Take a journey through the labyrinth of rooms and tunnels to

**BEST SCOUSE IN LIVERPOOL**

**The Welsford Bistro**
Hearty scouse (Liverpudlian stew) served with homemade bread and pickled cabbage; there's a blind scouse version for veggies. Located at the foot of Liverpool Cathedral. £

**Lady Lever Art Gallery Cafe**
Good-sized portions of the local stew served in the cosy gallery cafe in the basement of the Lady Lever Art Gallery in Port Sunlight. £

**Maggie May's Cafe Bar**
Freshly made scouse served daily with crusty bread and butter and beetroot or cabbage. A favourite with locals. £

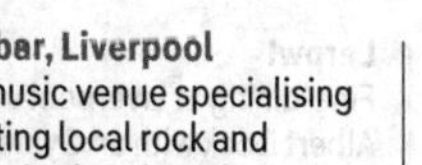

**WHERE TO FIND LIVE MUSIC**

**Zanzibar, Liverpool**
Live-music venue specialising in hosting local rock and alternative bands and musicians.

**Future Yard CIC, Birkenhead**
Venue supporting emerging local talent, and bringing national and international acts to the Wirral.

**The Jackaranda, Liverpool**
Longstanding live-music bar whose previous regulars included the Beatles. Regular new-talent and open-mic nights.

**BEST BEATLES-THEMED BARS**

**The Cavern Club** Liverpool's most famous bar on Matthew St. It's an intimate live-music venue with vaulted cellars, 1960s Beatles memorabilia and live tribute acts.

**Sgt Peppers** Cheap and cheerful Beatles-themed bar on Matthew St serving 2-for-1 cocktails and hosting regular live bands that play into the early hours.

**Yellow Submarine Bar** Quirky yellow-submarine-styled bar based on the Beatles' song of the same name in the chilled-out drinking capital of Caines Brewery.

Sculpture from *Another Place*, Crosby beach

get a feel for the command's nerve-wracking role during the Battle of the Atlantic, ensuring pinpoint accuracy to destroy the enemy. The operations room remains as it was on the day the doors closed on 15 August 1945 when the 300 personnel left the bunker at the end of the war.

## Music, Football, Community & War

LOOKING AT LIFE IN LIVERPOOL

The **Museum of Liverpool** chronicles the social and community history of the diverse people who make up this strong and resilient city. Each exhibit shares stories of real Liverpudlian people and their memories of events that have brought people together, from the Blitz to the African music festival. Listen to stories, look at photographs and get under the skin of the people who make Liverpool what it is.

## Liverpool's Fab Four

THE ORIGINAL BOY BAND

The Beatles, Liverpool's most famous export, play a significant role in the city's musical heritage. **The Beatles Story**, one of Liverpool's most popular museums, won't illumi-

**WHERE TO EAT SEAFOOD DISHES**

**The Seafood Kitchen, Crosby** Highly recommended across Merseyside, serving fresh seafood from lobster to oysters and everything between. **££**

**Lansdowne Bistro** Classic family favourites seasoned with French inspiration; has the best lobster thermidor in Southport. **££**

**Lerpwl** Fine-dining at Liverpool's Royal Albert Dock with an Oyster Bar serving sustainable Welsh produce. **£££**

nate any dark, juicy corners in the turbulent history of the world's most famous foursome, but there's plenty of genuine memorabilia to keep a Beatles fan happy. Also take a visit to the suburban **childhood homes** of **John Lennon** and **Paul McCartney** (National Trust entry applies), then check out the **Beatlemania gallery** at the Museum of Liverpool. Finish off with a walk along the waterfront to grab a photo with the **Fab Four statues** and offer some company to the lonely **Eleanor Rigby** statue on Stanley St.

## Wildlife Haven

WALK WITH THE RED SQUIRRELS

Relish in the natural beauty of **Formby beach**, just north of Liverpool. Long sandy beaches; precious wildlife habitat in the dunes; and a natural woodland, home to the native red squirrels, make this an excellent day out away from the city and a lovely spot for a picnic. The area is protected by National Trust (meaning there is a parking charge), ensuring that it is looked after and clean.

### BEST TEAROOMS NEAR FORMBY

**The Tea Rooms**
Down-to-earth, friendly cafe serving teatime favourites like crumpets and tea cakes. **££**

**SunShine Tea Rooms**
Quaint, bright and welcoming cafe and outdoor seating serving bean-to-cup coffee, afternoon tea, homemade food and delicious cakes **££**

**Delish**
Family-run designer dessert bar and cafe selling luxurious pancake stacks, light lunches and decadent ice creams with vegan options. **££**

## Sculpture, Sand & Sunsets

GOLDEN HOUR OVER THE WIRRAL

*Another Place* is a series of 100 cast-iron human sculptures along the 1.5-mile coast at **Crosby beach**, created by internationally renowned artist Anthony Gormley. Ghostly figures stand proud of the sand and sea, staring at the horizon. Catch a haunting sunset from the promenade with the figures silhouetted against the golden-hour sky.

## A Proper Seaside Town

CANDYFLOSS, FUNFAIRS, FISH AND CHIPS

**Southport** has all you need for a fun-filled day at the seaside. Funfair rides, crazy gold and parks along the front and splendid Victorian gardens tucked away from the beach revellers. The air is filled with the sweet scent of fried food and sugar, which makes it all the more appealing. Wander along the second-longest pier in the country to try your luck on the vintage arcade machines, visit the **National Lawnmower Museum** or grab a drink at **The Lakeside Inn**, Britain's smallest pub.

## The Home of Sunlight Soap

A VILLAGE FOR THE WORKERS

**Port Sunlight Museum**, at the heart of Port Sunlight Village

### WHERE TO GET AFTERNOON TEA IN THE WIRRAL

**Isabelle's**
Small, friendly, independent teashop in Heswall, serving delightful afternoon-tea stands and light-lunch options. **££**

**Benty Tea Rooms**
Ideally located for walks at Thurstaston common, with a delicious selection of cakes and sandwiches. **££**

**Thornton Hall Hotel and Spa, Thornton Hough**
Delightful afternoon-tea experience at the former residence of Sunlight Soap's William Lever. **£££**

### SCENIC CYCLES WITH COFFEE

**Edward Lamb**, from the Traffic Reduction Campaign at Low Traffic Futures, shares his favourite scenic cycle routes and coffee stops.

**Wirral Way**
From West Kirby Concourse, follow the trail until it runs out! Aim for Willaston for a drink at the **Station Master's House** or turn off at Neston to follow the River Dee to Chester.

**Landican Lane**
Start at Little Storeton Lane, and follow the track as it winds under the M53. A quick mile of tarmac, and you get to enjoy Arrowe Park in time for tea at the **Red Rooms Cafe.**

**Port Sunlight Greenway**
Start behind the Gladstone Theatre for plain sailing to the Croft Retail Park. From here, hit the Wirral Circular Trail and pedal on to **Mimosa Tea Garden** at Eastham Country Park.

Wirral Way

Conservation Area, tells the story of William Lever of Sunlight Soap. The son of a grocer, he grew his wealth and company in the 19th century by producing individual soap bars and advertising them to housewives. He was also known for building a village to house his workers to ensure shared prosperity. Today you can explore the old factory, hear stories from past workers and inhabitants of the village, see a typical worker's house, and learn about the brand's modern incarnation: Unilever, which makes Dove soap and many other recognised products.

## Collections from around the Globe

ART AS INSPIRATION FOR ALL

With the wealth from his soap-making empire, William Lever became an avid collector of art, furniture and cultural objects, filling his many homes. He opened the **Lady Lever Art Gallery**, named in memory of his late wife Elizabeth, to showcase his collections. From Roman sculpture to Chinese ceramics and quilled furniture, the vast collection is varied and extensive.

## Celebrating Northern Waterways

LIFE ON THE CANALS

Where the Shropshire Union Canal meets the Manchester Ship Canal is the **National Waterways Museum**. Here you

### WHERE TO EAT ON THE WIRRAL

**107 Dining Room**
Warm and welcoming restaurant in Heswall with ramp access, a wholesome menu and delicious vegan options. **££**

**Port & Anchor**
Understated restaurant in Ellesmere Port with exciting menu choices, vegan options and delightful desserts. **££**

**Atrium Restaurant & Coffee Shop**
Garden-centre restaurant in Meols with excellent food choices, vegan burgers and a selection of cakes. **£**

can see everything from domed conical boats and the dirty working horse-drawn barges of the industrial period, to the leisure aspect we know and love today. Work up a sweat as you try to work the interactive Ice Breaker boat, and squeeze inside the tiny cabins of the working boats.

## A Geological Curiosity

SANDSTONE LANDSCAPE AND COUNTRYSIDE WALKS

**Thurstaston Common** is a vast area of woodland, parks and heath along the coast of the Wirral. The winding paths will take you to local curiosity **Thor's Rock**, a 30ft-high outcrop of sandstone. Legend has it that the name comes from Thor striking his hammer upon the rock, although the more believable story is that it comes from the Viking settlers in the 9th century (Thurstaston meaning 'village of a man called Thorsteinn'). Linked to the wider Wirral by the **Wirral Way** walking and cycling route, it is an excellent location to spend the day.

## Wildlife Walk by the Marshes

LOCAL ICE CREAM AND SEAFOOD

Once a crucial 18th-century seaport, as an embarkation point for Ireland, the silted up waterfront at **Parkgate** is now a nature reserve and pretty coastal village. Managed by the Royal Society for the Protection of Birds (RSPB), the salt marshes are a beautiful spot for enjoying local wildlife like the little egrets and meadow pipits. In summer, locals and visitors flock here to enjoy a Nicholl's ice cream or local potted shrimp on the walls of the marshes.

## A Seaside Town on the Mersey

OVER THE WATER FROM LIVERPOOL

Holidaymakers have been ascending on the beach at **New Brighton** and **Wallasey** since the Victorian era. Walk along the promenade, past the remnants of the Black Pearl Pirate Ship, for views directly over the Mersey from Liverpool; it offers the perfect vantage point for seeing the impressive city skyline. With long sandy beaches, fairground rides and the aroma of freshly fried seafood, it still captivates the imagination of walkers, bike riders and beach bums alike.

### BEST ICE CREAM

**Nicholls**
A family-run ice cream parlour on Parkgate front since the 1930s, making the velvetiest ice cream on-site in their Art Deco premises. **££**

**Maizy's Ice cream Parlour, Brimstage**
Little ice cream shop next to the Brimstage Maze, with 16 flavours to choose from, including some inventive British favourites like Werther's Originals caramel flavour. **£**

**Artisan Gelato**
Fresh, creamy ice cream made on the premises without too many flavour choices. Perfectly located to enjoy on a walk around West Kirby boating lake. **££**

### GETTING AROUND

Merseyrail covers the Liverpool City Region, across the Wirral and down to Chester meaning you can easily move around the region on a day pass.

The Wirral is primarily flat and easy to walk and cycle. There are specific car-free routes like the Wirral Way to connect you to different areas, but they can be muddy in the winter.

Driving isn't really necessary around Liverpool and the Wirral, but if you do need to bring the car, it's better to park outside the busy central locations and take public transport in as the one-way systems and Mersey Tunnel can be confusing to non-locals.

# ISLE OF MAN

Nestled between Britain and Ireland in the the Irish Sea is the Isle of Man, home to rural countryside, water sports, motorbike racing, fairies and wildlife, including the tailless cat, the Manx. It has an unhurried pace of life and a unique culture, making it a fascinating destination. The weather might be somewhat inclement, but like the rest of the northwest, the Isle of Man makes up for it with its affable community. In the north, there's the impressive Laxey Wheel that pumps water from the mines the pretty seaside town of Ramsey, with a backdrop of green tree-crusted hills; and Snaefell, the island's tallest mountain. In the south, the cute and characterful fishing villages of Port Erin and Port St Mary await. Today the island attracts nature lovers, walkers and railway enthusiasts, as well as those wanting a seaside escape away from the mainland.

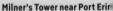

## TOP TIP

Pack for the wind and rain – being an island, it gets weather in the extremes! Even in the summer months it isn't particularly hot and sunny.

Milner's Tower near Port Erin

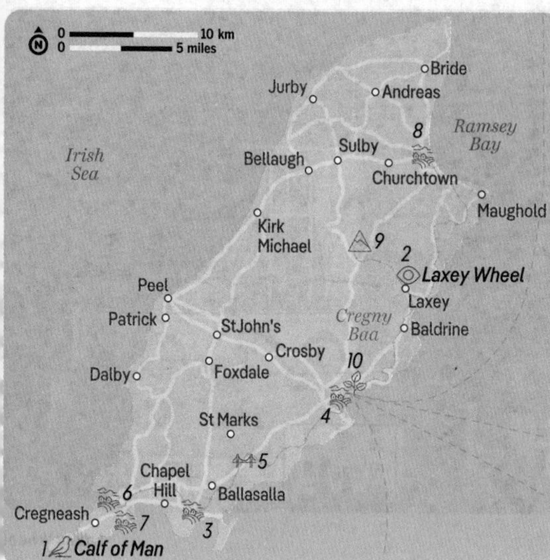


**HIGHLIGHTS**
1 Calf of Man
2 Laxey Wheel

**SIGHTS**
3 Castletown
4 Douglas
5 Fairy Bridge
6 Port Erin
7 Port St Mary
8 Ramsey
9 Snaefell
10 Summerhill Glen

## The Island's Capital

STEAM, ELECTRIC AND HORSE-DRAWN TRANSPORT

The decorative redbrick **Manx Museum** is a great place to begin your visit to **Douglas**. Here you can learn about the natural world of this Unesco Biosphere island and find out where to get up close with seals. Sit back in the museum's deckchairs to enjoy videos of the sights and sounds of the Victorian 'holiday isle', then delve into the Norse beginnings of the island, the Tynwald Parliament, and the Manx language's origins.

There are a number of novel ways to get around. The hissing and puffing of the fire-driven **Steam Railway** evokes excitement as it heaves and snakes its way from Douglas to Port Erin through picturesque countryside and charming Victorian-era stations. Almost 200 years in operation, the **Victorian Electric Tramway** offers views of coastal cliffs as it makes its way up Snaefell mountain. Or ride on a **horse tram**, which has been running since 1876. The trammers (tram-pulling horses) work two hours a day in summer and get a pension scheme guaranteeing a place at the Home of Rest for Old Horses (open May to September),

### BEST HOT DRINKS & VIEWS

**The Sound Cafe**
Cosy Port Erin cafe serving local produce, including a Manx kipper sandwich, with front-row views of the Calf of Man. ££

**Victory Cafe**
Quirky canteen-style cafe located in an ex-Cold War Rotor Radar Station, in Snaefell, on the TT motorcycle racecourse. ££

**The Shed**
Laxey cafe famed for bringing inside dining onto the beachfront with the comfort of blankets, hot-water bottles and a piping hot drink. ££

### WHERE TO STAY ON THE ISLE OF MAN

**The Empress Hotel**
Traditional glass-fronted seafront hotel in Douglas with comfortable rooms. Upgrade for fantastic sea views. ££

**Langtoft Manor B&B**
A rural B&B located a 20-minute walk from Peel's centre. It's comfortable and cosy and serves local food. £

**Ramsey Park Hotel**
Modern hotel overlooking Mooragh Lake and the Ramsey coast with easy access into the island's second-largest town. £

## BEST LUNCHES IN DOUGLAS

**Junk Box**
Piled-high plant-based burgers, loaded fries and vegan chick'n wings to take out or eat in at the eclectically decorated and chilled-out venue close to the Sea Terminal. ££

**The Eatery**
Traditional vegan-friendly cafe on the high street, popular with all ages. The menu includes breakfast, lunch and delicious Hawaiian Waikiki bowls. £

**The Tea Junction**
The island's only dedicated tea shop, with over 20 varieties of loose-leaf tea, serving breakfast, lunch and afternoon tea in a flamboyant setting. ££

Laxey Wheel

An isle of folklore and fairies, you will soon be lured in by the magic. If travelling along the A5 to or from Douglas by bus, you'll be requested to observe the Manx tradition by saying 'Hello Fairies' when crossing the Fairy Bridge – it is considered unlucky not to. You can also wander into the fairies' natural habitat (best after dusk for the twinkling lights) at **Summerhill Glen**, a beautiful trail with woodland and waterfalls.

## Experience Isle of Man's North

SUNSETS OVER THE SEA

**Ramsey**, the second largest town on the island, has a slightly more relaxed approach to life than the capital, with a long sandy beach, seaside hotels, quaint shops on the narrow high street, boats lining the harbour and colourful tiny houses overlooking the water. An iron swing bridge from 1892 provides an interesting link from the town to the promenade by the shipyard. Located on the northern coast, Ramsey is the perfect place to catch the sunset over the horizon.

Along the route of the **Electric Tramway**, you'll see the largest surviving working waterwheel of its kind in the world, the Victorian **Laxey Wheel**. The Lady Isabella, as it is also known, was designed by Robert Casement and built in

### WHERE TO FIND A LOCAL BEER

**The Manx Arms**
A traditional pub in Onchan with a friendly buzz and locally brewed Okell's beer. ££

**The Shore Hotel**
Victorian charm with modern styling, this pub in Laxey serves Old Laxey Brewing Company Beer (made nextdoor!). ££

**The Rovers Return**
Tucked away on a side street, the oldest pub in Douglas has a lively atmosphere. Try the local Bushy's beer or Manx cider. ££

1864 to pump 250 gallons of floodwater per minute from the lucrative zinc mines below, spewing it out into the nearby river. It is an engineering feat.

Ramble your way to the island's highest point from the Steam Railway Station to savour the views and rugged terrain from **Snaefell** (2034ft). You can hike your way up or take a more leisurely journey on the Electric Tramway. The often-windy hike takes between 15 to 30 minutes from Bungalow station; at the summit cafe recharge with a hot drink and, if you're lucky, take in the views over England, Scotland, Wales, Ireland and the Isle of Mann, when Manannan's Cloak isn't obscuring the way. Manannan is the Manx sea god and island's namesake who hides behind a 'cloak of mist' when danger is afoot. To lay folk, this means it's a cloudy or misty day!

### WHY I LOVE THE ISLE OF MAN

**Sarah Irving**, Lonely Planet writer

Relatively unspoilt by the modern age, nurturing its historical past with the railways and trams, and the magical fairy superstitions, the island embraces a slower pace of life – something we mainlanders don't often appreciate. Rugged coastlines, nature-rich waters and breathtaking winds all add to the charm of this northwestern coastal cousin. It's easy to make friends on every corner, absorbing their enthusiasm and passion for the island into my own outlook on the place.

## Southern Isle of Man

DISCOVER THE SOUTH

A ride on the Steam Railway from Douglas takes you to the centre of **Port Erin**, where classic white houses and seaside hotels overlook the quiet bay, making it one of the most picturesque places on the island. This Victorian seaside resort is home to the **Railway Museum**, which charts the history of the island's steam railway from inception in 1873 to the present day.

Continue with the train to **Port St Mary**, a more sheltered part of the island thanks to the breakwater that keeps harsher waves at bay. Here you can dip your toes or (for the brave!) take a swim in the calmer waters.

Once the island's capital city, **Castletown** is dominated by the impressive 13th-century **Castle Rushen**. It is one of Europe's most complete medieval castles, allowing you to step inside the ancient kitchen, dungeon and great hall with thick stone walls, worn spiral staircases and impressive hanging tapestries.

Off the southern coast, you will find the small island Calf of Man, a bird sanctuary since 1939, which sits on the route of Britain's migrating birds. Take a boat trip to the island to see species like peregrines, zorbills and shags. On the mainland is the **Sound**, a natural area and scenic outlook that is abundant with wildlife (including schools of dolphins and sharks) and is the perfect spot to admire the sunbathing seals on the nearby rocky Kitterland. Named a Dark Sky Discovery site, it is also the perfect location for some stargazing.

### GETTING AROUND

The island is easily accessed by air and sea, with the Steam Packet Ferry from Liverpool taking you to the capital city of Douglas.

During peak season (April to October), you have the pick of transport, including buses, Electric Tramway and Steam Railway. In the off-peak months, bus is the primary mode of transport to get you around the island.

The many coastal promenades are easy for walking, cycling and wheeling, though it can be more challenging when heading further inland where it is more hilly.

It's easy to drive around the island, but parking can be at a premium with only on-street parking available for limited times.

JOHN FINNEY PHOTOGRAPHY/GETTY IMAGES ©

Above: Rostwaithe (p528); right: Newcastle (p555)

## THE MAIN AREAS

**KESWICK**
Gateway to the northern Lakes.
p522

**WINDERMERE & BOWNESS**
'Capital' of the most popular Lakes.
p533

**THE CUMBRIAN COAST**
Wild, windswept and teeming with birds.
p546

# THE LAKES, CUMBRIA & THE NORTHEAST

## THE BLEAK AND THE BEAUTIFUL

Lakes, fells, castles and a truly distinct culture: England's northernmost regions are sublimely stark and scenic.

The Lakes, Cumbria and Northumberland are England's wild northern frontier. Historically disputed between Britons, Saxons, Danes and Scots, their beauty can be as harsh as their history. And their variety is equally stunning: the Lakes remind visitors of the Scottish Highlands; only Cornwall is larger than the wild North Pennines among England's Areas of Outstanding Natural Beauty (AONB); and the sheer coastline and historic cities of Northumberland are captivating.

Cities such as Newcastle, Durham and Carlisle have serious historical pedigree, sometimes stretching back to the Romans. It was the Romans, too, who marked the northernmost extent of their British province with one of the ancient world's great engineering feats – Hadrian's Wall. Many choose to walk along the length of this once-mighty barrier, as they do on countless trails through the Lakes, the Pennine Way and the Northumberland Coast. This is truly a place for wanderers.

First-timers will know at once they're in a place unlike any other in the country. The accents aren't just different – entire dialects are unique to precise places. Where you'll hear a northwesterner use 'our' for 'mine', a Geordie (someone from Newcastle and around) will say 'wor'. So 'my wife' could be either 'our lass' or 'wor lass'. What you'll definitely notice is a fierce regionality overlying a welcoming warmth many feel they don't encounter so readily further south.

# Find Your Way

It's compact on the map, but England's north presents obstacles such as high fells, narrow roads and wild weather. Many of its most rewarding places are quite remote, so allow plenty of time to get around.

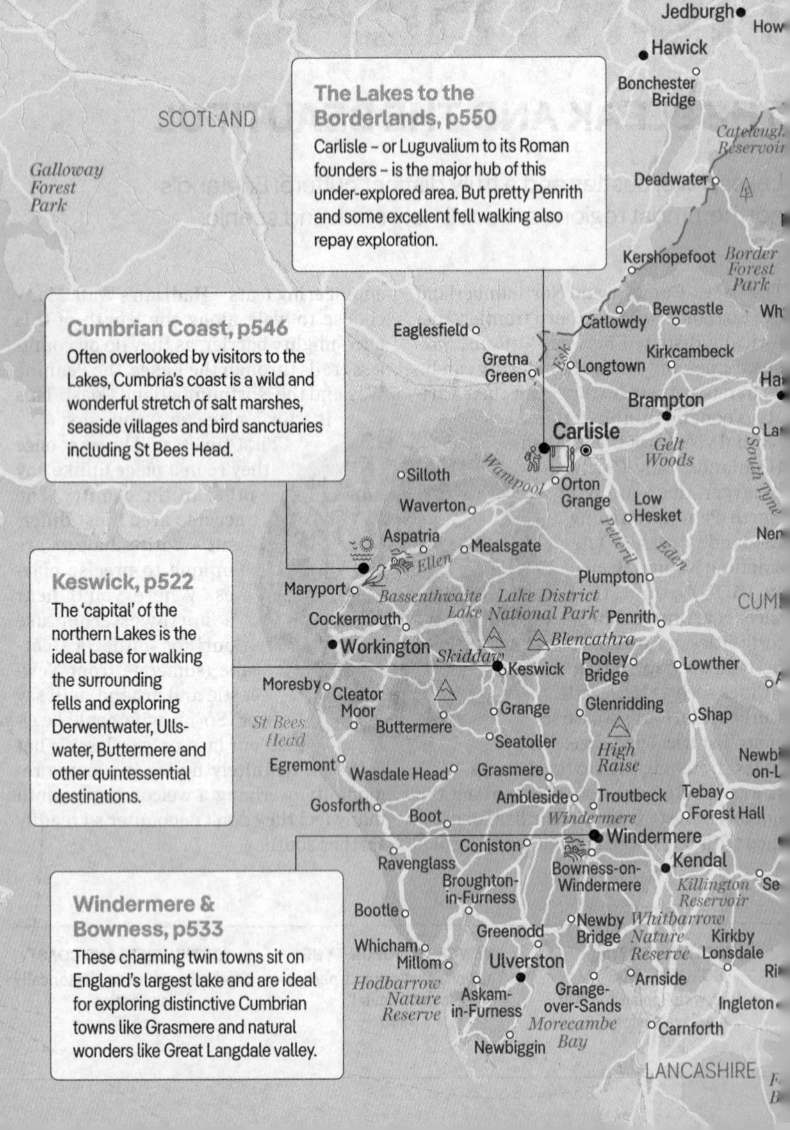

## The Lakes to the Borderlands, p550

Carlisle – or Luguvalium to its Roman founders – is the major hub of this under-explored area. But pretty Penrith and some excellent fell walking also repay exploration.

## Cumbrian Coast, p546

Often overlooked by visitors to the Lakes, Cumbria's coast is a wild and wonderful stretch of salt marshes, seaside villages and bird sanctuaries including St Bees Head.

## Keswick, p522

The 'capital' of the northern Lakes is the ideal base for walking the surrounding fells and exploring Derwentwater, Ullswater, Buttermere and other quintessential destinations.

## Windermere & Bowness, p533

These charming twin towns sit on England's largest lake and are ideal for exploring distinctive Cumbrian towns like Grasmere and natural wonders like Great Langdale valley.

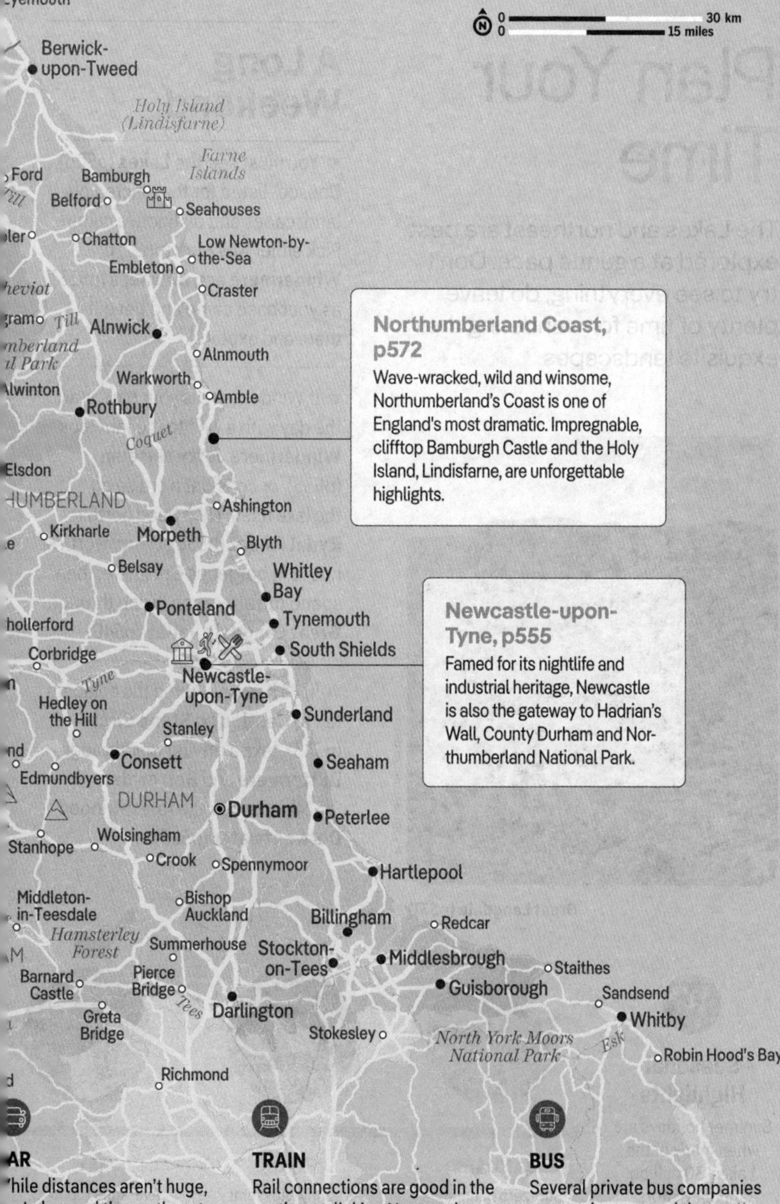


**Northumberland Coast, p572**

Wave-wracked, wild and winsome, Northumberland's Coast is one of England's most dramatic. Impregnable, clifftop Bamburgh Castle and the Holy Island, Lindisfarne, are unforgettable highlights.

**Newcastle-upon-Tyne, p555**

Famed for its nightlife and industrial heritage, Newcastle is also the gateway to Hadrian's Wall, County Durham and Northumberland National Park.

**AR**

'hile distances aren't huge, e Lakes and the northeast are est explored by car. The ast oast Line connects London to ewcastle in three hours; once ere, you'll do best with your wn wheels.

**TRAIN**

Rail connections are good in the northeast, linking Newcastle to London, Carlisle, Edinburgh, Berwick and Durham. In the Lakes, however, only Penrith, Windermere, Kendal and Oxenholme are on a branch of the West Coast Mainline. Local buses or cars are best for exploring.

**BUS**

Several private bus companies run services around the north. They're best for connecting major centres, but present problems for those trying to access remote parts of the Lakes, Northumberland National Park or Hadrian's Wall.

# Plan Your Time

The Lakes and northeast are best explored at a gentle pace. Don't try to see everything; do leave plenty of time for wandering their exquisite landscapes.

MNSTUDIO/SHUTTERSTOCK ©

Great Langdale (p531)

## A Long Weekend

- You must see **the Lakes** (p505), Unesco-listed for their incredible landscapes and distinctive culture. Pick either **Keswick** (p522) or **Windermere** and **Bowness** (p533) as your base camp and get out there and explore!

- If Windermere is your pick, start the day with a visit to the fabulous **Windermere Jetty Museum** (p535), or consider a cruise on the lake itself. Next head north to **Rydal Mount** (p536), Wordsworth's house in gorgeous Grasmere, then spend the afternoon hiking through **Great Langdale valley** (p540).

- If it's Keswick, climb the adjacent fell to **Castlerigg Stone Circle** (p543), take a driving tour through **Buttermere** and **Borrowdale** (p524), or cruise the forest-fringed **Derwentwater** (p525).

## Seasonal Highlights

Summer holidays are when many of the Lakes' 30 million annual visitors arrive. While Northumberland isn't as hectic, aim for the 'shoulder' seasons of spring and autumn in either region.

**JANUARY**

Sub-zero minimums bring snow to many areas, but this can be a magical season. Some attractions, accommodation and restaurants close.

**MARCH**

As spring blossoms, wildflowers, newborn lambs and slightly gentler weather appear. Some attractions and accommodation may still be closed.

**MAY**

Averages top 10°C, rainfall slackens and the crowds haven't yet arrived. One of the best times to visit.

MICHAEL HILTON/SHUTTERSTOCK ©, PHILIP BROOKES/SHUTTERSTOCK ©, LOVEMYDESIGNS/SHUTTERSTOCK ©

## If You Have a Week to Spare

- Try and see the best of both sides of the Pennines. Base yourself in **Newcastle-Upon-Tyne** (p535) and spend a day browsing the **Discovery Museum** (p558), **Life Science Centre** (p558), and the town's abundant pubs and restaurants.

- Next, head for **Northumberland National Park** (p564) and **Housesteads Roman Fort** (p567) on **Hadrian's Wall** (p567). After a day that big, you'll be happy to arrive in **Carlisle** (p553) for the night.

- After wandering the ramparts of **Carlisle Castle** (p553) the next morning, head south into **the Lakes** (p550), setting up base in **Keswick** (p522). From here you can spend the next few days exploring heathery fells, gleaming lakes and irresistible lakeside towns.

## If Time's Not a Problem

- If you can afford to take your time, you're in for a treat. Beyond the must-see attractions such as **Newcastle** (p535), Hadrian's Wall (p567) and **the Lakes** (p550) are gems such as **Durham** (p562), home to Britain's most beautiful Romanesque **cathedral** (p562) and a truly imposing **castle** (p563).

- You'll also be able to tour the **Northumberland Coast** (p572), walking skirting clifftops and photogenic redoubts such as **Alnwick** (p574) and **Bamburgh Castles** (p574).

- There's also the 'Holy Island' of **Lindisfarne** (p576); more remote corners of the Lakes like **Grizedale Forest** (p540) and **Coniston Water** (p544); and the teeming birdlife of **St Bees Head** on the **Cumbrian Coast** (p546).

**JULY**

Peak summer is delightful, but the Lakes can become Britain's most scenic traffic jam. Perfect for walking the Pennines.

**AUGUST**

High summer and school holidays. The weather can be enchanting across the north, but the crowds aren't.

**SEPTEMBER & OCTOBER**

Perhaps the best time to visit. Temperatures start to drop, but the autumn colours and dwindling of crowds easily compensate.

**DECEMBER**

The wettest and near-coldest month in the north is also the season of Christmas markets, gregarious pubs and snow-dusted hills.

Keswick

London

# KESWICK

Gateway to the northern Lakes, Keswick ('kezzick') is a major hub for walkers. A handsome town surrounded by fells, farms and ancient monuments, its twisting medieval layout and lakeside location make it lovely in its own right. While human inhabitation here reaches back to Neolithic times, it flourished from 1276, when Edward I granted it a market charter.

Lake District tourism began here in the 18th century, and Keswick now receives huge numbers of visitors. Expect to queue for lake cruises at busy times, and head out of town for peace and quiet. Keswick has abundant accommodation, pubs and nearby walks. Catbells is an easy ramble, while Skiddaw and Blencathra are harder. Castlerigg Stone Circle sits inscrutably among vistas of the Thirlmere Valley, High Seat and Helvellyn. Sitting on Derwentwater, Keswick is within easy distance of region-defining lakes, peaks and viewpoints such as Bassenthwaite, Thirlmere, Ullswater, Borrowdale and Lattrigg.

### TOP TIP

The Lakes are famous for dark skies, especially away from the light pollution of towns. A Dark Sky Discovery Pack, available online or from tourist offices, tells stargazers where best to scan the heavens. Apps such as the NASA app and GoSkyWatch Planetarium also enhance the experience.

Catbells

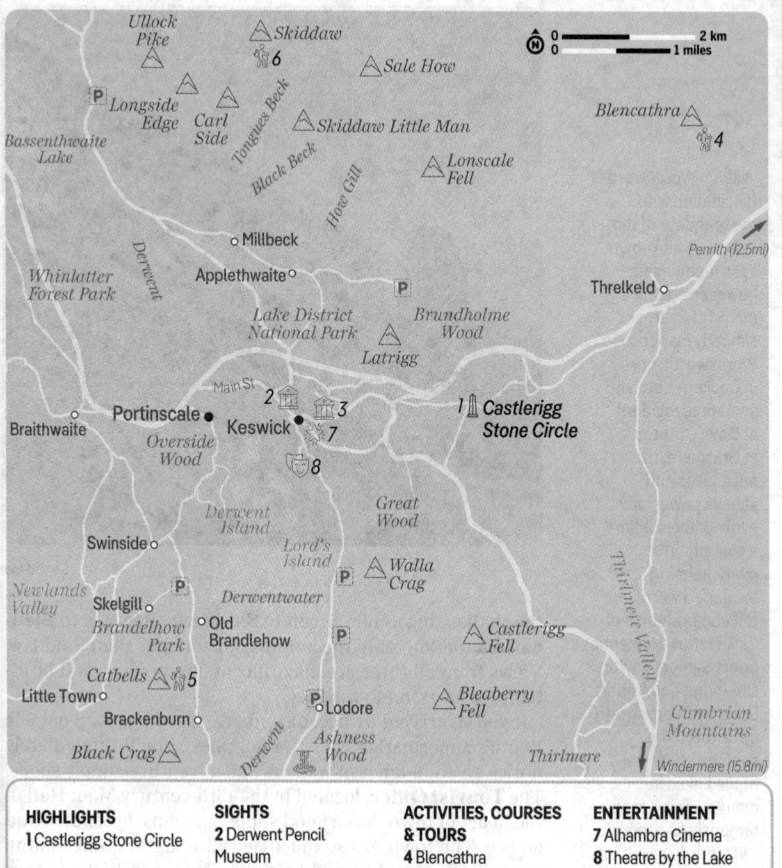


| HIGHLIGHTS | SIGHTS | ACTIVITIES, COURSES & TOURS | ENTERTAINMENT |
|---|---|---|---|
| **1** Castlerigg Stone Circle | **2** Derwent Pencil Museum | **4** Blencathra | **7** Alhambra Cinema |
| | **3** Keswick Museum | **5** Catbells | **8** Theatre by the Lake |
| | | **6** Skiddaw | |

## Climbing Keswick's Photogenic Fells

THE SCOTTISH HIGHLANDS IN MINIATURE

Walking is the best way to see the Lakes, and few places have such richness and variety of hiking as Keswick.

The town's historical importance in graphite mining and, from the 18th century onwards, tourism, has left a legacy of modest attractions. There's the locally focused **Keswick Museum**, the niche **Derwent Pencil Museum**, **Theatre by the Lake** and the handsome, red-brick **Alhambra Cinema**, in operation since 1913. To explore beyond town, first head east 1.5 miles for the short climb to **Castlerigg Stone Circle**. Erected some 4500 years ago, it's surely the most dramatically sited ancient monument in the country.

You may want to rest up for the night before attempting Keswick's more challenging slopes: **Catbells** (a steep 451m climb from Hawes End jetty on Derwentwater's west side);

Skiddaw

### ARTISTS & THE LAKES

William Wordsworth's fascination with the grandeur of the Lakes is well known. Less recognised, however, are the many other artists similarly inspired. To Wordsworth, born in Cockermouth and sometime resident at Dove Cottage in Grasmere, the fells, lakes and valleys powerfully evoked 'the sublime' – something so overwhelming it exceeded words or full comprehension.

Like fellow Romantic poets Samuel Taylor Coleridge and Robert Southey, Wordsworth celebrated the sublime character of the Lakes in many poems – most famously 'Daffodils'.

Writers were not the only artists drawn to the awesome natural beauty of the Lakes. Celebrated Romantic painters inspired by this country include John Constable and William Turner, whose *Buttermere Lake* (1798) hangs in London's Tate Gallery.

the challenging 8-mile circuit to **Skiddaw** (915m); or to **Blencathra** (868m), only the 5 miles but tougher than Skiddaw. Views from all three are magnificent, but none should be attempted in extreme weather.

If you've arrived by bus, disembark at the bus loop outside Booth's supermarket (best for supplies). You'll immediately notice an abundance of walkers and adventure-supply shops. The **Tourist Office**, located in the 16th-century Moot Hall in the heart of town, has a good supply of maps, brochures and advice. The town has so much accommodation that finding something central should be easy – except in high seasons when you should book early.

## Angling in Keswick

THE COMPLEAT ANGLING DESTINATION?

Keswick isn't just irresistible to fell walkers; it's like flypaper for anglers too. Sitting above Derwentwater and below Bassenthwaite, straddling the junction of the Rivers Greta and Derwent, and within easy reach of Buttermere, Loweswater and Crummock Water, there's almost too many fishing spots to choose between. With the right permits and equipment, plus respect for necessary regulations and restrictions, fish-

### WHERE TO GET A BEER IN KESWICK

**The Dog & Gun**
This congenial pub welcomes four-legged walkers and is famous for its goulash. £

**The Wainwright**
Serving eight local real ales, the Wainwright is a former West Cumbria CAMRA (Campaign for Real Ale) winner. £

**The Crafty Baa**
Serving over 100 craft beers, this gregarious inn does live music and good, locally sourced food. £

Crummock Water

ing can be one of the most satisfying, contemplative ways to enjoy Keswick's surrounding lakes.

**Bassenthwaite** and **Derwentwater** are two of the largest lakes in the region. The former, 4 miles long, quite shallow and bookended by two no-boating zones, promises pike, roach, brown trout, dace, eels and even salmon (best sought for in the Ouse Bridge overflow). The latter also has several no-boating zones, contains much the same species as Bassethwaite, and is dotted with leafy islands.

**Buttermere** holds perch, pike, trout and char; **Crummock Water** the same species plus ocean-salmon and -trout from July; and **Loweswater** pike, perch and brown trout (limited to a catch of three). All three have no launching facilities, prohibit powered craft and impose maximums (10 boats at a time on Buttermere and Crummock; four on Loweswater).

Fly fishing for trout and salmon is permitted on Greta and Derwent Rivers. Visit Keswick's Tourist Office or .lakedistrict.gov.uk for boating and fishing permits, maps and regulations.

## BEST PLACES TO EAT IN KESWICK

**Fellpack Kitchen**
This smart bistro's cosmopolitan menu might offer jerked local goat alongside vegetarian mushroom haché. ££

**Casa Bella**
A comforting, high-quality Italian restaurant serving dishes like lasagne made with local beef and venison stew. ££

**Thyme Bistro**
Ignore the serviceable pizzas and pastas for Cumberland sausage or lamb shank on truffled mash. ££

**Plant by Kat's Kitchen**
A cheery vegan café serving hearty plant-based dishes like bean chilli with rice. £

## LAKE CRUISES

Keswick (p522), like **Windermere** (p533) and **Coniston Water** (p544), offers seasonal boat trips on its adjacent lake, Derwentwater. Cruising a circuit of the lake's forested shores and tiny islands is a delight, especially in good weather.

## GETTING AROUND

Compact Keswick has a pedestrianised centre and 10 car parks, generally charging £4 to £10 for overnight parking. If you're staying longer than three nights it's worth applying to Allerdale Council for a monthly permit, valid at its Central, Lakeside and Otley Road long-stay car parks. Competition for space will be fierce in peak periods. Once established in Keswick, your feet are all you'll need to get around: the town's layout is easily learnt. Always be alert for traffic on Keswick's twisty streets, as there'll be plenty of it!

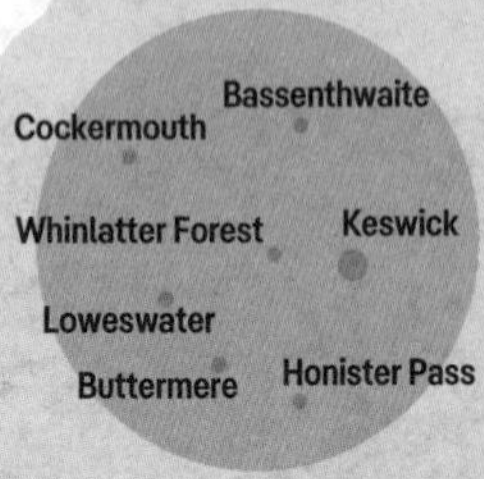

# Beyond Keswick

Cockermouth
Bassenthwaite
Whinlatter Forest
Keswick
Loweswater
Buttermere
Honister Pass

## Keswick is ringed by iconic fells, glacial lakes, charming towns and historic sights, all within easy striking distance.

Derwentwater, south of town, is scenic, shimmering and encircled by a moderately taxing 10-mile trail. Alternatively, explore its wooded islands and 360-degree fell vistas with Keswick Launch (March to November) leaving from Keswick Marina and a number of other jetties.

The bewitching lakes Buttermere, Ennerdale, Crummock, Loweswater and Bassenthwaite are all within 45 minutes' drive. Despite this, they can be quite remote – a relief after the hubbub of Keswick – and sometimes only accessible by foot.

Valleys and high passes such as Borrowdale and Honister Pass, also nearby, deliver quintessential Lakeland splendour. Borrowdale offers accommodation from traditional inns to youth hostels, while Honister's the place for activities like slate-mine tours and the via ferrata rock-face climb.

### TOP TIP

If travelling to Keswick's surrounding attractions and sights by bus, buy a Day Rover – an all-day, hop-on, hop-off ticket that costs less than basic returns.

**Buttermere (p529)**

Ullswater Steamers heritage boat

## Getting Out on the Water

LOVE THE LAKES AFLOAT

The principal attraction of the Lakes is, naturally, the lakes! While many are content to wander their sheep-nibbled shores, there are plenty of ways to experience the lakes that will truly float your boat.

Pleasure cruises are the way most visitors take to the water. **Keswick Launch** plies Derwentwater from March to November, leaving from Keswick Marina and visiting Ashness Gate, Lodore, High Brandelhow, Low Brandelhow, Hawes End, and Nichol End in a 50-minute circuit. **Ullswater Steamers** run the length of that lake all year, stopping at Glenridding, Howtown and Pooley Bridge.

If you'd prefer autonomy, Keswick Launch also rents rowboats and motorboats from Keswick Marina, while subsidiary **Platty+** provides kayaks, paddleboards and even sailing dinghies from the jetty at Lodore. **Derwentwater Marina** in Portinscale, a 15-minute walk from Keswick, also rents a good range of paddleboards, kayaks and the like.

The Lakes are also one of the UK's premier spots for **wild swimming**. Novices may want the reassurance of an or-

### BEST MOUNTAIN BIKING AROUND KESWICK

**Whinlatter Forest**
Whinlatter Forest offers four forest trails of varying difficulty – the most anywhere in the Lakes.

**The Skiddaw Loop**
This Skiddaw circuit has been legendary since 1920. Its 17 miles entail some stiff climbs.

**The Borrowdale Bash**
A challenging 17-mile loop, the 'Bash' connects some of the loveliest scenery south of Keswick.

**Bruntholm Wood and Skiddaw Circular**
This 6.5-mile circuit gains 721m and includes some tough, steep paths. For experienced riders only.

### WHERE TO PAMPER YOURSELF AROUND KESWICK

**The Falls Spa**
In the Lodore Falls Hotel overlooking Derwentwater, this spa has every treatment you could crave.

**The Spa at Underscar**
A luxurious full-treatment spa in a five-star retreat on the slopes of Skiddaw.

**Armathwaite Hall**
Overlooking Bassenthwaite Lake, this spa has all the treatments plus an outdoor hot tub.

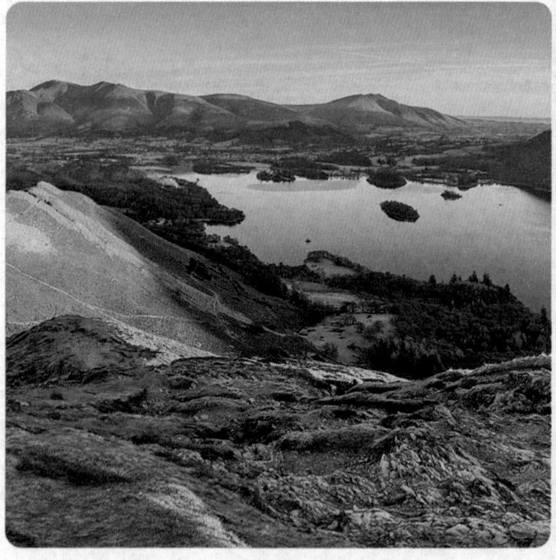
Derwentwater (p527)

**A LANDSCAPE SCULPTED BY WATER**

The sedimentary and igneous rock that forms the lakes and fells was sculpted by ice and water. Whether sedimentary, like the ancient Skiddaw Group, formed by compacted mud, silt and sand, or volcanic like Borrowdale and Eyecott, all were affected by the ice of the Devensian period, Britain's most recent ice age (usually dated to 70,000 years ago).

The Devensian glaciers transformed the Lakes, producing the distinctive landscape of today. Scouring away evidence of earlier glacial events, they left *arêtes* (narrow ridges between valleys), *roches mountonnées* (huge rocks rounded by glacial pressure), mountainside tarns, hanging valleys (smaller valleys sitting above larger ones) and all the features that make this landscape so arresting.

ganised swim with an outfit such as **Swim on the Wild Side** (in Millbeck on Derwentwater's southern end) while the more experienced can seek the best spots on websites like wildswimming.co.uk. **Rosthwaite** in Borrowdale offers a range of experiences – from shallow, family-friendly pools fed by cascades to deeper cliff dives and tarns on the heights of Scafell Pike.

## Fell Walking Around the Northern Lakes

GETTING HIGH ON NATURE

The northern fells are the ranges west of Bassenthwaite Lake and between Keswick and Caldbeck. We're including the north-western fells here too – bounded by Honister Pass, Lorton, Brathwaite and Borrowdale. Together, these regions abound in walkable fells.

Close to Keswick and Bassenthwaite, the easiest is **Lattrigg** (368m), a 2-mile circuit from Keswick, with views over Derwentwater. There's also a moderate 6-mile alternative and similarly gentle walks to **Friar's Crag** and **Castlerigg**,

### BOAT RENTALS ON THE NORTHERN LAKES

**Tall Bloke Adventures**
Guided kayak tours around Ullswater with an experienced instructor. Leaving from Glenridding.

**Glenridding Sailing Centre**
Cruise Ullswater in a hired dinghy or opt for lessons with experienced instructors.

**Derwentwater Marina, Portinscale**
Rents canoes, paddleboards, rowing boats, kayaks and even pedaloes from March to October.

both leaving from town.

At 931m, **Skiddaw** is the largest of Kewswick's encircling fells, with plenty of smaller peaks nearby. Walkers can choose a moderate 4-mile climb from Dodd's Wood to **Dodd** (502m) or other routes up Skiddaw from Millbeck: a difficult 8-mile trail or a punishing 15-mile one. Once there, drink in views of Bassenthwaite, Blencathra and the Dodds.

To the west, **Grasmoor** (852m) and **Eel Crag** (839m) are both accessible from Buttermere, and both moderately challenging. Easier is the 3-mile circuit from Buttermere to **Bleaberry Tarn**, perfect for families and still ravishingly scenic.

The **Honister Pass** has the advantage of height and a car park, so a 2-mile ramble to Dale Head's panoramic 752m peak is accessible to most. **Grange** offers possibly the highest concentration of peaks in the north, with **Catbells**, **Maiden Moor** (576m), **High Spy** (653m), **Grange Fell** (419m) and **Castle Crag** (only 290m but crowned by a prehistoric hill fort) all nearby.

## Visiting Villages Beyond Keswick

BRANCH OUT TO BEAUTIFUL BURGHS

Keswick makes a lovely base, but don't ignore the smaller settlements in its orbit. You'll deal with fewer visitors and fall in love with traditional villages soaked in true Cumbrian character.

Start with **Threlkeld**, 4 miles east, beneath Blencathra. Showing remnants of Neolithic and Anglo-Saxon habitation, its oldest buildings are now the inviting **Horse and Farrier** Inn (1688) and **Church of St Mary** (1777).

Northwest is **Bassenthwaite Lake**, the Georgian hamlet of **Applethwaite** (good for ascending Skiddaw), the unspoilt farming village of **Bassenthwaite** and, ultimately, **Ireby**. One of the loveliest Lakes villages, Ireby is also close to one of Britain's best-preserved **Romano-British farms** (on Aughertree Fell, it may even be Bronze Age) and the 12th-century **Ireby Old Church**.

Thirteen miles west is Georgian **Cockermouth**, where Wordsworth was born and where you'll find the **Wordsworth House & Garden** and the **Kirkgate Arts Centre**. Eleven miles south is **Buttermere** village and lake, then 5 miles further through dramatic Honister Pass, **Seatoller** (our recommended basecamp for climbing Scafell Pike).

One mile on is **Borrowdale**, flush with accommodation, hiking and boating options. Three miles further is **Grange**, entrance to the valley between Grange Fell and Castle Crag.

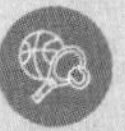

### BEST FUN FOR KIDS AROUND KESWICK

**Keswick Adventure Centre**
Wet and dry adventures including abseiling, paddleboarding and raft building should keep youthful energies engaged.

**Keswick Climbing Wall**
Near Castlerigg Stone Circle, this outdoor climbing centre also offers archery and high rope courses.

**Go Ape Whinlatter**
With Segway tours, treetop adventures and a WildPlay trail, all ages are catered to.

**Puzzling Place**
Puzzling Place's optical illusions include holograms, the Sideways Room, the Anti-Gravity Room and more.

### WHERE TO STAY IN KESWICK

**Howe Keld**
In central Keswick, this former guesthouse has been converted into six smart, self-contained apartments. **£££**

**Linnett Hill**
This handsome Georgian B&B in Fitz Park is recommended for more than its excellent breakfasts. **£££**

**Keswick YHA**
Centrally located and facing the rushing River Greta, this well-run hostel offers a bar and self-catering kitchen. **£**

## DRIVING TOUR OF THE LOVELIEST NORTHERN LAKES

This epic tour of obscure and lovely lakes can't be completed in a day. Narrow, indirect roads and the occasional hike mean it must be attempted in sections. However you approach it, you'll see things most Lakeland visitors never do.

Begin at the Kirkstone Pass Car Park, taking the path to Stony Cove and Thornthwaite Crags to reach the Royal Society for the Protection of Birds (RSPB) sanctuary at the southern tip of 1 **Haweswater**. The next stop, 16 miles south, is 2 **Esthwaite Water**. Visit Hill Top, Beatrix Potter's 17th-century farmhouse, before driving along Esthwaite Water's eastern shore.

Head north again for 3 **Tarn Hows**. The National Trust car park here is a short walk from some of the region's greatest fell views. Next, it's northwest to the immense, glacial Langdale valley, where 4 **Little Langdale**, 5 **Blea Tarn**, 6 **Stickle Tarn** and 7 **Easedale Tarn** are perfect examples of the region's miniature montane lakes. Both Stickle and Easedale do demand moderate hikes.

To explore some western lakes, drive north past majestic Helvellyn (950m), turn west at Keswick, and aim for the car park at the southern end of 8 **Loweswater**. Red squirrels can be seen in its forested fringes. Skirting the lake and its magnificent backdrop, Blake Fell (520m), turn south (perhaps diverting to Cogra Moss to see Blake's southern face reflected in its waters) and set your GPS for Bleach Green Car Park on 9 **Ennerdale Water**. The 7.5-mile circuit of this placid lake may be the best in the region.

As you head south to journey's end, 10 **Wast Water**, pause to visit restored Kinniside Stone Circle. Three miles long, Wast is backed by some of England's mightiest mountains: Great Gable (899m), Pillar (892m) and, tallest of the lot, Scafell Pike.

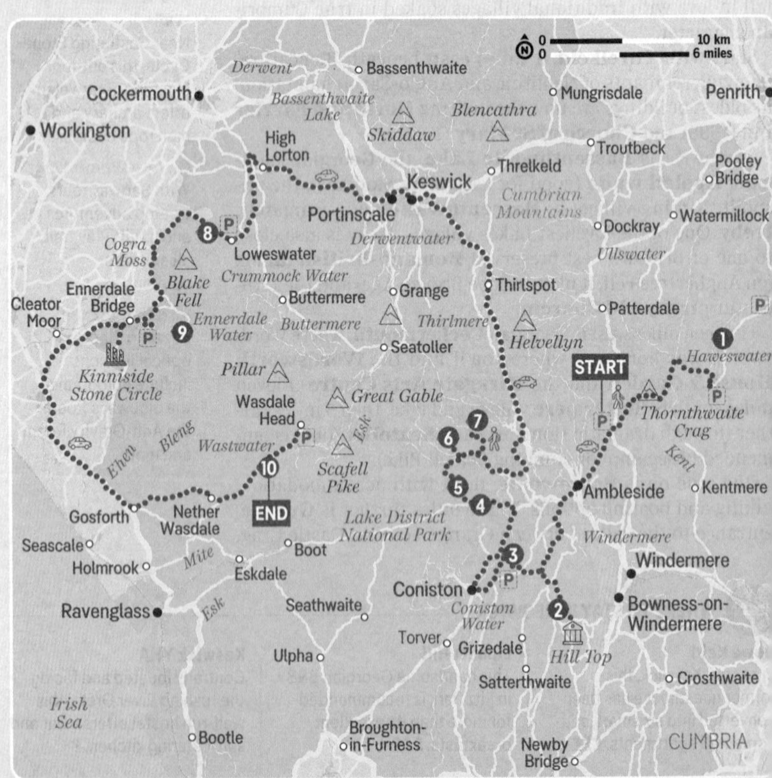

Keswick Market

Take the 21-mile scenic route to **Brathwaite**, starting point for walks through Whinlatter and Newlands Passes. Nearby are the evocative remains of Force Crag mine, the Lakes' last working metal mine.

## Historic Sights near Keswick

WALK IN ANCIENT FOOTSTEPS

The Lakes have been inhabited since Neolithic times, but naturally more survives from later eras. **Castlerigg Stone Circle** is famous, but the nearby remains of **Threlkeld Ancient Settlement** – seven stone huts, a well and agricultural network – receive less attention. The same could be said of **Aughertree Fell** – site of three of the best-preserved **Romano-British settlements** yet discovered.

Naturally the Romans, who built to last, have left intriguing vestiges of their 300-year rule. In the north, the most impressive is the 20-mile **High Street Roman Road** linking **Brougham** to **Ambleside**. It passes over high fells (including the eponymous, 828m **High Street Mountain**) and stone kerbs and metalling can be seen in places.

Grand houses and industrial vestiges mostly make up the remainder of the northern Lakes' historic sights. **Dalemain** – one of the finest properties in the northwest, with delightful gardens, is worth breaking a journey from Pen-

### BEST PHOTO OPPS NEAR KESWICK

**Castlerigg Stone Circle**
This 4500-year-old stone circle is the most photogenically situated in the UK.

**Bowder Stone**
Near Rosthwaite, this 2000-tonne megalith balances on one edge. Climb it for a great shot!

**Black Moss Pot**
Climb from Borrrowdale for the limpid waters, cascades and jaw-dropping backgrounds of Black Moss Pot.

**Great Langdale**
Towered over by the Langdale and Scafell Pikes, this hiker-friendly valley loves the camera.

### WHERE TO BUY LAKELAND PRODUCE

**Keswick Market**
Trading Saturday since 1246, Keswick Market has over 60 stalls selling local produce and handicrafts. £

**Keswick Cheese Deli**
Come to Keswick's historic Packhorse Court for artisanal Cumbrian cheeses and generous gift hampers. ££

**Basecamp North Lakes**
Basecamp's cheery café adjoins a farm shop selling local meats, cheeses, preserves and the like. ££

**NATIVE LAKELAND ANIMALS**

The Lakes, despite their eye-popping pulchritude, are by no means 'unspoilt'. This landscape is deeply affected by thousands of years of human activity, especially farming, felling, mining and building. Many species have vanished over that time; however, some do still remain.

This is the largest redoubt of the UK's 140,000 Eurasian red squirrels. More than 150 species of bird either live or migrate here, including ospreys and red kites, both successfully reintroduced. These remote waters also harbour three rare fish species: the schelly, the Arctic char and the vendace (found only in Derwentwater).

Farming has also bred domesticated species unique to the Lakes, including the fell pony and Herdwick, Rough Fell and Swaledale sheep.

rith to Keswick. Others have strong artistic connections: **Mirehouse** to Alfred, Lord Tennyson, and **Wordsworth House** to the foremost poet of the Lakes.

The industrial heritage of the region, which produced copper, graphite and slate, has not entirely vanished. Lovingly restored **Threlkeld Quarry & Mining Museum** is worth visiting, but is perhaps most popular for its scenic narrow-gauge railway, **Sir Tom**. The spectacularly sited **Honister Slate Mine** offers mine tours and thrill-seeking activities like the via ferrata rock-face climb.

## Industrial Heritage in the Northern Lakes

MANUFACTURING IN 'PARADISE'

Few think of factories when they consider the Lake District. Yet, belying its status as an icon of rural and wild England, it has a long and interesting industrial pedigree. The hammer blows of mining and manufacturing ring out through millennia of Lakeland history.

The earliest known manufacturing took place in the **Langdale Pikes**, where Neolithic craftspeople found the fine greenstone necessary to the Langdale Axe Industry (4000–3500 BCE). Polished, precision-made axes of Langdale stone have been found as far away as Lincolnshire and Ireland.

Other minerals – granite, slate, copper, lead and barites – brought mining to the northern Lakes. Slate from the **Honister Mine** (which is well worth visiting) has been found in local Roman and medieval sites. Slate and coal were carried on the Caldbeck Mines Railway – a vanished, wooden-railed 16th-century trolley system.

Lead and barites were extracted from the **Force Crag** mine near Brathwaite, while granite was extracted from **Threlkeld Quarry**, now an intriguing museum. **Ullswater's Myers Head** lead mine also left some scenic 19th-century remains.

Graphite, discovered in quantity in **Borrowdale**, led to the invention of the pencil in the 16th century – something to learn all about at the **Derwent Pencil Museum**. Caldbeck offers the remains of two mills: the **Howk Bobbin Mill** manufactured bobbins for textile manufacturing from 1857 to 1924, while **Priests Mill** ground corn from 1702 to 1933.

**GETTING AROUND**

Ideally, you'll have your own car and make your own schedule. But be warned that traffic can be intense in holiday periods (especially the August school holidays) and you'll need patience for tailbacks and reversing when meeting oncoming traffic in narrow lanes.

Stagecoach is the private bus network that runs your only other option for traversing Keswick and environs. It runs a variety of services connecting larger centres and popular sites along circuits, and offers Day Rovers – all-day, hop-on, hop-off tickets that usually represent better value than specific return tickets. Be aware that traffic can make bus schedules erratic, and reduced services operate between November and March. Visit stagecoachbus.com for maps and ticketing information.

# WINDERMERE & BOWNESS

Windermere and Bowness are conjoined towns on the eastern shore of England's largest lake. Windermere, 11 miles long and nearly a mile wide, is the glacier-carved ribbon lake at the heart of Lake District tourism.

Still served by trains, unlike most towns within the Lake District National Park, they're separated by just 1.5 miles of B&B-lined tarmac. The tourist economy is highly developed in both. Restaurants, hotels, adventure operators, boat-rental services, outdoor suppliers, pubs and many other businesses proliferate here, confident that the crowds will always come.

Accordingly, prices, vacancies and stress levels change with seasonal demand. Yet Windermere and Bowness retain abundant charm and make the perfect hub for exploring the southern half of the National Park. Throw in an excellent museum, the lure of the island-spangled lake and the proximity of abundant top-tier attractions, and it's clear why these towns remain the District's busiest gateway.

### TOP TIP

Some of Windermere and Bowness's top B&Bs line busy Lake Rd, which connects the two towns. If you're not set on waking up to lake views, getting the cheapest room near Windermere Station or sleeping next door to your dinner reservation, it's worth seeing what this stretch has to offer.

**Lake Windermere**

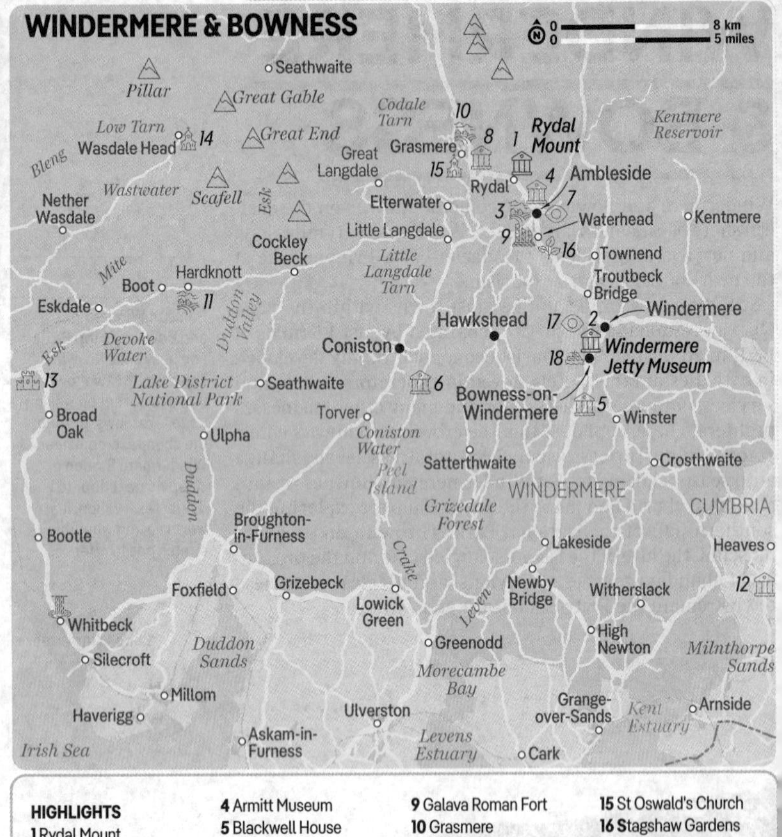


**HIGHLIGHTS**
**1** Rydal Mount
**2** Windermere Jetty Museum

**SIGHTS**
**3** Ambleside
**4** Armitt Museum
**5** Blackwell House
**6** Brantwood
**7** Bridge House
**8** Dove Cottage & Jerwood Museum
**9** Galava Roman Fort
**10** Grasmere
**11** Hardknott
**12** Levens Hall
**13** Muncaster Castle
**14** St Olaf's Church
**15** St Oswald's Church
**16** Stagshaw Gardens
**17** Windermere Lake

**ACTIVITIES & TOURS**
**18** Windermere Lake Cruises

## Wandering about Windermere

PLAY TOURIST FOR THE DAY

When in Windermere and Bowness, there's no sense trying t avoid all things commercial and touristic. Give in to it, and you've got the best chance of enjoying these genuinely appeal ing, if sometimes over-stuffed, towns.

Assuming you're starting in Windermere, having arrived by train on the branch line from Oxenholme, you'll find the won derfully helpful **Tourist Office** immediately on your way int town. Expert advice, reams of literature, permits for boatin and fishing, booking services and pamphlets outlining loca walks are only a fraction of what they can supply.

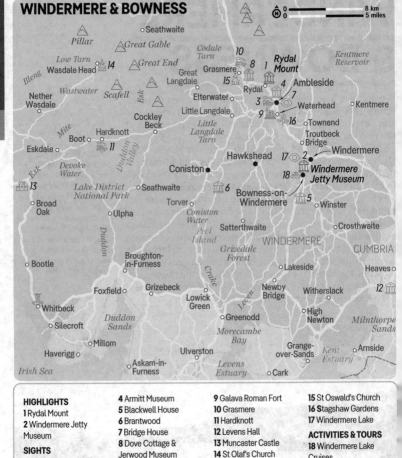

As gravity compels you down Main St (which becomes Nev Rd, then Lake Rd) B&Bs, hotels, cafes, pubs and local-foo

Hardknott Roman Fort

provedores present themselves in orderly procession. Drop your bags at your Windermere accommodation (or take the 599 or 755 bus if you're staying in Bowness and walking 1.5 miles isn't practical) and join the happy hordes.

While Windermere has good places to sleep, eat and drink, Bowness is the true tourist magnet. It's here you'll find **Windermere Lake** and operators like **Windermere Lake Cruises** to help you explore it; 200 years of boating exhibits at the top-notch **Windermere Jetty Museum**; and all the ice-cream parlours, confectioners, adventure outfitters, fish and chip shops, restaurants, parks and pubs you could possibly want. Set your pace to 'stroll', work with the crowds and get into the spirit of it all.

## The Southern Lakes' Historic Treasures

ROCKS, ROMANS AND ROMANTICS

Each successive wave of cultures, conquerors and settlers who made the southern Lakes their home left traces. Our Neolithic ancestors left stone circles at Burnmoor, Swinside, Blakeley Raise and many other places. Following them, the Britons, Romans, Anglo-Saxons, Vikings, Irish, Scots, Normans

### ROME'S LEGACY IN THE SOUTHERN LAKES

The Romans invaded Britain under the Emperor Claudius in 43 CE, but didn't begin to establish forts, roads and settlements in Cumbria until after 70 CE. Having governed 'Britannia' until the early 5th century, their legacy still shows in several places around the southern Lakes.

**Hardknott Roman Fort**, built under Hadrian in the second century CE, retains the footings of its symmetrical walls, bath house and several other buildings. Dramatically sited in the Hardknott Pass, it's a 2-mile walk from Cockley Beck and best accessed by car.

**Ravenglass Roman Bath House** retains the highest Roman walls remaining in Britain, and you can still see the gates and remains of several buildings at **Ambleside Roman Fort**.

### WHERE TO EAT IN WINDERMERE AND BOWNESS

**Bandito Burrito**
This friendly place serves authentic California-style burritos, quesadillas, spiced brisket and other good things. **£**

**Urban Food Kitchen**
Uphill from central Bowness, this contemporary cafe does fine brunch plus more sophisticated evening food. **££**

**Holbeck Ghyll**
Treat yourself to some of the finest dining in the north at this acclaimed restaurant. **£££**

## BEST MICHELIN-STARRED DINING IN THE LAKES

**The Cottage in the Wood**
This 17th-century hotel-restaurant in Whinlatter Forest turns out seasonal deliciousness using plenty of local produce. £££

**Old Stamp House**
Local venison and Herdwick Hogget exemplify a determination to show off the best Lakeland produce. £££

**Hrishi**
Expect Indian flourishes and a separate, wonderful, plant-based menu at the Gilpin Hotel's premier restaurant. £££

**Forest Side**
While Cumbrian beef and Morecambe Bay bass feature, there's equal emphasis on the vegetarian menus. £££

**Allium Ashkam Hall**
Fabulous produce from surrounding farms and woodlands and their kitchen garden build Allium's tasting menu. £££

Muncaster Castle

and subsequent English generations who trod these fells also left substantial legacies.

In the south, the Roman presence is most perceptible at **Hardknott**, a thoroughly excavated 2nd-century fort commanding the wild River Esk valley. Ambleside also displays the footings of a substantial military settlement, Galava (p537), while the bath house at **Ravenglass Fort** retains some of the highest Roman walls still standing in Britain.

Younger, and thus less diminished, are the region's medieval buildings. **Muncaster**, a 13th-century castle built on Roman foundations, is impressively intact. **Sizergh Castle**, set in spectacular gardens south of Kendal, has been home to the Strickland family since 1239.

Other notable houses include Elizabethan **Levens Hall** famed for its topiary, and **Blackwell House**, considered an Arts & Crafts masterpiece. The deep connections between artists and the southern Lakes live on in Wordsworth's **Rydal Mount** and **Dove Cottage**; in Brantwood, John Ruskin's former home on **Coniston Water**; and in Hill Top, Beatrix Potter's 17th-century **Near Sawrey** farmhouse.

Also worth visiting are several notable medieval churches – **St Oswald's** in Grasmere and tiny **St Olaf's** in Wasdale

## WHERE TO STAY IN WINDERMERE AND BOWNESS

**Windermere Boutique Hotel**
On Lake Rd, this handsome Victorian hotel has hot tubs in every en suite. £££

**Mere Lodge**
Wake up to the gentle lapping of Windermere at this modern, self-contained two-bedroom lodge. £££

**Lindeth Howe**
Once owned by Beatrix Potter, this historic, garden-wreathed Victorian hotel is a lakeside legend. £££

– and Troutbeck's **Townend**, where 400 years of farmhouse history are recreated.

## Exploring Ambleside & Grasmere

TWO QUINTESSENTIAL LAKELAND VILLAGES

Windermere's near neighbours, **Ambleside** and **Grasmere**, are two gems of the southern Lakes. Delightfully unspoilt, their stone-and-slate buildings perfectly complement the environment.

At the head of Windermere, Ambleside is a former mining town now irresistible to tourists. Highlights include: Wordsworth's **Rydal Mount**, beautifully preserved and set in delightful gardens; the **Armitt Museum** (where you can learn more about the poet and other local artistic luminaries including Beatrix Potter and John Ruskin); photogenic 17th-century **Bridge House**, straddling burbling Stock Ghyll; Galava Roman Fort, dating in part to the 1st century CE; and the 8 acres of landscaped loveliness at **Stagshaw Gardens**. In fine weather, the steep 5-mile circuit to **Loughrigg Fell** pays off with views of the Langdale Pikes, Bowfell (902m) and Crinkle Crags (859m).

Four miles further north, Grasmere might be the ideal Lake District village. Also closely associated with Wordsworth, is pretty **Dove Cottage**. The connected **Jerwood Centre** is essential for anyone interested in the Romantics, and austere 13th-century **St Oswald's Church** holds Wordsworth's tomb.

Hire boats (from Ableside's Low Wood) to glide cross tranquil **Grasmere Lake** or **Rydal Water** and contemplate the perfect fell scenery. For an invigorating walk, the 4-mile circuit to **Helm Crag** climbs 360m quite steeply, but rewards your effort with the jagged summit rock formation known as the Lion and the Lamb and more peerless views.

**KESWICK'S URBAN ATTRACTION**

ˌou're looking for other Lake District ˌntres with plenty of shopping and a ad selection of pubs and restaurants, **Keswick** (p522) is your best bet. **Derwentwater cruises** (p524) and other non-demanding diversions are also on offer.

**BEST WALKS AROUND WINDERMERE**

**Orest Head**
A gentle 2-mile circuit from Windermere, this rocky prominence promises delectable 360-degree views. Easy.

**Ferry Ride and West-Coast Scenic Loop**
A 5-mile circuit from Bowness to Ferry Nab with a cruise and west-coast panoramas. Moderate

**Stock Ghyll Waterfall from Ambleside**
This 5-mile circuit visits Ambleside, Galava Roman fort and several waterfalls. Park at Waterhead. Moderate.

**Troutbeck Tongue Height**
A 4.5-mile return hike along rural Troutbeck Valley leads to this bucolic, grassy prominence (364m). Moderate.

**GETTING AROUND**

A comfortable 1.5 miles apart, Windermere and Bowness are so close as to be practically one place. They're easily explored on foot. For those with restricted mobility, Stagecoach's 555 (Keswick to Lancaster) and 599 (Kendal to Grasmere) connect the two, with frequent stops around town and connections to Ambleside, Grasmere and other appealing towns nearby. There are at least a dozen car parks among Windermere, Bowness, Ambleside and Grasmere, but they fill up quickly in peak times, when tailbacks and slow progress should be anticipated. Windermere has a station on a branch of the West Coast Main Line, operated by Northern Railway and rejoining the main route at Oxenholme via Kendal.

# Beyond Windermere & Bowness

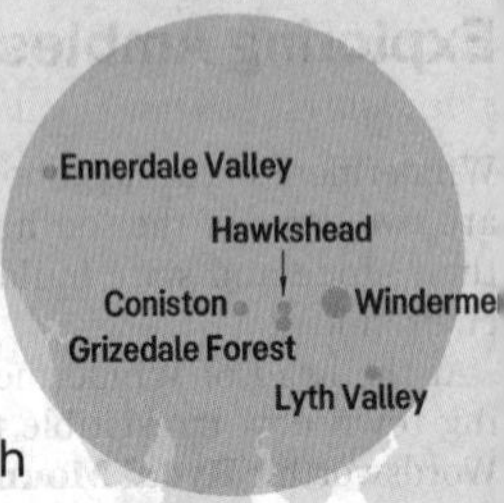

## Windermere and Bowness are within easy reach of the best of the southern Lakes. Be sure to explore!

Beyond Windermere and Bowness lies a panoply of quintessential Lakeland countryside and attractions. The major southern Lakes include Coniston Water, Esthwaite Water and Wast Water, while smaller mountain tarns such as Seathwaite, Little Langdale and Tarn Hows sparkle in panoramic perfection. Adventure seekers, those in need of rural R&R and families will all find what they need in this unique corner of England.

Walkers are drawn to Great Langland valley and its surrounding Pikes; lovers of literature can trace the heritage of Wordsworth, Coleridge, Potter and Southey; art lovers can experience sublime vistas painted by Turner, Constable, Ruskin and William Heaton Cooper; and those simply seeking beauty and tranquillity will find them in abundance.

**TOP TIP**

Base yourself in villages like Coniston and Hawkshead. Deep in the southern Lakes, they are less frenetic than Windermere or Grasmere.

**Coniston Wate**

Wasdale Head Inn

## BEST COUNTRY PUBS IN THE SOUTHERN LAKES

**Masons Arms**
Set on Cartmell Fell overlooking bucolic Winster Valley, the Masons does great locally sourced food. ££

**Drunken Duck Inn & Barngates Brewery**
Walkers returning from Black Fell Peak (323m) love this gastropub serving ales from the adjoining brewery. ££

**Wasdale Head Inn**
A legendary walkers' pub, the cosy Wasdale Head sits below Scafell Pike and Great Gable. £

**The Punch Bowl Inn**
Originally a Georgian smithy, this gregarious inn offers snug rooms and excellent modern British food. ££



# Adventure Activities in the Southern Lakes

AN OUTDOOR ADVENTURE PLAYGROUD

All those fells, rock faces, gills and forests make the southern Lakes one of the UK's best destinations for thrill seekers. Whatever the season, you won't lack for opportunities to get your adrenaline pumping.

**Windermere Outdoor Adventure Centre** hires kayaks, stand-up paddleboards and sailboats for Lake Windermere, and can organise guided tours. **West Lakes Adventures** offers everything from gill scrambling and canyoning in the rocky streams of Eskdale and Wasdale to archery and even raft building.

**Crags Adventures** and **Lake District Adventuring** offer vertical excitement with rock climbing and abseiling at sites including Coppermines Valley, Esk Ghyll, Devil's Canyon and Stickle Ghyll.

## THE NORTHERN FELLS

If you can possibly sate your appetite for altitude and adventure in the southern Lakes, consider tackling the northern fells around **Keswick** (p522), **Ullswater** and **Bassenthwaite Lake** (p528). **Skiddaw** (p529), **Grasmoor** (p529), **Eel Crag** (p529), **Helvellyn** (p543) and **Blencathra** (p524) are all significant climbs that should suffice.

## WHERE TO FIND HOSTELS IN THE SOUTHERN LAKES

**YHA Grasmere Butharlyp Howe**
Near central Grasmere, Burtharlyp offers great-value twins in a Victorian mansion. £

**Hawkshead YHA**
Private rooms sleeping three are a bargain at this listed Regency house above Esthwaite Water. £

**YHA Wasdale Hall**
Perfectly situated for walkers tackling the Lakes' highest peaks, this hostel was a 19th-century manor. ££

**WINNING UNESCO LISTING**

The Lake District won World Heritage Site listing in 2017 – recognition for a unique combination of glorious geology and specially adapted human activity.

Spectacular highlands and limpid lakes are obvious winning criteria. But the region's distinctive farming history, working with a challenging landscape to adapt endemic livestock such as Herdwick sheep (bred from Scandinavian species introduced by Norse settlers over 1000 years ago) is as important. Together, nature and agriculture earned recognition of the Lakes' unique significance.

Naturally, the slopes surrounding Windermere and Bowness also offer plenty of great mountain biking. The **Kentmere Horseshoe Circular** is a tough 12-mile loop gaining over 1000m in height and crossing some rough and rocky patches. On Windermere's western shore the **High Wray and Wray Castle Circular** is a much easier, flatter 6-mile circuit offering the chance to visit 19th-century Wray Castle. **Country Lanes Cycle Centre** near Windermere Station can supply bikes, maps and advice.

Even the onset of winter, despite the snow and wild weather, doesn't mean the fun has to stop. Experienced operators like the **Lakes Mountaineer** organise expeditions into Great Langdale, where you can scale Scafell Pike from Wasdale Head or the Langdale Pikes.

## Cycling in the Southern Lakes

FIND FREEDOM ON TWO WHEELS

If cycling is your thing, don't be daunted by the hills of the southern Lakes. Cycling infrastructure is excellent, and it can be the most rewarding way to explore this exceptional landscape. Whether it's a challenging fell climb or a laidback family ride you're after, you'll find it. See visitlakedistrict.com for details of the cycle routes and shops below.

The pastoral **Lyth Valley**, famous for its spring damsons and daffodils, offers a flat,13-mile circuit from Sizergh Castle through woodland and typical Lakeland farms. The 20-mile circuit from Ravenglass to Eskdale mostly follows a bridleway and demands more cycling experience and fitness.

The **Ennerdale Valley** offers trails of up to 10 miles, with a 350m climb from Bowness Knott car park to the trail head. Peaceful forest cycling and views of the lake, Pillar and Great Gable reward your efforts. It's suitable for mountain bikes, as is **Grizedale Forest**, which has seven purpose built trails catering to all abilities.

Park at Egremont's Beck Green car park for the undulating eight-mile **Under Cold Fell Circuit**. Views over the Irish Sea can be incredible on clear days, but be aware the route is all on-road. **Windermere to Staveley** (11 miles) is a good choice for families.

You'll find bikes, gear, maps and advice at **Total Adventure** (Windermere), **West Lakes Adventure** (Eskdale), **Lake District Bikes** (Lowick) and many other providers.

**PENNINE HIKING**

If you crave a different landscape to roam, the nearby **North Pennines AONB** (p564) offers heights and hikes aplenty. The Pennine Way weaves through here, while ascents to Cross Fell and the astonishing High Cup Gill will satisfy any amount of wanderlust.

### WHERE TO FIND ACCESSIBLE ACCOMMODATION IN THE SOUTHERN LAKES

**Foxglove Nook, Calder Bridge**
Step-free access, wide doors and other wheelchair-friendly features distinguish this rural cottage for four. £

**The Daffodil, Grasmere**
Roll-in showers, wheelchair-accessible parking and other touches make this stately hotel appealing. £££

**Burnside Apartments and Spa, Bowness**
Fully accessible luxe lodging near the Windermere waterfront. £££

Torver Bridge, near Coniston

## Quintessential Villages of the Southern Lakes

THE REGION'S 'REAL DEALS'

Much-loved Bowness, Grasmere and Ambleside are wonderful destinations – that's not in doubt. But some may feel they're missing the 'real' southern Lakes – the villages where Beatrix Potter–themed cafes and high-end outdoor outfitters don't dominate the main street. While these villages are by no means 'secret', they exist to serve local needs first, preserving the Lakeland character that's so closely cherished.

**Coniston** can be packed with sightseers and walkers, but it's unmistakably a 'real' Cumbrian town. Its stone-and-slate cottages, traditional pubs (notably **the Black Bull** and **the Sun**, both over 400 years old) and farmhouse B&Bs (**Bank Ground Farm**, used by Arthur Ransome as the model for Holly Howe Farm in *Swallows and Amazons*, published in 1930 epitomise Lake District beauty. Take a lake cruise on the **Steam Yacht Gondola**, brush up on John Ruskin at **Brantwood** and the **Ruskin Museum**, or climb the **Old Man of Coniston** (803m) while you're here.

### BEST LAKELAND HERITAGE RAILWAYS

**Ravenglass and Eskdale Railway**
One of the world's oldest narrow-gauge railways runs steam trains along this scenic 7-mile route.

**Lakeside and Haverthwaite Railway**
This restored passenger railway connects with the Windermere ferry from Lakeside to Bowness and Ambleside.

**Threlkeld Quarry & Mining Museum Railway**
'Sir Tom' and two other locos run a half-mile circuit around this former quarry.

**Millerbeck Light Railway**
Several light engines run a meandering mile circuit through Millerbeck House's charming woods and meadows.

### WHERE TO EAT BEYOND WINDERMERE AND BOWNESS

**Mortal Man, Troutbeck**
This beloved inn, dating to 1689 and with character to burn, does British pub food brilliantly. ££

**The Yan, Grasmere**
An exceptional bistro in a charming former farmhouse, the Yan concentrates on hearty, pleasing dishes. ££

**Herdwick's Cafe, Coniston**
Locally run, Herdwicks has the carbs you need to tackle the Old Man of Coniston. £

## BEST ACCOMMODATION FOR HIKERS

**Lingmell House, Wasdale**
This cosy B&B is run by nearby, legendary walkers' rest the Wasdale Head Inn. ££

**Langdale Hotel & Spa, Great Langdale**
Seeking luxury after a strenuous day up the Langdale Pikes? This is the place. £££

**YHA Black Sail, Ennerdale Bridge**
Remote and handy for peaks including Great Gable, Pillar, Red Pike (755m) and Steeple (819m). £

**Hows Wood B&B, Holmrook**
On Eskdale's 400-year-old Hollins Farm, this B&B is perfect for Scafell and the western fells. ££

Hiking trail, Scafell Pike

**Hawkshead**, 4 miles east, is similarly 'authentic' and nc less photogenic. Visit Beatrix Potter's 17th-century farmhouse **Hill Top**, see her watercolours at the **Beatrix Potter Gallery**, walk an enchanting 4 miles to **Tarn Hows** and spend a night at Victorian B&B **Yewfield**.

Other equally distinctive villages in the southern Lakes include **Troutbeck** (home to restored farmhouse Townend c 1700), **Cartmel** (for 12th-century Cartmel Priory), **Nether Wasdale** (don't miss the excellent Strands Inn & Brewery) and **Eskdale Green**.

## Tackling the Southern Peaks

AS HIGH AS ENGLAND GETS

While the northern Lakes abound with towering fells, the very highest lie further south. The southern and western fells and heights around Great Langland valley are a continuous procession of intimidating peaks, some the result of volcanoes and all shaped by millennia of weathering and glacial action.

Those with the climbing bug often have to tackle the biggest – and in England, that's **Scafell Pike** (978m). On a clear day, Snowdon (1085M) in Wales and Slieve Donard (850m) in Northern Ireland are visible from its summit. The mos

### ADVENTURE OPERATORS BEYOND WINDERMERE

**Outdoor Adventure Company, Kendal**
This do-it-all outfit offers everything from axe throwing to quad biking and archery. ££

**Coniston Boating Centre, Coniston**
Rents kayaks, paddleboards, motorboats and bicycles from Coniston Landing. Closed over winter. £

**Lake District Climbing, Ambleside**
Climbing and mountaineering expeditions are led by Jim Evans, who has over 30 years' experience. ££

popular route up is from Wasdale, although Seatoller to the north offers a more interesting approach. From the summit, paths lead to the grassy bowl of **Lingmell Col** (734m), the ridge of **Mickledore** (840m) – which then leads to **Sca Fell** (964m) and **Great End** (910m) – **Esk Pike** (885m) and **Allen Crags** (785m) via **Esk Hause** pass.

The **Langdale Pikes** run along the northern fringe of Great Langland valley, east of Scafell. The most prominent are **Bow Fell** (902m), **Harrison Stickle** (736m), **Pike o'Stickle** (709m) and **Pavey Ark** (700m). Other notable peaks in the Coniston region include the **Old Man of Coniston** (803m), **Brim Fell** (796m) and the comparatively wee **Black Fell** (323m), north of Tarn Hows.

All these fells *can* be climbed, but should obviously only be attempted by fit, experienced, well-prepared hikers, when conditions are good.

## Painting in the Lakes

A LANDSCAPE ARTIST'S DREAM

The Lakes are inspirational – that much is agreed! From the Neolithic people who erected stone circles whose purpose we may never decipher to the amateurs seeking the perfect spot to produce their easels and watercolours, there's something about this country that moves humans to express deep feelings.

The most famous painters associated with The Lakes are the Romantics: JMW Turner and John Constable. But there are many others: William Heaton Cooper, famous for his impressionistic Lakeland landscapes; Sheila Fell, who used oils to convey the melancholy and awe of her native Cumbrian mountains; the critic and painter John Ruskin (who lived here but rarely painted it); and Beatrix Potter, whose also had a talent with watercolours.

If you're moved to imitate these luminaries, consider a painting course or holiday with **Art Painting Holidays**. Sites that may inspire are listed at lakedistrict.gov.uk. There's **Packhorse bridge** at Wasdale Head; **Castlerigg Stone Circle**, with its awe-inspiring backdrop of High Seat (608m), **Helvellyn** and **the Thirlmere Valley**; **Yew Tree Tarn** near Coniston; and **Rather Heath Tarn** near Kendal.

Of course, there's no need to fall in with others' tastes. The Lakes are so abundant in glorious vistas, changing with the light and seasons, that you're sure to find something worthy of your brushes. Keep your materials to hand and your eyes open, and you'll definitely stumble across *your* inspiration.

### BEST GALLERIES IN THE SOUTHERN LAKES

**Armitt Museum, Ambleside**
Wonderful for Abraham Brothers Lakeland photographs, Potter watercolours, work by Kurt Schwitters and landscape exhibitions. £

**Ruskin Museum, Coniston**
Dedicated to Coniston and Ruskin, this small collection contains some of his sketches and watercolours. £

**Jerwood Centre, Ambleside**
Next to Dove Cottage, this major collection of 9000 Lake District works includes Turners and Constables. ££

**Beatrix Potter Gallery, Hawkshead**
In charming Hawkshead, this 17th-century building displays the writer's sketches and watercolours, composed for her books. £

### WHERE TO FIND WALKERS' PUBS IN THE SOUTHERN LAKES

**The Old Dungeon Ghyll Hotel, Great Langdale**
This venerable hikers' inn in Great Langdale does packed lunches for climbing the Langdale Pikes. £

**The Langstrath Country Inn, Stonethwaite**
North of Langdale, this secluded hikers' inn was built as a miner's cottage in 1590. ££

**The Boot Inn, Holmrook**
Perfect for Eskdale valley walks, you'll find great value rooms and excellent cooking at the Boot. ££

## Camping in the Southern Lakes

DON'T FORGET YOUR THERMALS!

Getting away from cars, crowds and creature comforts can be the best way to enjoy the Lakes. Camping at a designated site is the surest way to achieve that. Wild camping isn't allowed anywhere in the national park (unless you have permission from a private landowner).

While weather conditions can always be extreme at altitude, and many might avoid camping in the colder months, it's possible to camp here year-round. Each season brings its own delights (and difficulties): winter is the quietist season, and you may be rewarded with bright days and stirring snow-clad scenery; spring brings damsons, daffodils, bluebells and the beginning of warmer days; summer means long walking hours, occasional glorious weather, and more chance of striking up a conversation with fellow walkers over a well-earned pint; and in autumn you'll be treated to stunning colours and the dwindling of crowds.

The most popular areas to camp around the southern Lakes are: **Eskdale** (with campsites in Boot and Fisherground); **Langdale** (one site: Great Langdale near Dungeon Ghyll); **Wasdale** (one site on Wast Water); and near **Coniston Water** (three sites).

Being properly prepared is essential. You should have: accurate maps; warm, waterproof walking clothes; comfortable, broken-in boots; food and water, including emergency supplies; a decent tent capable of withstanding mountain weather; a torch, mobile phone and power pack; sun protection; and a comfortable pack.

### ALFRED WAINWRIGHT

Hero to many a Lake District hiker, Alfred Wainwright (1907-91) – AW to his fans – was an author, artist, cartographer and inveterate hill-walker whose classic seven-volume guidebook series, *The Pictorial Guides to the Lakeland Fells,* remains the bible for many walkers. Filled with hand-illustrated maps, painstaking route descriptions and quirky, sometimes poetic writing, they are the record of a lifelong love affair with the Lake Distric landscape.

The first guide was published in 1955, and six decades later they've sold well over a million copies. Second revised editions were published in 2011 by author Chris Jesty, followed by the third updated edition in 2020 by Clive Hutchby.

## Festivals in the Southern Lakes

FUN TIMES BENEATH THE FELLS

The southern Lakes, like their northern counterparts, offer a crammed calendar of festivals and events.

Music festivals are especially popular, and are held in both larger centres and across the region. Based in Ambleside every August, the **Lake District Summer Music Festival** includes performances from aspiring and established classical musicians. July's **Kendall Calling** entices young festival goers with four days of camping and music in Lowther Deer Park, 22 miles north of Kendal. More sedate (and closer to Kendal) is Staveley's three-day **Lake District Folk Weekend** in August. There's even live music at November's **Kendal Mountain Festival**, the UK's largest 'gathering of outdoor enthusiasts'.

### WHERE TO FIND CAMPSITES IN THE SOUTHERN LAKES

**Howthwaite Campsite, Coniston**
A National Trust site perfectly positioned for Coniston village, the Old Man and Tarn Hows. £

**Great Langdale Campsite, Great Langdale**
An ideal spot for Langland Valley and Pike walks, and near an excellent hikers' pub. £

**Wasdale Campsite, Wasdale Head**
Gloriously located between Wast Water and Scafell Pike; has pitches for campervans. £

Kendal Calling

Country fairs are long-established highlights in the ruggedly rural southern Lakes. Highlights of the agricultural calendar include: July's **Coniston Country Fair** (featuring trade stalls, a fell race and traditional Cumberland wrestling) and, all in August, **Hawkshead Show** (focusing more on agricultural displays); Bootle's **Black Combe Country Fair** (dog shows, fell-pony displays and kids' activities); and Torver's **Lakeland Country Fair** (more dogs and wresting, plus craft-making displays).

Competitive meetings over July and August include the **Rydal Sheepdog & Hound Show** and jamborees of Lake District sports at the Ambleside and Grasmere sports festivals. Less typical are the **Dark Skies Festival**, where attention turns heavenwards every autumn, and **The Lakes International Comic Art Festival**, held in Bowness in September.

## BEST BEER FESTIVALS IN THE SOUTHERN LAKES

**Northern Craft Beer Festival, Staveley**
At Hawkshead Brewery in Staveley each July, this festival caters to ale aficionados and is family friendly.

**The Strands Inn & Brewery Beer Festival, Wasdale Head**
Music, food and beer adorn this three-day May festival at the legendary Wasdale walkers' inn.

**Grasmere Guzzler, Grasmere**
Grasmere erupts each September for this celebration of beer and gaiety centred on Tweedie's Bar.

**Broughton Festival of Beer, Broughton-in-Furness**
Pubs in and around Broughton host four days of tastings and events every autumn.

## GETTING AROUND

The southern Lakes, like the northern, are not necessarily straightforward to explore. Your own car promises the greatest freedom and access, but comes with the unavoidable problems of high traffic (especially in holiday periods), narrow roads that are twisting, indirect and sometimes rough and steep, and the hassle of parking.

The bus network run by Stagecoach is the resort of choice for many. The 555 from Keswick to Lancaster, the major north–south route, is good for Windermere, Ambleside, Rydal, Grasmere and Staveley and Burneside, which are also on the minor branch railway running to Kendal and Oxenholme.

# THE CUMBRIAN COAST

Cumbrian Coast

Lond

Despite its proximity to the Lake District, the Cumbrian Coast welcomes a comparative trickle of visitors. This is regrettable, as the coast displays a distinctive, fascinating alternative side to the tourist-oriented Lakes. A now-defunct swathe of heavy industries has left its mark, both on the coastal landscape and on its towns, whose people can no longer rely on the mines, shipyards and steel plants for guaranteed employment.

Dry gallows humour and a lack of pretension characterise the local 'character', if such a thing can be defined. You'll encounter it in once-popular Victorian seaside resorts like Allonby, Seascale, St Bees and Silloth. And, from the Solway Firth to Arnside & Silverdale, there are several Areas of Outstanding Natural Beauty that are never awash with tourists. Add Roman remains, medieval castles and thriving bird sanctuaries, and you've got a fistful of reasons to visit this little-known corner of England.

**TOP TIP**

You'll probably make good use of the Cumbrian Coast Line, which connects Carlisle with Barrow-in-Furness via Maryport, Whitehaven, St Be Ravenglass and other towns of interest. It's wonderfully scenic, with views of Lakelan fells, coastal reserves and th Irish Sea. If you plan on makir several stops it's worth inves in a Cumbrian Coast Day Ran (adult/child £22.70/£11.35) rather than forking out for individual tickets.

**Solway Firth (p548**

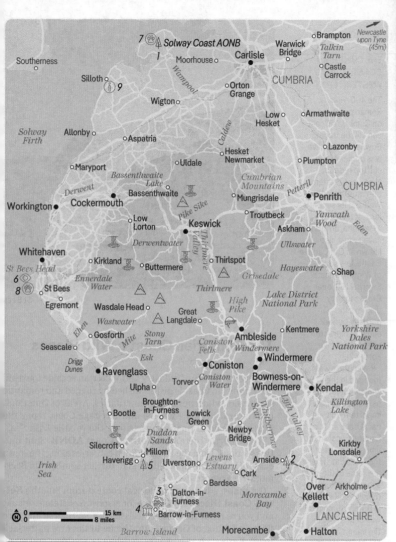

Solway Coast AONB
Newcastle upon Tyne (45mi)
Brampton
Warwick Bridge
Talkin Tarn
Carlisle
Moorhouse
Southerness
Castle Carrock
Silloth
CUMBRIA
Wampool
Orton Grange
Wigton
Low Hesket
Armathwaite
Solway Firth
Allonby
Aspatria
Caldew
Lazonby
Hesket Newmarket
Uldale
Plumpton
Maryport
Bassenthwaite Lake
Cumbrian Mountains
Derwent
Bassenthwaite
Petteril
CUMBRIA
Cockermouth
Mungrisdale
Penrith
Workington
Pike Sike
Troutbeck
Yanwath Wood
Low Lorton
Keswick
Eden
Askham
Derwentwater
Thirlmere Valley
Ullswater
Whitehaven
Kirkland
Thirlspot
St Bees Head
Buttermere
Hayeswater
Shap
Ennerdale Water
Grisedale
St Bees
Thirlmere
Lake District National Park
Egremont
High Pike
Wasdale Head
Great Langdale
Wastwater
Ambleside
Kentmere
Yorkshire Dales National Park
Ehen
Gosforth
Stony Tarn
Mite
Coniston Fells
Windermere
Seascale
Windermere
Esk
Drigg Dunes
Coniston
Ravenglass
Bowness-on-Windermere
Torver
Coniston Water
Ulpha
Kendal
Broughton-in-Furness
Lyth Valley
Killington Lake
Bootle
Lowick Green
Scar
Whitbarrow
Duddon Sands
Newby Bridge
Silecroft
Kirkby Lonsdale
Millom
Haverigg
Ulverston
Levens Estuary
Arnside
Irish Sea
Cark
Bardsea
Over Kellett
Arkholme
Dalton-in-Furness
Morecambe Bay
0 15 km
0 8 miles
Barrow-in-Furness
LANCASHIRE
Barrow Island
Morecambe
Halton

**HIGHLIGHTS**
1 Solway Coast AONB

**SIGHTS**
2 Arnside & Silverdale AONB
3 Barrow-in-Furness
4 Dock Museum
5 RSPB Hodbarrow
6 St Bees Head

**ACTIVITIES & TOURS**
7 Campfield Marsh RSPB
8 St Bees Heritage Coast

**INFORMATION**
9 Solway Coast Discovery Centre

**Arnside (p549)**

St Bees

**THE CUMBRIAN COAST: ROME'S WESTERN LIMIT**

The 400-year Roman presence on Cumbria's Coast can still be traced. Bowness-on-Solway was originally the clifftop redoubt Maia – the western terminus of Hadrian's Wall and its second-largest fort.

Maglona, an inland cavalry fort also known as Old Carlisle Castle, lies south of Wigton. Coastal Swarthy Hill, near Crosscanonby, displays the partially buried and reconstructed remnants of Mile Fortlet 21.

Ravenglass was founded in the 2nd century CE as Itunocelum, an important Roman naval base and the Empire's westernmost limit. The walls of the fort's bath house are some of the most substantial Roman remains still standing in Britain. Itunocelum was connected to the inland forts at Hardknott and Ambleside by a road through Hardknott Pass.

## The Cumbrian Coast's Wild Places

SEA, SANDS AND SOLITUDE

Despite its history of industry and Victorian seaside tourism, the Cumbrian Coast is distinguished by rugged and romantic sections of wilderness. Bird sanctuaries, Areas of Outstanding Natural Beauty (AONBs) and Heritage Coast repay the intrepid, as do dramatic sunsets over the volatile Irish Sea.

To the north, there's the **Solway Coast AONB**. Split into two sections: from the Esk and Eden estuaries along the south coast of Solway Firth to Silloth and, further south, from Beckfoot to Maryport.

Get maps, advice and historical context from Silloth's **Solway Coast Discovery Centre** (or atsolwaycoastaonb.org.uk) and you're ready to explore the estuaries, saltmarsh and rare flora and fauna of Grune Point (home to the rare natterjack toad). Birds such as lapwings, redshanks, warblers and many others can be spotted both here and at **Campfield Marsh RSPB sanctuary**, further north.

**WHERE TO STAY IN CUMBRIAN COASTAL VILLAGES**

**Cartmel**
Stay in tiny Cartmel for its 12th-century priory and excellent restaurants and food shops.

**Ravenglass**
Second-century Ravenglass offers Muncaster Castle, a heritage railway to Eskdale and substantial Roman ruins.

**Maryport**
You'll find the Lake District Coast Aquarium, an 1846 lighthouse and Senhouse Roman Museum here.

To the south is **St Bees Heritage Coast**, an important RSPB sanctuary for puffins, terns and the UK's only black guillemot colony. There's also 2 miles of spectacular coastal walking and a broad, sandy beach.

Ravenglass to Silecroft, the only coastal section of the Lake District National Park, contains the Esk Estuary – a world of dunes, saltmarsh and abundant birdlife. Morecambe Bay's glorious **Arnside & Silverdale AONB** is grossly underappreciated. Its varied coastline, ancient woodlands, limestone pavements and undulating meadows promise those elusive goals: solitude and serenity.

## Cumbrian Coastal Industry

CENTURIES OF MANUFACTURING AND MINING

It's quiet today, but the Cumbrian Coast once rang loud with many industries. Coal-, iron- and slate-mines; shipyards; steelworks; mills; quarries; goods trains; and industrial harbours all operated here. It's almost all defunct now, leaving crumbling remains that can be fascinating and forlorn.

**Barrow-in-Furness** was one the area's busiest industrial ports. Railways were built to transport iron and slate here, and by the 1870s it could boast the world's largest steelworks. Docks and shipyards were constructed, and from the mid-19th century a thriving shipbuilding industry grew. Today only BAE Submarine shipyards still operate, and you'll need the **Dock Museum** to get some sense of Barrow's heyday.

**Hodbarrow Iron Mine** operated in Haverigg from 1850, building a sea wall for its harbour. The mine is now an **RSPB sanctuary**. Other now-silent steelworks can be seen at **Workington** and **Broughton-in-Furness**, where the evocative remains of the 18th-century **Duddon Furnace** are worth visiting. **Whitehaven** thrived on its colliery and has a harbour and lime kiln dating to the 17th century. Ravenglass's **Muncaster Mill** operated from the 15th to the 20th centuries, leaving substantial remains.

The big industry today is power. The 'Energy Coast' is home to **Sellafield** nuclear power station and numerous wind farms, and there are plans for a new colliery near Whitehaven.

### BEST VICTORIAN RESORTS OF THE CUMBRIAN COAST

**Seascale**
Close to Sellafield nuclear power station, once-popular Seascale retains some 19th-century elegance.

**Allonby**
Allonby is distinguished by its long, sandy beach and lovely prospects of Solway Firth.

**Silloth**
Gateway to the both sections of the Solway Coast AONB, Silloth still has its Victorian promenade.

**St Bees**
Blessed with a stretch of sandy beach, dignified centre and proximity to St Bees Head.

### GETTING AROUND

The Cumbrian Coast is served by the Cumbrian Coast Line from Carlisle to Barrow-in-Furness via the principal coastal towns between. An unlimited day ticket costs £22.70/11.35 for adults/children. Driving along the coast is nowhere near the ordeal it can be in the Lake District National park – the A595 runs just inland from the coast and parking should never be too difficult. Barrow, Workington and Whitehaven all have local bus networks and longer-distance services connect most towns. Visit cumbria.gov.uk for maps, timetables and fares.

# THE LAKES TO THE BORDERLANDS

Lakes to the Borderlands

London

For many simply a distance to be covered between the box-office sights of the Lakes and Hadrian's Wall, this region in fact offers plenty of reasons to linger. You'll discover historic border cities, dignified market towns, a rolling, photogenic landscape of farms and forests and plenty more.

Carlisle, Cumbria's county town (there are no cities here) is historically significant, while Penrith is a solidly handsome market town sitting just outside the Lake District National Park. Farm stays, rambling through fields and woods on public footpaths, exploring the idyllic uplands of the North Pennines Area of Natural Beauty – there's a surprising amount to see and do in this under-recognised pocket of Britain.

This was once the terrain of border *reivers* (Scots and English raiders who took turns slaughtering each other and stealing cattle). Fear and strife drove many away, and it has remained one of England's most sparsely populated areas.

### TOP TIP

There are plenty of reasonably priced places to stay in the North Pennines AONB. They're usually great bases for walking and there's nowhere more beautiful to wake up in the region. Choose between sleeping in a tiny town like Alston or Bishop Auckland, or find the true rural heart of the North Pennines by camping or staying on a working farm.

**High Cup Nick**

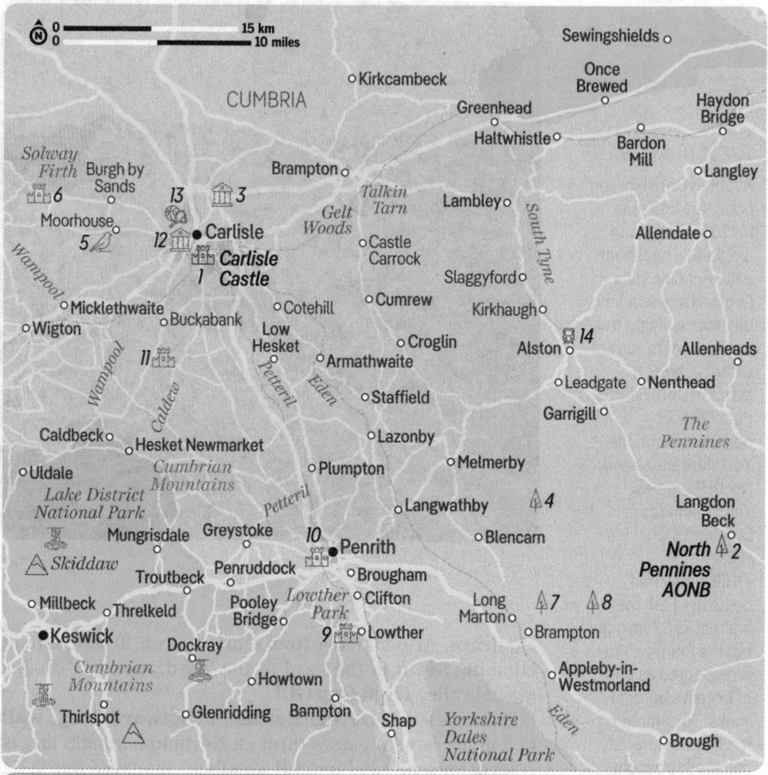

**HIGHLIGHTS**
1 Carlisle Castle
2 North Pennines AONB

**SIGHTS**
3 A World in Miniature
4 Cross Fell
5 Cumberland Bird of Prey Centre
6 Drumburgh Castle
7 Dufton Pike
8 High Cup Nick
9 Lowther Castle
10 Penrith Castle
11 Rose Castle
12 Tullie House Museum

**ACTIVITIES**
13 Fusion Trampoline Centre

**TRANSPORT**
14 South Tynedale Railway

## Hiking the North Pennines

FEEL SHIVERS TRAVERSING 'ENGLAND'S BACKBONE'

A Unesco Global Geopark, the North Pennines AONB is characterised by swelling peaks, heather moors, rushing watercourses and remote hamlets. Walking this landscape is much more rewarding than seeing it rush past your car window in 2D. The AONB is webbed with trails, including **the Pennine Way**.

The walk to **Dufton Pike** (481m) begins in the ancient village of Dufton on the AONB's southwestern fringe. A 4.5-mile circuit rising 293m, it unfurls a gorgeous panorama of Pennine farms and nearby peaks. **High Cup Nick**, a high, symmetrical, glacial chasm, is a stricter

**COASTAL WALKING IN NORTHUMBERLAND**

If wild coastal scenery and obscure nature reserves supporting plenty of native species are your thing, you'll love the **Northumberland Coast Path** (p576). Just hop across to the northeast, begin your journey at Creswell, and you'll be richly rewarded.

### THE PENNINE WAY

A fabled British hiking path, this trail runs for 268 miles along 'England's backbone' – the Pennine Hills. England's oldest long-distance walking trail, it achieved its current extent in 1965. It starts in Derbyshire's Peak District, passes through the Yorkshire Dales and North Pennines, and concludes in Scotland's Cheviot Hills.

'Hills' they may be (Cross Fell, the highest, is 893m high), but the Pennine Way is respected as one of Britain's hardest walks. To complete it requires more cumulative ascent than summiting Everest, and conditions are often energy sapping. The North Pennine section, including the U-shaped glacial valley High Cup Gill, crashing waterfalls and the peaks surrounding Cross Fell, is generally considered the most scenic.

Cross Fell

challenge. Also starting from Dufton, it's a 10-mile circuit, climbing 544m to the head of the jaw-dropping, U-shaped glacial valley **High Cup Gill**.

The more leisurely **Allen Banks and Staward Gorge walk** (5.3 miles return) passes through Northumberland's largest tract of ancient, semi-natural woodland, managed by the National Trust. Ascents of the North Pennines' acme, **Cross Fell** (893m), start from Kirkland, involve an 8.5-mile circuit and a 700m ascent. Boggy terrain and increasingly steep summit approaches make it challenging. Unimprovable views over the Pennines and Lake District fells are your reward.

The demanding **Green Route** from Kirkby Stephen to Keld begins is Cumbria and ends in the Yorkshire section of the Pennines. Over 12 miles long, it ascends nearly 500m through moorland and dry-stone-walled farms before reaching Keld in Swaledale.

### ACCOMMODATION FOR WALKERS TACKLING THE NORTH PENNINES

**Dufton Barn Holidays, Dufton**
These cosy, scenic cottage conversions include one designed especially for walkers – the Potting Shed. ££

**Lord Crewe Arms, Blanchland**
In the eastern Pennines, this unique hotel occupies the guesthouse of 12th-century Blanchland Abbey. £££

**The Inn at Brough, Kirkby Stephen**
This former 18th-century coaching inn offers immaculate, value-for-money rooms in the Eden Valley. ££

## Castle Spotting Around Carlisle & Penrith

VESTIGES OF A VIOLENT PAST

Carlisle, Penrith and the surrounding border areas have been on a war footing for much of their past. Occupying the 'debatable lands' between England and Scotland, internecine border raiding ('reiving') and full-scale battles have plagued this area for centuries. And, before there even was an 'England' or a 'Scotland', Danish and Norse raiders, Anglo-Saxons, Britons, Romans and others came to blows frequently in these parts. One legacy of al this confliect is a lot of castles!

**Carlisle Castle** was built by the Normans in 1112 CE on a strategic site previously fortified by Romans, Britons and Anglo-Saxons. A bastion against the Scots, it's a formidable red-stone fortress that's impressively intact. Fourteenth-century **Penrith Castle**, sadly, is not in such good shape, but is worth inspecting if you're in town. Nearby **Lowther Castle**, an extravagant 19th-century folly, is in better condition.

**Rose Castle**, given to the bishops of Carlisle by Henry III in 1230, is now a boutique hotel. Centuries of alterations obscure the fact that this front-line fortress saw plenty of action, especially during the Scottish Wars of Independence in the 13th and 14th centuries.

Robert le Brun, like many in these parts, pinched expertly dressed stone from Hadrian's Wall to build **Drumburgh Castle** in 1307. Along with Dacre, it's one of the more complete forts to be found here. More romantically ruinous castles include Lammerside, Kirkoswald, Bewcastle and Brougham.

## Keeping Kids Content

FAMILIES NEEDN'T FEAR

The joys of long moorland hikes, spotting golden plovers or sinking craft ales cut no mustard with the kids. Happily, the region from the Lakes to the Borderlands has an abundance of ways to keep them amused.

**Carlisle** has the most to see and do. Aside from visiting captivating Carlisle Castle, there's the **Tullie House Museum** (three permanent galleries telling the story of Carlisle and northern Cumbria, plus two temporary exhibitions spaces), the **Fusion Trampoline Centre** (a whole barn of bouncy surfaces guaranteed to burn off excess juvenile energy) and, in the Houghton Hall Garden Centre 2.5 miles to the north,

### BEST BIRD-WATCHING WALKS IN THE NORTH PENNINES

**Burnhope Head**
Look for red grouse (year-round), plovers, snipe and merlin on this circuit of Burnhope Reservoir.

**Wellhope Moor**
Skylarks, pipit and greenfinch may be spotted on this boggy 3-mile circuit in the Nent Valley.

**Blanchland**
You may see woodpeckers and tits on this 1.5-mile circuit around lovely Blanchland.

**Lambley & the South Tyne**
An 8-mile circuit beside the Tyne promises dippers, sandpipers, oystercatchers and grey wagtails.

**Chimneys on Dryburn Moor**
Moorland and abandoned lead-mining chimneys are the backdrop for spotting curlews, plovers and skylarks.

### WHERE TO EAT AROUND CARLISLE AND PENRITH

**Four and Twenty, Penrith**
Penrith's best bistro does imaginative things with Cumbrian lamb, beef and pork. ££

**Lounge on the Green, Houghton**
This highly regarded restaurant just north of Carlisle serves innovative prix-fixe menus. £££

**The Dog and Gun, Skelton**
This superb, Michelin-starred gastropub is worth the detour to the rural hamlet of Skelton. £££

**BEST PLACES TO STAY AROUND CARLISLE & PENRITH**

**Hidden River Cafe & Cabins, Longtown**
These superior luxury log cabins occupy a rural setting on the River Lyme. ££

**Halston Aparthotel, Carlisle**
A clutch of wonderful self-catering apartments in Carlisle's former General Post Office. ££

**The George Hotel, Penrith**
A red-brick coaching inn offering perfectly appointed rooms in Penrith's centre. £££

**Augill Castle, Kirkby Stephen**
A 25-mile drive southeast from Penrith is this Victorian 'castle' with gorgeous contemporary interiors. £££

South Tynedale Railway

the painstakingly tiny dioramas of **A World in Miniature**.

If the weather's fine, there's plenty to do outdoors. The **South Tynedale Railway** runs heritage stream trains through the exceptional landscape of the South Tyne Valley from Alston in the North Pennines, through Kirkhaugh and Lintley to the village of Slaggyford. At 300m, picturesque Alston is officially the highest market town in England. Those in thrall to all things locomotive should visit the **Hub Museum** at Alston Goods Shed.

There's also the **Cumberland Bird of Prey Centre**, the joyfully named **Killhope Lead Mine** (offering mine trips, a play park and informative exhibits) and plenty of interesting remnants of **Hadrian's Wall**, especially **Birdoswald fort**, **Harrow's Scar** and other milecastles, and the **Bridge at Willowford**.

**GETTING AROUND**

Avanti's West Coast Main Line connects Carlisle with Penrith and Oxenholme (for the branch to Windermere). Northern Railway connects Carlisle with Newcastle, stopping at Wetheral, Brampton, Haltwhistle and Bardon Mill. Northern services also run south from Carlisle to Kirkby Stephen via Appleby on the fringe of the North Pennines AONB.

Driving is easy here, especially after the congestion of the Lakes. Cycling is also a rewarding way to explore smaller distances. Hadrian Cycling in Haltwhistle, Arragons Cycle Hire in Penrith and Carlisle's Border City Cycle Hire all rent bikes.

# NEWCASTLE-UPON-TYNE

Founded by the Romans as Pons Aelius, a fort on the eastern extremity of Hadrian's Wall, Newcastle owes its present grandeur to shipbuilding and coal wealth. The metropolis of the northeast, its steep, curving streets and quayside are dignified by handsome Georgian and Victorian factories and warehouses, now occupied by museums, galleries, some excellent restaurants and plenty of nightclubs. Newcastle's exuberant nightlife is legendary.

Newcastle retains deep-rooted traditions, embodied by the no-nonsense, likeable locals – the 'Geordies', who know their city simply as 'Toon'. Ideally, you'll have at least a couple of days to explore the historic city centre and quayside areas along the Tyne and across the river in Gateshead, site of the famous Angel of the North. There's also the rejuvenated industrial Ouseburn Valley to the east, gentrified Jesmond to the north, and the buzzing coastal centres of Tynemouth and Whitley Bay. Plus, Newcastle is the ideal gateway for exploring the northeast's wild, starkly beautiful countryside.

**TOP TIP**

Bigg Market and Nicholas Square offer some of central Newcastle's cheaper accommodation. However, there's also a high concentration of bars and clubs here. Unless you plan on partying, be advised that the thumping beats, shouts and drunken singing won't stop until around 4am, even during the middle of the week.

**Newcastle**

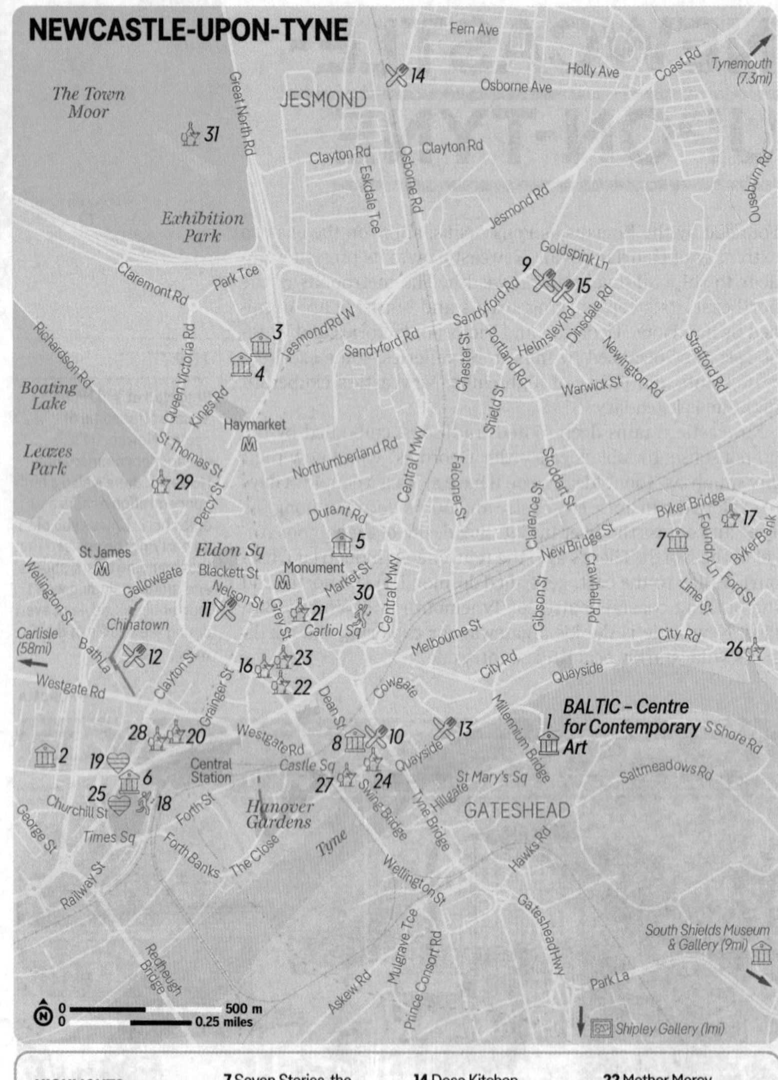


**HIGHLIGHTS**
1 BALTIC – Centre for Contemporary Art

**SIGHTS**
2 Discovery Museum
3 Great North Museum
4 Hatton Gallery
5 Laing Art Gallery
6 Life Science Centre
7 Seven Stories, the National Centre for Children's Books
8 Side

**EATING**
9 Aidan's Kitchen
10 Bangrak Thai
11 Biang Biang Noodles
12 Blackfriars
13 Broad Chare
14 Dosa Kitchen
15 Small Canteen

**DRINKING & NIGHTLIFE**
16 Beehive
17 Cumberland Arms
18 Digital
19 Eazy Street
20 Forth
21 Lola Jeans
22 Mother Mercy
23 Old George Inn
24 Redhouse
25 Rusty's
26 The Tyne Bar
27 Tiger Hornsby
28 Town Wall
29 Trent House
30 World HQ
31 Wylam Brewery

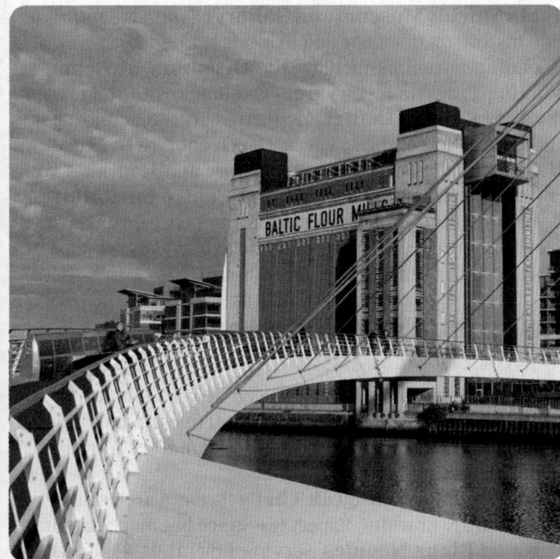


BALTIC – Centre for Contemporary Art

## Newcastle's Galleries & Museums

ENGLAND'S NORTHEASTERN CULTURAL CAPITAL

Beyond Newcastle's architecture, restaurants and nightlife lies one of the most compelling concentrations of cultural institutions in any British regional city. Museums and galleries mushroom among former warehouses and factories on both sides of the Tyne.

Foremost is Gateshead's **BALTIC – Centre for Contemporary Art**. Behind the 1950s facade of the former BALTIC flour mill lies 2600 sq metres of free, accessible space, home to wonderful permanent and temporary exhibitions. On the north bank is the Grade II–listed baroque/art nouveau **Laing Art Gallery**, purpose built in 1904 and showing paintings, ceramics, Newcastle glass and silverware, and temporary exhibits. Nearby is **Side**, the UK's only gallery of documentary photography.

Further afield, Newcastle University's **Hatton Gallery** exhibits paintings from the 14th century to the present, including work by Kurt Schwitters and Francis Bacon; Gateshead's **Shipley Gallery** is dedicated to craft and design; while the

### COALS TO NEWCASTLE

You may wonder where the phrase 'bringing coals to Newcastle' – meaning to attempt something futile – originated. There are two contending explanations.

The first points to a 1530 Royal Act that bestowed a monopoly on **Tyne River** coal shipments to the **Newcastle Quayside**, enriching **'The Hostmen'** – the group of middlemen who controlled the quays. While this arrangement helped this *entrepôt* to the northeastern coalfields prosper, it made it pointless for anyone outside the cartel to attempt shipping coal here.

The second explanation, more generally accepted, is that since coal was so abundant in Newcastle, it would be foolish for any importer to hope to supply the city with more.

### WHERE TO FIND NEWCASTLE MARKETS

**Grainger Market**
Dating to 1835, this Grade I-listed covered market is a Newcastle institution. Closed Sundays.

**Quayside Market**
This vibrant bazaar of food and local handicrafts animates Quayside. Sundays from 9.30am to 4pm.

**Tynemouth Market**
Just outside Tynemouth Station, this huge flea market attracts 150 stallholders every Saturday and Sunday.

**South Shields Museum and Gallery** examines South Tyneside history on one floor and exhibits art on another.

Leading museums include: the **Discovery Museum**, examining Tyneside history from the Romans to the present; the **Life Science Centre**, dedicated to the achievements and fascination of the sciences; the **Great North Museum: Hancock**, focusing on natural history and Hadrian's Wall; and **Seven Stories, the National Centre for Children's Books**, exhibiting artefacts from the last century of children's literature and offering participatory programmes in a repurposed, seven-storey Victorian mill.

### GEORDIE DIALECT

Visitors may hear the term 'Geordie' and wonder to whom it applies. Basically, it indicates a native of Newcastle and Tyneside, speaking in an unmistakeable accent the dialect that defines them. It's a relic of Northumbrian Old English, spoken here when English was divided into multiple regional versions.

The most accepted etymology of 'Geordie' is as a derivation of 'George' – a common name among the miners working the area's many coal pits. Linguists define their distinct speech as 'Tyneside English', but some would extend Geordie territory further into Northumberland and even County Durham. No matter the territory, it's words like *gan* (for 'go'),'*reet* (right) and *haddaway* (expressing disbelief) that make Geordie speech unique.

## Newcastle's Dining Scene

TIME TO LOOSEN YOUR WAISTBAND

As the metropolis of the northeast, Newcastle naturally offers its best dining. From experimental fine diners to gastropubs, brunch cafes and a galaxy of regional restaurants, it's a gourmand's playground.

On central Side, **Bangrak Thai's** flavours are as assertive as its staff are graceful. Expect less grace but much happiness at **Biang Biang Noodles**, serving lunchtime deliciousness from Shaanxi and Sichuan in Grainger Market. In upmarket Jesmond, **Dosa Kitchen** does exceptional South Indian food.

For inspired brunches and lunches, **Aidan's Kitchen** is another Jesmond gem. Vegetarians and vegans can trust the Italian-inspired plant-based menu at **Vegano**, near the Discovery Centre.

**Blackfriars** dishes up 'modern medieval' cooking in 'the oldest purpose-built dining room in the UK' – a refectory built for Dominican friars in 1239. The **Small Canteen** is just that – a tiny 15-seater pumping out fantastic modern British food in Jesmond. The **Broad Chare**, a gastropub in a converted quayside warehouse where over 50 quality beers are poured, is universally recommended.

Towards the very fine end of the dining spectrum are Gateshead's 'seasonal and ethical' **Träkol**; **21**, offering a separate plant-based menu; Ouseburn's **Cook House**, for simple, seasonal quality and a convivial atmosphere; and Jesmond's Italian bistro, **the Patricia**. At the top of the table sit **Fern** at Jesmond Dene House and the Michelin-starred **House of Tides**.

## A Night Out in Newcastle

TIME TO HIT THE TOON!

If you're keen to join the locals and enjoy Newcastle's renowned, rambunctious nightlife, you can throw yourself into

### WHERE TO SLEEP IN NEWCASTLE

**Albatross Hostel**
If centrality and value-for-money are important, book a twin at the Albatross on Grainger St. **£**

**Grey Street Hotel**
In a Grade II-listed Georgian building with 49 en suites, Grey St is charming and restful. **££**

**Jesmond Dene House**
Boutique luxury in a listed, Victorian Arts-and-Crafts mansion 3 miles north of central Newcastle. **£££**

Beehive

a huge night out without straying far from the city centre.

Centrally, the area around Tyne Bridge, Quayside, Bigg Market, Side and Central Station offers pubs aplenty. Near the station there's the **Forth**, a traditional boozer with a rooftop terrace; superior pub food and craft-beer selection at the **Town Wall**; and **Redhouse**, which also does food (pies) alongside an interesting beer selection.

The Bigg Market area is awash with average venues: exceptions include after-work favourite **the Beehive** and the 16th-century **Old George Inn**, which may be the city's oldest.

Near Newcastle United's St James's Park is the old-school atmosphere and superior jukebox of the **Trent House** and, further north, gigs and craft beer at **Wylam Brewery**. East of the centre you'll find live music and comedy at the Tyne Bar and the Cumberland Arms.

If you're intro cocktails, centrally located **Tiger Hornsby**, **Mother Mercy** and **Lola Jeans** all take their mixology seriously. Once it's time to hit the dance floor, try **World HQ** (in Curtis Mayfield House), while **Digital** is the place for top-notch house and techno. Gay clubs with an inclusive vibe include **Eazy Street** and **Rusty's**, among many venues in the 'Pink Triangle' bounded by Waterloo, Neville and Collingwood Sts.

### VIZ: NEWCASTLE'S OUTRAGEOUS CULTURAL ICON

*Viz* magazine could only have come from Newcastle. Founded by Jesmond local Chris Donald in 1979, this scabrous parody of wholesome British children's comics such as *The Beano* and *Dandy* (and the less wholesome British tabloids) is still available on the 'adult shelf' of newsagents today.

Donald produced the first, photocopied edition in his bedroom, alongside brother Simon and friend Jim Brownlow. Initially popular only in the northeast, where Geordie characters speaking their own dialect such as Sid the Sexist and Biffa Bacon were most recognisable, it reached peak sales of 1.2 million by the early 1990s. No longer so popular, or edited by Donald, it remains a testament to the British flair for scurrilous satire, toilet humour and nakedly outrageous silliness.

### NEWCASTLES ENTERTAINMENT VENUES

**St James' Park**
The home ground of Newcastle United, one of the country's most fervently supported football clubs.

**Sage Gateshead**
Full-scale performances from Northern Sinfonia and other diverse artists grace two stages at this eye-catching venue.

**Theatre Royal**
This 1837 venue hosts Royal Shakespeare Company productions, musicals, opera, comedy, ballet and more.

### TYNESIDE'S SAINTS & SCHOLARS

Tyneside has an exalted place in the story of British Christianity. This is the country of St Bede (672–735 CE), author of the *Ecclesiastical History of the English People* (a precious source of knowledge about Anglo-Saxon England), one of the leading European scholars of his time and a monk at Monkwearmouth–Jarrow Abbey.

This Unesco-listed religious foundation, the bastion of Anglo-Saxon clerical scholarship in the 7th century CE, can still be visited. Sections of the Anglo-Saxon abbey were incorporated into the 11th-century St Paul's Church, built by the Normans. Jarrow Abbey's founder was another revered saint, Benedict Biscop (c 628–90 CE), granted the land by King Ecgfrith of Northumbria in 681 CE.

## Exploring Tynemouth & South Shields

YOU'LL LOVE THE 'NEWCASTLE RIVIERA'

Less than 10 miles from central Newcastle, coastal Tynemout and South Shields have plenty to recommend a day trip or eve overnight visit. Easily accessible on the yellow metro line fro Newcastle Central, they've got medieval and Roman mon ments, aquariums, museums, great places to eat and drin and even outdoor adventures like surfing to lure you east.

**Tynemouth**, north of the Tyne estuary, offers 150 stalls craft and bric-a-brac each Saturday and Sunday at **Tynemout Market**. Beyond that, there are aquatic attractions at **Tyn mouth Aquarium** and the 11th-century T**ynemouth Pri ry and Castle**, looming over King Edward's Bay. Long San beach and North Sea swells support surfing, kayaking ar paddleboarding with experienced outfits such as **Longsan Surf School** and **CBK Adventures** (based in North Shield

**South Shields** tempts families and history buffs with **A beia Roman Fort**, the plunging cliffs and broad sands **Marsden and Sandhaven Beaches**, **South Shields M seum & Art Gallery** and the National Trust's historic **Sou er Lighthouse**. Consider stopping off at **Jarrow**, where Paul's Monastery was home to the Venerable Bede, and explc ing recreated Anglo-Saxon Northumbrian life at nearby **Ja row Hall Anglo-Saxon Farm, Village & Bede Museun**

Places to eat and drink well are plentiful: Harbour Ligh and **Sand Dancer** are wonderful South Shields seaside o tions, while Tynemouth's best includes the **Head of Steam** (f local craft beers) and **Riley's Fish Shack**.

Tynemouth Priory and Castle

### GETTING AROUND

While often steep, Newcastle's centre is best explored on foot. It's also served by a metro system, ferries and a comprehensive bus network. The Tyne and Wear Metro, a combination of underground and overground lines, connects Newcastle's grand neoclassical Central Station with the airport, Tynemouth, Gateshead, Sunderland and places within the city such as Jesmond and Haymarket.

If you're driving, you'll pay to park in central Newcastle, which further discourages cars with one-way systems and pedestrianised streets. If you're staying in a quieter place like Jesmond, your car becomes less of a liability.

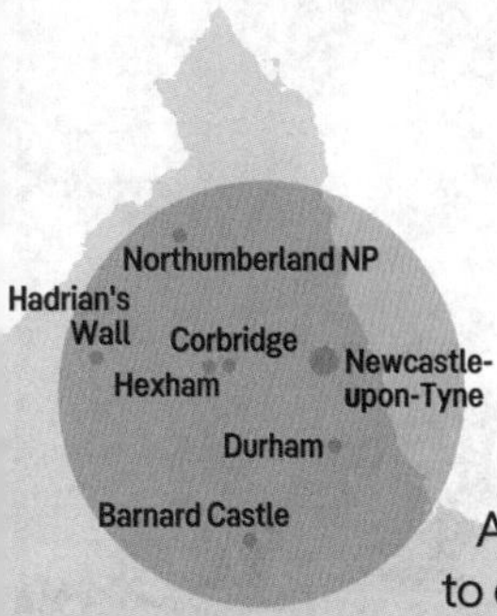

Northumberland NP
Hadrian's Wall
Corbridge
Hexham
Newcastle-upon-Tyne
Durham
Barnard Castle

# Beyond Newcastle-upon-Tyne

## Absorbing as it is, Newcastle is also a gateway: to delightful County Durham, Hadrian's Wall and Northumberland National Park.

### TOP TIP

Walking the 84-mile Hadrian's Wall Path may be the best way to experience this country. Try to time your attempt for May to June or September – you'll hopefully enjoy decent weather, and often have the trail to yourself. Allow seven days to complete the trail, prebooking accommodation at feasible intervals.

Newcastle's environs offer very different experiences to those of that energetic, post-industrial city. South lies County Durham – rich with architectural and scenic pleasures. Northwest lies Northumberland National Park (NP) – England's greatest remaining wilderness – and Hadrian's Wall, a feat of engineering and imperial power that still astonishes nearly two millennia after its first stones were cut and laid.

Accessing these wonders is surprisingly straightforward. Trains link Durham with Newcastle in the time you'd allow for short hops on London's tube. Points of access to Northumberland NP like Bellingham, Otterburn and Wooler connect with Newcastle and Alnwick by bus. Still, some highlights, such as Barnard Castle, are more easily accessed driving.

**Walltown, near Hadrian's Wall (p567)**

### BEST PLACES TO STAY IN DURHAM

**Hotel Indigo**
A gym, stylish public areas and tastefully decorated suites make this central hotel a bargain. ££

**The Kingslodge Inn**
A much-awarded pub-with-rooms set on the fringe of Flass Vale's woodlands, near Durham station. £££

**OYO The Townhouse**
This boutique hotel in a listed Georgian townhouse is one of Durham's most charming options. £££

**Lumley Castle**
Superior rooms in a 14th-century castle in Chester-le-Street, 8 miles north of Durham. £££

Durham Castle and Cathedral

## A Pilgrimage to Durham Cathedral

BRITAIN'S MOST COMELY CATHEDRAL?

No visit to the northeast is complete without visiting **Durham Cathedral**. A mere 25 minutes by train from Newcastle (or slightly longer by car), Durham is the capital of the ceremonial County Durham. Its monumental place of worship is one of the region's defining sights and ranked by many as the most beautiful Romanesque Anglo-Norman cathedral in the country.

Commenced shortly after the Norman conquest in 1093, it's the first European cathedral roofed with stone-ribbed vaulting, enabling the overpowering scale of its construction. Highlights include the 13th-century western and central towers (the latter, rebuilt in 1470, should be climbed for spectacular views over Durham); the tombs of St Cuthbert and St Bede; and the beautiful stone Neville Screen (1372–80).

### ROME'S LAKELAND LEGACY

For more Roman remains, head to the Lake District and Cumbrian Coast for sites such as **Ravenglass bath house** (p535), **Hardknott Roman fort** (p535)and **Galava Roman fort** (p547) in Ambleside.

### WHERE TO EAT IN DURHAM

**Tia's**
Durham is an unlikely place to find good Tex-Mex, but that's exactly what Tia's delivers. £

**Cellar Door**
Toothsome modern British dishes served in a 13th-century cellar with picture windows overlooking the Wear. ££

**The Garden House**
A superior pub-with-food sitting about a mile northwest of central Durham. £

Sitting on the same prominence above a horseshoe bend in the River Wear is **Durham Castle**. Commenced in 1072, it was the home of the Prince Bishops of Durham until 1837, when Durham University moved in. Book 50-minute tours in advance by phone, at the Palace Green Library or the Tourist Office. Highlights include the 17th-century Black Staircase and the beautifully preserved Norman chapel (1080).

Nearby is **Durham Museum**, housed in the former parish church of St Mary-le-Bow. You might also consider cruising the Wear for great perspectives on the cathedral above – either with **Prince Bishop River Cruises** or in a rental from **Browns Rowing Boats**.

## Delving Deeper into County Durham

DELIGHTS BEYOND DURHAM

Spectacular Durham is by no means the county's only appealing destination. Fifty miles southwest of Newcastle by car or by train and bus is the Tees-side market town of Barnard Castle, while seaside Hartlepool is 42 miles southeast, either by car or train.

**Barnard Castle**, 'Barney' to the locals, offers a perfect mix of castles, antique shops and pubs. Fourteenth-century **Raby Castle** was seized from the Catholic Neville family after their participation in the Rising of the North (1569), a failed attempt to depose Elizabeth I in favour of Mary, Queens of Scots. Its original exterior is wonderfully preserved, while the interior mostly dates to the 18th and 19th centuries.

**Barnard Castle** itself, once one of England's largest, is a sprawling, evocative 12th-century ruin overlooking the Tees. The **Bowes Museum** displays the collection of 19th-century industrialist John Bowes in an ornate purpose-built 'château'. Expect works by Goya, Canaletto and El Greco, alongside ceramics, tapestries and more.

**Hartlepool**, a former steel-smelting and shipbuilding town, offers fascinating wartime and maritime heritage. Following the closure of its industries in the 20th century, it reimagined itself as a tourist destination. The **Heugh Gun Battery Museum** and **National Museum of the Royal Navy Hartlepool** are both excellently curated and intriguing. There's also the diverting **Hartlepool Art Museum**, occupying a Victorian church. **Navigation Point**, above the marina, is lined with restaurants, cafes and bars.

### GREAT EATING AROUND BARNARD CASTLE

Well-heeled Barnard Castle and its surrounding area present gourmands with some of County Durham's best food. **Raby Hunt**, 11 miles east, won two Michelin stars for its exceptional tasting menus. The **Bay Horse**, 19 miles east, is a superior gastropub marrying classic French technique to local and European ingredients.

One of the best options in Barney itself is **Blagrave House**, a 15th-century building now housing a shop, cocktail bar and restaurant serving small plates such as lime-and-chilli fish tacos and flatiron steak with chimichurri. **Cross Lanes Organic Farm** offers both a restaurant serving organic breakfasts and lunches and a bountiful farm shop with a butcher's, delicatessen, bakery, frozen restaurant meals and fresh produce.

### HISTORIC HOTELS IN COUNTY DURHAM

**Beamish Hall Country House Hotel, Beamish**
Dating partly to the 12th century, Beamish Hall offers a very modern standard of luxury. **£££**

**Redworth Hall Hotel, Newton Aycliffe**
Acres of surrounding parkland and surviving period features distinguish this former Elizabethan manor. **££**

**Manor House Hotel, Bishop Auckland**
Built on 11th-century foundations, this handsome 13th-century manor offers 30 inviting rooms. **££**

## Exploring Northumberland National Park

A NORTHERN EXPOSURE TO NATURE

**Northumberland National Park**, England's northernmost, is furthest from any city and the least inhabited (Elsdon, with just 50 homes, is the largest village). It's also the least visited, which is both a shame, given its heritage value and stunning beauty, and a boon, as you're much more likely to find solitude. It's a 27-mile drive from Newcastle to the park's southeastern extremity at Walwick. Keep your eyes open for red squirrels, golden plovers or wild Cheviot goats while you're there.

Northumberland NP is also the second largest of England's 13 national parks. It comprises 410 sq miles of rolling moorland, *peles* (defensive towers), farms, forest and low peaks running from the Scottish border to south of Hadrian's Wall. **Chillingham Castle** and **Cragside House** are other rewarding sights.

The northern **Cheviot Hills**, a swelling series of peaks culminating in the Cheviot, highest of all at 815m, is one of many excellent places to walk. Visit **The Sill: National Landscape Discovery Centre** near the village of **Once Brewed** or northumberlandnationalpark.org.uk for inspiration. Cycling is also delightful in **Kielder** and **Harwood Forests**; visit **The Bike Place** near Kielder for rentals and information.

**Kielder Water**, England's largest artificial lake, is surrounded by another superlative – England's largest plantation of spruce and fir trees. There's plenty to do and see here: boating, walking, the **Kielder Observatory**, the **Minotaur Maze**, ruined **Kielder Castle** and **Kielder Bird of Prey Centre**.

### WALKING SOLO IN NORTHUMBERLAND NATIONAL PARK

**James Gingell** is a writer and avid walker. *@james.gingell.walks*

True wilderness is hard to come by in England. On Dartmoor, or in the Lakes, those thrilling senses of isolation do arrive, but they are fleeting. Every lip of a hill seems to hide a pub or a farmhouse.

But try walking from **Byrness** to **Kirk Yetholm** – the last stage of the Pennine Way – and you'll almost forget humans exist. If you have any breath by the time you make the top of **the Cheviot**, it will be taken by the views all around. In all directions are lush green verges and sparkling rivers, nature dancing in the absence of humankind.

## Wildlife Spotting beyond Newcastle

WHERE TO SEEK WILD ENCOUNTERS

The abundance of wild and sparsely inhabited territory within Newcastle's reach makes the chances of spotting birds and other wildlife higher than in almost any other area of Britain. The vast 'emptiness' of Northumberland National Park, the eastern section of the **North Pennines AONB**, and less remote places like the **Durham Heritage Coast** and the **Thrislington**, **Castle Eden Dene**, **Derwent Gorge** and **Muggleswick Woods**, and **Moor House – Upper Teesdale National Nature Reserves** all promise encounters with native fauna.

**Northumberland NP** retains populations of threatened red squirrels, while badgers, roe deer and wild Cheviot goats (descended from pre-modern species) can all be found. Adders (Britain's only poisonous snake), slow worms and common lizards also survive here. Birdlife, some seasonal, includes barn

### WHERE TO SLEEP IN NORTHUMBERLAND NATIONAL PARK

**Kielder Campsite, Kielder**
This remote campsite above Kielder Water rents pitches for camping and motor homes. £

**The Pheasant Inn, Stannersburn**
This pub in Stannersburn, below Kielder Water, offers bed and breakfast in bright, freshly decorated twins. ££

**Otterburn Castle Hotel, Otterburn**
Dating to the Norman conquest, this castle-hotel promises luxury amid its 13-hectare landscaped grounds. £££

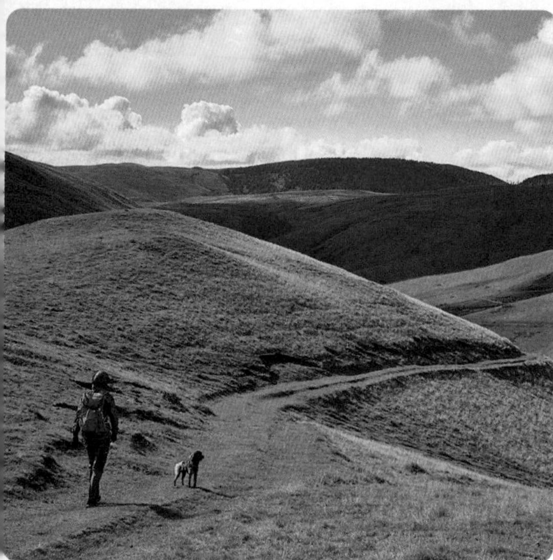

Cheviot Hills

owls, red- and black-grouse, snipe, redshanks, lapwings, curlews, dippers, oystercatchers and golden plovers.

The nearby **North Pennines** attract many of the same bird species, plus birds of prey such as kestrels, merlins and buzzards. You might see badgers and roe deer here, too, and perhaps hares or water voles. **Castle Eden Dene**'s 221 hectares of woodland and lowland grassland support roe deer, foxes and an abundance of bird species. Along the **Durham Heritage Coast** and other, less developed coastal regions there are little terns, sandpipers, glow worms, green tiger beetles and marine mammals like bottlenose dolphins, porpoises and both grey and common seals.

## Corbridge & the Villages of the Northeast

NEWCASTLE'S CHARMING SATELLITE SETTLEMENTS

Northumberland and County Durham abound in delightful, distinctive villages, and Newcastle's hinterland is no exception. Take the 19-mile trip to Corbridge either by car, the Newcastle & Carlisle Railway or Tyne Valley bus to discover the first of the region's many quiet, picturesque settlements.

### BEST CYCLE ROUTES IN NORTHUMBERLAND NP

Northumberland National Park should be flypaper for those who love lonely, rural cycling.

**College Valley and Yeltholm**
A 42-mile circuit traversing quiet roads from Wooler over the Scottish border through captivating Cheviot scenery.

**Otterburn & Coquetdale**
A demanding 38-mile circuit from Alwinton encompassing Roman forts and 'bastle houses' – fortified farms unique to the Borders.

**Curlew Cycle Route**
A gorgeous 18-mile circuit from Bellingham via Birtley and Wark. There are some long (but never-acute) climbs involved.

**Wooler to Bamburgh**
Two-wheeled tourists will also love this long-but-leisurely 32-mile circuit. While not a Northumberland NP ride in the strict sense, it nonetheless unveils many aspects of this region's distinctive charm.

### BIRD-WATCHING SITES NEAR NEWCASTLE

**Big Waters Nature Reserve, Newcastle**
See waterbirds such as grebes, swans and herons at this reed-fringed, water-filled former mine.

**Gosforth Nature Reserve, Gosforth**
Bitterns, barn owls, reed warblers and other species inhabit 61 acres of wetland and woodland.

**Cresswell Pond and Foreshore, Morpeth**
A network of paths and hides promises glimpses of sandpipers, sanderlings and ringed plovers.

Blanchland

Corbridge entered history as **Coria**, the Roman Empire's most northerly town. Today it's a harmonious collection of stone cottages, churches and local shops with nary a high-street chain store to be seen. You can visit the excavated **Roman Town**, the **Church of St Andrews**, consecrated in the 7th century and built of stone from Hadrian's Wall, and the 14th-century fortified **Vicar's Pele**.

More distinctively charming northeastern villages lie in every direction. In the North Pennines are **Blanchland**, built of stone from 12th-century Blanchland Abbey in a forested section of the Derwent Valley, and **Allendale**, surrounded by *peles* (the fortified towers testifying to centuries of border raiding).

To the north are **Bellingham**, **Otterburn** and **Elsdon**, three delightful settlements bordering Northumberland NP. In the Morpeth area are **Rothbury** (thought by some Northumberland's loveliest village), **Harbottle** and **Wooler** – 'Gateway to the Cheviots'.

In Durham there's **Brancepeth**, a harmonious ensemble of mellow stone dominated by a spectacular castle; **Staindrop**, near **Raby Castle**; and **Gainford** on the River Tees. Closer to Newcastle is **Beamish**, home to the ersatz Georgian-Victorian village, **The Living Museum of the North**.

## BEST COUNTRY PUBS IN NORTHUMBERLAND

**The Black Bull, Corbridge**
Very much the town's unofficial heart, this gregarious, stone-built village inn dates to 1755. £

**Carts Bog Inn, Langley**
Run by the offspring of local farmers, this 1775 country inn serves locally sourced food. £

**The Narrow Nick, Rothbury**
This friendly micropub in adorable Rothbury takes its craft ale and beer seriously. £

**The Beehive, Earsdon**
Low ceilings, wooden floors, rural views and great food all join hands at the Beehive. ££

## VILLAGE SLEEPS AROUND NEWCASTLE

**Dilston Cottage, Corbridge**
Usually rented by the week, this pretty rural cottage is ideal for exploring the area. £

**The Golden Lion, Allendale**
The social hub of this lovely North Pennine village, the Lion offers newly renovated rooms. ££

**Westfield House Farm, Rothbury**
Choose from bed and breakfast in the stone Georgian farmhouse, or self-catering in a 'shepherd's hut'. ££

# Discovering Hadrian's Wall

ROME'S NORTHERN LIMIT

This engineering marvel of the ancient world marks the point at which the Roman Empire stopped its northward march. Stretching 73 miles between Wallsend and Solway Firth, the Emperor Hadrian ordered its construction in 122 CE, keeping the unconquered Picts of Caledonia from the settled province of Britannia. Unesco-listed, it's an evoca-tive and unmissable icon of the north.

The fort and museum of **Segedunum** at Wallsend are 22 minutes east of central Newcastle on the yellow metro line. From there, a procession of excavated forts, milecastles, ob-servation turrets, temples and notable sections of remaining stone wall stretches east, often through lonely landscapes of haunting beauty. Those with the time and fitness can walk the 84-mile **Hadrian's Wall Path**, usually over seven days.

Reduced over time by the repurposing of its locally quar-ried sandstone for churches, *peles* and other buildings, some sights and sections remain more impressive than others. Travelling east-to-west, those include the forts and settle-ments of **Coria** (outside Corbridge), **Vindolanda**, **Chesters**, **Brocolitia** (with its **Mithraic Temple**), **Housesteads** and **Birdoswald**.

Some of the most complete remaining sections of the wall are at **Heddon-on-the-Wall**, **Planetrees**, **Sewingshields** to **Sycamore Gap** and **Walltown Country Park**. Museums rich with relics of life on the Wall are found at some forts; Greenhead's **Roman Army Museum**; Newcastle's **Great North Museum Hancock**; and **Tullie House** and **Senhouse Museums** at the Carlisle end.

### NORTHUMBERLAND'S VIOLENT HISTORY

Northumberland has seen its fair share of strife. Hadrian's Wall was built to keep out the warlike Picts to the north. The post-imperial Romano-Britons were then displaced by the Angles, who formed Northumbria in 654 CE by merging the smaller kingdoms of Bernicia and Deria (in present-day Yorkshire).

The Vikings commenced centuries of raiding and settling by sacking Lindisfarne monastery in 793 CE. Northumbria eventually became part of a united England in 973, but the Norsemen enjoyed ultimate victory when, as the Normans, they conquered the Anglo-Saxons. Buttressing England against Scottish invasions, the Earldom of Northumberland became a semi-autonomous, sometimes-rebellious power. For centuries, *reivers* on both sides of Scottish/Northumbrian border indulged in internecine raiding.

# Whitley Bay & Other Seaside Favourites

NORTH SEA SAND BETWEEN YOUR TOES

**Whitley Bay** is a favourite seaside retreat for Novocastrians. Just a 12-mile drive from Newcastle, or 43 minutes on the yellow metro line from Central Station, it's fish and chips, promenades, arcades, buckets and spades and everything else you'd associate with British seaside holidays.

Its most obvious attraction is the long, sandy **beach** stretching 1.7 miles south from Curry's Point. **St Mary's Island**, a nature reserve supporting an historic **lighthouse**, is accessible by a rocky causeway at low tide. There's also indoor swimming at **Waves Leisure Centre**; coasteering with **High Tide**

### SEASIDE SLEEPS NEAR NEWCASTLE

**Grand Hotel, Tynemouth**
Built by Northumberland's duke for his wife, this grand hotel has epitomised elegance since 1877. **££**

**Marsden Grotto, South Shields**
Reputedly once a smugglers' inn blasted from the cliffside, the Grotto is eccentric but inviting. **££**

**Park Lodge Guest House, Whitley Bay**
Inland from Whitley Bay's beach, this professionally run guesthouse is an ideal British seaside retreat. **££**

# Hadrian's Wall

## ROME'S FINAL FRONTIER

Of all Britain's Roman ruins, Emperor Hadrian's 2nd-century wall, cutting across northern England from the Irish Sea to the North Sea, is by far the most spectacular; Unesco awarded it World Heritage status in 1987.

We've picked out the highlights, one of which is the prime remaining Roman fort on the wall, Housesteads, which we've reconstructed here.

GANNET77 / GETTY IMAGES ©

### Housesteads' Granaries

Nothing like the clever underground ventilation system, which kept vital supplies of grain dry in Northumberland's damp and drizzly climate, would be seen again in these parts for 1500 years.

STEPHEN DOREY / GETTY IMAGES ©

### Birdoswald Roman Fort

Explore the longest intact stretch of the wall, scramble over the remains of a large fort then head indoors to wonder at a full-scale model of the wall at its zenith. Great fun for the kids.

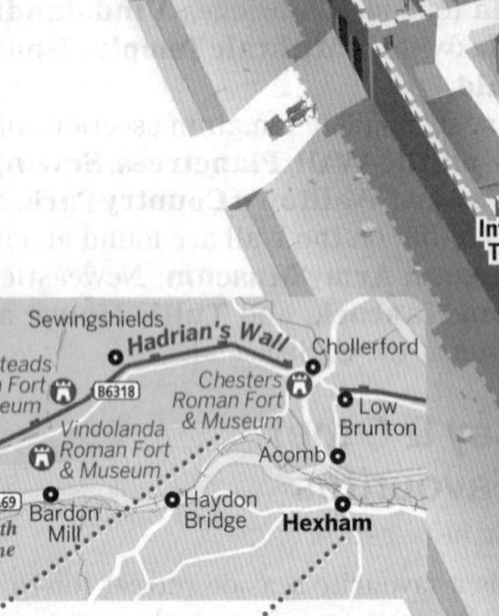


### Chesters Roman Fort

Built to keep watch over a bridge spanning the River North Tyne, Britain's best-preserved Roman cavalry fort has a terrific bathhouse, essential if you have months of nippy northern winter ahead.

### Hexham Abbey

This may be the finest non-Roman sight near Hadrian's Wall, but the 7th-century parts of this magnificent church were built with stone quarried by the Romans for use in their forts.

### Housesteads' Hospital

Operations performed at the hospital would have been surprisingly effective, even without anaesthetics; religious rituals and prayers to Aesculapius, the Roman god of healing, were possibly less helpful for a hernia or appendicitis.

STEPHAN GOERLICH / GETTY IMAGES ©

VERITYJOHNSON / SHUTTERSTOCK ©

**Housesteads' Latrines**
Communal toilets were the norm in Roman times and Housesteads' are remarkably well preserved – fortunately no traces remain of the vinegar-soaked sponges that were used instead of toilet paper.

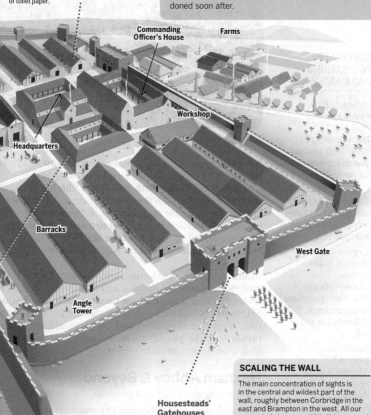

## QUICK WALL FACTS & FIGURES

**Latin name** Vallum Aelium

**Length** 73.5 miles (80 Roman miles)

**Construction date** 122–128 CE

**Manpower for construction**
Three legions (around 16,000 men)

**Features** At least 16 forts, 80 milecastles, 160 turrets

**Did you know** Hadrian's wasn't the only Roman wall in Britain – the Antonine Wall was built across what is now central Scotland in c140 CE, but it was abandoned soon after.

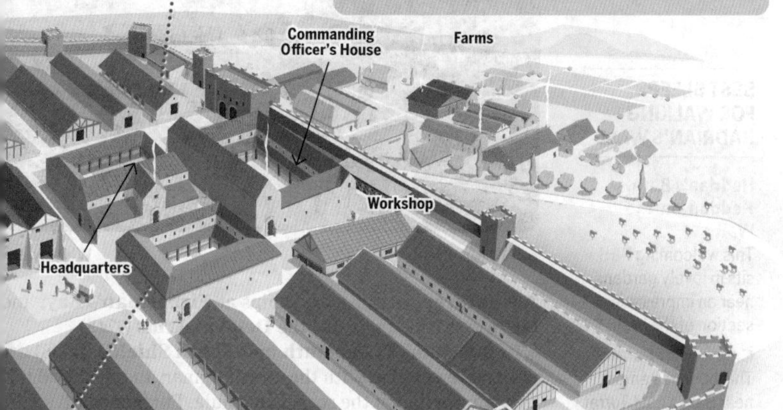

Commanding Officer's House

Farms

Workshop

Headquarters

Barracks

West Gate

Angle Tower

## SCALING THE WALL

The main concentration of sights is in the central and wildest part of the wall, roughly between Corbridge in the east and Brampton in the west. All our suggested stops are within this area and follow an east–west route. The easiest way to travel is by car, scooting along the B6318, but special bus AD122 will also get you there. Allow 7 days and book accommodation in advance. Hiking along the designated Hadrian's Wall Path (84 miles) allows you to appreciate the achievement up close.

**Housesteads' Gatehouses**
Unusually at Housesteads neither of the gates faces the enemy, as was the norm at Roman forts; builders aligned them east–west. Ruts worn by cart wheels are still visible in the stone.

## FREE GUIDES

At some sites, knowledgeable volunteer heritage guides are on hand to answer questions and add context and interesting details to what you're seeing.

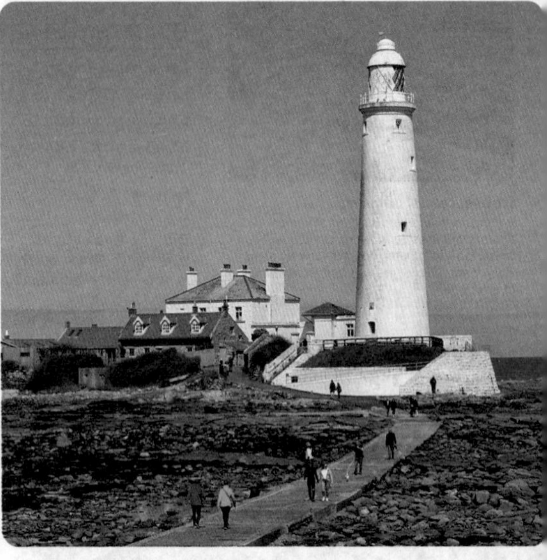

Whitely Bay

### BEST SLEEPS FOR WALKING HADRIAN'S WALL

**Hadrian's Barn, Heddon-on-the-Wall**
This welcoming B&B sits in lovely gardens near an impressive section of the Wall. ££

**Camping at Banks**
This bucolic campsite near Banks East Turret only accepts walkers and cyclists. £

**The Old Repeater Station, Haydon Bridge**
A lovely old stone B&B offering excellent value, just south of Turrets 34a and 33b. ££

**Dacre House, Gilsland**
A former Temperance House built in 1860, this welcoming B&B is close to Milecastle 48. ££

**Adventure**; great fish and chips at **Fisherman's Bay**; and historic seaside pubs like the **Delaval Arms** (1748).

To the south, **Tynemouth** and **South Shields** (p558) are even more popular, with the lure of Roman and medieval history improving on the seaside formula. Further south again you reach Sunderland's sandy **Seaburn** and **Roker Beaches**; the wave-carved rocks of **Seaham Hall's** sand-and-shingle beach; then **Hartlepool** at the southern end of the Durham Heritage Coast.

Once industrial, the Heritage Coast is dotted with former collieries at Easington, Horden and Blackhall. Threaded together by the 11-mile **Durham Coastal Path** from Seaham to Crimdon (where the two best beaches are found) is a beautiful, rehabilitated coastline and the flora and fauna that returned once the pits fell silent. Walking, rock-pooling and bird-spotting are the main recreations.

## Hexham Abbey & Beyond

THE NORTHEAST'S CHRISTIAN HERITAGE

The northeast has long been an important centre for British Christianity. The Romano-British culture had converted be

### INFORMATION POINTS ALONG HADRIAN'S WALL

**Housesteads Visitor Centre, Housesteads**
Open daily, Housesteads' Visitor Centre offers information, exhibitions and accessible facilities..

**The Sill: National Landscape Discovery Centre, Once Brewed**
Information, exhibitions and even a hostel, between Sycamore Gap and Vindolanda (thesill.org.uk).

**Hexham Tourist Office, Hexham**
Housed in Hexham's library, this tourist office is open Monday to Saturday (visitnorthumberland.com).

fore the Romans left, and the pagan Anglo-Saxons and Danes eventually followed suit. One of the most impressive churches to survive Henry VIII's dissolution of the monasteries (1536–41) is **Hexham Abbey**, 22 miles west of Newcastle by car or Northern's Tyne Valley rail service.

Built in the 12th century over a 7th-century predecessor, the Abbey survived dissolution as Hexham's parish church, and is a stately example of Anglo-Norman sacred architecture. The crypt of **St Wilfrid's**, the Anglo-Saxon church over which it was built, can still be visited. The crypt's stonework shows friezes and inscriptions indicating it was taken from a fine Roman house, almost certainly from nearby Coria (Corbridge). The tombstone of a 1st-century standard bearer, Flavinus, can also be seen.

Other notable religious sites within reach of Newcastle include **St Paul's monastery** in Jarrow (once one of Europe's great centres of religious scholarship); the moody ruins of **Finchale Priory** in County Durham; Blanchland's intact abbey church; and, sitting in a loop of the River Coquet near Rothbury, stately **Brinkburn Priory and Manor**. Like Hexham, Brinkburn and Blanchland both date to the 12th century and both survived as Anglican parish churches. Ruined Tynemouth Priory, founded in the 7th century, was the burial place of Northumbrian kings.

Hexham Abbey

## THE MOORLAND GROUP OF CHURCHES

Blanchland Abbey is the most prominent of the eight members of the Moorland Group of Churches. These parish churches, some ancient, some younger, all serve small communities in the North Pennines' eastern moors.

St Edmunds in Edmundbyers shows earlier features beneath its 12th-century edifice; All Saints in Muggleswick is early 18th century; St Philip & St James in Whittonstall is Georgian, as is Slaley's St Mary the Virgin and St John's in Healey. St Matthews in Waskerley and St James' in Hunstanworth are all mid-Victorian. While perhaps only Blanchland and St Edmunds are of great historical interest, a tour of these closely situated Pennine churches is a lovely way to see the landscape and its villages.

## GETTING AROUND

The easiest way to see all you'd like to in the country beyond Newcastle is by car. Once outside the metropolis, traffic is light by English standards, and parking is rarely a problem in smaller centres.

The Northern Rail network is extensive, connecting Newcastle with Durham, Hartlepool, Bishop Auckland, and Carlisle (via centres for Hadrian's Wall). Arriva runs a bus network throughout the northeast, connecting Newcastle with Whitley Bay and smaller centres throughout Tyne and Wear that aren't accessible by train.

But best of all is walking. Sparsely populated, often untroubled of other visitors, this physical, enduring archive of a wild England that's vanished in most other places promises something very special to those with the will to find it.

Northumberland Coast

London

# NORTHUMBER-LAND COAST

The Northumberland Coast is one of the most austere yet captivating corners of England. Characterised by dramatic coastline, rain-scoured farms, dignified market towns and some truly impressive castles, it's a region which is rarely plagued by tourist hordes.

Its 'capital' is Berwick-upon-Tweed, England's northernmost city and frequently a Scottish possession. Other notable centres include Alnwick, anchored by the incredible castle that's still home to the Dukes of Northumberland; Craster, a comely coastal centre near Dunstanburgh (another memorable fortress); and Bamburgh – home to the most awe-inspiring castle in the northeast. Wonderful walking, forested valleys, birdlife and sand dunes complete an alluring picture.

This coast is also a place of great spiritual significance. The monastery on Lindisfarne (the 'Holy Island') was sometime home to St Cuthbert, the favourite saint of the northeast. It's also where the first Viking longship broke the horizon, presaging centuries of raids and territorial struggles.

## TOP TIP

Taking the train north from Newcastle to Berwick, it's easy to overlook many exceptional stretches of this coastline. If you're to hire a car anywhere in the northeast, make it here. it's relatively hassle-free and you'll be able to access much more than you might if relying on buses and the single train line that hugs the coast.

Dunstanburgh Castle (p575)

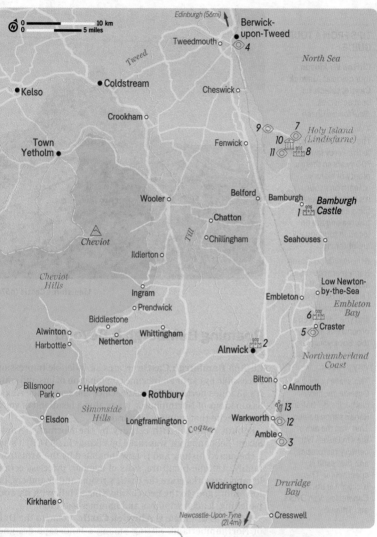

0 10 km
0 5 miles
Edinburgh (56mi)
Berwick-upon-Tweed
Tweedmouth
4
Tweed
North Sea
Coldstream
Kelso
Cheswick
Crookham
9
7
Holy Island (Lindisfarne)
10
Fenwick
11
8
Town Yetholm
Belford
Bamburgh
Bamburgh Castle
1
Wooler
Chatton
Till
Cheviot
Chillingham
Seahouses
Ildlerton
Cheviot Hills
Low Newton-by-the-Sea
Ingram
Embleton
Embleton Bay
Prendwick
6
Biddlestone
Craster
5
Alwinton
Whittingham
Netherton
2
Harbottle
Alnwick
Northumberland Coast
Bilton
Alnmouth
Billsmoor Park
Holystone
Rothbury
13
Simonside Hills
Elsdon
Longframlington
Warkworth
12
Coquet
Amble
3
Widdrington
Druridge Bay
Kirkharle
Newcastle-Upon-Tyne (21.4mi)
Cresswell

**HIGHLIGHTS**
**1** Bamburgh Castle

**SIGHTS**
**2** Alnwick Castle
**3** Amble
**4** Berwick-upon-Tweed
**5** Craster
**6** Dunstanburgh Castle
**7** Lindisfarne
**8** Lindisfarne Castle
**9** Lindisfarne Causeway
**10** Old Lifeboat House
**11** St Cuthbert Island
**12** Warkworth

**ACTIVITIES**
**13** Northumberland Coast Path

**Bamburgh Castle (p574)**

### TIPS FROM A TOUR GUIDE

**Clifton Wilkinson**, tour guide at **Alnwick Castle**, selects its best activities. *@clifton.wilkinson*

**Take a tour**
The castle belonged to the Percy family for 700 years so there's plenty of history to learn on a tour. It's been in several films and TV shows too, making the on-location tour equally enlightening.

**Broomstick training**
Harry learnt quidditch at Alnwick Castle ('Hogwarts' in the first two movies) and you can get on a broomstick and 'fly' too. Book your free ticket on arrival – it's very popular.

**The state rooms**
Outside, medieval castle; inside, Italian Renaissance palace. That was the aim of the 4th Duke's 19th-century restoration, and the result is spectacular. The highlight is the art: Canalettos, Van Dycks and Titians.

Lindisfarne Castle (p576)

## Roaming Bamburgh & Beyond

COUNTING COASTAL CASTLES

Clifftop **Bamburgh Castle** creates an indelible impression. Accessible by car or an irksome combination of bus and train, it's 53 miles north of Newcastle. Once the seat of the Anglo-Saxon kings of Northumbria, it sits atop a headland of volcanic dolerite that amplifies its drama.

Rebuilt from the 11th century by the Normans (Anglo-Saxon 'Bebbanburgh' was razed by Vikings in 993 CE) it's had a chequered history and is now inhabited by the Armstrong family. Antique furniture, suits of armour, priceless ceramics and artworks cram the castle's rooms and chambers, but top billing goes to the neo-Gothic King's Hall, with its wood panelling, leaded windows and hammerbeam roof.

Almost as dramatic is **Alnwick Castle**, home to the Duke of Northumberland. Sitting among a landscape designed by Lancelot 'Capability' Brown, it's largely unaltered since the 14th century. It too is stuffed with treasures, including

### WHERE TO STAY NEAR BAMBURGH, ALNWICK OR DUNSTANBURGH

**Alnwick Lodge, Alnwick**
This restful, 15-room B&B sits in the countryside 3 miles south of Alnwick. ££

**Lindisfarne Inn, Berwick-upon-Tweed**
Situated on the mainland facing the Holy Island, this delightful pub does food and rooms. ££

**Crasterway, Craster**
This four-room, eight-bed cottage is great for families basing themselves here longer than one night. ££

paintings by Canaletto, Titian and Van Dyck. **Alnwick** itself is an appealing market town with great pubs, cafes and shops selling local produce.

**Dunstanburgh Castle**, near the handsome fishing port **Craster**, is the third in a trinity of unforgettable fortresses. The scenic 1.5-mile clifftop walk to this 14th-century redoubt is one of Craster's greatest pleasures. Seafood lovers should seek out Craster's famous kippers, perhaps at **Craster Seafood Restaurant**, supplied by renowned smokehouse Robson & Sons.

## Experience England's Northern Extremity

BERWICK'S BARE-BONES BEAUTY

**Berwick-upon-Tweed** has one foot in England and another in Scotland. It's recognised as the most fought-over town in European history: between 1174 and 1482 it passed between the Scots and the English 14 times. The local dialect – a mixture of North Northumbrian and East Scots dialects – is one legacy of this tug-of-war.

Possessed of austere appeal, Berwick has long been part of England's coastal defences. Imposing Elizabethan walls and bastions encircle the town, frowning over the Tweed and the sea beyond. They're complete and make for a delightful 1-mile **walking circuit**. Along the way, inspect **Berwick Barracks**, designed in 1717 by Nicholas Hawksmoor and the oldest of their type surviving. **Time to Explore Tours** offers two-hour excursions of these and other Berwick highlights, including the 18th-century **Gunpowder Magazine** and **Bankhill Icehouse**.

The Grade I–listed **Berwick Bridge**, built between 1611 and 1624, and the **Royal Tweed** (1925–28) both span the river with picturesque precision. Beyond, the broad **estuary** is an ever-changing prospect of shimmering water and tidal mudflats. The **Town Hall**, once an 18th-century-century tollbooth replacing older predecessors, is home to the **Cell Block Museum**.

Lining **Bridge St**, Berwick's modern attractions include convivial pubs like the **Barrels Ale House** (craft beer and basement performances); intimate **Curfew Micropub** (four rotating ales and great standard choices); **Audela** (contemporary British food); and **Atelier** (charcuterie and wine).

### WHY I LOVE THE NORTHUMBERLAND COAST

**Hugh McNaughtan**, Lonely Planet writer

While I love the gentle, rural perfection of iconic English landscapes like the Cotswolds, there's something about the wild, rain-wracked Northumberland Coast that leaves me in happy, helpless wonder. The collision of ragged coastline and grim, hardscrabble farms creates a bleak beauty unlike anywhere else.

The unceasing sea, cutting coastal sandstone and shale, has produced a procession of headlands, overhanging cliffs, wave-tormented reefs, and lonely islands that is genuinely sublime. England's longest stretches of sand dunes also occur here. Human contributions to the northeast – the spray-slicked stones of Berwick, the awesome bulk of Bamburgh and Alnwick castles – provide the final flourish. Austere and resilient, they're part of a harmony that always touches me with awe.

### WHERE TO STAY IN BERWICK

**Berwick YHA**
Occupying multiple floors of an 18th-century granary, this superior hostel houses a gallery and bistro. £

**The Walls**
Perched above the Tweed, this delightful period B&B is close to Berwick's best sights. ££

**Marshall Meadows Manor House**
This seaside Georgian manor, 3 miles north of Berwick, is now a charismatic luxury hotel. £££

# The Pilgrimage to Lindisfarne

THE HOLY ISLAND'S INEFFABLE ATTRACTION

**Lindisfarne** is one of Britain's most historic Christian sites. The Holy Island's importance predates the creation of England – its first Priory was founded in 634 CE by Irish missionary St Aidan, who is credited with converting the Northumbrian Angles to the 'true faith'. Under successors like St Cuthbert, the Priory grew into a centre of Christian learning and evangelism. Famously and repeatedly ravaged by the Vikings from 793 CE, it was eventually abandoned by the terrorised monks, who fled with St Cuthbert's bones and the *Lindisfarne Gospels* in 875 CE.

The present remains are of the Norman Benedictine Priory founded in the 11th century. Now accompanying them are 16th-century **Lindisfarne Castle**, once the fabulously romantic home of Sir Edwin Lutyens, and the Georgian **Old Lifeboat House**, today a museum dedicated to the boats and their altruistic endeavours.

Information and exhibits are plentiful at the **Heritage Centre** (open mid-March to October). Lindisfarne is reached via a tidal causeway – check the day's tidal times (tidetimes.co.uk/holy-island-tide-times) to avoid getting stranded. When it's out, you can also walk to tiny **St Cuthbert Island**, where the saint sought solitude from even his fellow monks.

Places to stay and/or refresh yourself on Lindisfarne include the **Manor House** and **Crown & Anchor**, both right by the Priory; the convivial, timber-beamed **Ship Inn**; and **Lindisfarne Mead**, selling various meads, fruit wines and spirits.

### THE LINDISFARNE GOSPELS

The illuminated manuscript known as the *Lindisfarne Gospels* is perhaps the most beautiful relic of Anglo-Saxon Christianity there is. A work of painstaking intricacy, it's thought to have been created between 715 and 720 CE by the monk Eadfrith – Bishop of Lindisfarne Priory from 698 to 722 CE. Alongside the four gospels, it includes letters from St Jerome and other revered writings.

Combining Anglo-Saxon, Celtic and Mediterranean decorative styles, the Gospels include five densely illuminated 'carpet pages' – named for their resemblance to the intricate carpets woven in the eastern Mediterranean. The manuscript was one treasure the monks managed to carry with them when they fled Lindisfarne, indicating the value they accorded it.

# The Northumberland Coast Path

A WILD, WAVE-WRACKED WALK

The Northumberland Coast Path allows you to experience this unique landscape at your leisure, missing none of its ever-changing detail. Running 62 miles from Cresswell to Berwick-upon-Tweed, it passes above lonely sand-strewn bays and wave-battered clifftops, into coastal grass-

### WEST COAST CASTLES

If castles tickle your fancy, there ar plenty more to be discovered on th west coast. Head to **Carlisle Cast** (p553) for one of the country's mightiest medieval forts, or spare some time for **Rose** and **Drumburgh Castles** (p553).

### TOUR OPERATORS ON THE NORTHUMBERLAND COAST

**Berwick Boat Trips, Berwick-upon-Tweed**
Boats head upriver or out on the North Sea in search of sea life and scenery.

**Serenity Farne Island Boat Tours, Seahouses**
This outfit takes boats around the Farne Islands to see wildlife and obscure beauty spots.

**Northern Experience Wildlife Tours, Choppington**
Otter safaris, Farne Islands trips, photography workshops, stargazing excursions and more

Royal Tweed Bridge, Berwick

lands and woodlands and through distinctive northeastern villages and fishing ports.

Walkers usually take between three and seven days to complete the path – there are frequent opportunities to rest, explore especially appealing places and find accommodation for the night. After beginning with the 8-mile sands of **Druridge Bay**, walkable when the tide's out, you'll next reach **Amble** (where boat tours head to the seabird colonies of RSPB reserve **Coquet Island**, although landing isn't permitted). Beyond that, **Warkworth** has a castle, scenic beach, and welcoming places to eat and sleep like the **Wellwood Arms**.

Warkworth to **Craster** entails some of the path's most dramatic coast, plus sweet villages like **Alnmouth**. Next, Craster to **Seahouses**, one of the UK's most striking coastal walks, takes in seaside cliffs and **Dunstanburgh Castle**. Seahouses to **Belford** is all about Bamburgh Castle and Farne Island views, while Belford to **Fenwick** heads inland through woods and fields. The last leg, Fenwick to **Berwick**, reveals some of the wildest, loneliest coast on the entire path. The **Potted Lobster** (Bamburgh), **Jolly Fisherman** (Craster) and **Joiners Arms** (Newton-by-the-Sea) are some superior places to eat or sleep along the way.

### THE COAST'S REBOUNDING FLORA & FAUNA

The Northumberland Coast has steadily regenerated since becoming an Area of Outstanding Natural Beauty and reparation of damage left by industries such as coal mining. It's increasingly salubrious for the region's endemic plants and animals.

All along the coast, but in particular in nature reserves such as Cresswell, Hauxley, Annstead Dunes, Coquet Island and Lindisfarne, bird species are present in numbers. Terns, coots, moorhens, sanderlings and ringed plovers can all be seen at different times of the year.

Native plants on the rebound include bloody cranesbill, lady's bedstraw, bird's-foot-trefoil and restharrow. Insects like common blue and wall brown butterflies and mammals including red squirrels, stoats and otters may be glimpsed in reserves like Hauxley.

### GETTING AROUND

The Northumberland Coast is best explored via a combination of driving and walking. A car will get you to places not serviced by public transport, and your feet will take you to the most striking and secluded spots on the Coast.

If you're relying on public transport, LNER, CrossCountry and TransPennine trains run regularly between Newcastle and Berwick-upon-Tweed, usually stopping at Morpeth and Alnmouth (for Alnwick). Buses reach many of the less frequented destinations, including Craster, Bamburgh and Amble-by-the-Sea. The region's routes are serviced by Arriva Northeast.

UNDERGROUND
SUBWAY

# TOOLKIT

The chapters in this section cover the most important topics you'll need to know about in England. They're full of nuts-and-bolts information and valuable insights to help you understand and navigate England and get the most out of your trip.



**London Underground**

# Arriving

London is a global transport hub and the main point of entry for most travellers visiting England. Most international flights arrive at Heathrow, 15 miles west of central London, or Gatwick, a 30-minute train journey south of the city centre. Eurostar international trains arrive at London's St Pancras station.

**Visas**

Citizens of the EU, Australia, Canada, New Zealand, Japan and the USA do not usually need a visa to enter the UK for stays of up to six months.

**SIM Cards**

Prepaid SIM cards with internet data are sold at convenience stores and vending machines in airport arrival halls. The major operators are Vodafone, EE, O2 and Three.

**Border Crossings**

British immigration authorities can be tough; stay calm and have your documents ready. Once you have entered the UK you can travel between England, Scotland and Wales without further border formalities.

**Wi-fi**

Free wi-fi is available at Heathrow and Gatwick airports, though it can be slow. Elsewhere in England, wi-fi access is widespread.

**Public Transport from Airport to City Centre**

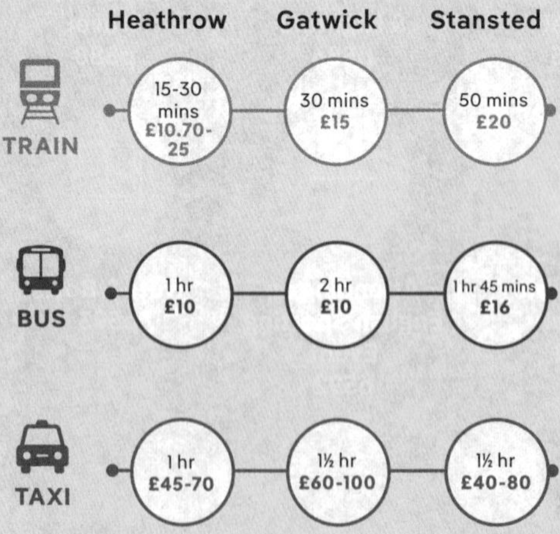

| | Heathrow | Gatwick | Stansted |
|---|---|---|---|
| TRAIN | 15-30 mins £10.70-25 | 30 mins £15 | 50 mins £20 |
| BUS | 1 hr £10 | 2 hr £10 | 1 hr 45 mins £16 |
| TAXI | 1 hr £45-70 | 1½ hr £60-100 | 1½ hr £40-80 |

## ARRIVING IN HEATHROW

Summer 2022 was marked by staff shortages and long delays at a number of European airports as passengers returned to the skies in almost pre-pandemic numbers. Heathrow was particularly badly affected, with long queues at security and passport control, cancelled flights, and lost and delayed baggage. The travel chaos has since subsided.

To get from Heathrow to central London, you can take the Heathrow Express train (the fastest but most expensive option), the Piccadilly underground line (a cheap but slow alternative), or the new Elizabeth line, which is the middle option in both price and journey length.

# Getting Around



England's towns and cities are well connected by road and train. However, transport in England can be expensive, and roads can be congested.

### TRAVEL COSTS

Rental
**From £35/day**

Petrol
**Approx £1.65/litre**

EV charging
**£1/hour**

Train ticket from London to Liverpool
**from £31**

## Hiring a Car

Car hire is available in every city. Having your own wheels helps you make the most of your time and makes it easier to reach remote places, but rental and fuel costs can be expensive. In cities, heavy traffic means public transport is often the better choice.

## Road Conditions

England's roads are generally in good condition but are often congested. Motorways and A-roads link major cities. Most roads are toll free (an exception is the M6 Toll in the West Midlands), but tolls are charged for a number of river crossings such as the Dartford Crossing.

**TIP**
The Traffic England website has live updates on congestion, incidents and closures affecting the country's motorways and major A-roads.

### GOING CAR FREE

Using a mix of train, bus, taxi, walking and hiring a bike, you can get almost anywhere in England without having to drive. There is no extra charge to bring bicycles onboard trains, but depending on the train company and route, you may need to reserve a space for your bike in advance, and bikes may only be permitted outside peak hours (usually defined as Monday to Friday before 10am and from 4pm to 7pm).

## Train & Bus

The main public transport options are trains and long-distance buses (coaches). Services between major towns and cities are generally good. At peak times you should book in advance to be sure of getting a ticket.

## Buying Tickets

Buses are usually slower – and cheaper – than trains. But if you book early and travel during off-peak periods, both train and coach tickets can be relatively inexpensive. In rural and remote places, buses may be the only public transport option available.

## Going by Plane

Though England hardly seems large enough to justify the carbon footprint of domestic flights, you can fly from London to Newcastle, Manchester and Newquay (in Cornwall), and from Newcastle to Bristol and Southampton.

### DRIVING ESSENTIALS

Drive on the left

**60**

Speed limit is 30mph in urban areas, 60mph on single carriageways and 70mph on dual carriageways and motorways.

**.05**

Blood alcohol limit is 0.08%

# Money

CURRENCY: **POUND (£)**

### Credit Cards

Visa and MasterCard are widely accepted in England. Other cards, including Amex, are not always accepted. Most businesses will assume your card is chip and PIN enabled. If it isn't, you should be able to sign instead.

### Parking Payments

It's often easiest to pay for car parking in England by downloading an app. The name of the app used locally will be displayed on parking payment machines.

### Contactless Payments

Nearly all business now accept card payments, and an increasing number no longer accept cash. Contactless payments – where you pay by tapping your card on the machine – are often preferred. If your card is not enabled for contactless payments, or for amounts exceeding the £100 contactless limit, you can use the chip and PIN payment method by inserting your card into the machine.

### Tipping

**Restaurants** 12.5% in restaurants with table service (usually added to your bill).

**Pubs & Bars** Not expected if you order drinks (or food) and pay at the bar; usually 10% if you order at the table.

**Taxis** Usually 10%, or rounded up to the nearest pound, especially in London.

### HOW MUCH FOR A...

Theme park entry
**£60**

City-centre car parking
**£2/hr**

Bicycle hire
**£25/day**

Surfing lesson
**£45**

### HOW TO... Save on Admission Costs...

Entrance to England's attractions can be expensive. Theme parks and other major attractions often sell reduced-price advance tickets online that offer discounts of up to 50%. For popular attractions, it's also worth buying tickets online to guarantee entry and to avoid ticket office queues on the day. If you are planning to visit several English Heritage or National Trust properties, you might save money by purchasing an annual membership.

### LOCAL TIP

Eating out is expensive. Staying in self-catering accommodation and buying food from supermarkets will save you money. Some restaurants offer cheaper set-price lunch and pre-theatre menus.

### COST-OF-LIVING CRISIS

England's cost-of-living crisis – prompted by a combination of factors including COVID-19–related supply-chain disruption, Brexit and the war in Ukraine – has seen restaurant and coffee prices rise by 26% between 2020 and 2022, huge hikes in rents and mortgage repayments, and spiralling fuel and energy costs, without a corresponding rise in wages. Between 2021 and 2022, domestic gas prices increased by 96% and domestic electricity prices by 54%. As millions of people feel the squeeze, it is England's poorest households that are experiencing the greatest hardship, since food and energy costs make up a higher proportion of their overall budget.

# Accommodation

## Find a Local B&B

Small, family-run B&Bs generally provide good value for money and a more personal experience. Hosts are usually happy to give recommendations for the local area, and you'll also be offered a traditional English breakfast in the morning. The most luxurious guesthouses are more like boutique hotels, with high-end toiletries and quality bedding. Prices start at around £80.

## Budget Beds

England has a selection of hostels, many housed in rustic farmhouses or historic buildings. Dorm beds cost between £10 and £30; private rooms start at £50. Bothies and bunkhouses can be found in remote areas for use by walkers. They are usually simple stone or wood buildings with a communal sleeping area. BYO sleeping bag.

## A Night on the Water

For something different, you can rent a narrowboat and cruise city canals or explore rural waterways on a quintessential English break. Most boats sleep four to eight people. You don't need a license to steer the boats, which travel at a leisurely 4 miles per hour. Prices for a three-night stay start at around £800.

**HOW MUCH FOR A NIGHT IN...**

a shepherd's hut
**£120**

a narrowboat
**£150**

a lighthouse
**£250**

## Historic Pubs & Inns

England's oldest pubs and inns make atmospheric places to stay, with creaking floors, wooden beams, cosy bars with crackling fires and even the occasional resident ghost. Some have outstanding restaurants that are destinations in themselves; after your meal you have only to climb the stairs to bed. Prices start at about £100.

## Camp Out

Camping ranges from simple farmers' fields to fully-furnished luxury bell tents with all the mod-cons. Possible lodgings include shepherd's huts, railway carriages, tree houses and cabins with outdoor bathtubs. Camping has become extremely popular recently, so book ahead. Prices start at around £20 for a pitch at a campsite, and upwards of £150 for a luxury glamping experience.

## ROOM WITH A VIEW

If you're a fan of English period dramas, you'll know there's usually a grand country house at the centre of the action. To get a taste of life on a country estate, you can book a stay in a palatial property such as Cliveden House in Berkshire, where Meghan Markle spent the night before her wedding, or Grantley Hall in Yorkshire. If you favour coast over country, consider a stay in one of England's romantic lighthouses, many of which offer self-catering or B&B accommodation. These spectacular buildings are usually in prime locations, with magnificent sea views.

# Family Travel

England's small size, good transport options and huge choice of attractions make it a fun and interesting destination for children of all ages. There are sandy beaches and wildlife-rich national parks to explore, historic castles with dress-up trunks to discover, and a reliable assortment of rainy day activities to keep the little ones occupied.

## Eating Out

- Nearly all family-friendly restaurants have kids' menus and highchairs.
- Many pubs will not allow children inside at night due to licensing rules, so check before planning a pub dinner with kids.
- Fine-dining restaurants are not usually suitable for children.
- Supermarkets sell good-value lunchtime meal deals that include a drink, sandwich and a snack, and are great for kids on the go.

## Getting Around

Most regions offer family tickets that give reductions on train and bus travel. If you are planning to make several journeys by train, you may save money with a Family and Friends Railcard (familyandfriends-railcard.co.uk).

If you're hiring a car, you should request a child's seat when booking. Not all rental firms guarantee that a car seat will be available, so be sure to check.

### TOP PICKS FOR KIDS

**BeWILDerwood, Norfolk (p352)**
Clamber through a tree-top world of zip wires, jungle bridges and tree houses.

**Lyme Regis (p274)**
Search for buried prehistoric treasure on a fossil walk with geologists from Lyme Regis Museum.

**York's museums (p442)**
Climb aboard a steam locomotive at the National Railway Museum and learn about Vikings at Jorvik.

**Whitby (p460)**
Teenagers can follow in the footsteps of Dracula; younger kids can take a boat trip and play on the beach.

## Facilities

Change tables are available in most restaurant bathrooms and public toilets, but not all. Most towns and beaches have signposted public toilets, but they can be harder to find in big cities. Try shopping centres, large supermarkets and train stations.

## Sights

Visitor attractions usually offer family tickets (for two adults and two children) for less than the sum of the individual entrance charges, as well as cheaper rates for solo parents and kids.

## EXPLORING THE PAST

England's castles and museums offer much to engage young minds, especially for children interested in history. Expect to find period costumes for dressing-up, interactive audiovisual displays, and themed children's playgrounds at many attractions. Guides at castles and other historic sites do a good job of making the facts entertaining.

Family travel in England can be expensive, but some of the country's best museums and galleries are free. There is no charge to see the life-size animatronics at London's Natural History Museum or the World Museum in Liverpool. Many museums and art galleries also offer organised activities for children during school holidays.

# Health & Safe Travel



## HEALTHCARE

Emergency medical treatment is available to all free of charge at National Health Service (NHS) hospital Accident & Emergency (A&E) departments. The European Health Insurance Card (EHIC), available to travellers from the EU, covers medically necessary healthcare in England. If you are not normally resident in the UK and don't have an EHIC, you will need to pay for most non-emergency medical treatment; make sure you have insurance.

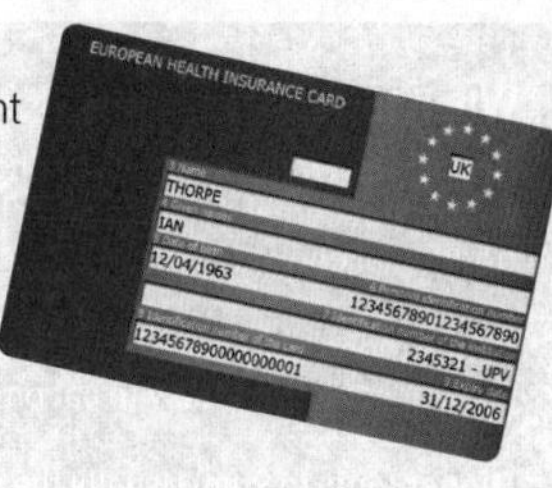


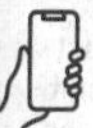

### Non-Emergencies

If you urgently need medical advice but the situation is not life-threatening, you can call NHS 111 (phone 111). Pharmacies can advise on minor ailments such as sore throats and earaches. The NHS website has a search function for pharmacies by area, including those with out-of-hours services.

### Terrorism

There is an ongoing threat of terror attacks by extremist groups in England. You can check the current UK government terrorism threat level, a five-point scale that rates the likelihood of a terrorist attack from low to critical based on intelligence reports.

### PICKPOCKETS

Watch out for pickpockets and hustlers in crowded areas popular with tourists, such as around Westminster Bridge in London.

## SWIM SAFELY

**Red and yellow flag**
Lifeguarded area. Swim between the flags.

**Black and white checkered flag**
Surfing area. No swimming.

**Red flag**
Danger. Do not enter the water.

**Orange wind sock**
Strong wind. Do not use inflatables.

### Drugs

Illegal drugs are widely available, especially in clubs. Cannabis possession is a criminal offence; punishment for carrying a small amount may be a warning, a fine or prosecution. Dealers face much stiffer penalties, as do people caught with other drugs. Police have the right to search anyone they suspect of possessing drugs.

### FLOODS

In recent years England has experienced heavy rainfall and an increasing number of floods, brought on by the climate crisis. Some coastal areas are particularly at risk, including Cornwall and parts of Kent and Sussex. The worst flooding occurs when a river bursts its banks. When this happens the water level rises quickly; in some cases emergency services have had to rescue people from their homes in boats.

# Food, Drink & Nightlif

## When to Eat

**Breakfast** (7am to 9am) Most English people eat cereal or toast rather than a traditional cooked breakfast.

**Lunch** (noon to 3pm) Often sandwiches, soup or something easy to eat on the go.

**Dinner** (6pm to 9pm) Usually the main meal of the day; also known as supper or tea. Often followed by dessert.

### MENU DECODER

**Pre-theatre menu** A fixed-price, two- or three-course menu served in the early evening; often good value for money.

**Wine pairings** Some fine-dining restaurants offer a glass of specially selected wine with each course.

**Cheese board** A plate of cheese and crackers, which is sometimes offered on dessert menus.

**Full English breakfast** Fried bacon, sausages, eggs, tomatoes, mushrooms and baked beans.

**Black pudding** Sausage made with pig's blood and oatmeal that is traditionally served for breakfast in northern England.

**Sunday roast** Roast beef, chicken or lamb served with roast and mashed potatoes, vegetables and gravy.

**Bangers and mash** A hearty dish of sausages, mashed potato and gravy.

**Chips** Like potato fries, but fatter and fluffier. Crisps are a potato snack sold in packets (known as chips in the US).

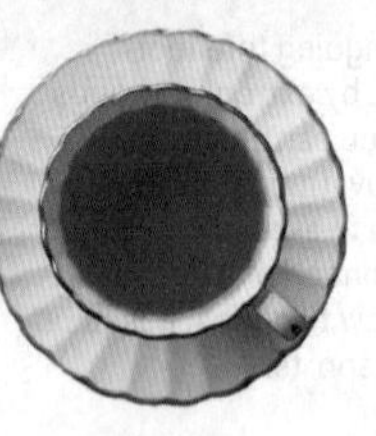

## Where to Eat

**Cafes** Also known as greasy spoons, traditional English cafes are basic, no-frills establishments serving fried breakfasts, sandwiches and baked potatoes.

**Coffee shops** Specialist coffee shops sell lattes, flat whites and drip coffees, as well as pastries.

**Tearooms** Old-fashioned tearooms are usually found in rural areas and have cosy decor and a menu of sandwiches and cakes.

**Pubs** Most pubs now sell meals, usually generous portions of comfort food like lasagne or pie and chips.

## HOW TO... Order Drinks

If you're in a pub with friends, it's polite to buy a round of drinks. Ask everybody in your party what they would like, then order and pay at the bar. Your friends will reciprocate. But if you're with a large group or on a tight budget it's not necessary to get a round; in this case you can order your own drink.

Draft beer is served by the pint and half pint; specify the quantity when you order. In England a standard measure of spirits is 25ml, but some bars use 35ml or 50ml measures.

Restaurants will always provide tap water to drink, but sometimes you need to request it. At the start of your meal, staff may offer you mineral water by asking the question 'still or sparking?' It's fine to ask for tap water if that's what you would prefer.

**HOW MUCH FOR A...**

99 ice cream
£4

Lunchtime sandwich
£4.50

Coffee
£3

Take-away fish and chips
£10

Dinner at a Michelin-starred restaurant
£50 to 300

Pint of beer
£4

Glass of wine
£4

HOW TO...

## Eat Curry

South Asian food is popular in England, and curry is the country's unofficial favourite meal. Having a curry doesn't refer to eating one specific dish; in fact, it's shorthand for a range of cuisines from India, Pakistan, Bangladesh and Sri Lanka. The dishes and flavours vary depending on the region the food is from.

**Where to eat curry** Though you'll find curry on many restaurant and pub menus, the best place to try it is at one of the country's numerous South Asian restaurants; there are particularly good places in Birmingham and Manchester.

**What to eat** The meal usually starts with poppadoms: crispy, fried flatbreads served with a selection of chutneys and pickles. Consider ordering a selection of curries to share. English curries are usually sweeter and thicker than curries in South Asia. Chicken tikka masala is based on the Indian dish butter chicken, made with chicken marinated in yogurt, cooked in a tandoori oven and served in a spicy, creamy tomato sauce. Other dishes to try include saag aloo (spinach and potato curry) and dahl, which is made with lentils. To accompany the curries, order basmati rice and naan bread to mop up the sauce.

**What to drink** In England curry is typically accompanied by a cold beer, but a lassi (a yogurt-based drink) is a more traditional South Asian refreshment.

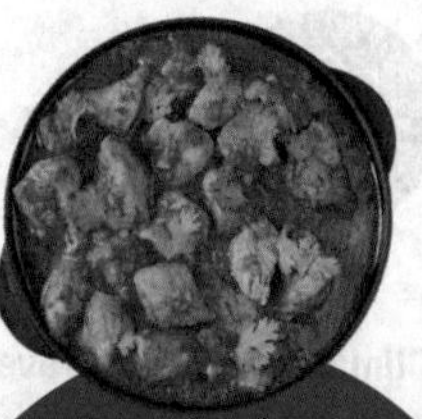

### South Asian Fine Dining

Eight Indian restaurants in England have been awarded a Michelin star, including chef Aktar Islam's restaurant Opheem in Birmingham, and seven London restaurants.

## AFTERNOON TEA

The tradition of taking afternoon tea began during the Victorian era, when it became fashionable for wealthy people to set up a table with tea, sandwiches and cakes between 4pm and 5pm. In summer, afternoon tea was taken in the garden.

How England came to be a nation of tea-with-sugar drinkers is a dark and murky story: the tea trade is rooted in colonial plantation. English tea traders facilitated the supply of opium to China, and used the military force of locally recruited soldiers to seize and control land for tea plantations in India, paving the way for British colonial rule. Even today, tea plantations are often exploitative workplaces.

Over the last 20 years, afternoon tea has become fashionable in England once again. An afternoon tea is often a form of celebration (for baby showers, birthdays and hen parties), during which elaborate tiered platters of crustless sandwiches, dainty cakes, and scones with jam and clotted cream are consumed. The tea served is typically Earl Grey, Darjeeling or English Breakfast, though these days it's not uncommon to see a bottle of Prosecco on the table.

Afternoon teas can be hosted at home or taken at a hotel (book ahead). The Ritz is famous for its afternoon tea, during which you can chose from 18 different teas and nibble on scones, sandwiches and cakes in the gilded opulence of the Amber Room, accompanied by a pianist, a small orchestra or sometimes a soprano. Look out for themed afternoon teas, where pastry chefs get creative. The Berkeley Hotel's Couture Cakewalk afternoon tea celebrates a fashion designer's latest collection.

# Responsible Travel

## Climate Change & Travel

It's impossible to ignore the impact we have when travelling, and the importance of making changes where we can. Lonely Planet urges all travellers to engage with their travel carbon footprint. There are many carbon calculators online that allow travellers to estimate the carbon emissions generated by their journey; try resurgence.org/resources/carbon-calculator.html. Many airlines and booking sites offer travellers the option of offsetting the impact of greenhouse gas emissions by contributing to climate-friendly initiatives around the world. We continue to offset the carbon footprint of all Lonely Planet staff travel, while recognising this is a mitigation more than a solution.

## Wildlife Safaris

In Yorkshire, take a Spurn point safari, a three-hour guided wildlife tour in a specially converted ex-military vehicle, for a chance to see harbour porpoises and seals. Tours help fund Yorkshire Wildlife Trust (ywt.org.uk) conservation projects.

## Stargazing

Thanks to efforts to limit light pollution, Exmoor National Park (p252) was designated Europe's first International Dark Sky Reserve in 2011. The Dark Sky Friendly accreditation scheme rewards local tourism providers who respect the region's dark skies.

## Fink Street Food

Fink (eatfinktalk.com) is a social enterprise with a mission to get people talking about mental health, while serving Middle Eastern–style street food. More than 50% of its profits go to mental health causes. Look for the Fink van in Reading or Heritage and at events.

## Kitchen Garden

Diners at the Ethicurian (theethicurean.com) near Bristol are taken on a tour of the fresh produce in the walled garden, before sitting down to a seasonal menu. The restaurant makes efforts to reduce food waste and uses sustainable local suppliers.

## Eden Project

Discover the planet's ecosystems at the Eden Project (p325) in Cornwall, a series of botanical gardens that showcase the natural world. A second Eden Project is planned for Morecambe in Lancashire.

Look for litter-picking stations all around the English coast and leave the beach cleaner than you found it, or join in with a community litter-picking event.

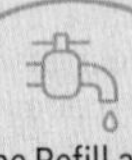

The Refill app shows the nearest places to refill your water bottle, get coffee in a reusable cup, bring your own lunchbox for takeaway food, and the location of shops offering plastic-free refills.

## Quiet Site

With a range of cabins, camping pods and cottages to choose from, the nearly carbon neutral the Quiet Site (thequietsite.co.uk) holiday park near Ullswater has been a pioneer in responsible tourism for more than 20 years.

## Seal Spotting at Blakeney Point

Take a boat trip out to see the grey seal colony and terns at Norfolk's Blakeney National Nature Reserve. Trips with family-run local operators depart from Morston Quay.

To buy fresh local produce direct from the farm, search the listings on Fabulous Farm shops (fabulousfarmshops.co.uk).

Brighton (p153) is a city that's big on all things green, from vegan restaurants to vintage clothes shops.

You can buy produce direct from growers at a farmers' market. One of the best is the Growing Communities (growingcommunities.org) Saturday morning market in London; all the farms with market stalls are organic or biodynamic.

## Carbon-Neutral Theatre

Pigfoot (pigfoottheatre.com) is a carbon-neutral theatre company staging plays across the country that address themes of climate change and eco-anxiety. In How to Save a Rock, actors generate electricity by cycling a bike live on stage.

## Off-Grid Camping

Stay in an architect-designed stilted cabin or Tipi in an abandoned quarry overlooking the sea at Kudhva (kudhva.com), an off-grid campsite in Cornwall. Activities include wild swimming and stargazing; food is prepared in a communal kitchen.

### RESOURCES

**naturevolunteers.uk**
Volunteering opportunities on a range of conservation projects.

**wildlifetrusts.org**
Wildlife conservation charity that manages nature reserves.

**nationalparks.uk**
Information on England's national parks.

# LGBTIQ+ Travellers

England is a generally welcoming place for the LGBTIQ+ community, and the UK was ranked joint fifth on the 2021 Spartacus Gay Travel Index list of community-friendly travel destinations. London, Brighton and Manchester are home to the country's biggest gay scenes.

## Pride

Between June and September, cities and towns across England celebrate Pride with parades, concerts and parties. The biggest events are in London and Brighton, with huge parades and performances from big-name acts, but there are Pride events across the country on different weekends. In 2022 the 50th anniversary London Pride parade was led by members of the Gay Liberation Front who organised the first UK Pride march in 1972. More than a million people turned out to show their support and join the party, including representatives from more than 600 different LGBTIQ+ community groups.

### HAPPY VALLEY PRIDE

The former mill town of Hebden Bridge in west Yorkshire is home to a vibrant LGBTIQ+ community. Prompted by the discovery of some homophobic graffiti in 2015, the community established Happy Valley Pride, a seven-day queer arts festival and celebration of LGBTIQ+ pride. Throughout the year look out for events at the Trades Club, a socialist members cooperative, club, bar and music venue.

### DISCRIMINATION

In England it's illegal to discriminate against someone based on their sexual orientation or because they are trans, which are protected characteristics under the Equality Act. It's unusual for same-sex couples to be treated with hostility at hotels in England.

## LGBTIQ+ City Scenes

In London the most established gay district is Soho, with further clusters of LGBTIQ+ venues in Vauxhall, East London and King's Cross. Manchester's gay scene is centred around Canal St, which is packed with gay bars and clubs. In Brighton you don't have to go far to find a gay bar; many venues are in Kemptown. There are also thriving LGBT districts in Birmingham, Leeds and Liverpool.

### RESOURCES

**Diva** (divamag.co.uk) Online magazine for LGBTIQ women and non-binary people.

**Gay Times** (gaytimes.co.uk) Covers culture, music, drag and fashion.

**Stonewall** (stonewall.org.uk) Advocates for the LGBTIQ+ community.

**Switchboard LGBT** (switchboard.lgbt) A listening service for LGBTIQ+ people. You can apply to help out as a listening volunteer; training is provided.

### Drag Brunches

You can catch drag shows at the Admiral Duncan, Karaoke Hole and Royal Vauxhall Tavern to name just a few London venues. Proud Cabaret hosts drag brunches and bingo in Brighton and London. In Leeds, check out Viaduct Showbar.

# Accessible Travel

While there is room for improvement, efforts have been made to enhance the accessibility of England's public spaces and buildings with ramps, lifts and other facilities.

## Cycling

Wheels for All (wheelsforall.org.uk) is a charity that offers adapted bikes for people with disabilities at centres across England. It also organises Pedal Away events, social bike rides that are open to all.

### Airport

Passengers with sensory, learning or physical disabilities are entitled to assistance at the airport. You should request airport assistance at least 48 hours in advance through your airline. However, there are also help points to call for assistance throughout the terminal building.

### Accommodation

All new hotels have wheelchair ramps and accessible bathrooms, but many places to stay still fall short when it comes to accommodating people with disabilities. England's National Accessible Scheme lists independently assessed accessible accommodation.

## RESOURCES

**Tourism For All** *(tourismforall.org.uk)* A charity that advocates for accessible travel and tourism in the UK. The website lists accessible accommodation, restaurants and attractions, and has a useful travel planner tool.
**Scope** *(scope.org.uk)* Offers advice and support for issues including using public transport as a person with a disability.
**Disability Rights UK** *(disabilityrightsuk.org)* Campaigns for equal opportunities for people with disabilities.

## WHEELYBOATS

Wheelyboats (wheelyboats.org) are specially designed craft with a ramp for wheelchair access. The boats are used for accessible trips on the River Tees (tees-wheelyboats.org.uk), Chichester Harbour and the Norfolk coast, among other locations.

## Guided Walks

Sense Adventures (senseadventures.co.uk) offers guided day walks and short breaks for blind and visually impaired people in the Malvern Hills. Sighted people are welcome too.

## Outdoor Adventure

People with physical, learning, behavioural and sensory disabilities can try zip lining, abseiling, archery and a host of other activities at the Calvert Trust (calvert-trust.org.uk) outdoor adventure centres in Exmoor, the Lake District and Northumberland.

## CANAL HOLIDAYS

CanalAbility (canalability.org.uk) provides specially adapted canal boats for people with disabilities and special needs. The boats can be hired for day trips or weekend breaks on the rivers Stort and Lee in Essex and Hertfordshire.

Beach wheelchairs with large pneumatic wheels can be hired free of charge at a number of England's beaches, including Great Yarmouth in Norfolk, Boscombe in Bournemouth, Brighton Beach and 19 places in Cornwall (see cornwallmobility.co.uk). Reserve in advance.

# Attending an English Sporting Event

From football matches to tennis tournaments, England hosts some world-class sporting events. Seeing a Premier League match or England play rugby could be one of the highlights of your trip, but getting hold of tickets is often far from easy.

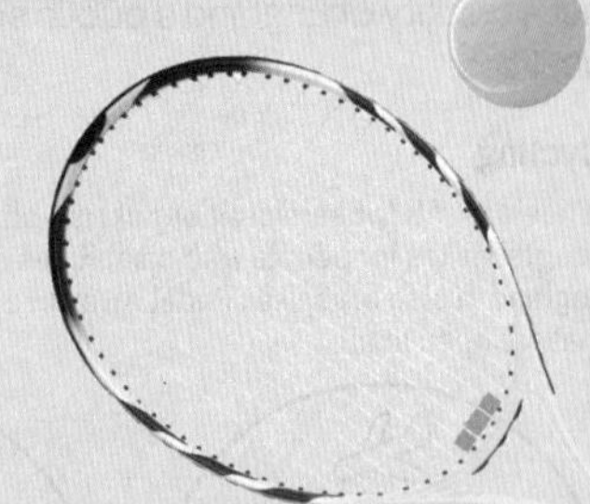

## Premier League Football

The best place to buy tickets is directly from the official club website or ticket office of the home team. Since tickets are made available to club members before the general public, it may be worth buying a club membership to have a better chance of success. Tickets usually go on sale around six weeks before the match. Derby games (games between clubs from the same city or local area) are extremely popular, and tickets may be allocated using a points system to give priority to fans who attend matches regularly. The Premier League website has a guide for how to buy tickets for every club. If you can't get tickets, you can take the edge off your disappointment with a stadium tour, available at most grounds.

## Wimbledon Tennis Championship

For two weeks in late June and early July, tennis takes centre stage in England as the country's attention turns to the Wimbledon. Tickets for Centre Court and Courts 1 to 3 are allocated by public ballot (random draw), which you can register for during a four-week window in late October and early November. If you don't get tickets in the ballot, you can still attend Wimbledon by joining the daily queue for a grounds pass; once in the grounds you can watch matches on the peripheral courts or see show court matches on the big screen. Tennis fanatics queue overnight to be sure of getting a grounds pass and to be in with a chance of buying a resale ticket to the show courts.

## Rugby at Twickenham

The England rugby team plays home games at Twickenham (twickenhamstadium.com), an 82,000-seater stadium 10 miles west of central London. Tickets are sold on the stadium website. One of the biggest events in the rugby calendar is the Six Nations tournament in February and March, during which England, Scotland, Wales, Ireland, France and Italy all play each other once, either home or away.

### TICKET TOUTS

One of the reasons tickets can be hard to get hold of in England is the proliferation of ticket touts, who buy up tickets to sell on at inflated prices, either online or outside the ground. If you buy from a tout, there is a risk that the ticket may be fake or have been cancelled.

# Nuts & Bolts

## OPENING HOURS

Opening hours may vary throughout the year in rural areas, where many places have shorter hours or close completely over winter.

**Banks** 9.30am–5pm Monday to Friday; some open 9.30am–1pm Saturday

**Pubs & bars** noon–11pm Monday to Saturday (some until midnight or 1am Friday and Saturday), 12.30pm–11pm Sunday

**Shops** 9am–5.30pm or 6pm Monday to Saturday, often 11am–5pm Sunday

**Restaurants** lunch noon–3pm, dinner 6pm–9pm or 10pm

### Smoking

Smoking is forbidden in all enclosed public places. Most pubs have an outdoor smoking area.

**Weights & Measures**

England uses a mix of metric and imperial measures. Petrol is sold by the litre but beer by the pint; mountain heights are in metres but road distances are in miles.

**Tap Water**

Tap water is safe to drink throughout England.

## GOOD TO KNOW

**Time Zone**
GMT in winter, GMT plus one hour in summer

**Country Code**
44

**Emergency Number**
999

**Population**
56.5 million

**Electricity** 240V/50Hz

**Type G**

Type G
230V/50Hz

## PUBLIC HOLIDAYS

If a public holiday falls on a weekend, the nearest Monday is usually taken instead. Banks and some businesses close on public holidays, but large attractions are usually open. Virtually everything – attractions, shops, banks, offices – closes on Christmas Day. There's no public transport on Christmas Day, and a minimal service on Boxing Day.

**New Year's Day**
1 January

**Easter** March/April (Good Friday to Easter Monday inclusive)

**May Day**
First Monday in May

**Spring Bank Holiday**
Last Monday in May

**Summer Bank Holiday** Last Monday in August

**Christmas Day**
25 December

**Boxing Day**
26 December

THE ENGLAND

# STORYBOOK

Our writers delve deep into different aspects of English life



**Fountains Abbey (p458)**

# A HISTORY OF ENGLAND IN 15 PLACES

For all the vainglory of its empire, England was conquered as often as it was conqueror. The Romans, French, Germans, Vikings and a string of other peoples stamped their identity on this green and pleasant island, fusing their cultures, customs and languages with the native traditions of the British Isles.

**THE FIRST PEOPLE** arrived on this island sometime before 500,000 BCE, but England only emerged as a distinct entity in the last millennia, replacing a patchwork of feuding kingdoms (most of them parts of other empires). Much of what is known about early England comes from religious manuscripts, with substantial gaps during the early Middle Ages.

Over the centuries, waves of invaders – Romans, Saxons, Angles, Vikings, Normans and more – left a lasting mark on the local culture and language. Even the Celts were newcomers from the Russian steppe. The English came together as one people in the 10th century, when rival Saxon kingdoms were unified by the descendants of King Alfred. This first incarnation lasted about a century before the French took over under William the Conqueror.

Despite being the victim of dozens of hostile empires, England wasted no time in forging an empire of its own – extending control across the British Isles and later across the world thanks to the rapacious ships of the Royal Navy. Even this didn't stop the outside influences – after centuries as a hub for global trade, locals see no inconsistency in speaking English, eating curry and drinking Indian tea.

### 1. Stonehenge

THE MOST FAMOUS STONE CIRCLE

England's most famous ancient monument has dominated Salisbury Plain for nearly 5000 years, but its story is still shrouded in mystery. The henge likely started life as a burial site for Neolithic peoples, but the mighty standing stones were stacked up in phases, with evidence suggesting some were hauled from as far away as north Wales. The stone circle was constructed to align with sunrise on the summer solstice and used for pagan ceremonies throughout the Bronze Age and into the Iron Age – the involvement of druids and the wizard Merlin, however, is purely latter-day conjecture.

*See p257 for more.*

### 2. Hadrian's Wall

ENGLAND'S GREAT DIVIDE

Few monuments tie as strongly to the national story as Hadrian's Wall, the mighty defensive barricade constructed by the Romans to protect their newly acquired foothold in the British Isles from the rebellious native people to the north. Indeed, the cultural divide between England and Scotland today partly has its roots in this 2nd century CE line of control between Roman Britain and independent Celtic Caledonia. These days, this 73-mile fortification is best explored on foot, stopping in at the ruins of a string of sentry posts, forts and temples between Bowness-on-Solway and Wallsend on the River Tyne.

*See p567 for more.*

### 3. Roman Bath

A TASTE OF ROMAN REFINEMENT

The invading Romans certainly brought brutality to their invasion of Britain in 43 CE, but they also imported modernity, including such cutting-edge inventions such as durable architecture, roads and warm bathing. Nowhere conjures up the refined life of Roman Britain quite like the bathhouse in the Somerset town of Bath, where well-to-do Roman ladies and gents came to bathe in heated mineral waters until the 5th century. Visitors are not permitted to take a dip in this Roman relic today, but you can drink a cup of the healing waters from a fountain in the Pump Room restaurant.

*See page 236 for more.*

### 4. Lindisfarne Priory

A MONUMENT TO TROUBLED TIMES

There are many Viking sites scattered around this oft-coveted isle, but perhaps the most evocative is the lonely island of Lindisfarne on the Northumberland coast. The monastic community founded by St Aidan in 634 CE became the focus for centuries of Viking raids, until its residents fled with their treasured books to the mainland. Wandering this wind-buffeted isle today, with its skeletal abbey ruins and tiny storybook castle, it's easy to imagine the monks' terror as the longships hauled up onto the beaches. After wandering the shoreline, warm your insides with a mug of mead at St Aidan's Winery.

*See p576 for more.*

**Lindisfarne Priory**

### 5. Westminster Abbey

THE NATION'S MOTHER CHURCH

Sky-piercing medieval cathedrals, abbeys and churches dot every corner of the English landscape, but if there's one mother church that defines the nation, it's London's Westminster Abbey. Founded in 960 CE, this Gothic masterpiece is the last resting place of 17 monarchs and the spot where almost every English ruler from William the Conqueror to Elizabeth II was crowned (King Charles III joins the roster in 2023). While the architecture dazzles, it's the tombs that capture the imagination – Darwin, Dickens, Sir Isaac Newton, William Wilberforce and Stephen Hawking all spend the centuries here, alongside sundry kings and queens.

*See p57 for more.*

### 6. The Tower of London

ONE CASTLE TO RULE THEM ALL

If you're after a date with history, head to the stone-cut castle where many of the most important events in English history actually happened. Founded by William the Conquerer in the 1070s, the Tower of London was the seat of power for a succession of English dynasties, as well as being a prison for everyone from William Wallace to Elizabeth I. The sprawling fortress is mobbed by visitors daily, but that does little to diminish the drama etched into these walls (literally, in the former cells). And yes, you can see the Crown Jewels – arguably the world's most extravagant collection of baubles and trinkets.

*See p73 for more.*

### 7. Fountains Abbey

A MONUMENT TO CHANGE

Rather than revelling in the excesses of Henry VIII, modern historians view his legacy with less rose-tinted spectacles. While Henry's impact on the lives of his spouses was brutally direct, his greatest influence on England was the Dissolution of the Monasteries, and the abandonment of Roman Catholicism in favour of the newly created Church of England. In the grounds of the Studley Royal estate in North Yorkshire, Fountains Abbey is the most impressive of dozens of ruined abbeys, monasteries and convents dotted around the country, whose ransacked remains reveal how the faith of the nation was savagely and forcefully remodelled.

*See p458 for more.*

## 8. Historic Stratford

THE BARD'S HOMETOWN

The historic Midlands city of Stratford-upon-Avon wears its Shakespeare connections on its sleeve – and on its stationary, and street signs, and just about anywhere else where you could slap a picture of the Bard. Nevertheless, Stratford's historical credentials stand up to scrutiny – indeed, it was Shakespeare who made English history known around the globe. Start the theatrical journey by wandering the half-timbered houses associated with the national playwright, including his birthplace on Henley St. Tack on a side trip to nearby Warwick Castle to see the real-life location for many events in Shakespeare's royal romps.

*See p380 for more.*

## 9. St Paul's Cathedral

THE MEASURE OF LONDON'S RESILIENCE

Sir Christopher Wren's magnum opus in Portland stone, St Paul's Cathedral is a powerful symbol of England's ability to bounce back from adversity. After a fire in a bakers' shop cremated 85% of the English capital in 1666, this newly constructed, elegantly symmetrical cathedral became a symbol of national resilience – a role only reinforced during WWII, when squadrons of home guards kept the cathedral safe from German incendiary bombs. Inside are monuments to great (and sometimes reappraised) national heroes and the tomb of Wren himself. The views from atop the dome are some of the most dizzyingly beautiful in the capital.

*See p76 for more.*

## 10. Portsmouth Historic Dockyards

WHERE EMPIRE SET SAIL

The British Empire is no longer viewed with quite the same unbridled enthusiasm, but the ships of the Royal Navy had an undeniable impact on the shape of the world. For a sense of England's seafaring history, head to Portsmouth's historic dockyards to explore such landmark vessels as Lord Nelson's flagship *HMS Victory* and the preserved wreck of Henry VIII's ill-fated *Mary Rose*, which sank during a battle with the French in 1545. Even if the historical context leaves you cold, the sight of these mighty tall ships will have you hankering for a life of sails and swashbuckling.

*See p168 for more.*

## 11. Ironbridge Gorge

CRADLE OF THE INDUSTRIAL REVOLUTION

The Industrial Revolution was the snowball that trigged an avalanche, dragging the world into the modern age. When Abraham Darby discovered the secret of smelting iron ore with coke in Ironbridge Gorge in 1709, the mass production of machines became possible for the first time. Within a generation, the countryside was transformed by heavy industry – a change alluded to by Tolkien in *The Two Towers* – bringing massive social change in its wake. Today the gorge is dotted with museums recalling this transformative time in history and you can wander across the Ironbridge – the first monumental iron structure ever constructed.

*See p396 for more.*

**St Paul's Cathedral**

Notting Hill Carnival

## 12. The Houses of Parliament

THE SEAT OF DEMOCRACY

The seat of the British government – home to England's twin Houses of Parliament, the Commons and the Lords – is inexorably tied to history and tradition, despite being several centuries younger than it first appears. The original medieval Palace of Westminster was destroyed by fire in 1834, so architect Charles Barry was commissioned to construct this mock-Gothic fantasy, dominated by the clocktower housing the famous Big Ben bell. While everything from cybersecurity to climate change is discussed inside, England's parliament is still legendary for its arcane traditions – for some government business, it is still mandatory to wear a top hat!

*See p61 for more.*

## 13. The Kensington Museums

TREASURE TROVES OF HISTORY

English empire-builders erected mighty memorials the world over to broadcast their power and status, but we prefer to single out the Victorian contribution to knowledge. At the Kensington museums, England's influence on modern culture is showcased in all its diversity. At the Natural History Museum, a statue of Darwin presides over specimens that inspired the theory of evolution. In the Science Museum, marvels such as the first steam train recall England's leading role in science and industry. And at the Victoria & Albert Museum, treasures gathered from around the world (not always with permission) stand alongside punk outfits and Elton John's stacked heels.

*See p124 for more.*

## 14. Imperial War Museum, Duxford

SEE WORLD WAR HISTORY UP CLOSE

There are many monuments, memorials and museums exploring the complex role of WWI and WWII in the British national psyche, but the Imperial War Museum campus at Duxford near Cambridge is one place where you can feel that history under your fingertips. The country's largest aviation museum lets you get within touching distance of a massive fleet of vintage combat aircraft, including the home-designed Hurricane and Spitfire fighters that tipped the balance during the Battle of Britain. It's not all military bombast – the collection also includes classic civilian aircraft, from the world's first jet airliner to Concorde.

*See p344 for more.*

## 15. Notting Hill Carnival

CELEBRATE ENGLAND'S DIVERSITY

England left an indelible mark on its many colonies, but immigration from those colonies also changed England. Every August, the London suburb of Notting Hill is reinvented as a continuation of the Caribbean, as outrageously colourful, feather-trimmed costumes, sensual dances, bone-shaking sound systems and the smells of 'herbal' cigarettes and grilling jerk chicken fill the streets. It's a testament to modern England's diversity and inclusivity, and a two-finger salute to the race riots in the 1950s that triggered its foundation. Come, imbibe, dance – but bring earplugs, as it gets loud!

*See p121 for more.*

# MEET THE ENGLISH

Joe Bindloss introduces his people.

**THE FIRST THING** to be aware of is the importance of manners in England. Politeness is the bond that ties people together on this densely populated island, and locals use all sorts of linguistic gymnastics to avoid causing offence – from pre-emptive apologies to the world's most inventive euphemisms for sex and bodily functions.

If a local finds you sitting in their seat on the train, for example, they may say, 'I'm sorry, you seem to be sitting in my seat,' but what they really mean, while obviously being far too polite to say it, is, 'I want you to immediately get out of my seat.'

The English use of politeness to circumvent difficult conversations is one of the traits you'll have to get used to. The love of queuing is another. Cutting in ahead in line is almost a capital offence. Locals' generous use of the words 'please' and 'thank you' can also feel like overkill, but it helps people get along on this small and (in places) crowded island.

Prejudice undeniably lingers in some quarters, but most people here are welcoming to folk from anywhere in the world – this is, after all, a country with a Hindu prime minister and a Muslim mayor in charge of its capital city. On LGBTIQ+ rights in particular, England has moved forward significantly since the 1980s.

What does exist is a sense of being slightly different to other Europeans, by virtue of geography, language and 20th-century history. So yes, people can seem hung-up on flags and traditions, but for the most part, it's out of habit not ill-will.

These days, you won't find many bowler hats or handlebar moustaches (except in hipster circles), but you will find lots of umbrellas and conversations about the weather – which is often more pleasant than locals acknowledge.

Demographically, England is an ageing society, but immigration is countering the falling birthrate, making the country ever more diverse. You'll spot this global influence instantly if you dine out – Indian, Chinese and Turkish restaurants pop up in the smallest towns and villages.

Another thing to note is the North-South Divide – a mostly good-natured rivalry between the north and south of the country. Some of it is political, some economic and some cultural, but you'll definitely hear the odd strong opinion about the merits of the other half of the country as you travel.

If London is your first stop, don't expect the rest of the country to be a mirror to the capital. As well as being pricey and crowded, London is a hub for people from all over the world, which locals love, as it ensures some of the best dining on the planet. Smaller places are often calmer, but not always so cosmopolitan.

### A Snapshot of the English

England is estimated to be home to around 56.5 million people, of whom 82% are white British, with significant populations from India, Pakistan, Bangladesh, China, Turkey, Eastern Europe, and countries in Africa and the Caribbean with colonial ties to the UK.

## WHAT DOES IT MEAN TO BE ENGLISH?

I'm nominally English, from an English family, but if you scratch the surface of that, my family are originally Norman French, from the forests of Normandy, with a little bit of Welsh and Cumbrian Anglo-Saxon thrown in for good measure.

And like 14.4% of residents, I was born overseas – in my case, in the eastern Mediterranean. In fact, the English are some of the most peripatetic people on the planet – some 200 million people around the world claim ancestry from this island, three times the number of people who actually live here today.

London was naturally where I gravitated, along with 16% of the English population. In my corner of the capital, you can find preserved vine leaves and Kalamata olives at 1am in the morning, and the default wines in local restaurants are Turkish Villa Doluca and Yakut. That's the glory of London – wherever you're from, you'll find a London enclave where you can plug in to the tastes of home!

Crown Jewels on the Queen's coffin

HOWARD CHENG/SHUTTERSTOCK ©

# GOD SAVE OUR KING

## Where does the monarchy go from here? By Keith Drew

**AT 6.30PM ON** 8 September 2022, Buckingham Palace released a short but seismic statement. Her Majesty Queen Elizabeth II had died peacefully that afternoon at Balmoral Castle, the favourite of her many royal residences. She was 96, had pared back her public engagements in recent years and was in increasingly deteriorating health. But it still came as a shock – the Queen had, after all, only sworn in Liz Truss as Prime Minister, the 15th of her reign, just two days before.

For the 250,000 people who queued up to see her coffin lying in state in Westminster Abbey – some of them waiting in line for 17 hours for the chance to file past for a few seconds – and the 29 million people who watched her funeral on TV and for many millions more across the UK and the Commonwealth, it felt like the end of an era. Which is exactly what it was.

Elizabeth II was never meant to have been queen. George VI, her father, was also never meant to have been king, but his brother, Edward VII, chose to abdicate in 1937 so that he could marry twice-divorced American socialite Wallis Simpson. Princess Elizabeth acceded to the throne on 6 February 1952. She was just 25. She would reign over the UK for the next 70 years, longer than any other British monarch in history.

In his address to the nation following the Queen's death, King Charles III described her reign as 'a promise with destiny kept' and talked of her 'dedication and devotion as Sovereign'. For many people in Britain and beyond, she had been a calm and constant presence in an ever-changing world. For more than 85% of the UK population, Elizabeth II was the only monarch they had ever known, a familiarity fortified from seeing her likeness on the back of banknotes and in the corner of letters, postcards and parcels. The Queen's first prime minister was Winston Churchill, and as such she represented a fast-fading link to WWII, the defining event in modern British history. Her reign spanned a period of unprecedented change: the recovery of post-war Britain, the end of the British Empire, the bitterly divisive Brexit vote and a global pandemic.

In a constitutional monarchy like the UK's, the sovereign's role is largely ceremonial – as Head of State, they have representational duties, but legislative power lies with parliament. During her reign, though, the Queen carved out a reputation as a diplomatic force and a wily advisor, able to 'encourage or warn' while remaining politically neutral. She was capable of making hugely symbolic gestures, such as the historic handshake she offered Sinn Féin's Martin McGuinness, a former IRA commander, on a visit to Northern Ireland in 2012. And on the rare occasions that she forayed into anything remotely approaching politics, like the time she publicly expressed the hope that Scottish voters would 'think very carefully about the future' before their independence referendum in 2014, her interventions carried enormous weight.

That's not to say that the Queen has enjoyed a consistently smooth ride. The raw lyrics of The Sex Pistols' God Save the Queen – 'God save the queen, the fascist regime' – released during the Silver Jubilee in 1977, struck a chord with a younger generation rebelling against what they felt was an antiquated monarchy. The Royal Family in general has often proved an easy, and intriguing, target for the British tabloid press, too, whether they've been hounding Princess Diana in the 1980s and '90s or Meghan Markle today.

*The Crown*, Netflix's fictionalised account of the Queen's reign, has evened things up a bit, and the series does a decent job at times of showing the Royal Family, if not ordinary people, then as an extended group of relatives facing their own challenges and issues. The show has been credited in some quarters with helping shift the public's perception of Charles, something of a controversial figure at one time, and it now falls upon the king to carry on his mother's work and to diplomatically tread the same fine lines. Aged 74 at the time of his coronation, Charles is the oldest person to become monarch in British history. He ascends to the throne at a time when his country is grappling with a cost-of-living crisis and inequality, driven by a widening gap among the social classes and a divide between North and South.

Questions are resurfacing around the monarchy's role and relevance in modern society. Republicans argue that a hereditary public office goes against the democratic principles that Britain stands for, while many bemoan the expense of sustaining the monarchy, which between its 23 official households and palaces cost the UK taxpayer £87.5m in 2021. To some, the Commonwealth is an institutional reminder of the British Empire, and several countries have gained independence in recent years, or are seeking independence today. Closer to home, a poll in June 2022 found that only 45% of people in Scotland wanted to keep the monarchy; it is not insignificant that Charles chose to hold his first official reception as king in Edinburgh.

In the coming years, Charles III will need to modernise the institution and repair the damage done by the recent Prince Andrew scandal (who settled a sexual-abuse case linked to his relationship with convicted paedophile Jeffrey Epstein in 2022) and the acrimonious way in which Harry, Duke of Sussex, and his wife Meghan Markle gave up their lives as working royals.

The King has long-championed environmental causes and sustainable farming – he made a speech about the dangers of pollution as far back as 1970 and has been practicing organic agriculture on his Highgrove estate since the 1980s – and holds strong opinions on a range of issues, from architecture to alternative medicine. But, as king, Charles will have to refrain from making the kind of outspoken comments he had become famous for in the past, keeping his thoughts and beliefs instead for the private weekly meetings with his Prime Minister.

If Charles III can tap into the goodwill afforded to his mother by her people, if he can follow the Queen's example of counselling from behind the scenes, and if he can refashion the Royal Family and prove that they still have a place and a purpose in 21st-century Britain, then the monarchy's future, for the time-being at least, will be assured.

# BOTTOMS UP

## Iow England's drinking culture and the role of its pubs ıas changed. By Isabel Albiston

**'HE ROMANTIC IDEAL** of the English pub vas perfectly captured by George Orwell n his 1946 essay 'The Moon Under Wa- er.' In it, Orwell describes the character- stics of a mythical London pub, painting ın appealing picture of regulars who al- vays sit in the same seats, warming win- er fires, a miraculous absence of rowdy lrunks, a convivial atmosphere and a gar- len filled with happy families. The fact hat the Moon Under Water is revealed to e fictional highlights the sentimentality urrounding the idea of the English pub, vhich could not exist in reality as it does n imagination.

Nonetheless, at least some of the qual- ties listed by Orwell do describe what nakes English pubs special. At their best, hey are places where people seek out com- ›any and conversation as well as beer and ;in, and many English pubs do have reg- ılars, roaring fires, fairy-lit gardens, and ›ub quizzes that bring people together to ocialise and have fun.

However, English pubs have been hav- ng a hard time of late; the number of pubs n the UK has been steadily decreasing for several decades. Between 2010 and 2020, the number of pubs fell by 15%, with small independent pubs the most likely to close. Pub landlords pointed to the rising costs of energy, goods and labour as well as lost business during the COVID-19 pandemic to explain the closures. The situation is made more tenuous by the English brewery system, in which landlords must pay rent to the brewery and adhere to the brewery's pricing structure. The sight of shuttered locals and news of the apparent decline of the English pub has caused much hand-wringing and calls for the government to do more to support the industry.

Ironically, rising energy costs might actually help some pubs stay in business. As more people in England are working from home, those reluctant to heat their homes all day can take advantage of 'working from the pub' workspaces, which offer power sockets and laptop space for a daily fee. Furthermore, English craft beer is thriving, with around 200 new independent breweries opening in the UK between 2021 and 2022. The increase in craft breweries coincides with the rise of the

CAT & MUTTON
COCKTAILS
HOUSE OF REVELRY
THE CAT & MUTTON
ESTD 1729

**Pub in East London**
ALENA VEASEY/SHUTTERSTOCK ©

nicropub, a small room with a bar that 'ocuses on serving local beers and ales. ?erhaps, then, the English pub scene is :hanging, rather than simply declining.

The nostalgia associated with English )ubs glosses over the issue of the coun-.ry's often troubling relationship with al-:ohol. In fact, England's drinking culture night also be characterised as a national lrinking problem. At weekends, pub 'last )rders' are often followed by ugly scenes n town centres as drunk people spill out nto the street. What's more, we might question why pubs are so often idealised ıs serving their local communities, when n reality their clientele doesn't represent England in all its diversity. For example, Muslims often don't drink alcohol for re-igious reasons, and men are more likely .o drink than women.

In fact, data indicates that young people n England are drinking less than the gen-:rations that came before them. A 2021 UK government report found that people aged .6 to 24 were least likely to drink more han the recommended limit of 14 units of alcohol per week, while adults aged 45 o 64 were most likely to exceed it. What's nore, 26% of the Gen Z age group don't lrink any alcohol at all. This trend sug-gests that the amount of alcohol consumed n England is set to decrease.

Of course, being teetotal doesn't mean 'ou can't go to the pub. These days many )ubs have top-of-the-range coffee machines and stock non-alcoholic beer; traditional non-alcoholic British drinks to try include dandelion and burdock soda and ginger )eer. And English pubs are places to go for a meal as well as a drink. A number of En-glish pubs serve food of such a high stan-dard they have been awarded a Michelin star; chef Tom Kerridge's pub the Hand & Flowers in Marlow has two.

Nonetheless, alcohol is what brings most people to England's pubs and bars. Indeed, pubs are the best places to sample English 'eal ales and local draught ciders. Beer remains the most popular order, but in 2018 gin overtook vodka to become the country's most popular spirit, with new gin distilleries opening all over the country: in 2022, there were 820 gin distilleries in the UK, up from 710 in 2020. The craft spirits craze follows hot on the tails of the craft beer boom in England, as people seek out more interesting flavours and drinks made by small independent distilleries rather than large corporations. The food trend for all things foraged and locally grown has also spilled over into the drinks world: small-batch gins are distilled with local ingredients such as bilberries, meadowsweet, hawthorn berries and heather, while Kent-grown hops are used in many craft beers.

Since 2021, cocktail sales have also increased, which may be linked to the fact that many people began drinking cocktails at home when pubs and restaurants were closed during the COVID pandemic. The classic English picnic cocktail is a jug of Pimms with lemonade, fresh mint and sliced strawberries, cucumber and oranges; it's associated with the Wimbledon Tennis Championships and the start of summer in the national consciousness.

Finally, although English wines were once the butt of jokes in France and Spain, vineyards in the southeast of the country have begun producing wines that can hold their own on the international stage. Some of the best English wines are sparkling, including those from Gusbourne and Nyetimber vineyards; the Kent and Sussex downs have a chalky soil that is similar to the Champagne region of France. The best way to try it is to do a tasting and buy direct from the vineyard. It's increasingly common to see English wines offered in restaurants, especially those with an emphasis on local produce, but its not that easy to find English wines in pubs, where it's best to stick to a pint.

# THE PEOPLE'S GAME?

How the Premier League has changed football in England.
By Keith Drew

**ENGLISH TOP-FLIGHT FOOTBALL** football has never been so popular. In a single season, the Premier League's exhilarating mix of star quality, competition, history and hype is lapped up by 3.2 billion people across the globe.

Football, in its simplest form, has been around since the Han Dynasty days of 3rd-century China, but the game as we know it today was invented in England. In 1863 the Football Association (FA) established the first standardised set of rules. They launched the FA Cup, now the oldest football competition in the world, in 1871, and created the first professional football league in 1888. A second, third and fourth tier were added, and the leagues played out, season after season, for over a hundred years. But in 1992 everything changed.

By then English football had been in steady decline for decades. Interest in the game was waning and the terraces had become a hotbed of hooliganism. In May 1985 the *Sunday Times* ran an editorial describing football in England as 'a slum sport played in slum stadiums and increasingly watched by slum people'. The nihilistic violence of this era, and the economic despair


Clockwise from top left: Emirates Stadium; fans at Stamford Bridge stadium; Premier League Flag; Sheffield Wednesday fans

that often fuelled it, is bleakly captured in films like *The Firm* (1988) and *The Football Factory* (2006).

By the early 1990s, the chairs of the 22 clubs in the English First Division, as it was then known, had decided that the game needed an overhaul if it was going to survive – and if they were going to have commercial independence, they needed to make serious money. In May 1992 the clubs broke away to form the Premier League.

Sky TV paid £191 million for the rights to broadcast the matches, nearly five times the amount public broadcaster ITV had been paying to show Football League games (as an example of how successful the Premier League has become, the most recent deal was worth £5.1 billion). With so much more money, the clubs were able to buy much better players, often from abroad. A cultural revolution, in both the dressing rooms and the stands, had begun.

When Arsène Wenger became manager of Arsenal in 1997, the London club was still holding midweek drinking sessions and the players struggled in matches if they hadn't had their pre-match Mars bars. The Frenchman introduced the idea of diet and nutrition to the players' lives and a possession-based approach to the way they played the game. In 1998 he became the first foreign manager to win the league in England.

Thanks to Wenger, and to other managers like Ruud Gullit at Chelsea and Gérard Houllier at Liverpool, there was a shift in emphasis from stamina and physicality to ball mastery and technique. Players like Dennis Bergkamp, Gianfranco Zola and David Ginola brought a style of play to English football, full of flair, creativity and panache, the likes of which the fans had never seen.

The demographics of the people watching from the stands changed, too. The FA was established by ex-public schoolboys in London, but the game itself developed quickest among the working class of the industrial North. Many clubs were born out of factory teams – Sheffield Wednesday, for example, is so named because that's the day its founding members were traditionally given time off work – and nearly half of the clubs that took part in the inaugural Football League were from mill towns like Accrington, Blackburn, Bolton and Burnley. Watching your team became a ritual among these working-class communities.

But the Premier League has become a premium product. And with the advent of all-seater stadiums following the Hillsborough disaster in 1989, when 96 Liverpool fans died in a crush due to overcrowding on the terraces, demand now outstrips supply. The cost of tickets has risen dramatically as a result – in some cases by 825% since 1990 – pricing many traditional fans out of the game.

For some older fans, the affinity they've always enjoyed with their club has diminished during the Premier League era. They point to fewer homegrown players coming through the youth academies and ownership of their clubs transferring from local businesspeople to Russian oligarchs, American sports moguls and even entire countries.

There has possibly never been a bigger disconnect between the players on the pitch and the people in the stands, either. Wage disparity is by no means unique to English football, but thanks to the riches of the Premier League it is probably not felt quite so keenly elsewhere as it can be here. In the 2022/2023 season Cristiano Ronaldo earned £515,385 a week at Manchester United, nearly 1000 times the average weekly salary in Greater Manchester that year.

There's also a gulf between the finances of clubs in the Premier League and those in the tiers below. Some money does drip down, in the form of so-called parachute payments for teams relegated to the Championship each season, and in other ad-hoc payments. But clubs in the lower leagues continually tread the fine line between investing in the players that will help them win promotion to the 'Promised Land' and making sure they don't extend themselves too far and spiral into debt.

Some don't get the balance right: Wimbledon, Coventry City and Portsmouth, all former FA Cup winners, have gone into administration at one time or another. They survived, but others have not been so fortunate: Bury FC, one of the oldest clubs in English football (they were founded in 1885), folded at the start of the 2019/2020 season. In 2022 a fans' group purchased the club's Gigg Lane ground in the hope of bringing football back to the north-west town. Now that would be fairytale revival worthy of the Premier League itself.

**Derwentwater (p525) and Catbells (p522), Lake District**
MARK HEWITT/GETTY IMAGES ©

# THE ENGLISH LANDSCAPE

How human activity has shaped England's environment. By Keith Drew

**WHEN IT COMES** to landscapes, England is not a place of extremes; there are no Alps or Himalayas here, no Amazon or Sahara. But the English landscape possesses a quality that, in the words of British writer Kazuo Ishiguro, marks it out as 'the most deeply satisfying in the world'.

The country may be small, but there's a diversity of environments that means even a relatively short journey can take you through surprising contrasts in scenery. England's green and pleasant land is most obvious in the West Country, particularly in Somerset's pastoral patchwork of fields and hedgerows, Wiltshire's ancient landscape of verdant plains, and the classic English countryside of the Cotswolds, which spreads into Oxfordshire and the West Midlands. In the South West, the heather-clad hills and wooded combes of Exmoor offer a softer juxtaposition to Dartmoor's weathered granite. The chalky uplands of the South Downs give way to the orchards of Kent and then the flat reed beds of the Fens. The landscape grows wilder, moodier moving north, through the limestone valleys and rocky moors of the Peak District and into the high hills and glassy meres of the Lake District. Cross the mountainous Pennines, the backbone of England, to reach the green valleys and drystone-walled hills of the Yorkshire Dales. Enclosing all of this are some 2750 miles of coastline: rugged cliffs, wide beaches, marshy estuaries, shingle spits and weather-beaten fishing villages.

With England's long history of human occupation, it's not surprising that the country's appearance is heavily the result of our interaction with the environment. Ever since humankind crossed the land bridge from mainland Europe to southeast Britain nearly a million years ago and left a few fossilised footprints on a beach at Happisburgh in Norfolk, we have been shaping and impacting England's landscape.

Mesolithic hunter-gatherers constructed the first dwellings in England at Star Carr in Yorkshire, dating back to around 9000 BCE, and at Howick in Northumberland, and with the introduction of farming to Britain in around 4500 BCE, forests were cleared and fields created for crops (wheat and barley) and grazing animals. Neolithic man started building wooden

walkways across the countryside – like the Sweet Track in Somerset – and carving earthwork enclosures into the Wiltshire landscape over 5500 years ago, while Iron Age settlements took this a step further, making rippled lines of earthen stockades around the contours of hills into huge forts.

Under the Romans, settlements expanded, with their capital of Londinium more than doubling in size from the time it was founded in around 47 CE to its peak a century later. Thousands of miles of paved roads were built to connect the towns, many of which – such as the Fosse Way, which linked Exeter with Lincoln – still survive in the form of modern highways like the A37 and the A46.

Towns encroached ever further into the English countryside, swelling in size during the Industrial Revolution, when coal mines, belching smokestacks and dark, satanic mills changed the look of northern England's landscape. The population of Manchester, the world's first industrial city, grew by 600% in just 50 years from the early 1770s, and England went from being a rural society in 1800 (with around 80% of the population living in the countryside) to an essentially urban one just a century later (with around 75% of the population living in its towns and cities).

Only 14.5% of England is now natural habitat. The changes to rural areas after WWII – when a drive to be self-reliant in food meant new (intensive and large-scale) agricultural methods – have been significant. Huge swathes of ancient woodland were lost, and in some areas patchworks of small meadows became vast prairie-like fields, as walls were demolished, ponds filled, wetlands drained and, most notably, hedgerows ripped out. Today 73% of England is farmland.

Perhaps prophetically, we have only really begun to appreciate England's countryside in the last 200 years. During the late 18th and early 19th centuries, a new generation of writers drew inspiration from the natural world, just as the foremost painters of the day also turned their attentions to the landscape – leading the public to do likewise. John Constable captured the romanticism of the Suffolk countryside where he lived in vividly realistic images in works such as *The Hay Wain* (1821), while JMW Turner used light and colour to reflect the power of nature in turbulent seascapes like the moonlit *Fishermen at Sea* (1796). One of England's most famous poems is focused on the experience William Wordsworth had as he wandered lonely as a cloud on a waterside walk in the Lake District, watching a host of daffodils 'beside the lake, beneath the trees, fluttering and dancing in the breeze'.

It was Wordsworth who suggested as early as 1810 that the Lake District should be 'a sort of national property, in which every man has a right and an interest'. It took well over a century for the first slice of England's landscape to be protected as such, when the Peak District was designated a national park in 1951, although Dartmoor, the North York Moors, the Yorkshire Dales, Exmoor, Northumberland and the Lake District itself all quickly followed before the end of the decade.

Despite the name, national parks in England are not owned by the nation: nearly all land is private, belonging to farmers, private estates and conservation organisations. And they are not the wilderness you might expect. In England's national parks, you'll see crop fields in lower areas and grazing sheep on the uplands, as well as roads, railways and villages, and even towns, quarries and factories in some. Over 120,000 people live in the South Downs National Park, England's newest; 85% of the park is farmed. It's a reminder of the balance that is struck in this crowded country between protecting the natural environment and catering

**South Downs National Park (p159)**

for the people who live in it.

In England, the great outdoors can be tantalisingly close. There are over 120,000 miles of public rights of way – public footpaths that run across private property, often on tracks that have been trodden for thousands of years. Just don't think about stepping off them. In 2000, the Countryside and Rights of Way (CRoW) Act gave the public a partial Right to Roam over about 8% of England without fear of trespass; ancient laws of ownership keep our footfall off the rest. It's a similar story on the rivers. Of the 42,700 miles of inland waterways in England, the public are allowed access to just 1400 miles of them, mostly canals and 'managed navigations'. That's around 4% – despite the fact that some groups argue there is an existing public right of navigation, enshrined in Magna Carta, on all navigable rivers in England.

The Right to Roam campaign hopes to extend the CRoW Act to include rivers, woods and green-belt land and to bring England in line with the more progressive access rights that exist north of the border. In Scotland, you are allowed onto most land to enjoy the outdoors (as long as you behave responsibly) and wild camp where you like. In England, the only place that wild camping has been permitted is in parts of Dartmoor – and local landowners are attempting to change even that.

Making the most of England's landscape seems more imperative than ever. According to the Met Office, average temperatures have increased by nearly 1°C since the 1980s. Spring is happening earlier in England, autumn leaf-fall later; animals are moving northwards and sometimes seeking higher altitudes. Sea levels around the UK have risen by over 3mm a year in the past decade and experts fear they could further rise between 40cm and 1m by the end of the century, accelerating coastal erosion and swamping salt marshes and mudflats. Scientists predict we are in store for hotter, drier summers, which will likely impact beech woodland and the lowland heath and fens of South East England, and warmer, wetter winters, resulting in a greater risk of flooding, particularly in the western areas of the country. The plants, trees and shrubs that can grow in England will change, as will the wildlife that lives among them.

Scafell Pike, Lake District (p542)

**IT WAS WORDSWORTH WHO SUGGESTED AS EARLY AS 1810 THAT THE LAKE DISTRICT SHOULD BE 'A SORT OF NATIONAL PROPERTY, IN WHICH EVERY MAN HAS A RIGHT AND AN INTEREST'**

In some parts of England, though, the landscape is changing for the better. Starting with a pioneering project on the Knepp estate in West Sussex in 2001, the rewilding movement – where the land is returned to nature and left for it to take care of itself – has gathered pace, particularly in the south. At Knepp, where traditional breeds such as Old English longhorn cattle and Tamworth pigs naturally manage the landscape, the restored habitat has seen an extraordinary increase in biodiversity. Elsewhere, keynote species that had become extinct have been reintroduced back into the wild, with beavers steadily revitalising local ecosystems in parts of Cornwall, Devon, Dorset and Cheshire, and, in the summer of 2022, bison released in Blean in Kent in a bid to restore the area's woodland. Maybe, after 11,000 years, we have learned that nature knows best?

# ENGLAND
## ON THE SMALL SCREEN

What fictional representations of England say about the country today. By Isabel Albiston

**ENGLISH PEOPLE WATCH** a lot of TV. In fact, in 2021 people in Britain spent an average of more than five hours a day watching TV or online video content. But what kind of reflection of themselves and their lives do they see on screen, and what can we tell about England and its people by how the country is depicted? When it comes to self reflection, it seems English screenwriters are best able to capture aspects of the national psyche and the realities of modern life when they use humour. Beyond the absurd situations that comically overblown characters in English sitcoms must navigate, there is often an underlying truth.

Phoebe Waller-Bridge's *Fleabag* (2016–19) swept the board at awards shows. The protagonist's fourth-wall breaking unreliable narration of what was happening in her life, and her often dark and taboo takes on events, captured a feeling of despondence, a longing for direction and meaning, and the contradictions of what it means to be a woman in England today. The use of sarcasm and humour to deflect from pain illustrates the tendency of some English people to respond in a light-hearted way when they are hurt and to hide their true feelings. *Fleabag*'s one-liners are funny, but they also reflect the thoughts that many English wom-

 **Clockwise from top left:** ***Mr Bean, Fleabag, Black Mirror, I May Destroy You***

en of her generation may secretly have had themselves. A similar fourth-wall breaking format was also used in *Peep Show* (2003–15), in which voice-over narration revealed the often despicable inner monologues of the main characters, Mark and Jeremy. In *Peep Show* the characters are dysfunctional and unlikeable but also very funny.

Although Waller-Bridge never claimed *Fleabag* represented anything more than one woman's story, the show was criticised by some for portraying a narrowly white, privileged version of life in modern England. In contrast, Michaela Coel's *I May Destroy You* (2020) depicted a more ethnically and culturally diverse London. The show's protagonist – the author of Twitter-feed-turned-book *Chronicles of a Fed-up Millennial* – deals with the aftermath of being drugged and raped. Subplots address themes of consent and race in modern England in an unflinching and nuanced way. Also dealing with issues of consent, *Sex Education* (2019–present) uses humour and warmth to show the awkwardness of teenage sex in a way that is generous to its characters and reflects how young people approach intimacy and sexual expression in England today.

When it comes to representation, English TV has not always done a good job of reflecting the country's diversity. One show that helped address the imbalance is the sitcom *We Are Lady Parts* (2021), which depicted an all-female Muslim punk band whose songs have titles like *'Ain't No One Gonna Honour Kill My Sister But Me.'* With stereotype-defying characters and plenty of silly jokes, the show challenged assumptions with its presentation of life for a group of Muslim students in modern England. In Jamie Demetriou's *Stath Lets Flats* (2018–21), the antics of an incompetent letting agent take place in the context of the miserable rental market of real-life London. The show is an affectionate portrayal of the Greek-Cypriot community in the north of the city.

The England depicted by some shows is difficult to characterise. Charlie Booker's *Black Mirror* (2011–present) is an unsettling anthology series. The stand-alone episodes mostly depict an imagined dystopian future, in which science and technology have continued to progress in a moral vacuum; some episodes are set in England. The show's themes of technological surveillance, individualism and consumerism are certainly issues affecting England today.

TV comedies of the recent past offer a glimpse into how the English have seen themselves in previous decades. One of the most enduring characters in English comedy is a man who behaves so embarrassingly that you might end up watching through your hands. These cringe-worthy anti-heroes can be seen in John Cleese's unlikable Basil Fawlty in *Fawlty Towers* (1975–79), Ricky Gervais's office manager David Brent in *The Office* (2001-03), Steve Coogan's sports commentator, talk-show host and radio DJ Alan Partridge – who has appeared in various guises since 1991 – and the broad comedy of Rowan Atkinson's *Mr Bean* (1990–95). Perhaps these characters reflect a general unease with the idea of breaking the social norms of politeness and repression of one's true thoughts. In *Absolutely Fabulous* (1992–95) it was a cast of female characters led by self-absorbed Eddie (Jennifer Saunders) and Patsy (Joanna Lumley) who pushed the boundaries of the socially acceptable in their superficial pursuit of the latest fad.

Political satire is another genre English TV has traditionally done well, from the memorably dark original *House of Cards* (1990) to the bureaucratic negotiations of *Yes, Minister* (1980–84) and *Yes, Prime Minister* (1986–88). In many ways, the craven behaviour and outlandish situations depicted in *The Thick of It* (2005–12) foreshadowed the political scandals, spin and cynicism of recent years.

Away from the London-centric world of political satire, several shows have offered affectionate representations of working-class families. In *The Royle Family* (1998–2012) nearly all the action takes place in the living room of a Manchester home, where a family sits on the sofa smoking, drinking, burping and watching TV. The show was a mirror for the way many ordinary English families interacted, with enough jokes and touching moments of intimacy to make it enthralling. Another enduringly popular depiction of working-class life is *Only Fools and Horses* (1981–91), in which the plucky protagonist Del Boy represented a wheeling-dealing optimism in the face of failure. Del Boy embodied the entrepreneurial pursuit of individual success promised by Thatcher's Britain, but his get-rich-quick schemes never paid off.

# POPULAR ACTION & ENGLISH DEMOCRACY

Don't 'keep calm and carry on' – how England was forged through a history of civil disobedience. By Tasmin Waby

**ENGLAND'S DEMOCRATIC MONARCHY,** with all its complexities and conventions, was forged through centuries of power struggles and protest. Here, politics has been a process of ongoing negotiation rather than violent revolution (although that doesn't mean radicalism doesn't exist). Instead, the English have a reputation for stoicism, patience and tolerance – famously manifested in their orderly queueing habits. Maintaining an even temper is respected, and is socially and tactically valuable in negotiating political change. But, when they've really had enough, the English will fight for a cause.

If serious popular grievances aren't addressed, then marches, disruptive protests and labour strikes have long, legitimate histories in England. Positive change for ordinary people doesn't always eventuate but innumerable rights have nevertheless been won through protests over the centuries. This is probably why – despite maintaining one the world's oldest parliamentary democracies – many of the statutes, common-law judgments and ancient rights that exist here seem quite nonsensical today.

Here's an example: a 1932 mass trespass in the Peak District's Kinder Scout secured the public's ancient 'right to roam' on designated moorland, heathland, coastline and other areas.

However, less than 2% of navigable waters are open to the public – an exclusion contested by public associations of anglers, swimmers and boaters. Incredibly, wild swimmers run the risk of a prosecution for entering inland waterways. In April 2022, a defiant group of swimmers held a mass 'swimpass' at Kinder reservoir, 90 years after their forebears did the same, arguing that the 'public right of navigation' for boats should be extended to swimmers as well. That fight continues.

Naturally, there are other curious aspects of England's ancient parliamentary democracy to understand. The two houses of the Westminster system have been reproduced in many countries. Yet few have an Upper House comprised of unelected representatives. The peers of the House of Lords are hereditary or political appointments, and yet they retain the power to veto laws written in the elected, accountable House of Commons.

Key rights and responsibilities wrung by rebellious barons from King John were written into Magna Carta (1215), while the triumph of parliament in the English Civil War (1642–51) paved the way for today's parliamentary democracy. Some unrest was less successful – all concessions 'granted' during the Peasants' Revolt (1381) were taken back once the uprising was brutally suppressed.

England (not quite yet the UK) passed the world's first Bill of Rights in 1689. It, and Magna Carta, are precursors to the US Bill of Rights (1789).

In the industrial era, waves of protests swept England as working-class populations grew, and traditional crafts and livings were swept away. The electoral franchise was a major source of unrest, as most workers were unrepresented in Westminster. Largely peaceful demonstrations calling for electoral reform were savagely repressed. The Peterloo Massacre of 1819, in which 60,000 workers protesting peacefully in Manchester's St Peter's Field were torn into by a sabre-wielding cavalry regiment, killing 18 and injuring 100s, is the best known.

The Reform Act of 1832 was a milestone of progress. The re-drawing of electoral boundaries and the creation of seats representing populous new industrial cities were two gains. Another was the extension of the franchise, although it was limited to 'any man who owned property worth £10 or more' at first.

The Chartists, a working class movement led by William Lovett and Francis Place, continued that fight for the next decade. Although their petitions were initially unsuccessful, further Reform Acts were passed in 1867 and 1884. By 1918 all but one of their demands were finally met.

Also in the late 19th century, a campaign to give women the vote gained momentum. The suffragettes protested publicly and sometimes violently. Bombings, vandalism and arson were tools encouraged by notable leaders like Emmeline Pankhurst (1858–1928). Other powerful actions – such as hunger strikes and Emily Davison's (1872–1913) suicide under the hooves of George V's horse at the 1913 Epsom Derby – pressed the point home. By 1928 all women over 21 were finally enfranchised. No one voluntarily 'gave' women the right to vote.

The 20th century saw the post-war introduction of the NHS and the welfare state. While initially supported by both Labour and Conservatives, the welfare state was aggressively diminished by the neoliberal Thatcher Government (1979–1990). Thatcher's radical programme of cuts and privatisation led to many confrontations between protestors and police at the time. In 1981 the Brixton riots broke out over racism and police brutality. The 1984–85 Miners' Strikes divided workers and communities and were sometimes violently dispersed. And the 1990 poll tax riots were vehement enough to see the scheme promptly abandoned.

In the 21st century, the causes and methods of popular protest have changed. Single-issue marches, like those protesting the 2003 invasion of Iraq, have been replaced with waves of continual societal disruption. First, the 2011 Occupy London movement saw the square outside St Paul's Cathedral taken over by activists for nine months. Occupy was a global movement protesting corporate influence over governments and increasing economic inequality.

The 2016 Brexit Referendum is undoubtedly Britain's most consequential recent expression of popular politics – a protest at the ballot box. A narrow majority in favour of leaving the EU ignited political chaos and divided the country, and its impact continues to reverberate across the region.

In recent times, Occupy London, Extinction Rebellion (XR), No To Oil and similar climate- and social-justice groups have been raising awareness through mass disruption and public spectacle. Their methods have included blocking busy motorways, 'vandalising' precious works of art and similar stunts to garner media attention. However, these tactics have also alienated potential supporters and in 2023 XR announced plans to change course.

A series of strikes held in late 2022 and early 2023 affected many public services. In response the government tabled legislation designed to keep essential services operating during industrial action, effectively hobbling the power of unions. Similarly, amendments to the 2022 Public Order Bill effectively criminalise many forms of political protest – even intended protest.

Some see these developments as presaging a new era of authoritarianism in a country that prides itself on its democratic traditions and protection of human rights. The question is: will the English 'keep calm and carry on', or will this be another flashpoint in the country's political history?

**Extinction Rebellion patch**

# INDEX

Map Pages **000**

Map Pages **000**

N

Map Pages **000**

"Beatles aficionados can't visit London without making a pilgrimageto the famous Abbey Road" (p107)

**LAUREN KEITH**

"This engineering marvel of the ancient world marks the point at which the Roman Empire stopped its northward march." (p567)

**HUGH MCNAUGHTAN**



## THIS BOOK

**Design Development**
Marc Backwell

**Content Development**
Mark Jones, Sandie Kestell, Anne Mason, Joana Taborda

**Cartography Development**
Katerina Pavkova

**Production Development**
Sandie Kestell, Fergal Condon

**Series Development Leadership**
Darren O'Connell, Piers Pickard, Chris Zeiher

**Commissioning Editor**
James Smart

**Production Editor**
Alison Killilea

**Book Designer**
Catalina Aragón

**Cartographers**
Chris Lee-Ack, Rachel Imeson

**Assisting Editors**
Karyn Noble

**Cover Researcher**
Gwen Cotter

**Thanks** James Appleton, Esteban Fernandez, Clare Healy, Gabby Innes, Gwen Cotter, Sandie Kestell

Paper in this book is certified against the Forest Stewardship Council™ standards. FSC™ promotes environmentally responsible, socially beneficial and economically viable management of the world's forests.

Published by Lonely Planet Global Limited
CRN 554153
12th edition - July 2023
ISBN 978 1 83869 352 7

10 9 8 7 6 5 4 3 2 1
Printed in China